THE
TORAH
AND ITS
GOD

THE
TORAH
AND ITS
GOD

A HUMANIST
INQUIRY

JORDAN JAY HILLMAN

Prometheus Books

59 John Glenn Drive
Amherst, New York 14228-2197

Published 2001 by Prometheus Books

Inquiries should be addressed to
Prometheus Books
59 John Glenn Drive
Amherst, New York 14228–2197
VOICE: 716–691–0133, ext. 207
FAX: 716–564–2711
WWW.PROMETHEUSBOOKS.COM

05 04 03 02 01   5 4 3 2 1

Library of Congress Cataloging-in-Publication Data

Hillman, Jordan Jay.
    The Torah and its God : a humanist inquiry / Jordan Jay Hillman.
        p. cm.
    Includes bibliographical references.
    ISBN 1–57392–820–8 (cloth)
        1. Humanistic Judaism. 2. Bible. O.T. Pentateuch—Commentaries. I. Title.

BM197.8 .H55 2000
222'.106—dc21   00–062515

Printed in the United States of America on acid-free paper

I dedicate this book, with love and respect, to

my parents, Louis and Della Miller Hillman,
who live yet in warm memories;

my daughters, Deborah and Amy,
each a source of pride in her own special way; and

my wife, Karen, whose unending patience and encouragement
throughout the past six years of my inquiry have been graced
even more by her keen eye for an errant phrase.

Jordan Jay Hillman

CONTENTS

TABLE OF COMMENTS

GENESIS

9

EXODUS

LEVITICUS

NUMBERS

DEUTERONOMY

A BRIEF PREFACE
TO JUDAISM, THEISM,
NATURALISM, AND
HUMANISM

What remains of the Torah when we openly acknowledge that its God exists in the human mind alone, having been created by human authors as the means, *in their time*, of guiding a people toward its highest human ends? To this question I bring my belief that human experience and our knowledge of the natural order argue against both the efficacy and reality of the Torah's heavenly means—even as they affirm the value of its earthly ends. Accordingly, after a close reading of the Torah to distinguish its means from its ends, I will consider how its humanist roots might be put to fuller use as a means toward its human ends.[1]

Because its God is central to the Torah and the Torah is central to Judaism, to question His separate existence as a transcendent Being might seem a rejection of Judaism itself. But even as I reject the reality of its God, I take pride in the many nontheistic ethical, social, and cultural values which the Torah has fostered apart from its God.

In acknowledgment of the power of the Torah's theistic rhetoric and imagery, I do not mean to challenge any theist with a socially constructive belief in the Torah's God—whether as first created, or as "humanized" over time by prophets, rabbis, theologians, and philosophers. But given the human purposes of the Torah's human authors, my hope, instead, is to foster a wider appreciation of the humanist values that underlie their creation of the Torah's God. So understood, this well-spring of Judaic culture might generate a greater pride of heritage in many who, like me, find no guidance in past or present incarnations of the Torah's God. Thus, while I respect the integrity of sincere and worthy believers who assert theistic claims to the Torah, my aim is to substantiate the equally valid claims of nontheistic humanists. The literary brilliance and vision of the Torah's authors and editors enable it to satisfy both.

In drawing on the spiritual traditions of an emergent people in a dangerous world, the human authors of the Torah created a single transcendent God as its protagonist. In time, He would become the spiritual foundation of the Judaism of their descendants, and of Christianity and Islam as well. These major monotheistic religions differ in many ways. But common to all is a belief in the reality of the one unique, supreme, and universal Being, whom humankind first encountered as the transcendent God of the Torah.

The Torah's grasp of a human need for spiritual inspiration has proved timeless and profound. However, the transcendent God created by its authors as Israel's spiritual "centerpiece" was a product of a particular time and place. That their creation would later become the spiritual focus of untold millions speaks to the brilliance of their psychological insights. Why, then, do I choose to focus on the Torah's spiritual qualities through the lens of "naturalism" rather than the traditional lens of "theism"? In a "word," because I cannot accept the customary premises of "theism."

As it derives from the Torah and relates to my inquiry, I understand "theism" as a belief in the existence of one godly entity—unique, supreme, and universal—*but with three additional attributes*. First, this entity, though Lord of the entire universe, has a special concern for earthly affairs, and for humankind in particular. Second, this entity is capable of exercising purposeful control over earthly events through powers that transcend the processes of natural causation. Third, starting with the creation of earth and its occupants, this entity has in fact intervened to control earthly events, and, as it wishes, can do so even now. By so defining "theism," I mean to avoid all metaphysical issues bearing on the origins of the wider universe, within which our earth is but a speck.

In turn, by "naturalism" I mean a disbelief in the god-idea that I associate with "theism." To accept "naturalism" as a "disbelief," however, is to assert the affirmative belief that all earthly phenomena, including those of the human spirit, reflect the operation of a natural order. Because "naturalism" rather than "theism" comports with my sense of reality, it is the perspective that I bring both to my Judaism and my reading of the Torah.

Being unable to commit humanity's destiny and my own to the transcendent God of monotheism, I turn instead to humanity itself—if not to what it always is, then to what it can be. In this regard, the following definition of "naturalistic humanism" from *Webster's New International Dictionary* (3d ed.) usefully summarizes my perspective: "a philosophy that rejects supernaturalism, regards [humankind] as a natural object, and asserts the essential dignity and worth of [humankind] and [its] capacity to achieve self-realization through the use of reason and scientific method." To knowledge and reason I would add empathy and compassion, whose seeds nature has long since planted in us. Our task is to provide a more fertile soil for their growth.

INTRODUCTION

A TRADITIONAL VIEW OF THE TORAH AS RECEIVED BY MOSES FROM ITS GOD

To Orthodox Jews in particular, the Torah remains sacred as God's Sinaitic revelation to Israel through His prophet and faithful transcriber, Moses. It was in this spirit that, Nachmanides (Rabbi Moses ben Nachman), the Ramban (1194–1270), introduced his thirteenth-century Torah Commentary: "Moses our teacher wrote this book of Genesis together with the *whole* Torah, from the mouth of the Holy One, blessed be He."[1]

Although Ramban cites Exod. 24:12 as his scriptural authority, the verse can also be read to cover something less than the "whole Torah." Thus, in the Jewish Publication Society's first translation (JPS1) the Lord tells Moses that he is to receive "the tables of stone, and the law and the commandment, which I have written, that thou mayest teach them." The Revised Standard Version (RSV) similarly refers to "the tables of stone, with the law and the commandment, which I have written for their instruction." However, the Society's second translation (JPS2) is more inclusive. Here Moses receives "the stone tablets with the *teachings* and commandments which I have inscribed to instruct them."[2]

In their rendering of Exod. 24:12, none of these twentieth-century translations explicitly include "the whole Torah," including its extensive nonlegal narrative. Ramban himself (as translated in his *Commentary on the Torah*) reads Exod. 24:12 as "the tablets of stone and the *Torah* and the commandment which I have written, to teach them." He then goes on to explain why his use of "Torah" includes narrative, as well as all laws and commands. "The expression 'and the Torah' includes the stories from the beginning of Genesis (and is called 'Torah' —teaching) because it teaches people the way of faith."[3]

The ambiguity of "Torah" in Hebrew is apparent in the following translation from a contemporary Hebrew/English dictionary: "Torah [i.e., the transliteral term in English]: the Pentateuch; Law; instruction, teaching; doctrine;

theory." By reading the Torah as "teaching" rather than "law," Ramban posits the intent of his God to reveal the "whole" Torah to Moses, including "non-legal" narrative.

Ramban then concludes that "upon descending from the mount," Moses wrote the entire books of Genesis and Exodus (i.e., "to the end of the account of the tabernacle"). From Deut. 31:26 he further concludes that the remaining books were revealed to Moses "at the end of wandering in the desert."[4] (But cf. Comments E–75 and 79.)

THEISM, NATURALISM, AND THE TORAH IN JUDAISM TODAY

As the two most "liberal" God-oriented denominations within contemporary Judaism, the Reform and Reconstructionist movements developed as modern accommodations to the literal orthodoxy of traditional Judaism. But in terms of formal doctrine, their responses were significantly different. Reform Judaism remains premised on a God of limited transcendence, as evolved from the Torah. As a matter of basic doctrine, it posits His existence as a separate Being, distinct from humanity itself. Yet Reform Judaism finds itself restive regarding the extent of His intervention in human affairs.

A prime example of such discomfort is the redefinition of God's role as author of the Torah. In this regard, consider the following statement by Rabbi Plaut, a major scholar and theologian of Reform Judaism: "The Torah is ancient Israel's distinctive record of its search for God. It attempts to record the meeting of the human and the Divine, the great moments of encounter. Therefore, the text is often touched by the ineffable Presence. The Torah tradition testifies to a people of extraordinary spiritual sensitivity. God is not the author of the text, the people are; but God's voice may be heard through theirs if we listen with open minds." [5]

This formal acceptance of the Torah's human authorship reflects the impact of naturalism on Reform Judaism. What else can account for this explicit departure from Judaism's traditional claim of direct divine revelation? It is both an honest and a necessary concession to modern perceptions of reality. To satisfy contemporary nonorthodox standards of credibility, Reform Judaism imposes limits on His capacity to intervene in human affairs. In this case, Rabbi Plaut is compelled to remove its God from His critical role as the Torah's author, even as he posits His continuing transcendence as a "Divine" or "ineffable Presence."

In the actual liturgy of Reform Judaism, however, such carefully crafted limitations of power are rarely, if ever, found. The following passage from the Rosh Hashonah Morning Service typifies the *liturgical* adherence of Reform Judaism to the traditional role of its God as author of the Torah. "In a cloud of glory, You spoke in holy address to Your people. We felt Your presence, a luminous mist. Your voice resounding from the very heavens. As all creation trembled, You revealed Your Torah to us at Sinai." Thus, what Reform Judaism purports to take from its God through "rational" commentary, it restores through vivid liturgical prose. Even if we assume that most congregants are familiar with the commentary, it is the liturgy that they repeat, and hear repeated, in the reverential atmosphere of a religious service. Whatever they "know" of the commentary, it is the liturgy that is meant to fill their spirits.

When reality compels a doctrinal transfer of Torah authorship from its God to humanity, it seems fair to ask, where does the accommodation end? Which Godly miracles of the Torah are to remain facts rather than metaphors? And if we come to regard all of His miraculous manifestations of power as metaphoric, then what is left of Him, as a Being? These are questions that Reform Judaism must yet address.

Rabbi Mordecai M. Kaplan, the founder of Jewish Reconstructionism, sought to relieve nonfundamentalist Judaism of such troubling tensions by discarding its traditional view of God. No longer would He exist as a transcendent Being, supremely independent of the natural order and humanity itself. Reconstructionism has been thus described as "the creative adaptation of the values of naturalism, pragmatism and functionalism for Jews who can no longer accept the inherited presuppositions and authority of supernaturalism."[6] Yet, although Reconstructionism formally discards the basic god-idea of Judaism, it looks to a conception of "God" as the ultimate foundation of human spirituality.

Rabbi Kaplan's verbal formulations of his god-idea include the following: (1) "It is sufficient that God should mean to us the sum of the animating, organizing forces and relationships which are forever making a cosmos out of chaos." (2) "What a Hallelujah would resound . . . if all peoples proclaimed that God was to be found in whatever there exists of man's urge to truth, honesty, empathy, loyalty, justice, freedom and goodwill!" (3) "The Torah may still be considered a divine revelation in the sense that it testifies to the reality of God as *the spirit that promotes righteousness in the world.*"[7]

For many Jews, Rabbi Kaplan's rejection of a separate transcendent Being as Judaism's God crossed the line between accommodation and apostasy. But his deep personal roots in Orthodox and Conservative Judaism, and his studies in sociology, committed him to the peoplehood and traditions of Judaism. It is this commitment that might explain both his creation of a naturalistic God *and* the pervasive presence of a transcendent God throughout Reconstructionist liturgy. ("Praises to God who rested from all labors of Creation! On the seventh day did God ascend, returning to the throne of glory."[8]) Here, too, the Godly vision of Reconstructionist congregants may be shaped more by the repetition of prayers than by formal doctrine. (I will comment further on Rabbi Kaplan's views in the conclusion.)

In recent years, my youthful fascination with the Torah was revived in many

Saturday morning minyan discussions at a major Reform congregation bordering Chicago. I was struck by the varied premises used by thoughtful congregants in regard to (1) divine or human Torah authorship and (2) the reality of Godly intervention in human and other earthly matters. Our discussions were too often blurred by the reluctance of congregants to acknowledge the differing premises and to address their interpretive implications. These impediments to more probing discussions reflected good manners rather than ignorance. Within this congregational setting there was a natural desire to avoid the disharmony that might follow a candid airing of doctrinal differences. Yet, even as I value good manners in social discourse, I was also perplexed by the resulting constraints on the substance of our discussions.

From these concerns a conviction emerged. As a people and a culture, Judaism could gain much by contemplating the full significance of the human origins of the Torah and its God.

TORAH AUTHORSHIP

On the premise of the Torah's human authorship, the identification of its particular sources has been the subject of much scholarly attention. As developed from the work of the late nineteenth-century German scholars Julian Wellhausen and Karl Graf, the so-called Documentary Hypothesis has provided a major structural framework for modern research.[9] It posits four principal sources of the written Torah. These are designated as "J," "E," "P" and "D."[10] Based on these early formulations, modern scholars have reached a measure of agreement on several important issues. These relate to (1) the order and approximate time periods in which the various sources were written; (2) certain perspectives and interests of each source and (3) the likely authorship of particular components of the Torah. Also widely accepted is the role of one or more final redactors ("R") who combined the texts of the separate sources into what we now know as the Torah.

Together with its acceptance of the human authorship of the Torah, Reform Judaism also largely accepts the basic tenets of the Documentary Hypothesis, as developed through continuing scholarship.[11] In drawing on this scholarship, I will rely both on a broad general consensus and the particular work of the eminent biblical scholar of the University of California, San Diego, Professor Richard Elliot Friedman.[12]

The designation of "J" as the earliest source derives mainly from its opening and continuing reference to God as *yahweh*, or *jahweh* in German. (This derives from the Hebrew letters that identify the Torah's God as *yehovah*, or "Lord.") "J" also identifies the source as oriented to Judah in the South, especially the Kingdom of Judah following the post-Solomon division of the United Monarchy into Israel and Judah, c. 922. J is thought to have written as early as 1000–900 B.C.E., but also as late as the eighth century. More generally, however, his work is attributed to the late tenth century B.C.E. (c. 950–900). Accordingly, even as the earliest source, J wrote centuries after the putative events of the Torah.

The "E" source derives its name from its early reference to God as *elohim* (to which might be added the dominance of the tribe of Ephraim in the north). As a voice for the concerns of the northern Kingdom of Israel, E is thought to have written between c. 922 and 722 B.C.E.—but more likely in the early or mid ninth century (c. 900–850). Among Israel's interests was the opposition of its kings and priests to the centralization of ritual sacrifices in the Jerusalem Temple.

"D" derives from Deuteronomy and is also widely viewed as author of the six books of Joshua through Kings. The High Priest Hilkiah reputedly "found" a draft of Deuteronomy which he gave to King Josiah of Judah in c. 622 B.C.E. Unique though it is in many respects, its format reads as a summary of post-Sinai (or Horeb) events. While Deuteronomy was not completed in large part much before its "discovery" in 622 B.C.E., its "Code of Law" likely dates back to c. 775–725 B.C.E. (As to a later "D2," see Comment D–38 pt. 3.)

"P," most likely the latest source, refers to the "Priestly" authors supportive of the Aaronide priesthood in Jerusalem. Of central importance to P was its unique ordained status (as distinguished from the northern Levitical priests and other priestly challengers in Jerusalem). P's emphasis on the centralization of ritual sacrifices in the Temple priesthood did much to mark it as the most "orthodox" of the four sources. The P source was likely written in stages, perhaps from as early as 750 to as late as 500 B.C.E.

The vital role of oral tradition in the creation of the Torah must also be noted. Many stories, episodes, and laws were not so much initiated within the various sources as they were assembled and restated by them.

Finally, there is R's critical role as redactor(s) or editor(s). Assuming a *general* pattern of Torah authorship like that suggested above, R's task was to meld the various sources, including different perspectives and nomenclature, into a reasonably coherent whole. This process was likely completed during the fifth century B.C.E. Scholars differ, however, on whether completion occurred before or after Ezra's return from the Babylonian exile, c. 450 B.C.E.

Coherence and consistency were among the principal editorial challenges to R. Whether from literary or liturgical respect, or political prudence, or all three, R sought to preserve the distinctive contributions and perspectives of each source. Because of his qualifications and imputed possession of the completed Torah, Ezra is widely regarded as, at least, the principal "R" (see 8 Neh. 1–18).

SOME PRINCIPLES OF INTERPRETATION

In approaching the Torah and its God from the perspectives of human author-ship and naturalism, we should first consider some basic principles of interpre-tation.

First, in searching for the substance of the Torah's God we should be mindful that His words and deeds are not "His," but are words and deeds attrib-uted to Him by His creators.

Second, from the style of the Torah it *usually* appears that events are being recorded as they occur. As previously noted, however, modern scholarship places its likely creation between c. 950 and 450 B.C.E. In comparison, the final events of the Torah, just preceding the Israelites' entry into Canaan, would have likely occurred c. 1300–1250 B.C.E.

Accordingly, the various authors wrote in the context of issues confronting Israel long after its entry into Canaan. As of 922 B.C.E. Israel's United Monarchy was divided into the separate Kingdoms of Israel and Judah. Even while "united," the North and South were beset by rivalries. Yet, there were also common concerns for the identity and perpetuation of the entire people.

One critical problem was the persistent challenge to *yahweh's* supremacy posed by the lure of the Canaanite deities, especially Baal and Asherah. That challenge became personified in Jezebel (c. 900–840 B.C.E.), the north Canaanite (Phoenician) wife of King Ahab of Israel. As queen, Jezebel would live in latter-day infamy as prime instigator in Israel of the worship of Baal and other Canaanite deities. It was amidst these and other concerns that the Torah's authors wrote from perspectives bearing on the social, political, and spiritual issues of their time and place. Thus, while we must first seek the Torah's mean-ings in its literal words (see principle 3, below), we may also ponder the "why" of those meanings. Our answers will often be found in the concerns of "later" periods in which the Torah was written.

In regard to its modern spiritual relevance, caution in reading the Torah is warranted. Most readers will view its social and cultural norms relating to women and war as anathemas. With but few exceptions, the status of women in the Torah varies between subordination and irrelevance. In this, the Torah mir-rors the societal standards of the Near East at the dawn of history. The same may be said of the wanton and quixotic mayhem that the Torah attributes to its God. In searching for any contemporary relevance in the Torah, a reader must be ever mindful that its God was meant to make His mark in a very different stage of history.

And on the subject of history, there is a further point to consider. Much of what the Torah's authors wrote was inevitably influenced by the turbulent events of the times *in which* they wrote. The much earlier events *of which* they wrote, however, were largely the product of myths, legends, and personal inspiration. As recorded in Exodus through Deuteronomy, the central narrative that brings Moses and the Israelites from Egypt to Moab, *whatever its possible factual roots*, lacks verification beyond the Torah. Thus, to regard this narrative as history requires a deep-rooted faith in the Torah as a repository of revealed truths.[13]

As for Genesis, historicity could only begin with Abraham, following the mythic tales that conclude with the Tower of Babel. However, as typically stated by one major scholar, and despite the paucity of evidence, the patriarchal narratives of Abraham, Isaac and Jacob (and his progeny) could well include a "*kernel* of authentic history."[14]

Third, our primary source of Torah interpretation will be the literal meaning of its words. Literalism in Torah interpretation is often identified with a quest for "truth," as revealed in the words of its God. Thus, as a sacred and perfect document revealed by God to Moses, each word of the Torah is thought to embody His precise meaning and purpose. Our quest for "truth," however, is not to establish the perfect consistency of a divinely revealed document. It is to determine the meaning of the text in light of its multiple human authorship over a span of some five hundred years.

The Torah's terseness inevitably imposes severe strains on its literal interpretation. Such difficulties would have added impetus to the fiction of the Oral Law. Its basis was that God had revealed not only the written Torah to Moses, but also a supplemental body of "Oral Law." In time, from the recordation of the "Oral Law" (as formulated in fact by human authority) came the Mishnah (as the Codified "Oral Law") and the Commentary (also known as the Talmud or Gemara). Together, they came to comprise the entire Talmud. Thus, the Talmud came to be revered as the fruits of a faithful intergenerational transmission of God's Oral Law, followed by its being written, organized, formally codified, and explained. These four processes were the work of the Scribes, the Tannaim, and the Amoraim. (Their ranks included such luminaries as Rabbis Hillel and Shammai and Judah ha-Nasi, as principal codifier of the Mishnah.) The era of the Scribes (as recorders of the "Oral Law" that would later be codified as the Mishnah) was basically that of the Second Temple (c. 450 B.C.E. to 70 C.E.). The period of the Tannaim (as organizers and codifiers of the Mishnah) extended to c. 200 C.E. The period of the Amoraim (as rabbinic commentators in Babylonia and Palestine) continued to as late as c. 500 C.E.[15]

In essence, then, the Mishnah, as such, was treated theologically as a divine supplement to the Torah, comprised of oral revelations that its God had chosen not to include in the written Torah. As the product of human authors, the Mishnah regularly addresses the Torah's many ambiguities and contradictions that plead for authoritative interpretation. Too often, however, its embellishments serve more to amend than to interpret the Torah.

Consider the thrice-stated Torah injunction: "You shall not boil a kid in its mother's milk." First found in Exod. 23:19, it is repeated in Exod. 34:26 and Deut. 14:21. From this ritualistic prohibition was launched a breathtaking rabbinic leap to a great defining principle of Jewish dietary law. Thus, in 8 Hullin 1 we find the following: "Every kind of flesh is forbidden to be cooked in milk, excepting the flesh of fish and locusts; and it is also forbidden to place flesh upon the table with cheese, excepting the flesh of fish and locusts." In this way, the Talmud seizes on a narrow Torah command to prohibit the simultaneous consumption of meat and dairy products. To the meat of mammals it adds the flesh of fowl. No less than "fish and locusts," however, fowl falls outside of any logically defensible expansion of the prohibition. Thus, if human sensibilities recoiled from the boiling of a young mammal in its mother's milk, it would make sense to consider the kid and its mother as representative of all *mammals*. But even under such a "rational" extension, the principle could never apply to milkless fowls.

The Torah's authors of this distinctive prohibition might well have been stunned by this later Talmudic reading. (Its possible relationship to pagan fertility rites was posited by Maimonides.[16]) In any case, this interpretive leap from Torah to Talmud presumably reflects a rabbinic effort to reshape this odd prohibition into a rule of common conduct that would help bind the people to each other and their God. Indeed, the entire Talmud was effectively directed to this purpose. *As a human interpretive document*, however, the Talmud's rightful role would not have been to amend the Torah, but to credibly resolve its *ambiguities and contradictions*. Nevertheless, in practice, Judaism has allowed such Talmudic interpretations to *supercede* the Torah's words without benefit of formal amendment. Such considerations limit the use of the Talmud to explain the Torah.

Similar considerations limit the use of Midrash. Midrash is variously described as (1) "the method by which the ancient Rabbis investigated Scripture in order to make it yield laws and teachings not apparent in a surface reading" and (2) "a sophisticated interpretive system that reconciled apparent biblical contradictions, established the scriptural basis of new laws, and enriched biblical content with new meaning."[17] Writing from a deep belief in theistic transcendence, Jacob Neusner, a leading scholar of Judaic biblical literature, vests Midrashic speculation with an even broader sweep: "In following Midrash into the inner structure of revelation . . . we enter into the mind of God—that one God who revealed the Torah and created the world and who thereby exposed for us the inner workings of God's mind."[18]

From such perspectives, Midrashic interpretations often take their readers on soaring flights of imagination involving both Halakhah (law) and Aggadah (narrative) in the Torah. Here I readily concede that a measure of speculation is both unavoidable and essential in Torah interpretation. And to this general principle, speculations that proceed from a "naturalistic" reading are no exception. But given my own reluctance to speculate from a premise of Godly transcendence, I will not rely (but once) on Midrashic explanations.

Here, however, I must pause to clarify an important point. It is one thing to limit one's recourse to the Talmud and Midrash where the particular aim is to interpret the Torah from a naturalistic assumption of human authorship. It is quite another thing, however, to ignore their vital roles in Judaic culture. For many, of course, both Talmud and Midrash are indispensable to any understanding of the Torah itself. But wherever one stands on the uses of Talmud and Midrash in Torah interpretation, there is a common ground on which all can stand. It is simply this: If we see the Torah as the fountainhead of Judaism, we can also envision the Talmud and Midrash as great rivers which flow from it to nourish Judaic culture in all of its many aspects.

From the rigor of Talmudic studies developed a cultural affinity for the process of learning. From the poetic imagery of Midrash came inspiration for Hasidic vibrance and Kabbalistic mysticism. In short, that my inquiry does not draw on Talmud and Midrash in no way lessens my respect for their rich and creative cultural endowments to Judaism.

Another characteristic of a humanist approach to the Torah is a welcoming receptivity to scholarship bearing on all of its human origins. Neither the authors of the Torah nor the Israelites of whom they were a part lived in isolation from the surrounding nations and peoples of the Near East. We should expect as a matter of course that the Torah would partake of the myths, legends, and cultures of those nations and peoples. Modern archeological discoveries and scholarship confirm such expectations.[19] Creation and the Great Flood, the early defining events of Genesis, clearly have earlier sources in the Babylonian epic of Enuma Elish and the Mesopotamian epic of Gilgamesh. The Garden of Eden would seem to be rooted in a legendary Sumerian theme of an earthly utopia. The story of the Tower of Babel alludes to the great Ziggarut Tower of Ur, or others, in Babylonia. The parallels continue as the Torah moves into the dawn of history. Elements of the Torah covenant between the people and their God resemble an early Hittite covenant between King and vassals. Egyptian circumcision preceded the role of Hebrew circumcision.

Other contributions to the Torah from neighboring cultures, past and present, could also be cited. But in this inquiry the fact of such "borrowings" is of limited import. The authors of the Torah were not plagiarists. What they "borrowed" from other cultures, they adapted to their own distinct purposes. The theme of godly creation may have been inspired by Enuma Elish, but the details and consequences as they appear in early Genesis were not. The Torah goes on to tell of a God whose attributes and relations with humankind are unique to the Torah. Accordingly, my inquiry will concern itself with the Torah's use of its borrowed materials, not on the fact they were borrowed.

CONCLUSION

Even as we seek to explore the relevance of the Torah's transcendent God to contemporary humanist principles and values, we can hardly ignore the monumental presence of Maimonides, the Rambam. (Nor should he be confused with his great Torah "colleague," Nachmanides, the Ramban). In his time (1135–1204) Maimonides sought to forge a complete identity between the Torah's God and his own. His was omnipotent, omniscient, omnipresent, incorporeal, inscrutable, and perfect. From his faith in both of these Gods, he viewed them as One.

Maimonides viewed the Torah's many troubling allusions to a seemingly anthropomorphic God as a practical necessity. For him, the God of the Torah effected His human physical manifestations and encounters as needful "competitive" responses to other gods whose realities were regularly evoked through idols and images. He regarded these manifestations and encounters as temporary psychological aids to give the people confidence that He existed. In this, Maimonides' God was a practical God.[20] I find support for my own efforts in his recognition that the Torah was shaped (in his case by God) to meet the needs of a given time, place, and people.

Being neither a biblical scholar, theologian, nor philosopher, I approach my inquiry from my training and experience as a lawyer and teacher of law. Accordingly, my method is that of induction. In reading a complex document, I first seek meaning in its words and their textual contexts. I thus limit my interpretive excursions beyond the text to the resolution of ambiguities or contradictions to which the entire text offers no adequate answers. But whenever possible, without undue strain on the text, I look for meaning in the document itself—in this case, the Torah.

Finally, I would again emphasize that any effort to establish the Torah's contribution to humanist values must allow for time. As humanity evolves, so, too, do its moral, ethical, and behavioral standards, together with its spiritual perceptions. In creating a God of the Torah, its human authors, in their time, wrote from the highest realms of the human spirit. In considering the humanist aspects of their Creation and the purposes He was meant to serve, we should strive as we can toward their heights, but in our time.

1.

GENESIS

INTRODUCTION

As an ancient literary masterpiece, Genesis quickly reveals an ancient literary truth. It is, simply put, that a good story, once told well, can often gain much and lose nothing in the retelling. It first makes the point in its two distinct versions of primal creation. The two versions then introduce us to the work of the redactor(s) ("R"), who wove the various strands of the Torah into its final fabric. I refer to the two distinct but inseparable creation stories as Creation I and II (Gen. 1:1–2:3 and 2:4–3:24).

Throughout the Torah we will encounter many varied versions of a single, or similar, event. Yet none ever equals the remarkable symbiosis of Creation I and II. Both were drawn from legendary mists by imaginative authors who wrote centuries apart. From R's artful union of these two versions, a mythic framework emerges within which humanity and the God of the Torah are meant to relate to each other.

The two versions of primal creation differ in mood and detail. But more important is a quality they share. Neither offers a theological nor metaphysical basis for its God. It is a simple "given" in both that primal creation arose solely from the purpose, power, and Being of its God.

CREATION I: "MAN IN THE IMAGE OF GOD"

In a clockwork sequence of events during the six days of creation, Creation I portrays a remote, but purposeful and well-ordered, God.

> *Note G–1: In Creation I (Gen. 1:1–2:3), P identifies the Creator as* elohim, *meaning "God." On P's general use of* elohim *and* yahweh, *see Note G–4.*

The powers required for His undertaking, and the ease of its accomplishment, can only be meant to imply His omnipotence. In the first four days of creation His purpose is to provide an earthly environment suited to all its inhabitants. On the first day He creates light and separates it from the darkness so that there may be day and night. On the second day He creates "an expanse" (or "firmament") to separate the waters below from those above. He calls the expanse "Sky," or "Heaven" (from the Hebrew *shamayim*). Having separated the earth, water, and sky, on the third day He creates every type of vegetation, followed by the sun, moon, and stars on the fourth day. Together they will mark the days, seasons, and years (1:1–19).

> *Note G–2: Nothing is said of the source of light or the measure of days before the creation of the sun.*

On the fifth day God creates every type of creature, from the minute to the monstrous, who are to fill the waters and sky (1:20–21). He then confers His blessing on them. "Be fertile and increase, fill the waters of the seas, and let the birds increase on the earth" (1:22).

On the sixth day, before turning to humankind as His final creation, God creates the lesser creatures of the land, that is, "every kind of living creature: cattle, creeping things, and wild beasts of every kind" (1:24).

Prior to His creation of humankind, the God of Creation I appraised His work at various stages. In each case He "saw [it] was good" (1:4, 10, 12, 18, 21, 25). He is now ready for the culmination of His creativity. To that end He proclaims His intent to "make man *in our image, after our likeness*," whose "mission," He declares, will be to "rule" all other earthly creatures and "the whole earth" (1:26). Accordingly, He then creates "man in His image, in the image of God He created him; *male and female He created them*" (1:27).

In conferring His blessing of fruitfulness on both great orders of earthly life, "God blessed them, saying 'Be fertile and increase' " (1:22, 28). For humans alone, however, He adds a charge to His initial blessing: " 'Be fertile and increase, fill the earth *and master it; and rule the fish of the sea, the birds of the sky, and all the living things that creep on earth*' " (1:28).

> *Note G–3: Land animals were not created until the sixth day. Thus, God's blessing of the fifth day on lesser animal life was technically limited to birds and fish. Surely, however, the author would have wished Him to bless all land animals no less than those of the waters and air.*

God then prescribes vegetarian diets for humans and animals alike. As food for humans, He designates "every seed bearing plant . . . and every tree that has seed bearing fruit" (1:29). To all other creatures, He gives "all the green plants"

(1:30). Having previously judged each stage of prehuman creation to be "good," on completing His creation of the sixth day, God then declares the totality of His work to be "very good" (1:31). On the seventh day, God "ceased from all the work of creation which He had done." He then blesses the day and declares it holy (2:1–3). Creation I is now ended, with no further word regarding His relations with the nameless male and female.

Comment G–1. On "man" in the image of God

The Torah's concept of humankind in the "image," or "likeness," of its God is basic to both the intended mission of humankind and its relations with its Creator. But with what qualities of its God does the Torah mean to endow human beings? What has it revealed of Him that is true of us?

Of His physical character and appearance (if any) Creation I says nothing. Accordingly, our first impulse might be to imagine P's God as a reverse image of "man." If humans are said to exist as images, or likenesses, of their Creator, will they not envision Him as they see themselves? Yet the passage includes an impediment to envisioning Him as "man's" reverse physical image. Recall the words of 1:27: "And God created man in His image, in the image of God He created him; *male and female He created them.*"

Is He to be "seen" as androgynous? In the context of Creation I, the passage is less than decisive on the point. From the several references to "man" in Creation I as "they," or "them" (1:26–28), it seems reasonable to construe the "man" of 1:27 as all humanity. Indeed the use of "them" and of "male and female" in 1:27 to modify "man" erases any doubt. If so, any reverse likeness of God as a physical image of the human male *and* female must either include, or exclude, all physical characteristics unique to either. Surely the author of Creation I did not mean to cast its God in such a bewildering physical image.

But the case can also be made that 1:27 was but a reflection of social realities. Thus, its reference to "man in His image," or "likeness," might well evoke visions of a male God. This would comport with the Torah's consistent portrayal of its God as a male. Thus, if "image" or "likeness" were construed as a "physical resemblance," the intent to portray an anthropomorphic male image of God is at least a possibility. Such a clear-cut physical likeness between God and "man" (politically correct in its time) would offer "visual" support for His reality. Nevertheless, the case for construing "image" and "likeness" as nonphysical metaphors finds stronger support in the point at which the critical pronouncement is made.

On reaching 1:27, we know nothing of the God of Creation I other than His role as Creator. Thus, as He is creative, so, too, is humanity. *The author, however, could not mean to confer God's full creativity on human beings. To do so would be to equate His creativity with the obvious limits of human cre-*

ativity. Instead, the author views human creativity as derivative from God's primal creative power. To humankind, therefore, the story of Creation I ascribes a lesser creative capacity, but one which will dominate life on earth. It is thus humanity's prime duty to exercise its unique creativity in pursuit of its unique earthly purpose.

But what is that purpose? It is revealed in the words of the God of Creation I. Having judged each stage of His work to be "good," He finds His total creation to be "very good." But "very good" is not perfect. It implies room for improvement. Given this all too apparent reality, the author posits a deliberate shortfall between the quality of primal creation and the goal of earthly perfection. As the purposeful core of God's plan in Creation I, the shortfall provides the purpose of humanity's existence. It is to complete the process of primal creation, that is, to raise the condition of earthly existence from "very good" to perfect. Thus, the Torah's first great charge to humanity is to perfect the quality of earthly existence.

It is humanity's unique capacity to strive for this purpose that enables the Torah to confirm its dominion over all other earthly creatures. *As envisioned in Creation I,* to the extent that humanity fails to fulfil its unique role, the entire earth is denied its sole source of purposeful improvement. In this lies the moral essence of Creation I.

But what particular qualities are included in humanity's derivative creativity? Ideally, they should encompass every quality of mind, spirit, and body necessary, or useful, to humanity's earthly purposes. Whether they should include free will is an issue left to Creation II.

Comment G–2. On human and animal fertility

As directed to humans, to "Be fertile and increase" constitutes God's first formal command, or *mitzvah.* As to animals, however, it can be no more than a blessing or wish. By their nature, they can neither comprehend nor obey a command that requires a future course of conduct. But if words directed to animals are understood as a laudatory blessing of their natural impulses, why should the same words directed to humankind not be understood in the same way?

Given the particular social value of fecundity to a people confronted by powerful foes, a flat command from Israel's God would have served them better than His good wishes. Nevertheless, whether as a command, a blessing, or a wish, the broader charge of Creation I is to consider reproduction in qualitative as well as quantitative terms. However compelling its claim and fulfillment, reproduction, like all human conduct, remains subject to humanity's basic responsibility for the overall quality of earthly existence.

Comment G–3. On animal vegetarianism and God's powers

In mandating animal vegetarianism, the Torah challenges the power of its God over the natural order. Knowing of the widespread consumption of meat by many animals, how will humans, knowing of their God's contrary purpose, interpret His inability to fulfil His plan for the natural order?

CREATION II: ADAM AND EVE AND THE MATTER OF FREE WILL

If the "God" of Creation I was purposeful but remote in creating humankind, the "Lord God" of Creation II may seem less decisive but more involved. If humanity was created in "God's" image, "Lord God" may seem to repay the compliment.

> *Note G–4: From Creation II through the banishment of Adam and Eve from Eden, elohim, the "God" of Creation I, becomes yahweh elohim, or "Lord God." Authorship of Creation I and II is attributed to P and J, respectively. Thus it is P who speaks of elohim, or "God," and J who speaks of yahweh elohim, or "the Lord God." As noted in the Introduction, J is characterized by the consistent use of yahweh, or "Lord" (both with and without elohim). To the contrary, however, P, in essence, continues to use elohim through Genesis to Exod. 6:2–3, where, in a "P" passage, P's elohim first reveals His name to Moses as yahweh. From there on, in referring to the Torah's God, P will typically combine yahweh and elohim (e.g., "I am the Lord, your God").*

Even before the creation of vegetation, Lord God of Creation II forms "man" (i.e., only "a" man), not in His image, but more modestly, "from the dust of the earth." "Man" then becomes alive when Lord God blows the "breath of life" through his nostrils (2:4–7). So that "the man" might "till it and tend it," Lord God sets him in a paradisical Garden of Eden (2:8, 15). He tells the man that he may eat of every tree (including the tree of life), but not of the "tree of knowledge of good and bad." As for that tree, "*as soon as you eat of it you shall die*" (2:16–17).

> *Note G–5: JPS1 and RSV convey a similar sense of instant death. Thus, Adam will die "in the day that you eat of it."*[1]

Comment G–4. On Lord God's "threat" of Adam's death

When told by Lord God not to eat from the tree of knowledge of good and bad, the man (now called Adam) is in a state of innocence. Lord God knows full well that Adam has no knowledge of right and wrong, and in particular that he knows of no moral obligation to obey Lord God. Accordingly, unless Lord God imposes physical barriers to Adam's access to the forbidden tree, He can only hope that Adam's fear of extinction exceeds the lure of the forbidden fruit. In effect, then, Lord God has chosen to gamble. His gamble is a second sign of His indecision on whether Adam should come to know of good and evil. The first, of course, was to place the tree in the path of temptation. The question, then, is whether fear alone can "save" Adam from temptation. Because of Adam's innocence, however, Lord God knows that He could never fulfil His threat of immediate death.

When Lord God goes on to create the "wild beasts" and "birds," He gives Adam the honor of naming them. So that he should not be alone and without a helpmate, Lord God makes a woman from Adam's rib (2:21–22). In their innocence, Adam and the woman feel no shame in being naked (2:25).

Although Lord God, Himself, does not directly forbid the woman from eating of the tree, Adam has apparently told her of His command and the penalty for disobedience. Though initially determined to obey, she meets a clever serpent endowed with human speech. It urges her to eat of the tree (3:1). She demurs, citing Lord God's warning that "you shall not eat of it or touch it, lest you die" (3:2–3). But the serpent is said to be the "shrewdest" of all beasts. "It" first assures Eve that even if she should eat of the forbidden tree, "you are not going to die" (3:4). To this it adds a beguiling non sequitur: "God knows that as soon as you eat of it your eyes will be opened and you will be like divine beings who know good and bad" (3:5).

The serpent's apparent purpose is to learn whether a promise to Eve to know of good and bad is tempting enough to overcome Lord God's threat of death. The assurance that she would not die (at least not at once) is meant to tip the scale.

Because Eve desires the knowledge of which the serpent spoke, she eats of the forbidden fruit (3:6). Having done so, she shares it with Adam. Now aware of their nakedness, they fashion loincloths from fig leaves (3:7). When Lord God asks, "Where are you?" and if they had eaten of the tree, they confess their disobedience (3:9–13).

Adam's fear proves greater than his appreciation of good and evil. He blames the woman, and even Lord God. He tells Him: "The woman You put at my side—she gave me of the tree and I ate" (3:12). The woman then blames the serpent. "The serpent duped me, and I ate" (3:13). (Knowing now of good and evil, they sense that to disobey Lord God is evil.)

Lord God then decrees consequences akin to punishments. He deals first with the serpent who, through his puzzling power of speech, had induced the woman to disobey Him. The serpent must forever crawl on its belly and eat dirt. In addition, Lord God declares eternal enmity between its "offspring" and those of the woman (3:14–15).

Comment G–5. On the serpent's "punishments"

Had the serpent truly possessed an independent power of speech, the most fitting punishment for its abuse would be its loss. Because its "punishment" lacks this element, we must ask if the serpent was indeed the actual source of its own words. Like other animals, serpents were not endowed with the capacity of human speech. *Within the theistic protocols of the Torah*, it could speak only through the will of Lord God. Thus, in "speaking" to Eve, the serpent did so as the voiceless instrument of another being with the power and purpose to use it as its agent. And who but Lord God, or a designated "divine being," could combine that ability and intent? What, then, can explain such Divine gamesmanship?

Lord God cannot decide whether Adam and Eve should know of good and evil. He thus resolves to let them choose. He then places the tree in their path and seeks to entice them through the serpent. By easing Eve's fear of death, He hopes to enhance the appeal of the forbidden fruit.

In telling his story, J had no wish to reveal the full measure of Lord God's anguished indecision. Thus, to hide His identity as the source of Eve's temptation, J knew He would have to rebuke the serpent. Justice, however, would allow no more than an appearance of punishment. That the serpent must crawl on its belly was merely a preexisting burden imposed by the act of creation. As for the enmity between humans and serpents, nature played no less a role. Therefore, in using the circumstances of nature to mask Lord God's equivocation, J asks us to acknowledge the serpent's innocence and to restore its good name among animals.

In responding to Eve's "disobedience," Lord God adds a complication to the *mitzvah* of fertility in Creation I. Eve will acquire a powerful disincentive to reproduction—"the most severe . . . pangs in child bearing." But to neutralize the disincentive, she will have an urge and desire for her husband, even as she remains subject to his "rule" (3:16). Lord God then responds to Adam's disobedience: "Cursed be the ground because of you; By toil shall you eat of it *all the days of your life. . . . By the sweat of your brow shall you get bread to eat until you return to the ground . . . for dust you are and to dust shall you return*" (3:17–19).

Comment G–6. On the "punishment" of Adam and "the woman": a preliminary view

By its terms the enmity between the serpent and the woman will extend to their offspring (3:15). In apparent contrast, the harshest realities of the human condition—pain, toil, and mortality are literally limited to "Adam" and "the woman" (3:16–19). But since these afflictions have been the lot of humanity ever since, we may assume that Lord God of Creation II meant them for their descendants as well. Thus, by attributing these harsh realities to human conduct rather than to flaws of original creation, J deftly shifts the responsibility from Lord God to humanity itself.

But what of the justice of imposing such consequences on Adam and Eve? Not only did they commit their acts in a state of innocence, they also did nothing other than what an equivocating Lord God had encouraged them to do. (For a final view on the "punishments" see Comment G-9.)

Adam now names his wife Eve, as "mother of all the living" (3:20) and Lord God makes them garments of skins before banishing them from Eden forever. Clearly, however, J's Lord God perceives a need for banishment that transcends mere punishment. Adam and Eve must be banished less for what they have done than for what Lord God fears they might do next—that is, eat from the "tree of life." He states his fear as follows: "Now that *the man* has become like one of us, knowing good and bad, what if he should . . . take from the tree of life and eat, and live forever!" (3:22). To prevent "him" from gaining immortality, Lord God "drove *the man* out" of Eden. He also barred the return of Adam and Eve by stationing "cherubim and the fiery ever-turning sword to guard the way to the tree of life" (3:24).

> Note G–6: In 3:22–24, JPS1 and RSV, as well as JPS2, *correctly speak of* "the man" (ha'adam) and "him" rather than "man" alone, which would include Eve as another human being. In this nod to "political correctness" in its time, the Torah converts the venturesome Eve from the true protagonist of Creation II into the man's passive mate.

Comment G–7. On "knowledge of good and bad" as either moral discernment or knowledge bordering on omniscience

The tree of knowledge is more fully described as "the tree of knowledge of good and bad" (2:17). The critical question is the meaning of "good and bad." Is it meant as moral discernment, or as wider knowledge, perhaps bordering on omniscience? On this Plaut observes that the Torah's occasional use of opposites such as "good and bad" and "moist and dry" are meant as merisms, that is, opposite extremes meaning "everything." (As to 3:22, Rashi speaks of "knowing of good and evil."[2] He says nothing of broader knowledge.)

There are practical problems in construing "knowledge of good and evil" as a "merism." Were it so, then Adam and Eve, on acquiring "knowledge of good and evil," would have gained knowledge of "everything," or omniscience. This, however, could not be the Torah's intent. To do so would equate humanity's knowledge with that of its God.

Another practical problem in equating the knowledge of good and evil with omniscience is that the knowledge, whatever it may be, is shared by other "divine beings." Thus, the serpent tells the woman that on eating of the tree she will be "like divine beings who know good and bad" (3:5). To the same effect, Lord God speaks of "man becoming like one of *us*" (3:22). The Torah will later reveal other divine beings, including angels, cherubim, and Nephilim. Do they all share the full measure of their God's knowledge? Is His knowledge to be no greater than that of His heavenly attendants?

Whether or not the Torah means to endow its God with omniscience, it surely means Him to have some measure of "cognitional" uniqueness. Thus far, we do not really know if the God of Creation I or Lord God of Creation II are meant to be omniscient. The text neither claims nor refutes it. However, unless "good and bad" is limited to moral discernment, the Torah must be understood to deny the uniqueness of its God's knowledge.

Here, however, we must consider that both JPS1 and RSV render the serpent's *elohim* as "God," rather than of "divine beings" (3:5). The Hebrew word for both is *elohim*. The absence of capitalization in Hebrew and the plural form of *elohim* permit this dual usage. However, JPS2's editor has a persuasive case for reading this *elohim* as "divine beings."[4]

Further support for reading "knowing good and evil" as moral discernment is the explicit shame of nakedness felt by Adam and Eve *after* eating of the tree of knowledge of good and evil (cf. 2:25 with 3:7,10). General knowledge is rarely a source of shame. Its source instead lies in the knowledge of one's own wrong (or of its exposure).

Gen. 3:6 might be thought to support the use of "good and bad" as a merism. Thus, when "the woman saw . . . that the tree was desireable as a source of wisdom, she took of its fruit and ate." (JPS1 and RSV also speak of her desire to be "wise.") But this reference to Eve's perception of the tree is broader than any prior description of the scope of knowledge to be gained from it. For Eve, in her innocence, knowledge of anything forbidden to her might well represent the very essence of wisdom. (Rashi also reads "making one wise," as it appears in 3:6, as "recognizing good and evil."[5])

Comment G–8. On Creation II and human free will

As revealed through its details, the parable of Adam and Eve offers a mythic approach to the dilemma of human free will. We start with the Lord God of Creation II who remains of two minds on whether Adam and Eve should eat of the tree of knowledge. Had He decided against it, He could have protected the tree from human intrusion. That He was at least partially prepared for Adam and Eve to learn of good and bad in support of human creativity was affirmed by His tempting of Eve through the serpent to eat the forbidden fruit. And once she ate, He knew the die was cast. She was sure to prevail on Adam, her mate, to share her knowledge.

Literally, of course, Adam and Eve acquired nothing more than an awareness of good and evil. Why, then, would their Creator wish to deny them this simple knowledge? The answer is that He knew enough of human nature to foresee the inevitable consequences. Human curiosity would not let the matter rest with the knowledge that good and evil existed. On learning of them, humanity would soon be impelled to learn of their differences. And as they learned of good and evil and right and wrong, they would soon realize that knowledge was of little use except as they applied it. It was for good reason, therefore, that Lord God hesitated to allow humanity to gain knowledge of good and evil. He understood that it could only lead to a human claim of decisional autonomy in choosing between right and wrong. If so, rather than *making* human choices, He would be reduced to *guiding and influencing* them. But in choosing for itself, would humanity remain aware of its responsibility for earthly perfection? And would it more likely value, or resent, the guidance of its Creator?

It was of course possible that human beings would come to cherish their free will as an invaluable element of human creativity. They might learn to direct it toward their highest goals. But mere possibilities could not ease Lord God's fears of the potential pitfalls of human free will. How easily might human free will succumb to indifference or arrogance? How often might it fall prey to clever rationalizations of right and wrong that mock the purposes of human creativity? How quickly might human perversity debase human free will to the level of human license?

And yet—however great the risks of granting human free will—were they not outweighed by the risks of its denial? Without it, could humanity draw on its other creative powers for their intended purpose? With all important choices affecting earthly well-being left to Lord God alone, could human beings ever rise above the level of moral and ethical robots, totally responsive to an external force? Could such human beings ever serve as creative stewards of earthly well-being? These were among the dilemmas faced by Lord God of Creation II as He pondered the final great issue of creation—that of human free will.

In truth, the decision was made neither by Lord God of Creation II nor Adam and Eve. Instead, it is the work of J as author and R as editor. It was R's judgment to reverse the order of antiquity between P's Creation I and J's Creation II. Thus, "together," J and R were able to confer free will on humanity as the final stage of creation.

Comment G–9. On Adam and Eve and the price of human free will

Though blameless in their state of innocence, Adam and Eve suffered consequences so much like punishment as to seem indistinguishable (see Comment G–6). Of particular interest is why Lord God was prepared to accept human immortality in the absence of human free will. As implied in His anguished outcry (3:22), His denial of immortality in the context of human free will reflected a social calculus broader than any mere wish to punish Adam and Eve. Guided by fears rather than hopes, He foresaw the growth of human arrogance and the decline of human introspection—and from both, the perversion of human free will.

This is why Lord God's initial warning to Adam not to eat of the tree of knowledge did not extend to the tree of life. Had they not eaten of the tree of knowledge, human immortality would have been theirs to keep. (But had they first eaten of the tree of life, J's Lord God would have physically barred them from the tree of knowledge.)

As with banishment, the requirement that man must toil for sustenance and woman must suffer pain in childbirth were for a purpose more compelling than punishment. Through these consequences, the parable of Adam and Eve makes three points. First, humanity's free will was acquired at a heavy price that each generation continues to pay. Second, despite the enormity of its ongoing price, its potential worth to humanity is even greater. Third, to realize that potential worth, humanity must apply its free will to the perfection of earthly existence.

However humanity chooses to exercise its free will, nothing can detract from Eve's initial courage in acquiring its potential for her descendants. Her spirit remains to remind humanity that the thirst for knowledge can prevail over the fear of death.

CAIN AND ABEL

Nowhere does the enigma of justice between the God of the Torah and humankind appear more starkly than in the story of Cain and Abel.

> Note G–7: The story continues the J narrative. Here, however, "Lord God" (the yahweh elohim of Gen. 2:4–3:24) becomes simply "the Lord" (or yahweh).

The telling of the story is simplicity itself. Cain, the first son of Adam and Eve, is a farmer. Abel, the second son, is a sheep herder. "In the course of time," *on his own initiative*, Cain brings an offering to the Lord. Only then does Abel bring an offering. Cain's offering, as a farmer, is "from the fruit of the soil"; Abel's, in turn, is from "the choicest of the firstlings of his flock" (4:3–4). Cain's knowledge of the Lord must have come from his parents. Indeed, Eve had attributed Cain's birth to "the help of the Lord" (4:1). Yet to Cain and his offering, the Lord "paid no heed," while to Abel and his, He "paid heed." Cain is "much distressed" by the Lord's rejection of his offering. In reply, the Lord offers a gratuitous homily on sin. "Why are you distressed? And why is your face fallen? Surely if you do right, there is uplift. But if you do not do right, sin couches at the door.

Its urge is toward you. Yet you can be its master" (4:7). Dispirited and bewildered, Cain then finds Abel in a field and slays him.

When the Lord asks Cain "Where is your brother Abel?" Cain answers in words forever associated with his name: "I do not know. Am I my brother's keeper?" (4:9). An angry Lord knows all, however, and responds accordingly: "What have you done? Hark, your brother's blood cries out to me from the ground. Therefore, you shall be more cursed than the ground" (4:10). Since the earth that received Abel's blood would "no longer yield its strength" to Cain, he was condemned to be a "ceaseless wanderer" (4:11–12). Cain expresses his fear that as "a restless wanderer on earth—*anyone* who meets me may kill me." The Lord then places a mark on Cain, "lest *anyone* who met him should kill him." He also promises "sevenfold vengeance . . . on him [who kills Cain]" (4:15). Cain then goes to the land of Nod, East of Eden. Though he is doomed to be a "ceaseless wanderer on earth," Cain "settled" there (4:16). Thereafter, "Cain knew his wife, and she conceived and bore Enoch" (4:17).

Comment G–10. On two aspects of the story of Cain

1. "Am I my brother's keeper?"

Cain's statement is generally taken as the apotheosis of human disregard for the life and well-being of other humans. This view ignores both Cain's intrinsic character and the circumstances that impelled him to his tragic deed. Both matters are addressed in Comment G–11.

2. The earthly presence of "anyone" and Cain's wife

The puzzle posed by the "anyone" feared by Cain is compounded by the presence of Cain's wife. Thus far we know of no humans other than Adam and Eve and Cain and Abel. Yet Cain's fears were hardly groundless. He had already found a wife. Moreover, by His "mark of Cain," J's Lord had taken his fears seriously. Could J possibly have known of an unrecorded Creation III as the source of a wife and "anyone"?

Following the birth of his son Enoch, Cain founded a city in Enoch's name. In time their descendants would lead useful and industrious lives. From Enoch there came Jabal, the "ancestor of those who dwell in tents and amidst herds"; Jabal's brother Jubal, "the ancestor of "all who play the lyre and pipe"; and Tubal-cain, "who forged all implements of copper and iron" (4:17–22).

> Note G–8: This genealogy, attributed to J, is notable for its inclusion of three women: two wives of Lamech (Adah and Zillah) and a sister to Tubal-cain (Naamah).

Comment G–11. On the story of Cain and Abel as the first post-Eden confrontation between a human and the Lord

What do Cain and Abel tell us of how the Lord proposes to relate to humanity? Of particular interest is the cause of Cain's desperation. Why did the Lord reject his offer, while accepting Abel's? The only stated distinction is that Cain brought "fruit of the soil" and Abel brought "the choicest of the firstlings of his flock."

By reasoning deductively from a fixed premise of God's "justice," Rashi suggests that Cain's offering was "from the inferior fruits."[6] While he does not comment on the quality of Abel's offering, JPS2's use of "choicest" may imply greater attention by Abel to the quality of his offering. In speaking of "firstlings" of the flock and of "the fat thereof," JPS1 and RSV also connote quality. At most, however, the Torah might credit Abel with an attention to quality greater than Cain's. But there is no suggestion that Cain had purposefully withheld the best of his produce. Indeed, it was Cain, not Abel, who brought the first offering. If not for Cain's example, would Abel have done so himself? As an "upstart" second son (in the model of Jacob to come), had Abel resolved to "outbid" Cain and thus gain the Lord's greater favor? We cannot know. Let us assume, however, that the Lord's rejection of Cain's offering reflected nothing more than a difference in the quality of the two offerings. If so, His response is that of a Being obsessed with His own dignity.

In His homily to Cain, the Lord might have been addressing the whole of humanity. In it He warns of the inherent perils of human free will. And who can protect humanity from itself? Only the Lord, Himself. Accordingly, when He chastises Cain for his distress at the rejection of his offering, He means to establish a human duty to accept His judgments with grace and resignation. It is as if He had said, "Accept My will as the source of justice. Do not pit yours against it." The well-meaning Cain cannot grasp such a standard of justice. Do his motives mean nothing?

When an anguished Cain cries out "Am I my brother's keeper?" he alludes to the despair that led him to murder. His outburst is less a disavowal of concern for Abel than an honest demand to know why his concern for his brother, or anyone, should be greater than the Lord's concern for him. Thus, his unspoken reproach to the Lord. "I came before You to acknowledge Your sanctity. How can You expect the victims of Your injustice to be more just than Yourself?"

Cain's slaying of Abel was a heinous wrong, however great the Lord's provocation. In the end, and at least for the moment, the Lord regrets the pride that prompted Him to reject Cain's offering. He thus spares Cain. *In turn, Cain has rightly learned that the Lord's injustice can never justify human injustice.* He accepts his guilt and his punishment. Cain and the Lord are then reconciled.

Meanwhile, having lost Abel by fratricide and Cain by banishment, Adam and Eve seek to fill their personal void by honoring the first *mitzvah* of Creation I. "Adam knew his wife again, and she bore him a son and named him Seth. . . . And to Seth in turn a son was born, and he named him Enosh" (4:25–26). With the birth of Enosh, "men began to invoke the Lord by name" (4:26). So it was that humanity had so far survived every test of the human spirit imposed by a proud, powerful, and sometimes all too human God of the Torah.

NOAH AND THE GREAT FLOOD

The Torah now sets out a second genealogy, or "record of Adam's line." It runs to the birth of Noah and his three sons, Shem, Ham, and Japheth (5:1–32).

> Note G–9: Friedman attributes this and other "mythic" genealogies to a larger "Book of Generations," possibly originating with P.[7] This one opens with familiar words from Creation I (cf. 1:26–27). "When God created man, He made him in the likeness of God; male and female He created them" (5:1–2). (The first of the line is Adam, a product of Creation II who is now linked to Creation I. This may illustrate why Friedman finds the hand of R in this and later genealogies.)
>
> While the genealogy alludes to various unnamed "sons and daughters," it identifies no daughters or wives by name. Notable in the long line of named sons (likely the firstborn in each case) is the "legendary" Methusaleh. Indeed, "legendary" best describes the entire genealogy. Typical among the life spans are: Adam, 930 years; Seth, 912 years; Jared, 962 years and Methusaleh, 969 years. Noah's father, Lamech, however, died at a relatively young age of 777. But even younger, was Enoch, son of Jared, who died at 365. It is said that "Enoch walked with God; then he was no more, for God took him" (5:24). The details are not given.

In time, "men began to increase on earth and daughters were born of them." Seeing their beauty "the divine beings . . . took wives from among those that pleased them" (6:1–2). It was then that "the Lord" said that "since [man] too is flesh; let [his] days be one hundred and twenty years" (6:3). "It was then, and later too, that the Nephilim appeared on earth—when the divine beings cohabited with the daughters of men who bore them offspring. They were "the heroes of old, the men of renown" (6:4).

Comment G–12. On "Nephilim," "cherubim," and other "divine beings"

The Torah's reference here to "Nephilim" and other "divine beings" (or "sons of God," per JPS1/RSV) recall earlier mythic conceptions of heavenly beings.

Thus, when Adam and Eve left Eden, their return was said to be barred by "cherubim" and the "fiery ever turning sword" (3:24).

Here the Torah tells of divine beings who cohabit and reproduce with human "daughters." This is the very stuff of mythology—a world of half-human/half-godly creatures moving freely between the heavenly habitat of the gods and the earthly habitat of humans. The gods then mate with humans to create demigods. (For whatever reason, among these "divine beings" only the "Nephilim" are capitalized.)

In the *Encyclopedia Britannica*, the word "cherubim" is traced to the Akkadian word *karibu*, meaning to pray or bless. It also notes the following: "Derived from Near Eastern mythology and iconography, these celestial beings serve important liturgical and intercessory functions in the hierarchy of angels." Cherubim are also found in Christian and Islamic literature. But in the long monotheistic tradition of heavenly beings, they first appear in the Torah.

The Torah's various categories of divine beings are portrayed as no less real than its God. As to "why," we might make a simple conjecture. From what Israelites knew of the divine assemblies of neighboring religions, how could their God alone be deprived of His own heavenly hosts?

The story of Noah and the great flood begins with J's introduction. Following the mythic tale of the divine beings and their earthly mates (6:4), it is said that "the Lord saw how great was man's wickedness . . . and how every plan devised his mind was nothing but evil." Indeed, He "regretted that He had made man on earth" (6:5–6). The intensity of His chagrin culminates in His resolve to destroy not only immoral humanity, but amoral beasts: "I will blot out from the earth . . . men together with beasts, creeping things, and the birds of the sky: for I regret that I made them" (6:7). The human exception, however, was Noah, who "found favor with the Lord" (6:8).

The disillusionment with humanity attributed by J to *yahweh* was then attributed by P to *elohim*. P then explains why, of all humanity, God will spare only the line of Noah. "Noah was a righteous man; he was blameless *in his age*; Noah walked with God" (6:9). It may also be pertinent that "Noah begot three sons: Shem, Ham, and Japheth" (6:10).

> Note G–10: *That Noah was only blameless "in his age" suggests the relativity of "blamelessness." But P also describes Noah as "righteous" in absolute terms (6:9).*

Whatever the causes of the rampant human perversity, P's God has no wish to test the possibility of human redemption. Amid the raging "lawlessness" and "corruption," He tells Noah, "I have decided to put an end to all flesh. . . . I am about to destroy them with the earth" (6:13).

His use of "all flesh," however, ignores an important exception. Thus, God proceeds to give Noah directions on the construction of a sturdy three-decked ark of "gopher wood" (6:14–16). The ark will save Noah and his line, and designated animals, from "the Flood," which will otherwise destroy "all flesh under the sky in which there is a breath of life" (6:17). He thus tells Noah: "I will establish My covenant with you, and you shall enter the ark with your sons, your wife, and your sons' wives" (6:18). "Of all that lives, of all flesh," Noah is to bring into the ark "two of each . . . to keep alive with you; they shall be male and female. From birds of every kind, cattle of every kind, every kind of creeping thing on earth, *two* of each shall come to you to stay alive" (6:19–20). And *"Noah did so; just as God commanded him, so he did"* (6:22).

> Note G–11: *"Flesh" of the waters are not among the creatures to be destroyed. Indeed, they might take a flood as a favor.*

> Note G–12: *God's revelation of His intent to Noah might be viewed as Noah's defining moment. That Noah asks no questions goes to the heart of their relations. Noah did indeed "walk with God" (6:9).*

The narrative is now J's. "Then the Lord said to Noah, 'Go into the ark with all your household, for you alone have I found righteous before Me in this generation' " (7:1).

> Note G–13: *Like P's "God," J's "Lord" deems Noah righteous at least "in this generation."*

As to Noah's "household," J's "Lord" repeats the instructions of P's "God." As to the animals, however, the instructions change: "Of every *clean* animal you shall take *seven* pairs, males and their mates, and of every animal which is *not clean,* two, a male and its mate; of the birds of the sky also, seven pairs, male and female, to keep seed alive upon all the earth" (7:1–3).

J's Lord then reveals the purpose and extent of His flood: "I will make it rain upon the earth, forty days and forty nights, and I will blot out from the earth all existence that I created." And true to form, *"Noah did just as the Lord commanded him"* (7:4–5).

> Note G–14: *The course of the flood and its completion is described in Gen. 7:6–8:19. It consists of an even more intricate and repetitive interweaving of J and P. Its wondrous and mythic details, however, are not important to our main concern of what the flood reveals of Noah and the Lord God.*

In brief, Gen. 7:6–8:19 passage tells of forty days and nights of continuous rain during the six hundreth year of Noah's life. From the flood that followed, "all existence on earth was blotted out—man, cattle, creeping things, and the birds of the sky. . . . Only Noah was left and those with him in the ark" (along with the "flesh of the waters") (7:23).

One hundred and fifty days later the flood waters began to subside. On the seventeenth day of the seventh month the ark came to rest "on the mountains of Ararat" (8:4). On the first day of the tenth month the mountain tops could be seen (8:5). Thereafter, "At the end of forty days," Noah began to send out birds to determine whether they could yet find a dry berth on which to rest. In time, a dove failed to return. The earth was dry (8:6–12).

Not long after, God instructs Noah to come out of the ark with his family and all the creatures of the earth and skies. Of fertility, God says nothing to the departing humans. Of all other creatures He says, "Let them swarm on the earth and be fertile and increase on earth" (8:17). The few survivors of the flood thus emerge from the ark to begin life anew (8:18–19). "Then Noah built an altar to the Lord and, taking of every clean animal and of every clean bird, he offered burnt offerings on the altar" (8:20).

In softening the image of its heavenly Assailant of earthly life, the Torah portrays J's Lord and P's God as a contrite Being Who seeks to be reconciled with humanity (8:15–9:29). He laments His past unrealistic expectations: *"Never again will I doom the earth because of man*, since the devisings of man's mind are evil from his youth; nor will I ever again destroy every living being as I have done" (8:21). The Lord also vows that "so long as the earth endures," He will "maintain the order of the seasons and of day and night" (8:22). P's God joins in to make a new "everlasting" covenant with Noah and "every living creature with you for all ages to come" (9:12). The covenant is stated and restated: (1) "never again shall all flesh be cut off by the waters of a flood, and never again shall there be a flood to destroy the earth" (9:11) and (2) "the waters shall never again become a flood to destroy all flesh" (9:15).

> Note G–15: It may be hoped that P's God meant any "natural" disaster having equivalent consequences.

God also assuages future humanity by easing its quest for food and reinforcing its dominance over all other creatures. To Noah and his sons He declares, "The fear and dread of you shall be upon all the [beasts, birds, and fish]. *Every creature that lives* shall be *yours* to eat." He then imposes a single condition on the consumption of meat. It is that all "life-blood" must be removed from it (9:4). *Left intact, however, is Creation I's limitation of animal food to "green plants"* (1:30). (See Comment G–3.)

Considering the flood and its consequences, there is a certain irony in God's warning of 9:5–6: "Whoever [animals included (9:5)] sheds the blood of man, by man shall His blood be shed; for in His image did God make man" (9:6).

And now, as His final act of reconciliation with humankind, God reextends the blessing of Creation I to Noah and his line: "Be fertile, then, and increase; abound on the earth and increase on it" (9:7).

Comment G–13. On the purpose of the flood in regard to human free will

Through these events, does the story of the great flood mean to say that of all humanity only Noah and his family were worth saving? And that every other human being was so unredeemably evil as to deserve death by drowning? How is it possible that any worthy Lord God could judge every adult, child, and newborn (other than Noah and his family) as deserving victims of mass extinction? The Torah must either justify the conduct of its God by a purpose that transcends justice, or it must disavow any pretense of His justice. *From the perspective of its God*, therefore, how might the Torah justify the great flood?

It might begin with the perception of its God that humanity's abuse of its free will had become irremediable. If humanity is to serve its purpose in perfecting earthly existence, it must learn to accept His guidance in the exercise of its free will. Because in all humanity, only Noah has totally subordinated His will to God's will, it is only Noah in whom J's Lord and P's God has total confidence. Of the factors that shape human character—as between genetics and environment, or nature and nurture—these authors of the Torah would have known very little. But through the acuity of their observations they may have sensed a lineal continuity of character arising from a mix of the two. If, in all humanity, only Noah had proved his total acceptance of God's will as his will, then *only Noah and his wife were fit parents for all humanity.*

For this, his credentials were beyond question. Who but Noah could remain utterly passive on being told of Lord God's intent to destroy humanity? Who but Noah could suppress all human compassion to the point of not crying out "Why?" Who but Noah, on hearing of God's plan to obliterate every earthly being (but for those on the ark), would respond mutely by doing "just as God commanded him . . ." (6:22)? Among all human beings, whose free will other than Noah's was so completely at Lord God's disposal?

The story of the flood, therefore, is a parable on the relationship between the wills of the Lord God and humanity. Having conceded free will to humanity, He could not dictate human choices. Left to His own resources, He could only punish or reward humanity for its choices. If further disasters were to be avoided, the need was for a compliant humanity more prepared to place its free will at the Lord God's disposal. To that end, the Lord God could look only to the line of Noah. To that end, all other humans must perish.

Comment G–14. On time and sequence in the Torah as reflected in the "clean" and "unclean" animals of the ark

The several references to "clean" and "unclean" animals in the story of Noah reveals some oddities of time and sequence resulting from the integration of materials written over several centuries.

Consider again the contradictory instructions of "seven" and "two" received by Noah in regard to the number of animals to be brought on the ark. Both instructions, however, distinguished between "clean" and "unclean" animals. In P's story, God tells Noah to bring "two . . . of all that lives . . . male and female" (6:19–20). Later, P describes the animals that entered the ark as follows: "Of the *clean* animals, of the animals that are *not clean*, of the birds, and of everything that creeps on the ground, *two* of each, male and female, came to Noah into the ark" (7:8–9).

In turn, J's Lord gives Noah this instruction: "Of every *clean* animal, you shall take *seven* pairs, males and their mates, and of every animal which is *not clean*, *two*, a male and its mate; of the birds of the sky also, seven pairs, male and female, to keep seed alive upon all the earth" (7:2–3).

The question, then, is how can Noah distinguish between clean and unclean animals? What does he know of the classification and its details? As yet, Genesis is silent.

Later, of course, the clean/unclean dichotomy, by type of animal, will become significant both as to food and sacrifice. (As to to food see Lev. 11:1–23 and Deut. 14:3–20.) As of Gen. 7:2–3 and 7:8–9, however, humankind is still vegetarian. Only after the flood does P's God revoke His Creation I decree of human vegetarianism. And then His permission for humans to eat of meat extends to "*every creature that lives*" (9:3). Absent any exceptions, it is possible that the clean/unclean dietary limitations of Leviticus and Deuteronomy were meant for post-Exodus Israelites. If so, the clean/unclean classification of animals *for food* is irrelevant to the Noah story.

It is of use, however, as to sacrificial animals. Thus, J observes that after the flood "Noah built an altar to the Lord and, taking of every *clean* animal and of every *clean* bird, he offered burnt offerings on the altar" (8:20).

How could Noah know which animals were clean or unclean for sacrifice? Since the Lord had not explained which was which, Noah, in making his burnt offerings as a spontaneous expression of gratitude (8:20–21), must have known one from the other. And so it would have been with the "clean" animals, of which seven pairs were needed, and the "unclean, of which only one pair was needed (7:2–3).

Torah passages dealing with the classification of animals for sacrifice are found at Lev. 1–5 and Num. 28 and 29. (Friedman attributes these to P and R, respectively.) Unlike the explicit designation of particular animals as clean or unclean for use as food, animals are not so designated in respect to sacrificial uses. Instead, the protocols for each type of sacrifice indicate the particular type of animal to be used.

Why does the clean/unclean dichotomy appear in the story of Noah for the first time? That it appears in P passages is less remarkable, given its importance in Leviticus. As author of the Levitical laws, P may have thought to give them added credibility by referring to them in the chronologically earlier Noah story—*even though (for reasons already stated) its presence in P passages of the flood serves no immediate purpose.* Conversely, as we have also noted, the only practical use of the clean/unclean dichotomy occurs in J's passage on Noah's burnt offerings (8:20). Yet, if J indeed wrote as long as two centuries before P, what could J have known of P's Levitical laws?

> Note G–16: *Presumably, P will defer all animal sacrifices until the ordination of Aaron and his sons (see, in general, Exod. 25–31 and Leviticus).*
>
> *In any case, two possibilities come to mind. First, that J knew of the clean/unclean dichotomy from oral traditions recorded years later by P. Second, that R, knowing of the Levitical laws, used it to embellish J's version of the Noah story.*
>
> *Writing as he did from a theistic perspective that viewed the Torah as a seamless web whose God is unconstrained by the factor of time, Rashi's comments are of interest. He views the clean/unclean dichotomy as applying both to food and sacrifice. As to its use for food, he takes note of the phrase "Of every clean animal you shall take seven pairs" (7:2). He then comments:* "[The cattle] which in the future would be considered clean to Israel [for food]. We thus learn that Noah studied the Torah."[8]
>
> *A related problem arises from God's permission for humans to eat of* "Every creature that lives," *on condition that all* "life-blood" *be removed (9:3–4).* "Later" *Levitical law will affirm the need to remove all* "life-blood" *from animals before eating. But what of the edibility of* "every creature that lives?" *What P's God allows to humanity in Genesis He will forbid to Israel in Leviticus.*

THE TOWER OF BABEL

Whether from pious obedience or natural bent, Noah's sons and their descendants were fruitful and increased. The lines of Shem, Ham, and Japeth sired many clans, tribes, nations, and peoples. (These are detailed in Gen. 10:1–31.) "From these [descendants of Noah and his sons] the nations branched out over the earth after the Flood" (10:32).

Note G–17: Plaut summarizes the geographic area said to be occupied by Noah's line as follows: "from the Caucasus mountains in the north to Ethiopia in the south, from the Aegean Sea in the west to the highlands of Iran in the east."[9]

Given this great proliferation of distinctive peoples, we might take pause on reading in 11:1 that "all the earth had the same language and the same words."

Note G–18: Our pause turns to wonderment in recalling the three summations in Gen. 10 of the ethnic descendants of Japheth (10:5), Ham (10:20), and Shem (10:31). As to each set of descendants, these three verses state the following: "These are the descendants of [each named son of Noah] according to their clans and languages, by their lands and nations." As we might surmise, the whimsy of the Tower of Babel marks it as quintessential J, who would not have known of these Gen. 10, verses that Friedman ascribes to P (including 5, 20, and 31). If so, we must be impressed by R's fidelity in preserving J's contradictory assertion in Gen. 11:1.

The story of The Tower of Babel is told in the nine brief verses of 11:1–9. "As men migrated from the east," they settled in Shinar (i.e., Sumer or Babylon). There they decide to "build us a city, and a tower with its top in the *sky*, to make a name for ourselves; else we shall be scattered all over the world" (11:4).

The Torah states no claim of human arrogance in this great joint undertaking. The thought is unavoidable, however, that a human effort to build a tower so high could strike the Lord as an arrogant and threatening intrusion.

Comment G–15. On the Hebrew *shamayim* as "heaven" or "sky" in regard to the motives of the "men" at the Tower

JPS1 and RSV place the top of the tower in "heaven," or "the heavens," rather than in the "sky." To use "heaven," of course, is to suggest a challenge to the Lord through a human "invasion" of His physical domain. Accordingly, the rendering of *shamayim* as "sky" or "heaven" is important in determining what the parable says of human motivation. Does it tell of a great human effort toward purposeful human cooperation? Does it look to an emerging millennium of human unity? Or does it reveal a rebellious human effort to challenge the Lord in His own domain?

Whatever the answer, the Lord will have none of it. "If, as one people with one language for all, this is how they have begun to act, then nothing they propose will be out of their reach" (11:6). In prompt response, He "confounded the speech of the whole earth" and scattered humanity "over the face of the whole earth" (11:7–8).

Comment G–16. On relations between the Creator and His creation in the wake of Adam and Eve, Cain and Abel, Noah and the Flood, and the Tower of Babel

Whether J intended the Tower as a human intrusion on the Lord's domain, we can never know for sure. In any case, the story of the Tower is more important for what it says of the Lord. In one sense it tells us that He has profited from the disaster of the flood. Though His judgment remains impulsive, His reaction is at least more restrained. The events at the Tower do not prompt Him to destroy humanity yet again. Now He is content to destroy its unity. But His "moderation" can only compound His problems in relating to humanity.

Before the events at the Tower, the God of the Torah could relate to a humanity whose "oneness" was nurtured by its common tongue. (Thus we decide the previously noted contradiction between Gen. 10 and 11 as to "language[s]" in favor of J.) Because of the Lord's rash reaction to the Tower, He must now forge a new relationship with a humanity divided by language, nation, and tribe. If the Torah would have its Lord serve as the God of all humanity, He must now learn to overcome human schisms and conflicts of His own making.

As the Torah moves on from the age of myth toward the dawn of history, the line of Noah's son Shem runs to Terah, and to his sons Abram, Nahor, and Haran (11:25–26).

ABRAHAM AND HIS GOD

It is through Abram and his line that a more serene relationship between the Lord and humankind is to develop. When the Lord first calls Abram (Abraham, as of 17:5), all we know of him is that the Lord called and he answered. Although married to Sarai (Sarah, as of 17:15), he was childless.

When we first meet Abram, he lives in Haran (today, in southern Turkey), to which he had first come with his father, Terah; his wife, Sarai; and his nephew Lot, the son of his deceased brother (also named Haran). The Torah states that Terah and his family (including Abram and Sarai) had "set out together from Ur of the Chaldeans *for the land of Canaan,* but when they came as far as Haran, they settled there" (11:31). Terah dies in Haran at the age of 205 (now by a "post-mythic" count) (11:32). Some time later, "the Lord said to Abram, 'Go forth from your native land and from your father's house to the land I will show you'" (12:1).

Comment G–17. On Abram's "point of departure" for the promised land

As rendered by JPS2, the Lord tells Abram, "Go forth from your *native land* and from your father's house" (12:1). But as stated in 11:31, the family was from "Ur of Chaldeans" (in southern Mesopotamia). Therefore, in the usual sense of "birth place," Ur, not Haran, was Abram's "native land." JPS1 (and RSV to the same effect) renders 12:1 as follows: "Get thee out of thy country [*mayartzcha*], and from thy kindred [*moladt'cha*], and from thy father's house [*bayt aviecha*]." The *moladt'cha* of 12:1 can mean both "native land" and "kindred." In the context of 12:1, "kindred" would seem the better choice. It both eliminates the ambiguity of "native land" and better reflects the reason for Abram's departure. It is not to leave his "native land," which he had left long ago, but to be free from the influence of his present life—his country, his household and his kinsmen. He is to make a new life.

If Abram could sense that the Lord who called him had the intent and ability to fulfil His promises, then he indeed had a powerful incentive to comply. "I will make of you a great nation, and I will bless you; I will make your name great, And you shall be a blessing. I will bless those who bless you and curse him that curse you; All the families of the earth shall bless themselves by you" (12:2–3).

Then, at the age of seventy-five, Abram took Sarai and Lot, his nephew, and "went forth *as the Lord had commanded him.*" With them were "all the wealth that they had amassed, and the persons that they had acquired in Haran" (12:2–5).

Comment G–18. On the Lord's choice of Abram and Abram's response to the Lord

When the Lord first speaks to him, Abram does not ask the obvious question: "Who are You to ask this of me?" Does the Torah mean to imply that Abram already knew of the Lord? Or did he accept the call from a perceived need to obey this "Lord" he did not know?

The uncertainty arises from the Lord's having told Abram of the rewards of acceptance before requiring him to answer. Only after hearing of the destiny of his descendants does Abram depart for the unknown land. Was Abram "inveigled" to depart by promise of reward or "inspired" to depart by the Presence of the Lord?

In either case, Abram's prompt decision suggests his considerable confidence in the Lord's sincerity and His power to fulfil His promise. J seems to imply, therefore, that Abram's innate spirituality prepared him to accept the Lord's actual Being and credibility. If so, JPS1/RSV must explain why Abram, rather than leaving his "kindred," took Lot, his nephew, with him" (see 12:1).[13]

The Lord has identified Abram's destination only as "the land I will show you" (12:1). Abram "then went forth as the Lord had commanded him." In fact, however, he sets out for "the land of Canaan" (12:4–5), *his father's intended destination on leaving Ur* (11:31). Abram proceeds through the land to Shechem (near the present Nablus, north of Jerusalem). There the Lord tells him, "I will give this land to your offspring." Abram then builds an altar to Him. En route to the Negev, he builds another at Bethel (12:7–8). By doing so, Abram confirms his commitment to the Lord. Yet, however great Abram's confidence in the Lord's sincerity and power was, we now learn of his self-reliance as well.

Still childless, Abram and Sarai are forced by a famine in the Negev to leave for Egypt (as would Jacob and his family at a later time) (12:10). Because of Sarai's great beauty, Abram fears that the Egyptians will kill him because he is her husband. He therefore asks her, "Please say that you are my sister, that it may go well with me because of you, and that I may remain alive thanks to you" (12:13). Sarai agrees. When her beauty is duly noted, she is brought to the Pharaoh, who then "took her as [his] wife" (12:19).

Thereafter, "because of her it went well with Abram; he acquired sheep, oxen, asses, male and female slaves, she-asses, and camels" (12:16). But in time, the Lord afflicts Pharaoh and his household "with mighty plagues on account of Sarai, the wife of Abram" (12:17). Through implied insight, Pharaoh senses the source of the plagues. He then berates Abram for representing Sarai as his sister. Perhaps from fear of the power behind the plagues, Pharaoh sends them off with "all that [Abram] possessed" (12:18–20).

Comment G–19. On the "sister" story as a reflection of Abram's faith and self-reliance

That Abram would willingly offer Sarai to Pharaoh as a wife suggests that he placed a higher value on his life than on Sarai's honor. But to be fair, we must consider his quandry. As yet being childless, Abram knew that his death would preclude realization of the Lord's promise regarding the destiny of his offspring. But rather than relying on the Lord to protect both his life and Sarai's honor, Abram chose to sacrifice Sarai's honor. In the "clutch," so to speak, Abram chose to rely on his own resources. Why does the Torah portray this failure of faith in Israel's founding patriarch? And how can Abram be excused for failing in his duty both to Sarai and the Lord?

Through this episode the ever realistic J may have intended to portray an early stage in the developing relationship between Abram and the Lord. Though impressed by the Lord's "Presence," he knows little of His powers. That the Lord was sincere, as Abram believed, would not save him from Pharaoh. Abram's natural self-reliance left him no choice but to take personal responsibility for his own life—the one vital human element of the Lord's promise.

If these were Abram's thoughts, what of the Lord's? Though concerned, He was not disillusioned. There was yet time for Abram to develop the total faith required of a patriarch. The Lord may also have recalled how His own past difficulties in dealing with humanity had led Him to Abram.

On returning with Sarai to the Negev, Abram is "very rich in cattle, gold, and silver" (13:2). With Sarai and Lot he goes on to Bethel (between Jerusalem and Shechem). To avoid problems of scarce feed and water for their flocks, Abram proposes to Lot: "Let there be no strife between you and me, between my herdsmen and yours, for we are kinsmen. Is not the whole land before you? Let us separate." Though speaking to Lot at Bethel, well within Canaan, Abram gives him a puzzling choice: "If you go north, I will go south; and if you go south, I will go north" (13:7–9). Lot then "looked about him and saw how well watered was the whole plain of Jordan, all of it . . . all the way to Zoar" (13:10). By way of anticipation, the narrator/author thoughtfully notes "that this [fertility] was before the Lord had destroyed Sodom and Gomorrah."

Lot then chose the "whole plain of Jordan" (which included Sodom and Gomorrah) and journeyed *eastward*. "Thus they parted from each other" (13:11).

> Note G–19: *Speaking to Lot, Abram bases his proposal that they separate on a shortage of "feed and water" for their animals. The text amply supports this reason (13:5–6). Yet Abram likely had other considerations in mind. Because Lot could not share the destiny of his line, Abram wanted no strife between them in regard to the Lord's commandments.*

Abram remains in "the land of Canaan." Indeed, from all that appears in the Torah, he had not yet moved from the site of the altar which he had "first built" near Bethel and to which he had returned from Egypt (13:3–4). It was also from there that Lot had "looked up" and saw the plain of Jordan (13:10). God then renews His promise. To further identify the land promised to his descendants, the Lord tells Abram, "look from where you are, to the north and south, to the east and west, for I give all the land that you see to you and your offspring forever" (13:14–15). To this, the Lord adds the promise that Abram's offspring will be as countless as "the dust of the earth" (13:16).

Comment G–20. On the scope of "the land" promised to the descendants of Abram

The Lord's first terse description at Shechem of the land promised to Abram's descendants as "this land" did little to define it (12:7). The Torah, however, had already twice alluded to "the land of Canaan" (11:31, 12:5). At the time of Abram (c. nineteenth century B.C.E.), Canaan was an area of uncertain scope. At Bethel the Lord first "defines" the promised land to Abram. In essence, it was as far as Abram could see in any direction. Were the boundaries of the promised land to be determined by the acuity of Abram's vision? Or, on a clear day chosen by the Lord, was Abram merely meant to gain an impression of its vastness?

In any case, by allowing Lot to choose first from any land in any direction, Abram seems quite prepared to cede him a part of Canaan. Was Abram then willing for Lot to share in the land promised to his descendants? Just as puzzling is this added consideration. If Lot, from Bethel, could see the plain of Jordan to the east, then why would Abram not have seen it from the same vantage point? Recall that the Lord had instructed Abram to look "to the east and west." Assuming he did, then the plain of Jordan was part of the promised land. Was it Abram's to cede to Lot?

Gen. 14 tells of Abram's military skills during the war of the kings in which Lot was taken prisoner (14:1–12). On hearing from a fugitive of his captivity, Abram quickly organized his retainers to effect a rescue (14:13–16).

> Note G–20: For the first time the Torah refers to Abram as "Abram the Hebrew" (14:13).

His pursuit of Lot's captors leads him to Hobah, north of Damascus. From there, Abram brings back Lot and all his "possessions" and "the women and the rest of the people" taken by the winners from the losers (among whom was the king of Sodom) (14:16).

> Note G–21: The identities of the invading and defending kings in the area of the Dead Sea involves questions of historical authenticity. Of greater import here is Abram's resourceful rescue of Lot, his still cherished kinsman.

En route home, Abram meets both Melchizedek, king of Salem (later Jerusalem and environs) and the king of Sodom. Of Melchizedek, it is said without explanation that "[he] brought out bread and wine; he was a priest of God Most High" (14:18). Melchizedek goes on to bless Abram, saying, "Blessed be Abram of God Most High, Creator of heaven and earth. And blessed be God Most High, Who has delivered your foes into your hand" (14:19–20). Abram then gives him "a tenth of everything" (i.e., the tithe owing to a priest).

Comment G–21. On God, Abram, and Melchizedek

Rashi comments: " 'A tenth of everything' he had since Melchizedek was a priest."[10] However, in addition to identifying Melchizedek as "king of Salem," to what purpose would the Torah identify him as priest of "God Most High"? Would the Torah place such a mantle of supremacy on a Being other than its own God? Would Abram so honor the priest of a God other than his own?

As yet, we know nothing of priests who serve the God of Abram, or of tithes to which they are entitled. (Priestly tithes in the Torah are the subject of Num. 18.) Apart from Abram's acceptance of the Lord's call, we know nothing of an "Abramic" religion. Were his tithes to a priest meant as a disguised tribute to a king? Or did he tithe out of respect for Melchizedek's personal worthiness? The former speaks to Abram's practicality, and the latter to his respectful religiosity. But what does the latter say of his views regarding the uniqueness and supremacy of his own God?

It is the Torah itself, of course, that identifies Melchizedek's God as "God Most High." Melchizedek returns the compliment by identifying Abram's God as "God Most High, Creator of heaven and earth." And he credits Him with Abram's defeat of the invader kings. As the priest of a Being known to the Torah as "God Most High," was Melchizedek now acknowledging that their respective Gods were one and the same? Or were his generous references to Abram's God merely a measure of his respect for Abram?

In truth, none of these conjectures can obscure the basic logic of this brief encounter between Abram and Melchizedek. Clearly, the Torah portrays the God(s) of Abram and Melchizedek as one. The encounter might thus be understood as an assertion of the universality of the God of the Torah. If so, while "God Most High" had chosen Abram for a special destiny, He did not mean to bar other worthy priests from honoring His supremacy and authority. And just as Noah, before the time of Abram, was said to have known both J's Lord and P's God, so, too, could Melchizedek have somehow known of Him in Abram's time.

But if Friedman's tentative attribution of Gen. 14 to J is correct, then there may have been another purpose being served. To Melchizedek, the passage attributes the dual status of king and priest in Salem. In portraying the site of Jerusalem as the early dwelling place of a priest of "God Most High," J may have sought to provide "early" credibility to King David's transference of the Ark of the Tabernacle to Jerusalem.[11]

Gen. 15 tells of a major encounter between Abram and the Lord, as experienced by Abram "in a vision." It begins "some time later" when the Lord appears to renew His promise. By now, however, Abram is troubled by prolonged childlessness: "O Lord God, what can You give me, seeing that I am childless, and the one in charge of my household is Dammesek Eliezer. Since you have granted me no offspring, my steward shall be my heir" (15:2–3). The Lord assures him, "None but your very own issue shall be your heir." He also reassures Abram that these descendants from his own issue will one day be as numerous as the stars (15:4–5). Abram was thus comforted. "And because he put his trust in the Lord, He reckoned it to his merit" (15:6).

The Lord then tells Abram that it was "I . . . who brought you out of Ur of the Chaldeans to give you this land as a possession" (15:7).

> Note G–22: The Lord first appeared to Abram in Haran rather than Ur (11:31–12:1), and it was from Haran that Abram departed to follow the Lord (12:4). Friedman ascribes Abram's departure from Haran to J and the family's departure from Ur to P (11:31). In turn, Gen. 15:7 is part of what he reads as the composite passage of 15:1–21. The reference to Ur in 15:7 as Abram's departure point for Canaan could result from different sources. Or it could imply that the Lord had somehow inspired the original move from Ur to Haran as the first leg of the final move to Canaan.

In response to Abram's plea "How shall I know that I am to possess [the land]?" the Lord instructs him on the precise details of a sacrifice involving a heifer, a she-goat, a ram, a turtle dove, and another young bird. When birds of prey come down on the carcasses, Abram drives them away (15:8–11). Then, "as the sun was about to set, a deep sleep fell upon Abram." He felt "a deep dark dread." The Lord then reveals the destiny of his descendants in Egypt. He is told of their enslavement for four hundred years; of their being freed to leave with "great wealth," following the Lord's execution of judgment on Egypt; and of their return to Canaan, but only when the iniquities of the Amorites (who will occupy Canaan) is "complete" (15:12–16).

> Note G–23: Through its God's knowledge of future events, the Torah could mean to imply either His prescience or His power to effectuate those events— or the two combined.

Another dream (or possibly another version of the same dream episode) then occurs. "When the sun set and it was very dark, there appeared a smoking oven, and a flaming torch which passed between those pieces" (15:17). Abram's vision concludes with the Lord's "making a covenant with Abram" in which He covenants a land far greater than anything visible from the hill at Bethel (see Comment G–20). Indeed, it will extend "from the river of Egypt, to the great river, the river Euphrates" (15:18).

Comment G–22. On the new scope of the promised land

Ignoring, as they did, any reference to Canaan, these new boundaries could literally include a territory "from the river of Egypt" in northeastern Sinai (and a later boundary between Egypt and Palestine), through northern Syria and a portion of Iraq, Jordan, and northern Saudi Arabia. Was it ever realistic to envision so vast a promise? While an eastern boundary of the entire Euphrates was surely fanciful, the Davidic/Solomonic empire would be said in time to have extended northward to the Euphrates in what now is Syria. Moreover, J, as Friedman's putative author of Gen. 15:1–18, would have known of the reported tenth-century B.C.E. conquests of David and Solomon. Thus, the Torah's descriptions of the promised land change over time with Israel's political boundaries.

In despair from her continued barrenness, Sarai asks Abram to take Hagar, her Egyptian maid, as concubine. "Look, the Lord has kept *me* from bearing. Consort with my maid; perhaps *I* shall have a son through her" (16:2).

When Hagar conceives, "her mistress was lowered in her esteem" (16:4).

> *Note G–24: By accomplishing what Sarai could not in this "defining" respect, Hagar felt superior to her mistress.*

Sarai then complains to Abram of Hagar's disrespect. He treats it as a household matter involving only Sarai and her maid. He thus tells Sarai: "Your maid is in your hands. Deal with her as you think right" (16:6). When Sarai treats Hagar "harshly," she runs away.

Comment G–23. On Abram's indifference to an expected child by Hagar

Abram's response to Sarai on hearing that Hagar bears his child seems devoid of feeling. Given Sarai's apparent infertility, Abram's disinterest in the fate of a potential heir by Hagar seems remarkable. *In none of His several promises to Abram of an heir had the Lord named the mother* (12:7, 13:14–16, 15:2–5, 15:13, 15:18). From all the Lord had said, Abram's covenantal heir could just as well come by Hagar as Sarai. Why, then, does the Torah portray Abram as indifferent to the fate of that possible heir? Why is it his main concern to be ridded of a household dispute?

Here we might assume that J would not likely portray Abram as indifferent to a son through whom his covenantal line would run. If so, we might also assume that Abram sensed from the logic of the situation that his covenantal heir must be by Sarai, and not a "proxy." Indeed, did he not consort with Hagar mainly to satisfy Sarai—that *she* might have a son (16:2). The disruption of his household only heightens Abram's frustration. Circumstances have conspired to mock his desperation for a covenantal heir.

An "angel" of the Lord comforts Hagar in her flight from Sarai and directs her to return (16:9). However, the angel also describes a destiny for Ishmael quite distinct from that of Abram's covenantal heir: "I will greatly increase your offspring, and they shall be too many to count. . . . [You] shall bear a son. You shall call him Ismhael." But Ishmael will not settle in the promised land. He is to be a "wild ass of a man" (i.e., a nomadic Bedouin). "His hand [will be] against everyone, and everyone's hand against him. He shall dwell alongside all of his kinsmen" (16:11–12). At Ishmael's birth, Abram is eighty-six (16:16).

Gen. 17 begins as follows: "When Abram was ninety-nine years old, the Lord appeared to Abram and said to him, 'I am *El Shaddai*. Walk in my ways and be blameless. I will establish My covenant between Me and you, and I will make you exceedingly numerous' " (17:1–2).

> Note G–25: *Plaut suggests that the meaning of* el shaddai *is in doubt. As its most frequent translation, he cites "God Almighty," with the additive that "some scholars" derive* Shaddai *from the Akkadian word for mountain (i.e., "shadu").* [12] *In considering both the events and nomenclature of Gen. 17, it seems important to note that Friedman and others attribute it entirely to P. Conversely, Gen. 16 is attributed mainly to J. Until now, P has used* elohim *to identify the Torah's God.*

Although J's Abram of Gen. 12–16 sometimes showed doubt of the fullness of the Lord's power, P's Abraham of Gen. 17 knows nothing of doubt. As God speaks to him, Abram, in a gesture of total subservience, "throws himself on his face" (17:3). God then renews his promise, *not to Abram, but to Abraham*. He adds to the Lord's earlier promises that Abram's progeny would be as numerous as "the dust of the earth" or "the stars" (13:16, 15:5). God will make Abraham the father of a "multitude of nations." From him "kings shall come forth" (17:4, 6). Less generous was His limitation of the promised land to "all the land of Canaan" (17:8). (Cf. Gen. 15:18 and Comment G–20.)

> Note G–26: *Rashi ascribes the name change from Abram to Abraham to his change of status as "father of Aram" (his home) to "father of a multitude of nations."* [13]

Comment G–24. On the "shrinking" promised land

The contraction of the promised land to Canaan itself speaks to the later date of the P author(s). By approximately the sixth century B.C.E., all aspirations to a broader empire beyond Canaan would surely have ended. Israel had already fallen to the Assyrians and Judah would soon fall to the great Babylonian colossus to the East. Circumstances required the revocation of any promise of a boundary on the Euphrates. But the "multitude of nations" still must be explained.

What had been the Lord's unilateral covenant with Abram now becomes bilateral through *el shaddai*'s pronouncement of the reciprocal obligation of circumcision. "Such shall be the covenant between Me and you and your offspring to follow. . . . You shall circumcise the flesh of your foreskin, and that shall be the sign of the covenant between Me and you. And throughout the generations, every male among you shall be circumcised at the age of eight days" (17:10–12). Also to be circumcised were slaves, whether "homeborn" or "bought from an outsider who is not of your offspring." If not circumcised as an infant, an adult male was charged to fulfil the covenant himself, lest he be "cut off from his kin" (17:14).

Comment G–25. On the punishment of being "cut off from his kin"

Rashi defines the metaphorical punishment of being "cut off from his kin" as that of "going childless" or suffering death "before his time."[14] Because it is seemingly the most pervasive punishment of the Torah, we will have other occasions to consider it.

What J's *yahweh* may have implied, P's *el shaddai* now makes explicit (see Comment G–23). The covenantal son of Abraham will be by Sarai, who now becomes Sarah. She is to be blessed "so that she shall give rise to nations; rulers of peoples shall issue from her" (17:15–16).

> Note G–27: Rashi attributes the name change from Sarai to Sarah to her change in status from being a "princess" for Abram alone to being a princess for Abraham, as "the father of a multitude of nations."[15]

Once again Abraham "threw himself on his face"—now from laughter rather than piety (17:17). He wonders "to himself" how a child can be born to a man of one hundred and a woman of ninety (17:17). But to God aloud, Abraham says, "Oh that Ishmael might live by your favor" (17:18).

El shaddai replies: "*Nevertheless*, Sarah your wife shall bear you a son, and you shall name him Isaac, and I will maintain my covenant with him" (17:19). Ishmael, however, will also receive God's blessing. He will be "fertile and exceedingly numerous"; he will father "twelve chieftains" (cf. Jacob's twelve sons). From him will come "a great nation" (17:20).

> Note G–28: When Abraham says, "Oh that Ishmael might live by your favor," el shaddai's next words are "Nevertheless, Sarah your wife shall bear you a son, and you shall name him Isaac, and I will maintain my covenant with him." Can we read el shaddai's "Nevertheless" as a rejection of what He mistook as Abraham's plea that Ishmael should be his covenantal heir? Or did He only refer to Abraham's laughter and apparent incredulity?

On the very day of *el shaddai*'s departure, Abraham circumcised himself, Ishmael, and all males included within the new covenantal obligation (17:23–27).

In Gen. 18:1, J's "Lord" appears to Abraham "by the terebinths [a Mediterranean tree] at Mamre . . . as the day grew hot." Thus, "looking up, [Abraham] saw three men standing near him" (18:2).

> Note G–29: *Following its initial use by P in Gen. 17, "Abraham" now appears for the first time in a J passage. We may assume that the transition was effected by R.*

Abraham responds to the presence of his visitors with the hospitality of a meal: "He took curds and milk and the calf that had been prepared, and set these before them; and he waited on them under the tree as they ate" (18:8).

Comment G–26. On Abraham's simultaneous serving of milk and meat to the Lord and His men

Abraham's service of milk and meat at the same meal may surprise a few readers familiar with Jewish dietary law. True enough, the Lord had not yet prescribed the basic laws of *kashrut*. But neither had He revealed the clean/unclean animal dichotomy of the Noah story (see Comment G–14). In that they knew of "clean and unclean" animals, we may assume that J or R would also have known of other basic dietary commands. Yet they both allow *Abraham* to bring meat and milk to *the Lord* in a single meal. They drew no contrary inference from the Torah's thrice stated ban on boiling a kid in its mother's milk. (Friedman also assigns the second statement of the ban [Ex. 34:26] to J.) The Talmudic gloss placed on the command is noted in the introduction. Gen. 18:8 surely suggests that the ban was unknown to the Torah.

The scene then turns to Sarah who, by now, "had stopped having the periods of women" (18:11). She hears "one [of the men]" tell Abraham that he will return when the son of Abraham and Sarah is due to be born (18:9–10). Unlike Abraham, who, in the P story, had laughed aloud at the thought of having a child, a more circumspect Sarah "laughed to herself." As she laughs she also says, "Now that I am withered, am I to have enjoyment—with my husband so old?" (18:12). While P's God said nothing of Abraham's laughter (17:16–20), J's Lord takes umbrage at Sarah's. He asks Abraham, "Why did Sarah laugh, saying, 'Shall I in truth bear a child, old as I am?' Is anything too wondrous for the Lord?" (18:13–14). To Sarah's fearful reply, "I did not laugh," the Lord retorts, "You did laugh" (18:12–15).

The balance of Gen. 18 (i.e., 17–33) deals with events immediately preceding the destruction of Sodom and Gomorrah. As the Lord ponders whether He should reveal His plans to Abraham, J undertakes to record His thoughts. "Shall I hide from Abraham what I am about to do, since Abraham is to become a great and populous nation *and all the nations of the earth are to bless themselves by him*? For I have singled him out, that he may instruct his children and his posterity to keep the way of the Lord by doing what is just and right, *in order that* the Lord may bring about for Abraham what He has promised him" (18:17–19).

Comment G–27. On two aspects of the Lord's thoughts as He contemplates the obliteration of Sodom and Gomorrah

1. On the implied conditionality of the Lord's covenant with Abraham's descendants

The Lord's soliloquy reveals an implicit condition of His promise to Abraham. Unlike P's *el shaddai*, Who had commanded a reciprocal covenantal condition of circumcision, J's *yahweh* has spoken only of a unilateral covenant. If J's Lord had ever contemplated a condition on His promise (other than the move from Haran to Canaan), He had never explicitly revealed it to Abraham. Nor does He do so now. Being who he was, Abraham may have assumed that a worthy God would require a worthy condition. Yet, only in His thoughts does J's Lord reveal to the reader that His promise to Abraham and his line will be honored only as they "keep the way of the Lord *by doing what is just and right.*"

2. On Abraham as "a great and populous nation" by whom "all the nations of the earth are to bless themselves"

Here J's Lord repeats His initial hope in having "chosen" Abraham. In time, his descendants will prove such powerful exemplars of humanity's potential for good as to cause other nations—as they come to recognize a common human potential—to bless themselves "by him" (12:3).

The Lord now confides in Abraham that He has heard that "the outrage of Sodom and Gomorrah is so great, and their sin so grave!" that He must verify its gravity (18:20–21). It is then said that "*the men* went on from there to Sodom, *while Abraham remained standing before the Lord*" (18:22).

As Abraham stands before the Lord, so that He may explain "what is just and right" in the pending destruction of Sodom and Gomorrah, an irony unfolds. It is the irony of how the Lord, having come to teach Abraham, instead has His own moral sensibilities awakened by Abraham. Recall Noah's mute acceptance of God's plan to destroy all humankind except for him and his family. Now compare how Abraham compels the Lord to consider the innocent in Sodom and Gomorrah.

As the dialogue begins, Abraham displays both the moral fervor and personal courage needed to inform the Lord of *his own* expectations of Godly justice: "Will you sweep away the innocent along with the guilty? What if there should be fifty innocent in the city; will you then wipe out the place and not forgive it for the sake of the innocent fifty who are in it? *Far be it from You to do such a thing, to bring death upon the innocent as well as the guilty, so that the innocent and guilty fare alike. Far be it from You! Shall not the Judge of all the earth deal justly?"* (18:23–25).

Through his sad disbelief and righteous anger, Abraham moves the Lord to rethink His standard of communal justice. He thus tells Abraham that on finding "fifty innocent ones" in Sodom, "I will forgive the whole place for their sake" (18:26). Having pared the number from fifty to twenty step by step (18:27–31), Abraham puts one more question to the Lord: "Let not the Lord be angry if I speak but this last time: What if ten should be found there?" Once again the Lord answers, "I will not destroy for the sake of the ten."

Comment G–28. On collective and individual justice as viewed by Abraham and the Lord

Abraham first pleads with the Lord to judge the guilt and innocence of individuals. "*Will you sweep away the innocent along with the guilty?"* (18:23). But his specific plea *to spare the guilty for the sake of the innocent* suggests that he somehow sensed the futility of his true position. When faced with rampant social evil, the Lord was inclined to judge the community as a single entity. As He allowed free will to humanity collectively, so, too, would He judge its use collectively. (That He had spared Noah and his family from the flood was not due to Noah's "blamelessness" alone. In beginning anew, the Lord's choice was between Noah and his family or an admission of total defeat.)

In Abraham's view, the surest sign of injustice was when "the innocent and guilty fare alike" (18:25). Yet to limit the mayhem, Abraham also knew that he must appeal to the Lord from the "second best" perspective of sparing the guilty in order to save the innocent.

The problem of individual versus collective justice will confront us throughout the Torah. (It is considered more fully in Comment L–59.) But quite apart from theory, Abraham's determination to confront the Lord on a matter of fundamental justice remains one of the Torah's greatest "revelations."

The story then turns to Sodom, where "two angels" arrived in the evening (19:1).

Comment G–29. On the Lord as the "third man"

The "three men" who had been with Abraham were said to have gone to Sodom (see 18:2, 16, 22). Yet, only "two angels" arrive there (19:1). No explicit explanation is given for the change of three "men" to two "angels" and the absence of one of the "three men." Clearly, however, the "third man" was the Lord, Himself, before whom Abraham continued to stand (18:22). Once again, the Torah draws on the mythology of divine beings who take human form at will.

As "the men" pass his house, Lot, like his uncle, proves a generous host. But for all the other "men of Sodom, young and old—*all the people to the last man*," there can be no hope (19:4–11). The men shout out to Lot: "Where are the men who came to you tonight? Bring them out to us that we may be intimate with them" (19:5). "I beg you," Lot replies, "do not commit such a wrong." He then tells "the men" of his own two daughters "who have not known a man." As an example of hospitality bordering on excess, Lot adds, "Let me bring [my daughters] out to you, and you may do to them as you please, but do not do anything to these men" (19:6–9). But for Lot's daughters, the men have no interest.

As Lot shelters his guests from harm, the men of Sodom scorn him as one who "*came here as an alien*" (19:9). But on reaching the entrance to Lots's house, they are struck with a blinding light that renders them helpless (19:10–11).

Comment G–30. On "the men" of Sodom as its moral representatives

Consistent with the culture of time and place, the moral quality of the entire community of Sodom and Gomorrah is measured by the conduct of its adult males. Yet every member of the community, women and children as well, will be among the victims of the Lord's response to that conduct.

Lot's guests now tell him to leave at once with his wife and "sons-in-law, your sons and daughters, or any one else that you have in the city" to avoid the destruction of all who remain. They identify themselves as agents of the Lord sent to "Sodom and Gomorrah . . . and the entire Plain." Lot urges his "sons-in-law" to leave, but they consider it a "jest." Together with their wives they remain (19:12–14).

Comment G–31. On the exemption of Lot and his family from death

In exempting Lot and his family, the Lord might seem to have made an exception to His standard of collective justice. Despite Lot's proposed sacrifice of his "maiden" daughters, his motives as a hospitable and protective host could have led the Lord to spare him and his family. But in fact his salvation was consistent with the strictest principles of collective justice. Having arrived but recently, Lot was viewed by the community as an "alien." As such, he and his family were not of the collectivity being judged.

Actually, from the only verse of Gen. 19 attributed by Friedman to P, we might derive another explanation of why Lot and his family were spared. It states that "*God* was mindful of Abraham" (19:29). If these were J's words, we might surmise that God was both mindful and respectful of Abraham's standard of individual justice. As P's words, however, the verse more likely portrays God's continuing protection of Lot, as Abraham's cherished nephew.

"As dawn broke, the *angels* urged Lot on" (19:15). As the family prepares to leave Sodom, one angel tells them, "Flee for your life! Do not look behind you, nor stop anywhere in the plain; flee to the hills, lest you be swept away. The Lord then rained a "sulfurous fire" on the two cities and "the entire Plain." Thus, "He annihilated . . . *all the inhabitants of the cities.*" But, alas, whether from terror or curiosity, Lot's wife looked back and "thereupon turned into a pillar of salt" (19:26).

> Note G–30: *The fate of Lot's wife is curious. The angel's words seem more an expression of concern than a command. Lot's wife could easily have taken them as a warning not to tarry. But knowing of J's delight in a good story, we might finally conclude that J contrived her harsh fate as an essential condition for the remarkable tale that follows.*

While Lot and his two unmarried daughters are resettled in a cave, the older observes to the younger, "Our father is old, and *there is not a man on earth to consort with us* in the way of the world. Come, let us make our father drink wine, and let us lie with him, that we may maintain life through our father" (19:31–32). Together, they implement her proposal. Their two sons, Moab and Ben-ammi, are then said to have fathered the Moabites and Ammonites (19:37–38).

Comment G–32. On the need for the "proactive" initiative by Lot's daughters

Why did Lot's daughters believe their father to be the only remaining male in the world? The three of them had in fact come to their cave from the town of Zoar, to which they had first fled from Sodom. At Lot's urging, the Lord had spared Zoar as a refuge for him and his family (19:21–22). But being "afraid to dwell in Zoar," Lot then "settled in the hill country" where he and his daughters "lived in a cave" (19:30). Why Lot feared to stay in Zoar, we do not know. But just as the backward look of Lot's wife provided the first condition of a good story, Lot's flight from Zoar to a cave provided the second. It is a tale on which the Torah imposes no judgment—neither on a benumbed Lot nor on his well-meaning daughters. Who can condemn an honest, though mistaken, effort to preserve humanity? But yet—what had become of the other men of Zoar?

Note G–31: Gen. 20, in which we return to Abraham and Sarah, is from a new source, E. This is noteworthy because the entire chapter consists of a retelling of the "sister" story first told by J. J's setting was the palatial court of Egypt's Pharaoh (12:10–20). E's is the more modest court of Abimelech, king of Gerar, in the Negev (20:1–18).

While "sojourning" in Gerar with Sarah, Abraham lets it be known that Sarah "is my sister" (20:2). When Abimelech then has Sarah brought to him, God (i.e., *elohim*) comes to him in a dream. He tells Abimelech that "you are to die because of the woman you have taken, *for she is a married woman*" (20:3). Abimelech protests his innocence. He tells God that Abraham had identified Sarah as his sister and that she had confirmed the "fact." Nor had he ever "approached" her. God replies, "I know that you did this with a blameless heart, and *so I kept you from sinning against Me. That is why I did not let you touch her*" (20:6). God assures Abimelech that all will be well if he returns Sarah to Abraham, who, being "a prophet," could intercede to save Abimelech's life. If not, God warns, "you shall die and all that are yours" (20:7). When Abimelech tells this to his servants they "were greatly frightened" (20:8). Then, as had Pharoah, Abimelech berates Abraham for so endangering him—and, indeed, his entire kingdom (20:9–10).

Note G–32: Contrary to relations between J's yahweh and Pharoah, E's elohim sought to protect Abimelech, and thus Sarah as well, from the sin of adulterous relations. (See Comment E–60 and cf. Lev. 18:20.)

Abraham then gives two reasons for his conduct. First, as he had in Egypt, he reveals his own fear of death: "I thought surely there is no fear of God in this place, and they will kill me because of my wife" (20:11). His second reason is more technical: "And besides, she is my sister, my father's daughter though not my mother's; and she became my wife" (20:12).

Comment G–33. On Sarah as Abraham's half-sister

If the Abimelech "sister" story is from E, it likely preceded the Holiness Code of the P source in Leviticus. Lev. 20:17 states the following in regard to the marriage of half-brothers and half-sisters: "If a man marries his sister, *the daughter of either his father or his mother* . . . it is a disgrace; they shall be excommunicated in the sight of their kinfolk" (see also, Lev. 18:9). If P wrote well after E and J, as is widely thought, neither would have known of the Levitical laws, as such. It is very possible therefore that neither E nor J knew of any bar to the marriage of Abraham and Sarah. In any case, R was content to accept E's explanation in full vindication of Abraham.

As had Pharaoh in Egypt, Abimelech showers flocks and herds and slaves on Abraham. But unlike Pharaoh who "sent him off with his wife," Abimelech invites Abraham and Sarah to settle in Gerar, "wherever you please." Abraham then prayed to God on Abimelech's behalf. In turn, Abimelech regained his fertility, and so, too, did his wife and his retinue, whose wombs had been "closed fast" (20:14–18).

Comment G–34. On the second "sister" story as it reflects on (1) Abraham's faith and self-reliance and (2) the problem of continuity among the sources

The same character traits that had shaped Abraham's conduct in Egypt were again evident in Gerar. Sometime after the events in Pharaoh's court, we were told that Abram had by then "put his trust in the Lord" and that God "had reckoned it to his merit" (15:6). Had his doubts now returned? If so, why? From the Lord's display of power at Sodom and Gemorrah, Abraham should have been reassured of His ability to fulfil his purposes. E, however, only told the story as drawn from tradition. Of Abraham's having been tested in the Egypt once before, E would not likely have known.

Comment G–35. On God, Abimelech, and human free will

The unconsummated wrong for which Abimelech might die is identified as sexual relations with "a married woman" (20:3). So far, no code of sexual morality has appeared in the Torah. Thus, Abimelech's potential sin may have reflected prevailing standards later included in the Seventh Commandment's prohibition of adultery. Note, however, that Abimelech's potential sin would not have arisen from his own marital status, but from relations with "a married woman." Were Sarah unmarried, there would have been no sin. Because he had been deceived as to Sarah's marital status, he would have been blameless until the truth was revealed.

Any decision by Abimelech to "approach" Sarah would have been made in ignorance of its moral ingredients (as was Pharaoh's in regard to Sarah). In turn, given her willing entry into his household, she could hardly object to any "approach" by Abimelech. *This dilemma could have prompted God's intervention, apart from any issue of Abimelech's free will. First, the honor of His peoples' future matriarch was at risk. Second, in that he believed Sarah to be unmarried, Abimelech could not have exercised his free will "sinfully."*

Of central importance in regard to God's possible intervention in the exercise of Abimelech's free will is His statement to Abimelech *in his dream.* "I know that you did this with a blameless heart, *and so I kept you from sinning against Me. That is why I did not let you touch her"* (20:6). Do these words imply that God had taken control of Abimelech's free will? While it might seem so, it was not God's purpose to modify an "informed" human choice. Rather, it was to avoid the dire consequences of an "uninformed" choice. And although the conduct would have been a "sin," as indicated by God, it would have been unintended, and therefore excusable—at least by the later recorded standards of Lev. 4:22–26 and 27–35.

The "Abimelech" sister story is immediately followed by the conception and birth of Isaac. The Torah gives Abraham's age at Isaac's birth as one hundred (21:5). In turn, Sarah, being ten years younger, was ninety (17:17).

Comment G–36. On Sarah's age in E's "sister" story

Sarah's age is pertinent to the Abimelech "sister" story. As she approached ninety (by P's count), Sarah's faded beauty was not likely to provide a credible basis for Abraham's fear of being killed because of her. Even before this episode, the Torah described her as "old, advanced in years" and she described herself as "withered." Further, she had "stopped having the periods of women" (18:11–12).

At the outset of the first sister story, we learn of "how very beautiful" Sarah was when she and Abraham came into Egypt to escape the famine in Canaan (12:11–16). By P's count (12:4b) (as applied to J's story), Abraham was then over seventy-five and Sarah over sixty-five. At sixty-five today Sarah could perhaps radiate a certain mature beauty. But what of the likelihood on approaching ninety? Though not revealed in the Abimelech story, Sarah's age is presumably appropriate to the occasion. The quandry arises, however, from R's placement of E's "sister" story just after P's focus on Sarah's age (cf. Comment G–38).

Now, "The Lord took note of Sarah as He had promised, and the Lord did for Sarah as He had spoken" (21:1).

Comment G–37. On the miraculous birth of Isaac

The manipulation and control of the forces of nature by the God of the Torah had long preceded the birth of Isaac. It began with creation itself and proceeded through the Great Flood, the events at the Tower and the destruction of Sodom. For people who knew little of the natural order, the dramatization of such events was well calculated to inspire awe in God's powers. But unlike a miraculous birth, these events were far removed from matters of personal well-being.

In a way, the creation of life through natural processes is a miracle in itself. But many humans find frustration rather than fulfillment in those processes. What could better replace despair with hope than a belief that the Lord, when He so chose, might "jump-start" nature? At least until experience created doubt, what belief could foster stronger ties between such aspirants and their God?

The joy with which the Torah tells of the birth of Isaac is diluted by the story of Hagar and Ishmael which follows (21:9–21). Although well aware by now of Isaac's destiny as Abraham's covenantal heir, Sarah seeks to remove its one possible impediment by evicting Hagar and Ishmael from the household: "Cast out that slave-woman and her son, for the son of that slave shall not share in the inheritance with my son Isaac" (21:10). Abraham, greatly "distressed" by Sarah's request, is now counseled by God. "Do not be distressed over the boy or your slave; whatever Sarah tells you, do as she says, for it is through Isaac that offspring shall be continued for you. As for the son of the slave-woman, I will make a nation of him, too, for he is your seed." With Sarah demanding and God commanding, Abraham gives Hagar bread and water and sends them off (21:12–14).

Hagar and Ishmael are now alone in the desert. With their water gone, Hagar "left the child under one of the bushes." She then sits down at a distance and cries. "Let me not look on as the child dies" (21:16). God then opens her eyes to a well of water. From then on Hagar and Ishmael do better. "God was with the boy and he grew up; he dwelt in the wilderness and became a bowman . . . his mother got a wife for him from the land of Egypt" (21:20).

Comment G–38. On Torah "years" as defined by Ishmael

P tells us that "Abram was eighty-six years old when Hagar bore Ishmael to Abram" (16:16). Since Abraham is now over one hundred, Ishmael is at least fourteen, as attested earlier by P in 17:25; that is, "Ishmael was thirteen years old when he was circumcised." The present passage, however, speaks of a much younger child. The image of a thirsty fourteen-year-old boy remaining quietly under a bush seems unreal. Would he simply remain there to die? At fourteen, would he not get up to look for water? Or is Ishmael's age anomaly, like Sarah's, a result of placing an "E age" (21:9–21) in the wake of ages recorded by other sources? (See 12:4b, 16:16, 17:17–25, 21:5, and Comment G–36.)

The balance of Gen. 21 tells of a pact between Abraham and Abimelech that appears to involve the ownership, or use, of water at the well of Beer-Sheba. "When they had completed the pact at Beer-sheba, Abimelech and Phicol, chief of his troops, departed and returned to the land of the Philistines" (21:32). The passage closes with Abraham's planting a tamarisk tree at the site, where he "invoked the name of the Lord, the Everlasting God" (21:33).

Gen. 22 tells of the *akedah*, the aborted sacrifice of Isaac, another defining event of the Torah. It is also a Torah masterpiece of terse compelling drama.

"Some time afterward, God put Abraham to the test. He said to him, 'Abraham,' and he answered, 'Here I am.' And God said, 'Take your son, your favored one Isaac, whom you love, and go to the land of Moriah, and offer him there as a burnt offering on one of the heights which I will point out to you'" (22:1–2).

We need not repeat Abraham's preparations in detail. It is sufficient to note that he makes them with dispatch and proceeds at once to Moriah with Isaac and his servants. There he builds an altar, lays out the wood, binds Isaac, lays him on the altar and picks up his knife to kill him (22:9–10). "An angel of the Lord" then tells him, "Do not raise your hand against the boy, or do anything to him. For now *I know that you fear* God, since you have not withheld your son, your favored one, from Me" (22:12).

Comment G–39. On the authorship of the *akedah* and on R's separate references to "the Lord" and "God"

1. *Authorship of the* akedah

The *akedah* (22:1–19) is generally attributed to E. Friedman surmises, however, that 22:11–16a may have been inserted by R to "undo" E's actual sacrifice of Isaac.[16] As evidence, he observes that "Isaac never again appears as a character in E." Literally, Friedman may be correct. But he then leaves to conjecture why, in at least four verses *that he attributes to E rather than R*, reference is made to Isaac as the father of Jacob (Gen. 31:53, 46:1, 48:15–16). As of the *akedah*, of course, Isaac, was a father to no one. If he had been sacrificed, with whom could E have replaced him as Jacob's father? There is the further point, however, that E speaks only of Abraham's return to his servants; and with them alone he is said to have returned to Beer-sheba (22:19).

2. *R's separate references to "the Lord" and "God"*

What first hints of the separate authorship of 22:11–16a is the appearance of *yahweh* amidst E's *elohim*. The insert might at first seem to portray "the Lord" and "God" as separate aspects of a single Being. Thus, "An angel of the Lord" tells Abraham, "I [the Lord] know that you fear God" (22:11–12). The reference, however, is not to "*your*" God, but to a God who, like the Lord, is a universal Being. But what of "the Lord's" further words to Abraham in 22:12? "*I* know that you fear *God*, since you have not withheld your son . . . *from Me.*" Who is "Me?" The Lord or God? Are *yahweh* and *elohim* one and the same? Or are they two distinct aspects of a unitary Being? Or is it possible to determine from R alone? (Cf. Exod. 6:5–7 and Comments G–43, G–56, L–43, and L–45.)

"An angel of the Lord" then tells Abraham of his reward for obedience. "Because you have done this and have not withheld your son, your favored one, I will bestow my blessing on you and make your descendants as numerous as the stars of heaven and the sands on the seashore; and your descendants shall seize the gates of their foes. All the nations of the earth shall bless themselves by your descendants, because you have obeyed my command" (22:16–18).

Comment G–40. On the internal logic of the *akedah*

Why was this emotionally wrenching narrative included in the Torah? As it relates to God and Abraham, the Torah tells us that "God put Abraham to the test" (22:1). But why? What doubts about Abraham's fitness to be the father of his people does the Torah mean to attribute to its God? Especially at this mature stage of relations between Abraham and its God, why must the Torah so test Abraham?

The answer lies in the Lord's statement regarding the standard by which He judges Abraham. Consider His words: "For now I know that you *fear* God, since you have not withheld your son, your favored one, from Me" (22:12). The Torah's concern was not that Abraham doubted the honest intent of its God to fulfil His promise. It was rather that Abraham's conduct had cast doubt on his "fear" of its God.

In this context what does the Torah mean by "fear"? Surely, something more than Abraham's abject fear of God's reprisal should he refuse to slay Isaac. If such were his "fear," then we must cringe at his moral fiber. How would we judge a father who would kill his son to save himself from punishment? How could the Torah fail to condemn him?

In fact, however, the Torah uses "fear" in a different sense directly related to Abraham's past conduct. In general, "fear" of a deity stems from the certainty of its power to fulfil its will. An especially critical aspect of Abraham's "fear" would be his certainty of God's power to fulfil His promise to Abraham and his descendants.

In what way had Abraham cast doubt on his "fear" of God? Recall that on at least three occasions, two being similar in nature, Abraham's conduct reflected his doubt of God's ability to fulfil His promises. The first, of course, was the "sister" episode in Egypt. Its meaning in regard to Abraham's faith in the Lord's powers have been noted (see Comment G–19). When Abraham repeated the process in Abimelech's court, God saw his problem all the more clearly (see Comment G–34). Moreover, Abraham had openly expressed incredulity on being told that a covenantal heir would yet be born to him and Sarah (17:17). Let us assume, then, that the *akedah* was meant to test Abraham's belief in God's power to work his will and fulfil His promises.

Here we should also consider what else God and Abraham knew at the time of the *akedah*. Both knew of God's repeated promises to Abraham that his descendants would proliferate and prosper. They knew as well of God's assurance that their descent would be through Isaac (17:15–21, 21:12).

In time, however, God's unilateral promise is replaced by a bilateral Covenant of Circumcision (17:9–14). In addition, we learn of a condition not yet revealed. It is the Lord's expectation that Abraham's descendants will do "what is just and right, *in order that the Lord may bring about for Abraham what He has promised him*" (18:19).

As yet both conditions have been honored. As for circumcision, Abraham had fully met his obligations (17:23–27, 21:4). As for the broader charge, it was Abraham's nature to do "what is just and right." Here we might wonder about his eviction of Ishmael and Hagar. But when he first resisted Sarah's request to send them away, God sided with Sarah. He then repeated His earlier assurance to Abraham that Ishmael's future would be worthy of his seed (21:9–13, 17:20). Accordingly, as of the *akedah*, all conditions had been met and God remained bound by His promise.

God and Abraham thus came to the "test" with the mutual knowledge that (1) God's several promises to Abraham were in full force and (2) that the other "party" knew so. Next to his love of Isaac, what overwhelmed Abraham's mind when God proposed His test was the added fear that God's promise would necessarily die along with Isaac. Thus, for Abraham, the ultimate irony would be that God's promise would fail for the reason of his obedience. As at Sodom and Gomorrah, Abraham was again compelled to question God's judgment. But to grasp the inner "realities" that guided both Abraham and his God in this matter, we must read the *akedah* as *midrash*.

Comment G–41. On the *akedah* as *midrash*

God appears to Abraham to tell him that he must take his son Isaac to Moriah "and offer him there as a burnt offering." Although Abraham is at first struck dumb by the horror of God's command, he finally contrives a reply. "My God, Whom I know to be just, and Whom I fear and hold in awe, how can You demand this of me? Who is to benefit from this sacrifice of my beloved son, Isaac? What good can come to You or anyone through the death of this innocent boy?"

God is shaken by Abraham's resistance. Was Abraham still afflicted by the same skepticism of His power that had twice caused him to place Sarah's honor in peril and then to doubt His promise of Isaac's birth? Realizing that Abraham or anyone worthy of having been chosen by Him must have an answer, God replies, "Abraham, you say you fear Me. But do you really? It is to prove your fear that I must test you." After recalling the three episodes of concern, God states His problem: "Such acts by the father of My people cannot be kept from his descendants. If you are to be their father, the people must know that I, Myself, have tested you. They must never doubt your total confidence in My power to fulfil My purposes."

In truth, despite all that he now knew of God's powers, Abraham's natural skepticism left him with doubts regarding the fulfillment of the covenant in the wake of Isaac's death. His task, therefore, was to assure God of his broad confidence in His powers while not disclosing his concerns about their limits. He answers accordingly: "My God, all that You say of me is true. But consider: You brought me from my father's house in Haran, a simple, untutored, and inexperienced man. Gradually, through Your guidance, I have come to learn of You and Your ways. But it was not until Isaac's conception and birth that I grasped the true breadth of your powers. If you demand his death because of my doubts before his birth, You must know that his birth has given me new faith in your powers. There is no need to test my fear of You. To require Isaac's death as proof of my fear would be a pointless injustice to him and his parents."

Abraham continued: "In truth, my God, I cannot obey Your command. If You do not deem me fit to be the father of Your people, then let me die so that Isaac may take my place. Let the people descend from Isaac, as their father. Am I, in fact, any more than my own father, the actual father of Isaac's descendants? What is important is that the father of Your people be worthy of You and that his descendants know him to be so. Isaac is truly a worthy lad, untroubled by questions regarding the limits of Your powers. In truth, the fear of you will be even more natural to his spirit than mine. As for myself, I fear You; I honor You; I know You to be unique. But Your request that I slay Isaac to prove my certainty that Your power suffices for all Your purposes only arouses my earlier doubts. Will Isaac not die in vain? How can even Your powers suffice to fulfil your promise to make a great nation of my descendants *through Isaac*? I ask, but I have no answers. My confidence is inadequate to assure me. The price You ask as a test of my faith is too much. No, My God, let me die instead."

God's answer did Him great honor. "Abraham, despite your doubts regarding the fullness of My powers, your words prove you to be a worthy father of my people. Your love of Isaac and your complete honesty justify my confidence in having chosen you. Neither Isaac nor you shall die before your time. My promise to you will be fulfilled.

"But there is a purpose, Abraham, *in making it appear* to your descendants that you had met the ultimate test of your certainty of my power. Without such a test, the doubts that they may perceive in you will come to weigh heavily on their spirits. And yet their own needs will require their fear of Me. Not all of your descendants will possess your wisdom, your self-reliance, your integrity and your respect for your fellows. It is essential, therefore, that you impart your fear of Me to them by your apparent readiness to obey my command to sacrifice your beloved son, Isaac.

"That such a test will create problems, I know. Some will fault you more for your readiness to sacrifice Isaac than they will praise you for your fear of

Me. I will deem them righteous. Others will question My justice in imposing such a test. I will also deem them righteous. But We must take these risks so that the people can harbor no doubts of your certainty of My power to fulfil My purposes."

Abraham's direct honesty gave him little patience for "staged" events. But as he had been honest with God, so God had been honest with him. And so Abraham replied, "I will do as You ask. I may lack confidence in some aspects of Your power, but not of your good intentions. I would ask only one favor of You. This terrible ordeal will haunt Isaac all his days. Give me wisdom, therefore, to explain its need, both to him and his mother." To which God replied, "I will try to add what little wisdom I can to your own." And so it was that Abraham accepted God's "test" and provided his descendants with "proof" of his "fear" of God.

Gen. 23 tells of Sarah's death in Hebron at the age of one hundred twenty-seven. Following his mourning, Abraham, as a "resident alien" among the Hittites, seeks permission to buy a burial site. He first asks to buy "a burial site among you, that I may remove my dead for burial" (23:4). The Hittites reply with generosity. "Hear us, my lord; you are the elect of God among us. Bury your dead in the choicest of our burial places; none of us will withhold his burial place from you for burying your dead" (23:6).

Abraham's response, however, reveals a broader purpose than the burial of Sarah—as important as that was to him. Having first "bowed low to the people of the land," he tells them, "If it is *your wish* that I remove my dead for burial, *you must agree* to intercede for me with Ephron son of Zohar" (23:7–8). Abraham's purpose will not be satisfied by one of the many public burial places offered to him as a gift. He wishes instead to pay "the full price" for a personal site at "the cave of Machpelah which [Ephron] owns, which is at the edge of his land" (23:9).

As it happened, Ephron the Hittite "was present among the Hittites" (23:10). On hearing Abraham's wish to buy his site, Ephron artfully responds with even greater generosity: "No my lord, hear me: I give you the field and I give you the cave that is in it; I give it to you in the presence of my people. Bury your dead" (23:11).

Abraham's refusal to accept the property as a gift soon reveals Ephron's astuteness. Bowing low to the Hittites, Abraham pleads: "If you would only hear me out! Let me pay the price of the land; accept it from me, that I may bury my dead there" (23:13). Ephron honors Abraham's anticipated wish at once. "My lord do hear me! A piece of land worth four hundred shekels of silver—what is that between you and me? Go and bury your dead" (23:15). Abraham then paid him "four hundred shekels of silver at the going merchants' rate." Thus, "Ephron's land in Machpelah, near Mamre—the field with its cave and all the trees anywhere within the confines of that field—passed to Abraham as his possession, in the presence of the Hittites" (23:17–18). And both parties were well served.

Abraham buried Sarah "in the cave of the field of Machpelah, facing Mamre—now Hebron—in the land of Canaan" (23:19). "Thus the field with its cave passed from the Hittites to Abraham, as a burial site" (23:20).

Note G–33: In regard to "now Hebron," see Comments G–63 and 65.

Comment G–42. On Abraham and the Cave at Machpelah

1. Abraham, as the "elect of God"

The term "elect of God," by which the Hittites address Abraham, is from the Hebrew *nesi elohim* (23:6). JPS1 and RSV render it as a secular "mighty prince." Literally, it could mean a "prince of God," a "prince of god," or, given the plural form of *elohim*, a "prince of the gods." Clearly, it is a term of high honor. But if, as implied by JPS2's capitalization of God, the Hittites are thought to mean a "prince of Abraham's God," we must wonder how they came to know of Him. Had Abraham told them of his God? If so, as implied by JPS2, did they mean to acknowledge his God as the Supreme Being? Or, since they knew Abraham to be of another people, could they have meant "prince of whatever divine being(s) you may serve?"

2. On Abraham as an exemplar of self-reliance and human responsibility

We have considered how the "sister" stories in the courts of Pharaoh in Egypt and Abimelech in Gerar reflected Abraham's commitment to self-reliance as a key element of human responsibility (see Comments G–19 and 34). His purchase of the cave of Machpelah and its field speaks admirably to the same truth. Beyond a burial place of sufficient dignity to hold the remains of his wife, what did Abraham seek? *His purpose, as related by P, was the permanent ownerhip of land in Canaan—as could be verified by the present occupants and owners of the surrounding land.* And so it was recorded: "Ephron's land in Machpelah, near Mamre—the field with its cave and all the trees anywhere within the confines of that field—passed to Abraham as his possession, in the presence of the Hittites" (23:18).

But why does Abraham attach such importance to his actual ownership of the land and cave? The Lord has not directed him to buy it. However, He has told Abraham that "your offspring shall be strangers in a land not theirs, and they shall be enslaved and oppressed four hundred years." But in time, "they shall return here" (15:13–16). True to character, in burying Sarah,

Abraham also took earthly responsibility for providing his descendants with a binding legal claim to land in Canaan pending their return.

Gen. 24 tells a warm human story of how Abraham's servant, "the Dammesek Eliezer" (15:2), the Torah's matchmaker *non pareil*, effects the marriage of Rebekah to Isaac. It is illuminated by repeated shafts of psychological insight. As the story begins, Abraham is planning for Isaac's marriage. He is determined not only to assure the fulfillment of the Lord's promise, but to launch it under optimal conditions. By now Abraham is even more "old [and] advanced in years" (cf. 18:11 and 24:1). He thus extracts two solemn promises from his trusted steward Eliezer. He requires him to swear by "the Lord the God of Heaven and the God of the earth" (24:2–3).

> *Note G–34: Here, to "the Dammesek Eliezer," J's Abraham portrays the "the Lord" as a universal God (cf. Comment G–39 pt. 2).*

He first swears that he will not "take a wife for my son" from among the daughters of Canaan, but only from "the land of my birth" (24:3–4). Abraham assures Eliezer that God will send "an angel before you." As always, however, he deems it prudent to make contingency plans (24:7). Abraham thus absolves Eliezer from his first promise if the woman he chooses "does not choose to follow you" (24:8). In that case, Eliezer asks, "Shall I take your son back to the land from which you came?" To this Abraham replies, by way of effecting a second sworn promise, "On no account must you take my son back there" (24:6). As a practical man, Abraham would do the best he could do without agonizing over what he could not do. And Isaac's remaining in Canaan would best assure his presence to fulfil the Lord's promise.

The story then tells of Eliezer's devoted and skillful efforts to identify a suitable young woman from the city of Abraham's brother, Nahor, and to gain her consent. On reaching his destination, he brings his camels to the well and prays: "O Lord, God of my master Abraham, grant me good fortune this day, and deal graciously with my master Abraham" (24:12). He then asks Lord God for a sign from the bride to be, so that he might choose accordingly (24:14).

Rebekah immediately appears at the well. In every way she seems an answer to Eliezer's prayer. She identifies herself as the granddaughter of Nahor. Her remarkable beauty is graced by qualities of modesty, self-assurance, kindness, hospitality, and quiet efficiency (24:15–28).

Out of deep gratitude, Eliezer bows in homage and speaks to Lord God: "Blessed be the Lord, the God of my master Abraham, who has not withheld His steadfast kindness from my master. For I have been guided on my errand by the Lord, to the house of my master's kinsmen" (24:27).

Comment G–43. On Eliezer's references to "the Lord" as the "God of Abraham"

While Abraham refers to the Lord as the universal God (24:3), Eliezer speaks of Him as "God of my master Abraham" (24:27). Whenever Eliezer seeks guidance from or gives thanks to Abraham's God, he never alludes to Him as his God. He prays that He deal "graciously with my master." His gratitude to Him is for His "steadfast kindness" to Abraham. But Eliezer never seeks guidance from, nor gives thanks to, Abraham's God as his God or for his own sake.

Why does J limit Eliezer's relationship with the Lord God to his role as Abraham's agent? J, of course, may have viewed Eliezer's relations with Abraham's God as an aspect of being Abraham's servant. As such, he would perhaps be expected to treat Abraham's God as his own. However, while actual spiritual adherence to Abraham's God was never explicitly attributed to Eliezer, his entire attitude suggests a relationship beyond a servant's obligation.

It is also possible that Eliezer viewed Abraham's God in a different sense, that is, as a "possession" of his master. As such, Abraham's God could be revered, but could not be shared without his master's leave. *Had Abraham ever encouraged Eliezer to accept his God? Or did Abraham regard his relations with his God as limited to himself and his descendants?* In either case, Eliezer's devotion, intelligence, competence, and character made him a worthy representative of both Abraham and his God.

Rebekah's brother Laban (later to become Jacob's duplicitous father-in-law) now appears. His flawed character is revealed at once. On learning of Eliezer from Rebekah and of his gifts of a heavy "gold nose ring" and "gold arm bands," Laban goes out at once to greet him. Moved by the possibility of further riches, Laban eagerly welcomes him with words of fawning hypocrisy: "Come in, O blessed of the Lord. . . . Why do you remain outside, when I have made ready the house and a place for the camels?" (24:31).

Before eating, Eliezer tells of his mission to find a suitable wife for Isaac, son of Abraham. He describes Abraham's wealth and his particular desire to find a wife for his son "from my kindred, from my father's house." Having credited his discovery of Rebekah to "the God of my master Abraham," he asks for her hand in marriage to Isaac. Laban and Bethuel (father of Rebekah and Laban) reply, "the matter is decreed by the Lord. . . . Let her be a wife to your master's son, as the Lord has spoken" (24:50–51).

Comment G–44. On Laban's and Bethuel's recourse to Lord God's will in agreeing to Rebekah's marriage to Isaac

Laban and Bethuel are quick to place the Lord's imprimatur on a match they ardently seek. The "Lord" to which they refer is none other than J's *yahweh*, or *adonai*, the God of Abraham and his offspring-to-be. Is it possible that Laban and Bethuel already knew and accepted Abraham's God as their God? Or does their invocation of the "Lord's decree" as the basis for their consent echo their initial self-serving hypocrisy? Their pretentious servility contrasts sharply with Eliezer's direct and honest words.

When the family waives its initial request for a customary premarital delay before departure, Eliezer and Rebekah depart at once. On arriving home Eliezer tells Isaac of his mission and of his return with Rebekah. "Isaac then brought her into the tent of his mother Sarah, and he took Rebekah as his wife. Isaac loved her, and thus found comfort after his mother's death" (24:67).

Comment G–45. On the absence of Abraham when Eliezer returns to "Sarah's" tent with Rebekah, the bride of Isaac

That Isaac brought Rebekah into "Sarah's" tent might suggest its current use by Sarah. But Sarah is dead and buried at Machpelah. Yet Isaac still thinks of the tent as hers. This seems natural. The *akedah* would have reinforced the strong bound between Isaac and Sarah that was first forged in the circumstances of his birth. The vivid memory of a father poised to kill him could only strengthen the attachment of a son to a loving mother. But if the aged Abraham still lives (24:1), where is he when Eliezer returns with a bride for Isaac that he had so eagerly wished?

As Gen. 25 opens, the closing bliss of Gen. 24 quickly gives way to shock. "Abraham took another wife [*ishah*], whose name was Keturah" (25:1–2). She bore him Zimran, Jokshan, Medan, Midian, Ishbak, and Shuah. Of these, the lines of descent from Jokshan, Dedan, and Midian are set out (25:3–4). Abraham is then said to have "willed all that he owned to Isaac"; but to his "sons by concubines" [*peelagshim*], he gave gifts while he lived and "sent them away from his son Isaac eastward, to the land of the East" (25:5–6). What he gave to, or where he sent, his six sons by Keturah, we are not told.

Comment G–46. On Abraham's new line of descendants

Compare carefully the texts of Gen. 25:1–4 and 5–6. The first states that Abraham took "another wife," Keturah by name. After the naming of their six sons, and the descendants of only three, it is said: "All these were the descendants of Keturah" (25:4). Gen. 25:5–6 then states that "Abraham willed all that he owned to Isaac," and gave living gifts to his sons by "concubines." The names and numbers of the concubines and their sons are not disclosed.

The combined verses portray a marvelously fruitful Abraham following Sarah's death. Recall that in 24:1 he was described as "old and advanced in years." Friedman assigns 25:1–4 to E and 25:5–6 to J. If so, the unidentified concubines and their sons, being of a separate source, are likely duplicative. But why are the descendants of only three of Keturah's sons named? Were the others without sons? Or, to better praise Abraham's adherence to the first *mitzvah*, did R choose to meld two sources into one story?

The commentators were hard pressed to interpret this passage. In regard to 25:1, Rashi minces no words. He states: "Keturah. This is Hagar. And she was called Keturah." On addressing 25:6, Rashi seeks to reconcile it with 25:1: "The concubines is written incompletely . . . for there was only one concubine, she was Hagar, the same as Keturah."[17] But Rashi does not explain how his Keturah/Hagar might be both wife and concubine. In naming her a concubine, Rashi might have relied on an identification of Keturah as "Abraham's concubine" in 1 Chron. 1:32. But this later source gives no hint of Keturah and Hagar as the same person.

Ramban rejects Rashi's view. He identifies Keturah as a true Canaanite wife of Abraham, sometimes called concubine because of her descent "from a family of slaves." As for the unnamed "concubines," Rambam says of Abraham, almost in passing, "all his consorts were concubines to him, not as wives since their children would not be among his heirs." Thus, "Hagar, Sarah's handmade, was his concubine."[18] By this test, however, since her sons were not Abraham's heirs, Keturah, would have been a concubine rather than a wife. Overall, these events in Abraham's old age are not easily explained.

The Torah then tells of Abraham's death at "a good ripe age" of one hundred seventy-five years (25:8). Reunited for the occasion, Isaac and Ishmael bury their father near Sarah "in the cave at Machpelah . . . in the field that Abraham had bought from the Hittites" (25:9–10). God then blesses Isaac (25:11). There is no mention of a blessing on Ishmael, but the names of his twelve sons are listed. They are identified as "twelve chieftains of as many tribes" (25:12–16). As the story of Abraham closes, we learn of the death of Ishmael at the age of one hundred thirty-seven years (25:17).

ISAAC, JACOB, ESAU, JOSEPH, AND THEIR GOD

Following its orderly presentation of the line of Ishmael, the Torah turns to the tumultuous origins of the line of Isaac. Sarah's inability to conceive until the Lord's miraculous intervention in her postmenstrual years is at least partially replicated in the story of Rebekah and her twins. Thus, "Isaac pleaded with the Lord on behalf of his wife, because she was barren; and the Lord responded to his plea, and his wife Rebekah conceived" (25:21).

Comment G–47. On the Lord's role in the births of Jacob and Esau

The manner of the Lord's "response" and of Rebekah's capacity to conceive "naturally" without His intervention are not known. His role in the conception and birth of Esau and Jacob is more whimsical than miraculous and perhaps less necessary than in Sarah's case. It may have been thought fitting, however, that the birth of this pivotal covenantal heir should receive no less Lordly attention than the birth of Isaac. Jacob was born to be the father of a mighty generation. Should the inheritance of his offspring be debased by the "natural" birth of their father?

The carriage and birth of Rebekah's twins proved no simple matter. When she sought an explanation for the tumult within her, the Lord answered: "Two nations are within your womb. Two separate peoples shall enter from your body; One people shall be mightier than the other. And the older shall serve the younger" (25:23). At their birth, the red and hairy Esau emerged first, followed by Jacob, grasping his brother's heel. Isaac was now sixty years old. As his first-born, Esau was his covenantal heir apparent. But with birth, only the venue of his struggle with Jacob had changed.

We are told that Isaac favored Esau, "a skillful hunter, a man of the out-doors" who could satisfy his "taste for game" (25:27–28). Rebekah favored Jacob, a milder and quieter man inclined to stay home (25:28). Once, when Esau returned home "famished" from hunting, he asked Jacob for some "red pottage" that he was cooking. Jacob replied: "First sell me your birthright" (25:31). Esau agrees, but Jacob seeks the greater assurance of Esau's swearing to the sale. Only then does Jacob allow Esau to eat his pottage. However, it is with Esau's indifference rather than Jacob's opportunism that the Torah finds fault. "Thus did Esau spurn his birthright" (25:34).

Comment G–48. On the Lord and the "sale" of Esau's birthright: some initial thoughts

Was Esau truly bound by the transaction? Could a first-born son, by his own accord, trade his "birthright" to a brother? Or was his transfer of this patrimony subject to Isaac's consent? Further, did Esau have any idea of the importance of his birthright? Did he, or indeed did Jacob, relate it to the covenantal heirship? Had Isaac explained the nature of his covenantal inheritance to either one? As yet, the text reveals nothing.

Jacob and Esau now give way to another story: "There was a famine in the land—aside from the previous famine that had occurred in the days of Abraham —and Isaac went to Abimelech, king of the Philistines, in Gerar" (26:1).

Note G–35: When Abraham first came to Gerar from Egypt, (an) Abim-elech ruled, not as the "king of the Philistines, in Gerar," but as "king of Gerar" (20:2). This is one of several variances between the E and J versions of Abraham and Isaac in the court of Abimelech in Gerar.

Comment G–49. On the presence of the Philistines in Canaan in the time of Abraham and Isaac

The Philistines are thought to have first arrived at the southern coast of Palestine from the Aegean area c. 1200, or "about the time of the arrival of the Israelites in Canaan from Egypt."[19] Similarly, they are said to have "first appear[ed] in history" in Egypt at "about 1190–1158 B.C.E."[20] In either case, the Philistines could not have reached Gerar until some 400 to 500 years after Isaac.

The Torah first refers to Philistines in regard to Abraham and Abimelech. It states that after the Beer-sheba water pact, "Abimelech and Phicol, chief of his troops, departed and returned to the land of the Philistines" (21:32). It then observes that "Abraham resided in the land of the Philistines a long time" (21:33). The Philistines (from which comes "Palestine") were especially prominent in the period of the early prophets during the reigns of Kings Saul and David (see, for example, 1 Sam. 4:1–10).

The anachronism of a Philistine presence in the time of Genesis must reflect a "misreading" of history by later authors. (Friedman ascribes Isaac/Abimelech to J, and Abraham/Abimelech to E.) If so, it is an interesting coincidence that both would have placed Philistines in Canaan long before their actual presence.

In theory we might conceive of an ambiguous oral tradition as confusing to E as to J. Perhaps earlier Aegean invaders were later misidentified as Philistines. What we know of more surely, however, are the Israelites' hostilities with the Philistines in the eras of J and E. By c. 1050 B.C.E., Philistines had moved eastward into the Judean hills. Defeated by King David, c. 1000 B.C.E., they retreated to their coastal cities. Their prominence at the time may have led J and E to place them in Canaan much earlier.[21]

Famine, or not, the Lord wants Isaac to remain in Canaan; and to that purpose He appears to him (26:2). "Do not go down to Egypt; stay in the land I point out to you. Reside in this land, and I will be with you and bless you; I will give all these lands to you and your offspring, fulfilling the oath that I swore to your father Abraham . . . *inasmuch as Abraham obeyed Me and kept My charge: My commandments, My laws and My teachings*" (26:3–5).

Note G–36: With this reminder of the "conditionality" of the Lord's covenant, Isaac then "stayed in Gerar."

And now with Isaac and Rebekah in the role of husband and wife, we encounter a third version of the wife/sister story (26:6–11). "When the men of [Gerar] asked him about his wife, [Isaac] said, 'She is my sister,' for he was afraid to say 'my wife,' thinking, 'The men of the place might kill me on account of Rebekah for she is beautiful.'"

> Note G–37: Isaac's claim, of course, lacked the technical "half-sister" support of Abraham's similar claim as to Sarah.

Isaac's dissembling is discovered when Abimelech, "looking out of the window, saw Isaac fondling his wife Rebekah" (26:8).

> Note G–38: Or "sporting with," per JPS1.

When Isaac tells Abimelech that it was from fear that he misrepresented his relationship with Rebekah, Abimelech chastises him: "One of the people might have lain with your wife, and you would have brought guilt upon us" (26:10). (Cf. Comment G–35 on the point of unwitting sins.) Abimelech then takes Isaac and Rebekah under his protection.

Thereafter, "the Lord blessed him," and through his skills with crops and animals Isaac amasses such great wealth that "the Philistines envied him" (26:13–14). When they stop up Isaac's wells, Abimelech tells him he must leave "for you have become too big for us" (26:15–16).

Isaac eventually arrives at the site he will name Beer-sheba. The Lord then appears to introduce Himself, not as a universal God, but as "the God of your father Abraham" (26:24). He assures Isaac that "I am with you, and I will bless you and increase your offspring for the sake of My servant Abraham" (26:24). Abimelech then arrives with Phicol, "chief of his troops" (26:26). To Isaac's complaint of Abimelech's past hostility in sending him away, the king answers, "We now see plainly that the Lord has been with you. . . . Let us make a pact with you, that you will not do us harm, just as we have not molested you, but have always dealt kindly with you and sent you away in peace." The pact was made and the parties feasted together (26:27–30).

When Abimelech leaves, Isaac's servants dig a well and find water (26:32). "He named it Shibab; therefore the name of the city is Beer-sheba to this day" (26:33).

> Note G–39: On "to this day" see Comments G–63 and 65, and Note G–47.

Comment G–50. On time and sequence in Gen. 25 and 26

1. On the order of Gen. 25:19–34 and 26

Immediately preceding Gen. 26, Gen. 25:19–34 tells of the births and birthrights of Jacob and Esau. Gen. 26:1–33 then tells of Isaac in Gerar. Friedman attributes both passages to J. Yet, during Isaac's stay in Gerar nothing is said of Jacob and Esau. Assuming Friedman is correct, it still seems unlikely that J would have placed the events in Gerar *after* the birth of the twins. Where were the boys, or young men, when Isaac identified Rebekah to Abimelech as his sister? Had Jacob and Esau been present, would J not have thought it necessary to take note of them? Whatever explains the sequence of Gen. 25:19–34 and 26, it was not likely J's sequence.

2. On the naming of Beer-sheba

In the concluding verses of Gen. 26, J tells how Isaac first named Beer-sheba as "Shibah" (26:32–33). A previous E passage tells of the naming of Beer-sheba by Abraham, along with Abimelech (21:31–32). This naming and renaming can be seen as one of the many variances drawn from broad traditions by different sources. Of further interest, however, is 26:23, which precedes Isaac's initial naming of Beer-sheba, as Shibah, in 26:33. When Isaac leaves Rehobeth because of ongoing water problems (26:22), where is he said to have gone? "From there he went up to Beer-sheba" (26:23). Although Isaac will not name Beer-sheba until 26:33, the Torah refers to it as such in 26:23. Here is the mark of a story teller. Look, he says, "You and I both know Beer-sheba. Wait a minute, and I'll tell you how it got its name." (Friedman ascribes both verses to J.)

Gen. 27 tells of the dubious conspiracy between Jacob and Rebekah to gain Isaac's blessing for Jacob. (Again, having gained Esau's birthright, what more can Jacob gain from Isaac's blessing?)

Now Isaac "was old and his eyes were too dim to see" (27:1). However, his taste for meat was as keen as ever. He tells Esau that he may soon die and, accordingly, that Esau should hunt some game and prepare "a dish for me such as I like." Esau should then "bring it to me to eat, so that I may give you my innermost blessing before I die" (27:4). Rebekah hears the conversation and tells Jacob of Isaac's plan to bless Esau "*with the Lord's approval*" (27:7).

As part of her plan to substitute second-born Jacob for first-born Esau, Rebekah tells Jacob to bring her choice kids from the flock. Jacob demurs—but only to note that his smooth skin will at once reveal his identity to Isaac. A resourceful Rebekah then prepares a disguise through use of Esau's clothes and kid skins. Jacob then brings Isaac the food she has prepared for him. He presents himself as "Esau, your first-born" and asks that Isaac eat the food so that "you may give me your innermost blessing" (27:19).

Isaac hesitates. He asks how Esau could have completed his hunting and food preparation so quickly. Jacob replies, "The Lord your God granted me good fortune" (27:20). A troubled and uncertain Isaac asks him to draw close so that "I may feel you, my son—whether you are really my son Esau or not" (27:21). The contradictions, ambiguities, and tensions are wonderfully set out in the verses that follow. They seem to imply the permanence of Isaac's blessing, once bestowed. (Despite several apparent contradictions within this passage, Friedman attributes all of 27:1–45 to J.)

Jacob draws close to Isaac, who feels him and wonders: " 'The voice is the voice of Jacob, yet the hands are the hands of Esau' " (27:22). The next verse clearly implies that Isaac had every intention of blessing Esau: "*He did not recognize him*, because his hands were hairy like those of his brother Esau; and *so* he blessed him" (27:23).

Note G–40: The Torah provides no text for this "first" blessing.

Despite the assertion in 27:23 that the blessing was already given, 27:24 portrays a dubious Isaac who has yet to give the blessing. He again asks Jacob, "Are you really my son Esau?" Jacob replies, "I am." Oddly enough, although he had been suspicious of Jacob's voice in 27:22, Isaac, in 27:25, now tells him, "Serve me . . . game that I might give you my innermost blessing." Isaac then partakes of the food and wine. But he again expresses doubts when he asks Jacob to kiss him (27:26–27). Isaac then smells the clothes of Esau that are now on Jacob. He finally seems convinced that he is dealing with Esau. "Ah, the smell of my son is like the smell of the field that the Lord has blessed" (27:27). He then bestows a second blessing on Jacob.

As we might expect, the blessing begins by looking to God for its fulfillment. "May God give you Of the dew of heaven and the fat of the earth, Abundance of new grain and wine. Let peoples serve you, and nations bow to you; Be master over your brothers, and let your mother's sons bow to you. Cursed be they who curse you, Blessed they who bless you" (27:28–29). (Cf. 12:2–3 on the Lord's words to Abram.)

Comment G–51. On the anomalies of Isaac's blessing

There is clearly an anomaly in the use of "brothers." Isaac is dying. Unless he anticipates Rebekah's remarriage and continuing fertility following his death, Esau and Jacob would each have only one brother. JPS1 (but not RSV) uses "brethren" for "brothers." However, unless "sons" is meant as "descendants" as well, the subsequent use of "your mother's *sons*" in all three translations to identify those who will "bow" to the son who is blessed also supports a literal meaning of "brothers." Why would Isaac refer only to Rebekah's descendants? Would his own not be among them?

Even more puzzling, however, *if Isaac's blessing is meant for Esau,* is why he reverses the Lord's prophecy to Rebekah in 25:23. Did he know that his blessing on Esau would contradict the Lord's plan? Had Rebecca told him of the prophecy? Finally, we must wonder if, in this single episode, we are not in fact dealing with multiple sources. This is suggested in the flat assertion of 27:23: "So he blessed him"—*prior to the contradictory dialogue and events of 27:24–29.* In all, this puzzling passage might best dramatize the inner tensions of an aged and confused Isaac torn between his love for Esau and his duty to the Lord.

On Esau's return, Isaac is "seized with violent trembling." He tells Esau, "I blessed him, now he must remain blessed. . . . Your brother came with guile and took away your blessing" (27:33). Whether his words are sincere or disingenuous is, of course, at the core of our mystery. In any case, Esau bitterly recalls his earlier loss as well: "First he took away my birthright and now he has taken away my blessing" (27:36). In response to Esau's tearful plea to "Bless me too, father," Isaac responds with a blessing that begins much like Jacob's—but for its failure to involve God. "See, your abode shall enjoy the fat of the earth and the dew of heaven above" (cf. 27:28). Esau's destiny, however, will be far more modest. "Yet by your sword shall you live, and you shall serve your brother, But when you grow restive, You shall break his yoke from your neck" (27:39–40).

Comment G–52. On the Lord's role in determining Isaac's heir— as possibly contemplated by J

What role does the Torah ascribe to the Lord in this most unbrotherly affair? That His "hand" was present in the birth order is clear enough. But why? We might readily assume that the Lord's purpose was to ordain Esau as Isaac's heir. But what of His puzzling response to Rebekah's inquiry in which He speaks of "two nations" in her womb, or of His final revelation that "the older shall serve the younger" (25:23)? Through the Lord's words to Rebekah and the subsequent birth order, the Torah clearly signals the certainty of Jacob's heirship. But if for his qualities of mind and spirit Jacob is the intended covenantal heir, why does the Lord complicate matters by reversing the birth order? And to whom does the Torah ascribe Jacob's ultimate displacement of a hale and hardy Esau? Do the human participants effect the result through contrivances of their own making? Or does the Torah mean to portray them as pawns whom J's Lord manipulates toward His preordained result?

In considering an answer to the puzzle, we must be mindful of J's insatiable and sometimes incorrigible whimsy. Through a tale of how the Lord's mischievous intervention in a birth process was finally put right, J manages to reveal the human frailties from which not even a patriarchal family is immune.

When Rebekah hears that Esau might kill Jacob (27:41–42), she tells him to flee at once to her brother, Laban, in Haran, until "your brother's fury subsides" (27:43–45). To Isaac, however, Rebekah gives a different reason for Jacob's departure. She refers to the marriages of Esau, at age forty, to the two Hittite women, Judith and Basemath. This, we know, was "a source of bitterness" to Isaac and Rebekah (26:34–35). She also tells Isaac of the sadness that would fill her life should Jacob also marry a Hittite (27:46).

Isaac needs no further prompting. He instructs Jacob, "You shall not take a wife from among the Canaanite women." Instead, Jacob is told to go to Haran and "take a wife there from among the daughters of Laban, your mother's brother" (28:1–2). If Isaac had truly resented Jacob's deception, it was not apparent from his words to Jacob on his departure. He now invokes the blessing, not of "the Lord," or *yahweh*, as before, but of *el shaddai*. "May He grant the blessing of Abraham to you and your offspring, that you may possess the land . . . which God [*elohim*] gave to Abraham" (28:4).

On hearing these words of Isaac to Jacob, Esau at last grasps the displeasure of his parents with his Hittite marriages. If Jacob is to marry a daughter of his mother's brother, Esau will marry a daughter of his father's brother. And so he marries Mahalath, daughter of Ishmael (28:6–8).

Comment G–53. On the measure of "years" as stated by P, and possibly J, in regard to the patriarchs' families

Abram left Haran for Canaan at the age of seventy-five. He lived to the age of one hundred seventy-five. Sarah lived to the age of one hundred twenty-seven. She give birth to Isaac at ninety. At sixty-six her beauty beguiled Pharaoh, and at eighty-nine, Ablimelech.

Now we are told that Isaac was forty when he married Rebekah (25:20), as was Esau when he first married (26:34). Isaac was sixty when his twins were born (25:26). Given the societal value and personal merit attached to reproduction, several of these occurences came remarkably late in life, as measured by years as we count them.

In thinking of more likely ages for marriages, births, and life-spans, we might note the effects of a simple division by two. Isaac and Esau would have married at twenty and Isaac would have become a father at thirty. As for Abraham, he would have lived to about eighty-seven and Sarah to about sixty-three. At Isaac's birth, Sarah would have been forty-five and Abraham fifty. (Although forty-five falls late in the child bearing years, it does not hint of miracles.) However, while such musings may fit J or P, the count seems different for E (see Comments G–36 and 38).

Comment G–54. On Esau and Jacob as viewed by J and P

While ascribing the greater part of the Jacob/Esau story to J, Friedman also regards P as the source of three short portions: 26:34–35, 27:46, and 28:1–9. If he is correct as to P, which seems likely, these portions tell us more of the distinctive perspectives of the two sources.

If the story of Isaac's family reveals J's penchant for psychological realism and whimsy, it offers a different view of P. This is revealed in the foolishness, or worse, of P's "villains" and the rigorous probity and faith of P's "heroes." In 26:34–35 P tells of Esau's marriages to two Hittite woman. They are "a source of bitterness to Isaac and Rebekah." P then confirms its portrayal of an inept Esau through his effort to placate his parents by marrying a daughter of Ishmael, his father's brother. Between Isaac and Rebekah, however, there is no discord and no intrigue. In all that matters, patriarch and matriarch are as one.

In comingling the J and P versions at the juncture of Gen. 27 and 28, R makes the best use of both. It is through P that Rebekah offers Isaac a compelling reason for Jacob to leave for Haran, without disclosing her fear that Esau will kill Jacob. In J's passage of 27:41–45 the question of Jacob's finding a wife in Haran had not occurred to Rebekah. Her aim was to protect Jacob from Esau's wrath. Thus, it is P who enables Rebekah to maintain harmony with Jacob.

The balance of Gen. 28 tells of Jacob's theophanic dream at Luz, en route to Haran. He first dreams of a stairway. It was "set on the ground and its top reached to the sky, and angels of God were going up and down on it" (28:12). He then dreams further that the Lord stands beside him and declares Himself to be "the Lord, the God of your father Abraham and the God of Isaac" (28:13). He repeats to Jacob the essence of His first covenantal promise to Abraham, but with an added promise of physical protection: "Remember, I am with you: I will protect you wherever you go and will bring you back to this land. I will not leave you until I have done what I promised you" (28:15).

On awakening, Jacob senses the presence of "the Lord" (28:16) and deems himself at the "abode of God" and the "gateway to heaven" (28:17). He renames Luz as Bethel ("House of God") (28:19).

> Note G–41: On arriving in Canaan, Abram built an altar to "the Lord" at a site called Bethel (12:8). Later, on returning to Bethel from Egypt, he "there . . . invoked the Lord by name" (13:3–4). Friedman divides Gen. 28:10–22 between J and E, in part based on the use of yahweh or elohim (see 28:13a, 17). But he also attributes to J and E verses in which yahweh and elohim are joined as one Being (J, 28:13b; E, 28:21; see Comments G–39 pt. 2 and G–43).

Abram, as noted, had known of Bethel, as such, in 12:8 and 13:3; Friedman attributes both verses to J. In 28:19, however, Jacob first renames Luz to Bethel. Given the interspersion of J and E in Gen. 28, we might assume that the renaming was by E. Yet Friedman assigns 28:19 to J. Whatever other reasons Friedman may have for attributing 28:19 to J, the result remains an anomaly.

Comment G–55. On "sky" or "heaven" in Jacob's dream

It was suggested in regard to the Tower of Babel that the varying translations of *shamayim* as "sky" or "heaven" might reflect different substantive views of the text by different translators (see Comment G–15). The same may be true of similar variances within a single translation. Thus, as rendered by JPS2, Jacob envisions a stairway during his dream on which angels were going up and down between ground and "*sky*" (28:12). But when he awakens after dreaming of an encounter with God, he is said to have sensed that the place was "the abode of God, and . . . the gateway to *heaven*" (28:17). Thus, within this one episode, JPS2 renders *shamayim* as both "sky" and "heaven." JPS1 and RSV render *shamayim* as heaven throughout the passage.

In effect, JPS2 shapes the story to Jacob's thoughts. Despite the "angels" on the ladder, Jacob did not at first think of "heaven." He had not anticipated God's presence prior to His appearance in the dream. Only on awakening did Jacob sense that he was at "the gateway to heaven itself." Conversely, the translator(s) of JPS1 and RSV may have viewed these events from God's perspective. Unlike Jacob, He knew throughout that Jacob's dream was of heaven itself.

The episode closes with Jacob's conditional acceptance of the Lord as his God. Far from embracing Him, however, Jacob will first put Him to the test. "*If* God remains with me, *if* he protects me on this journey that I am making, and gives me bread to eat and clothing to wear, and *if* I return safe to my father's house—*the Lord shall be my God* . . . and of all You give me, I will set aside a tithe for You" (28:20–22).

Comment G–56. On Jacob's conditional acceptance of the Lord as his God

What if Jacob finally chose not to accept "the Lord" as his "God?" Were there not other gods? Although the Torah can set matters right, Jacob's conditionality poses a risk. What kind of example does he set for the Israelites? Is their faith in the Lord, as their God, to be conditioned on His success as guarantor of their physical needs and safety? Was there no need for unconditional faith? Had the E of Jacob (28:20–22) forgotten the E of the *akedah*?

Once again we encounter a distinction between the fundamental Being of the Lord and the conditionality of His role as God. In relating to the Torah's God, the ever wary Jacob does not follow in the steps of Abram. Rather than "Here I am," his response to God is, "Here I will be—If."

The story of Jacob's arrival in Haran and the events that follow in Laban's household provide a morality tale for all times—the core of which lies in Gen. 29.

In brief, Jacob arrives in Haran where townsmen quickly point out Rachel, the younger daughter of his uncle Laban. Whether from sudden ardor or familial affection, Jacob sees her and cries. When he identifies himself, he is warmly greeted by Laban, also the father of Rachel's older sister Leah. After a month Laban suggests that Jacob be paid for his work. Jacob then professes his love for the "shapely and beautiful" Rachel. He offers to serve Laban for seven years in return for Rachel's hand. Laban agrees. "So Jacob served seven years for Rachel and they seemed to him but a few days because of his love of her" (29:20). When the time finally came, Laban gave a great wedding feast, after which he brought a heavily veiled Leah to Jacob. "He cohabited with her," but in the morning "there was Leah!" (29:23–25).

To Jacob's outraged inquiry, "Why did you deceive me?" Laban replies, "It is not the practice in our place to marry off the younger before the older" (29:26). Laban then proposes that in one week (when the marriage formalities are final), Jacob should marry Rachel, "provided you serve me another seven years" (29:27). Jacob agrees and thus he "cohabited with Rachel also." So much more did he love Rachel than Leah, that "the Lord saw that Leah was unloved and *he* opened her womb" (29:30–31). Over time (within the seven-year period) Leah gave birth to Reuben, Simeon, Levi, and Judah. Leah accepted her sons as a sign of the Lord's wish to awaken Jacob's love for her (29:31–35).

> Note G–42: *In referring to yahweh in 29:31, JPS2 uses a lower case "h" in "he." Given its presence in JPS1 and RSV as well, this rare usage might seem purposeful. However, in 29:33 RSV adheres to "he, while JPS1 reverts to "He" and JPS2 avoids the pronoun altogether. Since the difference between "He" and "he" lacks substance, this uniform exception to normal usage suggests a varied deference by later translators to what may have been an inadvertent use of "he" in Gen. 29:31 and 33 of the original King James version. In any case, for JPS1 and 2, once is enough. But for RSV, there is the added need to honor a parent.*

Wracked by envy of the fertile Leah, Rachel is determined to have her own son. Unlike Leah, however, she regards Jacob rather than God as the problem. To Jacob she says, "Give me children or I shall die" (30:1). An "incensed" Jacob denies responsibility. "Can I take the place of God, who has denied you the fruit of the womb?" (30:2). Like her great great uncle Abraham, Rachel then looks to her own resources for a solution. She decides to have a son through her maid, Bilhah (as Sarah had Ishmael through Hagar). With Jacob's cooperation, she actually acquires two sons through Bilhah. Now, for the moment, a grateful Rachel turns to God. She takes the birth of "her" first son, Dan, as a sign that "God has vindicated me; indeed, He has heeded my plea and given me a son" (30:6). With the birth of "her" second son, Napthtali, she considers herself to have "prevailed" in a "fateful contest" with Leah (30:8).

Not to be outdone Leah, through her maid, Zilpah, brings Jacob two more sons, Gad and Asher. This finally drives Rachel to seek an earthly rather than a Godly remedy for her personal barrenness. When Reuben brings his mother, Leah, some mandrakes from the field, Rachel asks for some. Leah then pours forth her feelings. "Was it not enough for you to take away my husband, that you would also take away my son's mandrakes?" (30:15). The clever Rachel then puts Leah's love for Jacob to good use. She promises, "[In] return for your son's mandrakes [Jacob] will lie with you tonight" (30:15). When Jacob returns from the field, Leah tells him that he is to sleep with her, "for I have hired you with my son's mandrakes." Thus, "he lay with her that night" (30:16).

God then "heeded Leah," who conceived and had her fifth son, Issachar. She regarded him as God's reward "for having given my maid to my husband." When Issachar was followed by her sixth and final son, Zebulun, Leah was confident that through this latest "choice gift" from God, "my husband will exalt me" (30:20). The Torah then takes rare note of a daughter's birth—in this case of Dinah to Leah (30:21).

In time, "God remembered Rachel; God heeded her and opened her womb." On giving birth to Joseph, Rachel readily acknowledges God's role: "God has taken away my disgrace" (30:23). But she also wishes for another son.

Comment G–57. On God, mandrakes, and fertility

The mandrake is an ancient plant with "a fancied resemblance to the human form."[22] As an aphrodisiac, it was also considered a source of fertility.

There is a another morality tale in these mandrakes. Leah, who views God as her true source of fertility, gives her mandrakes to Rachel. From her reliance on God, Leah is blessed with three additional births. What we do not know, of course, is whether Leah harbored a fear that mandrakes might cure Rachel's infertility. If she did, her concerns were groundless. The mandrakes proved of no use to Rachel. Only when she turned to God as her sole source of fertility was it said that "God heeded her and opened her womb."

The societal and familial virtues and values of bearing children is vividly portrayed in the fervent desires of the two sisters for children and in their related jealousies. Such prevailing virtues and values are surely mirrored in God's first *mitzvah* to humankind. "Be fertile and increase, fill the earth and master it." For us, a matriarch's desperate effort to fulfil her role by any means at hand more likely invites compassion than scorn. For the Torah, however, to rely on mandrakes rather than its God as a source of life was an insult to His sanctity. Thus, the moral of the story is clear enough. Only on turning from mandrakes to God was Rachel blessed with Joseph.

Gen. 30:1–24 was the product of E. Were it by J, we might expect a hint of admiration for Rachel's self-help efforts in the spirit of her great great uncle, Abraham. But whether as *elohim* or *yahweh*, God's role as the source of life and fertility was a vital element of the Torah. The idea of divinities as the source of fertility permeated Near East culture. The "principal goddess" among the Sumerian mythic gods was Ishtar/Inanna, "the embodiment of the generative force in nature." A Sumerian prayer describes her as "queen of the divine decrees, radiant light, life-giving woman, beloved of heaven and earth, supreme one."[23] More directly, the Israelites knew well of Baal, the Canaanite god, who, among its many gods, was worshipped as "the universal god of fertility." He was thus esteemed as "king of the gods."[24]

Given the high value and hard conditions of reproduction, it was essential to identify the God of the Torah as the ultimate source of fertility. If not, as denizens of the Near East, Israelites might well be tempted by other gods. The decisive role that the Torah attributed to its God in the fertility of Sarah, Rebekah, Leah, and Rachel was well calculated to counter the lure of Baal.

In Gen. 30:25–43 J expands on an ethical lesson by now well known to Jacob: that is, to gain by deceit is to lose by deceit. Following Joseph's birth, Jacob tells Laban of his wish to return home with his family. Laban (oddly out of character) professes a debt to Jacob for his valuable services from which he, Laban, has prospered. He asks Jacob, "What shall I pay you?" As his "wages," Jacob asks only that he might take from Laban's flock "every speckled and spotted animal—every dark colored sheep and every spotted and speckled goat." In return, he promises Laban, "I will again pasture and keep your flocks" (30:31–32). Laban agrees. (So rare were such colorations that Jacob knew that Laban would accept at once.)

Back in character, Laban sneakily removes from his flock the few animals of such colors to which Jacob was entitled. Jacob had no thought, however, of realizing his "wage" from the few spotted and speckled animals already in the flock. It would come instead from his skills in controlling animal coloration through manipulation of the breeding environment. Thus, by placing white rods where the animals came to drink and mate, he could breed large numbers of speckled and spotted animals. His agreement with Laban entitled Jacob to all such animals born during his extended stay. By choosing the "sturdier animals" of the flock as they mated, he was also able to acquire the strongest of the newborn. Jacob thus became "exceedingly prosperous," possessed of "large flocks, maidservants and menservants, camels and asses" (30:43). (Does the episode establish Jacob as the true founder of latter-day environmental evolutionism?[25])

Comment G–58. On white rods and mandrakes

Jacob's white rods and Rachel's mandrakes are kindred devices. Both are used as earthly alternatives to the Lord's natural order in reaching a desired end. But while Rachel's reliance on mandrakes for fertility fails, Jacob's reliance on the white rods proves invaluable. Why the difference? It would seem that because Jacob's rods involve mere coloration rather than actual birth, J does not regard them as unduly intrusive on the Lord's domain. In Rachel's case, it was a matter of challenging the Lord's unique role as the ultimate source of life and fertility.

As Jacob's wealth from his flocks increases, he faces growing jealousy from Laban's sons. The Lord then tells him to return to "the land of your fathers where you were born, and I will be with you" (31:3). In turn, Jacob tells Leah and Rachel of his increasing difficulties with Laban, and of his hard work, despite which "your father has cheated me, changing my wages time and again" (31:7).

But now we encounter E's version of Jacob's speckled and spotted animals, in which Jacob credits his success to God alone (31:6–13). He explains to Leah and Rachel that no matter what colorations had been agreed on as the measure of Jacob's wage, God would have provided accordingly. Thus, he assures them, "God has taken away your father's livestock and given it to me" (31:9). How can Jacob be sure? He tells his wives of a dream in which an angel of God said to him, "Note well that all the he-goats which are mating with the flock are streaked, speckled and mottled; for I have noted all that Laban has been doing to you" (31:12). This is followed by a command to Jacob from "the God of Beth-El" to return to "your native land" (31:13).

> Note G–43: Perhaps from a piety deeper than J's, E rejects the self-reliance that J ascribes to Jacob. As to any aspect of the birth process, E looks to God alone.

Leah and Rachel tell Jacob to "do just as God has told you" (31:16). Jacob, his wives, and his children then leave with "all his livestock and all the wealth he had amassed." He has not told Laban of his plans. Meanwhile, without telling Jacob, Rachel complicates matters by taking Laban's "household idols" (or "gods" or "teraphim") while Laban is away with his flock.

Before long, Jacob has crossed the Euphrates en route to Gilead. As Laban in pursuit nears Jacob's party, God warns him in a dream, "Beware of attempting anything with Jacob, good or bad" (31:24).

> *Note G–44: Unlike the use of "good and bad" by J's yahweh in regard to the Tree of Knowledge, this use of "good or bad" by E's elohim would seem to be a merism (cf. Comment G–7 as to "knowledge of good and bad") The sense of God's warning is that Laban should do nothing to Jacob.*

On reaching Jacob, Laban rebukes him for his furtive departure: "I would have sent you off with festive music, timbrel and lyre" (31:27). He tells Jacob of God's appearance in his dream. "I have it in my power to do you harm; but the God *of your father* said to me last night, 'Beware of attempting anything with Jacob, good or bad.' Very well, you had to leave because you were longing for your father's house; but why did you steal my gods?" (31:30).

Comment G–59. On Laban's use of "God of your father"

By use of "God of your father," Laban confirms that Jacob's God is not his God. Yet he knows well how Jacob has thrived under Him. Jacob's success alone would persuade the wily Laban that his God must be taken seriously. But Laban concedes nothing openly. Even as he tells Jacob of God's warning, Laban explains his own acceptance of Jacob's abrupt departure to his sympathy for Jacob's wish to return home.

Jacob tells Laban that he had left so quickly from fear that Laban would forcibly keep his daughters at home. But he rashly vows that "anyone with whom you find your gods shall not remain alive" (31:32). On failing to find his gods elsewhere, Laban finally enters Rachel's tent. She has hidden them in a camel cushion on which she is seated. As an apology for not rising, she tells him "the period of women is upon me." Laban leaves, his search a failure.

Jacob reacts to what he perceives as Laban's false accusation of theft by bitterly recounting the severe hardships endured over twenty years of tending his flocks. He accuses Laban of rewarding his work with penny-pinching meanness (31:38–41). He concludes: "Had not the God of my father, the God of Abraham and the Fear of Isaac been with me, you would have sent me away empty handed" (31:42).

Comment G–60. On Rachel and Laban's "household gods"

The Torah states no motive for Rachel's theft of Laban's household gods. One authority on Mesopotamian culture suggests the following: "The possession of the gods may have betokened clan leadership and spiritual power to an extent that made possessing them of paramount importance."[26] Although Rachel had discarded her mandrakes for Jacob's God as her accepted source of fertility, her impulse to self-help remained intact. It would have been like her to seek any benefits that might come from possessing her father's household gods. Grateful as she was to Jacob's God for Joseph's birth, she remained a daughter of her household and its traditions.

Laban then reminds Jacob that Leah and Rachel, their children and the flocks are still his own. But given his daughters determination to go, Laban knows that he lacks the power to stop them (31:43). With much grandiloquence, Jacob and Laban enter into a peace pact. Its site was marked by a stone pillar and a mound of stones. These will serve "as a witness" between Jacob and Laban that neither shall cross them "with hostile intent." As to their to their oaths and professions of good faith, Laban declares: "May the God of Abraham and the god of Nahor . . . judge between us" (31:44–54).

Laban returns home and Jacob proceeds toward Canaan. En route "angels of God encountered him." Jacob regards the site as "God's camp" (32:2–3). Whether from brotherhood or fear, Jacob now craves reconciliation with Esau. To that end he sends messengers to Esau in Edom. They are to address Esau as "my lord Esau." They are to tell him of Jacob's stay with Laban and of his wealth, including "cattle, asses, sheep and male and female slaves." Finally, they are to tell Esau of Jacob's "hope of gaining your favor" (32:6). The messengers return and tell Jacob that Esau is coming to meet him with four hundred men.

On hearing this, "Jacob was greatly frightened" (32:8). To avoid possible annihilation, he divides his party into two camps, so that at least one might escape. He then seeks God's help against Esau. He declares himself "unworthy of all the kindness that You have so steadfastly shown Your servant" (32:10). He then prays: "Deliver me, I pray, from the hand of my brother . . . ; else I fear he may come and strike me down, mothers and children alike" (32:12). Jacob also reminds God of His promise to "deal bountifully" with him and to make his off-spring "too numerous to count" (32:13). Not sure of his status with God as related to Esau, Jacob also seeks to appease Esau with gifts. He has five hundred fifty animals collected, among them, goats, sheep, camels, and cattle. His servants are to offer these as gifts from "Your servant," Jacob to "my lord," Esau. Jacob thinks, "If I propitiate him with presents in advance, and then face him, perhaps he will show me favor" (32:21).

Comment G–61. On Jacob's fear of Esau

This E passage vividly portrays Jacob's fear of Esau. It is so great, that even E causes Jacob to seek safety in Esau's mercy as well as God's protection. In part, his fear stems from ignorance. After twenty years, Jacob has no idea of Esau's feelings. Is he vengeful? Is he forgiving? Has he prospered despite the loss of birthright and blessing? Why does he come with four hundred men? Jacob's memory of his sordid conduct toward Esau weighs heavily on him. His fears are stoked by the knowledge that Esau has good cause for revenge. But Jacob's feelings transcend fear alone. He is honestly troubled by his treatment of Esau.

During the night Jacob sends his entire party of wives, children, and servants across the ford of the Jabbock, along with his possessions. A stark tale follows of Jacob's struggle with an unknown assailant (32:25–31).

"Jacob was left alone. And a man wrestled with him until the break of dawn. When he saw that he had not prevailed against him, he wrenched Jacob's hip at its socket, so that the socket of his hip was strained as he wrestled with him. Then the man said, 'Let me go, for dawn is breaking.' Jacob answered, 'I will not let you go unless you bless me.' Said the man, 'What is your name.' He replied, 'Jacob.' Said he, *Your name shall no longer be Jacob, but Israel, for you have striven with beings divine and human, and have prevailed.'* Jacob asked, 'Pray tell me your name.' But the man said, 'You must not ask *my* name! And he took leave of him there. Jacob then named the place Peniel, meaning, 'I have seen a divine being face to face, yet my life has been preserved' " (32:31).

Comment G–62. On Jacob's struggle with his conscience

Alone in the dark and tormented by recollections of Esau and their past, Jacob enters into a struggle with an unknown mystical entity or being. The nature of that entity or being is critical to an understanding of the awesome event. We may be aided by the interpretive differences between JPS2 (quoted above) and JPS1 and RSV. (Since the latter two are much the same, all references are to JPS1.)

In 32:25–26, JPS1 and 2 both refer in the lower case to "a man" or "he." However, where "the man" in JPS2 says, "you have striven with beings divine and human," in JPS1 he says, "with God and with men" (32:29). In translating *elohim*, of course, an editorial choice must be made between the God of the Torah or one or more godly beings. The same difference is found in the final verse of the quotation, in which JPS1 quotes Jacob as saying, "I have seen God face to face [in contrast to 'a divine being'in JPS2]" (32:31). No less puzzling is JPS2's statement, "And he took leave of him there," as compared to JPS1's, "And he blessed him there" (32:30). Yet their common use of the lowercase "h" in "he" and "m" in "my" suggests that neither regards "the man" with whom Jacob wrestled, and who either parted from or blessed him, as the Torah's God, Himself. But consider again JPS1's reference to God in 32:29.

In JPS2, the identity of the "man" remains unknown, except that his being is meant to partake of the divine. In JPS1 the "man" tells Jacob that he had "striven with God." *But he does not so identify himself.* Moreover, as noted, JPS1 later identifies the man who *blesses* Jacob with a nonsacred "he" and "my." In JPS2, the "he" simply "took leave" of Jacob (32:30). Different though they are, the blessing and the leave taking serve the same purpose. Each marks the end of Jacob's soul searing struggle. That struggle, however, is not a relatively simple two-party struggle between Jacob and "*a divine* being" or "God." Instead, we are told of Jacob's struggle with "beings divine *and* human" (JPS2) or "with God *and* with men" (JPS1; 32:29).

What are we to make of this strange struggle in which Jacob's antagonist is identified as an amalgam of divinity and humanity? If his struggle is not with his God alone, then with whom is it? *In effect, are we not being told of a conflict between the "divine" and "human" elements within Jacob himself?* Does his struggle not describe his anguished effort to resolve the tensions between them? Does the physical intensity of the encounter, including Jacob's physical impairment, not represent the intensity of Jacob's struggle for inner peace? Does the struggle not also symbolize the potential force of the human conscience?

From his much earlier dream of 28:10–15, Jacob has good reason to see himself as God's choice for his destined role as Isaac's covenantal heir. Yet he ponders the gap between the worthiness he must come to exemplify and the character revealed in his treatment of Isaac and Esau. Through his inner struggle, he grasps a simple truth—at least for the moment. Peace can not come from the mere abatement of fear. It must come from reconciliation. With this realization, Jacob's struggle for inner peace comes to an end. His lameness will testify to the intensity of his struggle. But can the name Israel bring Jacob new peace and integrity?

The story concludes with a fascinating appendage. In regard to the cause of Jacob's lameness, the Torah states: "That is why the children of Israel *to this day* do not eat the thigh muscle of the hip" (32:33).

Comment G–63. On "to this day"

What can we make of "to this day"? On a premise of human authorship, it is the author's reference to the time of recordation. On a premise of Godly origin, "this day" would refer to the revelation at Sinai (as is likely reflected in the silence of Rashi and Ramban).

On either premise, the joining of "children of Israel" with "this day" in Gen. 32:33 has further significance that RSV clarifies by use of "Israelites" for "children of Israel." Whether at the actual time of human transcription or the putative time of revelation at Sinai, the "children of Israel" would have become a people known as Israelites. Gen. 32:33 thus marks the Torah's first prospective identification of Israel as a people.

Gen. 33 tells of the meeting, reconciliation and parting of Jacob and Esau. On first seeing Esau and his four hundred men, Jacob is fearful of Esau's intent. He quickly positions his wives, maids, and children in the hierarchy of his affections. In front, and most exposed to any attack, were the maids and their children. Next were Leah and her children. Finally, to the rear in the safest of all positions, were Rachel and her children (33:1–3).

Comment G–64. On Jacob's placement of his family

In the wake of his great struggle of conscience, how can we construe Jacob's obvious preferences in exposing his family to danger? Had the struggle numbed all of his feelings for human sensibilities? Or, in the face of acute danger, did he simply act out of "blind instinct"? With more time to reflect, would he have grasped how deeply his children might be affected by his obvious favoritism?

Jacob's fears of Esau prove groundless. His "Laban-like" professions of subservience pale in the bright light of Esau's forgiving grace. When Jacob presses his rich gifts on him, Esau's acceptance of them reassures Jacob of his forgiveness (33:3–11). Esau then proposes that they go on together at a pace slow enough for Jacob's party (33:12). But Jacob dissembles and rejects Esau's offer of men to help. "Let my lord go on ahead of his servant, while I travel slowly, at the pace of the cattle before me, and . . . of the children, until I come to my lord in Seir" (33:13–15).

It seems that Esau erroneously assumed that Jacob meant to accompany him to his own home in Seir. Although Jacob had eagerly sought reconciliation with Esau, he also knew that their different destinies precluded their living together as brothers in Edom. Yet he had no wish to confront Esau with this truth at the moment of reconciliation. Rather than following Esau to Seir, Jacob proceeds through Succoth to Shechem "in the land of Canaan" (33:17).

Jacob settles in Shechem, buys land "from the children of Hamor, Shechem's father" and builds an altar to "the God of Israel" (33:19–20). Gen. 34 then tells of the rape of Dinah by Shechem, the king's son, and the events that followed.

> Note G–45: City and son are both named Shechem. Dinah, of course, was Jacob's daughter by Leah (30:21).

Shechem first takes Dinah by force as she walks in the city. But being "in love with the maiden," he says to his father, Hamor, the king, "Get me this girl as a wife." Meanwhile, as his sons were working in the fields, Jacob hears of Dinah's defilement. He does nothing until they return. When told of this "outrage in Israel," her brothers are "distressed and very angry" (34:7).

Comment G–65. On Dinah's rape as "an outrage in Israel"

Similar to Comment G–63, the use of "Israel" in "an outrage in Israel" refers to a collectivity of persons rather than to a single person. Here, however, in the absence of "to this day," the usage precedes Israel's development into a distinctive people. Thus, in context, the collectivity is limited to the extended household(s) of (J's) *Jacob* and his sons. But by referring to "Israel" rather than Jacob, J (or R) associates Jacob's present family with the future collectivity of Israel. (Cf. Note G–54 in regard to the Torah's first *contemporaneous* reference to "Israel" as a people [Gen. 47:27].)

Hamor then comes to tell Jacob and his sons of Shechem's love for Dinah and to ask that they give her to him in marriage. As king of Shechem, he goes further and proposes complete freedom of intermarriage with all "daughters." He also offers Jacob and his family full landholding rights. Finally, Shechem himself offers to pay any "bride price" the family might request.

The response to Hamor and Shechem comes not from Dinah's father, Jacob, but from "Jacob's sons" (presumably as one voice). (34:13). "We cannot do this thing, to give our sister to a man who is uncircumcised, for that is a disgrace among us" (34:14). In this, J describes them as "speaking with guile because he [Shechem] had defiled their sister" (34:13). Jacob's sons then agree to Shechem's proposal on the condition that "you will become like us in that every male among you is circumcised" (34:15).

On accepting the condition, Hamor and Shechem go to their townsmen to explain the added communal wealth, and other benefits, that could follow the circumcision of all the males. (However, they say nothing of the precipitating factor, i.e., Shechem's desire to marry Dinah.) The males all agree and are circumcised. On the third day, "when [the circumcised males] were in pain," Simeon and Levi, two of Dinah's six full brothers, came to the city and "slew all the males," including Hamor and Shechem. Then, "because their sister had been defiled, . . . the other sons of Jacob" plundered the town and seized "all their wealth . . . children and . . . wives . . . as captives and booty" (34:27–29).

Jacob complains of their conduct to Simeon and Levi. But his concerns are largely self-centered. "You have brought trouble on me, making me odious among the inhabitants of the land, the Canaanites and Perrizites; . . . if they unite against me and attack me, I and my house will be destroyed" (34:30). With utter indifference his two sons reply, "Should our sister be treated like a whore?" (34:31).

Comment G–66. On Jacob and his sons in Shechem

In Gen. 34 the Jacob of Peniel (32:25–33) gives way to the Jacob of Shechem. What has become of the chastened Jacob tormented by his youthful exploitation of Esau and Isaac? Have his emergent moral sensibilities slipped back to moral indifference? Is Jacob's conscience dead to his sons' hypocritical use of the Lord's covenantal command of circumcision to effect the wanton slaughter of the guiltless? It seems too soon for such a striking character change. More likely, we are dealing with two different Jacobs drawn from varying oral traditions. Friedman has good reason to ascribe the penitent

Jacob of Peniel to the more reverential E; and the self-pitying Jacob of Shechem to the psychological realist, J.

If Jacob's response to these events portray him as less than praiseworthy, what can be said of his sons? Evaluation is difficult without knowing of the societal standards of vengeance for the rape of a sister. Simeon and Levi, the slaughterers, were both full brothers of Dinah through Leah. But so were Reuben, Judah, Issachar and Zebulun. Under prevailing norms, should all of Dinah's brothers have joined in the slaying—at least of Shechem, the sole miscreant? In any case, consider how the standard of justice negotiated by Abraham with the Lord had now been perverted by Simeon and Levi in Shechem. Rather than sparing the guilty for the sake of the innocent, the killing of all the innocent was "justified" by the guilt of one man.

What, then, of Dinah's other brothers, both full or half? In the initial response to the proposals of Hamor and Shechem, it was "Jacob's sons . . . speaking in guile" (and with no stated exceptions) who proposed the mass circumcision of "every male" of Shechem (34:13–17). Although it was Simeon and Levi alone who then "slew all the [weakened] males," the "other sons" were quick to plunder the city of its wealth and to seize its women and children. Will the House of Jacob, including its father, be called to answer for these deeds? Are these descendants of Abraham fitting heirs to his covenant? Or did the norms of the time justify their contrived mayhem? (The fact that the "other sons" included J's exemplar, Judah, at least hints of an element of just retribution.)

In relating this tale, Gen. 34 avoids any mention of *yahweh* or *elohim*. His Being is evoked only by the brothers' hypocritical effort to enlist Him as a coconspirator through the covenant of circumcision. If there is any redeeming grace in this sordid story, it lies in the Torah's integrity in telling it.

In Gen. 35 God returns to tell Jacob to leave Shechem for Bethel. There he is to build an altar. In turn, Jacob tells his entire household, " 'Rid yourselves of the alien god(s) in your midst, purify yourselves, and change your clothes' " (35:1–2). Accordingly, they gave to Jacob for burial "all the alien gods they had, and the rings that were in their ears." God is then said to have brought down a "terror" on surrounding cities "so that *they* could not pursue the sons of Jacob" (35:5). (Whether "they" attributed the "terror" to Jacob's God is left unsaid.)

> Note G–46: Rashi suggests that the "alien gods" were "from the spoil of Shechem."[27]

Gen. 35:6–7 tells of Jacob's arrival at Bethel. "Thus Jacob came to Luz— that is Bethel—in the land of Canaan. . . . There he built an altar and named the site "El-Bethel, for it was there that God had revealed Himself to him when he was fleeing from his brother" (35:6–7).

Yet, just as we are told of Jacob's arrival at Bethel from Shechem, the Torah abruptly tells of God's appearance to him "*on his arrival from Paddan-aram*" (35:9). And now for a second time He is again renamed Israel. "You shall be called Jacob no more. But Israel shall be your name" (35:10). This new and repetitive God now identifies Himself to Jacob as *el shaddai*. As such, He confirms Jacob as covenantal heir to Abraham and Isaac (35:11–13). Jacob then erects a pillar of stone and anoints it with oil, and once again names the site "Bethel" (35:14–15).

Comment G–67. On a confluence of sources at Bethel

When Jacob arrives in Bethel (i.e., the "House of God") there seems little purpose in renaming it El-Bethel (i.e., God of Bethel), particularly since God has just directed Jacob to go to "Bethel" (35:1). Friedman ascribes Jacob's first naming of Bethel to J. "He named that site Bethel, but previously the name of the city had been Luz" (28:19). He ascribes 35:1–8, which includes the second naming, to E.

More notable, however, is the insertion at this point of Gen. 35:9–15, which, as might be expected, is ascribed to P. Jacob's abrupt arrival from Paddan-aram rather than Shechem clearly signals a different source. In an even sharper break from the preceding narrative, it also includes the second renaming of Jacob as Israel (see 32:25–33.) The promise now made by *el shaddai* to Jacob on renaming him closely tracks that made by *el shaddai* to Abram on his renaming (17:1–9). Finally, Jacob's erecting and anointing a pillar of stone at Bethel repeats what he first did on coming to Luz, or Bethel, en route to Laban, while fleeing Esau (see 28:18–19). (See Note G–41.)

As Jacob's party travels from Bethel to Ephrath, Rachel dies in "hard labor" while giving birth to her second son, Benjamin (35:16–19). The Torah adds: "Thus Rachel died. She was buried on the road to Ephrath—*now* Bethlehem" (35:19). Then, as Jacob camps at Migdal-eder, we encounter another example of the Torah's stark brevity. "Reuben went and laid with Bilhah, his father's concubine; and Israel found out" (35:22). No more is said of it here. A listing of Jacob's twelve sons by their mothers follows (35:23–26). Gen. 35 ends with Isaac's death at Mamre, "now Hebron," at the age of one hundred eighty. He was buried by "Esau and Jacob" (who are named in birth order) (35:27–29).

> *Note G–47: The phrases "now Hebron" and "now Bethlehem" serve much the same purpose as "to this day" in 32:33 (see Comments G–63 and 65). See also 23:19 and note later that 37:14 includes a contemporaneous reference to Hebron. As to "now Bethlehem," see Comment G–94 pt. 1.*

Comment G–68. On Esau—an appreciation

The Torah gives Esau his rightful due by listing his name in birth order. While Esau never rose to the spiritual heights of Jacob, neither, to our knowledge, had he fallen to his ethical depths. From all we know, Esau was a decent man who wished no one ill. His physical attributes happened to outweigh his mental and spiritual attributes. Although he was devoted to providing Isaac with fresh game, what had Isaac taught him of his lineage, destiny and birthright? Were his vexing marriages not more the result of ignorance than spite? Did he not use his abilities well? Did he not cherish his father's comfort? Did he not forgive Jacob?

Gen. 36 opens as follows: "This is the line of Esau—that is Edom." In order, Gen. 36:2–5 names the three wives of Esau and their sons; 36:6–8 narrates the move by Esau and family from Canaan to the "hill country of Seir—Esau being Edom"; 36:9–14 lists Esau's sons again, to which the names of his grandsons by each son are added (other than the sons of the sons of Esau's last listed wife, Oholibamah); 36:15–19 lists "the clans of the children of Esau" that in every respect conform to the prior list of Esau's grandsons (by sons of Anah and Basemath) and of his sons by Oholibamah, except for the addition of a second clan of Korah, which is now included among the "descendants" of Eliphaz; 36:20–21 lists the seven sons of Seir the Horite, who were also settled in the land of Seir, and identifies the Horite clans by their names; 36:22–30 lists the grandsons of Seir by their fathers, and repeats the names of the seven Horite clans as they first appeared; 36:31–39 names "the kings who reigned in the land of Edom *before any king reigned over the Israelites*"; 36:40–43, once more lists the clans of Esau, but differently than in 36:15–19.

Comment G–69. On various technicalities regarding Esau's credentials as the father of Edom

Friedman ascribes 36:1 to R and the balance of 36 to J and P. With some hesitance, he associates 36:2–30 with P, and with greater assurance, 36:31–43 with J. The mention of Edomite kings who reigned "before any king reigned over the Israelites" also calls to mind the Torah's inclusion of post-Torah references to events in the Torah (cf. Comments G–63, 65, and 94 pt. 1). The dates of the kings in Gen. 31–39 appear to be unknown, except for King Baalhanan, c. 1300 B.C.E.[28]

Friedman's hesitance as to P's authorship of 36:2–30 relates back to his earlier and more positive attributions of Gen. 26:34–35 and 28:9 to P. Both deal with Esau's wives. In Gen. 26:34–35 Esau at age forty took as wives Judith, daughter of Beeri the Hittite and Basemath, daughter of Elon the Hittite. Later, hoping to placate his father, he marries Mahalath, daughter of Ishmael (28:8–9). However, in Gen. 36:2–4, his wives are Adah, daughter of Elon the Hittite; Oholibamah, "daughter of Anah daughter of Zibeon the Hivite" and Basemath, daughter of Ishmael.

In effect, Adah has replaced Basemath as a daughter of Elon the Hittite; Basemath, no longer a daughter of Elon, is now a daughter of Ishmael, in which relationship she appears to have replaced Mahalath. Thus, in place of the three original wives, Judith, Basemath, and Mahalath, Esau's wives, according to Gen. 36, are Basemath, Adah, and Oholibamah. Of these, Basemath is now a daughter of Ishmael rather than of Elon the Hittite. Replacing Basemath as a daughter of Elon is Adah. Of the original wives, Judith, daughter of Beeri the Hittite, is gone, while Mahalath, daughter of Ishmael, is possibly known by a different name.

Also new among the wives, along with Adah, is Oholibamah, who is twice identified as "daughter of Anah daughter of Zibeon the Hittite" (36:2, 14). In 36:18 and 25 she is identified more simply as "the daughter of Anah"; and in 36:24 Anah is named as Zibeon's son. (Rashi identifies Zibeon as the actual father of Oholibamah by union with the wife of his son Anah.[29] Thus, he reads 36:2 as indicating Anah's *presumptive*, and Zibeon's *actual*, fatherhood. Gen. 36:20, however, names both Zibeon and Anah as sons of Seir the Horite. From this Rashi (in assuming Anah and Zibeon in 36:2, 14, and 20 to be the same persons) concludes that Anah was both a "brother" and son of Zibeon. With unerring logic he concludes that "this teaches that Zibeon had sexual relations with his mother and begot Anah."[30]

There are more direct contradictions in Gen. 36 in regard to Esau's sons and clans. In the (presumptive) P passage, *sons* are listed in 36:4–5 and 10–14 (with Esau's grandsons added). In 36:15–19 and 40–43, J lists the *clans* of the *children of Esau* and then of *Esau*, himself.

The listings of Esau's sons in 36:4–5 and 10–14 are identical. However, the list of the *clans* of Esau's sons in 36:15–19 varies from the list of Esau's *grandsons* in 36:10–14 in two respects. First, (as noted above) the clan-head, Korah, is named as a "descendant," but not as a son, of Esau's son Eliphaz (cf. 36:11, 15–16). Second, the clans of the "sons" of Esau by Oholibamah include only their own sons only. Conversely, as to Adah and Basemath, the clans of the "sons" of Esau include *only* grandsons. In all, fourteen clans are named. They take the names of (1) Esau's eleven *grandsons* from his sons Eliphaz and Reuel and (2) Esau's three *sons* by Oholibamah.

The passage ascribed to J has no listing of Esau's sons or wives (36:31–43). However, like the earlier P passage, it does list "the names of the clans of Esau" (36:40–43). Of these eleven clan names, only two appear among the fourteen clans of P in 36:15–19. Two of J's eleven clans of Esau bear the names of persons identified by P as women. In P, these are Timna, a concubine to Eliphaz, and mother of Amalek; and Oholibamah, a wife to Esau. P has also identified a Timna as a sister of Lotan (a son of Seir the Horite) (36:20–22). The two women are not otherwise identified by J.

In melding the P and J sources in Gen. 36, did R accept Timna and Ohilibamah as women in one and as men in the other? Or were J's Timna and Oholibamah earlier males with the same names as persons whom P later knew of as women? Or, indeed, were they both female clan heads? Are these names and identities that, in the time between J and P, became blurred in the mists of tradition? Yet, with all of its anomalies, Gen. 36 musters powerful support for Esau's credentials as the father of Edom. (Note also that R might have "resolved" the contradictions in Gen. 36 through excisions or other accomodations. But as recorded, it substantiates R's policy of inclusiveness.)

Gen. 37 begins the story of Joseph. Jacob and his family are now in Canaan, near Hebron, "in the land where his father had resided" (37:1). At seventeen, Joseph was the youngest son, but for Benjamin, his full brother from Rachel. Joseph tended flocks as a helper to the sons of Bilhah and Zilpah. The story opens with a vivid summation of his relations with his older half-brothers: "And Joseph brought bad reports of them to his father. Now Israel loved Joseph the best of all his sons, for he was a child of his old age; and he had made him an ornamented tunic. And when his brothers saw that their father loved him more than any of his brothers, they hated him so that they could not speak a friendly word to him" (37:2–4).

Joseph is then revealed as a dreamer of portentous dreams. His first is of grain sheaves in a field. Joseph's sheaf remains upright and the others bow down to it. Joseph is eager to share it with his brothers. "Hear this dream which I have dreamed" (37:6). Perceiving it to be Joseph's prediction, or claim, of future supremacy over them, they "hated him even more for his talk about dreams" (37:7–8).

Now Joseph tells them of a second dream, in which "the sun, the moon, and eleven stars were bowing down to me." This angers even Jacob. "Are we to come, I and *your mother* and your brothers, and bow low to you to the ground?" (37:10).

Comment G–70. On Joseph's dreams and the redaction of Gen. 37

The responses of the brothers and Jacob to Joseph's dreams attests to their presumed prophetic importance. That Joseph's dreams might reflect his wishes was perhaps excusable. But that he chose to flaunt those wishes as an implied prediction could only prove offensive. An even more puzzling aspect of the dreams is Jacob's reference to Joseph's mother, Rachel, as among those whom Joseph would expect to bow low to him. Rachel, of course, is dead. Yet the reference to the sun (Jacob), the moon (Rachel) and the eleven stars (the other brothers) seems to place his mother back among the living. The impression is confirmed in Jacob's angry response.

The actual presence of Rachel is never noted; but for that matter neither is that of Jacob's other wives (or concubines). Friedman attributes Rachel's death on the occasion of Benjamin's birth to E (35:16–20) and Joseph's dream to J (37:5–11). In such case, J, writing earlier than E, might have considered Rachel to be living despite E's later report of her death. Friedman reads Gen. 37 as a complex melding of verses and clauses by E and J.

Later, Jacob sends Joseph to where his brothers are pasturing the flock—"at Shechem" (of all places!). His mission is to "see how your brothers are and how the flocks are faring" (37:12–17). At Shechem "a man" tells Joseph that the brothers have gone to Dothan.

> Note G–48: Following the mayhem wreaked on Shechem by the brothers, how could they return so soon to pasture their flocks? Again, it is a matter of authors. Having ascribed the Shechem events of Gen. 34 to J, Friedman now ascribes the surprising return of the brothers to E.

As the brothers at Dothan saw Joseph approach "from afar," they said to each other, "Here comes the dreamer! Come now let us kill him and throw him into one of the pits; and we can say, 'A savage beast devoured him.' We shall see what becomes of his dreams" (37:18–20). But Reuben objects. "Let us not take his life." He proposes instead that they cast him into a pit, otherwise unharmed. In agreement, the brothers do so, after first removing his "ornamented tunic." Reuben's aim, however, is "to save him from them and restore him to his father" (37:21–24).

But now, as the brothers sit eating, their previous decision seems to have become undone. Looking up, they see "a caravan of Ishmaelites coming from Gilead" bound for Egypt with goods. Suddenly, Judah speaks up. "What do we gain by killing our brother . . . ? Come, let us sell him to the Ishmaelites, but let us not do away with him ourselves. After all, he is our brother, our own flesh." The brothers agree (37:25–27). Gen. 37:28, which follows, consists entirely of these two statements: (1) "When Midianite traders passed by *they* pulled Joseph out of the pit," and (2) "*They* sold Joseph for twenty pieces of silver to the Ishmaelites, who brought Joseph to Egypt." In (1), Joseph is taken from the pit. In (2), a pit is not mentioned. The story concludes in 37:36 as follows: "The Midianites, meanwhile, sold him in Egypt to Potiphar, a courtier of Pharaoh and his chief steward."

Comment G–71. On Reuben and Judah and Midianites and Ishmaelites

It is possible in 37:28 to read "Midianites" as the antecedent of "they," in both of its appearances. If so, the Midianites would have taken Joseph from the pit and sold him to the Ishmaelites. This possibility is foreclosed, however, by 37:36, in which the Midianites, on arriving in Egypt, still have Joseph in hand. Thus, the antecedent for the first "they" in 37:28 is "the Midianites," who take Joseph from the pit after the brothers have left. The antecedent for the second "they" can only be the brothers, who then sell Joseph to the Ishmaelites, as first proposed by Judah. Accordingly, the acquisition of Joseph by two different tribes in 37:28 would seem to result from R's having combined the J and E versions into one verse.

In the intervening verses of 37:29–35, Reuben had returned to the pit only to find it empty. Thinking of Jacob, he cried out, "Now what am I to do?" When he reports this to his brothers, they take Joseph's tunic and dip it in kid's blood (as they had first planned to do before the "Judah" episode) and bring it to Jacob. On hearing their story and receiving the bloody coat, Jacob "bewailed" Joseph's death. All "his sons *and daughters*" sought to comfort him, but he would not be comforted (37:35).

In effect, there is a coherent story in the E version which centers on Reuben's role. Thus, consistent with Reuben's plan to save Joseph's life, he is cast into a pit. But during Reuben's absence following the brothers' departure, Joseph is taken from the pit by the Midianites. In the J version, centered on Judah's protective role, Reuben is present throughout. It is in this version that the brothers, having agreed to Judah's proposal, sell Joseph to the Ishmaelites for twenty pieces of silver (37:27).

Why the versions vary between Joseph's acquisition by Ishmaelites or Midianites is not apparent. Ishmaelites were thought to comprise a group of twelve nomadic tribes founded by the sons of Ishmael (25:12–16). These twelve tribes did not include the Midianites, separately descended from Midian, a son of Abraham and Keturah (see 25:1–4). At the time, both tribes, or peoples, engaged in trade with Egypt.

Comment G–72. On Jacob's "daughters" in 37:35

If meant literally, we know of no "daughters" of Jacob other than Dinah. Ramban first posits that the plural form refers to Dinah and Jacob's granddaughter, Serah, by Asher (see 46:17). But he retains the possibility that "daughters" is meant to include "daughters-in-law."[31] Rashi first quotes Rabbi Judah as saying, " 'Twin sisters were born with each (founder of a) tribe [i.e., each son of Jacob], and they married them' (i.e., each brother married his brother's twin sister)." As a simpler explanation, Rashi cites Rabbi Nehemiah's view that "They were his daughters-in-law."[32] (For more on the meaning of "daughters" see Comments G–89A and 89B.)

Comment G–73. On Reuben or Judah as Joseph's protector from death at the hands of his other brothers

We know Reuben and Judah as the first and fourth of Leah's sons. Of Judah, as yet, we know very little more. Of Reuben we know that he "laid with Bilhah, his father's concubine" (35:22). (In the Hebrew text, Bilhah and Zilpah are variously designated as a wife or concubine. See 30:4 and 9, *ishah*-wife, and 35:22, *peelegesh*-concubine.) Friedman ascribes Reuben's dalliance with Bilhah to J, and Reuben's protection of Joseph to E (37:21:22). Thus the miscreant of one event becomes the hero of another. These distinctive views of Reuben and Judah by J and E will continue.

Comment G–74. On the fruits of Jacob's favoritism

Recall Jacob's insensitive display of favoritism in the placement of his family as the "unknown" Esau approached. Recall the "ornamented tunic" that he makes only for Joseph. Through such conduct, Jacob had nurtured arrogance in Joseph and resentment in his brothers. Jacob's lack of sensitivity to the developing tragedy then exacerbated his initial mistakes. It was only on hearing Joseph's second dream that Jacob could finally sense how his own overt favoritism had harmed his family. But it was too late. For Joseph's fate and for his own grief, Jacob could only blame himself. Yet Jacob, himself, was but a pawn in the unfolding saga of the Torah's plans for Israel.

Gen. 38 then turns from Joseph's arrival in Egypt to J's story of Tamar and her father-in-law, Judah.

> Note G–49: *The story focuses on the levirate marriage obligation. This required a brother-in-law to marry the widow of a brother who dies without a son. A son born of the marriage is then credited to the deceased husband rather than to the biological father. By this fiction, the line of the deceased husband continues, while the actual father gains no heir or offspring. Although a brother-in-law's wish to fulfill his obligation might vary with the person of his sister-in-law, the disincentive remained. It was the denial of fatherhood to the true father.*

Unlike his father, Judah had not returned to Haran to find a wife among his family's kin. He had instead married "the daughter of a certain Canaanite whose name was Shua," with whom he had three sons: Er, Onan, and Shelah. He had arranged for the marriage of Er and Tamar. But Er "was displeasing" to God, who then "took his life."

As a responsible father, Judah directed his second son, Onan, to marry Tamar "and do your duty by her as a brother-in-law, and provide offspring for your brother" (38:8). But Onan, "knowing that the seed would not count as his, let it go to waste whenever he joined with his brother's wife, so as not to provide offspring for his brother." This, too, displeased the Lord, who then "took his life also" (38:9–10).

Comment G–75. On Onan's death for wasting his seed

Creation I endows human sexuality with the sacred purpose of reproduction. Thus, the Torah might attribute sin to the waste of seed by any means. From the story alone, however, Onan's sin might have been limited to his waste of seed in the act of reproduction, or in his efforts to avoid his levirate obligation. Today, however, "Onanism" is more widely associated with masturbation.

Judah now feared that any husband of Tamar was marked for early death. Because his third son, Shelah, was too young to marry, Judah could yet buy time. Accordingly, Tamar was sent to her father's house until "Shelah grows up." "A long time afterward," Judah's own wife had died and Shelah was "grown up." Tamar now senses that Judah does not mean to honor the family's levirate obligation (34:14).

She then learns that Judah, now a widower, will travel through Enaim on his way to Timnah. She goes there, removes her widow's garb, covers her face with a veil, wraps herself, and waits for Judah. On seeing Tamar, Judah, did not recognize her and "took her for a harlot." He said, "Here, let me sleep with you." She agrees for the price of a kid, which Judah will send later. They also agree on the pledge of a "seal, cord and staff" as security for Tamar's receipt of the kid (38:14–18). Tamar then conceives.

Later, Judah sends "his friend the Adullamite" to Enaim with a kid to redeem his pledge. When he cannot find Tamar, he asks the townspeople if they know the whereabouts of a "cult prostitute." They tell him there has been none in Enaim. On hearing this, Judah gives up the search. "Let her keep them, lest we become a laughingstock" (38:23).

Some three months later Judah is told that Tamar "is with child by harlotry." When Judah orders that she be brought out and burned, she sends him the pledged items with the message that she is with child by their owner (38:25). He recognizes them and is remorseful. "She is more right than I, inasmuch as I did not give her to my son Shelah" (38:26). To Judah's words the Torah adds, "And he was not intimate with her again." In due course, the union of Judah and Tamar produces the twins, Perez and Zelah (38:29–30).

Comment G–76. On the Torah's emergent sexual mores

In telling of Judah's consorting with a harlot, J is totally nonjudgmental. Indeed, within marriage itself, both polygamy and concubines are acceptable (especially as aids to reproduction). Tamar's "scheme" clearly assumed that Judah (perhaps even more so as a widower) would resort to a harlot.

From his portrayal of Judah in Gen. 37, it is unlikely that J would impugn Judah's sexual morality. In any case, Judah's concern for his reputation was not that he might be thought immoral. His fear was that he might become a "laughingstock." But why is not so clear. Perhaps the people's laughter would come from thinking him to have been "hoodwinked"—that having bargained for a "cult prostitute," he had acquired a mere harlot.

Judah's ultimate approval of Tamar's conduct confirms that as her father-in-law, he felt responsible for the family's fulfillment of its levirate obligation. But what of his wrath on hearing of her "harlotry?" In fact, his concern was more for her adultery than her harlotry. In law, presumably, she remained married until the levirate birth of her deceased husband's son.

Whether based on adultery or harlotry, the matters of procedure and punishment should also be noted. As for procedure, Judah was both Tamar's father-in-law and judge. On his own, he could condemn her to death by burning. As for punishment, were Tamar to die at once, so, too, would the lives within her. Was the sin deemed so egregious as to require destruction of the actual "fruits" of the same seeds whose mere potentials for life were deemed sacred?

In Gen. 39 the narrative returns to Joseph as he arrives in Egypt. The balance of Genesis is the story of Joseph in Egypt.

JOSEPH IN EGYPT

In 37:36 it was Midianites who sold Joseph to Potiphar, "chief steward" to Pharaoh. In 39:1 it is Ishmaelites who do so (thus maintaining the "parity" between J and E.; see Comment G–71). As for relations between Joseph and the Lord in Egypt, they begin and continue on a quiet note. Absent are the direct and dramatic encounters, revelations and promises that so often attended His appearances to Abraham, Isaac, and Jacob. Instead, relations between Joseph and his God occur in an aura of serenity. "The Lord was with Joseph, and he was a successful man; and he stayed in the house of his Egyptian master." In turn, "when his master saw that the Lord was with him and that the Lord lent success to everything he undertook, he took a liking to Joseph . . . and put him in charge of his household." Then "from the time the Egyptian put him in charge of his household and of all that he owned, *the Lord blessed his house for Joseph's sake*, so that the blessing of the Lord was upon everything that he owned" (39:2–5).

Comment G–77. On the maturing of Joseph in Egypt

The Joseph of Egypt bears little resemblance to the Joseph of Canaan. A new spirit has arisen. Joseph is now free of Jacob's destructive favoritism, which had made him hateful to his brothers. The seed of Abraham, hitherto dormant within him, now springs forth. His natural gifts of self-reliance and practical wisdom combine to mark him for great achievement. Potiphar is said to have seen "that the Lord was with [Joseph]" (39:3). As an Egyptian at this time, Potiphar would have known little, if anything, of Jacob's God in Canaan. But just as Melchizedek had once sensed Abraham to be a most remarkable human being, so too did Potiphar come to regard Joseph.

Joseph soon discovers, however, that being "well built and handsome" could prove a mixed blessing (39:6). Potiphar's strong-willed wife is determined that Joseph must "Lie with me" (39:7). Joseph reminds her of Potiphar's generosity to, and trust in, him. He concludes: "How then could I do this wicked thing, and sin before God?" (39:9).

Her coaxing "day after day" fails to move Joseph. She then seeks the classic revenge of a woman scorned. She gains possession of his coat and uses it to give credence to her screams that Joseph had come "to dally with me" (39:17).

In Potiphar the feigned outrage of his wife becomes true outrage. He imprisons Joseph. "But even . . . there . . . the Lord was with Joseph." Without fanfare, "[The Lord] extended kindness to him and disposed the chief jailer favorably toward him" (39:21). Joseph became the chief jailer's deputy, in charge of all prisoners, and "the one to carry out everything that was done there." The chief jailer never supervised Joseph "because the Lord was with him, and whatever he did the Lord made successful" (39:23).

In Gen. 40 Joseph continues to serve as the chief jailer's deputy. But his skill in interpreting dreams soon enables him to fulfil his destiny as Pharaoh's trusted right hand. The dreams of the deposed chief baker and cupbearer will provide a "showcase" for his talents. For offenses to Pharaoh, they have been committed to the custody of his chief steward, who then "assigned Joseph to them" (40:4).

On finding them distraught one morning, Joseph asks why. They reply that "we had dreams and there is no one to interpret them." Saying, "Surely God can interpret," Joseph volunteers (40:8). When the chief cupbearer tells his dream, Joseph explains: "In three days Pharaoh will pardon you and restore you to your post." So complete is Joseph's confidence in his prediction that he asks a favor of the chief cupbearer: "think well of me when all is well with you again, [mention me] to Pharaoh, so as to free me from this place." He explains his predicament as a kidnapped "Hebrew" now imprisoned without cause (40:14–15).

On hearing such a favorable reading of the first dream, the chief baker tells Joseph his own. Joseph interprets this with equal candor, but less encouragment. "In three days Pharaoh will lift off your head and impale you upon a pole; and the birds will pick off your flesh" (40:19).

Three days later, on his birthday, Pharaoh summons the two dreamers to a banquet. He then deals with each of them just as Joseph had predicted. Nevertheless, "the chief cupbearer did not think of Joseph; he forgot him" (40:23).

Comment G–78. On Joseph as an interpreter of dreams

The two Egyptians were distraught because "there was no one to interpret [their dreams]. In his own confidence that his God could "surely" interpret the dreams, what role did Joseph attribute to Him? Did he believe that his God had endowed him with an *independent* capacity to interpret dreams? Or was he, as a chosen dream "diviner," to serve as a conduit, or "prophet," for God's revelations of dreams?

Thus far, Joseph's uncanny ability to prophesy from dreams has done little to improve his fortunes in Egypt. Although highly privleged, he remains a prisoner. But now, Pharaoh himself becomes the dreamer. He has two dreams with a common theme. In the first, seven "handsome and sturdy" cows, arisen from the Nile, are eaten by seven "ugly gaunt" cows (41:1–4). In the second, seven "solid and healthy" ears of grain are swallowed up by seven "thin and scorched" ears (41:5–7). The next morning Pharaoh's "spirit was agitated." Yet neither his "magicians" nor his "wise men" could interpret these dreams (41:8).

But now the chief cupbearer who had "forgotten" Joseph remembers him. He tells Pharaoh of the "Hebrew youth" who had truly prophesied the fates of himself and the chief baker. Pharaoh summons Joseph from the "dungeon" and tells him, "I have heard it said of you that for you to hear a dream is to tell its meaning." Joseph does not deny his skill, but places its source in God: "Not I! God will see to Pharaoh's welfare" (41:16).

Comment G–79. On Joseph's prophecy of Pharaoh's "welfare"

Even before Joseph hears Pharaoh's dream, he assures him that "God will see to Pharaoh's welfare." But how can he be sure it will serve Pharaoh's "welfare"? To have assured the well-being of the ill-fated chief baker would have been tragically delusional. ("Welfare" is from the Hebrew *shalom*, generally meaning "peace." JPS1 renders it as "an answer of peace" and RSV, as "a favorable answer.")

Now Pharaoh reveals his dreams. They closely follow those told to his courtiers. However, as Pharaoh first described them, the ugly images are even more vivid and intense; and he is more agitated (cf. 41:3–4, 19–21).

Joseph promptly tells Pharaoh that the two dreams are the same: "God has told Pharaoh what He is about to do" (41:25). The fact that Pharaoh had "the same dream twice . . . *means that the matter has been determined by God, and that God will soon carry it out*" (41:32).

Joseph then interprets the dreams. In Egypt, seven years of abundance will be followed by seven years of famine. Pharaoh must thus find "a man of discernment and wisdom, and set him over the land of Egypt" (41:33). During the years of abundance, grain must be gathered in the cities as a "food reserve" for the years of famine (41:34–36).

Pharaoh promptly picks Joseph as his "man of discernment and wisdom." He declares to his courtiers, "Could we find another like him, a man in whom is the spirit of God?" To Joseph he adds, "Since God has made this all known to you, there is none so discerning and wise as you" (41:37–40). Pharaoh then puts Joseph "in charge of all the land of Egypt" (41:44). He defines Joseph's authority as follows: "I am Pharaoh; yet without you, no one shall lift up hand or foot in all the land of Egypt" (41:44).

Pharaoh then names Joseph, Zaphenath-paneah, and gives him as a wife, Asenath, "daughter of Poti-phera, priest of On" (41:45). Joseph "was thirty years old" when he entered Pharaoh's service (41:46a).

> Note G–50: That a "Poti-phera" is now Joseph's father-in-law suggests that the initial "Potiphar" was a varietal form of a common Egyptian name. Also, that Joseph was thirty on assuming office suggests the current invalidity of the "two for one" Canaanite age formula suggested in Comment G–53. As de facto ruler of Egypt at fifteen, Joseph, or anyone, would seem impossibly precocious. Either the formula was off the mark originally, or by now, or in Egypt, years were measured differently. (Friedman ascribes 41:46a to P.)

The following years confirmed Joseph's predictions. During the seven years of plenty Joseph gathered such a reserve of grain that "it could not be measured" (41:49). These were years of personal fertility as well. Perhaps to imply Joseph's gradual acculturation to Egypt, the text is quite precise in stating that "Joseph became the father of two sons, whom Asenath daughter of Poti-phera, priest of On, bore to him." These were Manasseh, his first-born, and Ephraim, whose names were explained as follows: "Joseph named the first-born Manasseh meaning, 'God has made me forget completely my hardship and my parental home.' The second he named Ephraim meaning, 'God has made me fertile in the land of my affliction' " (41:50–52).

Comment G–80. On the names of Manasseh and Ephraim

The name of "Manasseh" clearly suggests Joseph's accomodation to his life in Egypt, while that of "Ephraim" may recall his earlier "affliction" in prison. The point is that he has succeeded in rising above it. In naming his sons, however, he credits his present well-being to the God of his youth. While the dominance of Egypt in Joseph's present life may have inevitably diluted the loyalties of his youth, it has not displaced them.

Then came the years of famine, which in time "spread over the whole world." On learning of the grain in Egypt, "all the world came to Joseph in Egypt to procure rations" (41:57). Those who came did not know him as Joseph, but as the Pharaoh's "vizier" (or "governor"). It was Joseph "who dispensed rations" from the grain reserves. As the famine deepened in Canaan, the brothers of Joseph, except for Benjamin, came to Egypt. So begins the family's physical, emotional, and spiritual reunification (Gen. 42).

As would befit Joseph's rank, when his brothers are brought before him to explain their presence in Egypt, they "bowed low to him, with their faces to the ground." He, of course, recognizes them at once, but in him they see nothing of their brother Joseph (42:6–8). This is fortunate in that Joseph is not ready to greet them as brothers. He recalls too well their having sold him into servitude. For the moment, he means to subject them to the same fears that he had experienced on first arriving in Egypt and being sold to an Egyptian master. He dismisses their story of having come from Canaan "to procure food." Instead, "recalling the dreams he had dreamed about them," he accuses them of having entered Egypt through unguarded areas of the Sinai as "spies . . . come to see the land in its nakedness" (42:9–14).

The brothers protest the charge. They identify themselves as ten of twelve bothers, one of whom "is no more" and the youngest of whom remains with their father in Canaan. In reply, Joseph merely repeats his accusation. Only one brother will be allowed to leave. He must return from Canaan with the youngest brother, whose presence will prove their honesty. Until then, the other brothers will be kept in custody (42:14–16).

Comment G–81. On the connection between Joseph's "reunion" with his brothers and his "recalling the dreams he had dreamed" about them

Of Joseph's past dreams, we know only of those in Canaan, in which his entire family bowed down to him. Triggering his recollection, of course, was the sight of his brothers bowing down to him. But why would the recollection of his dreams cause Joseph to accuse his brothers of being spies? In his wiser and kinder maturity, should he not finally realize that his youthful arrogance in revealing his dreams was a precipitating factor in his brothers' guilt? Why, then, such calculated spite?

Ramban suggests the following: "Now since he did not see Benjamin with them, he conceived of the strategy of devising a charge against them so that they would also bring his brother Benjamin to him, in order to fulfil the first dream." Ramban goes on to ascribe Jacob's ultimate arrival in Egypt as the means by which the second dream would be fulfilled.[33] This analysis, however, omits the problem of Rachel's role in the second dream following the report of her earlier death (see Comment G–70 and preceding text).

After three days, Joseph softens his demand. He will allow all the brothers but one to return to Canaan with grain rations—subject to the condition of their return to Egypt with their youngest brother. To assure their return, one brother must remain. As a sign of his own good faith, Joseph precedes his proposal with a profession: "Do this and you shall live, for I am a God-fearing man" (42:18).

Comment G–82. On Joseph as a "God-fearing" man

Joseph's professed fear is of "*ha-elohim*," meaning either "God," or the "the gods." Which did Joseph mean?

One answer might lie in Friedman's attribution of 42:8–20 to J, and with it the "*ha-elohim*" of 42:18. Given J's normal use of *yahweh* ("God"), or *yahweh elohim* ("Lord God"), is it possible that J has Joseph use *ha-elohim* as a calculated ambiguity? If so, it would be another example of J's disposition toward psychological realism—in this case predicated on the realities of Joseph's life in Egypt.

Although an alien in Egypt, Joseph stood second only to Pharaoh. The effective discharge of his duties undoubtedly required him to "fit in" both with other Egyptian officials and the highest levels of Egyptian society. Knowledge of the Egyptian gods would have seemed essential. Pharaoh's recognition of this need was reflected in his personal choice of a wife (and father-in-law) for Joseph. As the husband of a high born Egyptian wife and the son-in-law of "Poti-phera, the priest of On," Joseph could hardly remain indifferent to Egyptian society and culture. Was it not possible in time that even the sturdiest tie to his father's God might succumb to his isolation from his family and the demands of his new life? (Cf. Comment G–80.)

If so, Joseph's fear of "the gods," no less than of God, would have been a natural element of Egyptian religious beliefs. While fear of the God of Jacob might largely reflect a fear of earthly punishment for disobedience, the fear of the gods of Egypt centered on the quality of one's afterlife. That fear in itself could have been sufficient to discourage dishonesty and other failures of character.

One noted authority, Will Durant, summarizes Egyptian religious beliefs on good and evil and the afterlife as follows: "What distinguished this religion above everything else was its emphasis on immortality. . . . [The] Elysian Fields . . . could be reached only through the services of a ferryman, an Egyptian prototype of Charon; and this old gentleman would receive into his boat only such men and women as had done no evil in their lives. Or Osiris would question the dead, weighing each candidate's heart in the scale against a feather to test his truthfulness."[34]

In seeking to impress his brothers with his good faith, Joseph would have known the value of evoking their father's God. But he also knew that they would think it more natural for an Egyptian ruler to swear by his own gods. In using *ha-elohim*, J may have hoped to serve both purposes.

Despite Joseph's profession, the brothers cower at the thought of bringing Benjamin from Jacob to Egypt. Standing before him, they refer aloud to their present travail as punishment for their treatment of Joseph. "Alas . . . we looked on his anguish, yet paid no heed as he pleaded with us." On hearing them, Joseph turns away in tears. He orders that their bags be filled with grain, that "each one's money" be placed in their sacks, and that they be given food for their trip. Simeon will remain as hostage (42:21–25).

En route, *"one of them"* discovered the money "at the mouth of his bag." When he tells his brothers, "their hearts sank." Trembling, they ask, "What is this God has done to us?" (42:27–28).

Now back in Canaan, the brothers tell Jacob all that has occurred. Then, "as they were emptying their sacks, there, in each one's sack, was his money-bag!" (cf. 42:27–28). When they and their father saw their money bags, they were dismayed" (42:35). Jacob berates them for what has befallen him. "It is always me that you bereave: Joseph is no more and Simeon is no more, and now you would take away Benjamin. *These things always happen to me!*" (42:36).

In a moment of high emotion, Reuben gives Jacob leave (at least figuratively) to kill his [Reuben's] own sons should he fail to return with Benjamin. But Jacob remains adamant: "For his brother is dead and he alone is left. If he meets with disaster on the journey you are taking, you will send my white head down to Sheol in grief" (42:38).

Comment G–83. On "Sheol" and immortality

"Sheol," it has been said, "demonstrates a spiritualistic tendency in the belief of an afterlife in the Hebrew scriptures." Being neither heaven nor hell, however, it is more "an extension of the grave." As such, it is described as "an immense, underground place, deep, dark, and bolted shut, the abode of shadows—to lead lives that are shadows of their lives on earth."[35] Unlike the image of hell, "Sheol" was not intended as a post-mortal punishment that might influence earthly conduct through fear. Thus, "throughout nearly all of the Old Testament, the afterworld was considered a dreary underground place called Sheol, where the good and bad alike led an eventless existence. Indeed the later Jewish, Christian, and Islamic concept of the afterlife, as one in which the individual is rewarded or punished depending on his earthly record, is more akin to Egyptian views than to those of the Old Testament."[36]

As the famine deepens in Canaan (43:1), the Jacob of Gen. 42 is now the Israel of Gen. 43. And when he tells his sons to return to Egypt for food, it is Judah rather than Reuben who speaks for the brothers (43:2–3). In explaining the need to bring Benjamin, Judah makes much the same plea as had Reuben in Gen. 42. When Israel (again) refuses to send Benjamin, Judah, a bit less dramatically than Reuben, tells him, "I myself will be surety for him; . . . If I do not bring him back to you . . . I shall stand guilty before you forever" (43:9).

Seeing no alternative, Israel agrees. He instructs his sons to bring as gifts "some of the choice products of the land" and "double the money," should the money first paid for the grain have been mistakenly replaced in the bags (43:11–12). Israel then calls on *el shaddai* to aid his sons in gaining the release of "your other brother, as well as Benjamin" (43:14).

> Note G–51: Among the "choice products of the land" were "honey, pistachio nuts and almonds" (43:11). However severe the famine in Canaan (see 41:1), it may have been limited to grain.

Comment G–84. On the authorship of Gen. 42 and 43

As we might expect by now, Friedman ascribes 42:35–37 to E (in which *Reuben* offers to serve as guarantor of Benjamin's safe return from Egypt with Benjamin). In turn, he ascribes 43:8–10 to J (in which *Judah* assumes the same role; cf. Comment G–73). The ongoing melding of sources in these chapters is also evident in the brothers' discovery, and rediscovery, of the replaced purchase money in their sacks (cf. 42:27–28 and 35).

When "the men" (as the sons and brothers are now termed) return to Joseph, any further fears seem groundless. Joseph invites them to his house for a noon meal. In the interim they tell the steward of the money found in their sacks after their first visit. He eases their fears of being charged with theft: "Do not be afraid. Your God and the God of your father must have put treasure in your bags for you. I got your payment" (43:23).

> Note G–52: Joseph's steward shows great respect for the family's God. He knew, of course, that it was Joseph who had ordered the money to be placed in their sacks. Did he expect the brothers to accept his explanation of God's role? In any case, the steward's tact and grace testifies to Joseph's ability to choose worthy and competent aides.

Joined by Simeon, whom the steward had brought to them, the brothers enter Joseph's house for the noon meal. For the first time, Joseph inquires about Jacob's health (i.e., of "your aged father of whom you spoke") (43:27). As they tell him of Jacob's good health, Joseph looks about and sees Benjamin. He tries to hide his recognition by asking if he were the youngest brother of whom they had spoken. But with emotion, he impulsively adds "May God be gracious to you, my boy" (43:29). He then goes to another room to weep. On regaining his composure, he returns for the meal (43:30–31).

To their astonishment, Joseph seats the brothers in birth order. As was the practice in Egypt, however, he eats apart from them. (The Torah notes that Egyptians deemed it "abhorrent" to eat with strangers [43:32].) Yet all was convivial and "they drank their fill" (43:34).

In the morning, the brothers again prepare to leave with their animals and bags of grain. Yet, despite the festivities, Joseph had set in motion a Byzantine procedure that would lead to their return and the revelation of his identity. Once more he orders that the purchase money be placed in his brothers' bags. In Benjamin's bag he has added his silver divination goblet (44:1–2). Following their departure, he sends his steward in pursuit to accuse them of stealing the goblet and to bring them back (44:3–6).

The brothers protest their innocence and call for the death of anyone who has the goblet. If anyone does, they volunteer slavery for all (44:7–8). When the goblet is found, the brothers "threw themselves on the ground before [Joseph]" (44:14).

Joseph continues his game. He complains of the theft, not of a mere goblet, but of a "divination" cup. "Do you not know that a man like me practices divination?" (44:15). Judah responds from a deep-rooted sense of guilt. "God has uncovered the crime of your servants. Here we are, then, slaves of my lord, the rest of us as much as he in whose possession the goblet was found" (44:16). But Joseph tells them that only Benjamin "shall be my slave." The others will "go back in peace to your father" (44:17).

Judah pleads for Joseph to reconsider. He describes the grief that will overwhelm Jacob should his youngest son, Benjamin, not return. Judah tells him of Jacob's statement to the brothers regarding Joseph and Benjamin. "As you know, my wife bore me two sons. But one . . . was torn by a beast! If you take this one from me, too, and he meets with disaster, you will send my white head down to Sheol in grief." Judah then tells Joseph of his pledge to Jacob as the guarantor of Benjamin's safe return. He pleads to stay in Benjamin's place. "Let me not be the witness to the woe that would overtake my father" (44:34).

Comment G–85. On Judah's plea to Joseph

Judah also recalls a statement purportedly made by the brothers to Joseph on their first encounter. "We said to my lord, 'The boy cannot leave his father; if he were to leave him, his father would die' " (44:22). In the only passage bearing on their first meeting (where Reuben's presence, but not Judah's, is explicitly noted), no mention is made of Jacob's grief should Benjamin leave him (see 42:6–26). This creates an unusual editorial anomaly. Was another version of their first meeting somehow "lost?" In any case, Judah's plea in 44:22 seems to constitute a rare case of a missing antecedent—that is, a nonexistent passage which is alluded to in a later passage (cf. Comment G–97).

Judah's plea sparks a surge of compassion in Joseph for his family. Having ordered his attendants to leave, "His sobs were so loud that the Egyptians could hear, so the news reached Pharaoh's palace" (45:2). Joseph then reveals himself to his brothers and forgives them for what they had done. He assures them they had served God's will rather than their own. He speaks of the famine and God's purpose. "God sent me ahead of you to insure your survival on earth. . . . So it was not you who sent me here, but God; and He has made me . . . ruler over the whole land of Egypt" (45:7–8).

Comment G–86. On Joseph's view of God's uses of human evil

In declaring his brothers to have been the agents of God's will, Joseph speaks from a great burst of emotion. He expresses the most loving sentiments toward his entire family. Prior to this, however, there is little to suggest that Joseph has been of such a mind. His previous tears on seeing Benjamin were not for his brothers, as unknowing instruments of God. They were for Benjamin alone, "his mother's son," the youngest and least guilty (if guilty at all) (43:29–30). True, Joseph had also wept at his first meeting with the brothers (other than Benjamin). But if he had then viewed them as blameless agents of God, why would he have imposed such severe emotional distress on them and Jacob? Indeed, at the present meeting, prior to Judah's plea, why did he contrive to subject the brothers to the further travails resulting from the "theft" of his cup?

But let us accept Joseph's stated belief at face value; that is, it was God's will that provoked the brothers' evil deed. Where, then, would he begin the line of causation? Had God made Joseph the favored son of Jacob in order to foster his youthful arrogance? If so, was his arrogance meant to instill sufficient hatred in his brothers to sell him into slavery? Were the reasons for Jacob's "corruption" of Joseph (i.e., his love for Joseph's mother, Rachel, and her early death) also part of God's same plan?

But what if Joseph had not viewed his God as the cause of his brothers' conduct? Could he have forgiven them had they acted as totally free agents? If so, would he not have first had to concede his own provocative arrogance? By recourse to God's will, could Joseph better accept his own role in the chain of Godly causation? Could he then "be at greater peace" with the flaws of his youth?

Finally, consider Joseph's assurance to his brothers that "God sent me ahead of you to insure your survival on earth" (45:7). As for the famine itself, was it Joseph's belief that God had first ordained it for purposes unrelated to Jacob and his line? Or that He had devised it to effect a loving reunion of Jacob's family in Egypt? Or both?

Joseph tells his brothers to take the following message to Jacob: "God has made me lord of all Egypt; come down to me without delay." Jacob is to dwell in "the region of Goshen" with his entire family, his flocks and herds and all that is his (45:9–10). Joseph and Benjamin embrace and weep together. Joseph also kisses and weeps with his brothers. Only then were they "able to talk to him" (45:15).

On hearing of the presence of Joseph's brothers in Egypt, "Pharaoh and his courtiers were pleased" (45:16). Pharaoh tells Joseph that all the households of his father's family should "come to me." To Joseph's brothers, Pharaoh promises, "I will give you the best of the land of Egypt and you shall live off the fat of the land" (45:18). They then leave, well provisioned for the journey to Canaan and back.

Jacob at first could not believe that Joseph not only lived, but did so as Egypt's ruler. When he then sees the wagons Joseph had sent, "the spirit of their father *Jacob* revived. 'Enough,' said *Israel*, 'My son Joseph is still alive. I must go and see him before I die' " (45:27–28).

Comment G–87. On "Jacob" and "Israel"

In two juxtaposed phrases from 45:27–28, the father is both "Jacob" and "Israel" (thus, "the spirit of their father Jacob revived [45:27]). "Enough!" said Israel. "My son Joseph is still alive" (45:28). Friedman ascribes both verses to J. *If so, the names are used interchangeably without regard to context—*unless each name is somehow meant to denote a different aspect of Jacob/Israel's total being. Also, despite the earlier decisive reports of Joseph's death by his brothers, Jacob does not now ask "How can this be!" Does he sense that the subject might best be left alone?

Israel then sets out with "all that was his." At Beer-sheba, "*Israel*" stops to offer sacrifices to "the God of his father Isaac" (46:1). There, God called to "*Israel*" in a "vision by night": "*Jacob! Jacob!* . . . I am God, the God of your father. Fear not to go down to Egypt, for I will make you there into a great nation" (46:2–3).

Comment G–88. On the Godly visions of Israel/Jacob

How can we interpret Jacob's call from God through "a vision at night?" Is it a matter of *what is said* or *heard*? In this theophanic night vision is "God" portrayed as internal or external to Jacob? The question arises from Jacob's earlier theophanies. Friedman divides the first (i.e., Jacob's *dream* at Bethel enroute to Haran) between J and E (28:11–22). In the second, which he ascribes to E, Jacob tells Leah and Rachel of an "angel of God" who appeared in a *dream*. He identified Himself as "the God of Beth-el" and told Jacob to return to Canaan (a command which Jacob welcomed) (31:10–13). The third was Jacob's wrestling match with an unidentified "man," as he "was left alone" with his thoughts of meeting Esau. There, the man tells Jacob he will now be known as Israel and that he had "striven with beings divine and human" and had prevailed (32:25–32). The fourth occurred following the slaughter at Shechem, when Jacob heard God say, "Go up to Bethel and remain there" (35:1–4). This, too, is ascribed to E.

In none of these theophanies of E and J is it made clear that Jacob and the Torah's God actually confront each other. What befalls Jacob in each case (except perhaps for the lameness following the wrestling match) could be viewed as internal to him. The most recent "vision by night" is of the same character (46:2–3). Only in a theophany ascribed to P is it said that "God *appeared* again to Jacob" (on his arrival from Paddan-aram) (35:9–15). Only there does God speak at length to a fully conscious Jacob. *Only in P's theophany does the event center more on God than on Jacob.*

These episodes project a sense of two distinct types of Torah theophanies. The first is consistent with an internal perception of a spiritual encounter. The second asserts the actual presence of the Torah's God as a separate Being. At this point, however, I only note the possible distinction. It is clear enough that the Torah, through all its sources, means to project its God as a separate Being external to the human spirit. Thus, for example, at Shechem, as Jacob and his household left for Bethel, "a terror from God fell on the cities round about" (35:5).

Jacob (1) then proceeded to Egypt with "all his offspring," including "his sons and grandsons, his daughters and granddaughters—all his offspring" (46:7). The following are then listed by names: Reuben (Jacob's first son) and his four sons (5); Simeon (a son) and his six sons (7); Levi (a son) and his three sons (4); and Judah and his five sons (with the comment that of these, Er and Onan "had died in the land of Canaan" [as reported in the story of Tamar and Judah, Gen. 38]). (Thus [4], excluding Er and Onan.)

> *Note G–53: The five named sons of Judah include Perez and Zerah, who were born of Tamar. But recall that Tamar had enticed Judah into a union in order to fulfil his family's levirate duty to her deceased husband Er. Why, then, are Perez and Zerah not attributed to Er rather than Judah?*

Two sons of Perez (Hezron and Hamul) (2); Issachar (a son) and his four sons (5); Zebulun (a son) and his three sons (4). It is then said that these were all the sons "whom Leah bore to Jacob . . . in addition to his daughter Dinah" (46:15). No more is said of Dinah. Her presence in the group is not made explicit. However, this first group, consisting of Jacob and his descendants by Leah, concludes as follows: "Persons in all, male and female, 33" (46:15).

Comment G–89A. On who counts in a Torah count, as reflected in the count of Jacob's party

Two different descriptions of Jacob's entire party appear in two separate verses. First, "the sons of Israel put their father Jacob and their children and their wives in the wagons" (46:5). Second (as also noted at the outset of the journey), "Thus Jacob and all his offspring with him came to Egypt: he brought with him to Egypt his sons and grandsons, daughters and granddaughters—all his offspring" (46:7). We know that these two initial summaries do not literally include all persons within the party because the detailed listing of this first group that follows is said to include the two sons of Judah's son, Perez. These would be Jacob's great-grandsons and Judah's grandsons. Neither category of persons appear, as such, in the summaries. Since "grandsons" are distinguished from "sons," we might expect "great-grandsons" to be distinguished from "grandsons." It is possible, however, that the two "great-grandsons," Hezron and Hamul, are included in the catchall of "all his offspring." In any case, they are among the "33" who constitute to his "offspring" through Leah. Note, however, that with the possible exception of Dinah no daughters are named or counted. Consistent with the two initial summaries that do not include Jacob's wives (or concubines), Leah is not named.

Considering these facts, how do we arrive at "33" persons in this first group; and what is the significance of the number? Omitting Leah, for the reason noted, the underscored sub-totals above, including Jacob, add up to 32. The most logical way of reaching 33 is to include Dinah, despite the ambiguity surrounding her presence. In fact, but for Dinah, there is no named person to support the assertion that the group of "33" included "male and female."

What is the significance of the total of 33? It tells us that either none of Jacob's sons (or his grandson, Perez) had wives at the time, or that their wives were simply not counted. Since "their wives" are in fact mentioned in the initial summation (46:5), it must be that they were not counted. The same may be said of daughters, other than Dinah, whose birth was noted and who was central to the story of Shechem. Given Jacob's many sons by two wives and two concubines, it would be remarkable if Dinah were Jacob's only daughter. As for including "granddaughters" within the category of "daughters," note that among the categories of "offspring" in 46:7, "granddaughters" are listed apart from "daughters" (cf. Comment G–72).

The next group consists of Jacob's offspring by Zilpah. These were: Gad and his seven sons (8); Asher and his four sons and one named daughter (Serah) (6); two sons of Beriah (a son of Asher) (2). The stated total of "16 persons" corresponds to the underscored subtotals (46:18). Again, other than Serah, no wives and daughters are named or counted. (Nothing yet explains the listing of Serah.)

Next were Jacob's offspring by Rachel. These were: Joseph and his two sons (already in Egypt) (3) and Benjamin and his ten sons (11), or "(14) persons in all" (46:22).

The final group was of Jacob's offspring by Bilhah. These were: Dan and one son (2) and Napthali and four sons (5). These were "(7) persons in all" (46:25).

Once again, the names of these final two groups (by Rachel and Bilhah), include no wives or daughters. In all, however, the four groups, including Jacob and Joseph and his two sons in Egypt, totalled (70).

The count concludes with these verses: "All the *persons* belonging to Jacob who came to Egypt—*his own issue*, aside from the wives of Jacob's sons—all these persons numbered 66. And Joseph's sons who were born to him in Egypt were two in number. Thus the total of Jacob's household who came to Egypt was 70 persons" (46:26–27).

Comment G–89B. On who counts in a Torah count, as reflected in the count of Jacob's party

As the Torah now states, the count of 70 consists of all of Jacob's "own issue" (including Joseph and his two sons) and Jacob, himself. Also, for first time, the text explicitly notes the absence of "the wives of Jacob's sons" from the count. Since *nothing* similar is said of Jacob's wives or of other daughters of these generations, can we not assume the following? (1) Jacob's wives have all died. (2) All daughters of these generations, other than Dinah and Serah, if any, have married and left the household. If not, why is the noninclusion of Jacob's daughters-in-law expressly noted, but not that of any daughters?

The remainder of Gen. 46 (46:28–34) tells of Jacob's arrival in Egypt. Jacob sends Judah ahead "to point the way to Goshen." Their arrival in Goshen is marked by an emotional reunion between Joseph and Jacob. "Then Israel said to Joseph, 'Now I can die, having seen for myself that you are still alive.'"

Comment G–90. On Jacob's family as "sheepmen" or "cattlemen"*

Whether intended by J or not, the family's meeting with Pharaoh offers the reader a rare touch of levity. It also identifies Egypt as a primordial site of the age old conflict between sheepmen and cattlemen. (The Torah wisely removes its God from the scene of this early episode in the eternal human struggle for grass.)

Pharaoh had already assured Joseph that he would give his family "the best land in Egypt" (45:18). It would be in "Goshen" (a large fertile region in the rich northeast sector of the Nile delta). Joseph's present concern is that nothing should occur to cause Pharaoh to change his mind.

---

*Ed.—Because of a particular need to juxtapose text and commentary, this Comment combines both.

In "coaching" his family for their first meeting with Pharaoh, Joseph tells how he will describe them to Pharoah. "The men are *shepherds* (*roay tzone*); they have always been *breeders of livestock* (*anshay mikneh*); and they have brought . . . their flocks and herds" (46:32). Thus, Joseph will honestly, but artfully, equate their roles as keepers of "flocks" (i.e., sheep) and "herds" (i.e., cattle). He then tells the brothers how *they* should answer Pharaoh when he asks "What is your occupation?" (46:33). "You shall answer, '*Your servants have been breeders of livestock* (*anshay mikneh*) from the start until now, both we and our fathers'—so that you may stay in the region of Goshen. *For all shepherds* (*roay tzone*) *are abhorrent to the Egyptians*" (46:34). Thus, by referring to "livestock," they, like Joseph, will minimize their role as shepherds. (JPS1 and RSV render the Hebrew *mikneh* as "cattle" rather than "livestock." Depending on context, both are appropriate.)

On first telling Pharaoh of his family's presence in Egypt, Joseph says (consistent with the preceding scenario), "My father and my brothers with their *flocks and herds* . . . are now in the region of Goshen" (47:1). Joseph then introduces "a few of his brothers" to him (47:1). When Pharaoh promptly asks, "What is your occupation?" (47:3), their answer must have left Joseph dumbstruck. "We your servants are *shepherds* (*roay tzone*), as were our fathers. We have come . . . to sojourn in this land, *for there is no pasture for your servants' flocks.* . . . Pray, then, let your servants stay in the region of Goshen" (47:3–4; cf. 46:34). Luckily, Pharaoh's respect for Joseph exceeds his abhorrence of sheep. He then tells Joseph to "settle your father and your brothers in the best part of the land; let them stay in the region of Goshen. And if you know any capable men among them, put them in charge of my *livestock*" (47:6).

Although Joseph and his brothers are as "disintegrated" as ever before, Friedman ascribes the entire passage to J. Yet, by reading *mikneh* as "live-stock" rather than "cattle," JPS2 points the way for keepers of cattle and sheep to meet on common grazing grounds as "keepers of livestock."

Joseph then brings Jacob to meet Pharaoh. Answering his question, Jacob tells Pharaoh that his years are one hundred thirty. To this he adds a touch of self-pity: "Few and hard have been the years of my life, nor do they come up to the life spans of my fathers during their sojourns." Joseph then "settled his father and his brothers, with holdings in the choicest part of the land of Egypt, in the region of *Rameses*, as Pharaoh had commanded" (47:9–11).

Comment G–91. On "the region of Rameses"

Why is "the region of Rameses" named as the place in which the family set-tles? Pharaoh's words to Joseph were: "Settle your father and your brothers in the best part of the land; let them stay in the region of *Goshen*" (47:6).

The reigns of Rameses I and II during the thirteenth century B.C.E. roughly approximate the period of the Hebrew Exodus from Egypt (i.e., Rameses I, 1292–90; Rameses II, 1279–13).[37] (As appears from the Torah, this was some four hundred years after Jacob and Joseph. Exodus 1:11 later tells of the Hebrews having built the "garrison cities" of "Pithom and Raamses." Thus, a reference in Joseph's time to "the region of Rameses" may again reflect a "reordering" of earlier time relationships by later authors lacking accurate historical data (see Comment G–49).

Gen. 47:13–27 goes on to describe the Torah's version of the origins of tenant farming in Egypt. It also portrays Joseph as a master of economics and administration. And yet, though his aim may have been to improve the whole of Egyptian agriculture, it is Pharaoh who benefits most.

As the famine intensified, "there was no bread in all the world" (47:13). In time, through payments to Pharaoh for grain, "Joseph gathered in all the money that was to be found [in Egypt and Canaan]" (47:14). When desperate Egyptians came for grain, Joseph took their "livestock" to pay for food. He thus acquired "all their livestock for Pharaoh" (47:17). As the famine persisted, he took land for grain. In this way "Joseph gained possession of all the farm land of Egypt for Pharaoh" (47:20). Only the priests kept their lands for "they lived off the allotment which Pharaoh had made to them" (47:22).

When the people no longer owned property, Joseph proposed to give them seed so that they could farm the land as tenants. His terms were these: "And when the harvest comes, you shall give one-fifth to Pharaoh and four-fifths shall be yours as seed for the fields and as food for you . . . your households, and . . . your children" (42:24). For this the people are grateful. "You have saved our lives! . . . and we shall be serfs to Pharaoh" (47:25).

This epic tale of expropriation and nationalization concludes with a statement of Egyptian agricultural Law: "Joseph made it into a land law of Egypt, *which is still valid*, that a fifth should be Pharaoh's; only the land of the priests did not become Pharaoh's" (47:26). Of Joseph's family it is said: "Thus *Israel* settled in the country of Egypt, in the region of Goshen; *they* acquired holdings in it, and were fertile and increased greatly" (47:27).

> Note G–54: Having "increased greatly," the descendants of Jacob/Israel are now for the first time contemporaneously identified as the people of Israel (cf. Comments G–63 and 65).

Comment G–92. On Joseph's agricultural program

Comparisons of relative productivity under Joseph's "nationalized" system and the previous system can not be made. In distributive terms the allotment of four-fifths of the output to the "tenants" seems fair in the circumstances, while offering substantial productivity incentives. Also difficult to gauge, however, is whether Joseph's subsequent generosity justified his coercive use of bargaining leverage. Was it his main purpose to improve the efficiency of Egyptian agriculture? Or to increase Pharaoh's wealth and power? If both, as likely, Joseph's dual success again proved his talents. The farmers' professions of gratitude for their serfdom may actually have been heartfelt.

Gen. 47:26 states that Joseph's law "is still valid." (As to similar issues regarding the use of "still," see Comments G–63 and 65 and Note G–47.)

Having lived for seventeen years in Egypt, Jacob, at age one hundred forty-seven, now prepares for his death. Joseph swears to Israel that he will not be buried in Egypt, but in the burial place of his fathers in Canaan (47:28–31).

"Some time afterward," on hearing that Jacob was ill (48:1), Joseph brings his sons, Manasseh and Ephraim, to see him. Jacob first tells Joseph: "*El Shaddai* appeared to me at Luz in the land of Canaan, and He blessed me, and said to me, 'I will make you fertile and numerous, making of you a community of peoples; and I will give this land to your offspring for an everlasting possession'" (48:3–4).

Comment G–93. On *el shaddai* and Jacob at Luz

Why does Jacob tell Joseph of *el shaddai*'s earlier appearance to him at Luz (otherwise Bethel) (35:9–15), while saying nothing of his more recent vision of *elohim* at Beer-sheba (46:1–4). Once more, the oddity reflects the separate continuity of a particular source. This P passage of 48:3–6 alludes to the earlier P passage of 35:9–15, in which *el shaddai* actually appeared before Jacob. It was then that P recorded the second renaming of Jacob as Israel—on this occasion by *el shaddai* (see Comments G–67 and 88).

Jacob then tells Joseph that Ephraim and Manasseh are to become his own sons: "Now your two sons who were born to you in the land of Egypt . . . shall be mine; *Ephraim and Manasseh shall be mine no less than Reuben and Simeon.* But progeny born to you after them shall be yours; they shall be recorded instead of their brothers in their inheritance" (48:5–6). Jacob attributes his decision to Rachel's death "on the road to Ephrath"—now Bethlehem (48:7).

Comment G–94. On Rachel's death and Jacob's adoption of Joseph's sons

1. On Bethlehem as the site of Rachel's death

In 48:7 JPS2 places "now Bethlehem" *outside* the quotation of Jacob's statement that names Ephrath as the site of Rachel's death. This attribution of the phrase to an author, rather than to Jacob, suggests that Jacob himself did not know of Ephrath as Bethlehem. *Thus, if he had not renamed Ephrath as Bethlehem prior to departing for Egypt, it could not have been renamed by Israelites until their arrival in Canaan from Egypt.* This would have followed the traditional revelation of the Torah at Sinai by some forty years (see Note G–47).

Conversely, JPS1 renders the phrase as follows: "in the way to Ephrath—the same is Bethlehem." By attributing "the same is Bethlehem" to Jacob, JPS1 clearly implies that he had renamed Ephrath while still in Canaan. To confuse the matter further, consider the words (and punctuation) of RSV: "on the way to Ephrath (that is, Bethlehem)." Does RSV mean to read "that is, Bethlehem" as Jacob's or the author's thought? Friedman attributes Gen. 48:7 to the redactor ("R"). (See Note G–47.)

2. On Jacob's adoption of Joseph's sons

This is the Torah's first adoption of grandchildren by a grandfather (even more notably, while the father still lives). Joseph's immediate acceptance surely speaks to the respect and authority granted by a grown son to his father. But does the episode reveal a father's absolute authority or a son's loving obedience? In either case, does Jacob mean to gain through Joseph the additional sons denied him by Rachel's death?

But now we encounter an "Israel" totally at odds with the resolute "Jacob" who has just adopted "Ephraim and Manasseh" *by name.* "Noticing Joseph's sons, Israel asked, '"Who are these?'" Joseph replies: "They are my sons, whom God has given me here" (48:8–9).

Israel asks that the boys be brought to him to be blessed. "Now Israel's eyes were dim with age, he could not see." When Joseph brings them, Jacob kisses and embraces them and makes a statement that contradicts all that has just preceded it: "I never expected to see *you* again, and here God has let me see your children as well" (48:10–11).

Having "removed them from his knees," Joseph then places his sons before Israel in accordance with their seniority of birth: Manasseh at Israel's right hand and Ephraim at his left (48:12–13). Israel, however, crosses his own hands and places his right on Ephraim's head, his left on Manasseh's. In that "crossed" position, Israel gives his blessing: "And he blessed Joseph, saying, 'The God in whose ways my fathers Abraham and Isaac walked,/ The God who has been my shepherd from my birth to this day—/ . . . Bless the lads./ In them may my name be recalled,/ And the names of my fathers Abraham and Isaac,/ And may they be teeming multitudes upon the earth' " (48:15–16).

Comment G–95. On "Jacob and "Israel" in Gen. 48

How can the fast failing "Israel" to whom Joseph seems to bring his sons for their first visit be the same "Jacob" who has just adopted them. The "Jacob" who tells of *el shaddai's* appearance to him speaks knowingly of Ephraim and Manasseh. He refers to them by name. We gather that he has met them before. Jacob's words and conduct in adopting them are forthright and purposeful. To Israel, however, the boys are strangers who must be identified. Although said to be ill, the Jacob of 48:3–7 seems strong and coherent. In 48:8–11, Israel's eyes are "dim with age"; death is at hand.

How can we explain the anomalies between 48:1–7 and 48:8–20? Have the impediments of age caused Israel to forget about ever having met his adopted sons in the course of his seventeen years in Egypt? In fact, the boys seem younger on meeting Israel than on meeting Jacob. Joseph's identification of the boys in 48:9 as "my sons" ignores their prior adoption by Jacob. Having accepted Jacob's adoption of his sons, would Joseph, as a dutiful son, not feel bound by these words of Jacob: "Now, your two sons . . . shall be mine; Ephraim and Manasseh shall be mine no less than Reuben and Simeon" (48:5–6). Would Joseph have mocked his father by reclaiming his sons as Israel approached death? In truth, E's Joseph of 48:8–20 had no idea that P's Jacob of 48:3–6 had adopted his sons.

Joseph now intercedes to move Israel's hands to the proper heads so that his right hand is on Manasseh, the first-born. Israel objects and will not change the placement of his hands. He then explains why. Speaking first of Manasseh and then of Ephraim, Israel says, "He too shall become a people, and he too shall be great. Yet his younger brother shall be greater than he, and his offspring shall be plentiful enough for ages" (48:19).

Comment G–96. On Israel's reversal of the birth status of Joseph's sons

Why does Israel insist that Ephraim, rather than Manasseh, be blessed as Joseph's first son? Is the answer to be found in his troubled conscience? Does the episode reveal his desire to legitimize the accession of second sons to the status of first sons. Israel's stated reason for his choice is that Ephraim shall be "greater" than Manasseh. Not disclosed, however, is the basis of his prophecy.

As he did the birth of Joseph's sons (41:50–52), Friedman assigns this "*elohim*" episode to E (the "source of the north"). What was to Israel a prophecy of the future was for E a known reality that could explain E's need to "arrange" for Israel's elevation of Ephraim over Manasseh.

Consider these two typical descriptions of the tribe of Ephraim. (1)

"Joshua, an Ephraimite, lead the Israelites into the promised land. . . . In 930 [B.C.E.] the tribe of Ephraim led the 10 northern tribes in a successful revolt against the south and established the Kingdom of Israel, with Jeroboam I, an Ephraimite, as king."[38] (2) "They [the Ephraimites] were long the most warlike and most successful of the tribes of Israel, and the Ark and Tabernacle were at their capital, Shiloh. . . . After the division of the Israelite Kingdom into Israel and Judah, Ephraim was used as a synonym for the northern kingdom, Israel."[39]

It was not that E deemed the northern tribe of Manasseh to be unworthy. It was that E knew the need to square birth order with history. But in doing so, E enabled Jacob, the quintessential second son, to find virtue in necessity.

Telling Joseph "I am about to die . . . ," Israel assures him that "God will . . . bring you back to the land of your fathers" (48:21). Then, as a prelude to his testament, or blessing, which soon follows, Jacob declares: "And now, I give you one more portion than to your brothers, which I wrested from the Amorites with my sword and bow" (48:22).

Comment G–97. On "one more portion"

Why should Joseph receive "one more portion" than his brothers? When and where had Jacob "wrested" that extra portion from the Amorites with his "sword and bow"? The answers are found in a pun. (Though rarely so pertinent to our inquiry, such puns abound in the Torah.)

The phrase "one more portion" is from the Hebrew sh'chem achad ahl. This is generally presumed to place the episode of which Jacob speaks in the Shechem of Gen. 34 (where mayhem followed the rape of Dinah). It would thus have been at Shechem that Jacob, with "sword and bow," had "wrested" the "extra portion" from the Amorites, a major tribe of Canaan.

Jacob's passive role in the mayhem of Gen. 34 affords no support for his personal claim of victory. To give him the benefit of any doubt, however, we must take note that J's yahweh of Gen. 34 has become E's elohim in Gen. 48:8–22 (see Comment G–96). Variations in different versions of a similar episode are more the rule than the exception.

In bestowing a "double portion" on Joseph, E's Jacob serves two purposes. First, assuming Joseph will have no more sons, it assures a full portion to each of Joseph's two sons—and in particular to Ephraim (for the reasons noted in Comment G–96). Second, it will serve to formalize Jacob's effective displacement of Reuben by Joseph as "the elect of his brothers," thus entitled to the prerogatives of the first-born son" (see Gen. 49:26 in the context of Jacob's testament). The later reference in Deut. 21:15 to a first son's "double portion" likely confirms a general prevailing practice. But how would E have known of Joseph's double portion as a "first-born" son? Although he attributes Jacob's blessings of Gen. 49 to J, Friedman also suggests their origins elsewhere.[40] If only "borrowed" by J, this same tradition may have been known to E.

In Gen. 49 Jacob calls his sons together "that I may tell you what is to befall you in days to come."

> Note G–55: *I will limit my reprise of Jacob's lengthy testament to portions bearing on the known character and conduct of his more prominent sons. Also, his allocation of tribal lands largely, or wholly, reflect what was later known to J.*

A pervading quality of Jacob's testament is objectivity in regard to the character and conduct of his sons. The moral essence of the testament lies in the linkage between the quality of a son's character and conduct and the destiny of his tribe. The most dramatic expression of this essence is found in Jacob's testament to Reuben. "Reuben you are my first-born. . . . Unstable as water, *you shall excel no longer*; For when you mounted your father's bed, You brought disgrace—my couch he mounted!" (49:3–4). Thus, like Esau, Reuben was stripped of his birthright as a first-born son (but for the more obvious reason of dishonoring his father with Bilhah; see 35:22).

> Note G–56: *Located east of the Jordan River and Dead Sea, the tribe of Reuben would play a minor role in the affairs of Israel.*[41]

Given the slaughter which they precipitated at Shechem, Simeon and Levi fare no better (34:25–26). "Simeon and Levi are a pair. Their weapons are tools of lawlessness. . . . Cursed be their anger so fierce. . . . I will divide them in Jacob, Scatter them in Israel" (49:5–7). (Lacking any customary tribal territory, the Levites would indeed be scattered in Israel. First located in the south, the tribe of Simeon was absorbed by the tribe of Judah. Its remnants later moved north.[42])

For Judah, the fourth son of Leah, Jacob predicts a destiny of honor and success. In Judah and Reuben, the pattern of a worthy younger son preempting a less worthy first-born son is repeated. With Judah, however, it was necessary to descend further into the order of sons because of the flaws of Simeon and Levi. Jacob's praise of Judah marks his tribe for leadership. "You, O Judah, your brothers shall praise; . . . Your father's sons shall bow low to you. . . . Judah is a lion's whelp. . . . Like the king of beasts—who dare rouse him? The scepter shall not part from Judah. . . . So that tribute shall come to him. And the homage of people be his" (49:8–12).

What, then, is left for Joseph and Benjamin, Jacob's most cherished sons by

Rachel? The Torah's description of Joseph (i.e., *bayn porat yohsayf*, 49:22a) has spawned highly varied translations. JPS2 renders 49:22a as "Joseph is a wild ass," and the balance of the verse as "a wild ass by a spring—Wild colts on a hillside." In striking contrast, JPS1 describes Joseph as "a fruitful vine, A fruitful vine by a fountain; Its branches run over the wall." Similarly, RSV uses bough for vine and spring for fountain.

Comment G–98. On the description of Joseph in 49:22

JPS2's use of "wild ass" comes from reading *porath*, not as "fruitful," but "as a poetical feminine form of *pere*," or 'wild ass.'" Its editor also notes that Jacob describes his other sons as animals rather than plants.[43] I am not an etymologist. But I sense that "fruitful vine" better expresses Jacob's view of Joseph than "wild ass." Indeed, Rashi is said to read *bayn porath* as "fruitful son," that is, "endured with favor (grace)."[44]

Whether as "wild ass," "fruitful fountain" or "fruitful son," Joseph remains Jacob's most beloved son. As he showers *respect* on Judah, so he showers *love* on Joseph. For Judah's tribe, he foresees political leadership and public eminence. But for Joseph, he invokes the blessings of heaven: "The God of your father who helps you; And *Shaddai* who blesses you, With blessings of heaven above; Blessings of the deep that couches below, Blessings of the breast and womb; The blessings of your father surpass the blessings of my ancestors, To the utmost bounds of the eternal hills, May they rest upon the head of Joseph . . . the elect of his brothers" (49:25–26).

Because Jacob's testaments are in birth order, the last is for Benjamin. It is peculiar in that (1) we have learned nothing of Benjamin that supports it and (2) it runs counter to Jacob's characteristic tenderness toward Benjamin as Rachel's (and his) youngest son. Thus, "Benjamin is a ravenous wolf; In the morning he consumes the foe, and in the evening he divides the spoil" (49:27).

> Note G–57: With support from Judges 20 and 21, the tribe has been described as "very warlike."[45]

Comment G–99. On the source of Jacob's testament as viewed through Jacob's blessing on Joseph

Friedman attributes Jacob's testament to J, subject to the following *caveat*: "This song, known as the Blessing of Jacob, was probably not composed by the author of J, but was rather a source that this author used and then wove into the narrative."[46] Certain elements of the testament would seem to support J's major role in its final formulation.

First, consider the matter of Joseph's sons Manasseh and Ephraim, whom

Jacob adopts in the P passage of 48:3–6. Why does Jacob not "bless" them as his sons? To view them as "derivative" through Joseph contradicts Jacob's resolve to the contrary. Recall his words: "Ephraim and Manasseh shall be mine no less than Reuben and Simeon" (48:5–6). One answer may be that J, writing long before P, may not have known of the adoption. But even if J knew of such a tradition, given Ephraim's tribal dominance in the north, J might have preferred to bless Joseph alone.

Second, Judah's succession to the honors of Reuben's first-born status would also typify what we might call J's "political perspective." We have noted the consistently contradictory pattern of "hero identification" as between Judah and Reuben in various J and E passages.

If the entire testament of 49:1–27 was the final work of J, as adapted from another source, the presence of "*shaddai*" in Joseph's blessing must be explained (49:25). Although *shaddai* is associated with P, J could possibly have taken it from an earlier source used later and more fully by P.

On completing his testaments and blessings, Jacob instructs his sons to bury him in "the cave which is in the field of Machpelah," bought by his grandfather, Abraham—and where Abraham, Sarah, Isaac, Rebekah, and Leah already rest. Jacob was then "gathered to his people" (49:28–33).

Comment G–100. On Jacob's burial at Machpelah

Jacob might have chosen to be buried near Rachel "on the road to Ephrath," where she died giving birth to Benjamin (see 35:16–20). Instead, in this final wish, he chooses to be buried with his grandparents, parents and his first wife, the mother of six sons. With all his faults, he finally puts aside personal sentiment in deference to his destiny and descendants. This is the Torah's own testament to Jacob's role as covenantal heir to Abraham and Isaac.

Gen. 50 tells of the preparations for, and the burial of, Jacob at Machpelah. It closes with the death of Joseph. On Jacob's death, Joseph "flung himself on his father's face and wept over him and kissed him" (50:1). Jacob was embalmed over a "full period" of forty days and "the Egyptians bewailed him seventy days" (50:2–3). In giving Joseph permission to travel to Canaan to bury Jacob, Pharaoh displays his usual grace by noting the solemnity of Joseph's oath to Jacob: "Go up and bury your father, as he made you promise an oath" (50:6). In addition to his own and his father's entire households, Joseph is accompanied by a great Egyptian entourage. It includes "a very large troop" of chariots and horsemen, "all the officials of Pharaoh, the senior members of his court, and all of Egypt's dignitaries" (50:7–9). After further mourning en route, they bury Jacob at Machpelah and return to Egypt (50:10–14).

With Jacob dead, Joseph's brothers now fear his retribution for their cruelty

to him—their blood brother! They send him what they claim to be an "instruction" from Jacob: "Forgive, I urge you, the offense and guilt of your brothers who
treated you so harshly." As Joseph reads it, his brothers plead further that he forgive "the offense of the servants of the God of your father" (50:15–17).

Comment G–101. On Jacob's "instruction" to Joseph

Was Jacob's "instruction" that Joseph forgive his brothers of his or their
doing. If this were his wish, why had he not told Joseph directly? And what
had Joseph done to feed such fears? Following their reconciliation, he had
proved himself a loving brother, deeply committed to their well-being. Did
they attribute his conduct to nothing more lasting than a wish to please the
living Jacob?

To put their motives in a better light, however, we might attribute their
final quest for forgiveness to their deep-rooted sense of guilt. Indeed, it may
have been fed by Joseph's warmth and kindness. How could it be possible,
they might ask themselves, to atone sufficiently to deserve his forgiveness?
*More likely, however, the motives of the brothers in mounting this final plea
were as varied as their characters.* Some spoke from true remorse and others
from continuing fears of reprisal (as they contemplated the vengeance they
would have sought had roles been reversed).

When the brothers prostrate themselves before Joseph and offer to be his
slaves, Joseph assures them, much as he had earlier, that God's hand had guided
all these events. But his reassurance is preceded by a disavowal of his right or
capacity to be their judge. "Have no fear! Am I a substitute for God? Besides,
although you intended me harm, God intended it for good, so as to bring about
the present result—*the survival of many people.* And so, fear not. I will sustain you
and your children" (50:18–21).

Comment G–102. On the mature Joseph
as the worthiest descendant of Abraham

When Joseph first sought to assure his brothers of his forgiveness, he characterized their spiteful conduct as a manifestation of God's will. The purpose
he then attributed to God, however, was seemingly limited to the well-being
of his own family: "God sent me ahead of you to insure *your* survival on
earth" (45:7–8). Given the potential disaster of a famine throughout Egypt,
to judge God's beneficence by His protection of Joseph's family alone is to
cast Him as a tribal God with no broader concerns for humanity.

The limited "tribal" concerns that Joseph first seemed to impute to his
God were uttered amid the emotions of his family reunion. But Joseph now
imputes purposes to his God that marks him as Abraham's truest heir. It is not

only Joseph's family whom *his* God meant to preserve by bringing him to Egypt. The "good" of which Joseph now speaks involves "the survival of *many* people" (50:20). Joseph could not accept that the concern of *his* God was limited to the well-being of his own family, as descendants of Abraham and Sarah. But among them all, Joseph, in assuming that *his* God was concerned with all afflicted by famine, was the worthiest.

Thereafter, "Joseph and his father's household remained in Egypt" (50:22); Joseph would live to the age of "one hundred and ten years" (50:22, 26). This enabled him to see "children of the third generation of Ephraim"; the children of Machir, son of Manasseh, "were likewise born upon [his] knees" (50:22–23).

As death approaches, Joseph finally speaks to his brothers of their future and the future of their descendants in Egypt: "God will surely take notice of you and bring you up from this land to the land which he promised on oath to Abraham, to Isaac, and to Jacob." Joseph then made "the sons of Israel" swear that "*when God has taken notice of you, you shall carry up my bones from here*" (50:24–25). Joseph then dies. Until his God would "take notice," Joseph "was embalmed and placed in a coffin in Egypt" (50:26).

Comment G–103. On Joseph's instructions to his brothers in regard to God's "taking notice of you"

Joseph's instructions to his brothers to bring his "bones" to Canaan are directed to their descendants as well. The time would depend on God's "taking notice." Also, since Joseph was "the child of [Jacob's] old age" and the youngest but for Benjamin, many of his brothers may not yet be alive. It is unlikely that Joseph was the first to die (although in Canaan, if not in Egypt, one hundred ten years bespoke a relatively short life). As Jacob gave his final testament, he seemed to speak directly to each of his sons (Gen. 49). A lengthy period between the deaths of Jacob and Joseph is implied by the several generations of Ephraim and Manasseh whom Joseph lived to know.

But why must the brothers wait for God to "take notice"? What bars their immediate return to Canaan? Did Joseph foresee them as hostages in Egypt following his death? If so, as hostages to whom? To various Pharaohs, to their own preferences, or to their God?

> Note G–58: *Here we may recall that it was God, Himself, who had told Abram of four hundred years of slavery and oppression in Egypt (15:12–16).*

GOD AND HUMANITY IN GENESIS: AN OVERVIEW

The following *overview* of Genesis addresses four major topics: (1) the attributes and character of its God, (2) the attributes and goals of humanity, (3) relations between its God and humanity, and (4) societal good and evil in Genesis.

1. The Attributes and Character of the God of Genesis

We can only know of the God of Genesis, and of the entire Torah, from what His authors say of Him. His attributes are the endowments of His creators. His words and deeds do not serve His purposes, but rather their purposes—in a different time, place, and stage of human development. So understood, how might we describe the God of Genesis?

Consider first His possible omnipotence. Although Genesis never proclaims His omnipotence, as such, it quickly implies it. What else can we conclude from His role as Creator? Consider His precise and orderly creation of the earth and its atmosphere, of all life on earth and of all that is required to sustain life. Whether accomplished ex nihilo or by rearranging matter, the act of creation in Genesis implies a degree of power tantamount to omnipotence.

The omnipotence that He first manifested in creating the natural order is amply confirmed in His continuing manipulation of it: the great flood, the events at the Tower of Babel, the plagues that beset an earlier Pharaoh because of Sarai, the destruction of Sodom and Gommorah, the salinization of Lot's wife—each portrays His total dominion over His own natural order. Indeed, quite apart from Isaiah's imagery of a future Messianic king (Isa. 7:14), Christianity's "immaculate conception" is but a natural culmination of the role of the God of Genesis in matriarchal birthing. From the miracle of Isaac's birth after Sarah "had stopped having the periods of women," it is but a short step to a virgin birth (18:11–15).

Two other aspects of transcendence with which Genesis might seem to endow its God are omniscience and omnipresence. In Genesis, however, neither is independently established. The initial ambiguity in Genesis on the omniscience of its God (i.e., His infinite knowledge) is partially addressed in Comment G–7. Thereafter, Genesis endows its God with knowledge of certain future events—including the future of the Hebrews in Egypt, as revealed to Abraham (15:13–16) and Jacob (46:2–3).

Rather than being an aspect of omniscience, however, such prescience might reflect His power to effect His will. That is to say, the prescience of the God of Genesis may be limited to future events that He Himself will cause to occur. Consider His words to Jacob: "Fear not to go down to Egypt, for I will make you there into a great nation. I myself will go down with you to Egypt, and I myself will also bring you back" (46:3–4). More broadly, however, while Genesis does not openly assert its God's omniscience, it implies His *potential* to be so. Can omnipotence be such without a power to know whatever one wants to know?

Godly omnipresence is even more easily envisioned as a derivative from Godly omnipotence. The ability of the God of Genesis to be in any one place, as He wishes, is clear. But the matter of His simultaneous presence everywhere is less clear. Yet from the *power* to be anywhere at anytime, it is but another short step to be everywhere at anytime. In effect, God's presence in Genesis is a function of His will. Were He unable to effect His will, He would be less than omnipotent.

The qualities of mercy and compassion are widely regarded as the moral essence of the Torah's God. Genesis, however, offers little evidence of either. That He spared Adam and Eve from His threat of immediate death stemmed neither from mercy or compassion. His threat in their state of innocence was only intended to frighten them into compliance. Having allowed Eve and Adam to gain free will for humanity, He then chose, for a time (until Noah), to allow humanity to develop, while He monitored the consequences.

In sparing Cain for having killed Abel, the God of Genesis acted from remorse for his senseless dismissal of Cain's offer. Later, He again feels remorse for the wanton destruction of His flood—*the need for which His more sympathetic guidance might have averted.*

In time, repeated remorse for one's repeated injustice may nurture a preventive compassion before the fact. But as to its God, the possibility seems no greater when Genesis closes than when it opens. Most perplexing of all was the aborted sacrifice of Isaac. In their time, the *akedah*'s author(s) perceived a compelling need to demonstrate Abraham's "fear" of their God. For whatever its purpose, in our time we must decry the needless denigration of Abraham's humanity and the heartless searing of Isaac's soul. The true sacrifice of the *akedah* was of Godly compassion to Godly pride. (See Comment G–41.)

Finally, we should take note of an emergent intimation in Genesis concerning the "Being" of its God. It is the sense of a possible distinction between the Being of the Lord, as Creator, and His separate role as God. We should remain alert to how this yet faint intimation might develop beyond Genesis (see Comments G–39 pt. 2, G–43, and G–56).

2. The Attributes and Goals of Humanity

While the first great purpose of the God of Genesis was to create an earthly environment and its inhabitants, He chooses to stop short of perfection. Having limited the quality of His earthly creation to "very good," He then endows humankind with a portion of His creativity so that it might bring His creation to perfection. *To that ultimate end, the Lord, as Creator, vests humanity with all necessary qualities of mind, spirit, and body.*

However, a decision on human free will, as the vital core of humanity's creative potential, is deferred to Creation II. In it, a perplexed Lord of Creation II finally resolves His troubled uncertainty by allowing humankind to acquire this awesome potential for good or evil. The die is cast. And it is from this decision that Genesis derives the great remaining purpose for its omnipotent Lord of Creation. He is charged with guiding humanity toward the highest and best use of its free will. It is this intended relationship between human ends and Godly means that constitutes the spiritual core of Genesis. By virtue of this relationship, each party becomes subject to a basic disability. Having caused humanity to pay a heavy "price" for its free will, the Lord cannot reclaim it. In turn, having freely sought and obtained free will, neither as individuals nor collectively can humanity renounce its use or avoid responsibility for how it is used.

3. Relations between the God of Genesis and Humanity

a. Between the God of Genesis and all humanity

As with most new and untested relationships, the two parties have much to learn of each other. Until both come to understand and fulfil their respective roles and responsibilities, their differing perceptions of themselves and each other will lead to errors and miscalculations. Humanity must come to recognize the value of constructive affirmative guidance in the exercise of its free will. In turn, the God of Genesis must come to recognize that whatever its value in *preventive* guidance, power alone is a poor source of *constructive affirmative* guidance.

Of the two parties, the God of Genesis may have the most to learn. Why did He reject Cain's first offering, only to accept Abel's later offering? In the time of Noah, why did He equate mindless obedience with human "blamelessness"? At Babel, why did He destroy humanity's cooperative unity as it sought to build a city and a tower "to make a name for us, else we be scattered all over the world"? Did He fear the self-sufficiency of a unified humanity? In Sodom and Gomorrah, why did he "annihilate" an entire community for conduct unique to its men?

But just as Genesis portrays human beings who come to understand and regret their failings, it also portrays its God as capable of acknowledging errors and making amends. Indeed, His principal mitigating grace is a capacity for occasional remorse. Following His devastating flood, it is from remorse that He resolves never again to afflict earth and its inhabitants with such a calamity. In observing that "the devisings of man's mind are evil from his youth," He professes His understanding that human perfection itself is but part of humanity's quest for earthly perfection. And yet, at Babel, His fear of a unified and purposeful humanity leads Him to destroy its unity.

But in truth, it could not have been easy for the Torah's God to relate to humankind. Among the human characters of Genesis, both mythic and post-mythic, we encounter the full gamut of human qualities: from deep compassion to utter indifference, from the highest integrity to the meanest deception, and from the moral dignity of forgiveness to the moral squalor of hypocritical vengeance for personal gain. Of the rich variety of human characters in Genesis, some would respond best to the "humanity" of a concerned and compassionate God. Others, however, would scorn any influence less compelling than an omnipotent and vengeful God.

The Torah's remaining work now seems evident. It must develop the capacity of its God to guide and influence an endless variety of human beings toward the highest and best use of their free will. How it addresses and meets the task awaits our consideration of the four remaining books. Will the measure of human worth be found in the mutely obedient and "blameless" Noah and the "reconstructed" Abraham of the *akedah*? Or will it be measured by the quality of human choices made through the exercise of human free will?

b. Between the God of Genesis and His "Chosen People"

The most difficult questions posed by Genesis involve the Lord's choice of Abraham and his descendants as covenantal partners. The question is "*Whose God is He to be?*" We first encounter Him as the Creator of a single unified humankind. Yet, at Babel, to avoid the threat He perceived in human unity, the Lord "confounded the speech of the whole earth . . . and . . . scattered [the people] over the face of the whole earth." Must the Lord of all Creation thus choose among them whom He will also serve as God?

As Genesis concludes with the death of Joseph in Egypt, the covenant between Abraham and the God of Genesis remains in full force. It carries God's promise of an eternal relationship—one that, in His own words, is to be taken as unique and exclusive: "I will maintain my covenant between Me and you, and your offspring to come, as an everlasting covenant throughout the ages, *to be God to you and your offspring to come*" (17:7). For good reason, He says nothing of serving any other people as its God. Could Israel, or any people in that time, accept a God whom its foes might also claim as their own?

Does Genesis mean to tell us, therefore, that its Creator of all humankind has permanently reduced Himself to the status of a tribal God for a single people? Or does it mean to tell us that He has made a "tactical" decision to reformulate His relations with all humanity through an intensely intimate relationship with one people? Because Genesis includes intimations of both, we must await further evidence for any meaningful answer.

As for Genesis itself, however, who are these people He has chosen? And of all peoples, why them? In fact, He could not have chosen Israel for its qualities as a people. His "simpler" choice was for a "father" of a people yet to be.

Together with, or as an aspect of, his willingness to be chosen, Abraham presumably possessed qualities which the Lord thought would suit him to his role. But not even Abraham's personal qualities could assure the quality of his line. Whether his descendants would strive to emulate their father was a matter that the Torah's God was meant to influence, but not control. Indeed, as Genesis tells us, neither Isaac nor Jacob ever rose to the level of Abraham's sense of personal responsibility and passion for justice.

It is in Jacob's sons, however, that we encounter the full gamut of virtue and vice. From the heights of decency, wisdom, compassion, and tact that mark the *adult* Joseph, we descend to the depths of the hypocritical self-serving wrath of Simeon and Levi. In short, to the limited extent that Abraham's descendants were "chosen" at all, they were never meant to serve as exemplars. As portrayed in Genesis, they represent a moral and ethical microcosm of humanity, whose task is to strive toward perfecting themselves and their earthly abode.

4. Societal Good and Evil in Genesis

Perhaps as an offset to His own proclivity toward mass annihilation, the God of Genesis first urges humanity to "be fertile and increase." Subject to such exceptions as He, Himself, decrees or allows, human life, as His final and finest creation, constitutes humanity's highest value. And so it is that the first societal sin of Genesis involves the taking of a life—Cain's murder of Abel. But in remorseful recognition of His own responsibility, the Lord, to His great credit, spares and protects him.

So great are God's further frustrations in seeking to influence humankind that He resolves to destroy it by flood in order to save it. Genesis defines the endemic "evil" as "corruption before God" and "lawlessness." *But the story of Noah is less about the elements of sin than about the power of the Torah's God to punish it.* Conversely, in Sodom and Gomorrah, His wrath is provoked by a particular form of sexual conduct that He deems especially egregious.

In general, responses to good and evil in Genesis run the gamut from poetic justice to no-nonsense death. For having deceived Isaac, Jacob was subjected to Laban's deceit (and, in time, a deeply troubled conscience). Reuben's chastisement for "mounting Jacob's couch" with Bilhah must await the bitter words of Jacob's testament, as must Simeon's and Levi's contrived mayhem in Shechem. Yet, in having wasted his seed with Tamar, Onan, son of Judah, was slain by God, Himself. Before that, He had taken the life of Onan's brother, Er, because he had "displeased" Him in some unspecified manner, However, the widowed Tamar would have been "justly" slain by Judah had she been of child through other than a levirate union.

In all, while Genesis leaves the subject of societal good and evil largely unexplored, it places it high on the Torah's future agenda. Thus, to validate the covenantal promise, Abraham's descendants must strive to learn of "good and evil" in order to choose what is "just and right." And how better could they honor the intrepid Eve than by doing just that.

THE PATRIARCHS: A BRIEF RETROSPECTIVE

Among the many human characters of Genesis, the three patriarchs of Israel, Abraham, Isaac, and Jacob, enjoy a unique status in Jewish liturgy and tradition. The story of each has been followed at some length in the main text. My purpose here is to summarize the unique role of each in the Torah's saga of a people and its God.

Abraham stands as a just, wise and honest human being whose self-reliance impels him to supplement the Lord's powers as an aid in fulfilling His purposes. Unless the resulting impression of his doubts of those powers can be erased, it could undercut his role as an exemplar of total faith in God's ability to achieve His purposes. Genesis addresses the need through the *akedah*, in which Abraham's failure as Isaac's father proves necessary to qualify him as a father to his people. Putting aside the contrivance of the *akedah*, Abraham's integrity, decency, and resourcefulness mark him as a worthy model for Israel and all humankind.

Isaac is transitional, both in time and character. He has neither his father's towering probity nor his son's moral and spiritual equivocation. He will make his greatest mark on Israel as a passive agent of his father's God. That He effects Isaac's birth "beyond the time" of Sarah enables Genesis to reaffirm its God as the ultimate source of life. But what the God of Genesis gives, He may also take back. And so, by His command that Abraham sacrifice Isaac, the God of Genesis puts to test the very fear and faith that Isaac's birth had inspired in Abraham. Thus, through the searing of his soul by the apparent imminence of death at the hand of his father, a quiet and gentle Isaac came to serve Israel as an instrument of its God. Despite the horror of his aborted sacrifice, Isaac's travail, as intended, would come to serve Israel as a riveting symbol of its father's perfect faith.

We first encounter young Jacob as a flawed human being. With his mother's help, he undertakes to defraud his father and, through him, his brother. Later, as a father himself, he allows his emotions to dominate his common sense, thereby creating pain and conflict within his own family. In time, he is partially redeemed by a troubled conscience and a deepening piety for his God. In the end, as the father of twelve sons who will give birth to an entire nation, Genesis grants him total redemption. With his flaws faded in the glowing piety of old age, Jacob will serve as an exemplar of the Torah's first *mitzvah*—"Be fertile and increase."

2.

EXODUS

Exodus opens with a brief recapitulation of the "sons of Israel who came to Egypt with Jacob, each coming with his household" (Exod. 1:1). As in Genesis 46:26, "the total number of persons *that were of Jacob's issue* came to seventy, Joseph being already in Egypt" (1:5).

Joseph, his brothers, and "all that generation" had died, "but the Israelites were fertile and prolific; they multiplied and increased very greatly, so that the land was filled with them" (1:6–7). There then arose in Egypt "a new king . . . who did not know Joseph." He feared that the many Israelites might join Egypt's enemies in war. He thus "set taskmasters over them to oppress them with forced labor." It was under such conditions that they built the garrison cities of Pithon and Raamses (1:8–11). But despite the rigors of life, the Israelites "increased and spread out." The Egyptians now came to "dread" them (1:12).

Comment E–1. On Israelites "filling the land" and "spreading out"

That "the land was filled with them" (1:7) and they "spread out" (1:12) suggests the dispersion of Israelites from Goshen throughout Egypt. Their possible presence in areas of Egypt other than Goshen may bear on whether any of them were afflicted by several of the great plagues yet to come. That the "land was filled with them, JPS1 and 2 and RSV all agree." In 1:12, however, what JPS2 renders as "spread out" (*v'chayn yiphrohtz*), JPS1 and RSV render as "they spread abroad." But given the context, "abroad" must mean from "Goshen" rather than "Egypt."

As the Israelites continued to multiply, the Egyptians increased their burdens. "Ruthlessly they made life bitter for them with harsh labor at mortar and bricks and with all sorts of tasks in the fields" (1:14). Later, when harshness failed to reduce their fertility, the "king of Egypt" directed the two "Hebrew midwives," Shiphrah and Puah, to kill all sons (but not daughters) of "Hebrew women" (1:15–16). "Fearing God," however, the midwives let the boys live

(1:17). They explained to an angry king that "Hebrew women" were "vigorous"; thus, "Before the midwife can come to them, they have given birth." Because of their bravery, "God dealt well with the midwives; and the people multiplied and increased greatly" (1:20). Pharaoh then commanded "*all* his people" that "*every boy that is born* you shall throw into the Nile, but every girl shall live" (1:22).

Comment E–2. On Pharaoh's command to "*all* his people" to drown *every* newborn boy in the Nile

All three translations apply Pharaoh's command to "all his people." JPS1/2 both read *kol habayn hahyilohd* literally to include "every boy" (or "son"). This would require drowning "every" new born "boy" of any nationality. (A more dubious RSV limits the drownings to "Hebrew" sons.)

The text does not explain why Pharaoh would order the death of all new born Egyptian boys. Although Rashi reads the command literally, he restricts it to a single day on his personal surmise that Pharaoh's astrologers had told him that "Today, there was born their deliverer." But what they could not tell him was "whether (he is) of the Egyptians or of Israel."[1]

Comment E–3. On the descendants of Jacob in Exodus 1 as "Israelites" or "Hebrews"

In Exod. 1 the descendants of Jacob are primarily identified by the Hebrew phrase "*b'nai yisrael*." JPS2 renders the phrase as "Israelites" (except in 1:1, where the context requires a more literal translation, i.e., "*sons of Israel* who came to Egypt with Jacob"). Following the use of "Israel" based terms in Exod. 1:1–14, the reference to "Hebrew" midwives and women in 1:15–21 seems odd. To add to the puzzle, Friedman ascribes both 1:8–12 and 1:15–21 to E.

Were the "Hebrew" midwives and women descended from "Abram the Hebrew"? (See Gen. 14:13.) If so, was it through his "covenantal" grandson, Jacob/Israel? With regard to the midwives, Shiphrah and Puah, Plaut states, "Their names are of northwest Semitic type, suggesting they were Hebrews. 'Hebrew' is a term generally agreed to come from the name of a group called Habiru (or Apiru), people who had lost their status in the community to which they had originally belonged.[2] But if he is correct, we must assume different lineages for the "Hebrew midwives" and the "Hebrew women." Are the "Hebrew women" of Exod. 1:16 and 19 not among the Israelites of 1:8–12? Accordingly, in addition to their names, we might best consider the identity of the "Hebrew midwives" from the total context of Exod. 1:8–22.

Among the six references to the midwives, only the first is preceded by "Hebrew" (1:15). The two references to the "women," however, are both preceded by "Hebrew." Also, by the repeated use of "they" in 1:19, the midwives seem to place themselves apart from the "Hebrew women." Thus, whatever their lineage, the initial use of "Hebrew" to describe the midwives may simply describe their status as midwives to the "Hebrew women." If so, and as such, they were the "righteous gentiles" of their time.

As for the use of "Hebrew women," from 1:15–21 we might speculate that E used "Hebrew" in referring to "the people" *from Pharaoh's perspective*. But what then can explain the reference to "Israelite people" by the "king of Egypt" in 1:9.

Comment E–4. On the "Hebrew midwives" and their fear of God

Who is the "God" (*elohim*) whom the Hebrew midwives are said to fear? By capitalizing "God," the translators of JPS1, JPS2 and RSV indicate it to be the Torah's God. And rightly so, since God "dealt well with [them]." Granted that the midwives fear the Torah's God, what do they know of Him that the "women," and other Israelites, do not? And if many, or all, fear Him from a belief in His power, why had they not already sought His help so He might "take notice" of them? (Cf. Comment G–103.)

The story now turns to the birth of Moses. Of his parents the Torah simply states that "a certain man of the house of Levi went and married a Levite woman" (2:1). On his birth, "*when* she saw how beautiful [or "goodly" (JPS1/RSV)] he was," his mother hid Moses for three months to avoid the death decree. She then placed him in a wicker basket among the reeds in the Nile. "His sister" (Miriam) stood near enough to see what would become of him (2:1–4).

> *Note E–1: The phrase "when she saw how beautiful [or goodly] he was" suggests that had his mother not discerned these special qualities, she would have worried less about Moses' fate. On this Ramban states that "the meaning of goodliness is that she saw in him some unique quality which, in her opinion, foreshadowed that a miracle would happen to him and he would be saved. Therefore she applied herself and thought of ways to save him." Ramban softens her somewhat elitist view, however, with a kinder view of motherhood: "It is a known fact that all mothers love their children, and all would save them from harm with all their might."*[3]

Having come to the Nile to bathe, Pharaoh's daughter finds the infant crying. She says at once, "This must be a Hebrew child!" She then accepts the sister's offer to find "a Hebrew nurse to suckle the child." To the nurse, she says, "Take this child and nurse it for me, and I will pay your wages." And so Moses is returned to his own mother to be suckled (2:6–9). In time, when the child "*grew up*," his mother returned him to Pharaoh's daughter. Thereupon, the daughter "made him her son" and "named him Moses" (meaning "I drew him out of the water") (2:10).

Comment E–5. On Pharaoh's daughter, Moses, and his mother

Although Pharaoh's daughter immediately identifies Moses as "a Hebrew child," the text offers no clear reason for her conclusion. As noted in Comment E–2, Egyptians boys were also included in the king's death decree (of whatever duration it was). And since Egyptians, too, were circumcised, the *possible* circumcision of Moses would not be the unique mark of a "Hebrew" (except as timing or manner might vary).

Also, consider the promise by Pharaoh's daughter to a Hebrew nurse she did not know to "pay your wages." Would an Egyptian princess be expected to pay a Hebrew woman? Or did she do so from kindness or to encourage attentive care? *If payment was expected, then the Hebrews were hardly slaves. If not, the offer speaks well of Pharaoh's daughter.*

"Some time after that, when Moses had grown up, he went out to his kinsfolk and witnessed their toil." There he saw "an Egyptian" beating "a Hebrew, one of his kinsman" (2:11). Seeing no one else around, "He struck down the Egyptian and hid him in the sand" (2:12). The next day, on finding "two Hebrews fighting," he asked the "offender" why he had struck "your fellow." The offender then asked Moses, "Who made you chief and ruler over us?" He also mocks Moses by asking if he means to kill him as he did the Egyptian. On hearing of the slaying, Pharaoh "sought to kill Moses," who then flees to Midian (2:13–15).

Comment E–6. On self-identification by the "grown-up" Moses

JPS2 states that Moses returned to Pharaoh's daughter when he "grew *up*" (*yigdal*) (2:10), while JPS1 and RSV use only "grew." The difference is obviously significant. If Moses' return was delayed until he "grew up," he might have learned of his identity as an Israelite/Hebrew before entering Pharaoh's court. But if he "returned" to Pharaoh's daughter immediately on being weaned, his formative years would have been as her favored ward in Pharaoh's court.

As of the threatening events of 2:11–15, however, all three translations describe Moses as "grown up." The question, then, is: Did Moses, on seeing an Egyptian "beating a Hebrew," kill the Egyptian in order to protect a known "kinsman" from an oppressor? Or, kinsman or not, on seeing the beating, did Moses kill from anger and compassion for what appeared to be a gross injustice to a fellow human being? And what of his intrusion into the fight between two Hebrews? Did either know Moses as a Hebrew? ("Who made you chief and ruler over us?") Did he intrude on the impulse of a born peacemaker? Or was it his special concern that two fellow Hebrews were fighting? As yet, the extent to which Moses knows of his heritage remains uncertain.

At a well in Midian, Moses meets the seven daughters of Reuel, "the priest of Midian." He then drives off the shepherds who had first driven off the daughters. At home, they tell Reuel that "*an Egyptian* rescued us from the shepherds." After "breaking bread," Moses agrees to stay and Reuel gives him "his daughter Zipporah as wife." A son is born to them, whom Moses names Gershom, saying "I have been a stranger in a foreign land" (2:16–22).

Comment E–7. On the sisters' identification of Moses as an Egyptian

Had Moses identified himself to the sisters as an Egyptian? If so, why? From actual belief? Or from concern for his safety among the Midianites? Or, from his dress and speech, had the daughters assumed him to be an Egyptian? If Moses knew that they thought him to be an Egyptian, did he verify it, correct it, or remain silent?

"A long time after that, the king of Egypt died. The Israelites were groaning under the bondage and cried out; and their cry for help from bondage rose up to God." On hearing their moaning, "*God remembered His covenant with Abraham, Isaac, and Jacob.*" And now (as foretold by Joseph) "God took notice of them" (2:23–25).

> Note E–2: Exodus 1 and 2 refer to the ruler of Egypt as both "king of Egypt" and "Pharaoh." As with "Israelites" and "Hebrews," the varied usages are not explained. Yet the parties are clearly one and the same (cf. 5:4–5).

Comment E–8. On the current status of God's covenant with Abraham and his descendants

Exodus 2:23–25 speaks to the remoteness that developed over time between the Israelites and their God. It is not said that their groans and cries for help from bondage were directed specifically to Him. On hearing their groans, however, He "remembered" His covenant with Abraham and his descendants. Whether His "notice of them" resulted from their initiative or His remains uncertain.

Of particular interest is whether the Israelites had maintained the covenant of circumcision. Was it possible under the burdens of forced labor and bondage? Or did they do so fortuitously, that is, together with the Egyptians?

Exodus 3 tells of Moses' first stark encounter with Lord God. It occurs as he "[tends] the flock of his father-in-law Jethro, the priest of Midian" in the wilderness at "Horeb, the mountain of God" (3:1).

Comment E–9. On the separate traditions of Reuel and Jethro and Horeb and Sinai

The "Reuel" of Exod. 2:18 is now the "Jethro" of Exodus 3:1. Both verses identify him as Moses' father-in-law and as a "priest of Midian." These dual names,
together with this initial identification of "Horeb," rather than Sinai, as "the
mountain of God" tells of more than one source at work (as do the "melded"
appearances of *yahweh* and *elohim*). J pairs Reuel, the person, and Sinai, the
sacred mountain, with *yahweh*. E pairs Jethro and Horeb with *elohim*.

It is at Horeb then, "the mountain *of God*" (3:1), that "an angel *of the Lord*"
appears to Moses out of a blazing bush that remains untouched by the fire (3:2).
Then, from the bush, God, Himself (i.e., not the angel), calls "Moses! Moses!"
Moses replies, "Here I am (*hinaynee*)" (3:4).

Note E–3: So said E's Abraham in the akedah *(Gen. 22:1).*

God tells Moses to stay back and to remove his sandals, "for the place on
which you stand is holy ground" (3:5). God identifies Himself as "the God of
your father, the God of Abraham, the God of Isaac, and the God of Jacob."
Moses hid his face, "for he was afraid to look at God" (3:6).

Now it is "the Lord," rather than "God," who tells Moses that He has
"marked well the plight of My People in Egypt." He is "mindful of their suffer-
ings" (3:7). Therefore, He has come to "rescue them" and to bring them from
Egypt to "a good and spacious land . . . flowing with milk and honey" (3:8). He
notes that the land is now "the home of the Canaanites, the Hittites, the Amorites, the Perizzites, the Hivites, and the Jebusites" (3:8). Then, in a command
couched as an invitation, the Lord tells Moses: "Come, therefore, I will send you
to Pharaoh, and you shall free My people, the Israelites, from Egypt" (3:10).

Whether from modesty, curiosity or doubt, Moses asks God, "Who am I that
I should go to Pharaoh and free the Israelites from Egypt?" (3:11). God replies, "I
will be with you, and it shall be your sign that it was I who sent you" (3:12). In
anticipation of His future revelations at Horeb/Sinai, He adds, "When you have
freed the people from Egypt, you shall worship God at this mountain" (3:12).

Comment E–10. On the matter of the "Burning Bush"

God's flamboyant appearance to Moses in a blazing bush is a far cry from the
serenity of His first appearance to Abraham (Gen. 12:1–3). Does the Torah
mean to attribute the manner of His appearances to differences in the character of Abraham and Moses? Perhaps in part. But a more compelling reason
is found in the distinctive characters of their missions. Since Abraham's task
was to initiate a process of "quiet" growth in the absence of organized

opposition, the Lord would have felt no need to overwhelm him at once with His awesome powers. Abraham was not indifferent to whether the Lord had power to fulfil His promise, but there was time enough to learn more of this initially impressive Being.

In contrast, Moses, from the outset of his mission, will face the power of Pharaoh and the vast forces at his command. God would thus think it essential for Moses to grasp a sense of His power at once. Only with knowlege of it might he hope to prevail against Pharaoh. And so God chooses to stun Moses by His Presence in a blazing bush that would not burn. That Moses was "afraid to look at God" testifies to His success. But in resisting God's "invitation," Moses reveals his doubts notwithstanding. He knows the difficulties—including Pharaoh's own powers.

Also, Moses' reference to "the Israelites" rather than to "my people," implies his lack of any close affinity with them. True enough, God reveals Himself to Moses as "the God of your father." But what could this cryptic revelation mean to him? What did he actually know of his own father, let alone of Abraham, Isaac, and Jacob?

In answering Moses' question "Why me?" (3:11), God offers little help. He identifies no personal qualities that might especially qualify Moses for the task. Instead, His answer, "I will be with you," suggests the irrelevance of Moses' human qualities (3:12). It was as if He had answered, "Why not you? Given My Presence, anyone will do."

With the die seemingly cast, Moses goes to the heart of his problem. "When I come to the Israelites and say to them, 'The God of *your* fathers has sent me to you,' and they ask me, 'What is His name?' what shall I say to them?" (3:13).

As His "name forever" and "appellation for all eternity," God answers "Ehyeh-Asher-Ehyeh." And further, "Thus shall you speak to the Israelites: 'The Lord, the God of your fathers [Abraham, Isaac and Jacob] has sent me to you'" (3:14–15).

> Note E–4: Even now, Moses does not speak of "my people," or "my brethern" or "my kinsmen." He speaks instead of another people, "the Israelites," whose God he refers to as God of "your," rather than "our," fathers (3:13).

Comment E–11. On God's "Name" as God's Being

In rendering God's revelation of His name as "Ehyeh-Asher-Ehyeh," JSP2 simply uses the transliteration from the Hebrew. Consistent in each case with Hebrew grammar, it appears as (1) "I AM WHO I AM" (RSV), (2) "I AM THAT I AM" (JPS1), or (3) "I WILL BE WHAT I WILL BE."[4] However it is rendered, the name revealed by God speaks to His total inscrutability.

In asking for God's "name," Moses presumably hoped as well to identify Him to the people. What he is told in essence, however, is this: "You must accept me for who I am and what I am; or for who or what I choose to be. You may know of Me only as I choose to reveal Myself. Do not ask why I do what I do. My reasons are known only to Me, except as I may choose to reveal them. Know that I will be and do what I choose to be and do." While this explanation of God's "Name" expresses the spirit of Ehyeh-Asher-Ehyeh, it will of little help to Moses in explaining their God to the Israelites.

God then gives Moses his instructions (3:16–22). In brief, he is to tell the "elders of Israel" that he is sent by "the Lord, the God of your fathers, the God of Abraham, Isaac and Jacob"; and that He will take the Israelites from their "misery in Egypt" to "the land of the Canaanites [and other named tribes] . . . a land flowing with milk and honey" (3:17). Together, they will tell the "king of Egypt" that "the Lord, the God of the Hebrews has come to us. They will ask the king to "let us go a distance of three days in the wilderness to sacrifice to [Him]" (3:18). God tells Moses that the king will refuse until forced by a "greater might" to agree. To that end, God will "smite Egypt with various wonders," after which the king will let the Israelites go (3:19–20). But they will not leave in need. Instead God will "dispose the Egyptians favorably toward this people, so that when you go, you will not go away empty handed" (3:21). Thus, "each woman shall borrow from her neighbor and the lodger in *her* house objects of silver and gold, and clothing, and you shall put these on your sons and daughters, thus stripping the Egyptians" (3:22).

> Note E–5: If "neighbor" is taken literally, then the Israelites, rather than being segregated, were living amidst the Egyptians, presumably under similar conditions. However, that God should "dispose the Egyptians favorably" to the Israelites also poses the problem of human free will. On this issue, see Comments E–30, 31, and 32.

Comment E–12. On the request of Moses and the elders of Israel to the king of Egypt

God's instructions hint of the "gamesmanship" to come. The Israelites will know for sure that their destination is Canaan. However, they are to ask the king that he let them go but "a distance of three days into the wilderness to sacrifice to [their God]" (3:18). God "predicts" that the king, until faced with a greater force than his own, will refuse. He already has in mind the "various wonders," or plagues, by which He will "smite Egypt." Given God's knowledge of His own intentions and of His power to fulfil them, why are Moses and the elders not told to demand full and immediate freedom? Moreover, if the Israelites have indeed "spread out" and "filled" the land, how are they to be assembled for a three-day journey to the wilderness? (See Comment E–1.)

Moses then observes that the elders might not believe the Lord had appeared to him. In reply, the Lord turns Moses' rod, after being cast down, into a snake. When Moses grasps its tail, it again becomes a rod. As further evidence of the Lord's miracles, Moses is told to put his hand into his bosom. It then emerges "encrusted with snowy scales!" When reinserted and withdrawn, "it was again like the rest of his body." If these acts were not enough for the elders, Moses was to "take *some* water from the Nile," It would then "turn to blood on the dry ground" (4:1–9).

But Moses still feels that his own role must be a factor in the outcome—for better or worse. He thus reminds the Lord of his speech impediments: "I am slow of speech and slow of tongue" (4:10). The Lord replies that it is He Who "gives man speech" and Who "makes him dumb or deaf, seeing or blind" (4:11). He assures Moses, "I will be with you as you speak and will instruct you what to say" (4:12). Outwardly, Moses is a modest man. But inwardly he could never assume the role of a spiritless robot who can merely speak the Lord's words and act through His powers. Thus his final plea: "Make someone else your agent" (4:13).

Now the Lord "became angry with Moses." He tells him that "even now," his brother, "Aaron the Levite," who "speaks readily," is setting out to meet him. Aaron will speak the words that Moses is to "put . . . in his mouth" (4:14–15). "I will be with you and with him as you speak, and tell both of you what to do." Aaron will thus serve "as your spokesman, with you playing the role of God to him" (4:16). Moses now accepts the inevitable. He returns to "his father-in-law" and asks leave "to go back to my kinsmen in Egypt and see how they are faring." Jethro's reply is "Go in peace" (4:18).

> *Note E–6: The Lord has just identified "Aaron the Levite" as Moses' brother. From this, we can now assume that in referring to "my kinsmen," Moses means Israelites. Even though raised as an "Egyptian," Moses would likely have known of the Levites as an Israelite tribe. Is it not this sudden revelation of his identity as an Israelite that now binds Moses to their liberation and destiny?*

Comment E–13. On the final reconciliation of Moses and the Lord on leading the people from Egypt

Why does the Torah ascribe anger to the Lord over the initial reluctance of Moses to agree to the task? Is He affronted by the importance that Moses attaches to the personal qualities of anyone who, as the Lord's agent, is to lead a people from slavery to freedom? Will Moses prove another Abraham who by nature must retain a degree of personal responsibility in fulfilling his duties? Thus, the root of the problem lies in the Lord's insistence on the total sufficiency of His own powers. But now He may be at ease. Moses' newfound identification with his people enables him to dispel his doubts and misgivings.

The Lord now tells Moses, "Go back to Egypt, for all the men who sought to kill you are dead" (4:19). So Moses placed "his wife and sons" on an ass, took the Lord's rod in his hand and returned to Egypt (4:20).

Note E–7: As yet, we know of the birth of only one son, Gershom (2:22).

Comment E–14. On the Lord's assurance of Moses' safety

Why does the Lord wait until 4:19 to advise Moses that the Egyptian king and the courtiers from whom he had fled were now dead? In 4:18 Moses was already fully committed to go. Clearly, His purpose was not to persuade Moses to go, but to offer added assurance of his safety. Perhaps the Lord could sense that Moses, like Abram before Isaac's birth, remained less than certain of His powers.

The Lord then tells Moses that he is to perform before Pharaoh "all the marvels that I have put within your power." (These are presumably the same miracles by which Moses is to convince the elders of Israel that he had come from their God.) But He also tells Moses that He "will stiffen [Pharaoh's] heart so that he will not let the people go" (4:21). Moses is then to identify "Israel" to Pharaoh as the Lord's "first-born son"; since Pharaoh will not honor the Lord's request to "let My son go, that he may worship Me," the Lord will then "slay [his] first-born son" (4:21–23).

Comment E–15. On the "stiffening" of Pharaoh's heart

Now we learn why the Lord could confidently predict Pharaoh's refusal to "let the people go." He means to "stiffen" Pharaoh's heart so that not even miracles will move him to do so. In the plagues to come, several of Pharaoh's refusals will be explicitly attributed to the Lord's stiffening of his heart. This possible intrusion on Pharaoh's free will is akin to the Lord's earlier revelation to Moses of His intent to "dispose the Egyptians favorably toward this people" (3:21). In freeing Israel from Egypt, does the Torah also mean to "free" the Lord from His first commitment to humankind? Or is the human free will, first acquired through Eve, now to be limited to Israel?

In Exod. 4:24–26, as Moses and his family move toward Egypt, we abruptly confront one of the Torah's most enigmatic verses: "At a night encampment on the way, the Lord encountered him and sought to kill him. So Zipporah took a flint and cut off her son's foreskin, and touched his legs with it, saying, 'You are truly a bridegroom of blood to me!' And when 'He let him [Moses] alone' she added, 'A bridegroom of blood because of the circumcision.'"

Comment E–16. On the meaning of Exod. 4:24–26

RSV and JPS1 render the passage much the same as JPS2. Why the Lord sought to kill Moses is revealed in Zipporah's prompt circumcision of "her son's foreskin." But how did she know of the problem, and which of the "sons" of Exod. 4:20 did she circumcise? As for "sons," Ramban speculates that at the time of departure, Zipporah was pregnant with "Eliezer," who was born en route to Egypt.[5] Rashi, however, omitting all speculation, simply asserts that the newly circumcised son was Eliezer.[6] The Torah itself, however, does not identify the circumcised son.

Assuming a second son, Eliezer, there is still a troubling question of which one Zipporah circumcised. Was it Eliezer? As to his birth, of course, the Torah has yet said nothing. Nevertheless, consistent with the views of Rambam (and possibly Rashi), should we assume that the haste of his sudden journey had caused Moses to overlook his circumcisional duties to Eliezer?

Or was it Gershom he had failed to circumcise? Because the Lord would have long since known of this failure, it was surely an odd time for the Lord to slay Moses as a heretic—having finally persuaded him to accept his destiny. But whichever son the quick-witted Zipporah circumcised, she must be honored for having rescued both Moses and Israel from the consequences of his death. Absent any other "logical" explanation, we might view the episode as a frightening, but timely, reminder of the continuing vitality of Abraham's covenant of circumcision.

Now the Lord arranges for Moses and Aaron to meet "in the wilderness . . . at the mountain of God" (4:27). After no more ado than Aaron's kiss of greeting, Moses relays all of the Lord's instructions regarding the mission (4:28). On arriving in Egypt the two brothers "assembled all the elders of the Israelites (4:29). Aaron tells them all that the Lord had said to Moses and "*he* performed the signs in the sight of the people" (4:30). The people were convinced. They bowed "low in homage . . . that the Lord had taken note of the Israelites and that He had seen their plight" (4:31).

> Note E–8: *Aaron not only speaks for Moses, as directed, but he also performs the "signs" that the Lord had directed Moses to perform (4:17). Contrary to later events in which dire consequences follow lesser errors, the Lord is silent. Had the people not known of His prior commands, neither His authority nor dignity would have been demeaned. However, before performing "the signs" of 4:17, as told to Moses to perform, Aaron "repeated all the words that the Lord had spoken to Moses" (4:30).*

Moses and Aaron now go to Pharaoh to tell him that "the Lord, the God of Israel" wishes him to "let My people go that they may celebrate a festival for Me in the wilderness" (5:1). Professing to know nothing of "the Lord," Pharaoh refuses (5:2). Moses and Aaron reply, "The God of the Hebrews has manifested Himself to us. Let us go we pray, a distance of three days into the wilderness to sacrifice to the Lord our God, lest He strike *us* with pestilence or sword" (5:3). But "the king of Egypt" replied, " 'Moses and Aaron, why do you distract the people from their tasks? Get to your labors!' And *Pharoah* continued, 'The people of the land are already so numerous, and you would have them cease from their labors!' " (5:4–5).

Comment E–17. On further alternative uses of "Israelites" and "Hebrews"

Comment E–3 notes the varied use of "Israel" and "Hebrews" in Exod. 1. In Exod. 5:2, following *their* use of the term in 5:1, the king speaks of "Israel" to Moses and Aaron. Yet in next speaking to Pharaoh in 5:3, Moses and Aaron refer to "the God of the Hebrews." A consistent pattern in the use "Israel" or "Hebrews" has yet to emerge.

Comment E–18. On the threat of "the Lord, the God of Israel" to strike "us" with "pestilence and sword"

1. The threat to the Israelites as a threat to Pharaoh

Pharaoh may have wondered initially why "the Lord, the God of Israel" would strike His own people with pestilence for not being allowed to sacrifice to Him in the wilderness. What manner of God would punish His people for having been forcibly prevented from fulfilling His command?

Neither Rashi nor Ramban accept the literal implication of the passage. Both regard the use of "us" by Moses and Aaron as a euphemism for "you," so stated "out of respect for royalty." Both view the threat of "pestilence and sword" as directed against Egyptians.[7]

But Pharaoh, being well acquainted with the uses of power himself, would soon grasp the Lord's Machiavellian threat. Once struck with pestilence, Israel will be forever lost to Pharaoh. Thus begins a fateful battle of wits between two manipulators of power—the Lord and Pharaoh.

2. On Pharaoh's statement that "the people of the land are already so numerous, and you would have them cease from their labors!" (5:5)

Here Pharaoh associates rest with increased fecundity. (Cf. JPS1, 5:5: "Behold the people of the land are now many, and will ye make them rest from their burdens?") Does this imply a Pharaonic policy of relying on hard labor to stem Israel's growth? (See Exod. 1:7.)

A god in his own right, the proud Pharaoh will as yet concede nothing. Having rejected Moses and Aaron with words, he then does so with deeds. While prohibiting any reduction in their "quota of bricks," Pharaoh orders "the taskmasters and foremen" to stop providing workers with the straw needed to make them. The straw is to now be gathered by the people, but with no reduction in output (5:6–9).

When the orders were relayed to them, " the people scattered *throughout the land of Egypt* to gather stubble for straw" (5:12). As the people fell behind in their quotas, Pharaoh's taskmasters beat the Israelite foremen (5:13–14). When the foremen complain to Pharaoh of their impossible work loads, he calls them shirkers. He accuses them of seeking to go to the wilderness to sacrifice to their God only to avoid work. He again demands that they maintain their quotas while searching for straw as well (5:15–18).

The Israelite foremen blame Moses and Aaron alone for their plight. "May the Lord look upon you and punish you for making us loathsome to Pharaoh and his courtiers" (5:21). In turn, a sad but passionate Moses remonstrates with the Lord: "Why did You bring harm upon this people? Why did you send me? Ever since I came to Pharaoh to speak in your name, he has dealt worse with the people; and still you have not delivered Your people" (5:23).

The Lord then assures Moses that on being faced with His "greater might," Pharaoh shall not only "let them go," but shall "drive them from his land" (6:1).

Exodus 6:2–13 briefly summarizes what has already transpired between the Lord and Moses and between Moses and the people. It begins: "God [i.e., *elohim*] spoke to Moses and said to him "I am the Lord" [i.e., *yahweh*] (6:2). *To this He adds: "I appeared to Abraham, Isaac and Jacob as El Shaddai, but I did not make Myself known to them by My name yahweh"* (6:3). He then tells Moses of His earlier relations with the Israelites. These include: (1) His covenant with Abraham in Canaan, (2) His having heard the moaning of the Israelites now held in bondage by the Egyptians, and (3) His having "remembered" the covenant (6:4–5).

The Lord then instructs Moses to bring a threefold message to the Israelites: (1) I am the Lord. I will free you from bondage and will redeem you "through extraordinary chastisements." (2) You will be My people and I will be your God; and you shall know that I freed you from Egypt. (3) I will bring you to the land I promised to the patriarchs and "give it" to you as a possession (6:6–8).

When Moses spoke the Lord's words to the Israelites, "they would not listen to Moses, their spirits crushed by cruel bondage" (6:9). The Lord then sends Moses to "Pharaoh king of Egypt" to tell him "to let the Israelites depart from his land" (6:10–11). Moses again appeals to the Lord. Since the Israelites would not listen to him, "how then should Pharaoh heed me, a man of impeded speech!" (6:12).

The passage concludes with the appearance of Aaron. "So the Lord spoke to both Moses and Aaron in regard to the Israelites and Pharaoh king of Egypt, instructing them to deliver the Israelites from the land of Egypt" (6:13).

Comment E–19. On 6:2–13 and the Torah's structure and Godly nomenclature

On reading 6:2–13, an attentive reader will experience a sense of *déjà vu*. The passage is a précis of events following the first encounter of the Lord and Moses. Despite the omission of details and a varied ordering of events, *the following core remains*: God appears to Moses. He presses him to serve as His human agent in freeing the Israelites from bondage and in bringing them to the promised land. Because their spirits are crushed from their burdens, the people will not heed Moses, who then pleads his speech impediment as reason not to approach Pharaoh. The Lord then tells "both Moses and Aaron" of their joint mission.

Friedman is surely correct in ascribing 6:2–12 to P and the transitional appearance of Aaron in 6:13 to R. With its penchant for narrational distillation, P has unknowingly reduced the previous three J and E chapters to twelve brief verses—in part by the exclusion of Aaron until R's 6:13.

Note as well in 6:2–3 that while *el shaddai* initially tells Moses of His previous appearances, *as such*, to the three patriarchs, He ignores the similar appearances of *yahweh*. Thus, it was *yahweh* whom Abraham first encountered and accepted as the Lord (Gen. 12:1 and 7–8). (Similarly as to Isaac and Jacob, see Gen. 26:24–25; 28:13, 16.) Nor does *el shaddai* speak of the recent revelation of the Lord's "name" as *ehyeh-asher-ehyeh*, Who then identifies Himself as the God (*elohim*) of Abraham, Isaac, and Jacob. (Exod. 3:13–15). In all, we find reference to J's yahweh, E's elohim and P's *el shaddai*.

Also of interest in 6:3 is the unique rendering by JPS1 and 2 of the hebrew *yahweh*. Rather than the customary "Lord," here they use the Hebrew letters of *yahweh* (*yod, heh, vau, heh*) without its vowels. As a tradition derived from the Third Commandment, these four letters alone are pronounced *adonai* in order to avoid pronouncing or writing the name of *yahweh*. Thus, the inscrutability of *ehyeh-asher-ehyeh* is matched by the ineffability of *yahweh*. From its Christian perspective, RSV reads this same *yahweh* as "the Lord."

Exodus 6:14–25 sets out the genealogy of the clans of the three oldest sons of Jacob, these being Reuben, Simeon, and Levi. The lines of Reuben and Simeon are shown only through their sons, while that of Levi extends two and three generations beyond. But the centerpiece of the passage is the parentage of Moses and Aaron within the line of Levi.

The cosanguinity of their parents is of particular interest (6:20). Amram, their father, was a son of Kohath, one of the three sons of Levi. Amram married Jochebed, "his father's sister," and thus his aunt. Thus, Moses and Aaron were both sons and great nephews of their mother. Could many other Levites claim equally impeccable credentials?

> Note E–9: In closing the genealogy with Nadab, Abihu, Eleazar, and Ithamar, sons of Aaron by Elisheba, P ignores the sons of Moses by Zipporah, the Midianite.

Exodus 6:26–30 offers a second selective summary of earlier episodes. It begins: "It is the same Aaron and Moses to whom the Lord said, 'Bring forth the Israelites from the land of Egypt, troop by troop' " (6:26). It continues: "The same Moses and Aaron" spoke to Pharaoh to free the Israelites (6:27). They did this because "in the land of Egypt" the Lord had said to Moses, "I am the Lord; speak to Pharaoh king of Egypt all that I tell you" (6:28–29). Moses then appealed to the Lord saying, "See, I am impeded of speech; how then should Pharaoh heed me?" (6:30).

Comment E–20. On certain editorial aspects of 6:26–30

Friedman attributes 6:26–30 to R. This seems logical. The passage adds no substance to the narrative. In brevity and selectivity it outdoes even P's concise summary in 6:2–13. R's inclusion of 6:26–30 probably results from the prior "parenthetical" insertion of 6:14–25, in which P traces the Levite lineage of Moses and Aaron. R's purpose in 6:26–30 may be to establish a firmer base from which to move on with the "main" narrative. Thus, 6:26 repeats the essence of R's transitional verse of 6:13 while 6:30 repeats 6:12, which concludes P's initial passage. P's ongoing narrative then jumps to 7:1 from 6:12, having been interrupted by R's 6:13 and 26–30 and P's own genealogy in 6:14–25.

The Lord now instructs Moses on how to deal with Pharaoh. "I place you in the role of God to Pharaoh, with your brother Aaron as your prophet" (7:1). As such, Moses "shall repeat" to Aaron all that God commands him, and Aaron "shall speak to Pharaoh to let the Israelites depart from the land" (7:2). Then, having first told Moses that He would "stiffen" Pharaoh's heart "so that he will not let the people go" (4:21), the Lord now explains why He will "harden" it (7:3). It is so "that I may multiply my signs and marvels in the land of Egypt" (7:3). Through "extraordinary chastisements . . . the Egyptians shall know that I am the Lord" (7:4–5). At the time of their demand on Pharaoh, "Moses was eighty years old and Aaron eighty-three" (7:7).

Comment E–21. On the Lord's "hardening" of Pharaoh's heart

In explaining why He will prolong the general agony by "stiffening," or "hardening," Pharaoh's heart, the Lord's saving grace lies more in His candor than His reason. He will harden Pharaoh's heart so "that I may multiply My signs and marvels in the land of Egypt . . . with extraordinary chastisements. And the Egyptians shall know that I am the Lord" (7:3–5). (While JPS1 and RSV use "harden" in 4:21 and 7:3, JPS2 uses "will stiffen" for *ahchahzayk* [4:21] and "will harden" for "*ahksheh*" [7:3].)

The Lord's first effort to impress Pharoah and his court develops into a skirmish between Aaron and the Egyptian "wise men . . . sorcerers . . . and magicians." As directed by the Lord, Aaron casts down his rod before Pharaoh and his servants. It becomes a serpent! But the Egyptian wise men, sorcerers, and magicians quickly do the same with their rods. The deadlock ends when Aaron's rod swallows theirs. But "Pharaoh's heart *stiffened* and he did not heed them" (7:8–13).

Comment E–22. On Pharaoh's "stiffened" heart in 7:13

In JPS1/RSV Pharaoh's heart does not "stiffen" from within, as in JPS2. Instead, it "*was* hardened." Here lies a question. Does the author mean to ascribe Pharaoh's reaction to the Lord, or to Pharaoh himself. Consider the Lord's words in 7:14. "Pharaoh *is* stubborn; he refuses to let the people go." *Is Pharaoh's stubborness a product of his own nature or the Lord's bidding?*

The moment for Plague One now arrives. In this case the standoff between Aaron and the magicians will not be so decisively resolved. Before calling down the plague, Moses and Aaron remind Pharaoh why they are yet again before him. They are sent by the "the Lord, the God of the Hebrews" whom Pharaoh spurned when He first asked him to "let My people go so that they may worship me in the wilderness" (7:16, 20). As instructed, Moses warns Pharaoh of what is now to happen because of his refusal. Then, when Aaron struck the rod on the Nile, "all the water in the Nile was turned into blood and the fish in the Nile died. The Nile stank so that *the Egyptians* could not drink water from the Nile; and there was blood *throughout the land of Egypt*" (7:19–21).

As before, the "Egyptian magicians" excelled in replication. "When [they] did the same thing with their spells, Pharaoh's heart stiffened and he did not heed them—as the Lord had spoken" (7:23). Thereafter, "*all the Egyptians* had to dig around the Nile for drinking water, because they could not drink the water of the Nile" (7:24).

Comment E–23. On some puzzlements of Plague One

1. The invocation of Plague One: who does what?

Speaking to Moses alone in 7:14–18, the Lord tells him of *his* role as wielder of the rod. He directs Moses "to strike the water in the Nile with the rod." The Nile will then be "turned into blood" (with the consequences noted above). In 7:14–18 Aaron is to have no role. But in 7:19 we find a second version in which, by the Lord's instruction to Moses, only Aaron is to take the rod. But rather than striking the Nile with it, Aaron is to hold up his arm, not only over the Nile, but "the waters of Egypt—its rivers its canals, its ponds and all its bodies of water—that they may turn to blood . . . throughout the land of Egypt, even in vessels of wood and stone" (7:19). Then in 7:20, "*Moses and Aaron* did just as the Lord commanded: *he* lifted up the rod and struck the water of the Nile." Thus, an unidentified "he" (as between Moses and Aaron) now wields the rod in the manner the Lord had first instructed Moses to do.

An accomodation of the differing sets of consequences then appears in 7:21. In accord with the first version, the fish in the Nile died, the Nile stank, and "Egyptians" could not drink water from the Nile (see 7:18). In accord with the second version, "there was blood throughout the land of Egypt, even in vessels of stone and vessels of wood" (7:19). It is helpful in understanding these events to consider Friedman's scalpular division of 7:14–21 between J (7:14–18, 7:20b–21a) and P (7:10–13, 7:19:20a). Does it all portend an emerging "brotherly rivalry" between Moses and Aaron, as fostered by J and P?

2. The replication by Egyptian magicians

Why would the Torah demean the power of its God by allowing the Egyptian magicians the same power to turn water to blood? Did the Lord know of their powers? Could He have nullified them had He wished? Or did He facilitate their success as the means of "stiffening" Pharaoh's heart? However, if Moses/Aaron had actually removed all water from Egypt (7:19), what was left for Pharaoh's magicians to turn into blood? But even if some water remained (7:24), their success would only compound the disaster.

3. The impact of Plague One on the Israelites

Did the God of the Israelites mean to afflict His own people with His plagues? If His power could not save them from the disasters that were to befall their oppressors, would not a prolonged process of gaining freedom simply add to their own suffering? *Other than by the most subtle of implications, the Torah leaves no more water for the Israelites "throughout the land of Egypt" than*

for the Egyptians. These might be found in three references to the unavail-
ability of water to "the Egyptians (7:18, 21, 24). Nothing, however, is said of
the Israelites. Presumably, they shared the same sources.

Seven days later, the Lord instructs only Moses in regard to Plague Two. Again, Pharaoh is to be asked to "Let my people go that they *may worship me*" (7:26). Should he again refuse, "the whole country" is to be plagued with frogs (7:27). They will swarm forth from the Nile and enter Pharaoh's palace, and "the houses of your courtiers and *your* people, and *your* ovens and *your* kneading bowls" (7:28). When Aaron evoked the plague by holding out his arm with the rod over the waters of Egypt, "frogs came up and covered the land of Egypt" (8:1–2). And again, the magicians "with their spells" did the same (8:3). But now a less confident Pharaoh summons Moses and Aaron to plead with the Lord "to *remove* the frogs from me and *my* people" (see Comment E–24 pt. 2). If He does, said Pharaoh, "I will let the people go *to sacrifice to the Lord*" (8:4). Moses replies, "That you may know that there is no one like the Lord our God; the frogs *shall retreat* from you . . . and *your* people; they shall remain only *in* the Nile" (8:7).

Moses then cries out to the Lord "in the matter of the frogs which He had inflicted upon Pharaoh" (8:8). The Lord did "as Moses asked" (8:9). The frogs "died" everywhere. "And they piled them up in heaps, till the land stank" (8:10). "But when Pharaoh saw there was relief, *he became stubborn* and would not heed them" (8:11).

Comment E–24. On some puzzlements in Plague Two

1. For what purpose must Pharaoh "let the people go"?

We have already noted the "gamesmanship" involved in the reason given Pharaoh by the Lord, through Moses, for asking that he let His people go. The Lord's true intent is that His people be freed to go to Canaan. But Pharaoh is to be told of a more "benign" purpose. As instructed, Moses and Aaron first tell Pharaoh of the Lord's wish that he "let us go a distance of three days into the wilderness to sacrifice to the Lord our God" (3:18, 5:3). (See Comment E–12.) Just before Plague One, however, the Lord omits any time limit. Moses is to remind Pharaoh that he should let the people go "that they may worship their God *in the wilderness*" (7:16 and 26).

By omitting any limit of time or distance in 7:16 and by broadening "sac-rifice" to "worship" is the Lord gradually preparing Pharaoh for the real pur-pose for which he must let the people go? From His statement of purpose preceding Plague Two, the plague of frogs, it would seem so. There, His instructions to Moses remove the spatial limits by omitting "the wilderness." The people are to be let go "that they may worship Me" (7:26). This demand, unlimited by time and distance, should have alerted Pharaoh to the Lord's possible intent of a permanent departure. (By rendering *v'ya'ahvduhny* as "that they may serve me" rather than "worship me," JSP1/RSV add to this impression. "Service" would seem to imply a broader and more continuing relationship than a single worship episode.

In the end, such subtleties were lost on Pharaoh. His focus remained on the "three-day" departure "to sacrifice," as first proposed by Moses: that is, if the Lord will "remove the frogs," he in turn will "let the people go *to sacrifice to the Lord*"—and only for "three days" (5:3).

2. On Moses' mixed signals and Pharaoh's modest expectations in regard to the nonremoval of the frogs

In the wake of the plague of frogs Pharaoh asks Moses and Aaron to "Plead with the Lord to *remove* the frogs . . . and I will let the people go to sacrifice to the Lord." Given the vast inundation of frogs, their actual "removal" must have been a condition of Pharaoh's agreement. Knowing this, Moses assures Pharaoh "the frogs *shall retreat* . . . they shall remain only *in* the Nile [i.e., where they belong]" (8:7). Although the Torah then states that "the Lord did as Moses asked" (8:9), in fact He only kills the frogs. Thus, they "piled . . . up in heaps, till the land stank" (8:10). Yet, the surcease from live frogs satisfied Pharaoh. "When he saw there was relief, he became stubborn" (8:11).

3. The impact of Plague Two on the Israelites

The Torah may be a bit more direct in Plague Two than in Plague One as to sparing the Israelites from its blight (see Comment E–23 pt. 3). While the frogs of Plague Two would inundate the "whole country," the Lord directs Moses to tell Pharaoh that they will invade the house, ovens, and kneading bowls of *"your* people" (7:27–29).

Plague Three was evoked by Aaron's striking his rod "on the dust of the earth." As he did so, "*vermin* came upon man and beast; all the dust of the earth turned to *lice* throughout the land of Egypt" (8:12–13). The magicians again drew on their "spells" to "produce *lice*" (8:14). This time (perhaps by now to Pharaoh's relief) their efforts failed. But "the *vermin* remained." The magicians attribute both the plague and their failure to repeat it to "the finger of God!" Plague Three ends as follows: "*But Pharaoh's heart stiffened* and he would not heed them" (8:15).

Comment E–25. On the brief narrative of Plague Three

The stylistic differences between Plague Three and the preceding two plagues is striking. Its bare-bones brevity immediately suggests a different source. This may one reason why Friedman attributes the entire Plague to P. Another might be the inability of the Egyptian magicians to replicate the "signs and marvels" of Israel's God.

As for the source of Pharaoh's "stiffened" heart in 8:15, JPS1 again states that "Pharaoh's heart *was* hardened," while RSV states that "*he* [i.e., Pharaoh] hardened his heart." Of the three translations, JPS2 reveals the least concerning the source of its "stiffening," as between the Lord or Pharaoh. RSV is the most precise in treating it as internal to Pharaoh. In turn, by use of the passive "was hardened," JPS1 most clearly alludes to the Lord as the source. Do such differences reflect a basic indifference by one or more translators to the source of the "hardening"? Or does each translation reflect internal consistency? And what of the Torah itself? Is it consistent throughout? Or do the sources vary? And if so, consistently, as among themselves?

Also, JPS1 and RSV render the Hebrew *kinnim* as "gnats" rather than as "lice" or "vermin." But by whatever such torment, the plague afflicted "man and beast . . . throughout the land of Egypt." *Thus, in Plague Three, there is nothing to suggest that the Israelites were spared* (8:12–15).

Plague Four again reflects J's broader narrational style. It is the plague of "swarms of insects" (or "flies" in JPS1/RSV). It repeats the potential ambiguity of Plague Two regarding Pharaoh's understanding of the purpose for which he is to let the people go. Once more, the Lord states the purpose "that they may *worship* Me" (8:16). Again, as in Plague Two, JSP1/RSV render *v'ya'avduhny* as "that they may *serve* Me" (see Comment E–24 pt. 1). Now, however, by excepting Goshen from the plague, the Torah for the first time states an explicit intent to spare Israelites. Thus, Moses is to tell Pharaoh: "If you do not let My people go I will loose swarms of insects against you, your courtiers and your people and your houses. . . . But on that day I will set apart the region of Goshen, where my people dwell, so that no swarms of insects shall be there. . . . And I will make a distinction between your people and My people" (8:19). But the actual exclusion of Goshen *from Plague Four* is put in question when "swarms of insects" ruin the land "throughout the country of Egypt" (8:20).

As the full force of Plague Four afflicts all of Egypt, Pharaoh again seeks to bargain with Moses and Aaron. He thus proposes: "Go and sacrifice to your God *within the land*" (8:21). By "within the land," Pharaoh seemingly means a distance short of "the wilderness." But Moses again stresses the need to "go a distance of three days into the wilderness and sacrifice [to God]." Otherwise, he claims, Egyptians offended by their mode of sacrifice would stone the Israelites. To his reluctant agreement ("I will let you go to sacrifice . . . in the wilderness") Pharaoh adds, "but do not go very far" (8:23–24). In agreeing to plead with the Lord "that the swarms of insects depart," Moses warns, "Let not Pharaoh again act deceitfully" (8:24–25).

The Lord accepts Pharaoh's plea to "undo" the plague. "He removed the swarms of insects; . . . [and unlike the frogs] not one remained" (8:27). But Pharaoh "became stubborn this time also, and would not let the people go" (8:28).

Comment E–26. On the exemption of Goshen from Plague Four

The Lord is said to have exempted the region of Goshen from Plague Four in order to "make a distinction between My people and your people" (8:18–19). This is the first *explicit* statement of such a purpose. (However, the Lord's distinction in 8:18–19 between "My people" and "your people" could imply that His sole reference to "your people" in Plague Two implies the same distinction. (See Comment E–24 pt. 3 and 7:28–29. As for Plague One's impact on the Israelites, see Comment E–23 pt. 3.)

The use of "the region of Goshen" as the basis for distinguishing between the impact of the plague on Israelites and Egyptians presents a problem. Separation by geography rather than ethnicity would likely preclude the mutual exclusivity that the Torah intends (i.e., that the plague impacts on *all* Egyptians and *no* Israelites).

Consider the problem in relation to "the region of Goshen." To establish mutual exclusivity, it must be assumed that all Israelites, and only Israelites, live in Goshen. If the first is not true, then Israelites living in Egypt outside of Goshen will suffer the plagues. If the second is not true, then Egyptians living in Goshen will be spared the plague. The Israelites, of course, are said to have built the "garrison cities" of Pithon and Raamses in Goshen (Exod. 1:12). While their work might imply that many, perhaps most, Israelites lived in Goshen, what of those who had "filled the land" and "spread out" (1:7, 12)? Was there not a single Israelite in Egypt outside of Goshen? And what of the garrison cities of Goshen? Were they not occupied by Pharaoh's troops? And would their presence not involve the presence of other Egyptians? Does the Torah intend that the many Egyptians living in Goshen were to be spared from the plagues? Note also that in 11:2, the Israelites and Egyptians are portrayed as "neighbors."

The question, then, concerns the distinction the Torah means to make as to the differential impact of the plagues. Does it mean to separate the people by geography, ethnicity, or by whatever seems most appropriate to a given plague? Or, as is more likely, did R accept each formulation as he found it, with little concern for consistency? In any case, this all ignores the *uncontradicted* report of swarms of insects "throughout the country of Egypt" (8:20).

As a prelude to Plague Five (9:1–7), the Lord gives Moses a message to Pharaoh: "Thus says the Lord, the God of the Hebrews; Let My people go to worship Me." If Pharaoh does not do so, then his "livestock in the fields" will be stricken with "a very severe pestilence." This will include every type of live-stock—"*the horses, the asses, the camels, the cattle, and the sheep.*" In this case, however, the Lord will distinguish "between the livestock of Israel and the live-stock of the Egyptians, so that nothing shall die of all that belongs to the Israelites." On the next day "all the livestock of the Egyptians died." Of the "livestock of the Israelites not a beast died." But "Pharaoh remained stubborn, and he would not let the people go."

Comment E–27. On "cattle" and "livestock" again

1. On mikneh *as "cattle" or "livestock"*

As in Gen. 46 and 47, JPS2 again renders *mikneh* as "livestock" while JPS1/RSV use cattle (see Comment G–90). Here, in the context of Exod. 9:1–7, the need to read *mikneh* as "livestock" seems indisputable. Note that every type of "farm animal" is to be afflicted. These include "*the horses, the asses, the camels, the cattle, and the sheep*" (9:3). Thus, in identifying the slain animals in 9:6 as "cattle" rather than "livestock," JPS1/RSV would spare only the "cattle" of the Israelites, while slaying all their other livestock (9:6). Is this their intent?

2. *The status of Israelites as owners of livestock*

Also of interest in Plague Five is the portrayal of the Israelites as owners, or possessors, of livestock. Did the "forced laborers" who built the garrison cities of Pithom and Raamses maintain their own livestock (1:11)? If so, were they protected by the applicable property laws of Egypt? Or did they hold their flocks and herds at Pharaoh's sufferance—as possibly related to their capacity for work?

In preparing for Plague Six (9:8–12) the Lord speaks once more to Moses *and* Aaron. This plague will be a "of an inflammation breaking out in boils on man and *beast* throughout the land of Egypt" (9:9). The Lord instructs them both to take "handfuls of soot from the kiln." But only Moses is to throw his into the sky "in the sight of Pharaoh." The resulting "fine dust all over the land of Egypt" will cause an inflammation of boils "on man and *beast*" (9:10). In due course, the magicians, like "all other Egyptians," were afflicted by boils. Thus, they "were unable to confront Moses." But now "*the Lord stiffened the heart of Pharaoh,* and he would not heed [Moses and Aaron], just as the Lord had told Moses" (9:12).

Comment E–28. On the plagues of the P source

1. On the "discontinuity" of Plague Six

The appearance of "beasts" in the plague of boils, *following the slaying of all Egyptian livestock in Plague Five*, might, but need not, constitute evidence of a discontinuity between Plagues Five and Six (see Comment E–27 pt. 1). The class of domesticated animals in 9:6 (covering the several animals named in 9:3) are all from the Hebrew *mikneh*. Thus, the "beast" (from *b'haymah*) of 9:10 might cover only non-domesticated animals. More likely, P would have used "man and beast" to distinguish between the two great classes of animal life.

2. On the source of Pharaoh's "stiffened" heart

This is the first Plague as to which JPS2, JPS1, and RSV all state, "*And the Lord stiffened [or hardened] the heart of the Pharaoh.*" In 9:12, P's statement of the source of the stiffening (i.e., *vahy'chahzayk yahweh et-layv paroh*) is more decisive than P's use of *vahyehchehzak layv-paroh* in 8:15. From it, our three translators derived three different translations (see Comment E–25 pts. 1, 2).

3. On the region of Goshen and the exclusion of Israelites from the plagues of the P source

Regarding the possible impact of the plague of boils on the Israelites, the text states only that the magicians "as well as all other Egyptians" were stricken (9:12). This might be construed to exclude all Israelites (cf. Comments E–23 pt. 3 and E–24 pt. 3 in regard to the same issue in previous plagues). Especially puzzling, however, is the fact that Moses took the soot from "the kiln" (seemingly the only kiln) and threw it into the sky "in the sight of Pharaoh." The kiln would have been where bricks were made; and the bricks would have been made in a region heavily populated with Israelite laborers. From all other accounts, that region was Goshen. Yet the kiln was in Pharaoh's sight. This suggests that P placed Pharaoh in Goshen, not far from such centers of Israelite labor as the garrison cities of Pithom and Raamses. *This is consistent with P's overall failure to exclude the region of Goshen from "its" plagues.*

If P means to spare the Israelites from its plagues, why so indirectly? Or did P assume that the Lord's exception of Israelites from the Plagues was too obvious to require comment? P's narrative on the plague of vermin (Plague Three, 8:12–15) offers no clue as to its impact on Israelites (see Comments E–25 and 26).

Plague Seven takes the form of "a very heavy hail such as has not been in Egypt from the day it was founded" (9:18–26). The Lord again speaks only to Moses; and once more He requests that Pharaoh "Let My people go to worship Me" (9:13). He also directs Moses to tell Pharaoh why He has chosen to send plagues. It is so that the Egyptians may know "that there is none like Me in all the world" (9:14). The Lord notes that had He so wished, He could have "effaced" Pharaoh and his people "from the earth" (9:15). That He did not do so was "to show you My power . . . that My fame may resound throughout the world" (9:16).

By warning Pharaoh and his courtiers to bring all their possessions under shelter, the Lord enables those "who feared [His] word" to protect "their slaves and livestock" from the hail (9:20). When Moses holds out his rod to the sky, the Lord sends a "very heavy" hail, with "fire flashing" in its midst. Here the exclusion of Israelites is again made explicit. "Throughout the land of Egypt the hail struck down all that were in the open, both man and beast" (9:25). All the grasses of the field were struck down and the trees were shattered. "Only in the region of Goshen, where the Israelites were, there was no hail" (9:26).

Now Pharaoh confesses his guilt and swears penance: "I stand guilty this time. The Lord is in the right, and I and my people are in the wrong" (9:27). He promises that if the Lord will end His thunder and hail, "I will let you go; you need stay no longer" (9:28). As Moses spreads out his arms to the Lord to signal Pharaoh's promise, the thunder and hail cease. At this point, "he [Pharaoh] reverted to his guilty ways, as did his courtiers. So Pharoah's heart stiffened and he would not let the Israelites go, just as the Lord had foretold to Moses" (9:34–35 per JPS2).

Comment E–29. On prior ambiguities in Plague Seven

1. On the exemption of Goshen from certain plagues

For the first time an explicit statement that a plague struck "throughout the land of Egypt" is limited by an equally explicit exclusion of "Goshen, where the Israelites were" (cf. Comment E–26). But again, what of the Egyptians who lived in Goshen? Were they also spared?

2. On Pharaoh's "stiffened" heart

The "stiffening" of Pharaoh's heart by the Lord, Himself, was explicitly stated for the first time in Plague Six. In previous plagues, the source of Pharaoh's "stiffened" heart, as internal or external, is implied mainly by use of the active or passive voice, that is, Pharaoh's heart "stiffened" or "was stiffened" (cf. Comments E–21, 22, 25, and 28 pt. 2).

In Plague Seven, however, the earlier ambiguities return. Consider this rendering of 9:34 by JPS1/RSV: "[Pharaoh] sinned yet more (JPS1) [or "again" (RSV)], and hardened his heart." What could be more descriptive of the operation of human free will? That Pharaoh "sinned" was the result of own choice. As a mere conduit for implementing the Lord's will, He could not have "sinned." However, in the very next verse (9:35), JPS1/RSV again use the passive form in stating that "the heart of Pharaoh, himself, *was* hardened." Here, however, "was hardened" could indicate "tense" rather than "causation"; that is, having been hardened by Pharaoh in 9:34, his heart remained so in 9:35. Although 9:34 and 9:35 read as a continuum, Friedman ascribes the latter to R.

But now consider the 9:34–35 in JPS2: "He [Pharaoh] reverted to his guilty ways, as did his courtiers. So Pharoah's heart stiffened and he would not let the Israelites go, just as the Lord had foretold to Moses." The reference to "guilty ways" in 9:34, absent any attribution of sin, could describe wrongful conduct per se, as such, regardless of guilt. Nor is this ambiguity in JPS2's rendering of 9:34 entirely resolved by its rendition of 9:35, in which "Pharoah's heart stiffened." As noted, however, the use of the active form is *generally* more suggestive of internal than external causation. As for the Hebrew itself, the relevant phrases are *vahyohseph lahchat vahyachbayd liboh* (9:34) and *vahyehchehzak layv paroh* (9:35). (For some final thoughts on the vagaries of Pharaoh's heart, see Comments E–30 and E–32.)

The introductory passage to Plague Eight, of locusts (10:1–20), again speaks decisively of the Lord's role in the "stiffening," or "hardening," of Pharaoh's heart. It begins with His further explanation to Moses of why He has not yet effected the Israelites' departure from bondage: "*I have hardened [Pharaoh's] heart and the hearts of his courtiers, in order that I may display My signs among them*, and that you may recount in the hearing of your sons and of your sons' sons how I made a mockery of the Egyptians and how I displayed My signs among them— in order that you may know that I am the Lord" (10:1–2).

Comment E–30. On the Lord's claim to have "hardened" Pharaoh's heart: a tentative *deductive* view

From a reading of "Creation I and II," this inquiry has proceeded on three related premises: (1) that J's Lord God of Creation II allowed humanity to acquire free will; (2) that given the price He required for humanity's free will, the Lord is forclosed from unilaterally reclaiming it; and (3) that accordingly, *His remaining role is to guide humanity in applying its free will* toward the perfection of earthly existence (see Comments G–1, 7, 8, and 9).

The question posed by the Lord's "stiffening" of Pharaoh's heart primarily involves the second premise; that is, in "stiffening," or "hardening," Pharaoh's heart, must the Lord displace Pharaoh's free will by His own will? Just to state the issue is to posit a need to intrude on Pharaoh's will. Yet, Exod. 9:34 is equally decisive in declaring Pharaoh's "sin," thus attributing the "stiffening," or "hardening," to his own free will (see Comment E–29 pt. 2).

As we know Him, however, the Lord would not necessarily have needed to displace Pharaoh's free will in order to stiffen or harden his heart. Since He knew of Pharaoh's overriding arrogance, His task was to create a set of external circumstances that would evoke Pharaoh's arrogance rather than his common sense. Thus, by combining His knowledge of Pharaoh with His total control of external events, the Lord could assure Moses He would "stiffen [Pharaoh's] heart so that he will not let the people go" (4:21).

Moses and Aaron return to Pharaoh with the Lord's demand that he " 'let My people go that they may worship Me' " (10:3). If not, a vividly described plague of locusts will come to devastate any "surviving remnant" from the plague of hail. They will "fill your palaces and the houses of all your courtiers and of all the Egyptians" (10:4–6).

The courtiers advise Pharaoh to "let the men go to worship the Lord their God!" To that they add, "Are you not yet aware that Egypt is lost?" (10:7). Pharaoh accepts their advice. He first tells Moses and Aaron, " 'Go, worship the Lord your God!' " But then a question presents itself: " 'Who are the ones to go?' " (10:8). Moses replies, " 'Young and old . . . sons and daughters . . . flocks and herds; for we must observe the Lord's festival' " (10:9). Knowing that only men worshipped, an irate Pharaoh tells them, " 'Clearly, you are bent on mischief. No! You menfolk go and worship the Lord, since that is what you want' " (10:10–11).

As instructed by the Lord, Moses brings on the plague of locusts by holding out his rod over Egypt. Blown in on a powerful east wind, hordes of locusts invade the entire land (10:13–14). Soon, "nothing green was left, of tree or grass of the field, *in all the land of Egypt*" (10:15).

A desperate Pharaoh now professes his guilt and pleads for relief. His demeanor clearly conveys an intent to meet the Lord's demand (10:16–17). Accordingly, the Lord sends "a very strong west wind" so that "not a single locust remained in all the territory of Egypt" (10:19). "But the Lord stiffened Pharaoh's heart, and he would not let the Israelites go" (10:20).

> Note E–10: As with 9:35, Friedman attributes 10:20 to R. See Comment E–29 pt. 2.

As for Plague Nine (10:21–29), the Lord directs Moses to bring forth a darkness so thick that it can be "touched" (10:21–22). For three days people "could not see another," nor could anyone "get up from where he was." "All the Israelites," however, "enjoyed light in their dwellings" (10:23). A desperate Pharaoh now tells Moses, "Go, worship the Lord . . . even your children may go with you." Only the "flocks and herds" need be left behind (10:24).

But as Pharaoh is moved to soften his position, Moses is moved to harden his own. He now tells Pharaoh, "You yourself must provide us with sacrifices and burnt offerings for . . . God" (10:25). As for Israelite livestock, "not a hoof shall remain behind." Why? Because the Israelites "will not know with what we are to worship the Lord until we arrive there" (10:26).

Once again "the Lord stiffened Pharaoh's heart and he would not consent to let them go" (10:27).

Note E–11: As he does 9:35 and 10:20, Friedman attributes 10:27 to R.

Pharaoh then banishes Moses from his presence and warns him that should they again meet face to face, "you shall die" (10:28). Confident in the Lord's control of future events, Moses replies, "You have spoken rightly. I shall not see your face again!" (10:29).

The Lord now tells Moses of the final plague to come, after which Pharaoh will not only let the Israelites go, but "will drive you out of here one and all" (11:1). But first, each Israelite man and woman is to "borrow" from his and her "neighbor" objects (or jewels) of silver and gold. To this purpose, "the Lord disposed the Egyptians favorably toward the people" (11:3). "Moreover," the Torah adds, "Moses himself was much esteemed in the land of Egypt, among Pharaoh's courtiers and among the people" (11:3).

Comment E–31. On the "favorable disposition" of the Egyptians toward the people and their "esteem" for Moses

In a prior passage tentatively attributed by Friedman to J, the Lord told Moses, "I will dispose the Egyptians favorably toward this people" (3:21). Now, in a passage Friedman attributes to J without reservation, "the Lord disposed the Egyptians favorably toward the people" (11:3). Here the matter of J's authorship is especially critical. It was J's Lord of Creation II who offered humanity the choice of free will. And it was J's Abraham whose own free will compelled him to challenge the will of the Lord (Gen. 18:17–33). What, then, is J's purpose here? Does J now posit an independent power in the Lord to control the feelings of Egyptians toward the Israelites? Or does J mean to attribute their favorable disposition to the same processes through which the Lord may have been able to "stiffen" Pharaoh's heart, that is, through a set of external circumstances calculated to evoke an anticipated response drawn from a "subject's" natural propensities? (See Comment E–30.)

While Rashi does not comment on Exod. 11:3, Ramban looks to "internal" rather than "external" processes for an explanation.

3. AND THE ETERNAL GAVE THE PEOPLE FAVOR IN THE SIGHT OF THE EGYPTIANS. The purport thereof is that the Egyptians did not hate them because of the plagues. Instead they conceived affection for them, and the

Israelites found favor in their eyes, the Egyptians acknowledging, "we are the wicked ones. There is violence in our hands, and you merit that G–d be gracious to you."[8]

Is Ramban in this case too idealistic? Could guilt feelings alone inspire the Egyptians to comply with the Israelites' requests for "silver and gold, and clothing"? Would such generosity not require Godly manipulation?

In "naturalistic" terms, any expectation that the Egyptians would become favorably disposed to the Israelites seems unlikely. *But our question is how J's Lord might achieve this result without impairing human free will.*

Rather than as a source of Egyptian hatred, J would look to the powers of its Lord as a source of admiration and awe. Did His powers not mock those of any gods known to the Egyptians? Moreover, like the Israelites, most Egyptians were also victims of the harsh regime of a Pharaoh who ruled as a god. Would that a God such as Israel's might emerge to ease *their* hardships! But would such a God ever serve a people unworthy of Him? If not, how might they too become worthy of Him? Should they not begin by showing favor to His people—whom He clearly deems worthy? Thus, *in the spirit of J*, the Egyptians came to look "favorably" on the Israelites as a natural response to the powers of Israel's God (cf. Comments E–30 and 32).

And so Moses also "became much esteemed in the land of Egypt" (11:3). Just as the power of Israel's God led the Egyptians to look with favor on His people, so they esteemed Moses even more as His known prophet. (Cf. Potiphar in regard to Joseph [Gen. 39:2–5].)

In 11:4–7, Moses tells Pharaoh of the Lord's final plague. At midnight God will go among the Egyptians "and every first-born in . . . Egypt shall die, from the first-born of Pharaoh . . . to the first-born of the slave girl who is behind the millstones . . . and all the first-born of the cattle" (11:4–5). Despite the "loud cry" arising in Egypt "not a dog shall snarl at any of the Israelites." You shall thus know "that the Lord makes a distinction between Israel and Egypt" (11:6–7). The courtiers will then come and bow low to "me" (i.e., Moses) saying, "Depart, *you and all the people who follow you.* After that I will depart" (11:8a).

Thus, despite the mutual resolve of Moses and Pharaoh not to meet again (10:28–29), they have. And so it was that Moses "left Pharaoh's presence in hot anger" (11:8b).

The Lord once more tells Moses, "Pharaoh will not heed you, in order that my marvels may be multiplied in the land of Egypt" (11:9). Although "Moses and Aaron had performed all these marvels . . . *the Lord had stiffened the heart of Pharaoh* so that he would not let the Israelites go from his land" (11:10).

Comment E-32. On the Lord's "stiffening," or "hardening," of Pharaoh's heart: a final "*inductive*" view

As drawn from the "inductively" derived premise of Creation II regarding human free will, Comment E-30 offers a "deductive" explanation of God's "stiffening" of Pharaoh's heart. But since my entire inquiry is primarily inductive, we must address the issue without benefit of a premise.

Before and during the plagues, there are thirteen distinct references to some manner of some external influence imposed by the Lord on Pharaoh. In seeking to determine the intent of Exodus from its text I have considered these passages in relation to the following variables: (1) the Hebrew text; (2) the translations of JPS2, JPS1, and RSV; and (3) the likely authorship of the relevant passages. The passages so considered, together with Friedman's views on authorship (as among J, P and R) are as follows: 4:21b (R) (which by error appears as 4:2b), 7:3 (P), 7:13 (P), 7:22b (P), 8:15 (P), 9:12 (P), 9:34 (J), 9:35 (R), 10:1 (J), 10:20 (R), 10:27 (R), and 11:10 (R).

In three of the twelve passages, the Lord Himself claims responsibility for "stiffening" (or "hardening") Pharaoh's heart. These are 4:21b (R), 7:3 (P), and 10:1 (J).

In four other passages, 7:13 (P), 7:22b (P), 8:15 (P), and 9:35 (R), no particular source of the "stiffening" or "hardening" is identified. In each case Pharaoh's heart either "stiffened" (JPS2) or "was hardened" (JPS1/RSV).

In a third group of four, a narrator attributes the "stiffenings," or "hardenings," of Pharaoh's heart to the Lord. These are 9:12 (P), 10:20 (R), 10:27 (R), and 11:10 (R).

The remaining passage of Exod. 9:34 is most explicit in ascribing Pharaoh's "stiffened" heart to his own free will. Here, the relevant Hebrew text (*vahyosef lachat vahyachbayd libo*) reads much the same in all three translations. JPS1 states that "he [Pharaoh] sinned *yet more*, and hardened his heart." So, too, RSV: "He sinned *yet again*, and hardened his heart." More figuratively, JPS2 states that "he reverted to his guilty ways."

Overall, in all three translations, Exod. 4:21b (R), 7:3 (P), 9:12 (P), 10:1 (J), 10:20 (R), 10:27 (R), and 11:10 (R) project the clearest sense of the Lord's tinkering with Pharaoh's free will.

Nevertheless, there is a possible tension in other P/R passages regarding Pharaoh's free will that arises more from translational differences than from the original text. This occurs in connection with the four passages in which no particular source of the "stiffening," or "hardening," is identified: 7:13 (P), 7:22b (P), 8:15 (P), and 9:35 (R). The tension, if any, arises from the differing translations of *vahyechezak layv paroh* as "Pharaoh's heart stiffened" (JPS2) or "[it] was hardened" (JPS1 and RSV). Whatever the translator's intent, the active form is generally more suggestive of internal causation and the passive, of external causation.

The critical tension, however, is between J and P/R. It arises primarily from J's explicit attribution of "sin" to Pharaoh (9:34). To sin, in the tradition of J, is to abuse one's own free will by choosing to do evil. Absent the exercise of one's free will, there may be wrongful conduct, but not sin. But what of the possible tension within the J source itself, as suggested in 10:1, in which J's Lord tells Moses, "Go to Pharaoh. For I have hardened his heart"?

The J of 10:1 does not mean to disavow the J of 9:34. In light of 9:34, 10:1 may fully comport with the conclusions of Comment E–31. It, too, alludes to the Lord's having contrived "a set of external circumstances" calculated to evoke a response that expresses a "subject's" natural propensities (see also, Comment E–30).

From the many "stiffenings" and "hardenings" of Pharaoh's heart, what can be said of the Lord's intent to assume control over Pharaoh's free will? In truth, the textual ambiguities of the plagues neither affirm nor negate the great premise of Creation II (that is, given the enduring cost imposed by the Lord on humanity as the price of its free will, He is barred from reclaiming it, both from the whole of humanity or from any human being). Whether, or how, the tensions between J and P/R are ever resolved must remain a matter of central interest in any humanist inquiry into to the Torah (see Comments G–8 and 35).

> Note E–12: The Lord's slaying of the "first-born in the land of Egypt" will span Egyptian society from the first-born of Pharaoh to that of the "slave girl [or maid-servant] . . . behind the millstones" (11:5). Thus, the Lord will not distinguish between the guilty and innocent, only "between Israel and Egypt" (11:7).
>
> Although he speaks of the "affection" of the Egyptians for the Israelites, Ramban says nothing to justify punishing the lowly "slave girl."[9] Conversely, after ignoring" the Egyptians' "favorable disposition" to the Israelites (11:3), Rashi would justify the death of the "maid-servant's" firstborn by her guilt: "And why were the sons of the maid-servant smitten? Because they also used to enslave [the Israelites] and rejoiced at their affliction."[10]
>
> From the perspective of Comment E–31, however, it is clear that the Lord knew that the "favorable disposition" of the Egyptians toward the Israelites could never survive the deaths of their firstborn. His timing, therefore, was born of vindictiveness rather than honor. Only after the Israelites had obtained the silver, gold, and clothing of the Egyptians did He proceed with his slaughter of the innocent firstborn.

Exodus 12 is an admixture of passages dealing with the origins of the "Feast of Unleavened Bread" (or Pesach, or Passover) and the implementation of the final plague.

Friedman attributes Exod. 12:1–20 to P. This finds support in its opening verse and the ritualistic details governing the preparation and consumption of the passover lamb. Following the final intense confrontation between Moses and Pharaoh, the passage begins with the Lord speaking to Moses and Aaron "in the land of Egypt. The time is during the month of "the beginning of months," or, as also stated, "the first of the months of the year for you" (12:2).

> Note E–13: Moses later places the day "in the month of Abib" (later to become Nisan) (13:4).

Preparations were to begin on the tenth of the month with the acquisition by each household of a lamb of specified quality and character (12:3–5). It was to be kept until slaughtered at twilight on the fourteenth day of the month (12:6). A connection is then made between the lamb and Plague Ten. The people must put "some [lamb] blood . . . on the two doorposts and the lintel of the houses" in which the lambs are to be eaten (12:7).

Exod. 12:8–11 prescribes the manner of cooking and eating the "roasted" lamb. As "a passover offering to the Lord," it must be eaten "hurriedly," with "loins girded . . . sandals on your feet" and "staff in . . . hand." Later that night the Lord will go through Egypt and strike down "every first-born in the land of Egypt, both man and beast." He will also "mete out punishments to all the gods of Egypt" (12:12). To this explanation of purpose, the Lord adds a thinly veiled threat. Israelites, as such, will not be spared. Instead it is only "when I see the blood," that "I will pass over you" (12:13).

Comment E–33. On the status of Israelites as slaves

The Lord assumes the immediate availability of lambs for sacrifices and meals. Given the Israelites' possession of "flocks and herds," it seems a reasonable expectation (see Comment E–27 pt. 2). Separate "household" dwellings with "doorposts" and "lintels" also suggest living standards that exceeded sheer poverty or abject slavery.

Comment E–34. On the possible implications of the Lord's punishments against "all the gods of Egypt"

Among the Lord's most remarkable words to Moses and Aaron were these: "I will mete out punishments to all the gods of Egypt, I the Lord" (12:12). And as the Lord openly acknowledges the existence of "the gods of Egypt," may the Israelites not do so as well? However, with His concluding identification as "I the Lord" (12:13), He asserts His supremacy over the other gods and His unique power to punish them. Yet, to punish or execute judgments on "the gods of Egypt" is not necessarily to extinguish them.

Rashi offers an alternative to this more literal view of the passage. He suggests that the punishments will not fall *directly* on "gods," as such, but on their idols. That is, "the (idol of) wood will rot, and that of metal will melt and be poured into the earth."[11] In regarding "idols" as material representations, Rashi also accepts the existence of the gods of Egypt. But he then exposes them to the ultimate form of extinction—that is, through rejection by humans. This would occur through the disfigurement or destruction of the idols and images to which the people look as a sign of their reality. Accordingly, the inability of their gods to protect the essential symbols of their existence would cause the Egyptians to deny them their only abodes, that is, in the minds and spirits of their Egyptian followers.

In this, perhaps, Rashi would distinguish the Torah's God from all other gods. Among all godly beings, only He who bars the worship of idols and images can exist independent of human belief.

The passover (or "this day") is then declared "a festival to the Lord throughout the ages; . . . an institution for all time" (12:14). For seven days "unleavened bread" shall be eaten and "leaven" shall be removed from all houses. Whoever eats leavened bread in the seven days of the festival "shall be cut off from Israel" (12:15).

Comment E–35. On being cut off from Israel

Plaut suggests that this recurring penalty of the Torah "may have been exile, or ostracism, or execution, but more probably . . . premature death."[12] (See Comment G–25.)

Exodus 12:16–20 prescribes further details for future annual celebrations of the seven-day "Feast of Unleavened Bread." It is to extend from the evening of the fourteenth day of Abib (now Nisan) to the evening of the twenty-first day. The ban on the keeping or eating of "leaven" is repeated. Any "stranger or a citizen of the country" who does so "shall be cut off from the assembly of Israel."

Comment E–36. On cutting off "strangers" from Israel

The rigidity of the command to banish leaven from the presence of all Israelites is reflected in its application to the "stranger" (12:19). The general rigidity of 12:1–20 supports Friedman's ascription of it to P. Its tone differs from the less didactic reprise of 12:21–27 which follows.

In 12:21–27 the Lord does not speak to and through "Moses and Aaron" as in 12:1–20. However, the sequence is not without its mysteries. In 12:21–23 the instructions to the Israelites are from Moses alone. They relate only to their conduct in respect to Plague Ten. As for the sacrificial lamb, the prior details of 12:1–20 are omitted. The Israelites are simply told, "Go, pick out lambs for your families, and slaughter the passover offering" (12:21). Here, however, a "bunch of hyssop" is to be used to apply the lamb's blood to the doorposts and lintel. As in the first version of 12:1–20, on seeing the blood the Lord "will pass over the door." But now His means of sparing the house of the plague will be to "not let the Destroyer enter and smite your home" (12:23; cf. 12:13). (This deemphasis of ritual supports Friedman's ascription of 12:21–23 to J rather than P.)

The final passage before Plague Ten injects another element of discontinuity into the narrative (12:24–27). It begins: "You shall observe *this* as an institution for all time, for you and your descendants" (12:24). It also speaks of a "rite" to be explained to children as "the passover sacrifice to the Lord" to mark His passing over the houses of the Israelites in Egypt (12:25–27). The preceding passage (12:21–23) calls for the application of "blood" to the doorposts and lintel of each home in Egypt. Were the Israelites thus meant to continue this as well as a rite "for all time"? In any case, the people "bowed low in homage" (12:27). In 12:28, as P restores Aaron to Moses' side, the people "[did] just as the Lord had commanded Moses and Aaron."

Comment E–37. On explaining the "rite" to children

Should a thoughtful parent not ponder the wisdom of telling an impressionable child why the Torah so cherishes the death of first-born Egyptians? To tell of the Lord's purpose to free the Israelites from physical and spiritual bondage is to extol His justice and compassion. But for a sensitive child, would the frightening inhumanity of His means not obscure the worth of His ends? Here, the primacy that Genesis accords to His power over His justice and compassion is extended into Exodus.

This final plague then came and "struck down *all* the first-born in the land of Egypt, from the first-born of Pharaoh . . . to the first-born of the captive who was in the dungeon, and all the first-born of the cattle" (12:29).

Comment E–38. On the impact of Plague Ten

In addition to the triumph of Godly power over Godly compassion in Plague Ten, two lesser issues regarding its impact are suggested by 12:29. The first involves the Pharaoh, who was not slain. We might presume that under the prevailing system of hereditary succession, Pharaoh would have been firstborn. But there could also have been a firstborn sister or a deceased firstborn brother. Rashi contends, however, that Pharaoh was indeed firstborn in his generation. That Pharaoh "alone remained of the firstborn," he predicates on Exod. 9:16.[13]

There Moses speaks to Pharaoh just before Plague Seven: "Nevertheless, I have saved you for this purpose: in order to show you my power." In context, however, the Lord merely observes that He has *so far* avoided striking "you [i.e., Pharaoh] *and your people* with pestilence" from which "you would have been effaced from the earth" (9:15). But He says nothing of Pharaoh's status as a firstborn child.

There also remains the question of whether the firstborn of the Israelites' "cattle" were spared along with the first-born Israelites (11:4–5). As to cattle, of course, the "Destroyer" lacked the identifying lambs' blood. However, any "Destroyer" able to identify unmarked firstborn Egyptian cattle could also identify firstborn Israelite cattle—and people. This confirms that the lambs' blood on doorposts was not meant to identify Israelite families as such. It was to withdraw protection from those who failed to follow the Lord's instructions (see 12:13).

As the full impact of Plague Ten becomes known to Pharaoh, he importunes Moses and Aaron to have their people leave at once. They are to take their flocks and herds and "begone!" Pharaoh's final request to Moses that "you bring a blessing on me also!" constitutes, at long last, his recognition of the Lord's powers (12:31–32).

The Egyptian people echo Pharaoh's demand for a quick Israelite departure. In the wake of the final plague, they now associate the Israelites with death (12:33). To prepare for their quick departure, the Israelites take up their unleavened dough. They had already done "Moses' bidding" by "borrowing" the "objects of silver and gold, and clothing" of their *then* "favorably disposed" neighbors, thus having "stripped" them (12:35–36; see Comment E–31).

The long journey to Canaan begins as follows: "The Israelites journeyed from Raamses to Succoth, *about six hundred thousand men on foot, aside from children*" (12:37). With them was a "mixed multitude" and "very much livestock, both flocks and herds." In their haste "they baked unleavened cakes of the dough . . . taken out of Egypt." They had prepared no other provisions (12:38–39).

Comment E–39. On the Israelites' departure from Egypt

Note the initial single quick departure from Raamses to Succoth. If all the Israelites of Egypt left hurriedly from this single staging area, then surely they were all in Goshen. Plaut suggests that the Hebrew *alef* (of which the Hebrew text states there to be six hundred) may refer to a "contingent" of "nine or ten" rather than to a "thousand."[14] Whatever the case, the total includes only men. Thus, adult women were not only not counted, but, unlike "children," they were not even mentioned as not having been counted. (On counting women in Genesis see Comments G–89A and 89B.)

As stated in Exod. 12:40, "the length of time that the Israelites lived in Egypt was four hundred and thirty years; at the end of the four hundred and thirtieth year, to the very day, all the ranks of the Lord departed . . . Egypt."

Comment E–40. On the length of the stay in Egypt

The statement in Exod. 12:40 of a four hundred thirty year stay in Egypt differs from the Lord's revelation to Abram in Gen. 15:13: "Your offspring shall be strangers in a land not theirs, and they shall be enslaved and oppressed four hundred years." Many efforts have been made to reconcile the difference.[15] Because two different periods are described, the thirty-year difference is not *necessarily* contradictory. While Exod. 12:40 covers the total "length of time that the Israelites lived in Egypt," Gen. 15:13 is limited to the period of oppression. However, based on the generations of Joseph's descendant's *during his lifetime* (Gen. 50:22–23) following Jacob's death after seventeen years in Egypt (Gen. 47:28), the period of oppression could not have begun only thirty years after the arrival of Jacob and his family from Canaan.

Exod. 12:43–49 prescribes additional rules of the "passover offering," as revealed by the Lord to Moses and Aaron: (1) no "foreigner" (or "alien") shall eat of it; (2) a circumcised purchased "slave" may eat of it; (3) a "resident hireling" (or "hired servant") shall not eat of it; (4) it must be eaten "in one house"; (5) "the whole assembly of Israel" (or "all the congregation of Israel") shall offer it; (6) if a stranger who "dwells" with you would "offer the passover" to the Lord, he may do so if all males with him are first circumcised, after which "he shall then be as a citizen of the country"; (7) no uncircumcised person may eat of it; and (8) the law shall be the same "for the citizen and for the stranger who dwells among you."

Comment E–41. On the rules of the passover offering

Given the relationships between Israelites and non-Israelites that it covers, this passage may be less relevant to the Israelites' departure from Egypt than to their "settled" existence in Canaan. The general thrust of the rules suggests two main purposes: (1) to preserve the "passover offering" as an event unique to Israelites, and (2) to favor the conversion into Israel of non-Israelites who are so inclined. The key to conversion is circumcision. But once converted, the "alien" (or "foreigner" or "stranger") is the same to the Lord as the native-born Israelite.

Despite the in futuro aura of the passover rules, "all the Israelites did so, as the Lord had commanded Moses and Aaron, so they did" (12:50). They did so on the "very day" that "the Lord freed the Israelites from the land of Egypt, troop by troop" (12:51).

But before their departure on the stated day, the Lord "spoke further" to Moses.

Note E–14: Friedman regards E as the likely source of 13:1–16.

"Consecrate to Me every first-born; man and beast, the first issue of every womb among the Israelites is Mine" (13:2). Before repeating this command to the people, however, Moses turns to some unfinished business. Thus, he tells them (13:3–16), (1) "Remember this day, on which you went free from Egypt, . . . *how the Lord freed you . . . with a mighty hand; no leavened bread shall be eaten*" (13:3). (2) "So, when the Lord [brings] you into the land . . . which He swore to your fathers to give you, a land flowing with milk and honey, you shall observe in this month the following practice: Seven days you shall eat unleavened bread, and on the seventh day there shall be a festival of the Lord. Throughout the seven days . . . no leavened bread . . . and no leaven shall be found in all your territory" (13:5–7). (3) *You shall explain to your son, " 'It is because of what the Lord did for me when I went free from Egypt'* " (13:8) Moses then goes on to prescribe the ritual use of phylacteries: (4) "And *this* shall serve you as a sign on your hand and as a reminder on your forehead—*in order that the teaching of the Lord may be in your mouth—that with a mighty hand the lord freed you from Egypt*" (13:9).

Moses now returns to the Lord's command of 13:2 on the consecration of "every first-born; man and beast" (13:11–15). (5) When in the land sworn by the Lord to you and your fathers, "you shall set apart for the Lord every first issue of the womb; every male firstling that your cattle drop shall be the Lord's" (13:12). However, the firstborn of an ass must be redeemed with sheep. If not, the asses' neck must be broken, so that no benefit can come to the owner from not having substituted a sheep. As for "every first-born male among your children," he must be redeemed (i.e., by payment in lieu of service) (13:13). When "your son" asks what this all means, you shall answer, "*It was with a mighty hand that the Lord brought us out from Egypt. . . . When Pharaoh stubbornly refused to let us go, the Lord slew every first-born in the land of Egypt . . . both man and beast. Therefore I sacrifice to the Lord every first male issue of the womb, but redeem every first-born among my sons*" (13:15).

Comment E–42. On the theme of Exodus 13:3–15

The aim of every command recited by Moses is to glorify the Lord whose "mighty hand" freed the Israelites from Egypt. The passover itself, the laying of phylacteries, and the consecration of every firstborn son and beast to the Lord all derive from this defining event. In addition, the earlier "sacred convocation" on the first and seventh days of passover becomes seven days of eating unleavened bread with a "festival of the Lord" on the seventh (cf. 12:16, 13:6). But this is only a variance among sources. The basic theme of gratitude to the Lord as the source of physical and spiritual freedom is common to all sources.

Of all firstborn animals, only the ass is spared from sacrifice. Plaut suggests that this may be due to its being "ritually unclean."[16] (Indeed the ass is not included among the sacrificial animals. See Leviticus 1–7.) While Plaut's view suffices, Rashi's is more idealized. He has a special solicitude for asses "because they aided Israel in their departure, for there was not even one Israelite who had not taken many asses from Egypt laden with the gold of the Egyptians."[17] But should a firstborn ass not be redeemed with a lamb, Rashi's solicitude would be for naught. (Recall its consequential broken neck in 13:13.)

Exod. 13:17–22 describes the Israelites' initial route as they begin their trek toward Canaan. The shortest route was east and north along the Mediterranean coast. "God," however, "did not lead them by way of the land of the Philistines." His concern was that "the people may have a change of heart when they see war, and return to Egypt." So He led them round-about "by way of the wilderness at the Sea of Reeds" (13:17–18).

Comment E–43. On the possible desire of the Israelites to return to Egypt when confronted by the Philistines

As of the exodus, Philistines may in fact have occupied various coastal areas of Egypt and Canaan. (As to their presence in the Eastern Mediterranean see Comment G–49.) But Exod. 13:17–18 suggests other related problems.

God fears that the Israelites may wish to return to Egypt at the first sign of danger from the Philistines. Are His fears well-founded? Would they accept Egypt as a "lesser evil"? *Apart from their freedom to worship*, would they have preferred the quality of their life in Egypt to the dangers posed by the Philistines? If so, why was their God not able or willing to deal with the Philistines as He had dealt, and will soon again deal, with Pharaoh?

In any case, as the Israelites went "*armed* out of the land of Egypt," true to his ancestors' oath (in Gen. 50:24–25), Moses took Joseph's bones with him (13:18–19).

Comment E–44. On the departure of "armed" Israelites with the bones of Joseph

How, and to what extent, were the Israelites "armed"? They had left in great haste. Before going, they had acquired "objects of silver and gold" from "favorably disposed" Egyptians. But when and how had they acquired and hidden a cache of arms? Even though armed, would they rather return to

Egypt than face the Philistines? (RSV describes them as "equipped for battle.")

In addressing this enigma, Rashi relies on faith alone. Absent any plausible "earthly" explanation, he attributes their being "armed" to God. Thus, "He [God] caused them to go up armed." Rashi then continues: "And *this verse [13:18] was written* only to make intelligible what follows so that you should not wonder regarding the war of Amalek and regarding the war of Sihon and Og and Midian whence did they have weapons of war."[18] However contrived his own may be, Rashi at least recognizes a need for *some* explanation.

Also, that the Israelites could recall after four hundred years their ancestors' oath regarding the bones of Joseph evokes a sense of the deep-rooted traditions of a unified people. But how was this possible under conditions of "slavery" and isolation from their God? And how could Moses know of it but for an "unrevealed" revelation from the Lord?

"Armed" as they were, "they set out from Succoth and encamped at Etham, at the edge of the wilderness." And the Lord "went before them in a pillar of cloud by day . . . and a pillar of fire by night" (13:21–22). He then instructs Moses to double back and encamp "before Pi-hahiroth, between Migdol and the sea, before Baal-zephon, you shall encamp facing it by the sea" (14:1–2). The Lord means to persuade Pharaoh that the Israelites are lost and entangled in the wilderness. Once again He tells Moses "*I will stiffen Pharaoh's heart* and he will pursue them." Why? So "that I may assert My authority against Pharaoh and all his host; and the Egyptians shall know that I am the Lord" (14:3–4).

Comment E–45. On the varied routes
of the Israelites in 13:17–18 and 14:1–2

Because the various locations are either difficult or impossible to identify today, the precise route described in the Torah is not known. "The Lord's" reference to an Israelite encampment facing the sea (14:1–2) could possibly run counter to "God's" prior decision to avoid the coastal territory occupied by the Philistines (13:17–18). However, even the location of the "sea" is uncertain. The seemingly different, but not clearly incompatible, route descriptions of 13:17–18 and 14:1–2 are likely from different sources. (Friedman suggests E and P, respectively.)

Exod. 14:4–8 offers two versions of how Pharaoh came to give chase to the Israelites. In 14:5–7, when "told that the people had fled, Pharaoh and his courtiers had a change of heart." They asked, "What is this we have done, releasing Israel from their service?" Then Pharaoh "took six hundred of his picked chariots, and the rest of the chariots of Egypt, with officers in all of them" (14:7). This version assigns no role to the Lord in Pharaoh's decision to pursue the

Israelites. Instead, he and his courtiers are quick to enter into the chase on their own. Conversely, Exod. 14:8 states that the Lord, *as He promised in 14:4,* "stiffened the heart of Pharaoh, king of Egypt, and he gave chase to the Israelites."

> *Note E–15: Exod. 14:8 continues the story line of 14:4, in which the Lord first states an intent to stiffen Pharaoh's heart and then does so. Pharaoh's self-induced "change of heart" in 14:5 is from a different source. Friedman ascribes 14:1–4 and 8 to P and 14:5–7 to J. This division continues to reflect the tension between J and P as to the "stiffening" of Pharaoh's heart (see Comment E–32).*
>
> *Pharaoh's heart aside, following Plague Five, from whence came Pharaoh's horses? Were they "recreated" just for Pharaoh's ill-fated chase? (Cf. 9:3, 6 to 14:7, 9; see also Comment E–27 pt. 1.)*

As Pharaoh and his troops draw near, the "greatly frightened Israelites cried out to the Lord" (14:10). They also berate Moses with a reminder of advice they had given to him in Egypt. "Is this not the very thing we told you in Egypt, saying, 'Let us be, and we will serve the Egyptians, for it is better for us to serve the Egyptians than to die in the wilderness'?" (14:12). But a steadfast Moses reassures them. "Have no fear! Stand by, and witness the deliverance which the Lord will work for you today" (14:13).

> *Note E–16: The peoples' "advice" has no direct antecedent. Through a noteworthy convolution, however, Rashi derives it mainly from their complaints of Exod. 5:21 and 16:3.[19]*

In His frustration the Lord ignores Moses' exemplary leadership and rebukes him for the peoples' fears and complaints. "Why do *you* cry out to Me? Tell the Israelites to go forward" (14:15). The Lord then explains how Moses is to "lift" up [his] rod" and thus "split" the sea so that the Israelites can proceed on dry ground (14:16). Then (for one last time) the Lord "will stiffen the hearts of the Egyptians so that they go in after them" (14:17). In this way the Lord "will assert [His] authority" to let the Egyptians know "that [He is] the Lord" (14:18).

At this point "the angel *of God,* who had been going ahead of the Israelite army, now moved and followed behind them; and the pillar of cloud shifted from in front of them and took up a place behind them" (14:19). The cloud cast a spell that kept apart "the army of the Egyptians and the army of Israel" (14:20).

Comment E–46. On the impact of the varying sources in 14:10–20

In 14:13–14 Moses reassures the people of the Lord's protective presence. But in 14:15 the Lord chastises him for their complaints. Why? Again the two passages reflect the distinctive approaches of J and P to Moses (14:13–14, J;

14:15, P). J is quick to recognize and portray the fidelity and leadership of Moses, while P hesitates to set him too far above Aaron in the Lord's esteem.

Exod. 14:21–30 tells of the demise of the Egyptian pursuers. It fulfils the Lord's intent "to assert [His] authority" against Pharaoh and his army (14:16–18). Thus, as Moses holds out his arm over the sea, the Lord causes a strong east wind to part the waters. The muddy sea bottom turns into dry ground with the parted waters forming a protective wall on either side. When the Israelites enter "the sea" on dry ground, the Egyptians follow in pursuit, including "all of Pharaoh's horse, chariots, and horsemen." At "the morning watch," as the Lord looked down from His pillar of fire and cloud, the Egyptians are thrown into panic. When He then locks the wheels of their chariots, they know they are defeated. "Let us flee from the Israelites, for the Lord is fighting for them against Egypt" (14:25).

As directed by the Lord, Moses again lifts his arm over the sea (14:26). The sea then returns to its normal state and the Egyptians are drowned. Of "Pharaoh's entire army that had followed after them into the sea; not one of them remained." Safe between protective walls of water, "the Israelites [had] marched through the sea on dry ground" (14:28–29). And so "when Israel saw the wondrous power which the Lord had wielded against the Egyptians, the people feared [Him]; they had faith in [Him] and in His servant Moses" (14:31).

Through an exultant "Song of Moses," the Israelites then memorialize their new feelings of awe and of faith in the Lord, as their God (15:1–19). The words and cadence of the poetry exude their overwhelmed sense of His overwhelming power. It includes five distinct themes:

1. *How the Lord, God thwarted the Egyptians* (15:1, 4, 5, 8, 9, 10, 12, 19): "Horse and driver He has hurled into the sea."

2. *The fearsome power of the Lord, God* (15:6, 7): "Your right hand, O Lord, glorious in power, . . . shatters the foe. You break your opponents; . . . Your fury consumes them like straw."

3. *The Israelites' acceptance of the Lord, as their God.* (15:2, 3, 11, 13, 18): "He is become my salvation. . . . I will enshrine . . . and exalt Him. Who is like You, majestic in holiness. In Your love You lead the people You redeemed. The Lord will reign for ever and ever."

4. *Confidence in the Lord God's future protection* (15:14, 15, 16): "Agony grips the dwellers in Philistia. Now are the clans of Edom dismayed; the tribes of Moab trembling. . . . All the dwellers in Canaan are aghast."

5. *An affirming vision of the Jerusalem Temple on Mount Moriah* (15:17): "You will bring [your people] and plant them in Your own mountain, the place You made to dwell in . . . the sanctuary . . . which Your hands established."

Following the song, "Miriam, the prophetess, Aaron's sister, led the women "in dance with timbrels" while chanting the first verse of the song: "Horse and driver He has hurled into the sea" (15:20–21).

Comment E–47. On the Song of Moses as visionary and historical

From a reader's perspective, the events of (4) and (5) are visions of the future, but from the author's, they are history. Friedman attributes the *inclusion* (but not the full authorship) of this earlier Song of Moses to J. As for (5), in particular, it was during his reign (c. 1000–962 B.C.E.) that King David brought the holy ark to Jerusalem. Following his death, the Temple itself was built (c. 950 B.C.E.) by his son, King Solomon, who died c. 922 B.C.E. As a true son of what became the Kingdom of Judah after Solomon's death, J would have been impelled to honor the Temple as destined by the Song of Moses.

Now Moses led the Israelites from the Sea of Reeds into the wilderness of Shur. For three days they could find no water, and at Marah it proved too bitter (15:22–23). In their thirst, the people "grumbled against Moses" (15:24). The Lord answered his cry with a piece of wood. When Moses threw it in the water, it became sweet. (15:25a). The Lord then made a "fixed rule" for the people and "put them to the test." *"If you will heed the Lord your God diligently, doing what is upright in His sight, giving ear to His commandments and keeping all His laws, then I will not bring upon you any of the diseases that I brought upon the Egyptians, for I the LORD am your healer"* (15:25b–26).

They next arrived and encamped at Elim, an oasis, with "twelve springs of water and seventy palm trees" (15:27).

Comment E–48. On the Lord God's modest commitment under His first "postdeparture" pact with the people

We need not ponder how twelve springs and seventy palm trees could meet the needs for food and water of six hundred thousand adult males (plus women, children, and livestock). The ensuing story of forty years in the wilderness was written neither as a treatise on logistics nor a manual for quartermasters. It is instead the Torah's metaphoric account of a developing relationship between its two great protagonists—its people and its God.

Their new postdeparture relationship takes root in a pact offered to the people by the Lord, their God. Its first charge to the people is simplicity itself. They must "heed [Him] diligently" and "give ear to His commandments." Given the circumstances that led to their departure from Egypt and their presence in the wilderness, a demand to "pay attention" seems modest enough. Furthermore, they must "keep all His laws." This, too, seems reasonable, since specifc laws that define right and wrong conduct are generally meant to be obeyed. And when the governed willingly accept the authority of the law maker, then all are obliged to obey.

It is the final expectation, however, that poses the greatest challenge to the relationship: The people must "do what is upright in [the Lord's] sight." Where no specific law governs a particular choice, how are the Israelites to discern what is "upright in [His] sight?"

And for obeying His laws and doing what is upright in his sight, what will Israel gain? Only that the Lord will not bring upon them "any of the diseases that I brought upon the Egyptians, for I the Lord am your healer." (Friedman ascribes 15:26 to E.)

On the fifteenth day of the second month after leaving Egypt, the Israelites came to the "wilderness of Sin," between Elim and Sinai (16:1). Their paucity of provisions is mirrored in their paucity of spirit. Hunger prompts them to grumble "against Moses and Aaron" (16:2). They recall their life in Egypt when they "sat by the fleshpots" [i.e., pots of meat] and ate their "fill of bread" (16:3).

> Note E–17: These memories, if real, are not of poverty or hardship (cf. Comments E–27 pt. 2 and E–33).

The Lord tells Moses He will "rain down bread from the sky" for the people to gather "that I may thus test them, to see whether they will follow My instructions or not" (16:4). As to these, He adds, "On the sixth day, when they prepare what they have brought in, it shall prove to be double the amount they gather each day" (16:5).

> Note E–18: The gathering of a double amount on the sixth day anticipates the Fourth (or Sabbath) Commandment (Exod. 20:8–11).

Moses and Aaron now tell the Israelites not that they will soon have bread but that they will see the Lord's Presence in the morning "because He has heard your grumblings against [Him]" (16:6–8). Moses and Aaron also tell the people that in grumbling against them, the people really grumble against their God: "For who are we that you should grumble against us?" (16:7).

They go on to tell the people not only of the Lord's promise of bread, but of "flesh to eat in the evening and bread in the morning." Then they "turned toward the wilderness, and there, in a cloud, appeared the Presence of the Lord" (16:10). He then reassures Moses. "I have heard the grumbling. . . . By evening you shall eat flesh, and in the morning you shall have your fill of bread; and you shall know that I the Lord am your God" (16:12).

As promised, quail appeared in the evening. And in the morning "a fine and flaky substance, as fine as frost on the ground" covered the wilderness

(16:14–15). Moses identifies it as the Lord's promised "bread." Each man was to gather "as much as each of you requires to eat"—that is, an "omer" each day for each person "in your tent" (16:16).

Exodus 16:17–18 describes the daily gathering of the bread: "When they measured it by the omer, he who had gathered much had no excess, and he who had gathered little had no deficiency: they had gathered as much as they needed to eat." Yet the next passage implies that some had taken more than their daily needs (16:19). When Moses cautions them not to "leave any of it over until morning," they ignore him. Next morning, the excess "became infested with maggots and stank." Moses was angry (16:20).

On the sixth day Moses explains the need for a double portion (16:21–22). "*This is what the Lord meant*: Tomorrow is a day of rest, a holy sabbath of the Lord. Bake what you would bake and boil what you would boil; and all that is left put aside to be kept until morning" (16:23). They did so "and it did not turn foul, and there were no maggots in it" (16:24).

> *Note E–19: Absent any revelation from the Lord, Moses "divines" what He means (16:23). In this the Torah portrays Moses as a prophet to whom the Lord reveals His intent not only through words, but also in some manner without words.*

When despite all, "some of the people went out on the seventh day to gather," the Lord equates Moses with them (16:27). "How long will *you men* refuse to obey my commandments and my teachings?" He warns Moses: " 'Let everyone remain where he is: Let no man leave his place on the seventh day.' So the people remained inactive on the seventh day" (16:29–30).

Comment E–49. On the Lord's rebuke to Moses for the failure of "some people" to rest on the sabbath

The episode foretells Moses' problems as intermediary between the Lord and His people. On his own initiative, Moses explains to the people *why* they must gather a double portion on the sixth day. By way of thanks, the Lord counts Moses among "you men" who "refuse to obey my commandments and my teachings." Can He not distinguish between Moses and the people? Must Moses now bear the brunt of their "sins"?

What had been known as the Lord's "bread," the "house of Israel" now names "manna." It is said to have been "like coriander seed, white, and it tasted like wafers in honey" (16:31).

> *Note E–20: On its appearance and taste cf. Num. 11:7–8.*

The passage then tells how Moses and Aaron implemented the Lord's command for preserving the miracle of His manna. One *omer* is put in a jar and placed before the Lord "to be kept throughout the ages" (16:33). The text then jumps forward some forty years. We are told that the Israelites ate manna "until they came to the border of the land of Canaan" (16:35). Exod. 16:36 then defines the *omer* as "a tenth of an *ephah*."

On the Lord's command at each stage, the Israelites moved from the wilder-ness of Sin to Rephidim. There "the people quarreled with Moses," because there was no water. Moses rebuked them for trying the Lord's patience (17:1–2). But the people "grumbled" even more for his having brought them from Egypt only "to kill us and our children and livestock with thirst" (17:3). Sensing them to be on the brink of open revolt, Moses "cried out to the Lord" that "before long they will be stoning me!" (17:4). The Lord directs Moses to go with some elders to "the rock at Horeb," on which "*I will be standing before you*" (17:6). Moses is to "strike the rock" with the rod he had used in the plagues, after which "water will issue from it" (17:6).

And so it flowed. The place was then named "Massah and Meribah." The names denoted that the people had quarreled with Moses and that they had "tried the Lord" by asking, "Is the Lord present among us or not?" (17:7).

Comment E–50. On the events at Meribah

The name of Meribah is more prominently identified with the miracle of water from a rock than that of Massah. A later version of the story will pro-foundly affect Moses' fate (see Num. 20:2–13, 24, 27–28; Deut. 32:51).

Compared to the plagues of Egypt, this miracle of water from a rock, *even in amounts sufficient to meet the needs of possibly two million persons (including women and children) and their livestock*, might seem modest. Nev-ertheless, it was to remove the peoples' doubts of His Presence and of His power and commitment to meet their needs that He told Moses that He "[would] stand" before Israel "on the rock at Horeb" (17:6).

JPS1 and 2 and RSV all read *omaid lephanecha* as stating the Lord's intent to stand on the rock before Moses and the elders. Does the statement imply that He will actually be seen? While rare, such a manifestation of His Presence would not be unique to J (see Gen. 18:1–2 and Comments G–29 and E–53). *How-ever, it is to E rather than J that Friedman attributes the "waters of Meribah."*

Rashi does not comment on the Lord's appearance on the rock, while Ramban regards it as a revelation of "Divine Glory."[20] Plaut reads *omaid lep-hanecha* as idiomatic for "I will be present."[21] These views reflect later per-ceptions of the Torah's God by prophets, psalmists, rabbis, and philosophers. As yet, however, the Torah has said nothing to preclude its God from revealing Himself in any form, even human, *that He might find useful to His purposes*. (see Comments E–53 and 91).

Now, "Amalek came and fought with Israel at Rephidim" (17:8). The episode introduces Joshua, whom Moses directs "to go out and do battle with Amalek" (17:9). Absent any stated instructions from the Lord, Moses, with rod in hand, overlooks the battle from atop a nearby hill. With him are Aaron and Hur (as yet, not otherwise identified). "Then, whenever Moses held up his hand, Israel prevailed; but whenever he let down his hand, Amalek prevailed" (17:11).

Clearly, the position of Moses' hand, as it grasped his rod, was a critical factor in the outcome. However, when Moses' hands "grew heavy," Aaron and Hur supported him so that "his hands remained steady until the sun set." So it was that "Joshua overwhelmed the people of Amalek with the sword" (17:12–13). Following the victory, the Lord has Moses inscribe the following words in a document to be read to Joshua: "I will utterly blot out the memory of Amalek from under heaven" (17:14). Moses then builds an altar to the Lord that he names *adonai-nissi*, meaning "Hand upon the throne of the Lord! The Lord will be at war with Amalek throughout the ages" (17:15–16).

Comment E–51. On Amalek and the roles in its defeat of the Lord, Moses, his rod, Aaron, Joshua, and his troops

Who is responsible for Israel's victory over Amalek? The Lord's direct intervention is never stated, although the transmission of His spirit through the rod of Moses is again implied. But the transmission depended entirely on Moses' ability to keep his hand raised. For that, the diligence of Aaron and Hur was essential. But what of Joshua's well honed military skills and the inspired state of the Israelite troops following the Lord's presence at Meribah and His miracle of the water? In effect, the Torah portrays the operation of an idealized relationship between each participating entity in Israel's victory over Amalek.

Why this encounter with Amalek? And why does the Lord denounce Amalek as an enemy with whom He will be at war "throughout the ages"? Five hundred years earlier, or more, Amalek was among the sons born in Edom to Eliphaz, a son of Esau, and his concubine, Timna (see Gen. 36:12 and Comment G–69). Amalek is also named as a "clan" of Eliphaz (see Gen. 36:16). By the time of the exodus, the people known as Amalek, or Amalekites, were a nomadic people who moved throughout southern Canaan and Sinai.[22]

As with the Philistines in Canaan (see Comment G–49), the appearance of Amalekites in early Genesis *may* involve an anachronism reflective of later events in the United Monarchy. Their presence in or near Sinai around the time of the "present" battle with the Israelites at Rephidim seems plausible. *However, their first appearance in Gen. 14:7 (during Abraham's war against the kings) occurs well before the reported birth of the Amalek in Gen. 36:12.*

Moses' father-in-law, Jethro, now hears of the exodus. Like J's Reuel, E's Jethro is "priest of Midian" (18:1). (See Comment E–9.) Together with Zipporah and Gershom and Eliezer, the wife and sons of Moses, Jethro comes to where Moses was encamped "at the mountain of God" (18:2–4).

> Note E–21: E is the first to identify Moses's second son, Eliezer, by name. J's Moses had named Gershom to signify "I have been a stranger in a foreign land" (2:22). Exod. 4:20a speaks only of Moses leaving Midian for Egypt with "his wife and sons." Thereafter, J says nothing to confirm Eliezer's name or actual existence (see Comment E–16).

Moses greets Jethro with warmth and respect and tells him of the intervening events since his departure for Egypt. He emphasizes the Lord's role in delivering the Israelites (18:7–8). Though still "the priest of Midian" in 18:1 as in 3:1, Jethro quickly acknowleges the greatness of Israel's God. He especially "rejoiced" in the "kindness" of the Lord in delivering Israel from the Egyptians" (18:9). And after saying, "Blessed be the Lord," he acknowledges His supremacy: "Now I know that the Lord is greater than all gods" (18:11). He then brought "a burnt offering and sacrifices for God," and Aaron came with the elders "to partake of the meal before God with Moses' father-in-law" (18:12).

Comment E–52. On Jethro's acknowledging the supremacy of the God of Moses

Unlike Melchizedek, priest of "God Most High," who somehow identified Abram's God as his own, Jethro is priest of the Midianites, with its own tribal pantheon of gods and idols.[23] The Torah thus portrays Jethro as a worthy and righteous priest of another people, who nevertheless acknowledges the supremacy of *yahweh*.

Worthy though he is, Jethro expresses no regret for the deaths of innocent Egyptians. Instead he is awed by the powers manifested by the Lord in Egypt. In accepting the power of Israel's God as proof of His supremacy, Jethro vindicates the Torah's aim to demonstrate those powers through the plagues and the parting of the "sea."

If Jethro's spiritual support could help to reassure all Israel of the Lord's supremacy his practical wisdom was of no less help to Moses (18:13–27). Jethro had observed the heavy demands on Moses in his capacity as "magistrate among the people." In addressing Jethro's concerns, Moses tells him of his unique role, in regard to all disputes, as interpreter of "the laws and teachings of God." But Jethro assures Moses that "the task is too heavy for you; you cannot do it alone."

He offers the following advice: First, rather than disclosing God's "laws and teachings" in the context of a single dispute, Moses should explain their basic principles to the people, so that they could act accordingly (i.e., he should "make known to them the way they are to go and the practices they are to follow" [18:20]). Second, all disputes should be decided initially by "capable men who fear God, trustworthy men who spurn ill-gotten gain" (18:21). Those chosen should be designated as "chiefs of thousands, hundreds, fifties, and tens." This delegation of judicial authority should be complete as to all disputes, however "minor" (or "small"). Only "major" (or "great") disputes should come to Moses. He would thus be relieved of an impossible work load, and the people would gain quicker justice. In agreeing to unclog his courts accordingly, Moses demonstrated his open mind. Jethro then went home.

Some three months after the departure from Egypt, "Israel" was encamped in the wilderness of Sinai "in front of the mountain" (19:1–2). The Lord God then called to Moses from the mountain. Moses must tell the "house of Jacob and . . . the children of Israel" what He, the Lord, "did to the Egyptians" and how He had brought them to Him on "eagles' wings" (19:3–4). If they will "obey [the Lord] faithfully and keep [His] covenant," [they] shall be "[His] treasured possession among all the peoples . . . and shall be to [Him] a kingdom of priests and a holy nation" (19:5–6). On hearing this from Moses, "the people answered as one, saying, 'All the Lord has spoken we will do!' " (19:8).

> *Note E–22: Of what import is the peoples' impulsive answer to the Lord? They know of His power and His professed but conditional commitment to Israel. They shout their willingness to do all that He "has spoken." But do they mean to include all that He will yet speak?*

The Lord then tells Moses of His appearance in three days "when I will come to you in a thick cloud, *in order that the people may hear when I speak with you* and so trust you ever after" (19:9). He will then come down on Mount Sinai *"in the sight of all the people"* (19:11).

In preparing for His appearance, the people are to "stay pure" and "wash their clothes" (19:9–11). Under penalty of death, no "beast or man" is to approach the mountain too closely (19:12–13a). "When [i.e., but *only* when] the ram's horn sounds a *long* blast, they may go up on the mountain" (19:13b). In addition to remaining pure and washing their clothes, Moses tells them, as a particular aspect of purification, "do not go near a woman" (19:14–15). On the morning of the third day there was thunder and lightning. A dense cloud marking God's presence was "upon the mountain" (19:9, 16). When the ram's horn sounded, Moses took the people "toward God." But they stopped at "the foot of the mountain" (19:16–17).

"Now Mount Sinai was all in smoke . . . and the whole mountain trembled violently." The blare of the horn grew ever louder (19:18–19). The Lord then descended to the top of Mount Sinai and called Moses to come there. He then tells

Moses to "warn *the people* not to break through to the Lord to gaze, lest many of them perish" (19:20–21). As for the priests, they first "must purify themselves" before they "come near the Lord" (19:22). Moses then reminds the Lord that He has already forbidden the people to "come up to Mount Sinai" (19:23; see also 19:12–13a). In turn, the Lord tells Moses to "Go down, and come back with Aaron." He then repeats that neither "priests nor the people" are to "break through to come up to the Lord" (19:24). So "Moses *went down to the people* and spoke to them" (19:25).

Comment E–53. On the Lord's appearance on Mount Sinai

In 19:21 the Lord echoes His warning of 19:12–13a. He tells Moses to "warn *the people* not to break through to the Lord to *gaze*, lest *many of them* perish." Who would be the "many"? "Many" of the whole of Israel? Or "many" of those who "break through" to "gaze" on Him? If "many" of all Israel, why "any" of the innocent? If "many" of those who "break through," why not "all" of the guilty? As for the priests of Israel (19:22), this is their first appearance in the Torah. These are J's priests, who must not be confused with P's Aaronide priesthood of Exod. 28–30, 38–40, and of Leviticus.

Also important is how J relates the Lord's "invisibility" to sanctity. Recall that it was J's Lord who stood before, and spoke with, Abraham at Mamre (Gen. 18:22–33). And it will be J's Lord who speaks "in the sight of the people" from "on Mount Sinai" (19:11). *From 19:11 and 21 together, we might conclude that J allows his Lord full latitude to determine when and how His sanctity is honored or demeaned by His visibility.*

In Exod. 20:1–14, the Lord speaks from Mount Sinai.

> Note E–23: His words constitute the text of the Ten Commandments, also known as the "Ten Words" (aseret hadevarim; see, e.g., Exod. 34:28, Deut. 4:13, 10:4). Literally, however, the "Ten Words," as such, are those inscribed on the two tablets of the commandments. The full text of the Ten Commandments, as set out in Exod. 20:1–14, is identified as "kahl hadevarim ha'ayleh," or "all these words" (20:1). D's version of the Ten Commandments appears in Deut. 5:6–19. While Friedman attributes Exod. 20:1–14 to P, he considers both versions to have been derived from an earlier formulation by E.

VERSES 1–6: THE FIRST AND SECOND COMMANDMENTS

1. God spoke all these words, saying:
2. I the Lord am your God who brought you out of the land of Egypt, the house of bondage:

3. You shall have no other gods beside Me.

4. "You shall not make for yourself a sculptured image, or any likeness of what is in the heavens above, or on the earth below, or in the waters under the earth. 5. You shall not bow down to them or serve them. For I the Lord your God am an impassioned God, visiting the guilt of the fathers upon the children, upon the third and upon the fourth generations of those who reject Me, 6. but showing kindness to the thousandth generation of those who love Me and keep My commandments.

Comment E–54. On Exod. 20:2–6 and the structure of the First and Second Commandments

1. On Exod. 20:1–2 and the Lord, as Israel's God

A demarcation of roles between of the Lord, as Lord, and as the God of Israel, is suggested in 20:1–2. *The Ten Commandments are spoken not by the Lord, as Lord, but as Israel's God* (20:1). In turn, it is not the Lord as God, but as the Lord," who brings Israel out from bondage in Egypt." This might suggest that *as its God*, the Lord will serve as Israel's moral and ethical compass. As God, therefore, it would be His role to instruct Israel in its quest for the perfection of the Lord's earthly creation. As Lord, however, His principal role would be to use His powers to (1) defend His sanctity, (2) protect Israel and (3) foster its commitment to Him—both as Lord and God.

2. On Exod. 20:2–6 as the source of two commandments

Since the remaining text of the Ten Commandments (20:7–14) is readily and logically divisible into precisely eight commandments, the text of 20:2–6 must be apportioned between two commandments. These verses, however, present several structural ambiguities. First, is 20:2 meant to constitute a complete command, a portion of a command or a preamble? (2. "I the Lord am your God who brought you out of the land of Egypt, the house of bondage.") Plaut suggests that the Ten Commandments are comprised of thirteen separate *"mitzvot"* that can be (and are) allocated in various ways.[24] He also notes that in the "prevailing Jewish division" 20:2 is regarded as the First Commandment, with 20:3–6 as the Second Commandment.

The basic structural question is whether Exod. 20:2 is meant to introduce all ten commandments, or whether it has a special implied relevance to 20:3 alone or to 20:3–6.

Read literally by itself, 20:2 commands nothing directly. In this it resembles the preamble of the United States Constitution, or others, which serve to establish the source of authority for what follows. Thus, *"We the people of the United States . . . do ordain and establish this Constitution. . . ."* If, as it might be, 20:2 were viewed as such a preamble to the Ten Commandments, then 20:3–6 would necessarily constitute the First and Second Commandments.

Exod. 20:2, however, can also be read to imply the following: "Know that I am the Lord who brought you out of bondage from Egypt; recall My many deeds in doing so. Through these deeds, I affirmed My role as your God and your role as My people. *From the honor and respect which you owe Me as the Lord, your God, My First Commandment is, simply, that you obey all My Commandments.*" This view of Exod. 20:2 would fully justify its treatment as the First Commandment under the "prevailing Jewish division" (as noted by Plaut).

But given the two possibilities of Exod. 20:2 as either a preamble or a command, its proper role depends largely on whether the texts of 20:3 and 20:4–6 are best read as one or two commandments. If two commandments are required, or preferable, then, in order to limit the total to ten, 20:2 must be treated as a preamble. Conversely, if 20:3 and 20:4–6 are best understood as a single command, then, 20:2 must be viewed as a command rather than as a preamble.

Structurally, 20:3 is complete in itself and can be read as a single command ("You shall have no other gods before me"). The same is true of the "mandate" of 20:4–6, set out in 4–5a. ("You shall not make for yourself a sculptured image, or any likeness of what is in the heavens above, or on the earth below, or in the waters under the earth. You shall not bow down to them or serve them"). Thus, 20:3 implies the supremacy of the God of Israel over all other gods and requires exclusive adherence to Him. In turn, 20:4–5a, read together, forbids the making and worship of any image or likeness of anything whatsoever. It thus serves two separate purposes, both of which in turn support the central and dominant purpose of 20:3.

The first purpose is to prohibit any portrayal of the "unportrayable" Being of the God of Israel through idols and images. The second purpose is to reinforce the prohibition of 20:3 against having "other gods beside Me." Together the structurally separable commands of 20:3 and 20:4–5a declare the *basic* incorporeality and supremacy of the God of Israel. Israelites must learn to know of God through their minds and spirits alone, without reliance on their physical senses. To that end, they may not worship images or idols that are thought to represent His Being—even if their purpose is but to feel closer to Him. Nor, for any reason, may they "have" or worship the images or idols of lesser gods. Logically, therefore, all these essential elements of His Being—His supremacy, His uniqueness and His inscrutability, should find expression in a single command.

This view finds support in the rationale for obedience set out in 20:5b–6: "For I the Lord your God am an impassioned God, visiting the guilt of the fathers upon the children, upon the third and the fourth generations of those who reject Me, but showing kindness to the thousandth generation of those who love Me and keep My commandments."

The promise of punishment and reward in 20:5b–6 might well apply to the entire Ten Commandments. That it appears where it does, however, suggests a special connection with the preceding command, which could be read as either 20:3–5a or 20:4–5a. The coverage of 20:5b–6 would be incomplete, however, were it to apply only to the implemental provisions of 20:4–5a, but not to the underlying substance of 20:3. This added consideration supports the logic of combining 20:3 and 20:4–6 into a single Second Commandment.

By similar reasoning the point can be made that 20:5–6 applies no less to 20:2, in regard to the respect, honor, and obedience owing to the God of the Torah. This would support the view that 20:2–6 does indeed comprise a single command. Again, however, this is possible only under two conditions. First, the Ten Commandments might be reduced to Nine, thus denying the clear intent of the Torah. Second, of the remaining eight commandments, one might be divided into two.

Here Plaut notes that the Augustinian division of the Roman Catholic and Lutheran churches does in fact combine 20:2–6 into one commandment.[25] Thereafter, in order to derive *Ten* Commandments from the text, it divides the prohibition of "covetnousness" into the separate objects of "thy neighbor's wife" and all others. My later comments on the Tenth Commandment will argue against such a division. Accordingly, I consider the "prevailing Jewish division" of 20:2–6 into the First (20:2) and Second (20:3–6) Commandments to be correct. (But I must also note that D's ordering of the components of the Tenth Commandment in Deut. 5:18 offers greater support to the Augustinian division than does P in Exod. 20:14.)

Comment E–55. On monotheism and monolatry in the Second Commandment

JPS2 renders 20:3 as "You shall have no other gods *beside* Me." JPS1 and RSV use the possibly less demanding term "no other gods *before* Me" (or *me*, as it appears in RSV). Notably absent in every translation is an unequivocal declaration of monotheism; for example, "There are no gods *other than Me*." The Hebrew source of "beside" or "before" Me is *ahl panai* ("before My face"). But this metaphoric vision sheds no light on whether "before" and "beside" *Me* can be read as "above" and "equal to" *Me*.

Does the Second Commandment, as such, accept the doctrine of monolatry (i.e., the worship of only One God among others who are thought to exist)? Does it assume the existence of "other gods" as independent entities? Or does it view their existence as human fabrications?

These questions recall God's punishment of the Egyptian gods in Plague Ten (see Comment E–34). Now, in the context of the Second Commandment, Rashi is even more explicit in stating that "other gods" exist only so long as they find human acceptance. Thus he comments: "Other gods—Which are not divine, but others made them gods over themselves."[26]

Ramban comments on the Second Commandment as follows: "[God] admonished us firstly that we should not accept ourselves a master from among all the gods excepting the Eternal." Who are these "gods"? He speaks of them as "the angels above" and "all the host of heaven who are called *elohim.*" Thus, the command is "a prohibition against believing in any of these things, accepting them as gods."[27] Unlike Rashi, Ramban does not address the matter of gods who are worshipped as such by non-Israelites. In accepting the "reality" of the Torah's lesser "elohim," he derives their status as gods from their services to the Lord. Their existence as such, however, is at His sufferance.

What, then, can we make of the role of monolatry in the Second Commandment? While the commandment can be read to accept the reality of other gods, it need not be. Equally consistent is the view that "other gods" exist only in the human mind and spirit. Or, as stated by Rashi, as human creations whom other peoples "made . . . gods over themselves."

VERSE 7: THE THIRD COMMANDMENT

7. You shall not swear falsely by the name of the Lord your God; for the Lord will not clear one who swears falsely by His name.

Comment E–56. On the meaning of the Third Commandment

The full thrust of the Third Commandment against the abuse of the Lord's authority has long been blunted by an unfortunate focus on His *name* rather than His *entire Being*. The problem is compounded by the literal translation of the Hebrew, *loh tisah et shaym yahweh elohechah lahshav.* With minor stylistic differences, RSV and JPS1 render the command as "You shall not take the name of the Lord your God in vain, for the Lord will not hold him guiltless who takes His name in vain."

So stated, the command seeks to the sanctify the Lord's "name" in itself. To do so, the view developed that to use His name in a secular context was to use it "in vain." But since references to Him in ordinary human discourse could also serve worthy purposes, Judaic conventions were adopted for referring to Him by other than His actual name. So it is that in Hebrew, *yahweh* becomes *"adonai";* in English, the written form of God becomes "G-d." In speech, one might also speak of "the holy one," or *hashaym* ("the name").

One effect of this practice is to elevate the "name," as a *symbol* of the substance, to a level no less sacred than the substance itself. Critical to the meaning of the Third Commandment, therefore, is the intended relationship between the "name" and "Being" of its God.

This relationship is expressed most dramatically in God's reply to Moses' plea that He reveal His name. His answer of *"Ehyeh-Asher-Ehyeh,"* or "I am who I am," in fact identifies His "name" with the very essence of His total Being (see Comment E–11). *And so it is in the Third Commandment as well. Beyond merely symbolizing His Being, His "name is meant to incorporate His entire Being.* And in this relationship lies the meaning of "You shall not swear falsely by the name of the Lord your God."

In general, to "swear falsely" is to proclaim as "truth," not only what one knows to be false, but what one does not know to be true. Through the Third Commandment, the Torah applies the principle to relations between its God and humanity. The Third Commandment declares in particular that to proclaim the will of God (as the fulfillment of His Being) *in the absence of certainty* is to "swear falsely" by His Being. It is to assume the role of a prophet.

Even more destructive of His sanctity are *acts* done in His "name," and thus by the authority of His "Being." The point was cogently stated by an Israeli judge in reply to the convicted killer of Yitzhak Rabin, who claimed to have acted under God's will: "There is no greater desecration of God's name [than the attempt] to justify the murder as a religious commandment or a moral mission."[28]

From such insights we can derive a restatement of the Third Commandment that embraces both its words and its essence: "DO NOT CLAIM TO JUSTIFY IN GOD'S NAME WHAT CANNOT BE JUSTIFIED IN HUMANITY'S NAME." *As viewed from the Torah,* such a reading of the Third Commandment serves the vital interests of its two great protagonists—the sanctity of its God and the dignity and responsibility of humankind. And it applies no less to the massacres, wars, pogroms, and other unspeakable cruelties "righteously" committed in His name.

VERSES 8–11: THE FOURTH COMMANDMENT

8. Remember the sabbath day and keep it holy.

9. Six days you shall labor and do all your work, 10. But the seventh day is a sabbath of the Lord your God; you shall not do any work—you, your son or daughter, your male or female slave, or your cattle, or the stranger who is within your settlements. 12. For in six days the Lord made heaven and earth and sea, and all that is in them, and He rested on the seventh day; therefore the Lord blessed the sabbath day and hallowed it.

Comment E–57. On remembering the sabbath and keeping it holy

Contrary to 20:2, which ignores Creation as a source of the Lord's authority for the entire Ten Commandments, the Fourth Commandment draws on the cycle of Creation as its sole rationale. Through it, the Israelites are to emulate the Lord, their God (20:11). (Other rationales are given in E's *mishpat* of Exod. 23:12 and in the Fourth of the Ten Commandments in Deuteronomy (Deut. 5:12–15).

Exod. 20:8 sets out two separate sabbath mandates. The first is to "remember" it and the second to "keep it holy." The balance of the Fourth Commandment provides that both be accomplished through a surcease of work. The work prohibition is applied to (1) all humans and animals attached to a household and (2) "strangers" in the community. *In construing the Fourth Commandment in its own terms, we need not consider the meaning of "work" and "rest." They remain to be defined.*

In that the God of Creation I rested on the Seventh Day, why should humans "created in His image" not do so as well? But what of cattle, not created in His image? Here it might follow that as humans may not labor, so may they not benefit from the labor of Godly creatures under their control. But why limit the command to "cattle" rather than "livestock"? In fact, P's use of *b'haymat* suggests animals other than livestock (see Comments G–90, E–27, and E–28 pt. 1). Although JPS1 and 2 and RSV all use "cattle," should we not read the term as a metaphor for all "work" animals under the family's control—including the lowly ass.

As for humans, the prohibition explicitly extends beyond male heads of households to a "son or daughter" and a "male or female slave." *Most notable among those not specified are wives.* But also expressly barred from work is "the stranger within your settlement."

The Fourth Commandment completes the first subset of commands covering relations between the Israelites and their God. The remaining commandments deal with standards of human relationships conducive to a peaceful, viable, cohesive, and productive community.

VERSE 12: THE FIFTH COMMANDMENT

12. Honor your father and mother, that you may long endure on the land your God is giving to you.

Comment E–58. On the Fifth Commandment

As confirmed in its final clause, the command looks to the family as the institution most responsible for the perpetuation of a successful society. Why should each generation honor its parents? Because it is parents who prepare each generation for its responsibilities. They do so by giving it life, by nurturing its bodies and minds, and by enriching its spirits through love.

The command to each generation to honor its parents places an implied reciprocal obligation on parents to be worthy of such honor. Through the fulfillment of these joint obligations, all may "long endure on the land."

The command to honor rather than love one's parents requires respectful and supportive conduct throughout the changing emotional climates of family relationships.

VERSE 13: THE SIXTH, SEVENTH, EIGHTH, AND NINTH COMMANDMENTS

13a. You shall not murder.

Comment E–59. On the Sixth Commandment

The prohibition of murder flows naturally from the creation of man in the image of God. It reflects the reverence for life expressed in the first *mitzvah* of Genesis to "be fertile and increase" (see also Gen. 9:1, 6–7). As it condemns the actual consummation of a murder, so, too, in theory, must it condemn every attempt to effect a murder. It is of interest, however, that murder (possibly including attempted murder) is the only act of physical violence prohibited by the Ten Commandments. In themselves, they impose no constraint against bodily injury and harm, except as they might result in murder.

But what is murder for the purposes of the Sixth Commandment? Although to murder is necessarily to kill, to kill is not necessarily to murder. To kill is to take a life. To murder is to kill without justifiable cause. To read *ratzach* in the command as "murder" is to draw a line between justifiable and wrongful killings. But on this point there is tension among the translations. JPS1 and 2 use "murder," while RSV uses "kill." But before assuming a moral divergence between Judaism and Christianity, we should note that "kill" appears in at least one "Jewish" translation. This is in JPS1, *as adapted by the editors of the interlineated Torah for use with Rashi's commentaries.*[29] But having read *ratzach* in the Torah as "kill, they proceed (without explanation) to read Rashi's own *ratzach* as "murder"!

With added support from E's later *mishpatim*, we can agree with JPS1 and 2 that P's Sixth Commandment condemns only nonjustified killings. But among all the motives and circumstances that result in killings, who is to judge which are just and unjust? Who but the God of the Torah?

If so, what remains of the post-Flood declaration of Genesis 9:6? Recall the words of a remorseful God in the wake of His human holocaust: "*Whoever sheds the blood* of man, by man shall His blood be shed; for in His image did God make man." Despite His passionate avowal of blood for blood, we will find that the Torah permits its God to make exceptions.

13b. You shall not commit adultery.

Comment E–60. On the Seventh Commandment

Rashi states that "adultery is only with a married woman."[30] The command, *in its time*, however, was meant to address one of most basic dilemmas of the human condition. It is, simply, that the very same sexual impulse that creates life can also debase life. Indeed, even more than greed or avarice, it may be the force of human sexuality that puts human free will to its greatest test. Coupled with the Torah's first wish for humanity to be "fertile and increase" is the primal human duty to avoid harm to others and oneself. Therefore, *within its cultural setting*, the Torah addressed humanity's need for sexual responsibility by prohibiting adultery.

Adultery today is generally defined as a consensual act of sexual relations (as defined for the purpose) by any married person, husband or wife, with a person other than one's spouse. But within its patriarchal culture, the Torah defined sexual responsibility in terms of the reality that "women were . . . virtually the chattel of their husbands."[31] Thus, its primary (but not exclusive) approach to sexual morality involved the husband's property right in his wife.

We might well be perplexed by the narrow social context in which the Commandment addresses the issue of sexual responsibility. But we cannot deny the validity of its concern for the social consequences of irresponsible sexual conduct. Therefore, *in our time*, we should read the Seventh Commandment, together with its related *mishpatim* and rules that follow, as a broad plea for sexual responsibility. Minimally, they require every human being to temper the urge for sexual gratification with a controlling regard for any potential harm in the circumstances to oneself or others.

13c. You shall not steal.

Comment E–61. On the Eighth Commandment

The stark simplicity of the command both belies and affirms its bedrock importance to the well-being of the entire community and all of its members. Just as the prohibition of murder speaks to the foundational sanctity of human life, the prohibition of theft speaks to the vital social importance of protecting lawful property rights. Absent the protection of such rights from theft, *by whatever means*, the community and its members will know neither justice, peace, nor economic well-being.

13d. You shall not bear false witness against your neighbor.

Comment E–62. On the Ninth Commandment

The command reads the same in JPS1 and RSV. As stated, the command might seem to do no more than prohibit perjury against a "neighbor" in trials or other official proceedings. But surely its broader thrust condemns all harmful lies uttered in any setting. Also, in its literal concern for lies *"against"* your neighbor, the command says nothing of lies that might favor him. Yet to bear false witness in *favor* of one "neighbor" might well harm another "neighbor." In order to protect all "neighbors" from the "false witness" of others, the command should be read to prohibit any lie from which anyone might be harmed.

VERSE 14: THE TENTH COMMANDMENT.

14. You shall not covet your neighbor's house; you shall not covet your neighbor's wife, or his male or female slave, or his ox or his ass, or anything that is your neighbor's.

Comment E–63. On the Tenth Commandment

In restricting thought rather than conduct, the Tenth Commandment differs from all others. Though covetousness is a "sin" of the mind alone, it can generate errant impulses toward "sins" of conduct. Such impulses can overpower the firmest resolve to obey all other commandments. And even where a resulting wrongful impulse is subdued, covetousness diverts the mind and spirit from worthier concerns.

The view that covetousness directed to a neighbor's wife constitutes a separate commandment in itself, apart from the balance of the Tenth Commandment, has been noted (see Comment E–54 pt. 2). In brief, however, the Tenth Commandment relates to adultery in the same way it relates to theft in general. Whether she is coveted for sexual pleasure or general household purposes, the command condemns the thought alone. To treat the coveting of a neighbor's wife as different from the coveting of other property is to disrupt the pyschological unity of the Tenth Commandment.

And so conclude these comments on the Torah's first rendering of the Ten Commandments. Following the drama of this first direct revelation, the Israelites are frightened by an awesome display of thunder and lightning, a blaring horn, and a smoking mountain (20:15). They vow to obey Moses, but fear death should God speak to them directly (20:16). Moses assures them that God means only to test them *"in order that the fear of Him may ever be with you, so that you do not go astray"* (20:17). With the people remaining at a distance, "Moses approached the thick cloud where God was" (20:18).

Comment E–64. On fear and gratitude as motivations for Israel's obedience to its God

While not consistently unique to P, Exod. 20:17 constitutes a "classic" expression of P's views on reflex obedience to the Torah's God as Israel's redeeming virtue. So that Israel will not "go astray," Moses invokes a fear of its God rather than a respect for the substance of His Commandments as the impetus for obedience.

The ultimate concern in "going astray," however, lies not in disobedience itself, but in its human consequences. In our time, the fear of punishment for disobedience to lawful authority continues to serve useful social purposes. But fear alone as an impetus to socially responsible conduct can also erode the development of the human conscience as a more fully informed and more reliable guide to such conduct. In *his time*, speaking for the authors of the Torah, Moses had good reason to invoke fear as the prime impetus for adhering to emergent standards of rightful conduct. In our time, however, we have the added human duty of a well-informed conscience—as *Eve knew intuitively from the beginning.*

The Lord then takes special note that the people, themselves, saw and heard His first revelation on Sinai (i.e., the *full text* of the Ten Commandments). Thus His words to Moses: "Say to the Israelites, 'You *yourselves* saw that I spoke to *you* from the very heavens' " (20:19).

E's *mishpatim*, which begin at 21:1, are preceded by the preliminary commands of 20:20–23. First, as an *apparent* echo of the Second Commandment, the people "shall not make any gods of silver, nor . . . gods of gold" (20:20).

Note E–24: On Exod. 20:20 as an aspect of E's earlier version of the Second Commandment, see Comments E–72 and 87.

For later comparisons of E with P's Exod. 25–31, 35–40, and Lev. 17:2–9, I quote 20:21 in full: "Make for me an altar of earth and sacrifice on it your burnt offerings and your sacrifices of well-being, your sheep and your oxen; *in every place where I cause my name to be mentioned I will come to you and bless you.*" (On the comparison of Exod. 20:21 and Lev. 17:3–7, see Comment L–38.) Next, altars of stone must be made from natural, not hewn, stones (20:22). Finally, as a matter of decorum, no one may expose his "nakedness" in ascending God's altar (20:23).

Comment E–65. On E's *mishpatim*: an editorial comment

The Lord's revelation of the Ten Commandments to Moses and the people at Sinai is now followed by His revelation of the *mishpatim* to Moses alone (20:19, 21:1). Also known as the book of the covenant or the Covenant Code, these civil laws extend from Exod 21:2 through Exod. 23:19. They are followed by a homily on the blessings of obedience (23:20–33) and the rituals of ratification (24:1–8).

Although the *mishpatim* reflect a degree of topical organization, they lack the systematic organization of most modern legal codes. With only a few deviations, the *mishpatim* fit into the following classifications suggested by Plaut (with my own added comments in brackets): "21:2–22:16: worship preamble, serfs [or slaves], capital and noncapital offenses [involving physical harm to persons], property [including harm to animals and the theft or misappropriation of animals and other property]; 22:17–23:9: moral and religious duties and justice [including obligations to the weak and disadvantaged and of fairness and honesty to all]."[32]

Given their greater detail, the *mishpatim* often lack the dramatic literary impact of the Ten Commandments. Many of the *mishpatim* are rooted in earlier Near East legal codes, including in particular the well-known Code of Hammurabi (c. 1750 B.C.E.). Other Near East Codes of possible relevance are: Laws of Eshunna (c. 1900–1800 B.C.E.), Law of the Hittites (c. 1400–1300 B.C.E.), and Law of the Assyrians (c. 1100 B.C.E.).[33] In drawing on such codes, the author(s) of the *mishpatim* selected, rejected, and created anew, in furtherance of their own purposes. And it is with their purposes, as they bear on the Torah's God and His relations with the Israelites, that we are concerned.

JPS2 renders the preface of Exod. 21:1 as follows: "These are the rules [i.e., the *mishpatim*] *that you shall set before them.*"

Note E–25: *JPS1 and RSV refer to the* mishpatim *as "ordinances."*

The first *mishpatim* of 21:2–11 cover relations between Hebrew masters and Hebrew slaves. The details suggest the presence of an established and highly structured institution for which a balance is sought between the master's authority and the "subject's" humanity. Most notably, a *male Hebrew* slave could claim absolute freedom after six years of service (21:2).

Note E–26: *The manner of acquiring slaves is not disclosed. In itself, the term limitation suggests a system of indentured service rather than slavery. Nevertheless, JPS2 and RSV translate the Hebrew* ehved *as slave. Conversely, JPS1 uses the more euphemistic "servant." Perhaps more protective of Israel's good name, JPS1 seeks to "humanize" an institution well accepted by the Torah and its God.*

A further rule of the master/slave relationship might deter the slave from departing after six years. Thus, "If he came single, he shall leave single; if he had a wife, his wife shall leave with him." However, if his master gave him a wife who had borne him children, "the wife and the children shall belong to the master, and he shall leave alone." In such a case, however, the slave could also choose to remain with his family, and thus with his master. Having fulfilled the prescribed declarations and protocols, "he shall then remain his slave for life" (21:3–6).

> Note E–27: A slave's prior knowledge of the consequences of marrying and having children in slavery might add a touch of "fairness" to his "Hobson's choice." However, we are not told if the slave could refuse a wife offered him by the master. If he could, his problem in part was of his own making. In any case, his choice was to go, thus leaving his family in servitude, or to remain in servitude himself.

Exod. 21:7–11 covers the different rules that apply in a master/female slave relationship "when a man sells his daughter as a slave" (or "maid-servant," JPS1). Unlike the male slave who had a basic right to freedom after six years, the future of this female slave varied with whether her sexual relationship was with her master or his son. As her master's concubine, if she "displeased" him, she could be "redeemed" (by her father or family). The master could not sell her to others "since he broke faith with her." If her relations were with a son who had married another woman, she was owed "food," "clothing" and "conjugal rights." Should the son "fail her in these ways," she was free "without payment" (21:10–11).

> Note E–28: The passage does not fix a redemption price.

Comment E–66. On the "prospective" or "contemporary" application of the laws of slavery and other *mishpatim*

The laws of slavery, like many other Sinaitic laws, look to Israel's future in Canaan. They seem socially and economically unsuited to a nomadic existence in the wilderness. These laws likely developed during the united and divided monarchies as Israel moved toward an established system of social norms and governance. As for the immediate effectiveness of the Sinaitic revelations, *neither Exodus nor Leviticus can, in the Torah's internal chronology, openly contemplate forty years of wandering in the wilderness.* Not until Numbers will the Lord require the death of a generation through wandering for thirty-eight more years in the wilderness.

Exod. 21:12–17 identifies several capital offenses. These include *intentionally* killing a "man" by assault or treacherous "schemes"; striking a mother or father, regardless of physical consequences; insulting (or cursing) a father or mother and kidnapping "a man." Conversely, any *unintentional* killing of a "man" is termed an "act of God." Rather than punishing the unintentional killer, God assigns a "place to which he can flee" (21:13).

> Note E–29: The provision of sanctuaries for unintentional killers is later explained and implemented through the creation of Levitical towns of refuge (see Num. 35:6, 13–15, Deut. 19:1–10).

Comment E–67. On slavery, the status of women and the cultural constraints of the Torah

Every *death* giving rise to a capital offense in 20:12–17 is said to be that of a "man." It is never the death of a "person." Did women not enjoy the protection of law against capital crimes? If not so protected, they may have been compensated for their vulnerability by the Torah's uniform reference to the perpetrators of offenses as "he." *We might assume, however, that the Torah intends neither to absolve women from capital offenses nor to abandon them as fair game for killers.* Nevertheless, just as the Torah accepts slavery, so, too, its "minimalization" of women reflects the most deeply ingrained social norms of time and place. These basic norms, apart from their details, would have been impervious to any challenge that the Torah's authors might have mounted (see also Comments G–89A and B).

Comment E–68. On unintentional killings as "acts of God"

JPS2 attributes death to "an act of God" when caused by a person who "did not do it by design" (21:13). JPS1 describes it as a death caused "if a man not lie in wait, but God cause it to come to hand"; and RSV, as death from "a man who did not lie in wait for him." In short, inadvertent or unintentional killings are regarded as "acts of God."

As yet, the Torah is vague in defining intent. Might a reckless or even negligent act leading to death constitute intent? Is it an "act of God" when the act resulting in death is intentional, but the death itself is not? But more to the point, why does the Torah assign responsibility to its God for deaths caused by humans who lack any "guilty" intent to kill? *Contrary to the random character of "acts of God" in modern parlance, the God of the Torah is eminently purposeful.* Although His purposes may be incomprehensible, He is portrayed as a purposeful God. Any "act of God," therefore, must have a purpose. Has He, Himself, marked the victim for a death that He means to implement through a human agent? If so, why? As yet, we do not know. But when He does so, the Torah, as an act of elemental justice, must protect an innocent agent of God's will from the victim's vengeful family.

But these same circumstances raise another question. If the Torah's God can effect "sanctified" deaths through the unintended acts of innocent human agents, why can He not prevent "unsanctified" deaths from the intentional acts of wilful miscreants? An answer might lie in His single sphere of incapacity—that is, His inability to control the exercise of human free will and its natural consequences. Thus, as a "price" of human free will, worthy persons may die through the intentional acts of evil killers. But the Lord God Himself, in effecting death through human agents, cannot intrude into their free will. His sole recourse, therefore, is through human acts that do not arise from human will.

Comment E–69. On the use of related *mishpatim* to interpret the meaning of Commandments: the particular case of the Sixth Commandment, "You shall not kill/murder"

This Comment considers the varied views in JPS1 and 2 and RSV as to whether the Sixth Commandment prohibits "murder" alone or a "killing" as well. Consider again that to kill is to take a life, but to murder is to kill without valid cause. Is this apparent ambiguity of the Sixth Commandment resolved in part by the *mishpat* of Exod. 21:13? By ascribing all unintentional killings to God, does it not exempt their human perpetrators from the Sixth Commandment?

But the question of whether a killing was intended or not differs from that of whether an intentional killing can ever be justified—as in the classic case of self-defense. Here, of course, we must ask why a person under lethal attack should accept death in order to avoid the sin of killing when to do so merely transfers the sin to the attacker. *Thus, on reading the Sixth Commandment in light of Exod. 21:13, we must conclude that it permits a class of "excusable" intentional killings.* It is therefore limited to "murder." Since the *mishpatim* and Ten Commandments are both laws of the Torah's God, both may be read to shed light on the other.

Exod. 21:18–27 prescribes penalties for a variety of assaults that, with only one exception, do not result in death. (1) In a quarrel among men leading to a fight in which one is injured and confined to bed, but is later ambulatory, the other must pay only for "his idleness and his cure" (21:18–19). (2) When death results from a man striking a male or female slave with a rod, "he must be avenged" (or, more generally, "punished"). But, "if he survives a day or two, he is not to be avenged, since he is the other's property" (21:20). (3) When a master strikes a slave and destroys an eye or knocks out a tooth, the slave must be freed (21:26).

> Note E–30: *The Torah again seeks a balance between what is excessive and acceptable in disciplining "slaves." The immediate death of a slave is taken as presumptive proof of the master's intent to kill.[34] But where death lingers "a day or two," the master, as such, is presumed to have exercised suitable restraint.*

A separate category involves the principle of "*lex talionis*." (4) "When men fight, and one of them pushes a pregnant woman and a miscarriage results, but no other damage ensues . . . the one responsible shall be fined . . . the payment to be based on reckoning [or 'as judges determine,' per JPS1/RSV]" (21:22). But for all other injuries to bystanders from the melee, the principle of *lex talionis* applies: "the penalty shall be life for life, eye for eye, tooth for tooth, hand for hand, foot for foot, burn for burn, wound for wound, bruise for bruise" (21:23–25).

Comment E–70. On the principle of *lex talionis*

Except for miscarriages, Exod. 21:22–25 applies the principle of *lex talionis* to all harm inflicted "when men fight." In commenting on this passage, neither Rashi nor Ramban would apply *lex talionis* literally. Based on prior rabbinic authority, both consider the stated examples to require monetary compensation in an amount equal to the loss incurred.[35] Such a reading of the Torah may comfort our humane sensibilities. Yet the full text of Exod. 21:22–25 requires us to reject it.

Note that "when men fight" (as in 21:22–25), monetary damages are expressly required for miscarriages alone. Only in the other circumstances does *lex talionis* apply. Since it is clearly an alternative to monetary compensation, to regard *lex talionis* as monetary compensation is to rewrite the text. If equivalent monetary damages were intended for all injuries resulting from street brawls, why would the Torah not simply include them in the monetary remedy for miscarriages? Does respect for the compassion of latter-day interpreters justify rewriting the Torah?

But why does the Torah except only miscarriages from the rule of *lex talionis*? The question answers itself. A physical injury unique to a pregnant woman would preclude the imposition of *lex talionis* on an offending male.

But if *lex talionis* was thought necessary to deter riotous street brawls, why did it fall out of use? Perhaps because it soon proved impractical and thus unfair. As the means of equating the punishment with the injury, it was inherently flawed. Consider the legal impediments to Shylock's exacting his contractual pound of flesh from Antonio in Shakespeare's *The Merchant of Venice*. Whether under private contract or public law, the enforcement of the principle of parity would soon prove impossible. The precision needed for a parity between injury and punishment would exceed all human capabilities. In short, while *lex talionis* had to be repealed, it was initially viewed as a fitting standard of retribution.

Exod. 21:28–32 involves death or injuries caused by animals. It first deals with the "goring of a man *or a woman* to death" by an ox. To strike a suitable balance between the interest of animal owners and injured persons, the rule incorporates the concept of fault, or negligence. Thus, an owner who knew that his ox "was in the habit of goring," but who failed to "guard it," must be put to death, subject to the possiblity of a redemptive ransom" (21:29–30). Absent such knowledge, an owner "is not to be punished." The goring of minors was dealt with "according to the same rule" (21:31). Where another person's slave is gored to death by an ox, the ox's owner was required to pay "thirty shekels" to the slave's owner (21:32).

> Note E–31: *Where the owner of an ox that gores a person to death had been warned of its propensity to gore, the owner could be put to death. Such situations would not normally involve the owner's actual intent to kill, but rather his negligence in failing to guard against a known peril. Thus, the principle is established that some degree of negligence was treated as actual intent rather than as mere inadvertence tantamount to an innocent "act of God." Yet, though the death of the ox's owner was a possibility, given the literal absence of "actual" intent, his life could be redeemed by suitable "ransom" (or compensation).*
>
> *Note as well, however, that where the deceased victim of goring was a slave, the ox's owner was subject neither to death nor, alternatively, compensation not limited by prior rule. Left unanswered is whether the life of a slave was of lesser societal concern than other lives, or whether a slave's property loss to an owner, as such, was thought to be inherently less than the loss of a family member.*

Finally, whenever a goring resulted in death (including the death of a slave), the ox was to be "stoned."

> Note E–32: *The Torah does not explicitly require a wayward ox's death. In general, however, stoning served as a means of execution. (See, e.g., Lev. 20:2; Deut. 13:11, 17:5.)*

In prescribing remedies for lesser offenses involving injuries *to* animals by persons or other animals, Exod. 21:33–36 speaks to the economic importance of farm animals.

Exod. 21:37–22:16 deals with a broad range of abuses against property rights, beginning with the theft of livestock (21:37–22:3). The emphasis on restitution by the thief to the owner again establishes the predominantly civil nature of the proceeding. The ratios of restitution attest further to the importance of livestock in post-exodus Israel. Thus, for slaughtering or selling stolen animals, the thief must restore five oxen for an ox and four sheep for a sheep. In certain cases in which restitution is not made, the thief "shall be sold for his theft." Yet, the rule also barred the purely spiteful killing of a thief. A thief who entered premises furtively in a manner to frighten its occupants could be "beaten to death" without "bloodguilt." But "bloodguilt" for killing a thief could result, if the time or manner of his entry into the premises created no fear of physical threat in its occupants (22:1–2).

For certain impairments to agricultural produce not involving theft, restitution was required without regard to negligence. These offenses included the destruction of the crops or vineyards of others through the grazing of one's own animals or by the spreading of a fire (22:4–5).

Exod. 22:6–14 covers four types of disputes involving property owned by one person, but held by another as bailee, custodian or borrower. (1) Exod. 22:6–7 applies "when a man gives money or goods to another *for safekeeping* [*lishmor*], and they are stolen from the man's house." (2) Exod. 22:8 involves "charges of misappropriation" against a bailee or custodian, including misappropriation of "an ox, an ass, a sheep, a garment, or any other loss, whereof one party alleges 'this is it' " (i.e., presumably claims it as his own). (3) Exod. 22:9–12 applies to "when a man gives to another an ass, an ox, a sheep, or any other animal *to guard* [*lishmor*] and it dies or is injured or is carried off, with no witness about." (4) Exod. 22:13–14 involves the death or injury of an animal which one man borrows from another.

As for (1), in regard to "money or goods" stolen and not recovered, the custodian could be absolved by "deposing" his innocence "before God."

As for (2), in which an owner charges property misappropriation by a bailee or custodian, "the case of both parties shall come before God; *he whom God declares guilty shall pay double to the other*" (22:8).

As for (3), "restitution" is an absolute requirement only when the animal is "stolen" (22:11). Should the animal die or be injured or "carried off" (22:9–10), restitution could be avoided by the custodian's oath of personal innocence "before the Lord."

> Note E–33: *Rather than JPS2's reading of* nishbah *as "carried off," JPS1 and RSV read it as "driven away," thus distinguishing it from "but if it is stolen"* (v'im ganohv yiganayv; 22:11).

Where the animal was "torn by beasts," the "guardian" was held harmless by bringing the torn body as evidence.

As for (4), responsibility for the death or injury of a borrowed animal fell on the borrower if the animal was actually in his custody. But if its owner retained custody (perhaps because he had been "borrowed," or hired, along with the animal), restitution was not required.

Comment E–71. On interpreting the rules of bailments

In construing these rules, we must first take note of the different subjects of bailment in 22:6–7 and 22:9–12. The former covers bailments of "money or goods" while the latter covers those of animals. Rashi and Ramban consider the two categories to differ on the basis of "unpaid" and "paid" bailees.[36] Plaut agrees on grounds that mere custodial bailments of "money or goods" warrant no pay, while those for animals requiring active oversight do.[37]

Plaut's rationale reflects JPS2's use of "for safekeeping" (22:6) in regard to inanimate property and "to guard" (22:9) in regard to animals. However, JPS1 and RSV read *lishmor* in both 22:6 and 9 as a common obligation, "to keep." The text is less than clear, therefore, as to any different standards of care and liability that E may have meant to establish between animate and inanimate property.

The penalty for seducing a virgin centers largely on her father's property rights (22:15–16). If "a bride price has not [yet] been paid" the seducer must offer to marry the daughter and pay her father the bride price. Should the father forbid the marriage, the seducer "must still weigh out silver *in accordance with the bride price for virgins*."

Exod. 22:17–19 turns from property rights to three aspects of the Lord's sanctity. The first forbids "toleration" of a "sorceress" (22:17)

Note E–34: JPS1/RSV read loh t'chahyeh *to require her death.*

Exod. 22:18 decrees death for "Whoever lies with a beast" and 22:19, the same, for "whoever sacrifices to a god other than the Lord."

Comment E–72. On the rules against sorcery, bestiality, and sacrifices to "a god other than the Lord"

Contrary to the text, Rashi construes the *mishpat* on sorcery to require the death of both a sorcerer and a sorceress. He regards the use of "sorceress" as reflecting the predominance of female practitioners.[38] Sorcery, of course, invites recourse to "extra human" powers other than the Lord's.

In that bestiality involves a waste of seed, it is an aspect of the sin for which God killed Onan. As such, it demeans the sanctity of God's gift of reproduction (see Comment G–75 and Lev. 18:23).

The powerful thrust of P's Second Commandment against other gods "before" or "beside me" finds expression in E's ban on sacrifices to *any* other god(s) (22:19). (Whether such gods were thought to exist independently or in minds and spirits alone remains an open issue. See Comments E–34 and 55.) (JPS2 and RSV render the *elohim* of 22:19 as god, while JPS1, like Rashi, refers to gods. More usually, the singular use of *elohim* relates to the Torah's God of Israel.) Together, Exod. 20:20 and 22:19 might be read as E's earlier formulation of what later became the Second Commandment of both P and D (see E–87).

The *mishpatim* of Exod. 22:20–26 deal with three aspects of human compassion. Recalling that Israelites had been "strangers in the land of Egypt," the first concerns "a stranger." In admonitions to be repeated throughout the Torah, the first of these declares, "You shall not wrong a stranger or oppress him" (cf. Lev. 19:18 and Comments L–40 and 42). The second decrees that "you shall not ill-treat any orphan or widow." Only as to this *mishpat* does the Torah express the wrath of its God for its violation. His anger will "blaze forth" and the miscreant will be put to the sword. In consequence, his own "*wives* shall become widows" and his children "orphans" (22:23).

The third *mishpat* of this group comes into force: "*If* you lend money to My people, to the poor who is in your power." The lender is admonished: "Do not act toward him as a creditor; exact no interest from him" (22:24). When a "garment" is pledged by a "neighbor" who borrows, "you must return it to him before the sun sets, it is his only clothing, the sole covering for his skin. In what shall he sleep?" (22:25–26). The passage concludes with God's "warning" that if the borrower "cries out to Me, *I will pay heed*, for I am compassionate" (22:26).

Comment E–73. On the *mishpat* of lending

More explicitly than anything yet said, the *mishpatim* of 22:20–26 imputes human compassion to the Torah's God. However, one problem in the third *mishpat* is the intended scope of the ban on interest. ("If you lend money *to My people*, to the poor who are in your power, do not act toward him as a creditor; exact no interest from him" [22:24].) Does the *mishpat* assume that only the poor would borrow?

JPS1 puts the matter in these terms: "If thou lend money to *any* of My people, *even to the poor with thee*, thou shalt not be to him as a creditor; neither shall ye lay upon him interest" (22:24). Here the prohibition on interest applies to all loans to Israelites, including those to the poor. This may be meant to emphasize that the prohibition applies to all loans, whatever the risk of repayment.

RSV most clearly limits the interest prohibition of 22:24 to loans to poor Israelites. "If you lend money *to any of my people* with you *who is poor*, you shall not be to him as a creditor, and you shall not exact interest from him." Literally, then, RSV would allow interest on other loans to others than the poor—thus providing incentives for commercial loans.

Of all three translations, RSV best satisfies the social need for both "charitable" and commercial lending. As for the Torah's intent, however, a question remains.

The final *mishpatim* of Exod. 22 also look to God's sanctity (22:27–30). The first, however, is notable for its literal equation of divine and civil authority: "You shall not revile God, nor put a curse upon a chieftain of your people"

(22:27). The need then is to honor "Caesar" no less than God. (But what of the "chieftain" who deviates from God's commands? Must his removal "be left to heaven?")

Exod. 22:28–29 repeats the basic Torah obligation to "give" God the first fruits from the cycle of harvests and births (cf. Exod. 13:2). Although the manner of effecting such gifts is not explained here, the basic requirement is clear enough. Included are "the skimming of the first yield of your vats" and the "first-born among your sons [and] your cattle and your flocks."

As to the harvest, JPS2 limits the command to the "the first yield of your vats" (22:28). However, to the "outflow of your presses," JPS1 and RSV add the "fulness of your harvest" (from *m'layahtchah v'dimachah*). Whatever their fate on separation, firstborn animals must not be taken from their mothers for eight days (22:29).

The third and final *mishpat* of 22:27–30 prohibits the eating of flesh from animals that have been killed by other animals: "You shall be men holy to Me; you must not eat flesh torn by beasts in the field; you shall cast it to the dogs" (22:30).

> *Note E–35: The command anticipates later rules of Leviticus and Deuteronomy on the consumption of meat.*

Exod. 23:1–9 returns to societal concerns. First, every Israelite must treat every party to a dispute with objectivity and fairness (23:1–3). It is forbidden to "carry false rumors" and to conspire with the guilty to serve as a "malicious witness." It is equally prohibited to "side with the mighty to do wrong" and to "show deference to a poor man in his dispute."

> *Note E–36: Justice and compassion are thus viewed as two distinct qualities, each with its own purpose.*

Illustrative of the consideration owed to an "enemy" as well as a friend are the duties to return an "enemy's ox or ass wandering" and to help an "enemy" in raising an ass "lying under its burden" (23:4–5).

Exod. 23:6–8 requires honesty and objectivity in resolving disputes. Just as "you" must not show deference to poor man in his dispute (23:3), neither shall "you subvert the rights of your needy in their disputes." And just as false charges against the "innocent and righteous" are prohibited, so, too, are bribes, which "upset the pleas of the just." Exod. 23:9 invokes the quality of empathy to support the essence of 22:20: "You shall not oppress a stranger, for you know the feelings of a stranger, having yourselves been strangers in the land of Egypt."

The concluding *mishpatim* deal mainly with time cycles (23:10–19). The agricultural cycle of Exod. 23:10–11 follows the theme of the sabbath. In every seventh year, farm lands, including "vineyards and olive groves," must be allowed to "rest and lie fallow." Thereafter, the "needy," followed by the "wild beast," are to eat the gleanings of the harvest (cf. Lev. 25:2–7).

Except for the substitution of rest for the cycle of creation as its rationale, Exod. 23:12 repeats the substance of the Fourth Commandment: "Six days you shall do your work, but on the seventh day you shall cease from labor, *in order that* your ox and your ass may rest, and that your bondman and the stranger may be refreshed."

Exod. 23:13 warns Israelites to "be on guard concerning all that I have told you." Akin once more again to the Second Commandment, they must "make no mention of the names of other gods; they shall not be heard on your lips."

Exod. 23:14–17 prescribes three yearly festivals. The first echoes the Feast of Unleavened Bread, or the Passover, as decreed in Exod. 12:14–15, prior to the Tenth Plague and the departure from Egypt. Two new festivals are the Feast of the Harvest (or spring harvest, later *shavuot*) and the Feast of the Ingathering (or fall harvest, later *sukot*).

Exod. 23:18 deals with the sacrifice of the Passover lamb. (See Exod. 12:21–26.) It is followed by the final two *mishpatim* of 23:19. The first requires that the "choice first fruits of your soil you shall bring to the house of the Lord your God."

> Note E–37: As yet, *"the house of the Lord your God"* has not been identified.

The final *mishpat* of Exod. 23:19 marks the first appearance of the Torah's thrice-stated injunction, "You shall not boil a kid in its mother's milk."

Comment E–74. On the injunction of the final *mishpat* against boiling a kid in its mother's milk

For a discussion of this command as it relates to later Talmudic law, see my introduction (pp. 35–36). As the final *mishpat* in a group of cultic, or ritualistic commands, however, its initial appearance warrants a further comment.

As implied in the introduction, Maimonides surmised that the ban was likely directed against a Canaanite rite in the worship of Baal. The introduction also tells of a dramatic episode from the early prophets regarding the importation of Baal worship into Israel (p. 34). Whether as history or fiction, it speaks of the challenge posed by the widespread cult of Baal to the Lord's supremacy, as God of Israel. It provides support for the view that this thrice-stated *mishpat* was directed against a particular cultic rite of Baal.

With the revelations of the Ten Commandments and *mishpatim* completed, the Torah now turns to the fruits of obedience. The Lord, their God, tells the people of an angel He will send "to guard you on the way and to bring you to the place which I have made ready" (23:20). His "Name" (and thus His authority) will be in the angel (23:21). Offenses against it will not be pardoned. But, "*if* you obey [the angel] *and* do all that I say, I will be an enemy to your enemies and a foe to your foes" (23:22).

The Lord then adds specifics to his conditional promise (23:23). For obeying the angel and doing "all that I say," He will "annihilate" the six named tribes of Canaan—but only on condition that the Israelites not bow to "their gods" or follow "their practices." Instead, they must "tear them down and smash their pillars" (23:24).

In 23:25–26, after promising to bless their bread and water, He makes a further *conditional* commitment: "And I will remove sickness from your midst. No woman in your land shall miscarry or be barren. I will let you enjoy the full count of your days."

> Note E–38: *The condition thus transfers responsibility for the inevitable failure of the promise from the Torah's God to the people.*

In 23:27–28 the "Lord God" commits Himself to "send forth My terror before you." The enemy will be thrown into panic and will "turn tail before you." A plague will "drive out [the tribes] before you."

A description of the displacement process, as it would have been known to E, is reserved for 23:29–30. Because a land devoid of all humans will "become desolate and the wild beasts will multiply to your hurt," the Lord God will not "drive out" the enemy tribes in a "single year." Rather, He states, "I will drive them out . . . little by little until you have increased and possess the land."

> Note E–39: *The gradual displacement of Exod. 23:29–30 seemingly contradicts the prompt annihilation implied in 23:23 and 27–28.*

The Lord God will then set Israel's borders from "the Sea of Reeds to the Sea of Philistia, and from the wilderness to the Euphrates" (23:31).

> Note E–40: *As noted in Comment G–22, the United Monarchy under David did extend to a northern portion of the Euphrates. As for the "Sea of Philistia," see Comment G–49 and E–43.) The identity of the body of water known here and elsewhere as the "Sea of Reeds" is more of a puzzle. (See Exod. 13:18, 14:21–30, Comment E–45, and Note N–52.)*[39]

In Exod. 23:31 the Lord God modifies His intended division of labor between Him and the Israelites in driving out the inhabitants of Canaan: "I will deliver the inhabitants of the land into your power, and you will drive them out before you."

Note E–41: In 23:29–30 Lord God says "I will drive them out before you little by little." But in 23:31 Lord God says "you will drive them out," after He has delivered all the Canaanite tribes into their power.

The passage ends with yet another warning against the dangerous lure of the Canaanite gods: "You shall make no covenant with them and their gods" (23:32). To that end, the Canaanites must go. "They shall not remain in your land, lest they cause you to sin against Me; *for you will serve their gods* and it will prove a snare to you" (23:33).

On completing His homilies and instructions of 23:20–33, the Lord tells Moses: *"Come up to the Lord, with Aaron, Nadab and Abihu, and seventy elders of Israel, and bow low from afar. But only Moses shall come near the Lord. The others shall not come near; and the people shall not come up with him at all"* (24:1–2).

But first there is a covenantal ratification in which the people vow to accept what they had received. After Moses "repeated to the people all the *commands* of the Lord and all the *rules*," they shouted "with one voice, 'All the *things* that the Lord has commanded we will do' " (24:3). On hearing these avowals, Moses "wrote down all the *commands* of the Lord" (24:4a).

Note E–42: These avowals to obey the mishpatim *echo the similar avowals preceding the Lord's revelation of the Ten Commandments (Exod. 19:8).*

Comment E–75. On the *mishpatim* as "mutable" emanations from the "immutable" *devarim*

JPS1 and RSV leave no doubt that in 24:3–4 Moses writes down the Ten Commandments alone. Both read *kol divray yahweh* as "all the *words* of the Lord" and *kol hamishpatim* as "all the *ordinances*," thus distinguishing between the Ten Commandments (or the "words," as they are commonly termed) and the *mishpatim* (or "ordinances"). In 24:3, Moses "tells" the people "all the words of the Lord *and* all the ordinances." (The people had heard the "words" directly from the Lord, but only Moses had heard the *mishpatim*.) On their first having accepted them, Moses "wrote all the *words* of the Lord"—*but not the "ordinances," which the people had not yet accepted.*

Because of its varied translations of *kol divray yahweh*, JPS2 is less clear on what the people accepted and what Moses "wrote down" (24:3–4). Yet, though less directly, JPS2 can be read to the same effect as JPS1/RSV.

As stated in JPS2, in 24:3 Moses repeats "all the commands [*kol divray*] of the Lord and all of the rules [*kol hamishpatim*]" to the people. The people then answer "all the things [*kol divray*] that the Lord *has commanded* we will do." Thus, having first read *kol divray* in 24:3 as "all the commands," JPS2 then reads the same term in the same verse as "*all the things.*" (In a more traditional and literal mode, JPS2 renders the first *kol divray* of 20:1, which introduces the Ten Commandments, as "all these words.")

Yet, as for 24:3–4, a certain consistency can be found in these varied translations. First, in 24:3b the reference to "all the things" is modified by "that the Lord has commanded." In this way JPS2 would seem to equate "all the things" of 24:3b with "all the commands" of 24:3a. The result, of course, is to exclude the "rules" of 24:3a from the "things" of 24:3b. Then, quite consistently in 24:4, JPS2 observes that Moses "wrote all the *commands* of the Lord" (24:4). By omitting the "rules" (or *mishpatim*), JPS2 has Moses write down only what the people had thus far accepted—that is, the Ten Commandments.

On this central issue, therefore, JPS2 and JPS1/RSV can all be said to agree: The *mishpatim* were not included with the Ten Commandments in what Moses wrote down in 24:4.Does this mean that the *mishpatim* were not a part of the Sinaitic covenant between the people and their God (as it is referred to in Exod. 19:5)? As yet, of course, the Lord has not told Moses to write down anything. Why, then, does Moses write down the Ten Commandments, but not the *mishpatim*?

Recall that in identifying the *mishpatim* to Moses, the Lord states, "These are the rules which you *shall set before them*" (21:1). The question then is whether "shall set before them" (as it also appears in JPS1 and RSV) should be read as "shall write them down." Neither Rashi nor Ramban accept the possibility.[40] Rashi, however, does suggest a meaning for "shall set before them." He views it as a requirement that Moses, beyond merely acquainting the people with the words of the *mishpatim*, is "to make them understand the reasons of the thing and its explanation."[41] Thus, while "writing them down" might be useful, Rashi would allow Moses a measure of discretion in deciding how the *mishpatim* are to be "set before" the people.

But an even more basic question remains. Having heard both the *mishpatim* from Moses and the Ten Commandments from the Lord, why did the people explicitly accept only the latter? Here, a later comment by Rashi on 24:12 may be helpful. He observes: "All the six hundred and thirteen commandments are included in the Ten Commandments."[42]

Rashi thus views the *mishpatim*, and all other *mitzvot*, as derivatives from the fundamental moral and ethical dictates of Ten Commandments. In this he seems to be affirmed by the events of 24:3–4, in which the people's binding acceptance of what they have heard is limited to the Ten Commandments. Thus, through E at least, the Torah views the Ten Commandments as the eternal spiritual and ethical foundation of Israel's laws. *In turn, it is for mishpatim, and other mitzvot, to accomodate the basic principles of the Ten Commandments into the changing circumstances of human existence. As Israel evolves, Exod. 24:3–4 charges it to perpetuate the Ten Commandments by adapting them, through* mishpatim *and other* mitzvot, *to changing circumstances.*

Because the derivative *mishpatim* were not intended to be eternal, there was a need to distinguish them from the Ten Commandments. In 24:3–4 the people mark the distinction by symbolically accepting the Ten Commandments alone. In turn Moses writes down the Ten Commandments alone. (But then see Exod. 24:7 and Comment E–77.)

Comment E–76. On the location of Moses during the first revelation of the Ten Commandments and of the *mishpatim*

By the close of Exod. 23, the Lord God has revealed the Ten Commandments to the people and Moses and the *mishpatim* to Moses. A common vision of the revelation places Moses *on* Mount Sinai during the entire process. But quite to the contrary, immediately before the revelation of the Ten Commandments (20:1–14), Moses "went down to the people [then at the base of Sinai] and spoke to them" (19:25). On Lord God's instructions he had gone down in order to "come back together with Aaron" (the only person who was to return with him; 19:24). But in 20:1 (the next verse), before any reported ascension, "God spoke all these words."

The Ten Commandments are then followed by awesome signs of His presence in the thick cloud on the mountain. Moses then "approached" the cloud (20:18). (See text preceding Comment E–64.) At this point, with Moses merely having "approached" the cloud, the Lord begins to recite the *mishpatim* to Moses. Moses remains there until their completion (23:33–24:1). The Torah does not specify how close to the cloud Moses had "approached," nor does it say anything of Aaron's presence. All it says, or implies, is that Moses, being aware of God's presence, came closer.

In sum, as God revealed the Ten Commandments, Moses was at the foot of the mountain with the people. Then, while the people "remained at a distance, . . . Moses approached the thick cloud where God was." As the *mishpatim* are revealed, Moses stands alone, somewhere between the thick cloud covering Mount Sinai and the people at its foot (20:18).

Following Exod. 24:4a in which Moses wrote down the Ten Commandments, the rituals of covenantal ratification began "early in the morning" (24:4b–8). These included building an altar at the foot of the mountain with twelve pillars representing the tribes (24:4b); and burnt offerings and offerings of well-being (24:5–6). Then, in the words of JPS2, Moses "took the record of the covenant and read it aloud to the people (24:7). To this the people reply, "*All that the Lord has spoken* we will faithfully do." The pact was "sealed" by the dashing of blood, first "against the altar" and then "on the people" (24:8).

Comment E–77. On the "record of the covenant"

What JPS2 renders as "record of the covenant" (i.e., *sefer hahb'reet*) JPS1/RSV render more traditionally and literally, as "*book* of the covenant." In that following the reading, the people accept "all that the Lord *has spoken*" (in JPS2 and JPS1/RSV alike), it would seem that "the book," or "record," is meant to cover both the "words" (*kol divray*) and "ordinances" (*mishpatim*) of 24:3–4. Perhaps so. But why would Moses read anew "*all* that the Lord has spoken?" Why would the Torah refer to the Ten Commandments in such unfamiliar terms? And why did the people in 24:3 not initially accept "*all that the Lord has spoken?*"

In recent years, the "record of the covenant" has become widely identified as the "ordinances," or *mishpatim* of 21:1–23:19, to the exclusion of the Ten Commandments.[43] Plaut, however, considers its use in 24:7 as ambiguous. He surmises that it might be the "Decalogue" or the "Code of the Covenant (beginning in chapter 21)."[44]

From the total context of Exod. 24:1–8, I conclude that the "record [or book] of the covenant" is meant to contain "all that the Lord has spoken." It is what Moses reads in 24:7 and what the people accept. In this way the people now accept the *mishpatim*, in addition to their earlier acceptance of the Ten Commandments. The reason for the separate acceptances rests on the considerations discussed in Comment E–75—that is, the difference intended between eternal law and evolving interpretive ordinances. If so, why does Moses repeat, and why do the people again accept, the Ten Commandments along with the *mishpatim*? As the basis for their informed acceptance of the *mishpatim* as contemporary derivatives of the Ten Commandments, the people must have the Ten Commandments fresh in mind. (Still to be explained, however, is how the "ordinances" that Moses "read" in 24:7 ever came to be "written" in the "record of the covenant." He himself is reported to have written down only the "words," or Ten Commandments (see Exod. 24:4 and Comment E–75.) Thus Plaut has good reason to suggest alternatives.[45]

On completing the ratification rituals of 24:4b–8, Moses turns to the Lord's instructions of 24:1–2 (24:9). Together with "Aaron, Nadab and Abihu, and seventy elders of Israel," Moses ascends to where "they *saw* the God of Israel" (24:9). "*Yet* He did not raise His hand against the leaders of the Israelites; *they beheld* God, and they ate and drank" (24:10–11).

Comment E–78. On beholding and eating and drinking with "the God of Israel"

That E's God permits Himself to be seen contradicts a major theme of the Torah that portrays Him as impervious to human senses. As to be expected, therefore, both Rashi and Ramban comment on 24:10–11. Indeed, it is to this event that Rashi attributes the sudden death of Aaron's sons, Nadab and Abihu, and the death of others in "a fire of the Lord" (see Lev. 10:1–2, Num. 11:1–3).[46] Ramban regards their "sight" of God to have been a mere "vision" within their minds.[47]

Nevertheless, the several "sources" of the Torah differ on the inevitability of an early death in consequence of seeing God (see Comment E–50 and Exod. 33:7–11; see also Comments E–91 and 92). Indeed, we have noted J's preference to leave the choice of being seen, or not, in the Lord's hands. And Exod. 24:1–15a suggests the same of E.

More diffiult to to reconcile is the variance between 24:2 and 24:10–11. In 24:2 God commands that "only Moses shall come near the Lord," while "the others shall not." Apart from their "seeing" God, even the nearness of the others to Him would be an act of disobedience. (On the possible sources of Exod. 24, see Note E–43.)

As noted, in 24:9–11 the entire party, including Nadab and Abihu, had already "ascended" the mountain to where they saw "God." In apparent communion, they "ate and drank" with Him to mark the covenantal ratification. But in 24:12, the "ascension" seems to start anew when "the Lord" tells Moses: "Come up to Me on the mountain and wait there, and *I will give you the stone tablets with the teachings and [the] commandment[s] which I have inscribed to instruct them.*" Thereupon, "Moses and his attendant Joshua arose, and Moses ascended the mountain of God." But before leaving he instructs "the elders." "Wait for us here until we return to you. You have Aaron and Hur with you; let anyone who has a legal matter approach them" (24:13–14).

> *Note E–43: Gone are Nadab and Abihu (24:9–11). Present instead are Joshua (24:13) and Hur (24:14). Friedman ascribes 24:1–15a to E. If so, the change in Moses' retinue and his further ascension from a meal with "God" to "the Lord . . . on the mountain" needs explaining. Note, too, that Moses tells the elders and Aaron and Hur to wait "here," that is, at the site on the mountain side to which they had ascended from the foot of the mountain (cf. 24:14, 9). (If 24:14 is by E, then Aaron's presence among the people at the mountain base in E's tale of the golden calf (Exod. 32) raises a question. Was it E or R who caused Aaron to descend prematurely from the mountain side to its base?*

Comment E–79. On the revelation of Exod. 24:12

As reflected in Ramban's commentary (see introduction, pp. xx), Exod. 24:12 is the verse most closely identified with the revelation of the "whole Torah" on Sinai. As also discussed, its text (i.e., *et luchot ha'evehn v'hatorah* v'hamitzvah) is less than clear because of the possible meanings of *hatorah* as "law" or "teaching."

In fact, in this second Sinaitic theophany, Moses will receive nothing in writing other than the "stone tablets," symbolizing the Ten Commandments. Nor are there suggestions of other oral revelations. Rashi, as noted, surmounts this strict limitation with his view that "all the six hundred and thirteen commandments are included in the Ten Commandments" (see Comment E–75).[48] In any case, as will become evident, by the close of this second Sinaitic revelation (Exod. 24:15–31:18), the "stone tablets" are the only "writings" that Moses will have received.

Meanwhile, the "ascension" continues. "*When Moses had ascended the mountain* [24:15a], the cloud covered the mountain" (24:15b). "The Presence of the Lord abode on *Mount Sinai*, and the cloud hid it for six days" (24:16). On the seventh day He called to Moses from the cloud (24:16). To the Israelites below, the Lord's Presence appeared "as a consuming fire on top of the mountain" (24:17). "*Moses went inside the cloud and ascended the mountain; and Moses remained on the mountain for forty days and forty nights*" (24:18). Thus, in 24:15b–18 the stage is set for P's version of Moses' second Sinaitic encounter with the Lord.

Comment E–80. On Moses and the mountain—a reprise

On the whereabouts of Moses vis-à-vis the mountain during the revelations of (1) the Ten Commandments and (2) the *mishpatim*, see Comment E–76. As of 24:1, Moses had received both (20:1–18, 21:1–23:19). In 24:1 the Lord had directed Moses to "Come up" to him with Aaron and the elders. Following the ratification rites of 24:3–8, Moses and the others ascend the mountain (24:9) to where they "beheld God, and ate and drank" (24:10–11). After beholding "God," Moses ascends to "the Lord," first in 24:15–16, in which he remains outside the cloud that "covered the mountain." In 24:18 he ascends further "inside the cloud" to a point "on the mountain" where he remained "forty days and forty nights." At the close of this period, the Lord will give Moses "the two tablets of the Pact, stone tablets inscribed with the finger of God" (31:18). (See Comment E–79.)

During the period of "forty days and forty nights," as described in Exod. 25:1 through 31:18, the Lord will also give Moses the most meticulous instructions on the building of a dwelling place for Him amidst the Israelites. It is to be a constant reminder of His Presence and His Being (29:45–46). And so His instructions to Moses begin.

Tell the Israelite people to bring Me gifts; *you shall accept gifts for Me from every person whose heart so moves him*. And these are the gifts that you shall accept from them: gold, silver and copper; blue, purple and crimson yarns, fine linen, goat's hair; tanned ram skins, dolphin skins and acacia wood; oil for lighting; spices for the anointing oil and for the aromatic incense; lapis lazuli and other stones for setting, for the ephod and for the breastpiece. *And let them make Me a sanctuary that I may dwell among them.* Exactly as I show you—the pattern of the Tabernacle and the pattern of all its furnishings—so shall you make it (25:2–9).

> *Note E–44: P's impeccable logic requires the Lord's dwelling place to be fashioned only from voluntary contributions. How could the Israelites deserve His Presence if they had not willingly met His needs?*

His instructions covering His dwelling place include the following elements: (1) the Ark of the Pact (also the Ark of the Testimony), including the two golden Cherubim who are to shield its cover (25:10–22); (2) the Table for the Bread of Display (25:23–30); (3) the Lampstand (i.e., Menorah) and Lamps (25:31–40); (4) the Tabernacle, 26:1–36 (also known as the "Tent of Meeting"; see, e.g., 30:36, 31:7, 39:40); (5) the Altar for offerings (27:1–8); (6) the Enclosure of the Tabernacle (27:9–19); (7) Instructions for Lighting the Lamps (27:20–21); (8) Priestly Vestments (28:1–43); (9) Priestly Investiture Rites (29:1–37); (10) Designated Offerings (for the "Main" Altar) (29:38–46); (11) Separate Altar for Burning Incense (30:1–10); (12) Census Expiation Payments (30:11–16); (13) Copper Laver (31:17–21); (14) Anointing Oil (30:22–33); (15) Incense (30:34–38); (16) Designation of Craftsmen (31:1–11).

> *Note E–45: The relevance of the census expiation payments at this point (see 12) derives from the intended use of its proceeds for "the service of the Tent of Meeting" (30:11–16). The payment consisted of "a half-shekel" by those of the age of "twenty years up" who are "entered in the records" of a census "of the Israelite people." "Rich" and "poor" alike are to pay the same amount "as expiation for your persons." That each person paid the same amount regardless of ability to pay presumably symbolized the equality of each person before God. The half-shekel was to be measured "by the sanctuary weight—twenty gerahs to the shekel." (Were such "sanctuary weights" known to the Israelites on leaving Egypt? Or were they more likely found, or developed, in Canaan?[49])*

The principal components of the Tabernacle and their contents are summarized in a passage described by the Lord as "everything I have commanded you."

The Tent of Meeting [i.e., the Tabernacle], the Ark for the Pact [or the Ark of Testimony], and the cover upon it, and all the furnishings of the Tent; the table and its utensils; the pure lampstand and all its fittings, and the altar of incense; the altar of burnt offering and all its utensils, and the laver and its stand; the service vestments, the sacral vestments of Aaron the priest and the vestments of his sons, for their service as priests; as well as the anointing oil and the aromatic incense for the sanctuary. (31:6–11)

On completing His specifications, the Lord identifies the sabbath "as a sign between Me and you throughout the ages." In effect, P repeats the substance of the Fourth Commandment (20:8–11), including its sabbath rationale—that is, the cycle of creation. (31:12–17; cf. Comment E–57 and E's sabbath *mishpat* of 23:12). But now punishments are prescribed for sabbath violations: "You shall keep the sabbath, for it is holy for you. *He who profanes it shall be put to death: whoever does work on it, that person shall be cut off from among his kin*" (31:14). Exod. 31:15 repeats the death penalty, but now applies it to "whoever does work on the sabbath day. . . ." This will be a "covenant for all time."

Comment E–81. On the sabbatical punishments, including a further insight into being "cut off from his kin"

In Exod. 31:14 the punishment *for sabbath work* is that a person "shall be cut off from among his kin." In 31:15 it is that a person "shall be put to death." If the punishment for sabbath work can be stated categorically in either form, then death and being "cut off" are either the same punishments; or minimally, being "cut off" includes the possibility of death (see Comments G–25 and E–35).

Exod. 31:14 also prescribes death for "profaning" the sabbath. The passage, however, says nothing of whether, or how, the sabbath might be profaned other than by work.

Comment E–82. On the feasibility of the Tabernacle

The Israelites left Egypt in great haste. In the wilderness they have wanted for food and water. They must look to the Lord for daily manna. From where would come the stunning variety of exotic materials needed for the Tabernacle and its contents? We do know of their having "borrowed . . . objects of silver and gold, and clothing" from the Egyptians (12:35). But the Torah speaks of no other largesse, as would be needed in the Tabernacle. Perhaps gold, silver, and clothing were meant as metaphors for a far wider range of wealth and valuables. But did the modest workaday Egyptian neighbors of the Israelites "just happen to have" all of the necessary materials? And if they did, how would the Israelites have known what would be needed? And if they had such prescience, in their final sudden haste to leave, how would they have found time to collect it all?

No summary can adequately describe the Tabernacle and its contents. Only a full direct reading can impart a sense of the rich exotica of its ingredients and the precision and complexity of its design. In sum, however, they would surely preclude the feasibility of the entire undertaking.

When P wrote of these events centuries later, however, such materials may have moved freely among the trading communities of the Near East. Also, more readily available were the skilled crafts and craftsmen required to meet the needs of the Tabernacle, its contents, and the priestly paraphenalia. In all, sufficient materials and craftsmen likely existed in c. 700–500 B.C.E. to enable a portion of them to be transported through P's imagination back to c. 1300 B.C.E.

The rich decor of the Tabernacle and the complexity of its rituals underscored a need for priests on whom the Lord could rely to maintain its sanctity. It is here, therefore, that P first speaks of the Lord's ordination of a hereditary line of Aaronide priests. He thus instructs Moses: "You shall bring forward your brother Aaron, with his sons, from among the Israelites, to serve Me as priests: Aaron, Nadab and Abihu, Eleazar and Ithamar, the sons of Aaron" (28:1).

Their exalted stature is symbolized in the design of their priestly attire, which, in the Lord's words, would serve as "sacral vestments . . . for Aaron and his brothers, for priestly service to Me" (28:4). Again, the ornamental richness of the components, which included "a breastpiece, an ephod, a robe, a fringed tunic, a headdress, and a sash" (28:4) can be fully "appreciated" only in a direct reading (28:4–40). Included also were the Urim and Thummim. These "symbols of special access to God's will" were to be placed in Aaron's "breastplate of decision over his heart" (28:30).[50] After placing the vestments on Aaron and his sons, Moses was to "anoint them, and ordain them and consecrate them to serve [the Lord] as priests" (28:41).

Amid this splendor, Aaron and his sons are charged as well to wear "linen breeches to cover their nakedness." These must extend "from the hips to the thighs." They are to be worn "when they enter the Tent of Meeting or when they approach the altar to officiate in the sanctuary, *so that they do not incur punishment and die*" (28:42–43).

> Note E–46: *In less threatening terms, E's Lord had earlier admonished the Israelites, when engaged in non-Tabernacle worship, against exposing their nakedness in ascending earthern altars "by steps" (20:20–23).*

Comment E–83. On the Tabernacle and the Aaronide priesthood

As noted, the consecration and ordination rites in the Tabernacle were meant to confirm the unique hereditary status of the Aaronide priesthood. In the words of the Lord, they will establish "priesthood as their right for all time" (29:9). (For related rituals, including anointment rites, sacrificial slaughters, and dissections and the attendant ubiquity of blood, see Exod. 29:1–46.)

This portrayal of the Tabernacle's origins might be explained by what is broadly surmised as the priestly politics of c. 600–450 B.C.E. In essence, the

Zadokites, also descended from a Levite branch, had prevailed as priests of the First Temple since the time of David. It would appear that sometime during the sixth century B.C.E. the Aaronides successfully challenged Zadokite claims to the Temple priesthood. Scholars differ as to whether these Aaronide claims were preexilic, relating in part to the First Jerusalem Temple, or postexilic, relating entirely to the Second Temple. (The Babylonian exile began in 587 B.C.E. and formally ended in 538.) In either case, P likely sought to strengthen the Aaronide claims by building on earlier lore regarding the Lord's abode, as Israel's God, in a simpler, but portable, wilderness "Tabernacle." This can also explain how the instructions of P's Lord regarding the Ark, the Tabernacle, and the consecration of the priestly line of Aaron came to dominate Moses' forty days and nights on Mount Sinai.[51]

But of what value was the priestly monopoly in the Jerusalem Temple that P sought to gain for the Aaronide priesthood through the earlier Tabernacle? In theory, as the situs of the ancient Ark of the Tabernacle, the Jerusalem Temple was viewed as the successor to the Tabernacle. In the words of P's Lord, therefore, it, too, like the original Tabernacle, " shall be sanctified by My Presence." It is there, He says, that "I will abide among the Israelites, and I will be their God. And they will know that I the Lord am their God, who brought them out of the land of Egypt *that I might abide among them, I the Lord their God*" (29:45–46).

Comment E–84. On the Lord's inability to abide as God among the Israelites in Egypt—a brief digression

The Lord's resolve to abide with the people in the Tabernacle raises a question. Was His failure to abide with them during their four hundred years of travail in Egypt attributable to Him or them?

Here we might recall the story of the wise Rabbi of Kotzk, as retold by Martin Buber in his Ten Rungs. When visiting scholars ask him, "Where does God abide?" the Rabbi dismisses their vision of a "whole universe filled with His Glory." Instead, he replies, "God dwells wherever He is allowed to enter." Would the Rabbi thus read the Lord's words of Exod. 29:45–46 as an acknowledgment that His presence anywhere (or that of any god) is contingent on a receptive human spirit? (Cf. Comment E–34.) If so, would the Rabbi regard such a spirit as merely a "necessary" condition for His presence that carried no guarantee, or as a "sufficient" condition in itself?

Comment E–85. On the Tabernacle and the "finger" of God as accomodations to the Second Commandment

We read in 31:18 that at the close of the forty days, "when He finished speaking with him on Mount Sinai," the Lord gave Moses "the two tablets of the Pact, stone tablets *inscribed with the finger of God*." Why would P so personify its God other than to foster a sense of His reality? Does a finger not imply a hand, and a hand an arm, and an arm a body?

The point can be made, of course, that the "finger of God" is simply a metaphor for the "miraculous" powers that the Torah attributes to Him. But for this it would suffice to say that "God caused the tablets to be inscribed with His words." It is likely, however, that the Israelites were no more prepared than their neighbors to place their destiny in the "hands" of an incorporeal Essence. (On the Lord's physical appearance see Comments G–29 and E–50, 53, and 78.)

Meanwhile, at the base of Sinai, a fear of abandonment infects the people who await the return of Moses from his prolonged absence. And in many of them, fear gives way to despair and anger. Amidst this emotional turmoil, they "gathered *against* Aaron" and implored him as follows: "Come make us *a god* [or "gods," from *elohim*] who shall go before us, for *that man* Moses, who brought us from the land of Egypt—we do not know what has happened to him" (32:1).

Aaron then tells "them" (i.e., the men) to take "the gold rings that are on the ears of your wives, your sons, and your daughters, and bring them to me" (32:2). In response, "*all the people* took off the gold rings that were in their ears and brought them to Aaron" (32:3). "This he took from them and cast in a mold and made it into a molten calf" (32:4). On seeing it the people cried out, "This is *your god*, O Israel, who brought you out of the land of Egypt!" (32:4). "When Aaron saw this, he built an altar before it," and announced, " 'Tomorrow shall be a festival of *the* Lord (i.e., *yahweh*)' " (32:5). The next day, "the people offered burnt offerings and brought sacrifices of well-being." Then they ate, drank, and danced (32:6).

> *Note E–47: RSV states, "These are your gods." Perhaps with the thought that one calf better represents one god, JPS1 and 2 read the plural* ayleh elo-hehchah *as "This is your god."*[52] *In fact, the singular form better suits the logic of the story.*
>
> *From E's perspective, as the author of the earlier related verses of Exod. 20:20 and 22:19, apostasy does not hinge on a "god" or "gods," but on whether the molten images of Exod. 20:20 and the object of sacrifices in 22:19 are of a god "other than the Lord" (see Comments E–72 and 87). (For good reason, Friedman attributes Exod. 32:1–33:6, the full episode of the golden calf, to E, together with Exod. 20:20 and 22:19.)*

Having observed the events of Exod. 32:1–6, an irate Lord tells Moses that the peoples "made themselves a molten calf and bowed low to it and sacrificed to it" (32:7–8). (But of Aaron's having declared a "festival to the Lord" in which he made the prescribed burnt offerings and sacrifices of well-being, the Lord says nothing; 32:5–6). He then tells Moses, "Hurry down, for *your* people, whom *you* brought out of the land of Egypt have acted basely."

Note E–48: In effect, the Lord disavows His role in bringing Israel from Egypt and commits the people to Moses.

As he had with Noah in regard to all humanity, the Lord plans to start anew with Moses in regard to Israel. Thus, He says to Moses, "I see that this is a stiff-necked people. *Now let Me be,* that My anger may blaze forth against them and *that I may destroy them, and make of you a great nation*" (32:9–10).

Note E–49: By "Now let Me be," God warns Moses against any "Abra-hamic" plea for the innocent.

Comment E–86. On the psychological setting of Exod. 32

It was in the presence of Moses that the people had heard the Lord's Ten Commandments and it was through Moses they had learned of His *mish-patim*. In a spate of emotion they had eagerly accepted both; they further affirmed their mutual covenant with "burnt offerings" and "sacrifices of well-being" (see 24:3–8). But now, without the presence of their one link to the Lord, the peoples' hopes erode.

On the mountainside the Lord had told Moses alone why he was to "come up on the mountain" (24:12). In turn, as he departed from Aaron and the elders on the mountainside, Moses said nothing to them of his destina-tion or mission. They were simply told to wait there, and for Aaron and Hur to deal with any disputes that the people might bring up to them. Nor had anything been said to them previously, as they "ate and drank" with the "God of Israel" (24:10–11).

On departing with Joshua, Moses did not yet know that he would remain on the mountain for "forty days and forty nights" (24:18), or that he would first wait outside the cloud for seven days until he was summoned by the Lord (24:16). Although the "Presence of the Lord" appeared to the people as a "consuming fire" (24:17), they knew nothing of His purpose. And because the people did not know why Moses had left them or when he might return, many took his prolonged absence as a sign of abandonment—both by him and the Lord, their God.

Comment E–87. On Aaron, the people, and the golden calf

Apart from all other considerations, the logic of the episode of the golden calf affirms Friedman's judgment in ascribing it to E. Of special significance in judging the relationship of Aaron and the people to the golden calf is the fact that E wrote well in advance of P or D. In particular, there is strong evi-dence that E's version of the Second Commandment, unlike its final formula-tion by P and D, did not prohibit the worship of images of *Israel's God*. Also, because of earlier authorship, E knew nothing of P's later ordination of Aaron and his line as priests of the Tabernacle (and of the Jerusalem Temple as its successor). *Therefore, in writing of the golden calf, E had no reason to denigrate Aaron as a rival to the northern priests.*

First, as recorded by P and D at least a century after E, the Second Commandment prohibits a "sculptured image, or any likeness of what is in the heavens above, or on the earth below, or in the waters under the earth"— *including any image of yahweh.* While he attributes the formal codified texts of the Ten Commandments to P and D (Exod. 20:1–14, Deut. 5:6–18), Friedman also suggests that an earlier "original text . . . appears to have been a part of E originally."[53]

Elements of E's Second Commandment appear in Exod. 20:20 and 22:19: "With Me, therefore, you shall not make any gods of silver, nor shall you make for yourselves any gods of gold" (20:20), and "whoever sacrifices to a god other than the Lord shall be proscribed [or destroyed]" (22:19).

As to 20:20, JPS1, 2, and RSV all refer to the silver and gold images of the "gods" as just that—that is, of gods and not *the elohim* of the Torah. (The Hebrew phrases are *elohay chesef* and *elohay zahav.*) But should the gloss of P and D's Second Commandment impart a sense of ambiguity to 20:20, consider the following translation, as used by Rabbi Hertz with his well-known Orthodox commentaries: "Ye shall not make *other* gods with me; gods of silver, or gods of gold, ye shall not make unto you."[54]

In effect, just as E in 22:19 prohibits sacrifices only to "other gods," so, too, in 20:20 did E mean to limit the use of silver and gold images or idols to those of "other gods." But why does E stand apart from all other sources by impliedly tolerating the creation of images or idols in connection with the worship of Elohim, the God of the North?

As dramatically revealed in Exod. 20:21–22, E supported the independence of the northern priests, in opposition to the centralization of ritual in Jerusalem (see text preceding Comment E–65). Indeed, the doctrinal differences between north and south were such that Jeroboam, the first king of the northern Kingdom of Israel (c. 922–901), felt free to worship Israel's God, as "embodied" in his golden calves at Bethel and Dan. As stated in *The Anchor Bible Dictionary,* "The calf images thus served as the N[orthern] counterpart of the cherubim and Ark iconography in Solomon's Temple."[55]

Writing later, the author of 1 Kings viewed this use of the golden calves as a "sin" (see 1 Kings 12:28–30). Regarding 1 and 2 Kings, however, the *Encyclopedia Brittanica* states that "all of the kings of the northern kingdom are presented in a bad light because they did not recognize the exclusive legitimacy of the cult in Jerusalem."[56] As a supportive compatriot of the Northern Kingdom, would E not have wished to legitimize its distinctive cultic practices? And if only in retrospect, would E not have wished to vindicate Jeroboam's two calves?

E was able to accomplish all this through Aaron's resourceful use of the golden calf *to represent Israel's God* (who E as well now identifies as *yahweh*). *Within the strictures of E's Second Commandment,* Aaron could in good conscience proclaim "a festival of the Lord." And so great was their joy in once again sensing the reality of their God through the golden calf that the many who worshipped Him "ate, drank and danced." (Rather than "danced," JPS1 and RSV render *vahyahkumoo l'tzahchayk,* respectively, as "rose to make merry" and "rose up to play" (32:6). Yet, in his efforts to revive the peoples' morale, Aaron had no choice but to accept the risk that many of them would indeed worship the calf as an image of other gods. *It thus became E's task to limit the Lord's wrath to them alone* (32:7–10).

Although the Lord had evinced no special anger toward Aaron, Moses, being unaware of Aaron's dilemma, will later ask, "What did the people do to you that you have brought such sin on them?" (32:21). To this, a troubled Aaron, having been well aware of possible sin in the circumstances (32:22–23), offered an inartful reply: "I said to them, 'Whoever has gold, take it off!' They gave it to me and I hurled it into the fire and out came this calf" (32:24).

Now faced with the Lord's wrath against the entire people, Moses, like Abraham, pleads for restraint. He implores the Lord, "Let not Your anger . . . blaze forth against Your people" (32:11). In supporting his plea with two arguments, Moses directs them both to the Lord's pride. First, the Egyptians will say that "it was with evil intent that He delivered them, only to kill them off in the mountains and annihilate them from the face of the earth" (32:12). Second, by destroying the Israelites, the Lord will break His promises to Abraham, Isaac and Jacob: "I will give to your offspring this whole land of which I spoke, to possess forever" (32:13). And so "the Lord renounced the punishment He had planned to bring upon His people" (32:14).

Comment E–88. On the rhetoric of Moses' appeal that the Lord not destroy Israel

Moses was able to persuade the Lord that His obliteration of Israel would only be evidence of impotence rather than power. Laid bare would be (1) the Lord's failure, having delivered Israel from bondage in Egypt, to gain its fidelity, and (2) His ultimate failure to guide Abraham's descendants to the destiny He had planned.

Less successful, however, was Moses' appeal to the Lord's self-image of His integrity and honor, based on His promise to Abraham and his descendants. The Lord feels no reflection on His honor in revoking His covenant with all Israel because of the egregious sins of some of them. In what we have read and will read in the Torah, its God is impelled by an ethic of Israel's collective responsibility for the sins of some (see, e.g., Comment L–59). In this case some number, as yet not identified, had sinned egregiously against the Lord by worshipping the golden calf not as an embodiment of Him, but of other gods. For this, in His initial wrath, the Lord was quite ready to obliterate all Israel. It was not from a sense of justice that He would now desist, but from the force of Moses' argument as to how He would look to others.

As Moses descends the mountain "bearing the two tablets of the Pact," Joshua, who is now with him, hears the "boisterousness" of the peoples' singing (32:15–18). On witnessing "the calf and the dancing," Moses himself became so "enraged" that "he hurled the tablets from his hands and shattered them at the foot of the mountain." He then "burned" the calf, ground it to powder, strewed it on the water, "and so made the people drink of it" (32:19–20). After reproaching Aaron, Moses then fears that the people had become "a menace to anyone who might oppose them" (32:25).

> Note E–50: Moses' initial confrontation with Aaron and Aaron's disingenuous explanation (32:21–24) are included in Comment E–87.

Moses now calls out, "Whoever is for the Lord come here." At once "all the Levites rallied to him" (32:25–26). Under the authority he claims from "the Lord, the God of Israel," Moses directs the Levites to "go back and forth from gate to gate *throughout the camp*, and slay brother, neighbor and kin" (32:27).

> Note E–51: On viewing the "scene of the crime" from closer quarters, Moses is overwhelmed with the same passionate anger that had first afflicted the Lord. Thus, his explicit instructions to the Levites make no distinction between the truly guilty worshippers of other gods and the well-intended worshippers of yahweh (but see Comment E–89).

At the hands of the Levites, however, the modest amount of "some three thousand . . . fell that day" (32:28). For their having avenged the Lord, Moses directs the Levites to prepare themselves to receive His blessing "for each of you has been against son and brother" (32:29).

Comment E–89. On the Levites as avengers of the Lord in the slaying of three thousand Israelites

When Moses calls out, "Whoever is for the Lord come here," it is "all the Levites," and *only* the Levites, who respond. Despite the unlimited sweep of Moses' directive (32:27), the resulting mayhem proves modest indeed. In all, they slay only three thousand men (of the more than six hundred thousand *adult males* who recently left Egypt)! (See Exod. 12:37 and Comment E–39.)

Consider as well that "*all* the people" had brought their gold jewelry to Aaron (32:3) and that, without any stated exception, "they" joined in the ritual worship of the the golden calf—*whatever each Israelite might have thought it to represent* (32:4–6).

Because "all the people" were participants, so, too, were the Levites among them. And yet they answered Moses' call. And having done so, among "all the people," *they slayed only three thousand.*

Why did they spare the greater multitude of Israelites? And why were they, themselves, guiltless? The logic of the story admits only one answer: *From E's apparent perspective, the Levites killed only those whom they thought had used the golden calf as the means of worshipping other gods.* But why? Clearly, for the same reason that the Lord had not condemned Aaron. Only those who envisioned and worshipped the golden calf as an idol of "other gods" had violated the Second Commandment, *as E knew it* (see Comment E–87). Conversely, those who viewed and worshipped the golden calf as an image of *yahweh* had not violated the Second Commandment, *as E knew it.*

This is not a story by P or D, or even J. It is by E. And as such, it must be judged by E's standards of piety and apostasy. If the story defies "logic," it is because of E's unique view of the Second Commandment. But it is this very view that resolves the anomalies of the story in regard to guilt or innocence in the worship of the golden calf. To worship it as an image of "other gods" was a sin. To worship it as an image of *yahweh* was a pious act.

The next day, following the slaying of only three thousand Israelites by the Levites, Moses tells the great preponderance who still live that they, too, "have been guilty of a great sin." Nevertheless, he again invokes the Lord's forgiveness. Moses first concedes that "this people is guilty of a great sin in making for themselves *gods of gold*" (32:31). To add substance to his plea for the people to be spared, Moses then makes a plea for himself: If the Lord will not "forgive their sin," then may He "erase me from the record which [He has] written"(32:32).

> Note E–52: *What was the sin of those not already slain? It was that they had encouraged the creation of the golden calf in an emotional climate that could lead many others to profane it, and themselves, in the worship of other gods.*

In the end, the Lord tells Moses to continue to lead His people toward their covenantal destiny—but not without a final reckoning. And so He declares, " 'He who has sinned against Me, him only will I erase from my record. Go now, lead the people where I told you. See, My angel will go before you. But when I make an accounting, I will bring them to account for their sins.' Then the Lord sent a plague upon the people, for *what they did with the calf* that Aaron made" (32:33–35).

Comment E–90. On the enigma of Exod. 32:33–35

Rashi's comment on 32:35 says nothing of "why" the Lord smote the people, but only "how" (i.e., "death at the hands of Heaven"). He attempts no reconciliation between 32:35 and 32:33–34.[57]

Ramban, however, offers two reasons why the great body of Israelites were not slain.[58] The first is that despite the Lord's intent to defer any punishment of the guilty, "He wanted to take away from them part of the great sin, in order that they should be worthy [to go up to the land]." As another possibility, Ramban observes: "Or it may be that He had decreed the plague upon them [before Moses' prayer] and the plague had already begun." More important, however, he accepts the need to reconcile the limited impact of the Lord's plague.

Although Ramban's first interpretation comes closest to the mark, it also misses the internal logic of the story. E means to portray the Lord's sudden plague as the prompt fulfillment of His promised accounting. On hearing Moses' final plea, the Lord (to avoid losing him) feels compelled to apply Abraham's principle of individual justice: "He who has sinned against Me, him only will I erase from my record" (32:33). The Levites, limited by less than divine knowledge, had identified only three thousand Israelites who had used the golden calf to worship other gods. In that the Lord's omniscience included human motives, only He could identify every sinner the Levites had missed. They, then, were punished through His plague.

Epilogue for Aaron and the Golden Calf

The foregoing interpretation of the high drama of Aaron and the golden calf runs counter to any traditional reading of the Second Commandment. But given the centrality of the Second Commandment to the relationship between Israel and its God, what else can account for the traditionally defined sins of so many and the punishment of so few? *In the circumstances, Aaron had enabled the great majority to adhere to the First Commandment at the cost of enabling a guilty minority to violate the Second Commandment.*

The Lord now tells Moses to set out for the land "which I swore to [to the offspring of] Abraham, Isaac and Jacob . . . a land flowing with milk and honey" (33:1–3). The Lord promises to "send an angel before you" and "to drive out [the six named tribes of Canaan]." But because they have themselves to be a "stiff-necked people," the Lord adds these words: *"But I will not go in your midst . . . lest I destroy you on the way"* (33:2–3).

> *Note E–53: Following P's Exod. 25–31, the Lord's refusal to join the Israelites enroute to Canaan would eliminate the very purpose of the portable*

Ark and Tabernacle. In His own words, it was to serve as "a sanctuary that I may dwell among them" (25:8). Thus, His avowal not to "go in your midst" (33:2–3) must be the work of E or J. As E's apparent denouement to the golden calf story, it might hint of the Lord's chagrin in having forgone the ethic of collective punishment.

On hearing the Lord's "harsh word," the people "went into mourning, and *none put on his finery*" (33:4). Through Moses, the Lord responds to their mourning, first by amending his "harsh word" of 33:2–3: " 'You are a stiffnecked people. If I were to go in your midst for one moment, I would destroy you. Now then, leave off your finery, and I will consider what to do to you.' So the people remained stripped of their finery from Mount Horeb on" (33:5–6).

The serenity of what follows speaks of a reconciliation between the people and the Lord, their God (33:7–11).

"Now Moses would take the Tent and pitch it outside the camp, at some distance from the camp. It was called the Tent of Meeting, and *whoever* sought the Lord would go out to the Tent of Meeting that was outside the camp. Whenever Moses went out to the Tent, all the people would rise and stand, each at the entrance of his tent, and gaze after Moses until he had entered the tent" (33:7–8). Then, "when Moses entered the Tent, the pillar of cloud would descend and stand at the entrance of the Tent, while He [the Lord] spoke with Moses. When all the people saw the pillar of cloud poised at the entrance of the Tent, [they] would rise and bow low" (33:9–10).

There, at the Tent, "the Lord would speak to Moses *face to face, as one man speaks to another.* And Moses would then return to the camp; but his attendant, Joshua son of Nun, a youth, would not stir out of the Tent" (33:11).

Comment E–91. On the tensions between Exod. 33:7–11 and other E passages of the Torah

Together with the Ten Commandments, the centerpiece of P's Sinaitic theophanies has been, and will be, a Tent and Tabernacle to serve as the Lord's dwelling place (see Exod. 25–31, 35–40). In 33:7–11, however, we encounter a simpler Tent that Moses himself "would pitch outside the camp, at some distance from the camp" (33:7). There he would meet the Lord "face to face." Gone is the central dominating presence of Aaron and his sons (see Exod. 28–30). Instead, when Moses returned to the camp, "Joshua would not stir out of the Tent."

Even more striking is the vision of the Lord speaking to Moses "face to face, as one man speaks to another." This phrase need not negate the fundamental concept of the Lord's inscrutability. Friedman, in fact, identifies E as the author of both the *"Ehyeh-Asher-Ehyeh"* of Exod. 3:14 and the "face to face" of 33:11 (see Comment E–11). E's purpose here is to "humanize" the

Lord externally, even as He remains internally inscrutable. Note, however, that He only appears to Moses. (For other references to the Lord's visibility, see Comments E–50, 53, and 78.)

In 33:12, following the "face to face" encounters of 33:11, Moses pleads with the Lord, "See, You say to me, 'Lead this people forward.' *But You have not made known to me whom You will send with me.* Further, You have said, 'I have singled you out by name, and you have indeed gained My favor.' Now, if I have truly gained Your favor, pray *let me know Your ways, that I may know You* and continue in Your favor" (33:13).

To the first plea, the Lord replies, "I will go in the lead and will lighten your load" (33:14). On hearing these words, Moses is encouraged to seek even greater assurance. "Unless You go in the lead, do not make us leave this place. For how shall it be known that Your people have gained Your favor unless You go with us, so that we may be distinguished, Your people and I, from every people on the face of the earth?" (33:15–16).

The Lord's reply is (ambiguously) reassuring: "I will also do this thing that you have asked; for you have truly gained My favor and I have singled you out by name" (33:17). But in seeking more, Moses asks too much. "Oh, let me behold Your Presence!" (33:18). The Lord's refusal is kind, but decisive: "I will make all of My goodness pass before you, and I will proclaim before you the name Lord, and the grace that I grant and the compassion that I show. *But you cannot see My face, for man may not see Me and live*" (33:19–20). To this, as He passes by a rock on which Moses is stationed, the Lord adds, "You will see My back, but My face must not be seen" (33:23).

Comment E–92. On the stark contradictions of Exod. 33:1–11 and 33:12–23 regarding the Lord's "face"

On reading 33:12 we might conclude at once that the E of 33:1–11 has given way to another source. How else can we comprehend Moses' gentle reminder to the Lord that He has not yet revealed "whom You will send with me" (33:12)? In 33:2–3 the Lord made it perfectly clear that the people would be led by an angel, lest "on the way" He Himself should "destroy" the "stiff-necked people." Would Moses have forgotten this revelation? But now, in a sudden reversal, the Lord reveals that He will lead in order to "lighten your burden." What has occurred in the interim?

But the major defining difference in 33:1–11 and 12–23 is in the intimacy which the Lord allows Moses. In 33:1–11 He speaks to Moses "face to face, as one man speaks to another" (33:11). In 33:20 He tells Moses "you cannot see My face." Instead, Moses may know Him only in His "goodness," "grace," and "compassion," that is, through what He does rather than through Who He is (33:19).

But what the two different portrayals of the Lord God do share is the inscrutability of His "inner Being," or His true essence. For both it must remain a mystery. In 33:11, however, His "face," as such, serves important spiritual and psychological needs. It provides a vivid impression of the reality of the Lord's Presence while honoring Moses as His only "intimate." In contrast, the Lord's "face" in 33:20 serves as a metaphor for His "inner Being." As such, not even the Moses of 33:11 may see it.

Withal, Friedman attributes all of Exod. 33:1–33 to E. I assume, therefore, that his judgment reflects other factors that override the "face to face," and other, disparities of 33:1–11 and 33:12–23. If he is correct, Exod. 33 offers a unique case of a major tension within a single source bearing on the visibility of the Torah's God. (In both Exod. 33:11 and 20 "face" is from the root word "pahnim.")

Comment E–93. On the authorship and structure of Exod. 34—a brief prospective comment

In Exod. 34 the Lord directs Moses to ascend Mount Sinai for what will prove a second forty day theophany. The Lord will again reveal "commandments" to him, including J's early formulation of the "Ten Commandments." These, too, will serve as a "covenant" between the Lord and His people.

Friedman attributes all of Exod. 34:1–28 to J, but for 34:1b, which he assigns to R. He attributes the mystical imagery of 34:29–35 to P. These attributions make good sense—assuming that Friedman means to include "like the first" in 34:1b. To this I would add "like the first," as it appears in 34:4. (See Comment E–94.)

In Exod. 34:1 the Lord tells Moses, "Carve two tablets of stone *like the first*, and I will inscribe upon the tablets *the words that were on the first tablets, which you shattered*" (34:1). On the next morning, Moses, is to come to the mountain top alone and present himself to the Lord. "No one else" is to be "anywhere" on the mountain, nor are "flocks and herds" to graze at its foot (34:2–3).

"So Moses carved two tablets of stone, *like the first*, and early in the morning he went up on Mount Sinai, as the Lord had commanded him, taking the two stone tablets with him" (34:4). The Lord then came down in a cloud to Moses and "stood there with him there." The Lord then "passed before him, and proclaimed: *'The Lord! The Lord! a God compassionate and gracious, slow to anger, abounding in kindness and faithfulness, extending kindness to the thousandth generation, forgiving iniquity, transgression and sin; yet He does not remit all punishment, but visits the iniquity of fathers upon children and children's children, upon the third and fourth generations'*" (34:5–7).

Moses then bowed "low to the ground in homage" and said in return, "If I have gained Your favor, O Lord, pray let the Lord go in our midst, even though this is a stiffnecked people. Pardon our iniquity and our sin, and take us for Your own!" (34:8–9). The Lord responds, "I hereby make a covenant. Before all your people I will work such wonders as have not been wrought on all the earth or in any nation; and all the people who are with you shall see how awesome are the Lord's deeds which I will perform for you" (34:10).

Comment E–94. On R's conversion of Exod. 34 from J's single sojourn of "forty days and forty nights" on Mount Sinai to the second of two such sojourns

Within itself, what suggests Exod. 34 as a second, rather than a first, forty-day visitation by Moses to the Lord on Mount Sinai? First, there are these italicized words of Exod. 34:1: "Carve two tablets of stone *like the first*, and I will inscribe upon the tablets words *that were on the first tablet, which you shattered*." Second is the same underscored phrase of 34:4: "So Moses carved two tablets of stone, *like the first*, and early in the morning he went up on Mount Sinai, as the Lord had commanded him, taking the two stone tablets with him."

Why does Friedman attribute 34:1b to R? It must be that he views this event as J's independent version of the Sinaitic revelation. Consider the three stages of the Sinaitic/Horeb revelations that precede Exod. 34.

1. It was in the P passage of 20:1–17 that Moses received the Ten Commandments orally from the Lord as he stood not far from the people near the base of the mountain.

2. There follows the E passage of *20:19–23:19*, in which the *mishpatim* were revealed to Moses after he had "approached" the thick cloud of the Lord in 20:18.

3. The *mishpatim* are followed by P's version of Moses' first forty day sojourn on Mount Sinai (24:15–31:18). It deals almost entirely with the Lord's instructions on the Ark and Tabernacle. To underscore the need to cease all Tabernacle work on the sabbath, the Lord concludes by repeating His earlier sabbath instructions. The sojourn ends when the Lord gives Moses "the two tablets of the Pact, stone tablets inscribed with the finger of God." They will symbolize the full text of the Ten Commandments.

Thus, of the three sources of Genesis and Exodus, only J, until now, has said nothing of the revelations on Sinai.

Because J's version of Moses' sojourn on Mount Sinai was written long before P's, we might expect to find J's "Ten Commandments" to be less structured than those of P in 20:1–17. And while J's *mishpatim* contain various elements of E's later *mishpatim* of 20:19–23:19, they also differ.

While the need to fit J's Sinaitic revelations into the Torah posed an editorial problem for R, it also offered a providential opportunity. The conversion of J's sojourn on Mount Sinai into a second ascension would enable R to replace the two smashed tablets of Exod. 32. As Friedman probably means to imply, this was done by the simple device of adding "like the first" to J's "two tablets of stone."

Comment E–95. On the Lord's self-proclaimed attributes of compassion, grace, and kindness

Exod. 34:5–7 constitutes the Torah's clearest reference yet to the Lord's internalized limits on His use of power. These He proclaims as qualities of character.

> The Lord! The Lord! a God compassionate and gracious, slow to anger, abounding in kindness and faithfulness, extending kindness to the thousandth generation, forgiving iniquity, transgression and sin; yet He does not remit all punishment, but visits the iniquity of fathers upon children and children's children, upon the third and fourth generations."

Throughout Genesis and Exodus the essence of the Torah's God has been His power. Now, by self-proclamation (as inspired by J), He lays claim to qualities more capable of human emulation. As for His power, however often the Torah's God speaks of it with pride, it is through its actual exercise that the Torah seeks to project its reality. In that He now proclaims kindness and compassion as constraints on His power, we must also await such evidence of their reality.

There would seem, however, to be little compassion in his closing words: "Yet He does not remit all punishment, but visits the iniquity of fathers upon children and children's children, upon the third and fourth generations." Why does J introduce this discordant tone into the Lord's initial claim of compassion? In fact, it may attest more to J's knowledge of the human condition than to any Godly purpose. It is a reminder that the quality of human life in following generations is shaped by the quality of human conduct in preceding generations.

Seeking to invoke the Lord's compassion, Moses pleads that the Lord forgive the people for their "iniquity" and "sin" and "and take us for Your own" (34:9). In turn, the Lord promises His fealty to Israel: "Before all your people I will work such wonders as have not been wrought on all the earth or in any nation; and all the people who are with you shall see how awesome are the Lord's deeds which I will perform for you" (34:10).

The covenantal promises, warnings, admonitions, and specific commands that follow 34:10 repeat the essence of many previous pronouncements (mainly in the *mishpatim* of E) (34:11–27). Conversely, many others, including most of E's *mishpatim*, are omitted. Without attempting a complete catalogue of prior pronouncements, the following identities, or similarites, can be noted:* **11/23:23;**

---

*The verses in boldface are those of Exodus 34. The corresponding chapter and verse citations that follow are to E's *mishpatim*.

12/23:32–33; 13/23:24; 14/23:24; 15/23:32–33; 16 (see next paragraph); 17/20:20; 18/12:14–15, 23:15; 19/13:12, 15, 22:28–29; 20/13:13; 21/23:12, 31:12–17; 22/23:16; 23/23:17; 24/23:27–31; 25/23:18; 26/23:19; 27/24:4.

Among the pronouncements of Exod. 34, only 34:16 lacks a direct antecedent in prior pronouncements. It warns against the corrosive impact of intermarriage on the loyalty of the Israelites to their God. "And when you take wives from among their daughters [i.e., of the inhabitants of the land] for your sons, their daughters will lust after their gods and will cause your sons to lust after their gods."

Note E–54: J later dramatizes the point in Num. 25:1–5.

As Moses' sojourn ends, the Lord tells him, "Write down these commandments [or "words"], for in accordance with [them] I make a covenant with you and Israel" (34:27). "And he was there with the Lord forty days and nights; he ate no bread and drank no water; and he wrote down on the tablets the terms of the covenant, the Ten Commandments" (*aseret hadevarim*; 34:28). (See Comment E–96, par. 3.)

Comment E–96. On comparing the several Sinaitic/Horeb theophanies of P(1), E, P(2), and J

In comparing Exod. 34 to previous Sinaitic theophanies, we must again consider what Moses wrote down. (Comment E–75, is a background to what follows. It deals with "what Moses wrote down" following the first two theophanies, P[1] and E, in which the full text of the Ten Commandments and E's *mishpatim* were revealed. See 20:1–23:19.)

Recall as well that during and following the first forty-day theophany *on* Mount Sinai (i.e., P[2]) Moses wrote nothing down. Having received the Lord's oral instructions regarding the Ark and Tabernacle (25:1–31:11), Moses was next told to "speak to the Israelite people" in regard to the sabbath instructions of 31:12–17. Then in 31:18, the Lord gives Moses the "two tablets of the Pact . . . inscribed with the finger of God."

At the close of J's forty-day theophany on Mount Sinai, the Lord tells Moses to write down "these words" (*hadevarim ha'ayleh*; 34:27). (JPS2 renders the phrase as "these commandments." Cf. Comment E–75 on related issues.) As instructed in 34:27, in 34:28 Moses *himself* writes down *ait divrai hahbreet aseret hahdevarim* (or "the words of the covenant, the Ten Commandments"). Oddly enough, however, the Lord's opening advice to Moses in 34:1 was that "*I* will inscribe upon the tablets the words that were on the first tablets, which you shattered."

"So Moses came down from Mount Sinai. And as Moses came down from the mountain bearing the two tablets of the Pact," he was not aware "that the skin of his face was radiant since he had spoken with Him" (34:29). So it was that "Aaron and all the Israelites saw that the skin of Moses' face was radiant; and they shrank from coming near him" (37:30). At his call, however, they drew closer and "he instructed them concerning all that the Lord had imparted to him on Mount Sinai (34:32).

> Note E–55: As with E's mishpatim, Moses orally instructs the people on "all that the Lord had imparted to Him on Mount Sinai." In addition, at the Lord's command, he had written down the "Ten Words," the aseret hadevarim (34:28).

Exod. 34:33–35 then tells of a mystical veil worn by Moses. "And when Moses had finished speaking with them, he put a veil over His face. Whenever Moses went in before the Lord to speak with Him, he would leave the veil off until he came out, and when he came out . . . the Israelites would see how radiant the skin of Moses was. Moses would then put the veil back over his face until he went in to speak with Him."

Comment E–97. On the authorship of Exod. 34:29–35

Here the Torah portrays Moses in a perfect state of grace "whenever" he spoke with the Lord. Friedman ascribes 34:33–35, as well as 34:29–32, to P. This, however, does not explain the puzzling reference 34:34 to "whenever Moses *went in* before the Lord to speak." "Went in" where? Only E tells of meetings between Moses and the Lord in the "Tent of Meeting" (33:1–11; see Comment E–92). For P, there is yet no Tent.

Following the "interlude" of Exod. 32–34, the Torah picks up the narrative of Exod. 25–31. In Exod. 35–40 the Torah tells of the completion of the Ark, the Tabernacle and the Tent of Meeting as the dwelling place for its God.

Comment E–98. On the "interlude" between Exod. 25–31 and 35–40 as it bears on the structure of the Torah

In what would become Exod. 25–31 and 35–40, the P authors (c. 750–500 B.C.E.?) had presumably recorded a single text of how the Lord's dwelling place had come into being. This seems evident from the conclusion of Exod. 31 and the beginning of Exod. 35. Exod. 31, of course, is the final chapter of six in which the Lord sets out the details of His dwelling place and consecrates the Aaronide priesthood). Having identified the complex architectural and ornamental tasks to be completed to perfection, the Lord then warns the people that their Tabernacle work must cease on the sabbaths (31:12–17). P's version of the first theophany *on* Mount Sinai then ends with the Lord's gift to Moses of the most sacred component of His dwelling place, that is, "the two tablets of the Pact . . . inscribed with the finger of God."

With unbroken cadence, Exod. 35 picks up the narrative of the Tabernacle from Exod. 31. Having received His instructions on Mount Sinai, "Moses then convoked the entire Israelite community and said to them: 'These are the things that the Lord has commanded you to do' " (35:1a, b). There follows a precis of the Lord's sabbath homily of 31:12–17, to which Moses adds his own special reminder: "You shall kindle no fire throughout your settlements on the sabbath day" (35:2–3). He then goes on to fulfil the Lord's instructions, including the placement of "the Pact [i.e., "the tablets of the Pact" (34:29)] in the Ark" (40:20).

Why are these closely knit P passages interrupted by three chapters of E and J? As suggested in Comments E–93 and 94, R could hardly have found a better setting for E's golden calf and J's Sinaitic revelations. Then, in order to relink Exod. 35 with 31, R inserts at the close of J's Exod. 34 theophany what was likely P's original Exod. 31 version of Moses' descent from atop Sinai, *prior to R's decision to insert the golden calf episode of Exod. 32.* To this end, Exod. 34:29–33 provides a perfect segue from Exod. 31:18 to 35:1. But the source and "logic" of 34:34–35 remains less certain (see Comment E–97).

Following the sabbath homily of Exod. 35:1–3, Exodus 35–40 opens with the peoples' enthusiastic response to the Lord's call, as related by Moses, for "free will" offerings of materials and labor. "This is what the Lord has commanded. Take from among you gifts to the Lord, everyone *whose heart so moves him* shall bring them" (35:5).

The fullness of the response by women and men alike is described in 35:20–29 and 36:2–7. Exod. 38:21–31 sets out the "records of the Tabernacle," consisting of the weights of gold, silver, and copper "used for the work . . . of the sanctuary." The measures of "sanctuary weight" are talents, shekels, and half-shekels. As the source of 100 talents and 1,775 shekels of silver, the text cites the offerings of "603,550 men . . . from the age of twenty years up" (38:26).

Note E–56: This compares to "about six hundred thousand men on foot, aside from children" who left Egypt (12:37).

The principal designer/artisan of the entire project is Bezalel, whom the Lord first identified to Moses in 31:2–4. To the people, Moses describes Bezalel as having been endowed by the Lord "with a divine spirit of skill, ability and knowledge of every kind of craft: to make designs for work in gold, silver and copper, to cut stones for setting and to carve wood—to work in every kind of craft—*and to give directions.*" The Lord had also told Moses, "I have assigned to [Bezalel] Oholiab . . . and I have also granted skill to all who are skillful, that they may make everything I have commanded you" (31:6). Thus, Moses identifies Oholiab as Bezalel's principal aide, whom the Lord has also specially endowed with all requisite skills (35:30–34).

Comment E–99. On the Lord's endowment of skill to Bezalel, Oholiab, and "all who are skillful"

What does the passage mean to say regarding the Lord's endowment of particular human beings with special talents and skills? Does it cast Him as the determinant of the nature and degree of abilities in every person? Perhaps not. P might answer that the need for perfection in the Lord's abode warrants His special intervention.

Just as a summary could never capture the complexity and richness of the Lord's specifications of material and design, neither could it do justice to Moses' implemental work instructions (cf. Comment E–82 and Exod. 35–39). And so the people completed their work. "Just as the Lord had commanded Moses, so the Israelites had done all the work. And when Moses saw that they had performed all the tasks—as the Lord had commanded . . . Moses blessed them" (39:41–42).

Two quotations in particular from Exod. 35–40 provide useful summaries of the physical aspects and "politics" of the "Tabernacle of the Tent of Meeting."

These were the components of the structure:

Then they brought the Tabernacle to Moses, with the tent and all its furnishings: its clasps, its planks, its poles, its posts and its sockets; the covering of tanned ram skins, the covering of dolphin skins, and the curtain for the screen; the Ark of the Pact and its poles, and the cover; the table and all its utensils, and the bread of display; the pure lampstand, its lamps—lamps in due order— and all its fittings, and the oil for lighting; the altar of gold, the oil for anointing, the aromatic incense, and the screen for the entrance of the Tent; the copper altar with its copper grating, its poles and all its utensils, and the laver and its stand; the hangings of the enclosure, its posts and its sockets, the screen for the gate of the enclosure, it cords and its pegs—all the furnishings for the service of the Tabernacle, the Tent of Meeting; the service vestments for officiating in the sanctuary, the sacral vestments of Aaron the priest, and the vestments of his sons for priestly service. (39:33–41)

> Note E–57: *Amid the many references to clasps, planks, posts, sockets, fittings, and pegs, the Torah's failure here to mention the two cherubim seems remarkable. Although the Bezalel's work in making the cherubim is described*

in 37:7–9, in this summary of components they are totally subsumed within "the Ark of the Pact and its poles, and the cover" (39:35). Prominent in the Lord's specifications were their composition ("hammered gold"), location ("at the two ends of the cover [of the Ark]") and posture ("wings spread out" with their "faces . . . turned toward the cover"; 25:18–20). Even more important, it was "there . . . from above the cover, from between the two cherubim that are on top of the ark of the Pact," that the Lord was to "meet with [Moses]" and "command [him] concerning the Israelite people."

The "political" aspects of Exod. 25–31 and 35–40 reach their climax in Exod. 40, the concluding chapter of Exodus. The centrality of the Aaronide priesthood to the future of Israel was portrayed in Exod. 28 and 29. These describe the richly ornamented vestments of Aaron and his sons and the solemn rituals of consecration and ordination. And all for a purpose. For the Lord had told Moses that "they shall have priesthood as their right for all time" (29:9). With their consecration in Exod. 40:12–16, their tenure begins.

Put the sacral vestments on Aaron, and anoint him and consecrate him, that he may serve Me as priest. Then bring his sons forward, put tunics on them, and anoint them as you have anointed their father, that they may serve Me as priests. This their anointing shall serve them for everlasting priesthood throughout the ages. This Moses did; just as the Lord had commanded him, so he did.

It now remained for the Lord to accept the completed Tabernacle as "a sanctuary that I might dwell among them." Only then could the priestly monopoly that P conferred on Aaron and his descendants achieve its purpose. Thus, the conclusion of Exodus:

When Moses had finished the work, the cloud covered the Tent of Meeting, and the Presence of the Lord filled the Tabernacle. Moses could not enter the Tent of Meeting, because the cloud had settled upon it and the Presence of the Lord filled the Tabernacle. When the cloud lifted from the Tabernacle, the Israelites would set out on their various journeys; but if the cloud did not lift, they would not set out until such time as it did lift. For over the Tabernacle a cloud of the Lord rested by day, and fire would appear in it by night, in view of all the house of Israel throughout their journeys. (40:33–38)

Comment E–100. On the revelations at Sinai and the human origins of the Torah

A common understanding of the revelations at Sinai has Moses on the mountain for a period of forty days and nights. In fact, of course, the Torah describes a revelatory process of remarkable complexity. The purpose here is to provide a final summary of episodal relationships previously discussed in considerable detail. It focuses on three questions: (1) What is Moses said to have received at, and on, Sinai? (2) Where was he when he is said to have received it? (3) Of what he thus received, what was written down by whom? Much of the following summary (which omits individual source attributions) is drawn from Comments E–94 and 96.

1. While remaining with Aaron at the base of the mountain, Moses *hears* the full text of the Ten Commandments (Setting, Exod. 19:1–25, 20:15–17; Text, 20:1–14).

2. On approaching "the thick cloud where God was," Moses *hears* God present His first set of *mishpatim*" (Setting, Exod. 20:18–23; Text, 21:1–23:19).

3. On returning to the people at the base of the mountain, Moses wrote down the Ten Commandments (not yet having received them from the Lord in writing; Setting and Text, Exod. 24:3–8; Recording, 24:4).

4. Moses now ascends the mountain in stages and enters "the cloud" on the mountain where he remains for "forty days and forty nights." There he receives detailed instructions for building an Ark and Tabernacle as an abode for the Lord, God of Israel, so the people can know of His Presence among them (Setting, Exod. 24:15–18; Text, 25:1–31:17). As this first encounter between the Lord and Moses *on* the mountain concludes, Moses receives "the two tablets of the Pact, stone tablets inscribed with the finger of God" (34:18).

Prior to his ascent, however, the Lord had told Moses he would receive "the stone tablets with the teachings [Torah] and the commandments which I have inscribed to instruct them" (24:12; see Comment E–79).

5. On descending and seeing the golden calf of Exod. 32, Moses "hurled the tablets from his hands and shattered them at the foot of the mountain" (32:19). Another ascent is now required so that the Lord may replace the two shattered tablets. For this, the Lord tells Moses to carve and bring the two blank tablets on which "*I* will inscribe . . . the words [of] the first tablets" (34:1).

6. Once again "on Mount Sinai," Moses encounters the Lord "in a cloud," from where He proclaims Himself to be "compassionate and gracious, slow to anger, abounding in kindness and faithfulness" (34:6). (See Comment E–95.) Before inscribing the two stone tablets, the Lord reveals another set of rules to Moses in a format much like E's *mishpatim*. Thereafter, contrary to the Lord's initial advice in 34:1 that He would inscribe the tablets, it is Moses who "wrote down on the tablets the terms of the covenant, the ten commandments [i.e., *aseret hadevarim*]" (34:28). At the close of his second sojourn of "forty days and forty nights" on Mount Sinai, Moses brings the second set of tablets down from the mountain.

7. Exod. 35–39 describes the implementation of the Lord's instructions on the construction of the Ark and Tabernacle. The final revelation to Moses

(at ground level) covers the consecration of the Ark and Tabernacle and the ordination of Aaron and his sons (40:1–15).

In all, the revelations at and on Sinai/Horeb had generated (1) the Lord's oral revelation of the full text of the Ten Commandments, which Moses recorded in full; (2) one set of tablets containing the "ten words," as "inscribed with the finger of God"—only to be smashed by an outraged Moses on seeing the golden calf; (3) a second set of tablets on which Moses "wrote down" the "ten words"; (4) two partially similar sets of *mishpatim*, which the Lord revealed orally and which Moses imparted to the people (24:3 and 34:32); and (5) instructions on the Ark and Tabernacle.

Taken together, the several Sinaitic revelations may mark the peak of R's genius in melding the writings of an uncoordinated human "committee," operating over centuries, into a coherent narrative. The task of redaction and transcription, *and especially with the tools at hand*, would have overwhelmed authors and editors of any lesser skill and dedication. The integrated saga of these revelations at Sinai remains today as a monument to the potentials of human endeavor. The spirit and dedication of its creators warrants our awe.

CONCLUSION: ON THE POWER AND COMPASSION OF THE LORD, AS ISRAEL'S GOD

As the revelations on the mountain draw to a close, the Lord, through J, tells Moses of His less apparent attributes. He describes Himself as "compassionate and gracious, slow to anger, abounding in kindness and faithfulness" (34:6). Here were qualities worthy of human emulation. And they are among the qualities that the Torah seeks to infuse into Israel. But from the world around them, the authors of the Torah knew that Godly compassion and kindness alone could neither compel nor inspire human emulation. Instead, what they forged in Exodus, as the necessary means for directing Israel toward its highest human goals, was the compelling Presence and awesome power of the Lord, as Israel's God.

3.

LEVITICUS

INTRODUCTION: THE SETTING AND RELEVANCE OF LEVITICUS

The close of Exodus and the opening of Leviticus read as a continuum. As Exodus ends, "the cloud covered the Tent of Meeting and the Presence of the Lord filled the Tabernacle." During the Lord's Presence (in keeping with P's strictures), "Moses could not enter the Tent of Meeting" (Exod. 40:34–38). Now, as Leviticus opens, "the Lord called to Moses and spoke to him from the Tent of Meeting, saying: Speak to the Israelite people, and say to them: . . ." (1:1).

The Lord then imparts His initial commands covering five sacrificial offerings: (1) the Burnt Offering (*olah*); (2) the Meal Offering (*minchah*); (3) the Sacrifice of Well-Being (or Sacrifice of Peace Offering) (*zevach shelamim*); (4) the Sin Offering (*chatat*); and (5) the Guilt Offering (*asham*) (Lev. 1–5).

For these and all other Levitical rites, the Tent of Meeting was the sacred site and Aaron and his sons were the sacred officiants. Leviticus thus confirms Aaron and his descendants as the sole anointed priesthood at the site of the Lord's earthly abode among the Israelites. As noted in Comment E–83, it bears heavily on rival claims to priestly status in the Jerusalem Temple. The "politics" of priestly rivalries, however, is not why we probe into the arcane rituals of Leviticus. Our ultimate concern is with their possible psychological relevance to latter-day humanist social values. In pursuing this concern, we may become sated, and resated, by the animal slaughter and bloodletting that dominate the rituals of atonement and expiation. The specifics of these ancient rituals rarely inspire a quest for social values. Yet, it may be of use to probe the archaic means of another age for any valid ends to which they may have been directed.

A final "structural" point should be noted on the relationship between the continuing Sinaitic revelations of Exodus and Leviticus. As ultimately structured, Exodus contains no P source *mishpatim* equivalent to those of J and E. Instead they appear in Leviticus, as the Lord's ongoing revelation to Moses from the Tent of Meeting, still in situ at the base of Mount Sinai where it was first constructed. In this way, P replaces the mountain with the Tent as the site of His continuing presence. Therefore, from P's perspective, the people could no more depart for Canaan without the laws of Leviticus than without those of Exodus.

1. THE BURNT OFFERING, OR OLAH (LEV. 1)

> *Note L–1: Oddly enough, all three of our translations of Lev. 1:2 create a needless confusion. Consider these words of the Lord to Moses: (1) "When any of you presents an offering of cattle to the Lord, he shall choose his offering from the herd or from the flock" (JPS2); (2) "ye shall bring your offering of the cattle, even of the herd or of the flock" (JPS1); and (3) "you shall bring your offering of cattle from the herd or from the flock" (RSV). The reference, of course, is to all four-legged sacrificial animals. Thus, the Hebrew behaymah (from whence comes "cattle" in Lev. 1:2) would better be rendered as "animal," with specifications in each case to follow (as they do).*

The first burnt offering illustrates the point of Note L–1 (1:3–9). "If his offering is a burnt offering *from the herd*, he shall make his offering a *male without blemish*" (1:3). The "male" of the "herd" is then fittingly identified as a "bull," from the Hebrew *ben hahbahkar* (1:5).

Comment L–1. On sacrificial animals without blemish

Here the required offering is not of *any* male, but of a "male without blemish." Other offerings, in due course, will permit the use of female animals and less-than-perfect male animals. Where the need for perfection is implied by the use of "without blemish," the sacrificial purpose is likely of special import to the Lords' sanctity. As a practical matter, however, the frequent "waiver" of "without blemish" may have been an accomodation of demand to supply.

The offeror would first bring the animal "to the entrance of the Tent of Meeting, for acceptance in his behalf before the Lord" (1:3). He would then "lay his hand upon the head of the burnt offering, that it may be acceptable in his behalf, *in expiation for him*" (1:4).

> *Note L–2: No more is said here of expiation (but see Comment L–2). As for the class of offerors, JPS2 suggests that "any of you" from among "the Israelite people" could have been an offeror (1:2). In reading the Hebrew adam more narrowly, however (and as more likely intended by P), JPS1 and RSV limit offerors to "any man of you."*

Next, "the bull shall be slaughtered before the Lord" (1:5; JPS2). All further rituals are conducted by "Aaron's sons, the priests."

> *Note L–3: By use of "He shall kill," JPS1 and RSV clearly assign the killing to the offeror.*

In turn (1) the priests "offer the blood . . . dashing [it] against all sides of the altar which is at the entrance of the Tent of Meeting" (1:5); (2) having "flayed [i.e., skinned] and cut up" the burnt offering, they prepare the fire on the altar and "lay out the sections, with the head and suet, on the wood in the fire" (1:6–8); (3) they then wash the "entrails and legs" with water; and (4) "turn *the whole* into smoke on the altar as a burnt offering, an offering by fire of pleasing odor to the Lord" (1:9).

> *Note L–4: Although averse to any physical materialization of its Lord (see Comment E–92), P evokes the imagery of a "pleasing odor to the Lord" throughout the rituals of sacrifice. As to P's use of "inscribed with the finger of God" in Exod. 31:38, see Comment E–85).*

Lev. 1:10–14 deals with burnt offerings *"from the flock, of sheep or goats"*— also requiring "a male without blemish." It closely replicates the rituals of 1:3–9, which deal with offerings "from the herd." Thus, the *"whole"* of an animal of the flock is also turned "into smoke" (1:13). But now there is an added requirement that the animal "be slaughtered before the Lord *on the north side of the altar.*"

> *Note L–5: In contrast, the bull was simply "slaughtered before the Lord" (1:5).*

A burnt offering from the "flock" was also "of pleasing odor to the Lord" (1:13).

The final category of acceptable sacrificial animals for burnt offerings was that of "birds." These were limited to nonpredatory "turtledoves or pigeons" (1:14–17). In accord with these anatomical differences, the rituals for offering birds differed from those for animals of the herd or flock. Due, perhaps, to the difficulties of preselection, there are no quality or sex requirements for captured birds. *Yet the Torah accords spiritual parity to offerings of all three categories of animals.* Like those from the "flock and herd," a burnt offering of a turtledove or pigeon was "of pleasing odor to the Lord" (1:17).

Comment L–2. On the purpose of burnt offerings, as reflected in Lev. 1

Except for the terse reference in 1:4 to "expiation," Lev. 1 (in itself) ascribes no purpose to the burnt offering. Rashi suggests that the voluntary offering of 1:4 (i.e., *lir'tzohnoh*, "according to his will") is meant to cover "atonement" for "transgressions of a positive command."[1] Conversely, Ramban contemplates a mental state only: "The burnt offering," he agrees (with Rabbi Shimon ben Yochai), "only comes to effect atonement for sinful thoughts of the heart."[2] (But their views do meet in the mental sin of covetousness.)

But what of the spiritual parity (i.e., of "pleasing odor to the Lord" that P accords to all burnt offerings—whether of highly valued bulls, lesser valued goats or sheep and least valued free-flying birds? Citing Sifra, Rashi observes "it matters not whether one (offer) much or one (offer) little, so long as he directs his heart to heaven."[3] ("Sifra" is an edited compilation of early rabbinic *midrashim* on Leviticus.) Does Rashi mean to disassociate an offeror's state of mind from the "generosity" of his "sacrifice"? Or would he say that the owner of many bulls who offers no more than a pigeon has not "[directed] his heart to heaven?"

The "generic" burnt offerings of Lev. 1 say nothing of a "means test" to explain the burnt offering of a bird in place of a bull. But in other offerings that initially mandate the use of more valuable animals, only a lack of "means" warrants the use of a less valuable offering (as designated; cf. Lev. 5:7 and 11 regarding sin offerings and 12:8 regarding postnatal purification rites.)

2. THE MEAL OFFERING, OR MINCHAH (LEV. 2)

A Meal Offering "to the Lord" consists of "choice flour" on which oil has been poured and frankincense has been laid (2:1). "The priest" then scoops out a "token portion," which he "turn[s] into smoke on the altar, as an offering by fire, of pleasing odor to the Lord" (2:2). The remainder is "for Aaron and his sons, a most holy portion from the Lord's offerings by fire" (2:3).

A meal offering could be baked in a variety of ways. An offering first "baked in an oven" might consist of unleavened cakes of choice flour with oil mixed in, or of unleavened wafers spread with oil. The choice flour and oil might also be prepared "on a griddle." On being broken into bits and covered with oil, the resulting thin crisp wafer would qualify as a meal offering (2:5–6). Finally, a meal offering "in a pan" would also consist of "choice flour in oil" (2:7). (Note that frankincense was not included in any of the prebaked offerings.) As with the "basic" uncooked offering, "the priest" takes a "token portion" of a prebaked offering to be turned into "smoke on the altar as an offering by fire, of pleasing odor to the Lord." Again, the remainder is "for Aaron and his sons, a most holy portion from the Lord's offerings by fire" (2:8–10). And while "leavened" grain products and honey were suitable offerings of "choice products" for the priests, neither could be "offered up on the altar for a pleasing odor" (2:11–12).

The ritual then exalts the use of salt: "You shall season your every offering of meal with salt; you shall not omit from your meal offering the salt of your covenant with God; with all your offerings you must offer salt" (2:13).

> Note L–6: In context, the "salt" clause of 2:13 might seem limited to meal offerings. In the end, however, it applies to all offerings, whether of meat or grain. Rashi reads it to require the use of salt in all "burnt offerings of cattle and fowl."[4]

Finally, "a meal offering of first fruits to the Lord" was to consist of "grain in season parched with fire, grits of the first ear, as your meal offering of first fruits." With oil and frankincense added, "it is a meal offering" (2:14–15). The rituals of this unique offering were much like those for other meal offerings burnt on the altar (see 2:2–3, 9–10). Here, however, the smoke is no more than "an offering by fire to the Lord."

Comment L–3. On the respective purposes of Burnt and Meal Offerings

Comment L–2 pt. 1 dicusses the possible use(s) of the burnt offering based on the minimal information from Lev. 1. Lev. 2, however, says even less of the purpose(s) of meal offerings. Rashi distinguishes the two offerings by offeror rather than purpose: "Who customarily brings a meal offering? A poor man. The Holy One Blessed Be He said, 'I consider him (credit him) as though he had offered his very soul.' "[5] An example of Rashi's "last resort" usage of a meal offering is found in the sin offering of Lev. 5:1–13. However, as Leviticus later reveals, the meal offering had far wider uses.

3. THE SACRIFICE OF WELL-BEING, OR ZEVACH SHELAMIM (LEV. 3)

An "offering" made as "a sacrifice of well-being" could be "of the herd" or "from the flock" and either "a male or a female" (3:1, 6). But any such animal of either sex must be "without blemish" (3:1, 6).

> Note L–7: Left for conjecture is why female animals were suitable for sacrifices of well-being, but not for burnt offerings.

Comment L–4. On the purpose of Sacrifices of Well-Being, or Peace-Offerings, as reflected in Lev. 3

The purpose of the sacrifice of well-being, or *zevach shelamim*, is found in its name. In Hebrew, *zevach* means "sacrifice," and "*shelamim*" (from *shalom*) connotes "inner-peace" or well-being. *Thus, the impetus for the sacrifice lies in gratitude rather than penance.*

But for their use of the "fatty" portions of the animals, the rituals of the sacrifice of well-being also resembled those for burnt offerings. Both bulls and cows required a separate burning of fats: (1) the fat "that covers" and "is about" the "entrails (3:3); (2) the two kidneys and their fat (3:4); (3) the fat at the loins (3:4); and (4) the "protuberance [or "lobe"] on the liver," which "[the offeror] shall remove with the kidneys" (3:4). "Aaron's sons" would turn this fat "into smoke on the altar." Together "with the burnt offering which is upon the wood that is on the fire," the fat was "an offering by fire, of pleasing odor to the Lord" (3:5).

The rituals regarding sheep and goats were similar. These included the removal and burning of corresponding fatty portions. (As to these, however, sheep were unique in possessing a "whole broad tail," which was also removed as a fatty portion.) Different in each case were the stated consequences of the burning. While the burning of bulls and cattle produced smoke of "pleasing odor to the Lord" (3:5), the smoke from burning goats was simply "of pleasing odor" (3:16). In contrast to both, but like the "meal offering of first fruits" (2:16), the smoke of a sheep was described merely as "an offering by fire to the Lord" (3:11). Sheep therefore lacked the spiritual confirmation "of pleasing odor *to the Lord*" (as with "animals of the herd" [3:5]) or "of pleasing odor" in general (as with "goats" [3:16]). Nor does Lev. 3 allocate offerings between the Lord and the priests (but cf. Lev. 7:11–34).

As can be inferred from Comment L–4, the sacrifice of well-being had the character of a voluntary offering made in gratitude to the Lord for good fortune, or from feelings of well-being. It also served, however, as a required offering in broader ceremonial rites such as those of priestly ordination (see Lev. 8, 9).

Comment L–5. On variations in the degree of the Lord's pleasure from the smoke of different animals

What accounts for seemingly "arbitrary" variations in how smoke from different animals is received by the Lord? Perhaps on encountering such textual differences in the materials at hand, R may have chosen to use them as he found them. As a human editor dealing with human authors over time whose purposes were often obscure, R may have rightly concluded that perfect symmetry was not a realistic goal.

Lev. 3 concludes with two dietary laws—two principles of kashrut. "All fat is the Lord's . . . you must not eat any fat or any blood." This will apply "for all time throughout the ages, in all your settlements" (3:16–17).

Note L–8: The passage does not indicate if these practices were perceived as entirely cultic, or partially hygienic.

4. THE SIN OFFERING, OR *CHATAT* (LEV. 4 AND 5:1–13)

As in Lev. 1:1–2, the Lord instructs Moses to "speak to the Israelite people thus." His first words reveal one major use of sin offerings. In general, a "sin offering" is mandated "when a person *unwittingly incurs guilt* in regard to any of the Lord's commandments *about things not to be done*, and does one of them" (4:2).

Comment L–6. On the meanings of "sin" and "guilt" in Lev. 4

In considering the meanings of "sin" and "guilt" in Lev. 4, we must first consult the Hebrew text that states the overall rationale for its offerings: *nefesh key-tehchetah vishgahgah* (4:2). Literally, then, the need for an offering is triggered "if one shall sin through error." The concept of "sin" is expressed in *tehchetah*, from the root *chata'ah*, the noun for "sin. The term "through error" is from *vishgahgah*. While modern dictionaries give "guilt" as a second meaning to noun and verb forms rooted in *chata'ah*, their principal root for the noun and verb forms of "guilt" is *ashmah*. (From *ashmah* also comes *asham*, the "guilt offering.") The Hebrew, *vishgahgah*, is variously translated as "through error," "by mistake," or "through inadvertence." These then suggest such adverbial terms as "unintentionally," "inadvertently," or "unwittingly."

In the defining verse of Lev. 4:2, JPS1 and RSV closely follow its Hebrew text. Thus, JPS1 and RSV (in turn) describe the basis for the sin offerings of Lev. 4 as (1) "If any one *shall sin through error* in any one of the things which the Lord hath commanded not to be done, and shall do any one of them" and (2) "*If any one sins unwittingly* in any of the things which the Lord has commanded not to be done, and does any one of them." JPS2, however, avoids the use of "sin" as follows: "When a person *unwittingly incurs guilt* in regard to any of the Lord's commandments about things not to be done, and does one of them."

In that the literal pattern of the passage is for guilt to result from sin, the two concepts are obviously related. As RSV rightly implies, to "sin" is to "incur guilt." Nevertheless, by reading the "sin" root *tehchetah* as "incurs guilt," JPS2 identifies the result as the cause. (To similar effect see 4:3, 14, 22, 27.)

In two verses of Lev. 4 the text explicitly states the intended causal relationship between "sin" and "guilt" (4:22, 27). By adhering to its original format in these two verses, JPS2 must then posit guilt as the result not of sin but of guilt itself. Lev. 4:22 illustrates the problem of both verses. Its relevant Hebrew text is as follows: "*asher nasi yehchetah . . . bishgahgah v'ashaym.*" As rendered by RSV, the text reads: "When a ruler [i.e., *nasi*] *sins* . . . unwittingly . . . and is *guilty*" (to similar effect see JPS1.) Here, as elsewhere, "sin" derives from the *chatat* root and "guilt" from the *asham* root. But compare

JPS2: "If any person . . . *incurs guilt* . . . and finds himself *culpable*." Having rendered the *chatat* root as "guilt" rather than sin, JPS2 avoids using "guilt" twice by reading *asham* as "culpable." Again, JPS2 obscures "sin," *as such*, as the trigger for the sin offerings of Lev. 4 (see Comment L–8 in regard to the "unwitting" sins of Lev. 4).

Lev. 4 prescribes the rituals applicable to four different categories of offenders whose conduct requires a sin offering. These are (per JPS2) (1) "*the anointed priest who has incurred guilt so that blame falls upon the people*" (4:3); (2) "*the whole community of Israel* . . . has erred and the matter escapes the notice of the congregation, so that they do any of the things [forbidden by the Lord], and thus find themselves culpable" (4:13); (3) "*a chieftain who incurs guilt by doing unwittingly any of the things [forbidden by the Lord], and finds himself culpable*" (4:22); and (4) "*any person from among the populace* [who] unwittingly incurs guilt by doing any of the things [forbidden by the Lord], and finds himself culpable" (4:27).

The sin offerings required in each case were these:

1. "*If it is the anointed priest who has incurred guilt, so that the blame falls upon the people*, he shall offer . . . a bull of the herd without blemish as a sin offering to the Lord" (4:3). When the bull has been slaughtered "before the Lord" at the Tent of Meeting, the "anointed priest" brings "some of [its] blood" into the Tent (4:4–5). (The various applications of the blood are described in 4:6–7.) The fatty portion(s) of the bull are then removed "just as it is removed from the ox of the sacrifice of well-being." These are turned "into smoke on the altar of burnt offering" (4:8–10). The remaining portions of the bull—"the hide . . . all its flesh . . . its head and legs, its entrails and dung"—are all brought outside the Tent. They are burned, with wood, "on the ash heap" at a "clean place outside the camp" (4:11–12).

Comment L–7. On the peoples' guilt and expiation for the unwitting priestly sins of Lev. 4

Contrary to the other categories of unwitting sins in Lev. 4, this first sin offering is not said to expiate either priests or people. But no less puzzling is why the people should incur guilt for the sins of their priests.

If the people had freely chosen their priests, we might find it easier to hold them responsible for priestly sins (even if unintended). But in the case of a hereditary priesthood that claims anointment from the Lord (Exod. 40:12–16), how could P justifiably place guilt on the people for priestly sins? Does P imply a divinely ordained communal responsibility for the conduct of priests? If so, Rashi explains it as follows: "When the high priest sins, it is the guilt of the people, for they are dependent upon him, to make atonement for them and to pray for them, and he has become impaired (wherefore they remain under guilt)."[6] In this view, the people are obliged to seek expiation for the priests' sins so that the priests may once more seek expiation for the peoples' sins. By sharing priestly guilt and by seeking communal expiation for *unwitting* priestly sins, the people acknowledge their need for expiated priests to seek their own expiation for the unwitting sins they will inevitably incur. It thus confirms the need for priests.

2. In this case "the whole community of Israel" errs and thereby causes the congregation to commit a forbidden act. "*When the sin through which they incurred guilt becomes known*, the congregation shall offer a bull of the herd as a sin offering" at the Tent of Meeting (4:13–14). It is offered by "the elders" of the community in its behalf. As in (1), "the anointed priest" brings "some of the blood" into the Tent (4:15–16). The ensuing blood rituals (4:17–18) closely follow those of category (1) (4:6–7). The removal and burning of fat at the altar is done "just as . . . with the [priest's] bull of sin offering" (4:19–20). The priest then carries the remainder of the bull outside the camp and burns it "as he burned the first bull." This is "the sin offering of the congregation" (4:21), in which "*the priest shall make expiation for them*, and they shall be forgiven" (4:20).

3. "*Once the sin of which he is guilty is brought to his knowledge*," a "chieftain" (or secular leader) who "unwittingly" commits a forbidden act "shall bring as his offering a male goat without blemish" (4:23). After the usual hand is laid on its head, the goat, as a sin offering, is "slaughtered at the spot where the burnt offering is slaughtered before the Lord" (4:24).

Unlike those of (1) and (2), the blood rituals of (3) did not require the priest to "dip his finger in the blood and sprinkle it seven times before the Lord, in front of the curtain." All the "fat" of the goat (not further specified) was turned "into smoke on the altar, like the fat of the sacrifice of well-being" (4:26). In this way the priest makes "expiation [on the chieftain's] behalf, and he "shall be forgiven" for his sin.

> *Note L–9: Expiation for priestly and community guilt in (1) and (2) required a bull without blemish. But for an individual chieftain, an unblemished male goat sufficed.*

4. Finally, "*once the sin of which he is guilty is brought to his knowledge*," the class (4) offender must offer a "*female* goat without blemish" (41:28). This category covered "any person from among the populace [who] unwittingly incurs guilt [through an act forbidden by the Lord] and finds himself culpable" (4:27).

Rituals for the sin offering of an ordinary layman were the same as those for a "chieftain" (4:27–31). Literally, however, their consequences differed in that the "smoke" of a layman's offering, not a chieftain's, was said to provide "a pleasing odor to the Lord" (cf. 4:31, 26). (See Comment L–5.) The priest then makes expiation for the offeror, and he is forgiven (4:31).

The singular requirement in 4:28 for the offering of a "female goat without blemish" for the sin of 4:27 is abruptly broadened in 4:32. With continuing reference to 4:27, 4:32 states as follows: "*If the offering he brings as a sin offering is a sheep, he shall bring a female without blemish.*" The rituals for a sheep were the same as those for a goat (4:33–35). However, while both offerings bring expiation and forgiveness, only the smoke of the goat is described as "a pleasing odor to the Lord" (4:35).

> *Note L–10: The difference must surely be attributable to editorial rather than substantive factors.*

> *Note L–11: Between category (1) and the other three, there is also a literal difference in the "triggering" of sin offerings. I have "flagged" it by underscoring the relevant phrases at the outset of categories (2), (3), and (4). Because all sin offerings in Lev. 4 involve the "unwitting" commission of an act forbidden by the Lord, the "sinner" can hardly proceed with a sin offering until he becomes aware of his sin. In categories (2), (3), and (4) the need for a sin offering is accordingly deferred pending such awareness (see 4:14, 23, 28). Only as to unwitting priestly sinner(s) of category (1) is the sin offering not explicitly conditioned on the "sinner's" awareness of the sin.*
>
> *Why the difference? We might hypothesize that Lev. 4 attributes a heightened sensitivity to its priests that would alert them at once to the possibility of having sinned unintentionally. Priestly holiness would then prompt an investigation that would reveal the presence or absence of sin. Clearly, however, "heightened sensitivity" was not always a reliable guide to the commission of unintended sins (see Comment L–8 below, as to mistakes of fact).*

Comment L–8. On human intent and the Lord's sanctity in regard to the sins of Lev. 4

The central interpretive issue in Lev. 4 involves the nature of the sinner's mental state while committing an act forbidden by the Lord. That such a sin was committed "unwittingly," or "through error," or "by mistake," or "unintentionally" or "inadvertently" admits of three main possibilities. *First,* not knowing that he is forbidden to eat "X," the "sinner" eats "X." Here the saving grace, if any, is ignorance of the law. But should ignorance of the law suffice for expiation and forgiveness without further punishment? In theory, P might well have charged the sinner with an obligation to know the Law. *Yet the fact remains that though the act itself was deliberate, there was no deliberate intent to violate a law* (but cf. Lev. 5:17–19, Comment L–14). *Second,* having been credibly assured that "X," a forbidden food, was in fact "Y," a permitted food, the hungry sinner eats "X." *This sin involves an ignorance of fact rather than law.* Again, *there was no deliberate intent to violate the law. Third,* as with an "act of God," an act innocent in itself leads to an unintended, but forbidden, result. Again, the sin may be forgiven (cf. Comment E–68).

Lev. 4 is more more precise than E's mishpatim in defining the mental state by which intent, or its absence, is to be measured (see Comment E–68 and Note E–31). How are we to judge wanton recklessness that too often leads to unintended deaths? The basic element, however, is a lack of intent to sin (i.e., to commit a forbidden act). And it is the absence of such intent that was presumably thought to justify the "mild" conditions for expiation through the Lev. 4 sin offerings.

But this leaves the question of why any act lacking evil intent should ever qualify as a sin (as distingished from a *civil* wrong). The answer, in P's view, is that the commission of any act resulting in consequences inimical to the Lord constitutes a trespass on His sanctity. Thus, while a lack of intent would not eliminate the "trespasser's" need for expiation, it would warrant an easier path to its realization.

Comment L–9. On the unintended sins of P's Lev. 4 as compared to the unintended killings of E's *mishpatim*

Lev. 4 invites comparison with the previous treatment of unintended killings in E's *mishpatim.* "He who fatally strikes a man shall be put to death. If he did not do it by design, *but it came about as an act of God,* I will assign you a place to which he can flee" (Exod. 21:12–13). (See Comment E–68.) In such circumstances would Lev. 4 require a sin offering? If so, where and when? At the Tent of Meeting before taking flight? Or at the place of refuge?

In any case, given the unique passions for revenge aroused by killings, R could have rightly viewed E's *mishpat* on unintended killings as the Lord's own exception to Lev. 4. Only as to the unintended killings of Exod. 21:13 did E's God place the urgent needs of human justice above the vindication of His sanctity. Only *these* unintentional acts does He declare to be "acts of God." And logically, when the Lord Himself takes responsibility for deaths effected by unwitting human agents, those agents are free both of sin and the need for expiation through a sin offering.

Lev. 5:1–4 identifies four additional "sins" that give rise to the sin offerings of 5:6–13. These involve the following conduct: (1) the failure to appear as a witness in a legal proceeding of which one knows and as to which one has evidence (5:1); (2) any touching of an "unclean *thing*," such as an unclean animal carcass (5:2); (3) any touching of "*human* uncleanness" (5:3); and (4) "when a person utters an oath to bad or good purpose—whatever a man may utter in an oath—and, though he has known it, the fact has escaped him, but later he finds himself culpable in any of these matters" (5:4).

Sin (1) deals with a person's responsibility to the community. Fairness in the administration of justice requires the full and honest participation of persons with knowledge of the matters in issue. Such participation is too often frustrated by a natural human reluctance to become involved in the disputes of others. This aversion is often keenest in the case of "local" disputes among friends and neighbors. The pronouncement of a sin and the need for an offering were meant to serve the needs of justice.

Unlike the communal purposes of sin (1), the three other sins involved the "well-being" of individuals. Sins (2) and (3) thus looked to the restoration of cleanness to an individual who becomes impaired by contacts deemed unclean. "Touching" an unclean thing or person might result from not knowing that the "object" was unclean or, if known, from carelessness or even necessity. In some cases, compassion itself might dictate such contacts. Thus, while it was not feasible to condemn all unclean contacts, it was thought essential, whatever the circumstance, to show regret and gain expiation through the required sin offering.

> Note L–12: Human "uncleanness" and contacts with "unclean things" are treated in Lev. 11:24–40 and Lev. 12–15.

Sin (4) (5:4) addresses the ease by which oaths are freely uttered and forgotten. An oath, however, is a solemn undertaking—not to be forgotten. And even if made for "bad," or otherwise unfulfillable, purposes, they remain as warnings against all idle oaths. To recall an unfulfilled oath, even if unfulfillable, is to recall a sin that needs expiation.

> Note L–13: Literally, at least, the sin of 5:4 does not address the failure to honor an oath, once taken and never forgotten. Num. 30 deals with other aspects of "vows and oaths." See Comment N–29 for thoughts on the relationship between Lev. 5:4 and Num. 30.

> Note L–14: As with the sins of Lev. 4, those of 5:1–4 are from the chatat root. In turn, the "guilt" that results from a sin is expressed through the asham root. JPS1 and RSV continue to express this cause and effect connection between sin and guilt; and JPS2 continues to merge the two concepts by associating tehchetah with "guilt" and v'ashaym with "culpability" (5:1–2). (See Comment L–6.)

Comment L–10. On the distinctive character of the sins of Lev. 4 and 5

The sins of Lev. 5:1–4 differ from those of Lev. 4 in that they deal with conduct not sinful in itself. They result instead from technically nonsinful conduct of such social importance as to be encouraged or discouraged, as appropriate. As such, the particular act, or failure to act, requires forgiveness through expiation. Also, while Lev. 5 sins are not wholly unintended, as in Lev. 4, neither are they planned. They may stem from sloth, indifference lack of care, and indeed, as noted, even unexpected necessity.

In general, because the precipitating conduct of Lev. 4 sins was not purposeful, deterrence was a minor element at most in the purpose of expiation through sin offerings. Instead, the dominant purpose was to vindicate the Lord's sanctity. Conversely, because Lev. 5 "sins" often (though not always) resulted from lesser human failings, the sin offerings were meant to encourage greater care and responsibility.

On realizing a "sin" of Lev. 5, the "sinner" was first required to confess it. Then, "as his penalty to the Lord," he must bring "a female from the flock, sheep or goat, as a sin offering" (5:5–6). Unlike those of Lev. 4, Lev. 5 offerings do not require animals "without blemish." On receiving the sacrificial sheep or goat from the confessed sinner, "the priest shall make expiation on his behalf for his sin" (5:6).

However, we now encounter the first explicit permission for an impecunious sinner to offer animals of lesser value (see Comment L–2). "But if his means do not suffice *for a sheep*, he shall bring two turtledoves or two pigeons, one for a sin offering and the other for a burnt offering" (5:7–8). The protocols for sin offerings of birds are in 5:8–9. They are said to be "according to regulation" (i.e., as in Lev. 1:14–17) (5:10).

Finally, an offeror whose "means do not suffice" for the offerings of birds may bring "a tenth of an *ephah* of choice flour." As the flour was technically for a sin offering rather than a general meal offering, the embellishments of oil and frankincense were omitted. (5:11). The priest then scooped a "handful" as a "token portion" to be "turn[ed] into smoke on the altar" (5:12). Also, though not technically a meal offering in itself, the unburned portion of flour "shall belong to the priest, like the meal offering" (5:13). Regardless of what was offered, each brought expiation and the Lord's forgiveness (5:10, 13). As to no offering, however, be it of goat or flour, does Lev. 5 portray its smoke as "a pleasing odor to the Lord."

> Note L–15: Although Lev. 5 includes protocols for offerings of birds and cereal (5:7–13), none are stated for the offerings of female goats or sheep (5:6). A possible model, however, is that of Lev. 4:29–35 covering the same animals.

Comment L–11. On the sin offerings of Lev. 4 and 5 as measures of the relative "sinfulness" of Lev. 4 and 5 sins

Does the "waiver" of animals "without blemish" in the sin offerings of Lev. 5:1–13 reflect the perception of a less egregious trespass on the Lord's sanctity than occurs through the sins of Lev. 4? A common element in the "sin offerings" of Lev. 4 and 5 is the absence of any penal purpose. Instead, both provide the means of expiation and forgiveness for wrongful conduct as to which the degree of moral culpability does not warrant punishment. But what light, if any, does a recapitulation of differences in the expiation protocols (mainly as to required offerings) shed on the relative "sinfulness" of the sins of Lev. 4 and 5?

As to all four categories of its "unwitting sinners," Lev. 4 requires an animal from the herd or the flock. By categories, these are: (1) a bull without blemish (4:3); (2) a bull, but with no mention of blemish (4:14); (3) a male goat without blemish (4:23); and (4) a female goat or sheep without blemish (4:28, 32). From the total context it would seem that the "without blemish" requirement of category (1) is meant to carry over to the bull of category (2). In any case, for all offerings in expiation of Lev. 4 sins, a valuable animal of the herd or flock is required. And even the poorest among the sinners of Lev. 4 are denied the option of a less valuable substitute.

Contrary to Lev. 4, none of the sins of Lev. 5:1–13 require the offering of a more valuable bull or a cow. Moreover, even for the less valuable initial offering of a "female . . . goat or sheep," the sinner could substitute birds or flour. Nor were the sacrificial animals of 5:1–13 required to be "without blemish."

In every respect, therefore, the conditions of forgiveness for the sins of Lev. 4 are greater than those for Lev. 5:1–13. The question then is whether the varied conditions of forgiveness for Lev. 4 and 5 sins correspond fairly to the relative seriousness of their respective sins.

Clearly, the distinction is not found in a comparison of the "unwitting sins" of Lev. 4 with the more deliberate sins of Lev. 5. If the degree of intent were decisive, logic would require more stringent conditions of forgiveness for Lev. 5 sins. For P, however, the critical difference lies in the absence from the sins of Lev. 5 of any direct affront to the Lord's dignity or sanctity. Thus, while the mishaps or behavorial lapses that characterize the sins of Lev. 5 are to be discouraged, they do not demean the Lord by disobedience to a Godly prohibition, intended or not.

5. THE GUILT OFFERING, OR ASHAM (LEV. 5:14–26)

Lev. 5:14 introduces the guilt offerings of Lev. 5 with "the Lord spoke to Moses, saying. . . ." The first *sin* to require a *guilt* offering is then defined as "When a person commits a trespass, being *unwittingly* remiss about any of the Lord's sacred things" (5:15).

Comment L–12. On the meaning of "the Lord's sacred things" in the first guilt offering of 5:15–16

Given the ambiguity of "the Lord's sacred things," we might note that JPS1 and RSV are no more specific in referring to the "holy things of the Lord." In theory, "sacred" or "holy" things might include (1) the Tabernacle and its contents, including the Ark and its "Pact" (Exod. 25:16), the altar and the many designated furnishings, artifacts, and sacral vestments, and (more likely) (2) offerings, or other gifts, in support of Tabernacle operations. An "unwitting trespass" or "breach of faith," therefore, could in theory involve a wrongful appropriation or use of any of these "sacred" things of the Lord.

It is the need for "restitution" as an element of the related guilt offering (5:16) that precludes the inclusion of category (1) items among the "sacred" things covered in 5:15. Given their unique sanctity, they could be neither valued nor replaced. Thus, the "sacred things" *of 5:15* were necessarily limited to category (2).

This limited view of "sacred things" is reinforced by the mandatory priestly portion of an added "fifth part" of every restitution payment (5:16). That the "added fifth" can be measured defines the restitution itself as a "finite" value intended to restore a "finite" loss. This could only apply to gifts and offerings brought to the priests, which, though "sacred" to a point, did not share the sanctity of what the Lord had consecrated as His abode with Israel.

The rituals of expiation in such case were as follows: "He shall bring as his penalty to the Lord a ram without blemish from the flock, *convertible into payment in silver by the sanctuary weight*, as a guilt offering. He shall make restitution for that wherein he was remiss about the sacred things, and he shall add a fifth part to it and give it to the priest. *The priest shall make expiation on his behalf with the ram of the guilt offering*, and he shall be forgiven" (5:15–16).

Comment L–13. On the problematic guilt offering of 5:15–16

As rendered by JPS2 above, the rituals of the guilt offering are ambiguous.

First, of what import is the ram's "convertibility"? *Must* the "ram without blemish" that is brought "as a penalty" be converted "into payment in silver." Or is a conversion optional? If so, by whose choice—offerer or priest?

Read literally and alone, JPS2's use of "or the equivalent" in 5:18 permits the substitution of a like value in silver for the ram. If so, would such a "guilt offering" not violate the later guilt offering protocols of Lev. 7:1–10.

Plaut explains the JPS2 translation as follows: "The present rendering reflects the fact, known from cuneiform sources, that in ancient Near Eastern practice a money payment could be substituted for a sacrificial animal."[7]

Given the ambiguities of 5:15–16, Plaut is justified in looking to extrinsic sources for a solution. But given the closing words of 5:16, i.e., "The priest *shall* make expiation on his behalf *with the ram* of the guilt offering," is a guilt offering possible *without* the ram? Or can *"with* the ram" be satisfied by its conversion into money? In any case, would Lev. 7:2 not require its "slaughter"?

JPS2 states the impetus for the guilt offering of 5:17–19 as follows: "When a person, without knowing it, sins in regard to any of the Lord's commandments about things not to be done, and then realizes his guilt, he shall be subject to punishment" (5:17).

Comment L–14. On the rationale for the guilt offering of 5:17–19

Although the guilt offering of 5:17 may seem to echo the sin offering of *4:27–28*, it differs in one important respect: the offering of 4:27–28 involves a sin committed "through error," or "unwittingly," as *tehchetah vishgahgah* is rendered respectively by JPS1 and JPS2/RSV. In distinction, the offering of 5:17 involves the commission of an act forbidden by the Lord "though he does not know it" (JPS1 and RSV) or "without knowing it" (JPS2) (From the phrase *v'ahstah ahchat mikal-mitzvot yahweh ahsher loh tayahsehnah v'loh-yahdah*).

To sin "unwittingly," or "through error," implies a lack of intent to commit the particular sin—as, for example, when an isolated person, having lost count of the days due to illness, mistakenly observes the sabbath on the sixth day, and thus fails to observe it on the seventh. Despite a blameless intent, he has "unwittingly," or "through error," violated the sabbath. He knew the law, but failed to comply.

Compare this with a lender who, having taken a garment as a pledge, fails to return it to the owner before the sun sets on the first day (Exod. 22:25–26). From the borrower's complaint, the lender first learns of the applicable law. Thus, the lender has acted intentionally in a manner that violated a law, but one that "he does not know."

To breach a known command "unwittingly," or "through error," at least includes the virtue of knowing what the Lord forbids. But to violate a law through ignorance of its existence could imply indifference to His requirements. In any case, P seems to require no greater expiation for acting in ignorance of the law than for "unwitting" violations of a law that is known. (Cf. 4:27–35, 5:18–19.)

> *Note L–16: For reasons not apparent, JPS2 and RSV both render the v'loh yahdah of 5:17 as "without knowing it," but go on to read the same phrase in 5:18 as "unwittingly." Conversely, by repeating "though he knew it not" in*

5:18, JPS1 *keeps a clear distinction between the offenses of 4:27–28 and 5:17, as discussed in Comment L–14.*

Comment L–15. On the equally problematic guilt offering of 5:17–19

Read literally, JPS2's use of "or the equivalent" in 5:18 permits the offeror to substitute an equivalent value in silver for the ram. If so, the passage again posits a form of "guilt offering" which requires no sacrificial offering of animals and which, in general, overrides the protocols of Lev. 7:1–10. (See Comment L–13.)

RSV reads 5:18 to require as a guilt offering "a ram without blemish out of the flock, valued by you at the price of the guilt offering." Similarly, JPS1 calls for "a ram . . . according to thy valuation." Unlike JPS2, neither JPS1 nor RSV explicitly provide for the substitution of an equivalent monetary value for the ram. Instead, both might be read to require a ram of adequate value to serve as liquidated damages (or a "fine") for the offense of having violated a command out of ignorance of the law. Even if we could assume a necessary range of valuations within the ram population, of what purpose is a ram of particular monetary value, if in any case it must be slaughtered and sacrificed? And how, if at all in such cases, can the value be related to the egregiousness of the offense? The question remains, therefore, of whether the guilt offerings of 5:15–16 and 17–19 constitute exceptions to the guilt offering protocols of Lev. 7:1–10.

In contrast to the previous sin and guilt offerings of Lev. 4 and 5, the final guilt offerings of 5:21–26 involve *intentional* wrongs, in this case against property rights.

Designated as "trespass[es] against the Lord," the following *intentional* conduct of 5:21–22 precipitates the guilt offerings of 5:23–26: "dealing deceitfully with his fellow in the matter of a deposit or pledge, or through robbery, or by defrauding, or by finding something lost and lying about it; if he swears falsely regarding anyone of the various things that one may do and sin thereby."

As in the first guilt offering of 5:15–16, repayment is an explicit condition for expiation—only here, to a lay person wrongfully deprived of property. Thus, "when one has sinned and, realizing his guilt, would *restore that which he has got through robbery or fraud, or the deposit that was entrusted, or the lost thing that he found, or anything else to which he swore falsely, he shall repay the principal amount and add a fifth part to it*" (5:23–24). Added to the squaring of accounts with the human victim is the guilt offering of a "ram without blemish." Yet the need to sacrifice a ram is again put in doubt by such phrases as "or the equivalent" (JPS2), or "according to thy valuation" (JPS1), or "valued by you for the price" (RSV). (See Comments L–13 and 15.)

Comment L–16. On the sins and penalties of 5:21–22

The text of 5:21–22 can be read to cover virtually every known means by which one person might gain, or retain, wrongful possession of another person's property whether by force, stealth, or deceit. *The overarching theme goes to the essence of the Eighth Commandment—"You shall not steal" by any means whatsoever.*

A more problematic element of the offense lies in the concluding intentional sin of 5:22: "If he swears falsely regarding anyone of the various things that one may do and sin thereby." In context, it can be read to apply to all the offenses of 5:21–22. Thus, Plaut has good grounds for citing Rashi to the effect that the phrase denotes a separate sin—"deny falsely on oath a money debt he has incurred."[8]

Such a "money debt" might well include the sinner's repayment obligation under 5:24, that is, "the principal amount and . . . a fifth part." Added to this basic obligation is the sinner's need to "restore *that which he got through robbery or fraud*" (5:23). To steal money, of course, is to steal as well the possible benefits of its use during the period prior to restitution. It thus follows that where repayment of stolen money is further delayed by the thief's false denials of having stolen it, 5:23 and 24, together, require an "accounting" and repayment of any profits realized from its use. This should include profits during the period in which repayment was delayed by false denials of guilt. In all, the procedures combine civil remedies and criminal punishment.

The Lord now turns to priestly rituals by first telling Moses, "Command Aaron and his sons thus . . ." (6:1–2).

Lev. 6:2–6 supplements the burnt offerings of Lev. 1 with an added requirement that "a perpetual fire shall be kept burning on the altar, not to go out" (6:6). The commands also cover the donning and doffing of priestly vestments and the disposal of ashes.

> *Note L–17: A "perpetual fire . . . at the altar" of the* portable *Tent of Meeting was hardly possible. Thus, the rituals look toward the Jerusalem Temple and its custodianship by the Aaronide priesthood.*

As to meal offerings, Lev. 6:7–11 largely repeats the rituals of Lev. 2, while saying nothing of their purposes (cf. Comment L–3). But they are declared "most holy, like the sin offering and the penalty [guilt] offering" (6:10). Lev. 2 provides that "the remainder of the meal offering [other than the Lord's 'token portion'] *shall be for Aaron and his sons.*" Lev 6:9 then requires their total consumption. "*What is left . . . shall be eaten* by Aaron and his sons . . . in . . . the Tent of Meeting." Further, "*Only the males among Aaron's descendants may eat of it as their due*" (6:11).

Note L–18: Limiting the offering to male descendants, or priests, presumably helps to confirm it as "most holy" (as confirmed in 6:22).

Lev. 6:12–16 looks toward the priestly anointment, ordination, and consecration rituals of Lev. 8–10. The instructions here, however, apply to the particular meal offering "that Aaron and his sons shall offer to the Lord on the occasion of his anointment" (6:13). It is to be a "*regular* meal offering" of "a tenth of an ephah of choice flour," half to be offered in the morning and half in the evening. As "a law for all time" it is to be prepared by each successor priest to Aaron. Unlike the usual meal offering, it is to be turned "entirely into smoke" (6:15). Similarly, "every meal offering *of a priest* [for whatever purpose] . . . shall not be eaten" (6:16).

The sin offering rituals of 6:17–23 add several requirements and give new emphasis to others. First, the slaughtering of animals for the sin offering was to be "at the spot" used for burnt offerings (6:18). Second, the officiating priest was required to eat of the offering in the "sacred precinct" (i.e., in the Tent of Meeting) (6:19). Third, procedures are spelled out for separating the blood of sacrificial animals from any contact with meat to be eaten. Thus, if porous earthen vessels in which blood might be absorbed were used to wash blood spattered garments in the "sacred precinct," the vessel must be "broken" (and discarded). However, a nonporous "copper vessel" could be "scoured and rinsed with water" (6:21). Also being "most holy," the sin offering could be eaten only by "males in the priestly line" (6:22). Sin offerings "from which any blood is brought into the Tent for expiation . . . shall be consumed in fire" (and thus not eaten) (6:23).

Lev. 7 adds supplemental details for the two offerings not covered in Lev. 6: the guilt offering (7:1–10) and the sacrifice of well-being (7:11–18, 28–36). However, the rules for the sacrifice of well-being are interrupted by the general prohibitions of 7:19–27.

Animals for the guilt offering of 7:1–10 are described in 7:1–5 as having the "broad tail" of a sheep or ram. Lev. 7:6–9 then takes up the allotment of guilt offerings among the "males in the priestly line" (7:6). "Like the sin offering," the guilt offering "shall belong to the priest who makes expiation thereby" (7:7). The same rule is applied to the "skin of the burnt offering" (the rest of which is for the Lord as "an offering by fire") (see 1:9, 15). The final verses of the guilt offering involve the allotment of meal offerings between the officiating priest and "the sons of Aaron all alike" (7:9–10).

Unlike the *detailed* rituals for guilt offerings which first appear in Lev. 7, those for the sacrifice of well-being first appear in Lev. 3. There, however, only animals are offered (i.e., a male or a female of the flock or herd, without blemish) and the purposes of "sacrifices of well-being" are not identified. Lev. 7:11–18 goes on to distinguish between "thanksgiving" offerings and "votive or freewill" offerings. The former (7:12–15) require an additional offering of "unleavened cakes with oil mixed in, unleavened wafers spread with oil, and cakes of choice flour, with oil mixed in, well soaked" (7:12). To these are added "cakes of *leavened* bread" (7:13). Provision is then made for (1) disposing of the cakes and wafers to the priest who performs the animal offering and (2) for eating the "flesh" of the sacrifice of well-being (7:14–15).

"Votive or freewill" offerings were of sacrificial animals alone, without added cereal offerings (7:16–18). Flesh of the sacrificial animal had to be eaten by the close of the second day following the sacrifice. Any remainder was burned on the third day. To eat of it was "offensive," thus requiring the consumer to "bear his guilt" (7:16–18).

> Note L–19: *Votive offerings relate in general to the making, breaking, or fulfillment of vows.*

Lev. 7:19–21 deals broadly with the cleanness of sacrificial flesh to be eaten and of the person who eats of flesh. First, flesh made unclean by physical contact with unclean objects (identified elsewhere) "shall not be eaten." Second, no otherwise edible flesh can be eaten by a person who becomes unclean by a similar contact. The penalty in both cases is to be "cut off from his kin." Lev. 7:22–27 then applies the same penalty to the consumption of *"fat from animals"* and the *"blood, either of bird or animal"* (7:25–27).

> Note L–20: *In that certain birds could be offered for sacrifice (1:14–17), we might assume them to be included among the sacrificial animals from which no fat could be eaten. Yet the inclusion of "bird or animal" in regard to blood and the exclusion of birds in regard to fat suggests the permissibility of eating the fat of birds.*

The rituals of the sacrifice of well-being are concluded in 7:28–34, in which the "wave" and "heave" offerings first appear in Leviticus (cf. Exod. 29:26–28). The offeror by "his own hands" presents "the fat with the breast" to the priest. (Lev. 3 allows for the offering of any male or female "without blemish" from the herd or flock.) The priest then burns the fat on the altar. Separately, the breast, which is for "Aaron and his sons," is first "waved as a wave offering before the Lord." The right thigh is reserved as a "gift" to the one "among Aaron's sons" who makes the offering. Reference to the heave offering then appears in 7:34: "For I have taken the *breast of wave offering and the thigh of heave offering* from the Israelites, from their sacrifices of well-being, and given them to Aaron . . . and . . . to his sons as their due . . . for all time." The point is then repeated in Lev. 7:35–36.

Comment L–17. On the "wave" and "heave" offerings

As elements of the sacrifice of well-being, the "wave" (*tenufah*) and "heave" (*terumah*) offerings were distinguished by Rashi according to their respective hand-propelled movements: of the breast, "forward and backward" and of the thigh, "upward and downward."[9]

Lev. 7 concludes with a sudden shift of locale. "These are the rituals of the burnt offering, the meal offering, the sin offering, the guilt offering, the offering of ordination, and the sacrifice of well-being, *with which the Lord charged Moses on Mount Sinai*, when he commanded that the Israelites present their offering to the Lord, in the wilderness of Sinai" (7:37–38).

Comment L–18. On reconciling Lev. 1:1 and 7:37–38

In Lev. 1:1, "The Lord . . . spoke to [Moses] from the Tent of Meeting." And there He and Moses remain throughout Lev. 1:1–7:36. But now, in 7:37–38, we are told that "the Lord" had "charged" Moses with the various offerings of Lev. 7 while "*on* Mount Sinai."

"On Mount Sinai" is from *behar sinai*. While, JPS2 and RSV read the phrase as "*on* Mount Sinai," JPS1 reads the *b'* of *behar* as "*in*" Mount Sinai. By reading "in Mount Sinai" as "in the vicinity of Mount Sinai," we could settle the matter—for that is where the Tent now sits. Indeed, Ramban views this approach as a useful textual solution.[10]

While I agree with Ramban that an answer lies within the Torah itself, I think it is better expressed in the particular purpose of Lev. 7:38. In short, while Lev. 7:38 can be read as a summary of the offerings of Lev. 7, its primary purpose is to introduce Lev. 8 and 9 by recalling the rites of anointment, ordination, and consecration revealed to Moses "on Mount Sinai" in Exod. 29. Thus, Lev. 7:38 tells of the imminent completion of a process begun in Exod. 39–40.

At the conclusion of Exod. 39, we are told (in regard to the Tent and tabernacle) that "the Israelites had done all the work . . . as the Lord had commanded" (Exod. 39:42–43). But three major tasks remain, as to which Moses receives the Lord's instructions in Exod. 40:1–15. These are: (1) the assemblage of the completed components of the Tabernacle of the Tent of Meeting into an actual structure (Exod. 40:2–8); (2) the anointment of the Tabernacle and its contents, including, in particular, the altar, and the laver (Exod. 40:9–11); and (3) the anointment and consecration of Aaron and his sons as priests, *according to the ordination rites of Exod. 29* (Exod. 40:12–15). As to all of these distinct tasks, Exod. 40:16 then states the following: "*This Moses did; just as the Lord had commanded him, so he did.*"

Despite its use of the past tense, it is clear that 40:16 looks to the future, that is, to what Moses will have done, rather than to what he has already done. Thus, it was not until "the first month of the second year, on the first of the month, the Tabernacle was set up" (as the Lord had directed in Exod. 40:2) (40:17–33). Similarly, the final verses of Exodus (40:34–38) set the scene for Lev. 1, when "the Presence of the Lord filled the Tabernacle" and "Moses could not enter the Tent of Meeting" (Exod. 40:35). *As Exodus ends, tasks (2) and (3) remain undone, that is, anointing the Tabernacle and its contents and anointing and consecrating Aaron and his sons. These will now be done in Lev. 8 and 9.*

That the named offerings of Lev. 7:37–38 refer mainly to those of Exod. 29 rather than Lev. 7 is first suggested by the inclusion of the "offering of ordination." Neither Lev. 7 nor Lev. 1–6 before it refers to an "offering of ordination." A reader might initially identify the priest's meal offering of 6:12–16 "on the occasion of his anointment" as an "ordination" offering. This simple meal offering, however, is but a small element among the offerings required by Exod. 29:1–37, and fulfilled in Lev. 8, in "ordaining," or "consecrating," the priests (29:1).

Also, with the two exceptions of "guilt" and "meal" offerings, each offering named in Lev. 7:37–38 is also named in Exod. 29 as components of the composite rituals of the "offering of ordination" (see 29:10–14 [sin]; 21:15–18 [burnt], 29:26–28 [sacrifice of well-being]). And though not named as such in the "ordination" offerings of Exod. 29, the "guilt" and "meal" offerings are clearly identified.

Thus, the offering of Exod. 29:19–22 can be compared to the guilt offering of Lev. 7:1–7. In both, the offering is of a "ram without blemish" (cf. Exod. 29:1; Lev. 5:15, 18, 25). Identical portions of the ram are offered (cf. Exod. 29:22, Lev. 7:3–4). *Only in its application of blood to the persons of Aaron and his sons* do the rituals of Exod. 29:19–22 differ from guilt offering of Lev. 7:1. *In effect, the unnamed guilt offering of Exod. 29 is simply adapted to its special use as a ritual of "ordination."*

As to meal offerings, Exod. 29:23–24 may be compared to Lev. 2 and 6:7–11. As is evident in Lev. 2, meal offerings may vary with their particular purposes. Thus, the "one flat loaf of bread, one cake of oil bread, and one wafer" of Exod. 29:42 was also adapted to the occasion of ordination.

This process of adaptation is best demonstrated in the sacrifice of well-being of Exod. 29. Lev. 3 allows the offering of an animal of either sex from the herd or the flock as a sacrifice of well-being. However, as part of the "ordination" offering, the sacrifice is limited to the "*ram* of ordination" (Exod. 29:26–28).

As a composite offering, the guilt and meal offerings of Exod. 29:19–25 are given the generic designation of an "offering by fire to the Lord" (Exod. 29:25). Before being "turned to smoke," however, the composite offering is made "as a wave offering" (29:24). Thereafter, the breast and thigh of the ram are incorporated into a designated "sacrifice of well-being." This is done through a second wave offering of "the breast of Aaron's ram of ordination" (29:26). Reference is also made to the consecration of "the thigh that was offered as a heave offering from the ram of ordination" (Exod. 29:27). From the central role of the "ram of ordination" in these integrated offerings, we can conclude that in combination they serve as a composite "ordination" offering.

Thus, as noted initially, apart from its possible use as an imperfect summary of Lev. 7, Lev. 7:37–38 serves primarily to recall the anointment, ordination and consecration rites of Exod. 29 and to preface their imminent fulfillment in Lev. 8. And it was "on Mount Sinai" that Moses was so "charged" and it will be "in the wilderness of Sinai" that the rites of Exod. 29 will now take place.

Lev. 8 marks the fulfillment of the Lord's commands to Moses on the ordination of Aaron (Exod. 29) and on the anointment of the Tabernacle (Exod. 40:9–15). For these events, the Lord tells Moses to "assemble the *whole community* at the entrance of the Tent of Meeting" (8:3).

Comment L–19. On the legitimizing presence of the "whole community" of Israel at the priestly ordination of Aaron and his sons

It was not customary for the community to witness the cultic rituals of priests in which it had no role. In general, Moses instructed "the Israelite people" only on their own roles in the various offerings (see Lev. 1:1–2 as to Lev. 1–5). Knowledge of rituals in which the people had no role was largely, or formally, limited to "Aaron and his sons." Yet, P would have the "whole community" of Israel witness these particular priestly rituals.

In the wilderness of Sinai, it could have sufficed for Moses to witness and validate the rituals for the people. In the era of the First (or Second) Temple, however, when P wrote of these matters, there was no Moses. Centuries later, the "fact" that the "whole community" had witnessed the ordination rites of Aaron and his sons could only strengthen the Aaronide claim to the Temple priesthood.

The rituals of anointment and ordination largely, if not precisely, track the instructions of Exod. 29 and 40. (Cf. Lev. 8:1–9/Exod. 29:1–9; Lev. 8:10–13/Exod. 30:26–30, 40:9–15; Lev. 8:14–17/Exod. 29:9d–14; Lev. 8:18–21/Exod. 29:15–18; Lev. 8:22–29/Exod. 29:19–20, 22–28; Lev. 8:30/Exod. 29:21, 29–30; Lev. 8:31–35/Exod. 29:29–30; and Exod. 29:31–37/Lev. 8:31–35.)

Comment L–20. On the locations of the altar of
(1) animal offerings within the Tent and
(2) Aaron and his sons during the seven days of ordination

On concluding His ordination instructions in Exod. 29, the Lord tells Moses, "Thus you shall do to Aaron and his sons, just as I have commanded you. You shall ordain them through seven days, and each day you shall prepare a bull as a sin offering for expiation; you shall purge the altar by performing purification on it, and you shall anoint and consecrate it. Seven days shall you perform purification for the altar to consecrate it" (29:35).

While Exod. 29 is silent on the location of Aaron and his sons during the seven days when they were not engaged in ordination rituals, Lev. 8:35 is not. It thus requires their presence *at the entrance* of the Tent of Meeting day and night for seven days, keeping the Lord's charge—that you may not die— for so I have commanded."

Given the location of the sacrificial altar at the entrance of the Tent of Meeting, the priests' continuing presence *at the entrance* seems theoretically possible. (For references to the location of the sacrificial altar see Lev. 1:5; 3:2, 4:18.) Possibly more permissive regarding their movements within the Tent, however, is 8:33: "You shall not go outside the entrance of the Tent of Meeting [until completion of the seven days of ordination rites]."

But even a wider freedom to move throughout the Tent (if intended) might not suffice to dispel the impact of the protocol of Exod. 29:14: "The rest of the bull, its hide and its dung, shall be put to the fire, outside the camp, it is a sin offering." *Unless this sin offering can be fulfilled by persons other than the priests within the Tent*, the removal of the "rest of the bull . . . and its dung" must await completion of the seven days of ordination rites. (Such work-a-day details were prudently omitted from the ordination rites of Exod. 29.)

Following the complex rites (to which the Torah's words alone can do justice) of (1) the anointment and consecration of the Tent and Tabernacle and their contents and (2) the anointment, consecration, and ordination of the priests, the Lord's earthly abode is complete. Lev. 9 then tells of the final preparations to effect His Presence.

On the day following the seven days of ordination rites, Moses instructed "Aaron and his sons" and "the elders of Israel" on ceremonies for the Lord's appearance on that day. Aaron was to offer as a *sin* and a *burnt offering*, respectively, "a [bull] calf of the herd and a ram . . . without blemish (9:2). In turn, the people were to bring as a *sin* and a *burnt offering*, respectively, "a he-goat" and "a calf and lamb, yearlings without blemish."; and, as an *offering of well-being for sacrifice*, "an ox and a ram . . . and a *meal offering* with oil mixed in" (9:3–4).

Note L–21: Of the various sacrificial offerings of Lev. 9:2–4, only the ox and ram of the peoples' "offering of well-being" are not explicitly required to be "without blemish." This differs from the general protocols for the sacrifice of well-being (see Lev. 3:1, 6). Either some particular purpose of Lev. 9:3–4 supercedes the rule of Lev. 3, or Lev. 3:1 and 6 is assumed to cover all such offerings. Given the purpose of welcoming the Lord's Presence, it seems unlikely that a "blemished" animal could meet the need.

Aaron and his sons and the people brought the animals to "the front of the Tent of Meeting," and "the whole community came forward and stood before the Lord" (9:5). Moses then reveals the purpose of the rituals to the people. "This is what the Lord has commanded that you do, *that the Presence of the Lord may appear to you*" (9:6). Moses then directed Aaron to "come forward to the altar and sacrifice your sin offering and your burnt offering, making expiation for yourself and for the people, and sacrifice the people's offering and make expiation for them" (9:7).

Comment L–21. On the Presence of the Lord

Awaiting the Lord's revealed Presence, as their God, the whole community of Israel now stood before Him at "the front of the Tent of Meeting." It was a moment of high tension, for as Moses had often told them, His Presence will be subject to their adequate obedience to His commands. If inadequate, will He quietly withdraw? Or will He make His Presence known, not as the Lord, *their God*, but solely as Lord of the universe?

Lev. 9:8–21 sets out the detailed rituals of the offerings of Aaron and his sons and of the people. These basically conform to previous instructions as to (1) the distribution of the blood of the animals at the altar and within the tent, (2) the burning (or "turning to smoke") of designated portions of the animals, and (3) the disposition of other portions. What varies, however, is the final wave offering of the sacrifice of well-being. Thus, "they laid these fat parts over the breasts [of the ox and ram]; and Aaron turned the fat parts into smoke on the altar, and waved the breasts and *the right thighs as a wave offering* before the Lord—*as Moses had commanded*" (9:20–21).

Comment L–22. On Moses' command to use the right thigh in a wave offering

As noted above, Lev. 7:28–34 repeatedly calls for use of the "breast" in the wave offering and the "thigh" in the heave offering (see also Comment L–17). As a further reminder of the use of thighs in heave offerings, Moses might have recalled the Lord's same instructions on wave and heave offerings as part of the ordination rituals "You shall consecrate *the breast that was offered as a wave offering* and *the thigh that was offered as a heave offering*" (Exod. 29:26–28). But to no effect. "[Aaron] waved the breasts *and the right thighs* as a wave offering before the Lord—*as Moses had commanded*" (9:20–21). What has become of the heave offering?

As preparations close for the Lord's Presence in the Tent of Meeting, Moses and Aaron enter the Tent and then reemerge to bless the people. At that point "the Presence of the Lord appeared to all the people" (9:23). It was not, however, a serene Presence. "Fire came forth from before the Lord and consumed the burnt offering and the fat parts on the altar." Then "all the people saw and shouted, and fell on their faces" (9:24).

> Note L–22: *Once again, the Lord revealed His Presence with frightening dramatic effect. Given the manner of His "appearance," the people could be excused for any confusion as to His appearance as a vengeful Lord, or a compassionate God (see Comment L–21). In any case, such confusion as there may have been was fully vindicated by what then followed.*

Not all is well within the Tent. "Now Aaron's sons, Nadab and Abihu, each took his fire pan, put fire in it, and laid incense on it, and they offered before the Lord *alien fire*, which He had not enjoined on them. And fire came forth from the Lord and consumed them; thus they died at the instance of the Lord" (10:1–2).

P's Lord need never explain His conduct. But by now (putting aside the use of a right thigh in a "wave offering") Moses has learned much more of His ways. To a grieving Aaron, he explains that the death of his sons only confirms the unique closeness of the priests to the Lord. "This is what the Lord meant when He said: 'Through those near to Me I show Myself holy, And assert My authority before all the people.' " And Aaron was silent (10:3).

Moses then cautions Aaron and his remaining sons, Eleazer and Ithamar, against any open expressions of grief. "Do not bare your heads and do not rend your clothes lest you die and anger strike the entire community" (10:6). Instead, "your kinsman, all the house of Israel, shall bewail the burning that the Lord has wrought" (10:6).

> Note L–23: *Why does Moses counsel against any display of personal grief by father and brothers, even as he welcomes expressions of communal grief? Does he sense a crisis in relations between the the Lord and His priests. If the Lord indeed feels that His sanctity has been affronted, Moses may sense that He would not look kindly on mere personal grief for the loss of sons and brothers. However, being less influenced by personal loss, "the house of*

Israel" will more likely focus on what P's Lord would regard as a proper basis for grief—that is, the misdeeds that compelled Him to kill.

Moses concludes his counsel by warning Aaron not to leave the Tent of Meeting, "lest you die, for the Lord's anointing oil is upon you" (10:7).

Now all seems forgiven as the Lord again speaks to Aaron: "Drink no wine or other intoxicant, you or your sons . . . when you enter the Tent of Meeting that you may not die—it is a law for all time. . . . For *you* must distinguish between the sacred and profane, and between the clean and unclean; and *you* must teach the Israelites all the laws which the Lord has imparted to them through Moses" (10:8–11).

Moses then instructs Aaron, Eleazar, and Ithamar, his remaining sons, on eating the meal offering and "the breast of wave offering and the thigh of heave offering." As before, the meal offering could only be eaten by priests while in the Tent. But "from the Israelites' sacrifices of well-being," they, and their "sons *and daughters*," may eat the breast and thigh "in any clean place" (10:12–15).

> Note L–24: For children to eat of the breast and thigh suggests the more relaxed atmosphere of the sacrifice of well-being. Literally, however, their privilege did not extend to wives and mothers. (As to "mothers and wives," see Note N–77.)

Lev. 10:16–20 completes the subject of offerings with an enigma. The passage involves a command regarding sin offerings, which Moses states as follows: "The priest who offers it as a sin offering *shall* eat of it; it shall be eaten in the sacred precinct, in the enclosure of the Tent of Meeting." But as the rituals drew to a close, "Moses inquired about the goat of the sin offering," only to find that "it had already been burned (beyond edibility)"! Rather than to Aaron, Moses directs his anger to Aaron's two remaining sons, Eleazar and Ithamar: "Why did you not eat the sin offering in the sacred area? *For it is most holy, and He has given it to you remove the guilt of the community and to make expiation before the Lord.* Since its blood was not brought inside the sanctuary, you should have certainly eaten in the sanctuary, as I commanded" (10:17–18). (Here Moses cites the command of Lev. 6:23: "But no sin offering may be eaten from which any blood is brought into the Tent of Meeting for expiation in the sanctuary; any such shall be consumed in fire" (10:18).

Aaron's reply recalled the day's tragedy. "See, this day they have brought their sin offering and their burnt offering before the Lord, and such things have befallen me! *Had I eaten sin offering today, would the Lord have approved?*" (10:19). "And when Moses heard this, he approved" (10:20).

Comment L–23. On the matter of the uneaten sin offering

Had Aaron pleaded no more than overwhelming grief as reason for not
having eaten the sin offering, we could easily sympathize. In an instant he
had lost his two eldest sons. Yet Moses, with his own responsibilities to a
demanding Lord God, chastised Aaron for a reason that (to him) transcended
all personal grief. For it was to "remove the guilt of the community and to
make expiation before the Lord" that Aaron was charged to "eat the sin
offering in the sacred area."

In fact, however, Aaron's words were not meant as a plea of grief in self-
defense. Instead, he tells Moses of his own concern for the Lord's holiness.
Surely the sin offering had been corrupted by the same "alien fire" for which
the Lord had slain his sons. How could Aaron then "remove the guilt of the
community" with a corrupted offering? And so he asks, "would the Lord
have approved?" In this, P's Moses must accede to P's Aaron.

Comment L–24. On animal sacrifice and the
conscience of Israel—Lev. 1–10

The prominence of animal slaughter and blood and of arcane rituals can
easily discourage any effort to identify positive elements in the Levitical sacrifices. Yet, in functional terms, the Levitical sacrifices could have served to
institutionalize the processes of atonement as the possible means of inter-
nalizing the principles of morality and ethics.

*For P, the conscience of Israel, both collectively and individually, was
embedded in the authority of the Lord, its God.* The source of a clear conscience was obedience to Him. The source of a troubled conscience was disobedience. For P, human free will offered little more than a choice between
obedience and disobedience.

But if the sacrificial system was meant to serve the worthy end of human
atonement, what can we be said of the chosen means? What worthy human
values could be vindicated by institutionalized animal slaughter? In truth,
none—except as such slaughter *at the time* might avert even worse alternatives.

As can be inferred from the Torah and contemporaneous biblical passages, the practice of child sacrifice may have been that alternative. If a
wrathful and quixotic Lord could be placated by the sacrifice of valuable livestock, how much more might He be appeased by the sacrifice of a child?
Indeed, it was just from such "logic" that the *akedah* myth emerged (cf. Comments G–39, 40, and 41).

In any case, the potential appeal of child sacrifice to the Israelites was perceived as a real threat. Consider this Deuteronomic warning to the Israelites as
they approach Canaan: "When the Lord your God has cut down before you the
nations which you are about to invade and dispossess . . . beware of being lured
into their ways after they have been wiped out before you! Do not inquire

about their gods, saying 'How did those nations worship their gods? I too will follow those practices.' You shall not act thus toward the Lord your God, for *they perform for their gods every abhorrent act that the Lord detests, they even offer up their sons and daughters in fire to their gods"* (Deut. 12:29–31).

Although less explicitly than Deuteronomy, Leviticus will also address the subject of child sacrifice. "Do not allow any of your offspring to be offered up to Molech" (18:21). ("Molech" is thought to come from "Moloch," widely regarded as another name for Baal, to whom burnt offerings of children were made.) After much deliberation, Ramban concluded that Lev. 18:21 alludes to a practice in which "the child was actually consumed by flames."[11]

Jeremiah (c. 640–587 B.C.E.) also tells of how Israelites had succumbed to the fantasies of child sacrifice. Through the words of "the Lord of hosts, the God of Israel," he reports the following: "For the children of Judah have done that which is evil in my sight. . . . They have built the high place of Topheth . . . to burn their sons and their daughters in the fire; which I commanded not, neither came it to My mind" (Jer. 7:30–31).[12]

But even as a "benign" alternative to the fiery sacrifices of children, the system of animal sacrifices was not immune to prophetical condemnation. For expressions of their varied concerns, see Isa. 1:11–17, Jer. 7:21–23, Hos. 6:6, Amos 5:21–24, Mic. 6:6–7, Mal. 1:14, and Prov. 21:3.

The most common concern was that sacrificial offerings, whether in repentance or gratitude, would become "proxies," or substitutes, for commitments to righteous conduct (see Isa. 1:11–17, Hos. 6:6, Amos 5:21–24, Mic. 6:6–7, and Prov. 21:3). The following brief statements are from Hosea and Proverbs: (1) "For I desire mercy and not sacrifice, and the knowledge of God rather than burnt-offerings." (2) "To do righteousness and justice is more acceptable to the Lord than sacrifice." The main concern of these authors was the hypothetical use of sacrifices as surrogates for righteous conduct.

In sharp contrast to these substantive concerns, Malachi decried the corruption of sacrifices through impurities. Thus, his scornful observation: "You offer polluted bread upon My altar. . . . And when you offer the blind for sacrifice, it is no evil! And when you offer the lame and sick, it is no evil!" (Mal. 1:7–80). Malachi's aim was not to abolish sacrifices, but to restore their purity of purpose and practice.

Among the prophetic critics of the sacrificial system, Jeremiah, above all, undertook to question their sacred foundation. In the words of his God: "I spoke not to your fathers, nor commanded them in the day that I brought them out of the land of Egypt, concerning burnt offerings or sacrifices; but this thing I commanded them, saying: 'Hearken to My voice and I will be your God, and you shall be My people; and walk in all the way that I command you, that it may be well with you' " (Jer. 7:22–23). (With the end of sacrifices following the destruction of the Second Temple in 70 C.E., this passage was aptly included in the *haftarah* for the *sidrah, Tsav,* covering Lev. 6–8.)

Having been incorporated in the Torah as the means of expiation through atonement, the sacrificial system served two other purposes. For P, it provided a vivid reminder of the Aaronide priests as God's anointed intermediaries between Him and His people. And as a proxy for *material* images of Israel's God, the sacrificial descriptions offered mental images through repeated allusions to His human sensory capabilities.

Lev. 11 now turns from the use of animals for sacrifice to their wider use for food. Lev. 11:1–23 distinguishes between the ritually edible and inedible by type. It covers four broad classifications: (1) "land animals," (2) "all that live in the water," (3) "the birds," and (4) "winged swarming things." And now, for the first time in Leviticus, the Lord speaks to "Moses and Aaron" (11:1).

Comment L–25. On Aaron as joint auditor with Moses

In Lev. 10:8–11 the Lord had warned Aaron alone against drinking intoxicants in the Tent of Meeting. This was followed by technical instructions to Aaron and his two remaining sons regarding the meal, and other, offerings (10:11–15). Otherwise, the revelations of Lev. 1–10 were to Moses alone. Citing Lev. 10:10, Plaut offers the following explanation for the revelation of the dietary laws of Lev. 11 to both Moses and Aaron: "Aaron was included . . . since the priests had the duty of teaching the people to distinguish clean from unclean."[13] If so, what of the balance of Lev. 10:10–11? "For you must distinguish between the sacred and the profane, and between the clean and unclean; *and you must teach the Israelites all the laws which the Lord has imparted to them through Moses.*"

Since the final charge would justify the direct revelation of all laws to Aaron, another factor might be Aaron's recent ordination as high priest (Lev. 10). In this first post-ordination revelation, P may wish to memorialize Aaron's enhanced status by including him as a joint auditor.

In Exodus, joint auditorship occurred primarily in episodes involving Moses, Aaron and Pharaoh. Yet, within them, various commands meant for Aaron's sole execution were spoken to Moses alone (e.g., see Exod. 7:19, 8:1). Overall, the Lord's direct revelations to both might seem sporadic. However, of those in Exod. 6:13, 7:8, 9:8, 12:1 and 12:43, Friedman attributes four to P and one to R.

The prohibitions against the consumption of particular animals are as follows:

1. As to "land animals" (11:2–8). The distinction between what is permitted and forbidden is stated in terms of the former, that is, "any animal that has true hoofs, with clefts through the hoofs, and that chews the cud." Several marginal animals, each possessed of two qualifying features but lacking a third,

are then disqualified. These include the camel, the daman (from Asia and southern Africa), the hare, and the swine. These are all described as "unclean." As with all forbidden animals, their flesh could not be eaten and contact with their carcasses was to be avoided.

2. As to "all that live in the water" (11:9–12). Once again a stated combination of physical qualities separates the edible from the inedible. The condition of edibility for all creatures of all waters is that they have both "fins and scales." All other creatures of the water were declared an "abomination." By implication, therefore, carcasses of "abominable" water creatures, like those of forbidden land animals, were also unclean and untouchable.

3. As to "the birds" (11:13–19). Rather than being identified as edible by virtue of particular physical characteristics, as were land animals and water creatures, birds are declared inedible by name alone. All unnamed birds could be eaten. The difficulties in classifying "birds" as edible or not is reflected in the identification of the "bat" (a flying mammal) as a bird (11:19).

As it appears in JPS2, the birds to be "abominated" consisted of "the eagle, the vulture and the black vulture; the kite, falcons of every variety; all varieties of ravens; the ostrich, the nighthawk, the sea gull; hawks of every variety; the little owl, the cormorant and the great owl; the white owl, the pelican and the bustard; the stork; herons of every variety; the hoopoe, and the bat."

> Note L–25: By designated name, the birds of JPS1/RSV sometimes vary from those of JPS2 and from each other. While many of the named birds would qualify as "birds of prey," some would not. In all, the classification standards can be discerned only by experts. But more important than the particular choices is that P chose to establish a class of ritually inedible birds (and other flying beings).

4. As to "winged swarming things" (11:20–23). The basis for identifying edible and inedible "winged swarming things" again differs from previous categories. After the entire class that "walk[s] on fours" is declared inedible, exceptions are made for "all that have, above their feet, jointed legs to leap with on the ground." But the "all" of the exception is then limited to "locusts of every variety; all varieties of bald locust; crickets of every variety; and all varieties of grasshopper."

Comment L–26. On the dietary prohibitions of Lev. 11

Recall once more the post-flood words of a remorseful God to Noah and his sons as He withdrew His initial edict of vegetarianism (see Gen. 1:29.) "*Every creature that lives shall be yours to eat*; as with the green grasses, I give you all these" (Gen. 9:3). This dispensation reflected His more realistic view of humankind. "Never again will I doom the earth because of man, since the devisings of man's mind are evil from his youth" (Gen. 8:21).

In distinguishing between edible and inedible animals, health concerns, as then perceived, were conceivably a factor. But surely more decisive in this repeal of God's pronouncement of Gen. 9:3 was the goal of Israel's cultic distinctiveness.

Lev. 11:24–47 describes contacts with dead animals that render a person unclean. As for land animals, the following carcasses are declared unclean: (1) "every animal that has true hoofs but without clefts through the hoofs, or that does not chew the cud," and (2) "all animals that walk on paws, among those that walk on fours" (11:24–27).

A two-part distinction is then made in regard to the consequences of such contacts. Merely to touch such a carcass would render a person unclean, but only "until evening," when the state of uncleanness would automatically terminate. However, a person who carried a carcass was also obliged to "wash his clothes" (11:27–28).

> Note L–26: While the touching of an unclean carcass might be inadvertent, its carriage would likely be intentional, for whatever reason. Yet no more opprobrium attaches to an intentional carriage than to unintended touching. The need to wash the clothes simply recognizes that carriage has also made them unclean. The aim is not to punish an intentional contact, but to restore the clothes to cleanliness. In an agricultural economy, the death of unclean beasts of burden (whether of asses or camels) would be commonplace. To carry off their carcasses could hardly be sinful.

Lev. 11:29–38 deals with uncleanness resulting from contacts with certain creatures "from among the things that swarm on the earth." These are said to include the following: "the mole [or weasel], the mouse, and great lizards of every variety; the gecko, the land crocodile, the lizard, the sand lizard, and the chameleon" (11:29–30).

> Note L–27: These specific references to the "mole" and "mouse" and the broad references to "great lizards of every variety" leaves the coverage of 11:29–30 uncertain. Indeed, what JPS2 identifies as a "mole," JPS1 and RSV identify as a "weasel." Their commonality today is as mammals. (On the role of 11:29–30 and 11:41–42 in defining the scope of such "swarming things" on earth, see Comment L–27.)

The touching of any dead creature thought to be covered by 11:29–38 would render a person unclean "until evening." Furthermore, "anything on which [such a dead creature] falls shall be unclean." Here the "anything" includes "any article of wood, or a cloth, or a skin, or a sack—any such article that can be put to use."

On becoming unclean, the "thing" must be dipped in water and "it shall remain unclean until evening; then it shall be clean." (Literally, a "thing" that falls on a carcass is not declared unclean.)

Any item that came in contact with water made unclean from a carcass would thereby become unclean. The special importance of water as a source of uncleanness was expressed as follows: "If such a carcass falls upon seed grain to be sown, it is clean; but if water is put on the seed and any part of a carcass falls on it, it shall be unclean for you."

Lev. 11:39–40 deals with carcasses of ritually edible animals that die without having been slaughtered for food. Thus, "if an animal that you may eat has died, anyone who touches its carcass shall be unclean until evening; anyone who eats of the carcass shall wash his clothes and remain unclean until evening; and anyone who carries its carcass shall wash his clothes and remain unclean until evening."

> Note L–28: Notable here is the edibility of an animal rendered unclean by manner of death.

Following the designation of various creatures "among the things that swarm on the earth" as unclean (11:29–30), Lev. 11:41–43 now takes up the edibility of "all the things that swarm on earth." Especially when compared to the selective identification of unclean animals in 11:29–38, the sweeping prohibition and projected horror of 11:41–43 warrants close consideration. Thus, "all the things that swarm upon the earth are an abomination; they shall not be eaten. You shall not eat, among all the things that swarm upon the earth, anything that crawls on its belly, or anything that walks on fours, or anything that has many legs; for they are an abomination. You shall not draw abomination upon yourselves through anything that swarms; you shall not make your self unclean therewith and thus become unclean" (11:41–43). The passage then concludes with a dramatic invocation of the Lord's sanctity and authority: "For I the Lord am your God; you shall sanctify yourself and be holy. You shall not make yourselves unclean through any swarming thing that moves upon the earth. For I the Lord am He who brought you up from the land of Egypt to be your God; you shall be holy for I am holy" (11:44–45).

Comment L–27. On the scope of "all things that swarm upon the earth" in 11:29–30 and 11:42–43

Lev. 11:41 declares that "all the things that swarm on the earth are an abomination." They are not to be eaten. In 11:42, however, from "among all the things that swarm upon the earth," JPS2 would prohibit only three designated categories. Literally, this admits the possibilty that other unnamed categories were edible and clean. JPS1/RSV, however omit the use of "among."

They assume instead that the three designated categories of "things" are representative of "all the swarming things that swarm upon the earth" (11:42) and of "any swarming thing that swarms" (11:43). In this way, JPS1/RSV maintain a symmetry between 11:41 and 11:42–44 in which "all" things that swarm on the earth are classified as both unclean and inedible.

However, in regard to 11:29–30, as it applies to contaminance rather than edibility, JPS2 and JPS1/RSV concur that the named animals are only "*among* the things that swarm on the earth." Here it should be noted that "*among* the swarming things" in 11:29 is from *basheretz*, while the "all" of 11:42 is from *l'chal hasheretz*. Are the different Hebrew terms of 11:29 and 11:42 meant to establish different scopes of coverage? Or is the distinction inadvertent?

Comment L–28. On the Lord as the self-appointed God of Israel

The final verse regarding "swarming things on earth" includes these words: "For I the Lord am He who brought you up from the land of Egypt to be your God" (11:45). These two distinct aspects of the Lord as (1) an innate "universal Being" and (2) the self-appointed God to Israel alone constitutes a continuing theme throughout the Torah. The idea of a powerful Lord who chooses to be the God of Israel is utilized to evoke the two great pillars of obedience. Toward the Lord there is the fear that flows from His power; and toward God there is the reverence that flows from His special concern. (See, for example, Comments G–39 pt. 2, G–43, G–56, E–54 pt. 1, and L–21.)

Lev. 12:1–8 deals with the "unclean" state of women following childbirth and the means of purification.

> Note L–29: This is the first occasion in which a person becomes unclean by fulfilling the will of God (see Comment G–2). It underscores the point that being "unclean" need imply neither fault nor opprobrium.

The process of birth offers no exception to the Torah's distinctive treatment of males and females. As stated by the Lord to Moses, when a woman bears a male, "she shall be unclean seven days; she shall be unclean as at the time of her menstrual infirmity."

> Note L–30: Uncleanness from "menstrual infirmity" is also the subject of Lev. 15:19–24.

Circumcision of the male child takes place "on the eighth day." The mother then remains "in a state of blood purification for thirty-three days." During that time she may not touch any "consecrated thing" or "enter the sanctuary." For daughters, the mother's unclean period and "state of blood purification" were doubled to "two weeks" and "sixty-six days" (12:5).

> *Note L–31: That postnatal mothers could not for a time "enter the sanctuary" implies that when "clean" they could. At the time portrayed in Leviticus, "the sanctuary" would have been the Tent and Tabernacle rather than the Jerusalem Temple. As yet, technically, it did not exist. From all that follows in the Torah, however, such entry seems unlikely.*

Following the appropriate purification period, the mother brought prescribed animal offerings to the priest at the entry of the Tent of Meeting. As a burnt offering, she brought "a lamb in its first year," and as a sin offering, "a pigeon or a turtledove" (12:6). As with the sins of Lev. 5:1–4, a means test is available to mothers of lesser means. As a burnt offering, a bird might be offered in place of the lamb. Similarly, the usual requirement of a lamb "without blemish" is waived (cf. Lev. 5:7–10; see Comment L–11). The priest then made expiation on her behalf and she was clean.

Comment L–29. On the double periods of purification for mothers of newborn female children

Why does the mother of a daughter remain unclean and in a state of blood purification for twice the time of the mother of a son? Rashi avoids the issue, while Ramban offers a medical solution.[14] "We must say that the reason is that the nature of the female is cold and moist, and the white [fluid] in the mother's womb is then exceedingly abundant and cold, this being the reason why she gave birth to a female child. Hence she needs a longer time to become clean [in a physical sense] on account of the abundant moisture in her which contain the ill-smelling blood, and on account of the coldness [of her body]." By positing the physiological views of his own time, does Ramban mean to discount the Torah's broader cultural orientation?

Comment L–30. On the generic affliction of *tzara'at*: a preface to Lev. 13 and 14

Tzara'at appears in Lev. 13 and 14 as a disease or abnormality that can afflict not only persons but also cloth, garments, and houses. To be so afflicted is to be unclean. The impact of *tzara'at* on persons is the subject of Lev. 13:1–46 and 14:1–32. The first passage deals with the diagnosis of skin conditions which were thought to indicate the possible presence of *tzara'at*. The second sets out the purification rites for afflicted persons later found to be free of *tzara'at*. Neither passage speaks of curative treatments. As will become evident, our three "standard" English translations of the Torah vary in their perceptions of the various afflictions known as *tzara'at*.

The two passages on *tzara'at* in persons are separated by Lev. 13:47–59, which deals with *tzara'at* in cloth, or garments. The final passage deals with *tzara'at* in houses (14:33–57). This passage is separated from its companion passage on *tzara'at* in inanimate objects by a passage on the purification of persons (14:1–32). As to both persons and inanimate objects, the Torah's general format is to deal with (1) diagnosis, (2) cure, and (3) purification.

In revealing His commands on *tzara'at*, "The Lord spoke to Moses and Aaron, saying" (13:1).

Comment L–31. On the intended audience for the Lord's instructions on *tzara'at*

Although the people are most directly affected by *tzara'at* in persons, the Lord speaks only to Moses and Aaron in 13:1. Nor are they to share His words with the people. Does P mean to exclude the people from any role involving *tzara'at*? Within all Israel was the detection of *tzara'at* in persons to be the sole responsibility of the Aaronide priests? If so, given their duties, would the detection of *tzara'at* be left to chance Tent or Temple encounters?

We might also consider a similar problem in Lev. 14:1, in which the Lord speaks only to Moses regarding the cleansing of persons cured of *tzara'at*. Although nothing is said of Aaron or the people, the cleansing process involves both critical priestly responsibilities and the cooperation of the "patient." If we therefore *infer* that 14:1 is meant to include Aaron, then why does the Lord speak explicitly "to Moses and Aaron" on *tzara'at* in houses (14:33)?

In regard to the diagnosis of *tzara'at* in persons, Lev. 13:1–46 describes seven separate skin conditions. As each is a possible sign of *tzara'at*, a priest must examine it. Overall, JPS1, JPS2, and RSV describe the first set of skin conditions as "swellings, discolorations, rashes, scabs and eruptions" (13:2–8). *But even before the necessary diagnosis, the Torah terms the "symptoms" alone as negah tzara'at, or literally a "plague of tzara'at" (13:2).*

> Note L–32: JPS1 renders negah tzara'at *as a "plague of leprosy," JPS2 as a "scaly affection," and RSV as "a leprous disease." But it is the Torah that invites such confusion. For example, having used* negah tzara'at *in 13:2 to identify a prediagnosed skin condition, it uses the same term in 13:3 to identify a condition later diagnosed as unclean. For further diagnostic details in 13:2–8, see Comment L–31 pt.2.*

Lev. 13:9–17 addresses a condition that JPS2 also terms "a scaly affection." In reliance on the Torah's continued use of the generic *negah tzara'at* for the nondiagnosed condition, RSV and JPS1 continue their "rush to judgment" by identifying the prediagnosed condition as "leprosy" or a "plague of leprosy." In fact, however, to be diagnosed as unclean, the "scaly infection" must first be found to consist of "a white swelling, which has turned some hair white, with a patch of undiscolored flesh in the swelling" (13:10).

In turn, the trigger for a priestly diagnosis in 13:18–23 is an "inflammation" (JPS2) or a "boil" (JPS1 and RSV). This develops into "a white discoloration streaked with red" (JPS2) or a "white rising [or swelling]," or a "bright reddish-white spot" (these being the composite of JPS1/RSV) (13:18). Following his diagnosis, the priest declares the person "clean" or "unclean." Here again, *negah tzara'at*, which in 13:2 and 9 describes a prediagnosed condition, is now used to describe a condition diagnosed as "unclean." JPS2 describes the unclean state as "a leprous affection," while JPS1 and RSV call it "leprosy."

> Note L–33: *Even as to an unclean condition, JPS2 prudently avoids the word "leprosy." Instead, it speaks of it as "leprous" (i.e., as having the nature of leprosy).*

The three translations vary slightly in identifying the condition of 13:24–28, but their substance is the same. The following is a fair composite: "a burning of the skin by fire that leads to a bright spot discolored by white and red streaks" (13:24). Where the priest diagnoses the person as unclean, both *tzara'at* and *negah tzara'at* are used to describe the condition. Here, however, JPS2 identifies *tzara'at* as leprosy—while continuing to render *negah tzara'at* as a "leprous affection." Conversely, however, JPS1 continues to render the term as "plague of leprosy" (thus following the Torah's continued usage of *negah tzara'at* for both potential and actual unclean conditions).

In 13:29–37 the condition requiring priestly diagnosis is termed a "simple" *negah*, rather than a *negah tzara'at*, as in 13:2 and 9 (13:29–30). It is variously said to be "an affection" (JPS2), "a plague" (JPS1), or "a disease" (RSV). Whichever, it is a condition that appears "on the head or in the beard" (13:29). When diagnosed as unclean, the Torah uses *tzara'at* to identify the condition (13:30). JPS2 reads this *tzara'at* as "a scall, a scaly eruption in the hair or beard." JPS1 identifies it as "a scall, it is leprosy of the head or of the beard." RSV terms it "a leprosy of the head or of the beard."

Lev. 13:38–39 speaks of "discolorations," or "white spots," on the skin, which an inspection by the priest reveals to be "dull white." It is termed a "tetter." In every case, however, the condition is said to be "clean."

> Note L–34: *Lev. 13:38–39 may have been meant to assuage fears of a common condition that appeared noxious, but which in fact was known, or thought, to be "benign." Given the immediate recognition of the "cleanness"*

of the conditions described in 13:38–39, the term tzara'at is not used. "Tetter," today, has no particular meaning. A modern dictionary includes in its former meaning "eruptive skin diseases, as herpes, eczema and impetigo."

Lev. 13:40–44 addresses a variety of skin conditions occurring on the bald head of a man. Baldness in itself was not unclean. But if, on final examination, the "bald part" displays a certain "swollen affection" along with white and red discoloration, the condition is diagnosed as *tzara'at* (13:42–44). JPS2 again describes the *undiagnosed* symptoms of an unclean state as a "scaly eruption." JPS1 and RSV both term it "leprosy" (13:42). Upon a finding of *tzara'at*, all three describe the afflicted person as "leprous" (or as a "leprous man") and "unclean."

The "diagnostic" section on *tzara'at* in a person concludes with commands that look to protect the community through quarantine procedures (13:45–46). (Here the term for an afflicted male is "*hatzaruah.*" JPS1/RSV refer to him as "the leper"; JPS2, a "person with a leprous affection.")

Whether as a "leper" or as one afflicted with a "leprous affection," the unclean person was marked for isolation. His clothes were torn, his hair was left to hang loose, his head was covered to include his upper lip, and he was to cry "Unclean! Unclean!" He remained unclean "as long as the disease [was] on him." He was also required to dwell "outside the camp" (13:45–46).

The other important element of 13:1–46 bearing on the nature of *tzara'at* was the process (as distinguished from the standards) of priestly diagnosis. The need for a diagnosis arose from the presence of any of the skin conditions just described. It is not always clear, however, on whose initiative diagnoses were instigated.

Comment L–32. On diagnosing *tzara'at* in a person

1. The identification of persons requiring diagnosis

Of the first of the seven skin conditions requiring diagnosis (13:2–8), JPS2 states that "*it shall be reported to Aaron the priest or to one of his sons, the priests*" (13:2). To the contrary, JPS1 and RSV both state that the affected person "shall be brought" to Aaron or a son. There is, however, an important similarity between these two versions. Neither imposes a direct duty on the affected person to present himself to a priest. Indeed, as compared to JPS1/RSV, JPS2 might imply a priestly obligation to seek out any person "reported" to be affected.

Of the next two (13:9–17 and 18–23), however, JPS2 says (1) that the condition shall be "reported to the priest" (13:9), and (2) that the affected person "present himself to the priest" (13:18–19). However, JPS1 and RSV again call for the affected person to be "brought to" a priest. But no translation requires a "suspect" person to appear before a priest on his own initiative (as distinguished from being induced or forced by others to appear).

The final four skin conditions (i.e., 13:24–28, 29–37, 38–39, 40–44) do not vary the foregoing process(es) for activating priestly diagnoses. Over time the people might learn to identify "suspicious" conditions. But their role ended with reporting their suspicions to the priests. Only a priest, by examination, could diagnose the presence or absence of actual *tzara'at*.

2. On the diagnostic details of various conditions

Recall that the first condition requiring a diagnosis of *tzara'at* was the presence of "swellings, discolorations, rashes, scabs and eruptions" (13:2). The priest would then decide whether "the hair in the affected patch has turned white *and* the affection appears to be deeper than the skin of the body.") If so, the condition was leprous. But where there was also "a white discoloration on the skin . . . which does not appear to be deeper than the skin and the hair in it has not turned white," the matter was not so easily resolved (13:4).

In such case as many as two additional exams could be required, each preceded by two seven-day periods of isolation (13:4–6). Absent any change following the first period, a second period was required (13:5). Following the second seven-day period of isolation, if the affection had faded and not spread, the priest pronounced the person "clean." He had but to "wash his clothes" (13:6). If later, however, the rash did spread, "he shall present himself again to the priest" (13:7). The "patient's" duty to "present himself" presumably results from the priest's having acquired prior "jurisdiction" over him and his condition.

JPS2 states the test for determining an unclean condition in 13:9–17 as follows: "If the eruption spreads out . . . so that it covers all the skin of the affected person from head to foot, wherever the priest can see . . . he shall pronounce the affected person clean, for he has turned white. *But as soon as undiscolored flesh appears in it, he shall be unclean*" (13:12–15). (JPS1 and RSV describe the condition of *bahshar chai* as "raw" rather than "undiscolored.")

The test for the "inflammation" of the third skin condition is much like the initial test of the first condition—but with only one period of isolation (13:18–23). Here the inquiry is whether the inflammation "appears lower than the rest of the skin *and* that the hair in it has turned white" (13:20). Should the test prove "negative" after the first seven days, the priest then applies a second test. "If [the inflammation] should spread in the skin, the priest shall pronounce him unclean" (13:22). If it has not spread, "the priest shall pronounce him clean" (13:23).

The fourth condition (13:24–28) arose from a body skin burn, from which the discolored "patch" was either "white streaked or red with white." This condition was "leprosy" (or a "leprous disease," and thus unclean) where "some hair has turned white in the discoloration, which itself appears to go deeper than the skin" (13:25).

Absent these existing conditions, a seven-day isolation was required even where there was no white hair within the "faded" discoloration, if, in any case, it "is not lower than the rest of the skin" (13:26). Then, ignoring hair or color, if, after seven days, the "patch" "has spread in the skin, it was a "leprous affection" (13:27). But if it has not spread *and* remains faded, it is the . . . scar of the burn." The person is clean (13:28).

The fifth condition involved scaly eruptions of the head and beard (13:29–37). Any "affections" that went below the skin and included a yellow hair was a "scall" and thus unclean (13:29–30). But should an "affection" not "deeper than the skin" contain no "black hair," an initial seven-day isolation was required (13:31). Thereafter, if the scall has spread and contains a yellow hair, it is (tacitly in the text) assumed to be unclean. But even though it not be found unclean, a second seven-day isolation follows. Then, "on the seventh day the priest shall examine the scall. If the scall has not spread upon the skin, *and does not appear to go deeper than the skin*, the priest shall pronounce him clean" (13:34). However, should the scall spread on the skin "*after* he has been pronounced clean," the priest need not be concerned with yellow hair; he is unclean.

A final embellishment follows: "If the scall has remained unchanged in color, *and* black hair has grown in it, the scall is healed; he is clean" (13:37).

The sixth condition simply notes the occasional presence of streaks of "dull white" discolorations (13:38–39). These were viewed as clean. (This information provided prior assurance regarding a common condition that might otherwise waste the time of priests and "patients." See Note L–34.)

Although prominent in the seventh and final condition, baldness itself was not the problem (13:40–44). The essence of the unclean condition relating to baldness was the appearance of a "white affection streaked with red" on the bald part in the front or at the back of the head" (13:42).

As noted in Comment L–30, Lev. 14:1–32 deals with the purification procedures for persons found to be unclean under the provisions of Lev. 13. Thus, "the Lord spoke to Moses saying: This shall be the ritual for a leper at the time that he is to be cleansed" (14:1–2).

On learning that "the leper" may be healed, "the priest shall go outside the camp. If the priest sees that the leper has been healed of his *scaly affection*," he commences the cleansing rituals (14:2–3).

These rituals appear to require communal resources as well as those from the person to be cleansed. Thus, at the outset, "the priest *shall order* two live clean birds, cedar wood, crimson stuff, and hyssop to be brought *for* him who is to be cleansed" (14:4).

Comment L–33. On the community's role in the cleansing rituals of the recovered leper

As implied in all three translations, the ingredients ordered by the priest in 14:4 are "*for* him that is to be cleansed." That the ingredients of purification were apparently brought by others "for" the person to be cleansed seems to vary from the usual protocol of "offerings" from those on whose behalf offerings are made. But there is a technical and substantive explanation for the variance.

First, the ingredients from within the community are not sacrificial offerings. Although one of the two birds is in fact slaughtered as a source of ritual blood, it is not burnt, or otherwise submitted, as an offering to the Lord. Nor are any of the other items provided by the community (14:6–7). Second, P's requirement of communal resources in this cleansing ritual could well reflect its importance to the community. Not only was a threat of contamination removed, but the newly cleansed *hatzaruah* was now restored to the community. It should have been a happy occasion for the community as well as the *hatzaruah*.

The physical cleansing that preceded the return of the *hatzaruah* to the "camp" included the washing of clothes, the shaving of "all his hair" (including head, beard, and eyebrows), and a body bath (14:8). Following his return to the camp, he still could not enter "his tent" for seven days.

> Note L–35: The delay was likely intended to avoid sexual relations pending the completion of the cleansing rituals.

On the seventh day he repeated the previous ablutions, and on the eighth, he brought his own offerings to the priest at the Tent of Meeting to be "presented before the Lord" (14:9–11).

From persons of sufficient means, the offerings were of "two male lambs without blemish, one ewe lamb in its first year without blemish, three tenths of a measure of choice flour with oil mixed in for a meal offering, and one *log* of oil" (14:10–11). The complex rituals are described in 14:12–20. They included (in part) (1) a wave offering of a live male lamb and a *log* of oil (14:12–13), (2) a guilt offering, (3) the placing of blood and oil on designated portions of the person to be cleansed, (4) a sin offering, (5) a burnt offering, and (6) a meal offering. At each stage of the rituals the priest made "expiation" (or "atonement," per JPS1/RSV) for the person to be cleansed. On completing the rituals, the person was declared "clean."

For the "poor" person whose means were "insufficient," the need for two male lambs and a ewe was reduced to one male lamb, and the need for three-tenths of a measure of choice flour to one-tenth. Finally, in place of the second male lamb and a ewe, he could bring either two turtledoves or two pigeons (14:21–22). So solemn was the ritual, however, that even the poorest offerer had to bring at least one lamb. The cleansing protocols for persons of insufficient means otherwise follow the "usual" rituals (14:24–32).

For the law of *negah tzara'at* in "a cloth of wool or linen fabric, in the warp or in the woof of the linen or the wool, or in a skin or anything made of [animal] skin" we return to 13:47–59. "If the affection in [any of the foregoing] is streaky green or red, it is an eruptive affection [i.e., *negah tzara'at*]. It shall be shown to the priest" (13:47–49).

On receiving the affected cloth or skin, the priest " shall isolate [it] for seven days. If the affection had then spread, it was a *tzara'at mahmeret*, that is, a "malignant eruption" and "unclean" (13:50–51).

Comment L–34. On the first appearance of *tzara'at mahmeret*— a "malignant eruption"

For the first time an unclean state is described as *tzara'at mahmeret*—a "malignant eruption." Of particular interest is any distinction that might be intended between *tzara'at mahmeret* and *negah tzara'at*. Is *mahmeret* (i.e., "malignant") meant to intensify or add virulence to the earlier use of *negah tzara'at* as an undiagnosed condition? Given the meaning of *negah tzara'at* as a "plague of leprosy," this seems unlikely. More likely, then, *tzara'at mahmeret* is meant to apply distinctively to "things."

An unclean cloth on which the affection has spread must be burned (13:52). If it has not spread, it must be washed (on order of the priest). There follows a second seven days of isolation, after which "if the diseased spot has not changed color, *though* the disease has not spread, it is unclean; you shall burn it in the fire" (13:55; RSV).

> Note L–36: JPS2 and JPS1 find the cloth unclean only when both of two conditions are met. Thus, "but if the priest sees that the affection has not changed color and that it is not spread, it is unclean" (JPS2) In that this second condition is contrary to logic and other protocols, RSV's reading of v'hanegah loh phahsah in 13:55 seems preferable.

If the affected part of the cloth itself has faded, the priest must remove it from the rest of the cloth. If an "affection" (or "plague," or "disease") then "occurs again" in the remaining cloth, it is a "wild growth" (13:57). Although not declared to be *tzara'at*, or unclean, the newly affected cloth, without further diagnosis, must also be burned (13:57). If no affection reappears in the remaining cloth, it is clean (but for a final wash) (13:58).

The final category of *tzara'at*, as it affects houses, appears in Lev. 14:33–57.

The Lord again speaks to "Moses and Aaron" (14:33). Here His opening words are unique in three particulars: *"When you enter the land of Canaan . . . , and I inflict an eruptive plague upon a house* in the land you possess, *the owner of the house shall come and tell the priest,* saying 'Something like a plague has appeared upon my house' " (13:34–35).

Comment L–35. On the distinctive elements of *tzara'at* in houses

1. On P's explicit and unique attribution of tzara'at *in houses to the Lord*

Why is it only for *tzara'at* in houses that P's Lord claims responsibility? While *tzara'at* in persons and cloth appear as "natural" products of His natural order, its appearance in houses will result from His manipulation of His natural order. In Sinai there were no houses that either the Lord or nature might afflict with *tzara'at*. But this hardly explains why P's Lord, while in Sinai, anticipates overriding His natural order in Canaan by placing *tzara'at* in houses.

A hard-pressed but irrepressible Rashi offers one explanation. Given the particular "cure" for *tzara'at* in houses (see 14:40–45), he sees it as a "good tiding." Why? "For the Amorites had hidden treasures of gold in the wall of their houses . . . and on account of the plague [the Israelites] broke down the house and found them [i.e., the treasures]."[15]

2. On an owner's unique responsibility to report the condition of tzara'at *in houses to the priest*

Comment L–32 deals with the ambiguities of the process by which priests were apprised of skin conditions that required a priestly diagnosis for *tzara'at* in persons. There, a duty to report the condition fell on no one. Only in regard to *tzara'at* in houses does the Torah impose a direct duty on the affected party to alert a priest to its possible presence (14:35). But who else would be more likely to know of it?

3. On the explicit deferral of the effectiveness of the command to when the Israelites had entered Canaan

In the absence of houses in the wilderness, any laws governing them would have no immediate use. Just as P created a wilderness Tent and Tabernacle in anticipation of the Jerusalem Temple and its priesthood, so, too, did many other Sinaitic commands look to the circumstances of life in Canaan. Yet, however unsuitable or irrelevant were many such laws in the wilderness, once revealed, the Torah treats them as effective. So, too, were those on *tzara'at* in persons and cloths, to which *tzara'at* in houses was a stated exception.

Diagnosis and treatment involved several stages. The owner was first required to describe nothing more definite than "something like a plague" (14:35).
On examining the house, which first was cleared, the priest looked for "greenish
or reddish streaks, which appear[ed] to go deep into the wall" (14:37). If found,
the house was closed for seven days. If the plague had meanwhile spread, all
affected stones were removed. Along with coating scraped from inside the house,
they were "dumped outside the city in an unclean place" (14:40–41). The old
stones were then replaced and the house was recoated and replastered (14:42).

At this point the house is deemed clean and habitable. But where "the
plague again breaks out," the priest must return to examine it. Then, "if the
plague has spread in the house, it is a *malignant eruption* in the house; it is
unclean" (14:43–44). The house is then "torn down" and taken to "an unclean
place outside the city" (14:45).

> Note L–37: Once in Canaan, "outside the city" replaces "outside the camp"
> (cf. 14:45 to 13:46 and 14:3).

Persons entering an unclean house during its initial closure would be
unclean until evening. And whoever slept or ate in it had to "wash his clothes"
(14:47–48).

If the plague had not spread after the replastering of the house, "the plague
has healed" and the house was "clean" (14:48). But once affected, the house had
to be "purged" (14:49). As with persons cured of *tzara'at* (14:4–8), the first stage
of cleansing rituals for a house called for "two birds, cedar wood, crimson stuff
and hyssop" (14:49). (As in 14:4, the source of these objects from within the
community is not identified.) The rituals again included seven sprinklings of
blood from the slaughtered bird on the "object" being cleansed. Having "set the
live bird free . . . in the open country," the priest has made expiation for the
house and it was "clean" (14:50–53).

The summary of the law of *tzara'at* (14:54–57) begins as follows: "This is the
law [or procedure] for every *negah tzara'at*." Again, *negah tzara'at* is variously rendered as "eruptive affection" (JPS2), "leprous disease" (RSV) or "plague of leprosy" (JPS1). The entire subject of *tzara'at* concludes with the declaration that
"this is the law [or procedure] for *tzara'at*" (14:57).

Comment L–36. On the hygienics and/or
spirituality of the law of *tzara'at*

JPS2 identifies undiagnosed *tzara'at*, whether of person, cloth or house, as
various abnormal "affections," which may yet prove clean or unclean. In
turn, by identifying undiagnosed *tzara'at* as "leprosy," JPS1 speaks of conditions presumed to be unclean. In labeling prediagnosed *tzara'at* as both "leprosy" and a "leprous disease," RSV may strike a balance between the two. In

general these differences fairly reflect the ambiguity of the Torah's own undifferentiated use of *tzara'at*, or *negah tzara'at*, to describe both prediagnosed conditions and conditions later diagnosed as "unclean." (As to persons, see 13:2–3, 9, 12–13; cloth, 13:47; and houses, 14:34.)

In any case, what directs us to the hygienic aspects of *tzara'at* is its identification by translation with "leprosy." Not even its appearance in cloth and houses can fully dispel a reader's initial perception of a specific egregious human disease. But even as a human condition, *tzara'at* takes seven different forms, thus complicating any effort to identify it as a single disease. The presence of *tzara'at* in cloths and houses suggests that it existed more as an impulsive human response to troubling abnormalities than as a syndrome of diseases.

That leprosy was not likely known in the Near East before c. 300 B.C.E. adds a special irony to the association of *tzara'at* with leprosy.[16] Yet, the diagnostics and procedures of *tzara'at* (including interim "quarantines") were directed to conditions plausibly indicative of human disease. Those relating to cloth and houses also posed plausible problems of noxious spoilage or rot. Offsetting such *personal* hygienic concerns, however, was the total absence of even the most rudimentary curative efforts.

If not mainly hygienic in purpose, then what other purpose might the law of *tzara'at* have been meant to serve? Was it not akin to P's purpose in dividing animals into clean and unclean for purposes of human consumption? Just as P had infused this spiritual dichotomy into so many other basic aspects of human existence, P also sought through the law of *tzara'at* to broaden the spirituality of cleanness. It may be in this sense that we can best understand P's remarkable fascination with *tzara'at*.

Lev. 15 concludes the subject of clean and unclean that began with the animals of Lev. 11. It deals with physical uncleanness arising from the functioning of sex organs. The particular sources of uncleanness were: (1) "when any man has a [bodily] discharge [other than semen]" (15:3–15); (2) "when a man has [any] emission of semen [including sexual intercourse]" (15:16–18); (3) "when a woman has a discharge, her discharge being blood from her body [in this case menstruation]," the period of impurity being seven days (15:19–24); and (4) "when a woman discharges blood for many days, not at the time of her impurity, or when she has a discharge beyond her period of impurity" (15:25–30).

> Note L–38: Notably, this passage does not prohibit intercourse during menstruation. However, "if a man lies with her, her impurity is communicated to him; he shall be unclean seven days" (15:24).

In regard to other sources of uncleanness in Lev. 11–15, cleanness was restored by personal ablutions, the washing or discarding of contaminated items and the passage of time. Only as to (1) childbirth (Lev. 12), (2) *tzara'at* (Lev. 13–14), (3) male discharges other than semen (Lev. 15), and (4) prolonged vaginal bleeding (Lev. 15) did cleansing require expiation through sacrificial offerings. (See Lev. 12:6–8 and 15:14–16, 29–30.)

Comment L–37. On Aaron as joint auditor with Moses—a further thought

In Lev. 15, "the Lord spoke to Moses and Aaron, saying: Speak to the Israelite people and say to them: . . ." In Lev. 11:1 (as to 11:1–47, on animals), the Lord also spoke to Moses and Aaron, but with no reference to the people. This latter arrangement also occurs in Lev. 13:1 as to *negah tzara'at* in persons and cloth) and Lev. 14:33 (as to *negah tzara'at* in houses). In Lev. 12:1 (as to childbirth) and Lev. 14:1 (as to cleansing rites for cured "lepers"), the Lord spoke to Moses alone. But only in 12:1 is Moses told to "speak to the Israelite people." What explains these differences? Given the priestly duties of 12:1–12 and 14:1–32, we must assume that Moses was expected to instruct Aaron in turn (cf. Comment L–25).

Lev. 16 now concludes the broad theme of expiation and atonement that permeates Lev. 1–16. It begins by recalling the earlier death of Aaron's sons in 10:1–2. Thus, "the Lord spoke to Moses after the death of the two sons of Aaron who died *too* close to the presence of the Lord" (16:1).

> *Note L–39: I italicize "too" in order to emphasize its absence in JPS1/RSV, in which Aaron's sons merely "drew near before the Lord." JPS2's use of "too close" may be meant to heighten what may have been a belated warning that follows in 16:2. "The Lord said to Moses: Tell your brother Aaron that he is not to come at will into the Shrine behind the curtain, in front of the cover that is upon the ark, lest he die; for I appear in the cloud over the cover." Nothing in Lev. 16, however, alludes to the "alien fire" to which the deaths of Nadab and Abihu were attributed in 10:1–2.*

Priestly rites of atonement then follow (16:3–28). In brief summation, they include:

1. Aaron's entry into the shrine, in sacral vestments, with a bull and ram for a sin and a burnt offering, and with two he-goats and a ram "from the Israelite community" for a sin and a burnt offering (16:3–5).
2. Aaron's expiation for himself and his household with the bull of the sin offering, and his choice of one goat by lot for the Lord as a sin offering and of another for "Azalel," to be left standing before the Lord and sent as expiation to the wilderness "for Azalel" (16:6–10).

3. Aaron's heating of incense in connection with the sin offering of the bull, and attendant blood rituals, so that the resulting cloud "screens the cover that is over the [Ark], lest he die," followed by his slaughtering the goat of the sin offering and attendant blood rituals (16:11–15).

Through these opening rituals Aaron would "purge the Shrine of the uncleanness and transgression of the Israelites, whatever their sins." Then he would do the same for the Tent of Meeting, "which abides with them in the midst of their uncleanness." All the preceding was done in total privacy. "Nobody else shall be in the Tent of Meeting until he comes out" (16:16–17a) In this way, Aaron made "expiation for himself and his household, and for the whole congregation of Israel."

Next, he was to "purge" the altar. This required further blood rituals involving sin offerings of a bull and goat. Aaron would thus "cleanse [the altar] of the uncleanness of the Israelites and consecrate it" (16:17–19).

On completing the purge of the Shrine, Tent, and altar, Aaron performed the rituals of the second live goat for Azalel. He first placed his hands on its head and confessed "all the iniquities and transgressions of the Israelites, whatever their sins, putting them on the head of the goat." The goat was then "sent off to the wilderness through a designated man." In this way the goat would "carry *on it* all their iniquities to an inaccessible region," where it would then be "set free" (16:20–22).

Aaron then returned to the Tent to remove his vestments, bathe, and put on his vestments before offering the two rams as burnt offerings. This was in "expiation for himself and the people" (16:23–24). Finally, he turned the fat of the sin offering into smoke (16:25), and "He who set the Azazel-goat free." washed his clothes and bathed before returning to camp (16:25–26).

Not until 16:29–31 do we learn of a "day of atonement." And while the detailed rituals of 16:1–28 were directed through Moses to Aaron alone, it is the entire community of Israel for whom the instructions of 16:29–31 are meant. Thus "to *you*" it will be a "law for all time" that this day shall occur each year "in the seventh month, on the tenth day." On this day "*you* shall practice self-denial; and *you* shall do no manner of work, neither the citizen nor the alien who resides among *you*. For on this day *atonement shall be made for you* to cleanse you of all your sins; you shall be clean before the Lord."

In summarizing 16:2–28, Lev. 16:32–34 turns again to the attendant responsibilities of the Aaronide priest, that is, "the priest who has been anointed and ordained to serve as priest in place of his father." He "shall purge the innermost Shrine; he shall purge the Tent of Meeting and the altar; and he shall make expiation for the priests and for all the people of the congregation" (16:32–33). Lev. 16 concludes by noting the unique importance of these priestly duties: "This shall be to you a law for all time; to make atonement for the Israelites for all their sins once a year" (16:34).

In Lev. 17* the Lord speaks through Moses to "Aaron and his sons and to all the Israelite people" (17:1–2). The subject involves the centralization of all animal offerings.

"If any [male Israelite] slaughters an ox or sheep or goat in the camp, or does so outside the camp, and does not bring it to the entrance of the Tent of Meeting to present as an offering to the Lord, before the Lord's Tabernacle, such man shall be cut off from among his people. This is in order that the Israelites may bring the sacrifices *which they have been making in the open*—that they may bring them before the Lord to the priest at the entrance of the Tent of Meeting, and offer them as sacrifices of well-being to the Lord: that the priest may dash the blood against the altar of the Lord at the entrance of the Tent of Meeting, and turn the fat into smoke as a pleasing odor to the Lord" (17:3–6). The stated reason for the centralization of sacrifices is "that they may offer their sacrifices no more to the goat-demons after whom they stray" (17:7).

Lev. 17:8–9 extends the command and punishment of being "cut off from among his people" to "strangers who reside among them." The passage also restates the basic command to require that every Israelite or stranger who "offers a burnt offering or a sacrifice [shall] bring it to the entrance of the Tent of Meeting to offer it to the Lord."

Comment L–38. On the sites of animal sacrifices in Exod. 20:21 and Lev. 17:3–7

To accommodate the offerings of some six hundred thousand adult males at the Tent of Meeting would surely have required a remarkable system of "rationing" and priorities. But more important to the overall scheme of the Torah is the relationship between Lev. 17:3–4 and Exod. 20:21. "Make for me an altar of earth and sacrifice on it your burnt offerings and your sacrifices of well-being, your sheep and your oxen; in every place where I cause My name to be mentioned I will come to you and bless you." (This, of course, could have eased matters at the Tent of Meeting.)

Unlike the movable Tent of Meeting, the site of any single "altar of earth" was fixed. And where might such "altars of earth" be raised as alternate sites to the Tent of Meeting for "burnt offerings and your sacrifices of well-being"? As stated in by E Exod. 20:21: "In every place where I cause My name to be mentioned I will come to you and bless you." And where will the Lord God cause His "name to be mentioned"? In the context of Exod. 20:21,

---

*Ed.—Modern biblical scholarship generally ascribes Lev. 17–27 to a subsource of P different than that of Lev. 1–16. This subsource is commonly identified as "H," representing the first letter of the "Holiness Code," by which name Lev. 17–26 has become known. (See, for example, Friedman, "Leviticus, Book of," *The Anchor Bible Dictionary*, vol. 4, pp. 315–16; Friedman, *Who Wrote the Bible?* pp. 172, 214; and Plaut, *The Torah: A Modern Commentary*, p. 872.) As a subsouce of P, H will be identified as P/h.

it seems reasonable to read these words as follows: "Wherever I inspire you to make sacrificial offerings to Me, I will be there to bless you."

To read the Torah as the composite work of separate human authors writing at different times and from different perspectives is to relish such inevitable variations. But to read the Torah as an integrated revelation of its God requires an accomodation of its "surface" contradictions. To this end, Rashi explained Exod. 20:21 as follows: "In every place where I cause My name to be mentioned—Where I shall give you permission to mention My Ineffable Name, there 'I will come unto thee and bless thee,' I will cause My Divine Presence to rest upon thee. *Hence you learn that permission was not given to mention the Ineffable Name save in the place where the Divine Presence comes, and that is the Temple.*"[17] Thus, Rashi first "accepts" the Temple as the successor to the Tent. He then proceeds to read E's text through the lens of P's incompatible doctrine. But not even Rashi can sweep away the doctrinal polarities of E and P, as revealed in Exod. 20:21 and Lev. 17:3–4.

The Levitical prohibition against consuming blood is repeated and explained in 17:10–12. "*For the life of the flesh is in the blood, and I have assigned it to you for making expiation for your lives upon the altar; it is blood, as life, that effects expiation.*"

Lev. 17:13–14 manifests a similar concern regarding the blood of edible game (i.e., "an animal or bird that may be eaten," other than domesticated animals from the "herd or flock"). The blood of all such animals (i.e., that were eaten and not brought to the Tent) was to be poured out and covered with earth (17:13). Also, it was allowed to eat "what has died [naturally] or has been torn by beasts." But to do so brought uncleanness. This required such a meat consumer to "wash his clothes, bathe in water, and remain unclean until evening." He who had not made himself clean in this way "shall bear his guilt" (17:15–16).

Before turning to additional laws on human sexuality in Lev. 18, the Lord first warns against all alien practices: "You shall not copy the practices of the Land of Egypt where you dwelt, or of the land of Canaan to which I am taking you; nor shall you follow their laws" (18:2–4). Instead, the Lord alone is Israel's model. "My rules alone shall you observe, and faithfully follow My laws: I the Lord am your God. You shall keep My laws and My rules, by the pursuit of which man shall live; I am the Lord" (18:5).

Lev. 18:6–23 deals with prohibited sexual intercourse. (These are discussed under verse citations.) The prohibitions include:

6. "Anyone of his own flesh"

Note L–40: JPS2's term, "anyone of his own flesh," is from kol sh'ayr b'saroh, which JPS1/RSV render as "[anyone] near of kin to him." In this,

JPS2 is more literal and JPS1/RSV, more inclusive. As a prelude to the relationships of 18:7–18, however, the Hebrew presents a problem for both. Since no other command prohibits father/daughter relations, a prohibition against intercourse with "anyone of his own flesh" will provide a more explicit prohibition. Moreover, greater precision is warranted, given the explicit prohibitions in 18:7 against son/mother, and in 18:10 against grandfather/ granddaughter, relations. Conversely, "flesh" alone fails to cover the several relationships by marriage that are addressed in 18:7–18.

If, however, 18:6 is viewed as a separate command, and not as an introduction to 18:7–18, then, either translation involves repetition. In any case, except for 18:23, all the commands of Lev. 18 are directed to males alone.

7. A mother ("Your father's nakedness, that is the nakedness of your mother, you shall not uncover; *she is your mother*—you shall not uncover her nakedness")

8. A stepmother ("Do not uncover the nakedness of your father's wife")

Note L–41: As just noted, Oedipal incest, or relations with a natural mother, is the separate subject of 18:7. Thus, the "nakedness of your father's wife" in 18:8 refers to a stepmother. Whether the prohibition survives the death of the father depends in part on the purpose of the command. Is it mainly intended to preserve the father's dignity? If so, while alive, or in memory as well? Or is its concern to prevent jealousy or other ill-will among siblings or half-siblings? What, if any, of these prohibitions can be inferred from the Fifth Commandment to "Honor your father and mother"? And what of the Seventh Commandment against adultery?

9. A sister ("your father's daughter [without regard to the identity of her mother] or your mother's [without regard to her father]").

Note L–42: Here lies the conflict between Genesis and the Holiness code of Leviticus regarding relations between half-brothers and half-sisters. Against Lev. 18:9 we must consider Abraham's explanation to Abimelech of why he had spoken truthfully in presenting Sarah as his sister. "She is in truth my sister, my father's daughter, though not my mother's; and she became my wife" (Gen. 20:12). But given that Abraham had married Sarah before being "called," even P/h might have granted forgiveness. How else could E's God look with favor on Abraham's line? (See Comment G–33.)

10. A granddaughter

Note L–43: The command covers relations between a man and his "son's daughter" and his "daughter's daughter." Nothing is said of his own daughter. (See Note L–40.)

11. A stepmother's daughter

> *Note L–44: There is no blood relationship between a stepmother's daughter born of a different father and her stepson on whom the prohibition falls. As a total nonblood relationship, its prohibition underscores the harmony of broader kinship groups as a major concern of Lev. 18.*

12. An aunt who is the sister of a father

> *Note L–45: Exod. 6:20 states that "Amram took to wife his father's sister Jochebed, and she bore him Aaron and Moses." So stated, the marriage of the parents of Aaron and Moses violated the prohibition of Lev. 18:12. Even if the marriage were valid at the time, would the author of Exod. 6:20 knowingly portray Aaron and Moses as sons of what all Israel would come to know as a prohibited union? There is good reason for Friedman's attribution of Exod. 6:14–25, dealing with Levite geneology, to P. Does this imply that P knew of the prohibition, but thought it not binding until "formally" revealed? This seems unlikely, given P's insertion of the Levitical clean/unclean animal dichotomy into the story of Noah. However, as a subsource of P and as author of Lev. 18, P/h may not have known of Exod. 6:20.*

13. An aunt who is the sister of a mother
14. The wife of a father's brother (or aunt "in-law")
15. A daughter-in-law (or the wife of a son)
16. A sister-in-law
17. A stepdaughter or stepgranddaughter

> *Note L–46: Like 18:11, the prohibitions of 18:13–17 include nonblood relationships. Again, the broader concerns may have been for the dangers in such relationships to the harmony and stability of the entire household or kinship group.*

18. The sister of a wife "as a rival to her" during the lifetime of the wife

> *Note L–47: But what of Jacob's simultaneous marriages to Leah and Rachel? Their dramas unfold in Genesis as the work of J and E. As they tell the story, such marriages occurred as a matter of course. Neither J nor E, however, would have known of P/h's later Levitical prohibitions.*

Four of the five remaining verses of 18:19–23 prohibit sexual relations unrelated to kinship concerns. I will consider these before turning to the one exception of 18:21. These prohibitions include:

19. A woman "during her period of [menstrual] uncleanness"

Note L–48: This prohibition contradicts Lev. 15:24, in which a man who has sexual relations with a menstruating woman is to be "unclean seven days." This, too, supports the view of a separate subsource of P within Leviticus.

20. "Carnal relations" with a "neighbor's wife"

Note L–49: This command is also directed to the male alone. Its reach, therefore, is narrower than that of the Seventh Commandment, which prohibits all adultery (as defined at the time; see Comment E–60). Again, what the Tenth Commandment seeks to discourage in thought, Lev. 18:20 prohibits in conduct (see Comment E–63).

22. Another male ("as one lies with a woman")

Note L–50: Logically, homosexual relations fall within the broad rubric of "Onanism" (see Comment G–75). To expend seed with no thought or possibility of creating life was to defile the purpose and sanctity of human sexuality. In addition to the factor of blood itself, this principle (at least today) could also explain P/h's absolute prohibition of relations with a menstruating woman (18:19).

23. Any beast (cf. Exod. 22:18)

Note L–51: This is the first and only sexual prohibition of Lev. 18 directed to women. After first prohibiting "carnal relations" between a man and a beast, 18:23 concludes as follows: "let no woman lend herself to a beast to mate with it, it is a perversion." A prime concern, for men and women alike, was that unions of humans and beasts defile the Lord's natural order. Moreover, as with homosexuality, it defiled the sanctity of human sexuality through a quest for pleasure with no possibility of creating human life. But even this aspect of bestiality does not explain why it alone was explicitly prohibited to women. The answer may lie in the identity of the sexual partner as a beast and not a man. As to sexual relations with men, Lev. 18 views women not as temptresses but as subservient or passive pawns. Not so, however, in regard to the perversity of bestiality.

Finally, given its ambiguity, I quote 18:21 in full:

21. "Do not allow any of your offspring to be offered up to Molech, and do not profane the name of your God; I am the Lord."

Note L–52: The meaning and significance of 18:21 is considered in Comment L–24.

In a climactic conclusion (18:24–30), Lev. 18 condemns each and all of its prohibited practices as "abhorrent things . . . done by the people who were in the land before you." Through them, "the land became defiled." Being equal in sinfulness, all violations are to be equally punished. "All who do any of those abhorrent things—*such persons shall be cut off from their people*" (18:27).

Note L–53: On being "cut off from their people" see Comments G–25, and E–35, and E–81. In essence, being "cut off" might include isolation (through ostracism or expulsion) or early death (whether at once or in God's "own good time").

Comment L–39. On Lev. 18 and human sexuality

Together with the Seventh Commandment against adultery, Lev. 18 addresses the need for the responsibile exercise of human sexuality (see Comment E–60).

Pleasure derived from the satisfaction of natural human drives and needs can hardly be an evil. Indeed, absent the impetus of pleasure in reproduction, could duty alone ever suffice? Sexual pleasure becomes an evil only when, in seeking it, we fail to consider, and respond accordingly, to its potential for harm to oneself or any other person(s).

In its time, Lev. 18 sought to respond to the truth that the destructive potential of human sexuality could rival its blessings as a source of life. It thus sought to protect kinships and communities from the havoc of unrestrained sexual license. As part of its broader sweep, it sought above all to deter males within a kinship group from utilizing physical strength or social dominance to pursue convenient "targets of opportunity." And added to the strife, discord, and jealousies that could result from unrestrained sexuality within the kinship group, there was also a matter of property rights and lineage.

Today, the proliferating abuse of human sexuality for instant and mindless gratification reinforces the need for a human commitment to sexual responsibility. In particular, the pleasure that sustains human reproduction should not be pursued through conduct that subverts the human dignity and self-respect on which every worthy society depends. It is to this broad principle that Lev. 18 is directed.

In Lev. 19 we reach the moral and ethical heights of the Holiness Code. In it, P/h draws on the sanctity of its God to foster respect for the potential worth and well-being of every human being. It is in Lev. 19 that P/h rekindles the vision in Gen. 1 of a united humanity committed to the task of perfecting the earth (see Comment G–1).

With the Lord speaking through Moses to "the whole Israelite community," Lev. 19 begins with this central theme of the Holiness Code: "You shall be holy, for I, the Lord your God, am holy" (19:1–2). While the Code (set out below one after another by verse) retains P's broad emphasis on the holiness of ritual, its substance lies in the holiness of human relationships. It also draws on, or incorporates, many previous commands, including those of the Ten Commandments.

3. "You shall each revere his mother and his father, and keep My sabbaths: I the Lord am your God."

> *Note L–54: Verse 3 thus repeats (in order) the Fifth, Fourth, and First Commandments (on the First, see Comment E–54). As for the Fifth, the command to "honor" appears in 19:3 as a command to "revere" (reflecting a change in the Hebrew from "kabayd" to "teerahou)." JPS1 renders teerahou as "fear," while RSV, like JPS2, retains the tone of the Fifth Commandment with "revere." Rashi bases his reading of teerahou as "fear" on the reverse order of "mother and father" in Lev. 19:3 (as compared to Exod. 20:12). Since children were thought to honor mothers for kindness and fear fathers for discipline, Rashi sees the reversal of order as the means of better enabling both parents to evoke both feelings.[18]*
>
> *The sabbath command of 19:3 includes no rationale. Rashi opines that placing the duty to keep the sabbath just after the duty to revere parents is meant to clarify the primacy of the Lord's sanctity over parental authority. Thus, "even though I have admonished you regarding fearing (your) father, if he shall say to you 'Profane the Sabbath,' do not listen to him; and similarly all other commandments."[19]*

4. "Do not turn to idols or make molten gods for yourselves: I the Lord am your God."

> *Note L–55: However differently P/h might interpret this command, it echoes E's command of Exod. 20:20 more closely than the Second Commandment. The broader reach of the latter extends beyond other "gods" to any "sculptured image or any likeness of what is in the heavens above, or on the earth below" (see Comments E–54 and 87).*

5–8. This is a "ritualistic" command that largely repeats the rules of Lev. 7:15–18 on consuming the sacrifice of well-being. In essence, the meat must be eaten on the day of, or the day after, the actual sacrifice. To eat of it on the third day and not burn it entirely, was to profane "what is sacred to the Lord." Thus, he who does so "shall bear his guilt" and "be cut off from his kin."

Note L–56: See Comment L–23 on Aaron's related problem.

9–10. A farmer may not "reap all the way to the edge of [a] field, or gather the gleanings of [a] harvest," nor "pick [a] vineyard bare, or gather [its] fallen fruit." What remains is for "the poor and the stranger."

Note L–57: Cf. Lev. 23:22 and Deut. 24:19–22.

11. "You shall not steal; you shall not deal deceitfully or falsely with one another."

Note L–58: Here the Eighth Commandment against theft is linked to the added fraud and deceit which require expiation through restitution and the guilt offering of Lev. 5:20–26.

12. "You shall not swear falsely by My name, profaning the name of your God: I am the Lord."

Note L–59: This embodies the Third Commandment. See Comment E–56.

13. "You shall not defraud your neighbor. You shall not commit robbery. The wages of a laborer shall not remain with you until morning."

Note L–60: JPS1/RSV render ta'ahshok as "oppress" rather the "defraud." While the two ideas differ in meaning, they both involve the taking of property by unfair advantage, whether by lies or relative bargaining power. Impliedly, by its separate listing, "robbery" (tigzohl) is meant to differ from the "stealing" of the Eighth Commandment and Lev. 19:11 (tignohvu). The intended difference may be between the use of force (robbery) and stealth (stealing). Their common essence, however, lies in unlawful appropriation. Nor can one "misappropriate" the use of money by keeping wages owed to a laborer. He who works should not be left in want.

14. "You shall not insult the deaf, or place a stumbling block before the blind. You shall fear your God: I am the Lord."

Note L–61: JPS1/RSV render the Hebrew "kahlayl" as "curse" rather than "insult." To curse the deaf who can not hear to reply is a sin in itself. But to speak of concern for the "deaf" and "blind" is to speak metaphorically of every human being beset by disabilities of body or mind. All who are so beset must be respected as fellow human beings whose burdens all others should seek to lighten.

15. "You shall not render an unfair decision: do not favor the poor or show deference to the rich; judge your neighbor fairly."

> *Note L–62: This admonition is both simple and profound. While it allows for compassion, justice comes first. We must be sensitive to any true need to temper justice with mercy. But we must never permit the ultimate role of compassion to preempt the initial role of justice.*

16. "Do not deal basely with your fellows. Do not profit by the blood of your neighbor. I am the Lord."

> *Note L–63: Avoiding the broader sweep of "dealing basely," RSV speaks of "slandering" and JPS1 of "talebearing." The common element of these terms lies in the unjust debasement of the reputation, and thus the well-being, of another person. But the second sentence is more problematic. JPS1 forbids one to "stand idly by the blood of thy neighbor." Contrary to the sense of JPS2 (quoted above) that one must not seek to gain from the misfortunes of others, JPS1 seems to call for help in time of need. RSV compounds the ambiguity: "You shall not stand forth against the life of your neighbor." The composite essence of the second sentence formulations might well be JPS2's warning against profiting from the misfortunes of others.*

17. "You shall not hate your kinsman in your heart. Reprove your neighbor, *but* incur no guilt because of him."

> *Note L–64: JPS1 states that "thou shalt surely rebuke thy neighbor, and not bear sin because of him." ("And not" reflects a literal meaning of v'loh). In turn, RSV warns that "you shall reason with your neighbor, lest you bear sin because of him." In all three translations the first sentence warns against hatred. But what of the second? Taken together, the translations address the destructiveness of hate. It is a hatred of one's "neighbor" that longs to be vindicated by wrongful conduct that can "justify" the morally vacuous triumph of "I told you so." To harbor the hope that one's hatred may yet be justified is to foster misdeeds that human warmth might have prevented.*

18. "You shall not take vengeance or bear a grudge against your kinsfolk. Love your neighbor as yourself: I am the Lord."

Comment L–40. On the meaning of "Love your neighbor as yourself"

From the *vau* of *v'loh* in the final clause of 19:17, JPS2 derives both the conjunction "but" and an imperative verb form. However, from the *vau* of *v'a-*

havtah in 19:18, JPS2 derives the same verb form, but in a separate sentence. In JPS2, therefore, the prohibition of vengeance and grudges against "kinsfolk" and the affirmative duty to "love your neighbor" appear as separate commands.

Gramatically, JPS2 is justified in these different uses of *vau*. *Vau* is regularly used (1) to denote "and," (2) to denote "but," *and* (3) as an imperative verb form. The question, then, goes to substance rather than grammar. Which use (or uses) of *vau* best states the intended relationship between the prohibitions and the affirmative duty of 19:18?

1. To structure "Love your neighbor as yourself" as a separate sentence is to remove it from the context of, and to place it on a parity with, the preceding prohibitions. The result is to diminish its value as a practical guide to human thought and conduct. What does it mean to love another as one loves oneself? Indeed, is it possible? Or does the boundless breadth of this utopian precept reduce it to the level of a well-meaning but ineffectual sentiment?

Ramban wisely rejected this literal admonition as self-defeating: "18. AND THOU SHALT LOVE THY NEIGHBOR AS THYSELF. This is an expression by way of overstatement, for a human heart is not able to accept a command to love one's neighbor as oneself. Moreover, Rabbi Akiba has already come and taught, 'Your life takes precedence over the life of your fellow-being.' *Rather [it] means that one is to love one's fellow-being in all matters, as one loves all good for oneself.*"[20] Ramban thus looks for a more realistic guide to thought and conduct than the literal sweep of a pithy phrase of hope.

2. By connecting the two precepts with "and," we maintain a parity between them: "You shall not take vengeance or bear a grudge against your kinsfolk, *and* love your neighbor as yourself." As in (1), the two precepts are placed on a parity. Although somewhat reduced in import by this compound sentence structure, "Love your neighbor as yourself" nevertheless retains the full utopian scope of a separate sentence. Thus, the use of *vau* as a conjunctive "and" is rightly avoided in all three translations.

3. By using *vau* as a conjunctive "but" (as does RSV/JPS1), we avoid the problems posed by the other alternatives. Thus, "You shall not take vengeance or bear any grudge against the sons of your own people, *but* you shall love your neighbor as yourself." (On JPS1/RSV's varied use of *vau* in 19:17, see Note L–64.)

The use of "but" places "Love your neighbor as yourself" in apposition to the preceding clause. Such love, therefore, is contrary to the vengeance and grudges of the first clause. Accordingly, to "love your neighbor as yourself" is *not* to be vengeful and *not* to bear grudges against others. To be vengeful and bear grudges is to judge others through a debased spirit of rancor, spite and bias. Antithetical as they are to fairness and objectivity, such qualities inevitably erode the foundation of human justice. *Indeed, to judge others from a fixed and irrational perspective of antagonism is to deny a*

*basic attribute of human dignity—the right to be judged fairly, as we claim
the right to be judged.* Thus, the teaching of Lev. 19:18: "As we wish others
to respect our own human dignity by judging us fairly, so must we respect the
dignity of others by judging them fairly." While "fairness" again speaks to
the primacy of justice, it looks as well to the leavening role of compassion (cf.
Lev. 19:15 and Note L–62.)

In itself, of course, the precept of Lev. 19:18 extends only to the
"neighbor" of 19:18b, initially defined in 19:18a as "kinsfolk" (JPS2), "your
own people" (RSV), or "children of thy people" (JPS1). P/h's commitment to
human dignity, however, is not confined to Israel. "The stranger who resides
with you shall be to you as one of your citizens; you shall love him as yourself, for you were strangers in the land of Egypt: I the Lord am your God" (see
Lev. 19:33–34 and Comment L–42).

19. "You shall not let your cattle mate with a different kind; you shall not
sow your field with two kinds of seed; you shall not put on cloth from two kinds
of material" (19:19).

> Note L–65: This command turns from human to nonhuman relationships
> within the natural order. It expresses reverence for the natural order, as it
> was thought to have been created. Animals should not be cross-bred; dif-
> ferent seeds should not be planted together and wool and flax had no proper
> place in a single cloth. Insofar as "possible, the natural order was to be pre-
> served in its natural state.

20–22. This passage applies when "a man has carnal relations with a woman
who is a slave and has been designated for another man, but has not been
redeemed or given her freedom." Since "she has not yet been freed" (and thus is
not yet the "property" of her betrothed), neither the man or woman would be
"put to death." The interloper into the contractual expectation could then gain
expiation (per JPS2) by payment of "indemnity" (19:20) and a guilt offering
(19:21).

> Note L–66: Neither the amount of indemnity nor its claimant (as between
> slave owner or "fiance") is identified. In place of "indemnity," JPS1 uses
> "inquisition" and RSV "an inquiry" (both perhaps leading to punishment).
> Whatever the punishment or recompense, the issue of adulterous injury to the
> future husband does not arise. As yet, he has no vested property right in the
> slave. Nor is his marital status of concern. Even if he were a husband, the
> "interloper" could only commit adultery with a married woman (see Com-
> ment E–60).

23–25. This passage deals with the use of fruit from newly planted trees. The produce of the first three years could not be eaten (19:23). In the fourth year all the fruit was "set aside for jubilation before the Lord" (19:24). Thereafter, in the fifth year and beyond, the fruit could be eaten. In this way "its yield to you may be increased: I the Lord am your God" (19:25).

Comment L–41. On the significance of Lev. 19:23–25

It is difficult to discern the horticultural benefits of not picking and eating the fruit for three years. Ramban explained the prohibition as follows: "Now the fruit of the first three years is not fit to be brought before the Glorious Name." It is "small" and without "good taste or flavor." The offering of first fruits must therefore await the fourth year. To these Godly concerns, Ramban adds a human health factor. The "abundance of moisture" in the early years renders the fruit "harmful to the body" and "not good to eat."[21]

26. An initial restatement of the prohibition against eating "anything with its blood" is followed by a ban on the practice of "divination and soothsaying."

> Note L–67: Only the Lord knew truly of the future. What He wished to share, He Himself would reveal or cause to be revealed (as through His Urim and Thummim, held by Aaron and his sons). To seek knowledge of the future from other sources was to demean the Lord's sanctity. See Exod. 28:30 and page 227.

27–28. By distinguishing Israelites from other peoples, these verses are essentially cultic in purpose. Lev. 19:27 forbids "you" to "round off the side-growth on your head" or to "destroy the side-growth of your beard." Lev. 19:28 also forbids "you" to "make gashes in your flesh for the dead, or incise any marks on yourselves."

> Note L–68: Rashi cites the "gashes" of 19:28 as "a custom of the Amorites."[22]

29. "Do not degrade your daughter, and make her a harlot, lest the land fall into harlotry and the land be filled with depravity."

> Note L–69: That J regarded harlotry, or prostitution, as common place in the time of Genesis seems clear from the story of Tamar and Judah (Gen. 39). And that E allowed regulated sales of daughters by their fathers as sexual partners is clear from the mishpat of Exod. 21:7–11. Whether the purpose here is to discourage prostitution in general or to ban the "regulated" arrangements of E's mishpat is not clear. In any case, the command runs only to the

father and not to the daughter. (In general, cf. Comment L–48 and Deut. 23:18.)

30. "You shall keep My sabbaths and venerate My sanctuary: I am the Lord."

> Note L–70: This is the second linkage in Lev. 19 of the sabbath command with another command (see 19:3). As to a priority, if any, between the sabbath and sanctuary commands of 19:30, Rashi treats these as he did the joint commands of 19:3 (see Note L–54): "And even though I admonish you regarding the sanctuary 'Ye shall keep my sabbaths,' the construction of the Temple does not supersede (the law of) sabbath (Sifra)."[23] (See also Exod. 31:12–17 for P's inclusion of a sabbath homily amid the Tabernacle instructions.)

31. "Do not turn to ghosts and do not inquire of familiar spirits, to be defiled by them: I the Lord am your God."

> Note L–71: The command prohibits efforts to contact the dead, thus implying a certain prevalence of the practice.

32. "You shall rise before the aged and show deference to the old; you shall fear your God: I am the Lord."

> Note L–72: This eloquently simple command calls for deference to a class of persons whose self-respect and self-image too often fall prey to the ills of age. It is a fitting segue into the powerful evocation of a single humanity which follows.

33–34. "When a stranger resides with you in your land, you shall not wrong him. The stranger who resides with you shall be to you as one of your citizens; you shall love him as yourself, for you were strangers in the land of Egypt: I the Lord am your God."

> Note L–73: Regarding "you shall love him as yourself," see Comment L–40 final par.

Comment L–42. On the significance of "for you were strangers in the land of Egypt"

P/h is not the first source to draw on Israel's experience in Egypt in support of the common humanity of the "stranger." Indeed, it permeates the Torah.

By appealing to the *empathy* of Israelites, as the source of their deepest compassion, E's great *mishpat* of Exod. 23:9 is even more directly compelling. "You shall not oppress a stranger, *for you know the feelings of a stranger,* having yourselves been strangers in the land of Egypt." (To similar effect see E's *mishpat* of Exod. 22:20.)

35–36. "You shall not falsify measures of length, weight or capacity. You shall have an honest balance, honest weights, an honest *ephah,* and an honest *hin:* I the Lord am your God who freed you from the land of Egypt. You shall faithfully observe all My laws and all My rules: I am the Lord."

> Note L–74: Lev. 19 thus concludes with (1) an emphasis on accurate weights as fundamental to the avoidance of all "false and deceitful" practices (19:11) and (2) a final evocation of the Lord's authority: "I am the Lord."

Comment L–43. On the uses and meaning of "Lord" and "God" in Lev. 19

The phrases "I the Lord am your God" and "I am the Lord" are repeated throughout Lev. 19. The purpose in each case is to emphasize the source of a command. Specifically, "I the Lord am your God" follows the separate substantive commands of 19:3, 4, 9–10, 23–25, 31, 33–34, and 35–36. The phrase "I am the Lord" follows the separate commands of 19:12, 16, 18, 28, and 30. Neither phrase, however, follows the commands of Lev. 19:5–8, 11, 13, 15, 17, 19, 20–22, and 29. The final appearance of "I the Lord am your God" in 19:36 likely relates back to the whole of Lev. 19.

How are the "Lord" and "God" meant to relate to each other? Here Lev. 19 adds new substance to the question posed in Comments G–39 pt. 2, G–43, and G–56. While both terms are embraced in a single Being, does the Torah mean to portray that Being as functionally *homogeneous*? Or are the two terms meant to identify two distinct but integrated aspects, or roles, within a single Being?

A duality of roles is most apparent in "I the *Lord* am your *God.*" Added to all else that we have encountered, its repeated use in Lev. 19 warrants at least a tentative hypothesis that P/h regards the duality as functionally distinctive. As Lord, the Being I have termed the God of the Torah exerts His dominion over the Heavens and Earth. Except for the "technical" freedom of human beings to choose between right and wrong, His rule is absolute, His power, without limits. But added to His *innate* status as "Lord" is His discretionary but *chosen* role as Israel's God. As such, He serves as its Law-Giver, Protector, and Teacher. As "Lord," His power knows no constraints other than His own unfettered will. But for as long as He remains Israel's God, His power is constrained by covenantal obligations.

But what of the repeated use in Lev. 19 of the utterly singular "I am the Lord"? Because it omits His role as Israel's God, it must be read as a warning. By its use, P/h means to remind the "whole Israelite community" that whether or not it accepts the Lord as *its God*, He will forever remain "*its Lord.*" As such, He will rule Israel, as He now rules all the rest of humanity— that is, free of all covenantal obligations and constraints. Should Israel reject its covenant, He will no longer lead and protect it as its God. Yet He will remain its Lord.

> Note L–75: Lev. 20 restates the substance, and expands on the punishments, of many of the offenses of Lev. 18 and a few others of Lev. 19. As in Lev. 18:2 and 19:2, Moses speaks in 20:2 to the whole Israelite community.

Lev. 20 again turns to Molech: "Any man [Israelites and strangers alike] who gives any of his offspring to Molech shall be put to death; the people of the land shall pelt him with stones" (20:2). (Cf. 20:2 and 18:21: "Do not allow any of your offspring to be offered up to Molech.")

Though the offenses are similar, the punishments for 20:2 violations are more explicit than the "generic" punishment of being "cut off from their people," as applied to all Lev. 18 violations (18:29). Thus, "Any man among the Israelites, or among the strangers residing in Israel, who gives any of his offspring to Molech, shall be put to death; the people of the land shall pelt him with stones. And I will set My face against that man and will cut him off from among his people. . . . And if the people of the land should shut their eyes to that man when he gives of his offspring to Molech, and should not put him to death, I myself will put My face against that man *and his kin*, and will cut off from among their people both him and all who follow him in going astray after Molech" (20:2–5). (As to child-sacrifice in worship of Molech, see Comment L–24.)

Comment L–44. On the punishment for allowing offspring "to be offered up to Molech"

The blasphemy of the offense was heightened by its duality. To slay an innocent child for any reason was vile beyond words. To do so as a ritual of "having other gods" was vile beyond comprehension. Only its commission on the sabbath could compound such evil.

As punishment, "the people" must slay the offender by pelting him with stones. When they do so, the Lord will then "set [His own] face" against the offender and will "cut him [or his memory?] off from among his people." Should the people fail in their duty, the Lord Himself will then "set [His] face" against the miscreant and all others of his kin "who follow him in going astray after Molech."

Why does P/h have the Lord "set His face" against the offender's kin only *after* the people fail to act against the offender? Does P/h imply that the miscreant's kin had dissuaded the people from fulfilling their duty?

Of greater import, however, is the fact that in punishing the offender's kin, the Lord will "cut off" only those who had followed the offender "in going astray after Molech." Had they already strayed, of course, they, too, would have been subject to being stoned to death by he people. In the circumstance, the Lord's point would seem to be that He could not and would not rely on the people *to deal in the future* with any kin of the miscreant who go astray. He, directly and alone, will deal with them as need be.

Lev. 20:6 would "cut off from among his people" anyone who "turns to ghosts and familiar spirits and goes astray after them." (Here the punishment corresponds to that of the similar offense of 19:31.)

Lev. 20:7–8 offers a notable variation on the possible functional duality between "Lord" and "God" (see Comment L–43). Its admonition is this: "You shall sanctify yourselves and be holy, for I the Lord am your God. You shall faithfully observe my laws: *I the Lord make you holy*."

Comment L–45. On Lev. 20:7–8 as it relates to Comment L–43 on the functional duality of "Lord" and "God"

A literal reading of Lev. 20:7–8 in JPS2 again suggests two distinct roles of the single Being of the Lord. The question here involves the Lord's claim to be the direct source of Israel's derived holiness. The Holiness Code includes repeated suggestions that the attribute of holiness within the Lord relates to His role *as Israel's God*. Consider: "You shall be holy, for I, the Lord *your God*, am holy" (19:2); "You shall sanctify yourselves and be holy, *for I the Lord am your God*." Nevertheless, in 20:8 the Lord claims to impart holiness to Israel not as *its God*, but as *the Lord*. And so He declares, "*I the Lord make you holy*." (Cf. JPS1/RSV: "*I am the Lord Who sanctify you*.")

Thus, in Lev. 20:7–8 P/h differentiates between Israel's *God as the source of holiness* and *the Lord as its purveyor*. It is the Lord's *power* that enables Him to induce Israel to share in His holiness as Israel's God. Absent His *power*, would Israel have accepted the Lord's demanding terms for partaking of His holiness as their God? From what we know of Him, the Lord's claim of having *made* Israel "holy" as "the Lord," rather as "its God," seems credible.

This "duality" issue is beclouded, however, by P's use, with few exceptions, of *elohim* throughout Genesis. This inevitably portrays God alone as the source of the power that, in Exodus, is increasingly associated with the Lord. Among the notable expressions of *God's* power in Genesis are: the first story of creation (1:1–31, 2:1–3) and portions of the Noah story (e.g 6:9–22, 9:1–17). But adding to the confusion in Genesis is the appearance of *el shaddai*. In Gen. 17:1 it is P's *yahweh* who reveals Himself as *el shaddai*—or, as commonly understood, "God Almighty." And in Gen. 35:10–11, it is P's *elohim* who does so again.

It is J's version of creation that first hints at a duality in the Being of the "Lord God" (*yahweh elohim*) (Gen. 2:4, 3). Later, J imparts a similar sense of duality to Jacob at Beth-el (while en route to Laban). There the Lord introduces Himself to Jacob in his dream: "I am the Lord, the God of your father Abraham and the God of Isaac" (Gen. 28:10). Jacob quickly grasps the point. "*If* God remains with me . . . and gives me bread to eat and clothing to wear . . . *the Lord shall be my God*" (Gen. 28:20–21). And if not, as Jacob might seem to imply, "The Lord may be the Lord, but He will not be my God."

In Exod. 6:5–7, P moves firmly from its "God" of Genesis to the Lord, as God of Israel. Thus, he tells Moses:

> Say . . . to the Israelite people: *I am the Lord. I* will free you from the burden of the Egyptians and deliver you from their bondage. *I* will redeem you with an outstretched arm and through extraordinary chastisements. And I will take you to be My people, *and I will be your God.* And you shall know that I the Lord, am *your* God who freed you from the labors of the Egyptians.

Combined here in the God of the Torah is the power of "the Lord" and the love of Israel's "God." What does the duality of an "innate" Lord and a "volitional" God imply about relations between *yahweh* and all humanity other than Israel? It is only Israel that the Lord will claim as His people and serve as its God. All others will know Him only as *yahweh*, the Lord. And yet, His commands to Israel tell of a continuing concern for that portion of humanity to whom He will not be God—at least as yet. "The stranger who resides with you shall be to you as one of your citizens; you shall love him as yourself, for you were strangers in the land of Egypt; I the Lord am your God" (Lev. 19:34). (See also Comments G–39 pt. 2, G–43, and G–56.)

Lev. 20:9 follows on Lev. 19:3: "If any man *insults* his father or mother, he shall be put to death. . . . His bloodguilt is upon him" (20:9). "You shall each *revere* his father and his mother" (19:3).

> *Note L–76: The conduct that comprises the "insult" of 20:9 is usually more apparent than the lack of reverence that violates 19:3. So it is with "sins" of the mind that are shrouded in politeness or hypocrisy.*

Lev. 20:10 repeats the punishment for the offense of adultery. "If a man commits adultery with a married woman, committing adultery with his neighbor's wife, the adulterer and the adulteress shall be put to death."

> *Note L–77: Lev. 18:20 is literally directed to the man alone. "Do not have carnal relations with your neighbor's wife and defile yourself with her." But*

like the Seventh Commandment, Lev. 20:10 applies alike to the aggrieved neighbor's wife and to the man who stole his property right.

Lev. 20:11, 12, and 13 prescribe death (by means unstated) for offenders "whose bloodguilt is upon them." Each involves a sexual union initially prohibited under Lev. 18: between (1) a man and his "father's wife" (18:8), (2) a man and his "daughter-in-law" (18:15), and (3) a man who lies with another man, "as . . . with a woman" (18:22).

Lev. 20:14, relating to 18:17, deals with the depravity of "marriages" between a man and both "a woman and her mother." In specifying yet another component of the generic "cut off" punishment of 18:29, Lev. 20:14 declares as the penalty for such marriages that "both he and they shall be put to the fire, that there be no depravity among you."

> *Note L–78: JPS1 and RSV render yikach as "take" rather than "marry." Rashi, however, treats such unions as marriages.[24] Given the innocence of the first union, we might ask why "they" (including the first wife) should be punished. Was it her duty to end her marriage on the occasion of the second marriage?*

Lev. 20:15 and 16 prescribe death for the offense of bestiality (18:23), whether by man (20:15) or woman (20:16). In both cases, the beast "shall be put to death" as well. In addition, however, 20:15–16 more clearly distinguishes the nature of the offense as committed by a man or woman. As to men: "If a man *has carnal relations* with a beast, he shall be put to death" (20:15). As for women: "If a woman *approaches any beast to mate with it,* you shall kill the woman and the beast" (20:16).

> *Note L–79: Whether or not due to anatomical differences, male guilt, according to JPS2, required consummation. Female guilt, however, required no more than the effort. However, both JPS1 and RSV include a clause from 20:16, which JPS2 omits: l'riv'ah ohtah, rendered by JPS1 as "and lie down thereto" and RSV as "and lies with it."*

Comment L–46. On the mandatory death of the beast in light of Lev. 4:27–35 and Exod. 21:13

In regard to bestiality, Rashi asks the obvious question: "If a man sinned, in what way did the animal sin?" But as a measure of justice, his answer is less obvious: "However, since there came to the man a downfall through it, therefore Scripture writes 'It shall be stoned.' "[25]

Plaut views the logic of the Torah in much the same way. "Though it is not morally responsible, it was the *unwitting* cause of a human life being destroyed."[26]

What then of the person, who, having "unwittingly" caused a human death, may then gain expiation through the protocols of Lev. 4:27–35 (as "arranged" by P)? Is it because the beast cannot atone? But what of E's "man" who kills another, though "he did not do it by design"? Because the Lord declares it an "act of God," He will provide "a place to which [the killer] can flee" (Exod. 21:13). Nor does E require atonement. True enough, P/h is faced here by a possibly "unknown" *mishpat* from another source. But if we (like Rashi and Ramban) were to view the Torah as a perfectly structured unity, how could we not absolve the "unwitting" beast "who did not do it by design"?

Lev. 20:17 deals with the offense of 18:9 involving the "marriage" of a man and "his sister, the daughter of either his father or his mother" (see Note L–42). Both offenders were to be "excommunicated" (JPS2) or "cut off" (JPS1/RSV) "in the sight of their kinsfolk."

> Note L–80: *It now becomes clear that despite the "male-directed" commands of Lev. 18, Lev. 20 punishments may apply to both parties of a prohibited relationship.*

Lev. 20:18 relates to the command of 18:19 to "not come near to a woman during her period of uncleanness [for the purpose of sexual relations]." It emphasizes the impurity of the act. To lay with a woman "in her infirmity" is to "[lay] bare her flow." In that way "she has exposed her blood flow." The punishment for both is to be "cut off from among their people."

> Note L–81: *But again, consider the apparent contradiction of Lev. 15:24 in which the same act merely renders the man temporarily unclean.*

Lev. 20:19 restates 18:12–13 (barring sexual relations between a man and a sister of his father or mother). Here, however, the punishment is "they shall bear their guilt."

Lev. 20:20–21 repeats the offenses of 18:14 (relations with the wife of a father's brother) and 18:16 (relations with a brother's wife). Both involve "in-laws" rather than the blood relationship of 20:19. But to the punishment of 20:19 that they "bear their guilt" is added "they shall *die* childless" (as to an uncle's wife) or "they shall *remain* childless" (as to a brother's wife) (20:20, 21).

> Note L–82: *The punishment of "childlessness" recalls the Lord's several interventions into the birth processes of Genesis. But given its absence in the presumably more egregious blood relationships of 20:19, why is the penalty of "childlessness" added to the "in-law" relationships of 20:20 and 21?*
>
> *Also of interest in the punishments of 20:20 and 21 is the distinction between to "die" childless and to "remain" (or "be") childless. To die childless allows for the birth of children who will predecease their parents. To*

remain (or be) *childless is never to have children. But in either case*, absent a marriage between the parents, *what appears as a punishment might be viewed by them as a good fortune.* Accordingly, logic might suggest that rather than being needlessly directed against particular forms of adultery (i.e., relations with the present wife of an uncle or brother), the prohibition applies instead to marriages by a nephew with a widowed aunt or a brother with a widowed sister-in-law.

Lev. 20:22–26 then moves from punishments to a broad invocation of the special relationship between Israel and the Lord, its God. Its foundation again is obedience. "You shall faithfully observe all My laws . . . lest the land to which I bring you to settle in spew you out" (20:22). The unique status of Israel is then recalled. "I the Lord am *your* God who has set you apart from other peoples" (20:24). The clean/unclean distinction among the various classes of animals is then recalled (20:25). The passage concludes with a *near* reiteration of "I, the Lord *your* God, am holy" (19:2). It differs, however, in ascribing holiness to the Lord alone. "You shall be holy to Me, for I *the Lord am holy*, and I have set you apart from other peoples to be Mine" (20:26).

> *Note L–83: This formulation should be considered in relation to the thesis of Comments L–43 and 45.*

Lev. 20:27 returns to the themes of 19:31 and 20:6. "A man or woman who *has* a ghost or a familar spirit shall be put to death: they shall be pelted with stones—their bloodguilt shall be upon them" (JPS2).

> *Note L–84: Based on the root* phanah, *the earlier verses speak of "turning" to "ghosts and familiar spirits" (20:6 and 19:31). The operative phrase of 20:27 is* v'eesh oh ishah key yi'yeh vahem ohv oh yidonee. *The possible difference is between an individual who turns to divination for his own purposes and a "professional" practitioner, who alone must suffer the "sure" punishment of being stoned to death.*

Comment L–47. On using the particular punishments of Lev. 20 to construe the "generic" punishment of Lev. 18:29— to be "cut off from their people"

That Lev. 18:29 applies the one punishment of being "cut off from their people" to every offense of Lev. 18 poses the broad question of its relationship to the varied punishments of Lev. 20 covering many of the same offenses. *If the author(s) intend(s) a consistency between Lev. 18 and 20, then each of the following punishments of Lev. 20 fall within the meaning of being "cut off from their people"*: death by stoning (20:2), death by unspecified means (20:9–13, 15–16), death by fire (20:14), excommunication (JPS2) or "cut off in the sight of the children of their people" (JPS1) (20:17), bearing one's guilt (20:17, 19), *dying* childless (20:20), and *remaining* childless (20:21).

The pattern is broken, however, by Lev. 20:18, which uniquely (in Lev. 20) applies the generic "cut off" punishment of 18:29 to sexual relations during menstruation. Given the previously noted conflict between Lev. 20:18 and 15:24 (see Note L–81), is it possible that R chose to leave the matter open?

In this regard we should note as well that Lev. 20 does not cover all the offenses of Lev. 18. Among the omissions are relations between mothers and sons (18:7), grandfathers and granddaughters (18:10), stepbrothers and stepsisters (18:11), and men with the sisters of living wives (18:18).

Lev. 21 turns from the people to the priests. As guardians of ritual purity, the priests were held to higher standards of personal purity. And it is only to "the priests, the sons of Aaron," that the Lord tells Moses to speak these commands (21:1).

> Note L–85: *Nevertheless, Lev. 21 closes with this contrary assertion: "Thus Moses spoke to Aaron and his sons and to all the Israelites" (21:24).*

Except for "his mother, his father, his son, his daughter, and his brother; also a virgin sister," a priest could not "defile himself for any dead person among his kin" (21:1–3). Expressly prohibited was his defilement "as a kinsman by marriage" (i.e., "in-laws").

> Note L–86: *While "defilement" results from "unclean" contacts with, or proximity to, the dead, nothing is said of the nature of such contacts or the degree of proximity. The closest analogy thus far is to the carcass of a ritually edible animal (see Lev. 11:39). In general, the rules seek to balance a priest's innate feelings for his kin with the "innate" impurity of corpses.*

Lev. 21:5 forbids the priests to "shave smooth any part of their heads, or cut the side-growth of their beards, or make gashes in their flesh."

> Note L–87: *Although not in identical words, these commands to the priests regarding head and facial hair and bodily mutilation read much like those to all Israelite males in Lev. 19:27–28. As Israelites, were the priests not already bound? (Cf. Deut. 14:1.)*

Lev. 21:6 explains the special status of the priests. "They shall be holy to their God and not profane the name of their God, *for they offer the Lord's offerings by fire, the food of their God,* and so must be holy."

Lev. 21:7 forbids the sons of Aaron to marry "a woman degraded by harlotry" or a divorcee. These constraints apply only to priests, "for they are holy to their God." Moreover, "you must treat them as holy, since they offer the food of your God; they shall be holy to you" (21:8).

> *Note L–88: The "you" of 21:7–8 who must treat the priests as holy can only be the Israelites, en masse, who Lev. 21:24 will identify for the first time as auditors of Moses' words (see Note L–85).*

Lev. 21:9 extends the obligations of priestly holiness to a priest's daughter. "When the daughter of a priest degrades herself though harlotry, it is her father whom she degrades; she shall be put to the fire."

Comment L–48. On the "degrading," but not generally forbidden, practice of harlotry

This Comment supplements Note L–69 following Lev. 19:29 with the added insights afforded by Lev. 21:9. As a father, the priest is already prohibited by 19:29 from turning his daughter to harlotry. Thus, the prohibition of 21:9 against harlotry and the punishment of death by fire applies only to his daughter. As Note L–69 suggests, harlotry, as such, has not yet been prohibited in the Torah. It is only in Lev. 21:9 of the Holiness Code that harlotry is has yet been characterized as "degrading." And though the entire thrust of 19:29 is to condemn harlotry, the Torah does not prohibit it. It is a striking example of the accomodation of moral and ethical ideals to social reality.

Lev. 21:10–15 tells of the unique holiness obligations of the *high* priest. He could neither "bare his head nor rend his vestments" (21:10). "He shall not go in where there is any dead body." Nor could he so defile himself "even for his mother and father." Nor could he attend their burial rites. "He shall not go outside the sanctuary and profane the sanctuary of his God, for upon him is the distinction of the anointing oil of his God" (21:11–12).

> *Note L–89: Now, in barring the high priest from the presence of a dead parent's body, P/h rejects all compromise between personal feelings and ritual requirements. The holiness required of the high priest must transcend every aspect of human sentiment. However, the very harshness of this self-imposed disability also added dramatic credence to the unique status of the high priest.*

Lev. 21:13–15 limits the marriage of the high priest to "a virgin of his own kin."

> *Note L–90: JPS1 and RSV read the the Hebrew root ahm as "people" rather than "kin." However, "kin" here may be meant to refer to all Israel as descendants of Abraham.*

Expressly barred as a wife was "a widow, or a divorced woman, or one who is degraded by harlotry" (21:14). To do so would "profane his offspring among his kin, for I the Lord have sanctified him" (21:15).

Lev. 21:16–23 details the physical characteristics which will disqualify Aaron's male "offspring" from offering rites. In general, "No man ... who has a defect shall be qualified to offer *the food of his God*; no one at all who has a defect shall be qualified" (21:17–18).

A listing of particulars follows. As stated in JPS2, they include: a man who is "blind, or lame or has a limb too short or too long"; a man who has "a broken leg or a broken arm"; a man who is "a hunchback or a dwarf"; or a man who has "a growth in his eye, or ... a boil-scar, or scurvy or crushed testes." The listing ends much as it began. "No man among the offspring of Aaron the priest who has *a defect* shall be qualified to offer the Lord's offerings by fire: having a defect, he [is not] qualified" (21:21).

Comment L–49. On the requirement of priests without "defects"

The prohibited defects, or blemishes, differ among the three translations. Being illustrative, however, rather than all-inclusive, the differences are not significant. The generic injunction of Lev. 21:21 as to "defects" bars all.

In general, the Torah expresses compassion for the disabled: "You shall not insult the deaf, or place a stumbling block before the blind. You shall fear your God: I am the Lord" (see Note L–61). But by the undeviating priority accorded by the P source to the Lord's sanctity, priestly purity and perfection transcend ordinary human values.

However, the Holiness Code does include lesser nonritualistic concessions. Although barred from rituals, a blemished "son of Aaron" could "eat of the food of his God, of the *most* holy as well as the holy" (21:22). But there were other limits. Thus, "he shall not enter behind the curtain or come near the altar, for he has a defect. "He shall not profane these places sacred to Me."

Lev. 22 addresses the priests' need for "cleanness" in making offerings. Moses is told to instruct Aaron and his sons to "be scrupulous about the sacred donations that the Israelite people consecrate to Me, lest they profane My holy name, Mine the Lord's. Say to *them*: 'Throughout the ages, *if any man among your offspring, while in a state of uncleanness partakes of any sacred donation that the Israelite people may consecrate to the Lord, that person shall be cut off from before Me*': I am the Lord" (22:1–3).

Lev. 22:4–8 sets out various sources of ritual uncleanness: for example, no priest could partake of any "sacred donation" while still unclean from "an eruption or discharge" [i.e., other than semen]; contact with "anything made unclean by a corpse"; "an emission of semen"; contact with "any swarming thing"; and, as a "catch all," contact with "any human being by whom he is made unclean." But there was added concern for the "sacred donation," itself. Thus, the priest "shall not eat anything that died or was torn by beasts, thereby becoming unclean."

> *Note L–91: These sources of uncleanness, both of priest and offering, derive from earlier portions of Leviticus. As to specific sources of uncleanness, whether general or priestly, see 11:20–28, 15:2–5, 15:16–17, 21:1–4.*

In every case, the period of disqualification from eating "sacred donations" because of personal uncleanness was brief. Following a complete washing of his body, the priest was restored to cleanness at sunset. He could then eat of the "sacred donations" that were "his food" (22:7).

In 22:9, however, the punishment of being "cut off from before Me" for eating "sacred donations" while unclean, as first stated in 22:3, is now explicitly equated with death. "They shall keep My charge, lest they incur guilt thereby and die for it, having committed profanation."

Lev. 22:10–16 distinguishes between persons (other than priests) who could or could not eat of the "sacred donations." A broad standard of *ineligibility* is expressed in the Hebrew *chal-ẓar*, for which our three translations offer the terms "lay person" (JPS2), "common man" (JPS1), and "an outsider" (RSV) (22:10).

Among the named "eligible" members of the household who could eat of the sacred donations were (1) permanent household slaves of the priest and (2) an unmarried daughter of the priest, or a widowed or divorced daughter *without offspring* who had returned to the household. Also named as ineligible were (1) a "bound or hired laborer" and (2) a daughter married to a "layman" (or "common man" or "outsider") (22:10–13).

> *Note L–92: The basic distinction suggested by 22:10–13 is between the two classes of (1) permanent or semipermanent resident members of a priest's household (both family and slaves, or servants) and (2) nonresident members of the priest's family and temporary hired help. If so, RSV comes closest to the intended substance by distinguishing between "outsiders" and, impliedly, "insiders." However, the categories named seem more descriptive of "marginal" cases. Surely, if slaves and unmarried daughters could eat the sacred portions, so, too, could nonmentioned resident wives and sons (see Lev. 10:12–15 and Note L–24).*

Lev. 22:14–16 deals with an ineligible man who "eats of a sacred donation unwittingly." He must pay the priest its value (however determined), "adding one-fifth." The fact of a penalty, however, did not relieve the priests of their duty not to "allow the Israelites to profane the sacred donations which they set aside for the Lord, or to incur guilt . . . by eating such sacred donations" (22:15–16).

In Lev. 22:17–18, Moses is again told to speak to "all the Israelite people" as well as to "Aaron and his sons."

Lev. 22:18–25 deals with (1) "burnt offerings . . . for any of the votive or any of the freewill offerings" and (2) "a sacrifice of well-being . . . for an explicit vow or as a freewill offering" (22:19–21).

> Note L–93: "Votive" and "freewill" offerings were made through sacrifices of well-being (see Lev. 3, 7:11–18).

Male animals of the herd or flock not "without blemish" would "not be accepted in your favor" (22:20). As a single exception in the case of freewill (but not votive) offerings "an ox or sheep with a limb extended or contracted" could be offered (22:23).

> Note L–94: Lev. 3:1 and 6 requires animals "without blemish" for all sacrifices of well-being, including votive and freewill offerings. At the least an "extended or contracted limb" suggests an abnormality. If so, the ox or sheep of Lev. 22:23 is either an exception to the rules for sacrifices of well-being, or "without blemish" allows for limited deviations from "normality."

Lev. 22:24 bars the offering of castrated animals. Such "mutilation" was apparently common among neighboring peoples. Thus, a second and related command: "Nor shall you accept such [animals] from a foreigner for offering as food for your God, for they are mutilated, they have a defect" (22:25).

Into the strict rituals of purposeful slaughter in making "sacred donations" to the Lord, Lev. 22:29–30 injects an element of respect for animal sensibilites. A newborn animal was to remain with its mother for seven days. Only "from the eighth on" was it "acceptable as an offering by fire to the Lord." In addition, no sacrificial animal could be "slaughtered on the same day with its young."

> Note L–95: Although such acts of consideration were meaningless to the animals, they should have reminded Israelites that animals, too, were living beings. As such, they deserved a measure of kindness, even though death by slaughter for sacrifice would prove their highest destiny.

Lev. 22:29–30 restates the requirement of 7:15 that "thanksgiving offerings" must be "eaten on the same day."

Lev. 22 concludes with a repeated delineation of the distinctive roles of *yahweh*, as Lord, and *elohim*, as God of Israel: "You shall faithfully observe My commandments: I am the Lord. You shall not profane My holy name. . . . I the Lord who sanctify you, I who brought you out of the land of Egypt *to be your* God, I the Lord" (22:31–33).

> Note L–96: Cf. Comments L–43 and 45.

Comment L–50. On *"the* Lord's offerings by fire" as the "food of *your* God"

Lev. 1 and 3, most notably, speak of "offerings by fire of pleasing odor to the Lord" (see 1:9, 13, 17; 3:5, 11). But in a manner more consistent with with the posited dichotomy between "Lord" and "God," Lev. 21 and 22 speak (in varied terms) of *"the* Lord's offering by fire" that are meant as "food for *your* God" (21:6, 17, 21–22: 22:24–25). Again it would seem that P/h looks to the Lord's compelling power to persuade Israel of His sanctity *as its God* (see Comments L–43 and 45).

In Lev. 23 the Lord instructs "the Israelite people, through Moses, regarding "the fixed times of the Lord, which you will proclaim as sacred occasions" (23:1–2).

> *Note L–97: Not every day of a "fixed time" is declared a "sacred occasion." For example, only the first and seventh days of the seven-day Feast of Unleavened Bread are declared as such.*

The "fixed times" and "sacred occasions" of Lev. 23 consist of (1) the weekly Sabbath (23:3); (2) the Passover and Feast of Unleavened Bread (23:5–8); (3) the Omer (or the "first sheaf" of the harvest) (23:9–14); (4) the fiftieth day following the offering of the Omer (23:15–21); (5) the first day of the seventh month (23:24–25); (6) the tenth day of the seventh month, identified in the Torah as *yom hakippurim*, the Day of Atonement (23:26–32); and (7) eight days beginning on the fifteenth day of the seventh month (or five days after *yom hakippurim*, named as the Feast of Booths, or Tabernacles (23:33–36 and 23:39–43). Needless to say, they do not include such post-Torah holy days, or festivals, such as Chanukah and Purim.

THE "FIXED TIMES" AND "SACRED OCCASIONS" OF LEV. 23

1. *The Weekly Sabbath* (23:3). Following six days of work, "the seventh day . . . shall be a *sabbath of complete rest* [i.e., a *shabat shabaton*], a sacred occasion. You shall do *no* work; it shall be a sabbath of the Lord throughout your settlements."

> *Note L–98: Of importance here are the requirements of complete rest and no work. (JPS1/RSV render shabat shabaton as a "sabbath of solemn rest.") As in the Sabbath reminders of Lev. 19:3 and 30, the command here states no rationale—neither the cycle of creation of the Fourth Commandment (see Exod. 20:8–11 and Comment E–57), nor E's cycle of rest (Exod. 23:12).*

2. *The Passover and Feast of Unleavened Bread* (23:5–8). As identified in Lev. 23:5–8, the Passover and Feast of Unleavened Bread are two separate, but closely related, "sacred occasions." "In the first month, on the fourteenth day of the month, at twilight, there shall be a passover offering to the Lord, *and* on the fifteenth day of that month the Lord's Feast of Unleavened Bread." During the seven-day Feast only "unleavened bread" could be eaten. Only the first and seventh days of the Feast are declared "sacred occasions" on which "you shall not work *at your occupations*."

> Note L–99: *JPS1 speaks of "servile work" and RSV of "laborious" work. JPS2 makes the most useful distinction between the* m'lechet avodah, *or "occupational" work, of the first and final Feast days and the* kol m'lachah, *or the "no" work of the Sabbath.*

The Torah first mentions the "passover" in the Lord's directions to Moses on preparating for the Tenth Plague (Exod. 12). The slaying of the firstborn would occur on the night of the fourteenth day of the first month. As "an institution for all time" (12:24), the passover was to be observed in accord with the rituals of Exod. 12 and 13. E's *mishpatim* also mentions the "Feast of Unleavened Bread" (Exod. 23:15). (See Comment E–41.)

3. *The Omer (or "first sheaf" of the harvest)* (23:9–14). The "fixed time" (or "appointed season" of the Omer relates to the first harvest offering of the year. It takes its name from the *omer* itself, that is, "the first sheaf of your harvest." From the text, however, its "fixed time" is not easily identified. "When you enter the land which I am giving you and you reap its harvest, you shall bring the first sheaf of your harvest to the priest. He shall wave the sheaf before the Lord . . . *on the day after the sabbath* [this being the day of the Omer]" (23:11).

On the day the sheaf was waved two offerings were also made to the Lord. These were the burnt offering of a lamb without blemish in its first year and a meal offering of flour and oil (of specified measure). (There is no explicit command, however, that the meal, or "cereal," offering should come from the grain of the new harvest.) A "libation" of a quarter *hin* of wine was also required for priestly use at such offerings. Until they were made, the Israelites were to eat "no bread or parched grain or fresh ears [i.e., from the new harvest]." Work was allowed and rest was not required.

> Note L–100: *As noted above, although the Omer was a designated "fixed time," the Torah is anything but precise in fixing its date. It was to occur "on the day after the sabbath" (23:11). But which sabbath? Was it the "sabbath" following the year's first harvest? If so, it could not possibly have been a "fixed time." The harvest was subject to weather conditions. Moreover, it would*

vary across the land. However, if the time of the preceding sabbath could be fixed, then so, too, would be the Omer.

In time, the Omer was "fixed," where it remains today— on the second day of the seven days of Passover. As stated in the Torah, the Omer falls on mimachahraht hahshabat. The root word shabat, however, is not limited to the "fixed time" of the weekly sabbath. It may also include any "day of rest." In this case it is the shabat of the first day of Passover, a "fixed time and a day of rest from "occupational" work." (This is also Rashi's view.[27])

In theory, this solution might still seem subject to the weather. What if the new harvest is not ready by the "fixed time" of Omer? Even so, at least its "first sheaf," or omer, should have ripened sufficiently for waving.

4. *The fiftieth day following the Omer* (23:15–21). The next "fixed time" came seven weeks and one day, or fifty days, following Omer. On that day the Israelites were to bring "an offering of *new grain* to the Lord" (23:16).

> Note L–101: *JPS2 derives "an offering of* new grain" *from* minchah chahdashah. *JPS1 terms it "a new meal offering" and RSV, "a cereal offering of new grain." Fifty days would have passed, thus providing greater assurance that the "new" grain would be harvested.*

The "new grain" offering was to be brought from "your settlements" in the form of "two loaves of bread as a wave offering; each . . . made of two-tenths of a measure of choice flour, baked after leavening, *as first fruits* to the Lord" (23:17).

This unnamed harvest festival fell within the established principle of offering, or dedicating the first fruits of nature to the Lord—whether of plants, animals, or humans (see Exod. 13:2, 11–16, 22:28–29). Of these, Exod. 22:28–29 is included among the *mishpatim* of E. To express the joy and gratitude of the harvest, there were burnt, sin, wave, and well-being offerings. Together, these called for the sacrifice of "seven yearling lambs without blemish, one bull of the herd, . . . and two rams, . . . one he-goat . . . and two yearling lambs" (23:18–19).

The day is termed both a "celebration" and a "sacred occasion" on which "you shall not work at your occupations" (23:18–21). As with the two "sacred occasions" of the Feast of Unleavened Bread, the command to rest is limited to occupational work.

As an added element of the harvest festival, the gist of Lev. 19:9–10 is restated. A portion of the crop was not to be reaped and harvest gleanings were to be left ungathered. Instead, "you shall leave them for the poor and the stranger; I the Lord am your God" (23:22).

Comment L–51. On the offerings of the fiftieth day following Omer as collective or individual duties

Thus far in Lev. 23 (including the present passage of 23:15–21) "the Lord" has spoken to "the Israelite people," with each command directed to "you." For the most part, the "you" of the commands applies to Israel, collectively, and to each Israelite, individually. Examples include the ban on occupational work and the need to leave portions of the harvest in the fields "for the poor and the stranger."

But what of the animal offerings? Were these to be individual or collective? Consider the offerings associated with the basic "offering of new grain to the Lord." *In itself*, it called for no more than "two loaves of bread" ritually prepared "as a wave offering." This charge alone could likely be fulfilled by each family. However, together with the loaves were to be presented the following: (1) as a burnt offerings, seven lambs, one bull, and two rams; (2) as a sin offering, one male goat; and (3) as a sacrifice of well-being, two lambs. Apart from the strain on family resources, contemplate, if possible, the carnage of this multiplicity of sacrifices together with the inconceivable burden on the priests.

Perhaps to strike a somewhat more realistic balance, JPS2 reads *mimoshvotaychem* as "from your settlements" rather than as "from your dwellings," as in JPS1/RSV (23:17). Literally, these offerings, whether from each dwelling or each settlement, are to be presented "with the bread." Accordingly, Lev. 23:20 seems to allude to a separate wave offering in connection with each offering of bread. "The priest shall wave these—the two lambs—together with the bread of first fruits as a wave offering."

Given the utter impossibility of effecting individual animal offerings for all Israelite families at the single site of the Tent or Temple, we must conclude that the "you" of animal offerings is the whole of Israel. Thus, a single symbolic set of animal offerings would have been made on behalf of all Israel. But one can envision individual offerings of new grain in the form of two loaves each.

> Note L–102: Today, the unnamed fiftieth day following the Omer is known as shavuot. It is variously celebrated in Israel or the diaspora on the sixth or seventh day of Sivan. Its primary character as a harvest festival was eventually displaced by a focus on its calendar proximity to the revelations at Sinai. This was derived in time from the words of Exod. 19:1 which places the arrival of the Israelites in the Sinai on "the third new moon" (or the first day of Sivan). E's mishpatim also include a "Feast of the Harvest" as one of the "three times" each year that "all your males shall appear before the Sovereign, the Lord" (Exod. 23:16).

5. *The first day of the seventh month* (23:23–25). A nameless "sacred occasion" is then decreed for the first day of the seventh month. Although a day of "complete [or solemn] rest" (i.e., *shaboton*), the explicit work ban covers only "*your occupations.*" It is to be marked "with a blast of horns." Also required is "an offering by fire to the Lord."

> *Note L–103: The "blast of horns" is the* teruah *of the ram's horn (or shofar). This "sacred occasion" is known today as Rosh Hashonah, or the "head" of the year. Although it occurs in the seventh month, it marks the Jewish New Year.*

6. *The tenth day of the seventh month* (23:26–32). It is in regard to the tenth day of the seventh month that Lev. 23 describes a "sacred occasion" of even greater solemnity than the weekly Sabbath itself (23:26–32). It is the Day of Atonement (i.e., *yom hakippurim*) (23:27–28).

The commands regarding its observance both include and add to those of the weekly Sabbath: (1) You shall practice self-denial, and you shall bring an offering by fire to the Lord. (2) "You shall do *no* work throughout that day . . . on which expiation is made on your behalf before the Lord your God." (3) "Any person who does not practice self-denial throughout that day shall be cut off from his kin; and whoever does any work throughout that day, I will cause . . . to perish from among his people." (4) "Do no work *whatever*, it is a law for all time." (5) It shall a sabbath of complete [or solemn] rest for you (here, a *shabat shabaton*), and you shall practice self-denial." In sum, "on the ninth day of the month at evening, from evening to evening, you shall observe this *your sabbath.*"

Thus, through its unique requirement of "self-denial," its stark recitation of the dire punishments for disobedience, and its general rhetoric, Lev. 23 accords even greater sanctity to the Day of Atonement than to the Sabbath itself.

7. *The seven (or eight) days beginning on the fifteenth day of the seventh month* (23:33–43). The final "sacred occasions" are the first and last days of an eight day period beginning on the fifteenth day of the seventh month. Of particular interest are the two differing versions of this one holiday (i.e 23:33–36 and 23:39–43, as separated by 23:37–38).

In its brevity, version (1) does not identify the seven-day Feast of Booths as a harvest festival. The festival concludes with the "solemn gathering" (or *atzaret*) of the eighth day. The first and eighth days are declared "sacred occasions" on which "you shall not work at your occupations." On each day there were "offerings by fire to the Lord" (not otherwise identified) (23:33–36).

Version (1) (i.e 23:33–36) is followed by these words of 23:37–38: "These are the set times of the Lord which you shall celebrate as sacred occasions, bringing offerings by fire to the Lord—burnt offerings, meal offerings, sacrifices, and libations, on each day what is proper to it—*apart from the sabbaths of the Lord*, and apart from your gifts . . . votive offerings and . . . freewill offerings that you give to the Lord" (23:37–38).

> Note L 104: As a summary of 23:1–36, 23:37–38 contradicts 23:2–3 in which the "sabbath of the Lord" is enshrined as the first of the "set times." (In JPS2 the "fixed times" of 23:2 and the "set times" of 23:37 are both from mohadai.) Friedman attributes both version (1) and 23:37–38 to the P source (including P/h). However, he attributes version (2) (i.e., 23:39–43) to R (as he does the recapitulation of all the occasions for offerings in Num. 28–29, including those of the "mohadai." While the evidence is too sparse to associate 23:37–38 with version (2) rather than version (1), its notable contradiction as a summary of version (1) poses a question of its source.

Version (2) describes the eight-day festival more fully (23:39–43). It is to be held "when you have gathered up the yield of your land." The first and eighth days were each to be a *shabaton* (i.e., a "solemn" or "complete" rest). Nothing is said of "occupational" work.

> Note L–105: In this latter respect, version (2) reverses version (1), in which occupational work is barred, but with no further requirement of rest (cf. 23:35–36). In both cases either command was regarded as sufficient in itself. Statements of only one or the other are found elsewhere among the "fixed times." The Feast of Unleavened Bread and the spring harvest festival fifty days following the Omer prohibit occupational work with no explicit mention of rest (23:7, 21). In both cases, however, the ban on occupational work at most implies a measure of rest. Only in regard to the more restrictive prohibition of all work is the correlative need for a total rest made explicit and not left to implication (23:3, 27–32).

In version (2) the first day is also designated as the first of seven days during which "you shall rejoice before the Lord your God." This required using the "product of *hadar* trees, branches of palm trees, boughs of leafy trees and willows of the brook" (23:40–41). For these seven days only, "all citizens in Israel" were to live in booths (23:42). Except as a day of rest, the eighth day is left with no stated purpose. The Lord's explanation for requiring "all citizens in Israel" to live in booths looks more to their descendants than themselves: that "future generations may know that I made the Israelite people live in booths when I brought them out of the land of Egypt, I the Lord your God" (23:43).

Comment L–52. On the "set times" and "sacred occasions" as elements in the ethos of Israel

In discussing the "ethos" of Israel as expressed in Lev. 23, I do not refer to the aspect of "spirituality" that bears on Israel's relations with its God. Instead, I refer to qualities of communal character that P/h may have sought to foster through the authority of its God. In speaking of Israel's "ethos," therefore, I refer to "the fundamental character or spirit of a culture, the underlying sentiment that informs the beliefs, customs or practices of a group or society." The solemn occasions and celebrations of a people tell us much of its ethos— and prominent among the ethos of Israel in the era of the Torah were the "fixed times" and "sacred occasions" of Lev. 23.

From those "fixed times" and "sacred occasions," four major themes emerge. In their order of appearance, they are: (1) A theme of introspection and contemplation (as expressed most fully in the weekly Sabbath) (23:3); (2) A theme of freedom as a people (as expressed in the Passover and the Feast of Unleavened Bread) (23:5–8); (3) A theme of harmony between humanity and its environment (as expressed in the Omer and the two harvest festivals) (23:10–22, 34–36, 39–43); and (4) A theme of communal responsibility, self-evaluation and atonement (as expressed in *rosh hashonah* and the Day of Atonement (23:24–32).

The relative primacy of these themes finds expression in the modalities of observance. These generally involve the following factors: (1) the scope of any work prohibition and rest requirement; (2) the number and character of required offerings; (3) the length of the occasion; (4) the stringency of any special requirements (e.g., unleavened bread, living in booths or the practice of self-denial); and (5) the emphasis on, and stringency of, the punishments for failure to observe the prohibitions and requirements.

No calculus of comparison is capable of defining a precise hierarchy among the thematic values noted above. However, some general observations are possible.

The highest status was seemingly accorded to the themes associated with (1) the first day of the seventh month and the Day of Atonement and (2) the weekly Sabbath. These are the themes of communal responsibility, self-evaluation and atonement, all requiring a degree of personal introspection and contemplation. These themes look to the ethical and moral well-being of the community, as inevitably influenced by that of its individual members. The weekly Sabbath would remind the Israelites of their broader human purposes, which were too easily forgotten under the pressures of daily toil. In turn, the structured processes of communal atonement served to foster a culture of personal atonement. From such internalization would come the ultimate fruits of atonement—a deeper appreciation of the need to consider the effects of our daily choices on the quality of human life.

Together with the theme of communal character, as affected by atonement and introspection, the theme of communal freedom and self-identity was also a vital aspect of Israel's spiritual character. Thus, the importance of its freedom to develop as a distinctive people was memorialized by the Passover and Feast of Unleavened Bread.

But freedom from domination by other human beings offered no freedom from the vagaries of humanity's earthly environment. In truth, the actual power of the natural order deserved no less reverence and respect than the power attributed by the Torah to its God. Through its harvest festivals, Israel sought to show respect for, and live in harmony with, its earthly environment—ever mindful that its fruits were to be shared "with the poor and the stranger."

From the singular focus of Lev. 23 on the "sacred occasions" of Israel, Lev. 24 turns to subjects as varied as priestly rituals, blasphemy, and *lex talionis*.

Lev. 24 first repeats the commands of Exod. 27:20–21 on the lighting of the lamps just outside the Ark in the Tent of Meeting. In essence, the people are to bring "clear oil of beaten olives . . . to maintain lights regularly" (or "continually," per JPS1/RSV). As a law "for all time throughout the ages," the lights are to burn "from evening to morning before the Lord regularly" (24:2–4).

> *Note L–106: The use of "regularly" or "continually" is important because the general image conveyed in the two verses (i.e., Exod. 27:21 and Lev. 24:3) so closely resembles that of the latter-day ritual of a "perpetual" ark light. In that in both cases the light is to burn only "from evening to morning" the need is for "regularity" rather than "continuity." While these verses may "anticipate" a latter-day "perpetual" light, they do not command it.*

Lev. 24:5–9 deals with the sabbath "bread of display" (so denominated in Exod. 25:30 but not in Lev. 24). While Exod. 25:23–30 sets out precise specifications for the Table on which the bread is displayed, it only briefly mentions the bread. In all, twelve loaves are to be placed "on the pure table before the Lord in two rows, six to a row." To complete "an offering by fire to the Lord," frankincense must be added. This bread ritual is to be repeated "regularly every sabbath day." Once offered, the bread is for Aaron and his sons. As the "most holy things from the Lord's offerings by fire," the bread must be eaten by the priests "in the sacred precinct" (or "holy place").

The subject now turns from the priestly rituals to the ultimate sin of blasphemy, of which a particular case is dramatized in a brief narrative (24:10–16).

> There came out among the Israelites one whose mother was an Israelite and whose father was Egyptian. And a fight broke out in the camp between that half Israelite and a certain Israelite. The son of the Israelite woman *pronounced*

the Name in blasphemy, and he was brought to Moses—now his mother's name was Shelomith daughter of Dibri of the tribe of Dan—and he was placed in custody, until the decision of the Lord should be made clear to them.

And the Lord spoke to Moses, saying: Take the blasphemer outside the camp; and let all who were within hearing lay their hands upon his head, and let the whole community stone him.

And to the Israelite people speak thus: Anyone who blasphemes his God shall bear his guilt; *if he also pronounces the name LORD, he shall be put to death.* The whole community shall stone him; stranger or citizen, *if he has thus pronounced the Name,* he shall be put to death. (24:10–16)

Much like E's *"mishpat"* of Exod. 21:12 and 23–25, Lev. 24:17–20 applies the maxim of *lex talionis* to a man who "kills any human being" or "maims a fellow." For the killing, "he shall be put to death" (24:17). For lesser harm, "as he has done, so shall it be done to him: fracture for fracture, eye for eye, tooth for tooth" (24:19). The exception is in the killing of a "beast." Rather than to kill a beast of the killer in *retribution*, the penalty is "restitution" (cf. Comment E–70.) The passage ends with the reminder that the *"mishpat"* is for "stranger and citizen alike" (24:22). (Cf. Lev. 19:33–34.)

Lev. 24:23 completes the chapter's unfinished business. "Moses spoke thus to the Israelites. And they took the blasphemer outside the camp and pelted him with stones. The Israelites did as the Lord had commanded Moses" (24:23).

Comment L–53. On two distinctive aspects of the P/h Holiness Code in relation to other Torah provisions

Recall that modern scholarship attributes Lev. 17–26, also known as the Holiness Code, to a distinctive subsource within the broader P source (see p. 296). Lev. 24:10–17 most notably attests to such distinctiveness in regard to the sins of blasphemy and the killing of another person.

1. The "bifurcated" sin of blasphemy in Lev. 24:10–16

First consider the offense and the punishment as they appear in JPS2 and JPS1/RSV.

First, JPS2: "The son . . . pronounced the Name in blasphemy" (24:11). Accordingly, the Lord directs Moses to "speak thus" to the Israelites: "Anyone who blasphemes his God shall bear his guilt; *if he also pronounces the name Lord, he shall be put to death.*"

Second, JPS1/RSV: The son "blasphemed the Name and cursed. . . ." Accordingly, Moses was to say to the people that "whoever curses his God shall bear his sin. *He who blasphemes the name of the Lord shall be put to death.*"

As portrayed in Lev. 24:10–16, therefore, blasphemy emerges as verbalized, or spoken, apostasy. Like apostasy expressed through physical conduct, blasphemy constitutes a renunication, but by word, of the Lord's sanctity. The sinner has thus passed beyond the pale of redemption. In this, blasphemy differs from the Third Commandment, which assumes a particular demeaning of the Lord's sanctity that, however expressed, carries with it no intent to deny His sanctity. It falls short of total renunciation and thus, *apart from any separate sinfulness of an act committed in His name*, remains redeemable. (See Comment E–56 on the Third Commandment.)

Most remarkable here, however, is the lesser punishment accorded (i8n all three translations) to a person who speaks to renounce God than to a person who speaks to renounce the Lord. JPS2 offers the most striking "bifurcation." To "curse" the Lord God as "God," alone, is to suffer a punishment potentially less than death (i.e., "shall bear his guilt.") But death is the certain punishment for anyone who merely "pronounces" the Lord's "name." In JPS1/RSV the same differential punishments apply to "cursing" God and "Blaspheming" the Lord's name. In all, the passage strongly reinforces the distinction which P/h seeks to establish, more than any other source thus far, between the Lord, as an eternal Being, and the Lord, as God, for a time by His choice. (See Comments G–39, 43, and 56 and L–28, 43, 45, and 50.)

2. On P/h's nonforgiveable sin of killing

Lev. 24:17 decrees that "If a man kills any human being, he shall be put to death" (JPS2). To this JPS1 adds "surely." Absent from P/h's calculus of guilt is any exception either for killings equivalent to E's "act of God" or for an "unwitting" killing (JPS2/RSV) or a killing "through error" (JPS1). (See Lev. 4:27–35 and Comments E–68 and 69 and L–9.) Such failure to include a concept of excusable, or redeemable, killings combines a unique value of one life with an utter disregard for the sanctity of another life. It is a matter for R to redress.

In Lev. 25:1, we are told once more that "the Lord spoke to Moses *on* Mount Sinai" (i.e., *behar sinai*).

Comment L–54. On the reappearance of the Lord and Moses "on Mount Sinai"

Once before during His Levitical revelations, "the Lord" is said to have spoken to Moses "*on* Mount Sinai" (JPS2; see Lev. 7:38, 1:1). The point is discussed at some length in Comment L–18, based on textual material uniquely related to the setting of Lev. 7. In the course of my own inquiry, however, I had no need to accept or reject Ramban's view that *behar sinai* could be read as "*in*" rather than "*on*" mount Sinai—thus denoting "in the vicinity of mount Sinai."[28] But now in the context of Lev. 25, I find his analysis especially (and conveniently) apt. In effect, the Lord's words from *behar sinai* could include all His Levitical revelations from the Tent near the base of Sinai.

In Lev. 25:2, P/h reveals the role to be assumed by the Lord in the conquest of Canaan: "Speak to the Israelite people and say to them: When you enter the land *that I give you*, the land shall observe a sabbath of the Lord."

Comment L–55. On the Lord's "giving" the land to the Israelites

In what sense can the Torah view Canaan as "a gift of God." Must Israel not "pay" for it by effectively subordinating its free will to His will? And before the gift is given, will its "price" not include the loss of an entire generation during forty years of wandering in the wilderness?

Or can the Lord's "gift" be viewed as something other than the fruits of His power? Indeed, might the Torah not view His greatest gift as the internal qualities of self-respect and confidence inspired by His moral and ethical guidance? If so, it is a possibility least easily perceived by P.

Lev. 25:2–7 then turns to the sabbatical year.

Note L–107: Cf. E's mishpat of Exod. 23:10–11.

The commands looks to "a sabbath of the Lord" (but not until "you enter the land that I give you.") "Six years you may sow your field . . . prune your vineyard and gather in the yield" (25:3). In the seventh year, however, there must be "a sabbath of complete rest, a sabbath of the Lord" in which "you shall not sow your field or prune your vineyard" (25:4). Also prohibited in this "year of complete rest for the land" was "reap[ing] the *aftergrowth* of your harvest or gather[ing] the grapes of your untrimmed vines" (25:5). However, the people were permitted to eat "whatever the land during its sabbath will produce [i.e., from the seeds of the prior year]— you, your male and female slaves, the hired and bound laborers who live with you, and your cattle and the beasts in your land may eat all its yield" (25:6–7).

Lev. 25:8–17 and 23–24 then tell of yet more remarkable jubilee year. Every fiftieth year it must be announced by "the horn sounded throughout your land" on the "Day of Atonement." And how shall it be marked? The more traditional translations (i.e., RSV/JPS1) include the still resonant proclamation, "And you shall hallow the fiftieth year, and *proclaim liberty throughout the land to all its inhabitants*; it shall be a jubilee for you, when each of you return to his property and each of you shall return to your family" (25:10). As in the sabbatical years however, the land was to rest. "You shall not sow, neither shall you reap the aftergrowth or harvest the untrimmed vines . . . you may only eat the growth direct from the field" (25:11–12).

In effect, the jubilee year placed a fifty-year limit on the possession of land by anyone other than the original owner. To assure "fair dealing" in the sale of interim possessory interests, the principle of "proportionality" was incorporated into a prescribed pricing formula.

When you sell property to your neighbor, or buy any from your neighbor, you shall not wrong one another. In buying from your neighbor you shall deduct only for the number of years since the jubilee; and in selling to you, he shall charge only for the remaining crop years; the more such years, the higher the price . . . ; the fewer such years, the lower the price; *for what he is selling you is a number of harvests*. (25:14–16)

To this is added the ever present reminder and warning of Leviticus: "Do not wrong one another, but fear your God, *for I the Lord am your God*" (25:17).

> Note L–108: *In effect, God is not to be feared simply as God, but as an aspect of "the Lord" (see Comments L–43 and 45).*

In Lev. 25:20–22 the Lord addresses what would be a recurring concern in regard to the sabbatical year (but even more so in regard to the consecutive forty-ninth, or "sabbatical," year and the fiftieth, or "jubilee," year). "'What are we to eat in the seventh year, if we may neither sow nor gather in our crops?" The Lord's answer looks to His power over the natural order. "I will ordain My blessing for you in the sixth year, so that *it shall yield a crop sufficient for three years*." This will assure grain "until the ninth year, until its crops come in."

> Note L–109: *If the "three year crop" is meant to suffice for only the period of the single sabbatical year, will more not be needed for the consecutive forty-ninth and fiftieth years?*

In Lev. 25:23–24 the Lord states His rationale for the jubilee year: "the land must not be sold beyond reclaim, *for the land is Mine; you are but strangers resident with me.* Throughout the land that you hold, you must provide for the redemption of the land."

Comment L–56. On the role of the "jubilee year" in relation to the Lord as owner of the land and the Israelites as "strangers resident with Me"

How does the Lord's reminder of His ownership of the land, in which the Israelites are "but strangers resident with Me," relate to the jubilee year? The jubilee year could not eliminate the many uncertainties arising from the Lord's "reversionary" interest in the land, but it could help. While revisions in land ownership rules might be affected by His quixotic will at any time, at least until then a reasonably stable system of continuing land ownership could be realized through the principles of the jubilee year.

Lev. 25:25–34 reflects the importance attached to both preserving family lands and preventing undue aggregations of land. But while the Torah looks to the jubilee year as the basic device for achieving these important purposes, it also prescribes related rules for the years in between. Thus, if a "brother . . . in straits" (i.e., a fellow Israelite) is forced to sell "part of his holding," it must be redeemed by "his nearest redeemer" (presumably a close kinsman) (25:25). If there is no redeemer, the seller himself, when financially able, is commanded to redeem the property at a price based on the value of its remaining use until the jubilee year (25:26–27). If the seller cannot redeem his holding any earlier, then "in the jubilee year it shall be released, and he shall return to his holding" (25:28).

Excluded from the basic law of redemption is "a dwelling house in a walled city." Here the seller has a right (rather than a duty) to redeem the house within a year. If not redeemed, "the house . . . shall pass to the purchaser beyond reclaim throughout the ages; *it shall not be released in the jubilee*" (25:29–30). But this exception does not apply to "houses in villages that have no encircling walls." In being classed as "open country," these houses remained within the general laws of redemption, including those of the "jubilee" year (25:31).

> Note L–110: *This right of land alienation in walled cities may reflect the pressures within more complex urban settings for a greater mobility of all economic assets.*

In the "cities of the Levites, however, "the Levites shall forever have the right of redemption," both the jubilee year, itself, and a general right of redemption in interim years. Consistent with this special concern for stability in the ownership of Levitical lands, the alienation of "unenclosed land about their cities" was totally forbidden." As "their holding for all time," such land could never be sold (25:34).

> Note L–111: *Both as to urban and agricultural lands, the desired stability of Levite land ownership held precedence over general economic practices.*

The balance of Lev. 25 involves relations between masters and slaves (or indentured servants).

Lev. 25:35–46 covers relations between Israelites, in which one, "being in straits," comes under the "authority" of the other. *If* he is to be held "as though a resident alien " (i.e., as an indentured servant, or slave), then "let him live by your side as your brother." Should he require "money" or "food," it must be given without interest in any form (25:37). The passage closes with another reminder of the Lord's distinctive "innate" and "volitional" roles. "*I the Lord am your God, who brought you out of the land of Egypt, to give you the land of Canaan, to be your God*" (25:38). (Cf. Comments L–43 and 45.)

Lev. 25:39–46 distinguishes between the indentured service of Israelites and non-Israelites. Thus, "If your brother [i.e., fellow Israelite] under you continues in straits and must give himself over to you, do not subject him to the treatment of a slave. He shall remain under you as a hired or bound laborer; he shall serve with you only until the jubilee year" (25:39–40). At that time, "he *shall* go back to his family and return to his ancestral holding" (25:41). The release of individual Israelites from bondage is then equated with the freeing of Israel in Egypt: "For they are my servants, whom I freed from the land of Egypt; they may not give themselves over into servitude. You shall not rule over him ruthlessly [or "with harshness" or "with rigor"]; you shall fear your God" (25:42–43).

> *Note L–112: These rules differ from E's related* mishpatim *(Exod. 21:2–11). As to maximum periods of indentureship, compare E's basic six year maximum (Exod. 21:2) and P/h's use of the jubilee year (Lev. 25:40–42).*

To underscore the prohibition of harsh treatment against indentured fellow Israelites, comparisons are made to the treatment of alien slaves. "*Such male and female slaves as you may have—it is from the nations around you that you may acquire male and female slaves.* You may also buy them from among the children of aliens resident with you, or from their families that are among you, whom they begot in your land. These shall become your property" (25:44–45). Once acquired, slaves could be kept as "a possession for your children after you, for them to inherit as property for all time" (25:46). The difference in the allowable treatment of indentured Israelites and alien slaves are summarized as follows: "Such [i.e., aliens] you may treat as slaves. But as for your Israelite brothers, no one shall rule ruthlessly over the other" (25:46).

Comment L–57. On the tensions between Lev. 19 and 25 regarding the treatment of "resident aliens" within Israel

How do we explain the differences in Lev. 25:43, 45, and 46 between the treatment of Israelites as indentured servants and aliens as slaves? How do we justify "harsh" (RSV), "ruthless" (JPS2) or "rigourous" (JPS1) treatment toward alien slaves as compared to the concern expressed for indentured Israelites? Does this fulfil the equalitarian ideal of Lev. 19:34? "The stranger who resides with you shall be to you as one of your citizens; you shall love him as yourself, for you were strangers in the land of Egypt."

Moreover, the status of "slaves," as distinguished from "indentured servants," was reserved for "the children of aliens resident with you." As slaves, these "strangers" (RSV/JPS1) were the chattels of their Israelite owners. For them, the jubilee year would bring no freedom (25:44–46). Sadly, just as their faith precluded any rebuke of the Lord for slaying the innocent among the firstborn of Egypt, so, too, Rashi and Ramban accept these disparities in silence.

Within limits, Lev. 25:47–55 allows "resident aliens" to hold Israelites as indentured servants. Specifically, it deals with "a resident alien among you [who] has prospered, and your brother [or fellow Israelite], being in straits, comes under his authority and gives himself over to the resident alien among you, or to an offshoot of an alien's family" (25:47). Such indentureships, however, were to be ended as promptly as possible through redemption by a kinsman.

Lev. 25:48–49 suggests an order of responsibility for redeeming an Israelite as follows: "One of his brothers shall redeem him, or his uncle or his uncle's son . . . or anyone of his family who is of his own flesh shall redeem him." Also, the indentured servant who eventually prospered could "redeem himself" (25:49).

> *Note L–113: By its use of "shall redeem," JPS2 suggests the family's absolute duty to redeem an indentured Israelite servant, and presumably as soon as possible. Conversely, by their use of "may redeem," RSV/JPS1 simply impose a duty on the non-Israelite master to permit redemption through debt repayment, if requested. In either case, since 25:48–49 fails to identify any precise order in which the duty falls on family members, or kinsmen, an actual mandate would be difficult to enforce. What remains, therefore, is a general obligation on the entire family to arrange for redemption.*

Lev. 25:50–52 sets the redemption price of an Israelite bound to a "resident alien." Absent his prior redemption, an Israelite's indenture would terminate by law in the jubilee year (25:54). Thus, the factors governing a prejubilee redemption price were: (1) the total amount first owed the master for discharging the servant's debts, (2) the number of years between the beginning of indenture and the jubilee year, and (3) the redemption date. The redemption price would thus reflect the original debt less the proportional value of preredemption services.

Just as an Israelite master was barred from treating his indentured Israelite servant "ruthlessly" as a "slave," so, too, was a "resident alien" master. The Lord explains the need for the kind treatment of Israelite servants and for their early redemption as follows: "For it is to Me that the Israelites are servants: they are My servants, whom I freed from the Land of Egypt, I the Lord your God" (25:55).

> *Note L–114: In theory, to view all Israelites as the Lord's "servants" might warrant a Torah ban on all master/servant arrangements—and especially those involving non-Israelite masters. That Israelites could possibly be indentured to non-Israelites for up to fifty years was surely a compromise between theory and practice (cf. Comment L–56).*

Lev. 26:1 reads as a continuum from Lev. 25. Absent any stated change, the Lord continues to speak to Moses "on Mount Sinai" (see 25:1–2 and Comment

L–54). In its entirety, Lev. 26 evokes visions of the ultimate bliss, or terror, to be visited by the Lord on Israel for obeying, or rejecting, His laws and commandments. We begin with the bliss of obedience (26:3–13).

> *Note L–115: Although the blessings of obedience and the terrors of disobedience deserve a full reading, their length warrants a written precis.*

In brief, "*If you follow My laws and faithfully observe My commandments . . .* , I, the Lord, your God, promise" (26:3):

1. sufficient and timely rains to assure such an abundance of produce from the earth and fruit from the trees as to eliminate all threats of hunger;
2. untroubled sleep that comes from peace in a land that knows neither vicious beasts nor hostile swords;
3. the assurance of victory over all enemies, so that they fall before your sword;
4. and, finally, the ultimate assurance of a lasting relationship in which "I will look with favor upon you and make you fertile . . . ; I will maintain My covenant with you . . . ; I will establish My abode in your midst, and I will never spurn you. . . . *I will be your God ["elohim"], and you shall be My people* (26:9–12).

> *Note L–116: Only as its God will the Lord bestow and maintain these blessings on Israel. (26:12).Following this sublime vision of the Lord's Presence as Israel's God, P/h then forcefully reminds the people that the Lord, as Lord, is forever, but that God, as Israel's God, is by the Lord's choice alone. Only He will judge if Israel deserves Him as its God (see Comments L–43 and 45).*

And so the alternative, "if you do not obey Me . . . if you reject My laws and spurn My rules, so that you do not observe *all* My commandments and you break My covenant, I in turn will do this to you" (26:14–15):

1. "I will wreak misery up on you" through every form of disease and bodily ailment; you need not plant seeds for "your enemies shall eat it."
2. "I [the Lord] will set My face against you," in consequence of which you shall be routed by your enemies and dominated by your foes.
3. As for Israel's morale, "you shall flee though none pursues."
4. "If, for all that, you do not obey Me, I will go on to discipline you sevenfold for your sins."
5. "I will break your proud glory . . . make your skies like iron and your earth like copper." Despite all your efforts, the land will neither "yield its produce" nor the trees "their fruit" (cf. 26:16b).

6. Should Israel remain hostile and disobedient, "I will go on smiting you sevenfold for your sins. I will loose wild beasts against you and they shall bereave you of your children and wipe out your cattle. They shall decimate you, and your roads shall be deserted."

7. Should all this prove fruitless, the Lord will yet again smite the Israelites "sevenfold" for their sins. "I will bring a sword against you *to wreak vengeance for the covenant.*" Pestilence and the delivery of the Israelites into enemy hands will follow. Bread will become so scarce as to be rationed in amounts too small to slake hunger.

8. Should Israel continue to "disobey" and "remain hostile" to the Lord, it will suffer a third sevenfold increase in the intensity of His punishments. "I will act against you in wrathful hostility . . . [and] "discipline you sevenfold for your sins." (Perhaps to retain their attention He adds this following particular.) "You shall eat the flesh of your sons and the flesh of your daughters."

9. The Lord now refers to Israel's rampant disregard of the Second Commandment. "I will destroy your cult places and cut down your incense stands, and I will heap your carcasses upon your lifeless fetishes. I will spurn you" (26:16a–26:30).

Note L–117: *Given a choice, at this point Israel might settle for being "spurned." JPS1/RSV render* gahalah naphshee etchem *as "My soul shall abhor you."*

The continuing litany of horrors that follow the cannibalization and heaped carcasses of 26:29–30 is almost anticlimactic. The Lord will lay cities "in ruin" and will "desolate" sanctuaries. As for Israel's sacrificial offerings, the Lord will no longer "savor your pleasing odors" (26:31). Further, "*I will make* the land desolate, so that your enemies who settle in it shall be appalled by it" (26:32). Having desolated its land and ruined its cities, the lord will then "scatter [Israel] among nations" and "will unsheath the sword" against it (26:33).

In Lev. 26:34–35 the Lord assumes that among its sins Israel will have failed to honor the "sabbatical" year (25:1–7). Thus, only when Israel "is in the land of [its] enemies, "shall [its] land make up for its sabbath years throughout the time that it is desolate [by means of] the rest that it did not observe in your sabbath years while your were dwelling on it."

The Lord then returns to the matter of Israel's morale. To those who somehow survive the horrors, He promises "to cast a faintness into their hearts in the land of their enemies." Indeed, "the sound of a driven leaf shall put them to flight." Though not pursued, they shall "flee" and "fall" (26:36). In fleeing from "no one," they shall "stumble over one another." They will be unable to stand their ground against enemies, and shall "perish among the nations," and be consumed in their land (26:37–38).

But even as the final and total degradation of Israel approaches, the Lord, its God, speaks of atonement and redemption. Through His words, P/h voices confidence in the healing powers of the human spirit, influenced by the Lord, as God of Israel:

> Those of you who survive shall be heartsick over their iniquity in the land of your enemies; more, they shall be heartsick over the iniquity of their fathers; *and they shall confess their iniquity and the iniquity of their fathers*, in that they trepassed against Me, yea, were hostile to Me. When I, in turn, have been hostile to them and have removed them into the land of their enemies, *then at last shall their obdurate heart humble itself, and they shall atone for their iniquity*. (26:39–41)

In response to their confession of guilt and atonement, the Lord, as Israel's God, will prove forgiving.

> Then I will remember My covenant with Jacob . . . with Isaac, and also My covenant with Abraham; and I will remember the land. For the land shall be forsaken of them . . . for the abundant reason that they rejected My rules and spurned My laws. Yet . . . I will not reject them or spurn them . . . for I the Lord am their God. I will remember the covenant with the ancients, whom I freed from the land of Egypt . . . to be their God: I the Lord. (26:42–45)

Comment L–58. On the permanence of the Lord's covenantal role as Israel's God, from His perspective

In 26:39–41 JPS2 confidently predicts Israel's eventual confession of guilt and its atonement for its sins against the Lord, their God. It portrays a Lord, Who, as Israel's God, looks with confidence to the return of His errant people to Him. In comparison, consider RSV.

> But *if* they confess their iniquity and the iniquity of their fathers in their treachery which they committed against me, and also in walking contrary to me, so that I walked contrary to them and brought them into the land of their enemies; *if* then their uncircumcised heart is humbled and they make amends for their iniquity, then I will remember my covenant with Jacob. (26:40–42)

Contrary to JPS2, RSV places "ifs" in 26:40 and 41. It thus portrays a Lord essentially uncertain of whether Israel will ever confess its guilt and atone. What, then, of JPS1?

> *And they shall confess their iniquity, and the iniquity of their fathers*, in their treachery which they committed against Me, and also that they have walked contrary to Me. I also will walk contrary to them, and bring them into the land of their enemies; *if then perchance their uncircumcised heart be humbled, and they then be paid the punishment of their iniquity*, then will I remember My covenant with Jacob. (26:40–42)

JPS1 offers the most literal reading of the text. The conditional Hebrew *oh*, suggesting "or if," appears only in 26:41. In all, the passage portrays a Lord who wavers between certainty and doubt of Israel's ultimate confession of guilt.

Comment L–59. On an Israelite's behavorial calculus under the Levitical version of collective justice

In a broader Levitical setting, this comment returns to the issue of Comment G–28. In Lev. 26, the Lord directs His promises of rewards and punishments, or of blessings and curses, to "you." For the antecedent of "you" we must return to 25:1–2, in which "the Lord" directs Moses to speak to the "Israelite people." Thus, it is to Israel, *collectively*, that the Lord speaks as its God. *But Israel will not respond to His commands collectively. In the end, it will be individual Israelites who either obey or violate them.* Yet the Lord will judge Israel as an entity.

By their very character, His rewards and punishments operate collectively on an entire people. It is the people, as one entity, that is being judged, and not its individual members. The rains that fall and the fertility of the fields will affect all Israel. The absence of "vicious beasts" and the assurance that "no sword shall cross your land" will bless the worthy and unworthy alike. Conversely, there is no curse—whether of infertility, pestilence, slow starvation, or death, that will not touch every Israelite, independent of his contribution to the Lord's view of the whole of Israel.

As we near the end of Leviticus, it seems increasingly possible to attribute two basic social goals to the Torah, and to the P source in particular. These are (1) to develop and maintain Israel as a worthy and cohesive community, and (2) to sustain Israel's worth and unity through the conscience and conduct of every Israelite. To inspire the conscience and influence the conduct of every Israelite, P projects a single Being who, as the Lord of the universe, chooses also to become the God of Israel. As such, His awesome, wrathful, and quixotic omnipotence as "the Lord" is tempered by a prideful concern for Israel, as its God.

In evaluating the likely effect of Lev. 26 in promoting the purposes of the P source, we start with the "knowledge" that the Lord, through Moses, had informed all Israel of its contents (25:1). Above all, the people understand that Israel is to be judged collectively. *What they do not know, however, is the Lord's measure of collective worthiness.* What degree of obedience will He require to judge Israel as collectively worthy? What degree of disobedience will cause Him to visit the whole of Israel with indescribable misery?

In attempting to calculate how their individual conduct might affect Israel, and thus themselves, most Israelites would likely start from certain presumptions. As His measure of Israel's collective worthiness, the Lord would surely not demand total obedience to every command by every Israelite. If so, the need for universal obedience to every command as a condition of "collective salvation" would create a crushing sense of futility.

His more realistic aim, therefore, would be for Israel to achieve a high degree of worthiness by enforcement of His laws and through atonement and expiation. In the end, Israel's success in "policing" itself would weigh heavily in His judgment of its collective worth. But given Israel's uncertainty as to the degree of good over evil needed to establish its collective worth, *how might "reasonable" Israelites respond*?

Their first effort would be to estimate where Israel stood in a spectrum from total obedience to total disobedience. The perception of a huge and seemingly irreversible preponderance of disobedience would likely diminish existing incentives for individual virtue. If the Lord's threats against the whole of Israel were on the brink of fulfillment, many would question the marginal value of their own obedience. Except in those for whom obedience was an internalized source of personal fulfillment, to forgo even the brief rewards of disobedience might seem pointless.

Conversely, if individual Israelites perceived a great preponderance of collective obedience over disobedience, their reactions would be less certain. Once again, the truly obedient would remain so through their internalized values. In general, however, to the extent that Israel's collective well-being seems assured by a great preponderance of communal obedience, the response of many others would be to opt for personal fulfillment by whatever means. (Here, however, such "opportunists," although not fearful of the Lord's apocalyptic judgment, would have to ponder the factor of human justice. If well directed to achieving high levels of obedience, it alone might give pause.)

In general, knowledge of Israel's *collective* destiny would most effectively promote individual obedience when the existing balance between collective obedience and disobedience was least readily discerned. Uncertainty regarding Israel's collective moral posture would prompt each Israelite to realize the importance of his or her own marginal influence. Thus, the total balance would shift toward obedience—with greater hope of "salvation" for all.

The particular genius of Lev. 26, therefore, lies in its constructive use of uncertainty. Israelites are thus left to ponder the levels of collective obedience or disobedience at which the Lord will judge Israel as an object of love or wrath. Amid a prevailing uncertainty that only the rare conditions of near total obedience or rampant disobedience could lessen, many Israelites would be moved to obey. Thus, an "average" Israelite with a penchant for playing the odds might harbor thoughts such as these: "I have no idea of what lies ahead. All I know is that my future is tied to Israel's future. My main concern, therefore, is not for how the Lord judges me, as myself, but how he judges all Israel. And yet, since I cannot really sense where Israel stands in His spectrum of obedience, I must act as if our joint destiny depends on *my* obedience to His laws."

It can be argued, of course, as did Abraham to J's Lord, that the goals of personal worth and human justice are best served by viewing each individual as a unit of justice (see Comment G–28). In Lev. 26, however, P/h writes (whatever the actual realities) of a people whose sense of community had been forged in their common Egyptian bondage, their common liberation and their common encounter with the Lord, as their God, at Sinai/Horeb. Whether rightly or wrongly, the focus of P/h is less on human justice than on the collective character of a people. To this end, in the strongest terms yet, the Lord God of Leviticus reveals His commitment to collective justice *in advance* of its implementation. Amid the rampant evil in Sodom and Gomorrah, His revelation would have had little impact. But in the more balanced social and moral context that P/h likely portrayed, the social calculus of Lev. 26 offered a realistic contribution to communal worthiness.

The impact of this social calculus on the development of Israel's character is difficult to assess. However, were we to undertake a search for the roots of modern "game theory," we should not overlook the contributions of Lev. 26.

Lev. 26 end with the following summation: "These are the laws, rules and directions that the Lord established, through Moses *on* Mount Sinai, between Himself and the Israelite people" (JPS2, 26:46).

> Note L–118: Once again JPS2 and RSV move Moses from the Tent of Meeting to "on" Mount Sinai, while JPS1 adheres to "in" (see Comments L–18 and 54). But as to 26:46, Rashi, himself, "throws in the towel" by replacing the Torah's behar sinai with b'sinai, which his translator renders as "at Sinai."[29]

Although seemingly anticlimactic in the wake of 26:46, Lev. 27 serves a "Levitical" purpose. It provides a final reminder of the dominant "institutional" theme of Leviticus, that is, the centrality of the sanctuary and its Aaronide priesthood as conduits of holiness between Israel and the Lord, its God. It achieves this purpose by fixing equivalent values for the redemption of persons or property previously dedicated for use in, or by, the sanctuary and its priests. In this it provides a major source of financial support for the sanctuary's operations.

Lev. 27:2–8 deals with equivalent values for persons who, although vowed to the Lord's service, are yet redeemable from it, that is, "When a man explicitly vows to the Lord the equivalent for a human being" (27:2).

A scale of equivalent values is then set out (27:3–7).

(1) twenty to sixty years old
   male—"fifty shekels of silver by the sanctuary weight"
   female—thirty shekels
(2) five to twenty years old
   male—twenty shekels

        female—ten shekels
- (3) one month to five years old
        male—five shekels
        female—three shekels
- (4) sixty years or over
        male—fifteen shekels
        female—ten shekels

If the person to be redeemed cannot afford the scale price, "the priest shall assess him accordingly to what the vower can afford" (27:8).

> Note L–119: *The value differences between males and females may reflect their relative physical capacity for service. Age related differences might reflect a likely balance between years of work and years of necessary support in "retirement." Most noteworthy, however, is the irrelevance of all individual attributes other than age and sex. Lev. 27 thus adopts a limited principle of equality; that is, within their respective categories, every person is considered to be of equal inherent worth—subject to the recognition, however, that the needy should be excused from providing a full redemption price equal to their intrinsic value.*

Lev. 27:9–13 deals with the redemption of animals vowed to the Lord. Every such animal is declared "holy," or, in effect, unredeemable. Thus, "One may not exchange or substitute another [animal] for it, either good for bad, bad for good." Should a substitution be attempted, then "the thing vowed and its substitute shall both be holy (i.e., forfeited)." A different rule applies to "unclean animals" not qualified "as [offerings] to the Lord." These were to be brought to the priest to be assessed. "Whether high or low, whatever assessment is set by the priest shall stand." As redemption price for an "unclean" animal, the priest "must add one-fifth to its assessment."

Lev. 27:14–15 covers the redemption protocols for when "a man consecrates his house to the Lord." Once again, "the priest shall assess it"; and once again, his valuation is final. To redeem the house, "he must add one-fifth to the sum at which it was assessed, and it shall be his."

Lev. 27:16–21 applies "if a man consecrates to the Lord any land that he holds" (JPS2) [or "of his possession" (JPS1), or "which is his by inheritance" (RSV)].

> Note L–120: *The differences are significant. JPS1 and 2 would allow the consecration of possessory interests (such as leaseholds). RSV would limit the consecration of land to ownership interests. However, 27:22–25 will provide a highly formalistic right of consecration on lessees of land.*

The land valuation, and thus the redemption price, was based on its total seed requirement for the period of consecration (as calculated by its size and the number of years remaining to the next jubilee year). The price was then fixed at "fifty shekels of silver to a *homer* of barley seed." The redemption price included this basic value plus an added "one-fifth" (27:16–19).

Lev. 27:20–21 then limits the right of land redemption. "But if he does not redeem the land, *and* the land is sold to another [i.e., by the priests(?), to raise funds for the sanctuary], it shall no longer be redeemable [by the owner who had consecrated it]: when it is released in the jubilee, the land shall be holy to the Lord, as land proscribed; it becomes the priest's holding" (JPS2).

> Note L–121: *In that a prior sale of land would extinguish an owner/consecrator's normal right of reversion, he might have a powerful incentive to redeem promptly. Apart from sentiment, of course, his decision would depend on whether he valued the land at more or less than the redemption price. Because the price formula did not include differences in agricultural quality, there could be substantial variances between price and value.*

Lev. 27:22–25 deals with land consecrated by a current *holder* other than the owner by inheritance. As the land would revert to the owner in the jubilee year, a "tenant in possession" could consecrate no greater interest in the land than he actually owned. Accordingly, "In the jubilee year the land shall revert to him from whom it was bought, whose holding the land is" (27:24). What rights in the land did the "tenant in possession" have to consecrate? They are described as follows. At the time of consecration "the priest shall compute for him the proportionate assessment up to the jubilee year, and he shall pay the assessment as of that day, a sacred donation to the Lord" (27:23).

> Note L–122: *Should the tenant remain in possession, the "consecration" was essentially a convoluted monetary donation.*

Although both deal with animals, the connection between Lev. 27:26 and 27 is hardly clear. "A firstling of animals, however, which—as a firstling—is the Lord's, cannot be consecrated by anybody; whether ox or sheep, it is the Lord's (27:26). *But if it* is of unclean animals, it may be ransomed at its assessment, with one-fifth added; if it is not redeemed, it shall be sold at its assessment" (27:27).

> Note L–123: *Lev. 27:26 is clear enough. Since "firstlings" of oxen and sheep are consecrated to the Lord by law, they cannot be reconsecrated. The second verse is more puzzling. The sole antecedent for the "it" of 27:27 is "a firstling of animals." In general, however, only firstlings of clean animals could be consecrated to the Lord. Thus, 27:27 may have allowed "unconsecrated"*

donations of unclean firstlings as a source of support for the priests, whether
by means of donor redemptions or sales to third parties.

In regard to asses, a complication arises from the E source, which allows
the consecration of "unclean" male asses, redeemable only by a lamb. If not
so redeemed, the ass must suffer a broken neck (Exod. 13:13), but not by
the protocols of P/h.

Lev. 27:28–29 adds emphasis to the status of dedicated "firstlings." Thus,
"But of all that a man owns, be it man or beast or land of his holding, nothing
that he has proscribed for the Lord may be sold or redeemed; every proscribed
thing is totally consecrated to the Lord. No human being who has been proscribed can be ransomed: he shall be put to death" (27:28–29).

> Note L–124: "Proscribed" in 27:28–29 is from chayrem. As to its meaning
> in 27:29, Rashi reads the verse literally; that is, death sentences cannot be
> redeemed.[30]

The final "substantive" passage of Lev. 27:30–33 deals with tithes. "All tithes
from the land, whether seed from the ground or fruit from the tree, are the Lord's;
they are holy to the Lord. If a man wishes to redeem any of his tithes, he must add
one-fifth to them. All tithes of the herd or flock—of all that passes under the
shepherd's staff, every tenth one—shall be holy to the Lord." To this is added the
command not to substitute "bad" animals for "good" animals among "every
tenth." If substitution is made, "then it [i.e., the tenth animal by count] and its substitute shall both be holy; it cannot be redeemed."

> Note L–125: Since they are said to be "holy," tithed animals and their substi-
> tutes cannot be redeemed (27:33). However, the state of being "holy" does not
> prevent redemption of the "plant" tithes of 27:30–31 (i.e., of grain and fruit).
> Another more puzzling aspect of Lev. 27:30–33, however, is its recital of
> tithing protocols absent any prior command to tithe. Nor does 27:30–33
> include such a command. Thus, the redemption provisions of 27:31 and 33,
> 27:30 and 32 are predicated on an unstated, but established, tithing obligation.
> Thus far, the Torah only assumes but never mandates such an obligation. The
> first occasion is in early Genesis, where Abraham tithes Melchizedek, king and
> priest in Salem (Gen. 14:17–20). (See Comment G–21 and preceding text.)
> The second involves Jacob's promise to "set aside a tithe for You" (should he
> later decide to accept "the Lord" as his "God") (Gen. 28:20–22).
> That these Genesis passages are generally attributed to J and E, respec-
> tively, suggests that a tradition of tithing was known to all of the four main
> sources. P speaks further of tithes in Num. 18:20–32. Various tithing com-
> mands from the D source are found in Deut. 12, 14, and 26.

Leviticus concludes with a phrase that by now is more common to P/h than P (see Lev. 25:1 and 26:46). "These are the commandments that the Lord gave Moses for the Israelite people on Mount Sinai" (27:34).

> Note L–126: On the possible meaning of behar sinai see Comments L–18 and 54, Lev. 26:46, and Note L–118. But by now it would seem that P/h had another view of its own. (See also Lev. 26:46.)

CONCLUSION

A central purpose of the Levitical authors was to shape Israel's character through the role of the Lord, as its God. But here we must separate "role" from "role model." Israel's duty was to obey His commands, not to emulate His conduct. *It was to do as He said, not as He did.* Were He to be emulated, rather than merely obeyed, humanity might well experience even greater earthly mayhem. The purpose of His Being was to inspire obedience to His commands. In this, the Levitical Lord, God of Israel, was created to serve a role much like that which Sigmund Freud would later attribute to parents in the development of a child's "superego." Consider these views of the "superego" in relation to what we have read of the Levitical Lord, God of Israel.

First, from *Encyclopedia Americana*:

> The superego is the internal representation of the values and ideals of the society. It is the moral part of the personality, representing the ideal rather than the actual and demanding goodness rather than pleasure.
>
> Freud held that the superego developed in response to parental rewards and punishments. Transgressions of this internalized code are felt, consciously or unconsciously, as deserving of punishment following a pattern of guilt and atonement. Children thus incorporate both the approving and the punishing features of the all-important parents as a powerful and enduring agency within their own personality.[31]

Next, from *Encyclopedia Britannica*:

> The superego is the ethical component of the personality and provides the moral standards by which the ego operates. . . . [It] develops . . . in response to parental punishments and approval. . . . Violations of the superego's standards results in feelings of guilt or anxiety and a need to atone for one's actions.[32]

This early creation of the Lord, God of Israel, as a parental overseer in the development of the human conscience was indeed a brilliant stroke of psychological insight. But while the themes of Leviticus resonate throughout these definitions, there are differences as well as similarities. In particular, while the child's superego is meant to mature into an *independent* source of moral and ethical direction, the Levitical Lord, as Israel's God, is forever. That Israelites should be free to accept or reject the commands of its God was essential. Absent such choice, an Israelite would lack moral and ethical responsibility. The Levitical Lord, God of Israel, however, was relentless in His insistence that Israel's sole choice was between obedience or disobedience to Him. Their choices were defined by His commands.

Particularly as products of their time, the social values of Leviticus in themselves compel our highest respect. Overall, they sought to foster a quality of human compassion and responsibility that was too often mocked by the efforts of Israel's Lord God to exalt His sanctity. These social values manifest a deep reverence for human life and an abiding concern for the hungry, the needy and the otherwise disadvantaged, whether Israelites or (within limits) "strangers." Yet, much of what these Levitical social values could contribute to human decency and dignity would seemingly have been eroded by endless rituals of obeisance to a proud and wrathful Lord. But insofar as such rituals *in their time* may have fostered introspective atonement and self-appraisal, they, too, could contribute to Israel's moral and ethical development.

The Levitical regard for human life also fostered a fixation on bodily processes—of which little was known, other than by inexact observation and conjecture. As the vessel of life, the body, and its "purity," became a cornerstone of Levitical concerns. Were we to accord equal respect to our own bodies, how greatly we might benefit in the context of our present knowledge of bodily well-being. Finally, the Levitical agricultural laws and seasonal observances served to foster communal reverence for Israel's earthly habitation, on whose bounty all human life depended.

But when all is said, the highly structured system of Levitical animal sacrifices and other rituals of obeisance continue to trouble us. Yet, what strikes us today as utterly repellent at worst and irrelevantly arcane at best, may have once been spiritually compelling. *Thus, Leviticus challenges us to extricate the timeless and universal values of its ends from the dated particularities of its means.*

However well we manage this extrication, Leviticus will remain the most troubling book of the Torah. For to speak of means and ends is to confront the abiding enigma of Leviticus. Having created and given purpose to their Lord, God of Israel, how did the Levitical authors finally come to view Him? Was the acknowledgement and glorification of His sanctity to become the embodiment of Israel's highest aspirations? Or, was He created as the means for guiding Israel toward its highest human potential? If we attempt to weigh the rituals that were devised to sustain His sanctity against the substance of His social values, we come to realize that the enigma of Leviticus cannot be easily resolved within itself alone.

4.

NUMBERS

INTRODUCTION:
THE TIME AND-PLACE OF NUMBERS 1:1

As from Exodus to Leviticus, there is a close continuity of time and place from Leviticus to Numbers. Once again the continuity is facilitated by P's authorship of the end and beginning of the two successive books. Numbers begins on "the first day of the second month, in the second year following the exodus from the land of Egypt." And in the same general setting of "the wilderness of Sinai," the Lord again speaks to Moses "in the Tent of Meeting" (1:1; cf. Lev. 1:1).

> Note N–1: What portion of the thirteen months between the exodus from Egypt and Numbers 1:1 can be attributed to the revelations and events of Leviticus? As detailed below, all the Torah tells us is that the time span of Leviticus could not have exceeded the one month between the completion of the Tabernacle (or Tent of Meeting) and the beginning of Numbers. What we do not know is the elapsed time, if any, between (1) the completion of the Tent and the Lord's initial Presence within it (i.e., between Exod. 40:17 and 33–34), (2) the Lord's initial Presence in the Tent and His first words to Moses from within it (i.e., between Exod. 40:33–34 and Lev. 1:1), and (3) the end of Leviticus (Lev. 27:29) and Numbers 1:1. To fix the time span of Leviticus, the time of these three periods, if any, must be subtracted from the one month between "the first month of the second year, on the first of the month" (i.e., Exod. 40:17) and "the first day of the second month," when Numbers begins. In Exod. 40:33–34, all three translations indicate the Lord's immediate presence upon completion of the Tent. If so, only the elapsed times of (2) and (3), if any, are relevant to any time span of Leviticus less than thirty days.

Numbers opens with the first of the events from which comes its name. From the Tent of Meeting, the Lord tells Moses: "Take a census of the whole Israelite community by the clans of its ancestral houses, listing the names, every male, head by head. You and Aaron shall record them by their groups, from the age of twenty years up, all those in Israel who are able to bear arms. Associated with you shall be a man from each tribe, each one the head of his ancestral house" (1:2–4).

> Note N–2: Clearly, males under twenty were not meant to bear arms. Less clear is whether all males twenty and over could be counted on to bear arms. What of those too old or too physically impaired for the task? To include them would defeat the purpose of the count (see Comment N–1).

In Num. 1:5–16 the Lord names a man from each tribe to assist Moses and Aaron in the count.

> Note N–3: Their names are not important here.

The Lord explains His choices as follows: "Those are the elected [or "elect" (JPS1)] of the assembly, the chieftains of their ancestral tribes: they are the heads of the contingents of Israel" (1:16).

Num. 1:17–19 tells of the convocation of the "whole community" on the very same day, that is, "the first day of the second month" (of the second year). In due course, the whole community "were registered by the clans of their ancestral houses."

The counts by tribes of "all males aged twenty years and over, all who were able to bear arms," were as follows (with verses in parentheses) (1:20–46):

> Reuben, 46,500 (21); Simeon, 59,300 (23); Gad, 45,650 (25); Judah, 74, 600 (26); Issachar, 54,400 (29); Zebulun, 57,400 (31); Joseph (i.e., Ephraim and Manasseh)—Ephraim, 40,500 (33); Manasseh, 32,200 (35); Benjamin, 35,400 (37); Dan, 62,700 (39); Asher, 41,500 (41); Naphtali, 53,400 (43).

In all, the enrollment was 603,550 (1:46).

> Note N–4: Twelve tribes are listed, including those of Ephraim and Manasseh (for Joseph). (See Gen. 48:5–7 and Comment G–94.) We will soon learn more of the Levites.

Comment N–1. On two aspects of the census of Num. 1

1. Its identity with the counts of Exod. 12:37 and 38:26

The count of 603,550 in Num. 1 compares with "about six hundred thousand men on foot, aside from children" who left Egypt (Exod. 12:37). (See Comment E–39.) Later, in the census required by Exod. 30:11–14, Exod. 38:26 reports that 603,550 men "from the age of twenty years up" had been "entered in the records" of the Tabernacle. This essential identity of counts invites questions as to the "populations" counted—especially since Exod. 38 says nothing of the ability of those "entered in the records" to "bear arms.

First, the Exod. 38 count literally included *every male* "from the age of twenty years up." Given the purpose of identifying males twenty and over for payment of a head tax of "half a shekel," the ability of a man to "bear arms" was not directly relevant. Conversely, the sole purpose of the Num. 1 census was to identify males "able to bear arms."

Second, the Exod. 38 census, unlike that of Num. 1, does not explicitly exclude the Levites. But here, on the basis of Num. 1:47–53, we may assume that the Levites were initially excluded from being "enrolled," or included in, "[any] census of . . . the Israelites." As stated in JPS2, this command "had been spoken" by "the Lord . . . to Moses" at some prior indeterminate time (Num. 1:48–49). If so, the Levites would not have been "entered in the records" of the Exod. 38 census (see Exod. 30:13–14, 38:26.)

Of the two possible differences as to those included in the two counts, only the first remains unresolved—*unless all men twenty and over were in fact "able to bear arms."*

2. On the preservation of tribal identities

More "miraculous" than the identical counts is Israel's preservation of its tribal identities and affiliations over some four hundred years of "slavery" and leaderless dispersion in Egypt. That an accurate census could be taken implies that over these four centuries, the Israelites had somehow managed to maintain their tribal identities.

In Num. 1:47–53 the Lord explains why "the Levites . . . were not recorded among [the others] by their ancestral tribe" (1:47). Not on "any account" was Moses to "enroll the tribe of Levi or take a census of them with the Israelites" (1:49). Their unique role would necessarily exclude them from any census for any other purpose. Moses was to put the Levites "in charge of the Tabernacle of the Pact, all its furnishings and everything that pertains to it." They were to "carry" it, "tend" it, and "camp around" it (1:50). As it moved about with the transient Israelites, they were to "take it down" and "set it up." So sacred were their responsibilities, that "any outsider who encroaches shall be put to death" (1:51).

All other tribes were to "encamp troop by troop, each man with his division and each under his standard" (1:52). Of necessity, however, groups of Levites would be separated from each other. So "that wrath may not strike the Israelite community," the Levites were to "stand guard *around* the Tabernacle of the Pact" (1:53).

Comment N–2. On the census and human self-reliance

Would it not have been a *mitzvah* for the Lord, as Israel's God, to have spared Moses, Aaron, the tribal chiefs and the people themselves the burden of a census. Surely His omniscience could avert any need for an actual count. But here, at least, P is wise enough to perceive a greater human purpose in having Israel "take stock" of itself.

In Num. 2 "the Lord" continues to speak to "Moses and Aaron"—now in regard to the grouping of tribes into divisions and their placement around the sides of the Tent of Meeting. Under the "standards" and "banners" of their "ancestral houses," these "troops" were to be placed "at a distance" from the Tent, rather than next to it (2:1–2).

The twelve non-Levitical tribes were divided into four "divisions" (or "camps"), each composed of a lead tribe and two others. Each division, as designated by the name of the lead tribe, is assigned to a particular side of the Tent.

> Note N–5: As in Num. 1, the counts are limited to "all males aged twenty years and over, all who were able to bear arms." Where the women, children, and males under twenty were to march is not clear.

Camped on "the front, or east side" was the division of Judah, comprised of the tribes of Judah, Issachar, and Zebulun. It totalled "186,400 for all troops." These were to "march first" (2:3–9).

Camped on the south was the division of Reuben, comprised of the tribes of Reuben, Simeon, and Gad. Totalling 151,450 troops, it would "march second" (2:10–16).

"Then, midway between the divisions, the Tent of Meeting, the division of the Levites shall move. As they camp, so shall they march, each in position, by their standards" (2:17). In all, four separate groups of Levites would stand between the Tent and the four divisions.

Camped on the west was the division of Ephraim, comprised of the tribes of Ephraim, Manasseh, and Benjamin. Totaling 108,100 troops, it would "march third" (2:18–24).

Camped on the north was the division of Dan, comprised of the tribes of Dan, Asher, and Naphtali. Totaling 157,300 troops, it would "march last" (2:25–31).

And so again, the Israelites did "just as the Lord had commanded Moses, so they camped by their standards, and so they marched, each with his clan according to his ancestral house" (2:34).

Comment N–3. On tribal groupings and tribal status

The questions here are: (1) Why did P (or traditions preceding P) prescribe the particular tribal assignments to each of the four divisions? and (2) In what way, if any, did the marching order of the divisions reflect their relative status (as among "first," "second," "third," and "last")?

First. The lead division located "on the front" of the Tent which was to "march first" was headed by the tribe of Judah and included the tribes of Issacher and Zebulun. In terms of group identity and morale, there was a natural affinity among these tribes, descended as they were from the fourth, fifth, and sixth sons of Leah. They were, in order, the fourth, ninth, and tenth born sons of Jacob.)

Second. The second division was led by the tribe of Reuben, the firstborn of Leah. Grouped with it were (1) the tribe of Simeon, from the second born son of Leah, and (2) the tribe of Gad, from the firstborn son of Zilpah, Leah's maid and Jacob's concubine (per Leah). Reuben, Simeon, and Gad were the first, second, and seventh born sons of Jacob. Their rank order within the second division thus followed their birth order.

Third. The three tribes of the third division reflect the most obvious tribal affinities; that is, Ephraim, Manasseh, and Benjamin all descended from Jacob and Rachel. That the tribe of Ephraim led the division might seem contrary to birth order in two ways. First, although Benjamin was the last (or twelfth) son born of Jacob, his birth preceded that of his nephews, Manasseh and Ephraim. That they both precede him reflects their status as "joint proxies" for their father Joseph. As Jacob's eleventh son, Joseph preceded Benjamin. Second, Manasseh, rather than Ephraim, was the firstborn of Joseph (Gen. 41:50–52). That the tribe of Ephraim gained precedence over the tribe of Manasseh resulted from the greatness foreseen by Jacob for the tribe of Ephraim. As their father through adoption, Jacob, by his blessing, had reversed their legal status, if not their actual birth order (Gen. 48:12–20). In effect, therefore, the order of tribal ranking in the third division followed the "legalities" of birth order.

Fourth. The fourth division includes the three tribes descended from Jacob and the two concubines. The lead tribe of Dan was descended from the firstborn of Rachel's maid, Bilhah (Jacob's concubine per Rachel). Second in order was the tribe of Asher, whose founder was the second born of Zilpah (Jacob's concubine per Leah). Third was the tribe of Naphtali, whose founder was the second born son of Bilhah. Of Jacob, Dan, Asher, and Naphtali were the fifth, *eighth*, and *sixth* born sons. Inasmuch as Jacob had two sons each by Zilpah and Bilhah, it became necessary to place one (i.e., Gad) in a division descended from two sons by Leah. Thus, the fourth division gave recognition to a likely affinity among the tribal descendants of the concubines.

With three exceptions of varying import, birth order and filial affinity were the dominant factors in determining precedence both within and among the divisions. The principal exception to birth order is the placement of the tribes of Judah, Issacher, and Zebulun in the first division. This might be explained by P's wish to accord highest precedence to the tribe of Judah, in whose territory Jerusalem and Its Temple were located. Thereafter, in the interest of divisional morale, P would necessarily place Judah over his younger rather than his older full brothers. In general, that Judah should rank as "the first of the first" is a measure of his general preeminence throughout the Torah, and particularly within the J and P sources.

The second exception is the placement of the older sons of concubines in the fourth division behind the last born sons of Rachel. Here the purpose was to accord precedence to the sons of Rachel over those of concubines (except as to Gad, in order to assign three tribes to each division).

The third and final exception in the fourth division is least easily explained. Why should Asher, the eighth born son of Jacob (and second born of Zilpah) precede Napthali, the sixth born of Jacob (and second born of Bilhah)? The reason may lie in tribal considerations not yet apparent.

Num. 3 and 4 deal with the lineage and work of the Levites in relation to the Tabernacle and Tent of Meeting. They also identify the tribal clans by names and duties.

Num. 3:1–5 supposedly sets out "the line of Aaron and Moses at the time that the Lord spoke with Moses on Mount Sinai." *Although nothing more is said of the sons of Moses,* Aaron's sons, as Israel's ordained priests, are again recalled. These were Nadab, Abihu, Eleazar, and Ithamar, of whom the Lord had slain Nadab and Abihu for having "offered before the Lord alien fire" (see Lev. 10:1–2).

Although Num. 3 focuses on the duties of Levites in assisting the priests, the Lord speaks only to Moses. He first lays out His broad charge to the Levites (3:5–10). They will be "in attendance on Aaron the priest to serve him." Also, "on behalf of the Israelites," the Levites are to "take charge of all the furnishings of the Tent of Meeting." The Lord directs Moses to "make Aaron and his sons responsible for observing their priestly duties; and any outsider who encroaches shall be put to death."

In place of Israel's firstborn who were to be consecrated to Him, the Lord now takes the Levites (3:11–13). "I hereby take the Levites from among the Israelites in place of all the firstborn, the first issue of the womb among the Israelites: the Levites shall be Mine. . . . For every firstborn is mine; at the time I smote every firstborn in the land of Egypt, I consecrated every firstborn in Israel, man and beast, to Myself, to be Mine, the Lord's."

In Num. 3:14–20 the Lord directs Moses to "record the Levites by ancestral house and by clan; record every male among them from the age of one month up."

Note N–6: One reason for recording males from the age of "one month up" may have been to foresee over time the likely number of male Levites who would be available as aids to the priests. That infants in the first month were not counted suggests a significant mortality rate within this critical period.

There follows a listing of Levite clans, as named for the grandsons of Levi. Thus, the sons of Levi were Gershon, Kohath, and Merari (3:17). The names of their sons "by clan" were Gershon—"Libni and Shimei"; Kohath—"Amram and Izhar, Hebron and Uzziel"; and Merari—"Mahli and Mushi" (3:18–19).

Note N–7: That the Levites were recorded by "ancestral houses" and "clans" suggests a general ordering of (1) "tribes" (named for sons of Jacob), (2) "ancestral houses" (or "father's houses," per JPS1/RSV) (grandsons), and (3) "clans" (or "families," per JPS1/RSV) (great-grandsons).

Num. 3:21–37 tells of the three ancestral houses of Gershon (3:21–26), Kohath (3:27–31) and Merari (3:33–37) and their respective clans. As to each house and their clans, the passage covers (1) the total count of males "from the age of one month up," (2) the site of the clan encampments in relation to the Tabernacle (or Tent of Meeting), (3) the current "chieftain" of the ancestral house, and (4) its duties in and about the Tabernacle and Tent.

The "recorded entries" for the ancestral house of Gershon were 7,500. It would camp "behind the Tabernacle to the west." Its chieftain was Eliasaph, son of Lael. "The duties of the Gershonites in the Tent of Meeting" covered "the tabernacle, the tent, its covering, and the screen for the entrance of the Tent of Meeting; the hangings of the enclosure, the screen for the entrance of the enclosure which surrounds the Tabernacle, the cords thereof, and the altar—all the service connected with these."

The "listed males" of Kohath were 8,600. Its clans would camp "along the south side of the Tabernacle." Its chieftain was Elizaphan son of Uzziel. The duties of its clans covered "the ark, the table, the lampstand, the altars and the sacred utensils that were used with them, and the screen—all the service connected with these."

Note N–8: As noted, the current chieftain of the ancestral house of Kohath was a son of Uzziel, the fourth listed son of Kohath, its founder. Under "normal" birth order protocols, it would seem that a son of Amram, the first listed son of Kohath, would follow Amram as chieftain of the entire ancestral house. As we know, however, Moses and Aaron were the sons of Amram (and thus the grandsons of Kohath) (Exod. 6:18–20). Also, in Exod. 6:18 Uzziel appears as the fourth son of Kohath. How a son of a fourth son became the chieftain of the entire ancestral house is not explained. In theory, of course, it could result from the absence of surviving sons of the older brothers.

Num. 3:32 interrupts the listing of the three ancestral houses by clarifying the role of Aaron's line. "The *head* chieftain of the Levites was Eleazer son of Aaron the priest, in charge of those attending to the duties of the sanctuary."

For Merari, the "recorded entries" were 6,200. Its clans, headed by Zuriel son of Abihail, were to camp "along the north side of the Tabernacle." Their duties covered "the planks of the Tabernacle, its bars, post and sockets, and all its furnishings—all the service connected with these; also the posts around the enclosure, and their sockets, pegs and cords."

As yet, no group of Levites have been assigned to the east, or front, of the Tent of Meeting (where the division of Judah would provide the troops). This responsibility and honor would of course fall to "Moses and Aaron and his sons, attending to the duties of the sanctuary, as a duty on behalf of the Israelites." Again, "any outsider who encroached was to be put to death" (3:38).

As set out in Num. 3:22, 28, and 34, the counts for the three ancestral houses were Gershon, 7,500; Kohath, 8,600; and Merari, 6,200. Accordingly, the recorded total for all the Levites was 22,300. Nevertheless, as stated in Num. 3:39, "All the Levites who were recorded, whom at the Lord's command Moses *and Aaron* recorded by their clans, all the males from the age of one month up, came to 22,000."

> Note N–9: *In addition to this overage of 300 in the count, Num 3:39 includes another contradiction from the previous text. Moses alone was commanded to conduct the count, with no authorized participation by Aaron (3:14–16).*

The Lord next tells Moses to "record every firstborn male of the Israelite people from the age of one month up, and make a list of their names" (Num. 3:40). It is so that He might "take the Levites . . . in place of every firstborn among the Israelite people, and the cattle of the Levites in place of every firstborn among the cattle of the Israelites" (3:41). Moses then did "as the Lord had commanded him" (3:42). His count of Israelites came to 22,273 "firstborn males . . . of one month up" (3:43). (The count of firstborn cattle is not reported.)

The Lord then instructs Moses to "take the Levites in place of all the firstborn among the Israelite people, and the cattle of the Levites in place of their cattle" (3:45). However, the exchange of Levite males "from the age of one month up" for firstborn Israelites males of the same age leaves the Lord with a net loss of 273 consecrated males as compared to the 22,000 Levites reported in Num. 3:39.

With a "shortfall" of 22,000 Levites, the Lord requires a "cash" redemption payment of "five shekels per head . . . by the sanctuary weight, twenty *gerahs* to the shekel," or "1,365 sanctuary shekels." Moses then obtained and "gave the redemption money to Aaron and his sons" (3:46–51). (*But as indicated in N–9, based on the recorded total of 22,300 for the three ancestral houses, the Lord would have had gained twenty-seven.)*

Comment N–4. On Aaron and the missing 300 Levites: some thoughts on an arithmetical problem

Clearly, Aaron had an interest in the counts of both the Levites and the first-born of all other tribes. It was in the gain that the sanctuary and its priests would realize from a lower count of male Levites and a higher count of first-born males of other tribes. As consecrated to the service of the Lord, the male Levites were to replace the firstborn males of all other tribes. Had the number been equal, both the Lord and His sanctuary would have been fully compensated. But a shortfall of Levite males would entitle Him and His sanctuary to added compensation.

What, then, do we make of the reduction in the count of the three ancestral houses from 22,300 to the 22,000? Do 3:15–16 and 39 suggest that Aaron had wrongfully intruded into a count in which he had a conflict? Had he contrived to alter the first count of 22,300 in order to lower the number of Levites? Given P's authorship, the answer must be *no*! Would P portray Aaron as a knave?

In defense of both Aaron and P (but contrary to 3:39), Rashi cites "our rabbis" to explain the disparity of 300 as the number of *firstborn* Levites. As such, they were already consecrated to the Lord and could not count as Levitical substitutes for the first born of other tribes.[1] In the hands of the good Rashi, Aaron's honor remains intact.

The Lord now directs "Moses and Aaron" to take a count of the Kohathites, by clans, all males from age thirty to fifty, these being "all who are subject to service, to perform tasks for the Tent of Meeting." The responsibility of the Kohathites for "the most sacred objects," however, was of limited intimacy. The ultimate responsibility for handling "the most sacred objects" *when uncovered* was reserved to Aaron and his sons. On the "breaking of camp," they alone could wrap such objects in blue or crimson cloth, as designated, and in dolphin skins (4:5–14). These objects included the Ark of the Pact itself; the table of display (including bowls, ladles, jars, and libation jugs, together with "the regular bread"); and the "lampstand for lighting," with its lamps, tongs, firepans, and oil vessels "that are used in its service." After covering these objects, the priests placed them on a carrying frame. Similarly, only priests could cover the "altar of gold" and "all the service vessels" and place them on a carrying frame. And only they could "remove the ashes from the altar and spread a purple cloth over it" on which they placed "all the vessels that are used in its service." These included firepans, flesh hooks, scrapers, and basins. The priests then covered these with dolphin skin and put the carrying poles in place.

Only when these "most sacred objects" were packed for transport did Kohathites begin their work. Thus, "When Aaron and his sons have finished . . . only then shall the Kohathites come and lift them, so that they do not come in contact with the sacred objects and die. These things in the Tent of Meeting shall be the porterage of the Kohathites" (4:15).

To Eleazar alone are given special duties involving "the lighting oil, the aromatic incense, the regular meal offering, and the anointing oil—responsibility for *the whole Tabernacle and for everything consecrated that is in it or its vessels*" (4:16).

> Note N–10: Cf. 4:16 to 4:5–15, in which Eleazar, as Aaron's son, shares a broad responsibility with Aaron and his other sons for "the whole Tabernacle and everything consecrated within it." Rashi reads 4:16 as granting to Eleazar alone the supervision of the Kohathites in their porterage of these items.[2]

The "deadly" importance of keeping a strict division of labor between priests and Kohathites is expressed in the Lord's dire warning to Moses and Aaron. "Do not let the group of Kohathite clans be cut off from the Levites. Do this with them, that they may live and not die when they approach the most sacred objects: let Aaron and his sons assign each of them to his duty and to his porterage. But let [them] not go inside and witness the dismantling of the sanctuary, lest they die" (4:18–20).

Comment N–5. On P's vindication of the Lord's sanctity through the potential annihilation of innocent Kohathites

Num. 4:18–20 poses the issue of group annihilation, not in consequence of the guilt of a few individuals within the clan, but in a context of *total innocence*. Were Aaron or his sons to inadvertently allow one or more Kohathites to gain sight of the "sacred objects," who must then die for defiling the Lord's sanctity? If anyone, we might ask, why not the guilty priest(s)? It was they who had ignored the Lord's warning by allowing the innocent Levites who relied on their instructions to see "sacred objects."

Assuming the Kohathite workers had been warned of their peril, was it their duty before entering the Tent to ask the priests if any "sacred objects" were in sight? But even if it were a duty the particular workers had failed to perform, why would P think it necessary to vindicate the Lord's sanctity through the death of *all* Kohathites? And what if, having first asked, the workers were misinformed? Would vindication of the Lord's sanctity then require the death of an entire ancestral house because a few had innocently seen the "sacred objects"? From Num. 4:18, it would seem so.

Of 8,600 male Kohathites "from the age of one month up," only 2,750 between thirty and fifty were "subject to service for work" (cf. 3:28, 4:35–36). Nor could all those "subject to service" enter the sanctuary at any one time to witness its dismantling. Yet the "they" or "them," which in 4:18–20 defines the class who must die, has no antecedent but "the group of Kohathite clans" of 4:18. In sum, if *any* Kohathite saw the "sacred objects," then *all* Kohathites must die—even if the workers' entry was allowed by the priests who were primarily responsible for hiding the "sacred objects" from the eyes of mere Levites.

As to the ancestral houses of the Gershonites and Merarites, the Lord speaks only to "Moses" rather than to "Moses and Aaron," as with the Kohathites (cf. 4:1, 21).

In Num. 4:21–28 the Lord calls for a census of the Gershonites and reveals their duties. These consist mainly of the porterage of what might be called the "soft goods" of the sanctuary. They include in all "the cloths of the Tabernacle, the Tent of Meeting [and its dolphin skin covering], the screen for the entrance of the Tent of Meeting, the hangings of the enclosure, the screen at the entrance of the gate of the enclosure that surrounds the Tabernacle, the cords thereof, and the altar, and all their service equipment, and all their accessories" (4:24–26).

> Note N–11: JPS2's use of a comma after "Tabernacle" adds to an ambiguity regarding a Gershonite role in the porterage of an altar. Two altars, of course, have already been assigned to the Kohathites (4:11, 13–14). Both JPS1 and RSV better reflect Rashi's view of 4:24–26 that only the screen around the Tabernacle and altar, rather than the altar itself, is for the Gershonites.[3]

As stated in Num. 4:27–28, "All the duties of the Gershonites, all their service and all their porterage, shall be performed on orders of Aaron and his sons. . . . Those are the duties of the Gershonite clans for the Tent of Meeting; they shall attend to them under the direction of Ithamar son of Aaron the priest."

Num. 4:29–33 deals with the work of the ancestral house of Merarites. Like the Gershonites, their work is also supervised by Ithamar (but unlike the Gershonites, without reference to Aaron and his sons). (Cf. 4:27–28, 33.) The work of the Merarites focused on the porterage of the structure's "hardware": "the planks, the bars, the posts, and the sockets of the Tabernacle; all the posts around the enclosure and their sockets, pegs and cords—all these furnishings and their service *you* shall list by name the objects that are their porterage tasks."

> Note N–12: As noted above, "you" now refers to Moses alone. Although the Lord spoke to Moses and Aaron of the Kohathites (4:1), He speaks only to Moses of the Gersonshites and Merarites (4:21). The difference reflects

the less "deadly" work of these latter two houses. Since the sight of what they handle would pose no threat to the Lord's sanctity, we might conclude that there is less need for Aaron to hear of their duties from the Lord himself (see Comment N–5 and 4:17–20).

In all, Num. 4:34–44 states the recorded count of those "from the age of thirty years up to the age of fifty, all who were subject to service for work relating to the Tent of Meeting." Of Kohathites, there were 2,750 (4:36); of Gershonites, 2,630 (4:40); and of Merarites, 3,200 (4:44). Accordingly, the total number of Levite workers was 8,580.

Note N–13: In Num. 4:1–2 both "Moses and Aaron" are told to "take a census" of the Kohathites. But in Num. 4:21–22, "Moses" alone is to "take a census" of the Gershonites, and in 4:29 only he is to "record" the Merarites. Yet Num. 4:41 and 45 state that "Moses and Aaron recorded" the Gershonites and Merarites "at the command of the Lord." (But here, at least, Rashi need not defend Aaron's honor. Cf. Comment N–4.)

As a change from the arithmetical focus of the census counts, Num. 5 returns to some earlier themes of Leviticus. Thus, "the Lord spoke to Moses saying: Instruct the Israelites to remove from camp anyone with an eruption or a discharge and anyone defiled by a corpse. Remove male and female alike; put them outside the camp so that they do not defile the camp of those in whose midst I dwell" (5:1–3).

Note N–14: "Eruption" is from tzara'at, from which JPS1/RSV again derive "leper" (see Comments L–30–36.) On discharges, see Lev. 15. On the defilement of a priest by the corpse of a relative, see Lev. 21:1–4 and Note L–86. Num. 19:11–20 deals further with defilement by corpses.

Num. 5:5–10 may be rooted in the guilt offering of Lev. 5:20–26. It applies to "when a man *or woman* commits any wrong toward a fellow man, thus breaking faith with the Lord, *and that person realizes his guilt.*" Rather than speak of forgiveness as in Leviticus, P speaks in Numbers of "confession" and "restitution" (Num. 5:6–7; cf. Lev. 5:20–26).

But there is an addendum when "the [deceased] man has no kinsman to whom restitution can be made" (5:8). As a forerunner to modern escheat laws, it provides for the transfer of the restitution to the Lord. Thus, absent any heir, "the amount [of restitution] repaid shall go to the Lord for the priest—in addition to the ram of expiation with which expiation is made on his behalf" (Num 5:8).

Note N–15: As for the ram of expiation, see Lev. 5:25–26. Presumably it is required here as well for initial forgiveness. Also, Lev. 5:21 speaks of the wrong as a "trespass against the Lord," while Num. 5:6 speaks of it as "breaking faith with the Lord." The Lord is thus perceived as the ultimate party deserving redress, but only where payment cannot be made to the victim, or his heirs.

Num. 5:9–10 provides that "any gift among the sacred donations that the Israelites offer shall be the priest's. And each shall retain his sacred donations: *each priest shall keep what is given to him.*"

Note N–16: In this the sanctuary operated on "capitalistic" rather than "socialistic" principles. Here the key to priestly harmony was "to each his own."

Num. 5:11–31 addresses a timeless threat to marital bliss and stability, namely, a jealous husband's suspicions of his wife's infidelity. Here, of course, Moses must "speak to the Israelite people." His specific subject is this: "If any man's wife has gone astray and broken faith with him in that a man has had carnal relations with her unbeknown to her husband, and she keeps secret the fact that she has defiled herself without being forced, *and there is no witness against her*—but a fit of jealousy comes over him and he is wrought up about a wife who has defiled herself; *or if a fit of jealousy comes over one and he is wrought up about his wife although she has not defiled herself*—the man shall bring his wife to the priest" (5:12–15). As an offering "for her," he must also bring "one-tenth of an *ephah* of barley flour." Because it was a "meal offering of jealousy, a meal offering of remembrance which recalls wrongdoing," it could not be embellished by "oil" or "frankincense" (5:15).

Note N–17: The protocols might hint of a stacked deck. A visit to the priest could be prompted by nothing more than a husband's "fit of jealousy" although "[the wife] has not defiled herself" (5:14). Yet, whether she has actually "gone astray" must yet be determined. And even before the "trial" begins, the meal offering "recalls wrongdoing." (JPS1 and RSV speak of "bringing iniquity to remembrance.") Is the meal offering meant to recall the wife's presumed sin, or to acknowledge endemic sin?

Num. 5:16–22 sets out the ominous preliminaries to the test of guilt or innocence. They begin as the priest brings the wife forward to "stand before the Lord" (5:16). He then places "earth" (or "dust") from "the floor of the tabernacle" into "sacral water" contained in an earthen vessel (5:17). The priest next "bares" (or "unloosens") the hair of the woman's head and puts in her hands "the meal offering of remembrance, which is a meal offering of jealousy." In his own hands the priest continues to hold "the water of bitterness that induces the spell" (5:18).

The priest then reveals the purpose of "the water of bitterness that induces the spell" (5:19–20). He first "adjures" her in regard to innocence. "If no man has lain with you, if you have not gone astray in defilement while married to your husband, be immune to harm from this water of bitterness that induces the spell" (5:19). He then speaks of guilt. "'But if you have gone astray while married to your husband and have defiled yourself, if a man other than your husband has had carnal relations with you'—here the priest shall administer the curse of adjuration to the woman." Just as the wife's innocence would be established by an absence of harm from the water, so guilt would be shown by the contrary: "May the Lord make you a curse and an imprecation among your people, as the Lord causes your thigh to sag and your belly to distend; may this water that induces the spell enter your body, causing the the belly to distend and the thigh to sag." To all this the wife would signify understanding by "Amen, amen!" (5:21–22).

The priest would then write down the curses in a book (or scroll; i.e., *bah-sayfehr*) and blot or dissolve its words into the water of bitterness (5:23). He would then take the meal offering from the wife to "wave . . . before the Lord and . . . present on the altar" (5:25). A "token part of it" was turned into smoke. And finally the test: "He shall make the woman drink the water."

> *Note N–18: The priest must "make" the wife drink the "water of bitterness." But who would more likely resist? The guilty or innocent? Would it not vary with the wife's faith in Godly justice? In a belief that the body's response to the water was a sign of the Lord's own judgment, innocent wives would eagerly drink while guilty ones might tarry. But lacking such faith and trusting to chance, the innocent would fear injustice, while the guilty would hope for the best. But given the two variables, neither cooperation nor resistance was a useful sign of guilt or innocence.*

The judgment and denouement following the test were true to the priest's "adjurations." As a sign of guilt, "the spell-inducing water shall enter into her to bring on bitterness, so that the belly shall distend and her thigh shall sag." In consequence of guilt, "the woman shall become a curse among her people" (5:27). As both a sign and consequence of innocence, "she shall be unharmed and able to retain seed" (5:28).

As it was in 5:12–14, the husband's dominance in the patriarchal society of ancient Israel is again affirmed in Num. 5:29–31. "This is the ritual in cases of jealousy, when a woman goes astray while married to her husband and defiles herself, *or when a fit of jealousy comes over the man and he is wrought up over his wife*: the woman shall be made to stand before the Lord and the priest shall carry out all the ritual with her. The man shall be clear of guilt; but that woman shall suffer for her guilt" (5:29–31).

Comment N–6. On male dominance, due process, and the water of bitterness

Indictments based on jealousy and the trials by ordeal that follow are poor sources of justice. *But within its own cultural context*, the water of bitterness cannot simply be dismissed as a crude expression of male dominance and a travesty of justice. *On the Torah's premise* of its God as an "objective" judge and jury, the water of bitterness would offer wives some recourse against vengeful husbands who would otherwise assume both roles.

First, it must be understood that the husband could freely divorce his wife without fault on her part. (For the presumably prevailing standard see Deut. 24:1.) Thus, the husband could at least be "ridded" of his wife without proof of adultery. It is possible, therefore, that a husband might charge his wife in good faith in order to rid himself of honest suspicions.

In any case, once the triggering conditions were met, the decision was taken from the husband: "the man *shall* bring his wife to the priest" (5:15). At that point "justice became the Lord's." But what of the two triggering conditions? The first speaks of the wife's actual adultery, which the husband, though lacking conclusive proof, has good grounds to suspect: "If a man's wife *has* gone astray and broken faith with him . . . and she keeps secret the fact that she has defiled herself . . . and there is no witness against her—but a fit of jealousy comes over [the husband and he is wrought up about the wife who has defiled herself" (5:12–14a). The second speaks of an innocent wife, whose husband, nevertheless, is consumed by "a fit of jealousy . . . and he is wrought up about his wife although she has not defiled herself" (5:14b). In other words, whether a husband has good reason, or none, to suspect adultery, a wife's fidelity must be tested by a priest through the water of bitterness. In this way a suspicious or vengeful husband could not act as judge and jury in establishing a wife's guilt.

Whether the wife was in fact guilty or innocent, the test itself exposed the husband and wife to sheer chance. The Lord aside, the water of bitterness itself, the impact of which was the prime determinant of innocence or guilt, contained "some of the earth that is on the floor of the Tabernacle" (5:17). On the one hand, the earth might contain remnants of animal slaughter and sacrifice. On the other, the priests may have scrupulously cleansed the Tabernacle to provide fit surroundings for the Lord's Presence. In any case, the contents of the earthen floor were likely the single most decisive factor in determining guilt or innocence. But consider what was required to establish guilt: "that her belly shall distend *and* her thigh shall sag" (5:27). The need for such distortions might well skew the results toward innocence.

In sum, as a measure of fairness, three points can be made for the waters of bitterness as a test of guilt or innocence. First, as a presumed manifestation of the Lord's judgment, it was at least *thought* to be fair. Second, by its nature, the test was not rigged against the wife. Indeed, it was possibly skewed toward findings of innocence. Third, at the very least, the test displaced spiteful or vindictive husbands as judges and juries of their wives. To a degree, the test honored a broader dictum that the weak were to be protected against the arbitrary exercise of power by the strong.

Num. 6 tells of the nazirites. "The Lord spoke to Moses saying: Speak to the Israelites and say to them: If anyone, *man or woman*, explicitly utters a nazirite's vow, to set himself apart for the Lord" (6:1–2).

> *Note N–19: As implied, "nazirites" took special vows of dedication to the service of the Lord. Parents might also dedicate newborn children as nazirites for periods from thirty days to a lifetime. The nazirites were early exemplars of a holy life of separation and self-discipline.*

They were subject to three basic rules of conduct:

1. Absention not only from "wine and any other intoxicant," but also from "anything in which grapes have been steeped" (perhaps meaning any form of fermentation, or even unfermented grape juice), and beyond grape beverages, any "grapes fresh or dried" (i.e., raisins), and beyond whole grapes, "even seeds or skin" (6:3–4)
2. Avoidance, during "the term of his vow as nazirite," of any "razor," so that the "hair of his head" is left "to grow untrimmed" (6:5)
3. Avoidance, "throughout the term that he has set apart for the Lord," of any place "where there is a dead person," including the dead body of a "father or mother," or "brother or sister," for "throughout his term as nazirite, he is consecrated to the Lord" (6:6–8)

> *Note N–20: The rules governing intoxicants, hair, and proximity to a corpse were stricter for nazirites than for priests. (Cf. as to intoxicants, Lev. 10:8–11; as to hair, Lev. 21:5; and as to corpses, Lev. 21:1–3.)*

So "pure" was the nazirite to remain that the sudden death of anyone "near him" would void all prior service as a nazirite (6:9–12). It was a "defiling [of] his sacred hair" (6:9). Thereafter, the nazirite was unclean for seven days. On the eighth day he brought two turtledoves or pigeons to the priest "at the entrance of the Tent of Meeting." These were for a burnt and a sin offering in expiation "for the guilt incurred through the corpse" (6:10–11). On the same day he reconsecrated "his head" and was rededicated "to the Lord . . . as nazirite" (6:11–12). Following a penalty offering of a lamb in its first year, the nazirite's full period of service began anew (6:12).

Num. 6:13–20 covers "the ritual for the nazirite." On the day his term ends, the nazirite must be brought "to the entrance of the Tent of Meeting" (6:13).

The rituals began with a burnt offering of "one male lamb in its first year, without blemish"; a sin offering of "one ewe lamb in its first year, without blemish"; and an offering of well-being of "one ram without blemish" (6:14). To these were added "a basket of unleavened cakes of choice flour with oil mixed in, and unleavened wafers spread with oil; and the proper meal offering and libations" (6:15). The priest then presented the offerings to the Lord (6:16–17), after which the nazirite shaved his consecrated hair and put it into the "fire that is under the sacrifice of well-being" (6:18).

The priest then "places on the hands" of the nazirite "the shoulder of the ram . . . , one unleavened cake from the basket, and one unleavened wafer." These were waved "as a wave offering before the Lord." It was a sacred donation for the priest, "in addition to the breast of the wave offering and the thigh of the heave offering" (6:19–20).

As a symbol of "normalcy" following the wave offering, "the nazirite may drink wine" (6:20). But the nazirite is also warned of the need to honor vows made to the Lord beyond the formal requirements. "He who vows an offering to the Lord of what he can afford beyond his nazirite requirements must do exactly according to the vow which he has made beyond his obligation as a nazirite" (6:21).

Num. 6 concludes with a simple blessing of great warmth and beauty. It is the priestly benediction.

> The Lord spoke to Moses: Speak to Aaron and his sons: Thus shall you bless the people of Israel. Say to them:
>
> The Lord bless you and keep you!
>
> The Lord deal kindly and graciously with you!
> [Also, "The Lord make his face to shine upon you, and be gracious to you:" (RSV/JPS1)]
>
> The Lord bestow His favor upon you and grant you peace!
> [Also, "The Lord lift his countenance upon you, and give you peace." (RSV/JPS1)]
>
> Thus, they shall link My name with the people of Israel, and I will bless them. (6:22–27)

Comment N–7. On the priestly benediction and its connection with Lev. 26

As dramatically "recorded" in Genesis, prior to His role as Israel's God, the Lord's unilateral rule over the whole of humanity had been marked by gross overreactions to human sin (as He judged and misjudged it). He may have wished to be fair—only to have His good intentions fall prey to the complexities of human nature and free will. Recall His curt rejection of the offering of Cain who had been first to come to praise Him, His destruction of the innocent along with the guilty in the Great Flood, and His jealous petulance at the Tower of Babel that led Him to recast a humanity unified by purpose and language into quarrelsome factions separated by the barriers of language.

As to Israel, its entire relationship with its God was founded on Abram's acceptance of the condition that he leave home for a new land (Gen. 12:1–3). To this was added the Covenant of Circumcision (Gen. 18), followed by the climactic setting of Lev. 26 in which we encounter the ultimate expression of the Torah's continuing theme of conditionality. Through contrasting destinies of bliss and doom, the Lord God of Israel delineates the consequences for "the Israelite people" of obedience and disobedience to His conditions. Fundamental to His pronouncements is His implied commitment to a more predictable standard of justice in allotting rewards and punishments. Thus, to reap the bliss and avoid the doom of Lev. 26, "the Israelite people" must "follow My laws and faithfully observe My commandments" (Lev. 26:3).

The three blessings of the priestly benediction poetically express the essence of the rewards of Lev. 26:3–13. And just as those rewards are conditioned on the quality of human conduct, so, too, are the blessings. In this equivalence we find the meaning of the priestly benediction.

Its dual essence lies in faith and hope. P's faith (despite the past) is that the Lord, both as Israel's God, and the Lord, Himself, will judge Israel fairly. P's hope is that Israel proves worthy of the rewards of Lev. 26:3–13. These relationships between Lev. 26 and the priestly benedictions are revealed more clearly by the explicit, rather than the implicit, inclusion of "may" in the latter.

May the Lord bless you and keep you:

May the Lord make his face to shine upon you,
     and be gracious to you:

May the Lord lift his countenance upon you,
     and give you peace. (6:24–26)

Thus, the blessings seek nothing from the Torah's Lord God, except, as presumed, that He will honor His commitment to judge Israel fairly. In turn, however, it is for the people, on whom the blessings are bestowed, to prove worthy of the *hope* of the blessings, in order to reap their substance. That substance lies in the rewards of Lev. 26:3–13, whose poetic essence, as noted, finds expression in the blessings. *In short, the hope of the blessings is not that "the people of Israel" should receive rewards beyond their worth. It is that their worth should warrant the rewards of Lev. 26:3–13.*

But the problem of Lev. 26 remains. Whose worth is being judged? And the answer from the priestly benediction is the same as that from Lev. 26: "You must act as if you and Israel share a common destiny that will be determined by the measure of *your* worthiness" (see Comment L–59).

Num. 7:1a states that "on the day that Moses finished setting up the Tabernacle, he anointed and consecrated it and all its furnishings, as well as the altar and its furnishings." When this was done (7:1b), "the chieftains of Israel, the heads of ancestral houses, namely, the chieftains of the tribes" drew near with their first "offering before the Lord" (7:2–3a). This consisted of six "draught carts" (or "covered wagons") and twelve oxen, or "a cart for every two chieftains and an ox for each one" (7:3). These were to be allotted among the Levite divisions "for use in the service of the Tent of Meeting . . . *according to their respective services*" (as set out in Num. 4) (7:4–5).

The Gershonites were given "two carts and four oxen" and the Merarites "four carts and eight oxen." As bearers of the most sacred objects, however, the Kohathites received nothing. "Their porterage was by shoulder" (7:6–9).

As an additional "dedication offering for the altar," each chieftain of the twelve tribes brought identical items of silver and gold and of cereal and sacrificial animals. Here, they consist of the tribal offerings and the order of presentation are of particular interest.

As the chieftains drew near the altar with their offerings, the Lord directs Moses to "let them present their offerings . . . one chieftain each day" (7:11). And so they were made on consecutive days, from the first through the twelfth (including at least one sabbath day).

Each tribal offering consisted of "one silver bowl weighing 130 shekels and one silver basin of 70 shekels by sanctuary weight, both filled with choice flour with oil mixed in, for a meal offering; one gold ladle of 10 shekels, filled with incense; one bull of the herd, one ram, and one lamb in its first year, for a burnt offering; one goat for a sin offering; and for his sacrifice of well-being: two oxen, five rams, five he-goats, and five yearling lambs."

With no stated directions from the Lord or Moses as to their order, the tribal chieftains present their offerings over twelve days in the following order: First, Judah; second, Issachar; third, Zebulun; fourth, Reuben; fifth, Simeon; sixth, Gad; seventh, Ephraim; eighth, Manasseh; ninth, Benjamin; tenth, Dan; eleventh, Asher; and twelfth, Naphtali.

Note N–21: The consecutive daily offerings for the anointment of the altar are made in 7:12–88. In all, the animals slaughtered at the Tent numbered 36 bulls, 72 rams, 72 yearling lambs, and 72 goats.

Thereafter, "*when Moses went into the Tent of Meeting to speak with Him, he* would hear the Voice addressing him from above the cover that was on top of the Ark of the Pact between the two cherubim" (7:89).

Note N–22: Cf. Num. 7:89 with Lev. 1:1, in which "the Lord called to Moses and spoke to him from the Tent of Meeting," into which "Moses could not enter . . . because . . . the Presence of the Lord filled the Tabernacle" (Exod. 40:35). Why is Moses now allowed (following anointment and consecration of the Tabernacle and priests in Lev. 8 and 9) to enter the Tent in the Lord's Presence?

Comment N–8. On the tribal presentations of Num. 7

1. On accommodating time to editorial purposes

Num. 7:1 states that "on the day that Moses finished *setting up* the Tabernacle, he anointed and consecrated it and all its furnishings, as well as the altar and utensils." Exod. 40:17 first identifies the day it was "set up" as "the *first* month of the second year [after leaving Egypt], on the first of the month." Num. 1 (following Leviticus) then begins as the Lord speaks to Moses "on the first day of the *second* month in the second year following the exodus." Clearly, the events *recalled* in Num. 7 preceded the events of Num. 1. Further complicating the time relationships are the anointment and consecration in Lev. 8 of the Tent and Tabernacle and their furnishings (Lev. 8:10–11, 15).

Lev. 8 would seem to have occurred on a day uncertain during the month between Exod. 40:17 and Num. 1. If so, the events of Num. 7, having occurred on the same day as Exod. 40:17, would also have preceded Lev. 8. Is it possible that at some point, as the Torah developed, the three episodes were at least meant to have *begun* on the same day (in that the events of Lev. 8 extended over eight days)?

We might take note, however, that Num. 2 serves as a useful background to Num. 7 as the initial source for the order of its tribal offerings (see Comment N–3). Accordingly, we might view Num. 7 as a conveniently located deferred "recollection" of earlier events.

2. On keeping the sabbath during twelve consecutive days of presentations by the tribal chieftains

The twelve days of tribal presentations are portrayed as consecutive. If so, at least one, and possibly two, would have fallen on a sabbath. That sabbath sacrificial offerings were not only permitted, but required, will be established in Num. 28:9–10. There, however, the sabbath offering requires, *but is limited to*, "two yearling lambs *without blemish*" and a meal offering. Given such specifics, could the different offerings of Num. 7 have been made on the sabbath without the Lord's approval? If so, when was it given? And if not given, would this ritual error have been any less egregious than that for which the Lord had caused Aaron's sons, Nadab and Abihu, to be consumed by fire (Lev. 10:1–2)? Consider as well the Lord's required observance of the sabbath in building the Tabernacle (Exod. 31:12–17).

Num. 8:1–4 turns to the mounting of the gold hammered lampstand and the kindling of its lamps (8:1–4).

Note N–23: These are first described in Exod. 25:31–40.

Although the instructions are for Aaron, the Lord speaks only to Moses (cf. Lev. 10:8–11; see also Comment L–25).

The balance of Num. 8 deals with the Levites. The basis for its unique tribal status appears earlier in Num. 3:11–12: "The Lord spoke to Moses saying: I hereby take the Levites from among the Israelites in place of all the firstborn, the first issue of the womb among the Israelites: the Levites shall be mine."

Num. 8:5–12 sets out the ordination protocols through which the Levites were dedicated to "the service of the Lord" (8:11). As the prelude to all else, the first concern was for their bodily cleanliness, This was achieved by (1) a sprinkling on them of the water of purification, (2) the application of a razor to their "whole body," and (3) the washing of their clothes (8:6–7). This was followed by offerings of "a bull of the herd, and with it a meal offering of choice flour with oil mixed in, and . . . a second bull of the herd for a sin offering" (8:8).

Note N–24: Exod. 8:12 indicates that the first bull is for a burnt offering.

Before the "whole Israelite community" assembled at the Tent of meeting, the Levites were brought forward "before the Lord" where "the Israelites" were directed to "lay their hands upon the Levites" (8:9–10).

Note N–25: Given the number of "hands" in all, "the Israelites" must have acted through representatives, whether priests or clan chiefs.

Aaron then designates the entire body of Levites as a symbolic "wave offering from the Israelites . . . to the Lord" (8:11, 13).

Note N–26: Comment L–17, briefly describes the more usual "wave offering" of animal parts.

"Thus you shall set the Levites apart from among the Israelites, and the Levites shall be Mine. And now, having been 'cleansed' and 'designated as a wave offering, . . . the Levites shall be qualified for the service of the Tent of Meeting' (8:15).

Num. 8:16–18 repeats the substance of Num. 3:11–13, 41, and 45 regarding the assignment of the Levites to the Lord, as His, in place of "every firstborn among the Israelites, man as well as beast."

As well as noting the Levites' first duty in performing "the service for the Israelites in the Tent of Meeting," Num. 8:19 recalls their second sacred duty. It is "to make expiation for the Israelites, *so that no plague may afflict the Israelites for coming too near the sanctuary.*"

Note N–27: The threat of a "plague" among the Israelites because some might come too near to the sanctuary is a further reminder of P's approach to collective justice (see Comment L–59 and N–5).

Num. 8:20–22 tells of the total compliance by "Moses, Aaron, and the whole Israelite community" with all "the Lord had commanded in regard to the Levites."

Num. 8 concludes with the following summation of "the rule for the Levites." It is most notable in its variance from Num. 4. "From twenty-five years of age up they shall participate in the work force in the service of the Tent of Meeting; but at the age of fifty they shall retire from the work force and serve no more. They may assist their brother Levites at the Tent of Meeting by standing guard, but they shall perform no labor" (8:23–26).

Note N–28: The Levite census of Num. 4 was of those "from the age of thirty years up to the age of fifty, all who are subject to service, to perform tasks for the Tent of Meeting" (4:3, 23, 30). This is contradicted by Num. 8:24, which requires a Levitical "work force" that begins at "twenty-five years." Both Rashi and Plaut suggest that the five years between twenty-five and thirty may have been a learning and probationary period."[4] However useful such an arrangement might prove, it would have required a separate identification of males between twenty-five and thirty.

Num. 9:1 states that "the Lord spoke to Moses in the wilderness of Sinai, *on the first new moon of the second year following the exodus*" (or the first day of the month).

Note N–29: This date and its problem of sequence recalls Num. 7 and its possible connection with Exod. 40:17 (see Comment N–8 pt. 1). Rashi opines that from this "you learn that there is no arrangement of 'before' and 'after' in the Torah."[5] Plaut suggests a different source for Num. 9.[6] As he does Num. 1–8, however, Friedman ascribes Num. 9 to P (except for 9:15–23, which he logically ascribes to R). (See Comment N–9.)

In Num. 9:2–5, the Lord commands the Israelites, through Moses, to "offer the passover sacrifice at its set time," that is, "in the first month, on the fourteenth day of the month, at twilight, in the wilderness of Sinai."

Note N–30: JPS2 derives "offer the passover sacrifice at its set time" from v'yahahsu v'nai-yisrael et-hahpasach b'mohahdoh. JPS1 and RSV read the clause as "keeping the passover at its appointed time or season." That JPS2 speaks of the sacrifice rather than the general observance reflects its centrality to the occasion.

Moses is then questioned by "some men who were unclean by reason of a corpse and could not offer the passover sacrifice on that day" (9:6). They ask why they, too, cannot present "the Lord's offering at its set time with the rest of the Israelites" (9:7). Knowing it to be an important question, Moses tells them, "Stand by, and let me hear what instructions the Lord gives about you" (9:8).

Together with more general instructions (9:9–13), the Lord's answer to the specific question is a clearly implied "yes." Thus, "when any of you who are defiled by a corpse or are on a long journey *would offer* a passover sacrifice to the Lord, they shall offer it in the second month, on the fourteenth day of the month at twilight [i.e., one month after the date prescribed for all others]" (9:10–11).

Note N–31: JPS2's use of "would offer" suggests that for persons "defiled by a corpse" or "on a long journey," the passover sacrifice, in itself, was voluntary. This view gains support from 9:13, which limits its basic obligatory command and corresponding punishments for neglect to a man "who is clean and not on a journey" and who "refrains from offering the passover sacrifice."

Num. 9:11–12 commands that the offering be made "in strict accord with the law of the passover sacrifice" and that it be eaten with "unleavened bread and bitter herbs."

Num. 9:14 deals with the offering of a passover sacrifice by "a stranger who resides with you and would offer a passover sacrifice to the Lord." If he so chooses, "he must offer it in accordance with the rules and rites of the passover sacrifice. There shall be one law for you, whether stranger or citizen of the country."

Note N–32: Exod. 12:48–49 (ascribed to P) specifically conditions a "stranger's" passover observance on prior circumcision.

As the Israelites are about to leave the wilderness of Sinai for Canaan, Num. 9:15–23 tells of how their travels will be guided by the "cloud" that manifests the Lord's Presence. Once again, as in Num. 7:1, the narrative begins "on the day that the Tabernacle was set up" (9:15). (See Comment N–8 pt. 1.) On that day, "the cloud covered the Tabernacle, the Tent of the Pact; and in the evening it rested over the Tabernacle in the likeness of fire until morning. It was always so: the cloud covered it, appearing as fire by night" (9:15–16).

Num. 9:17–23 relates the movements of the Israelites to those of the cloud (9:17–23). In essence, "whenever the cloud lifted from the Tent, the Israelites would set out accordingly; and at the spot where the cloud settled, there the Israelites would make camp" (9:17). The Israelites regarded each movement of the cloud as "a sign from the Lord" (9:18). Whether the cloud lingered at great length in any one location, or quickly moved on, they would encamp or decamp accordingly (9:19–23). In being guided by the cloud alone, "they accepted the Lord's mandate at the Lord's bidding through Moses" (9:23).

Comment N–9. On the time and purpose of "the cloud" in Num. 9:15–23

Plaut writes of "the cloud" as follows: "Other biblical passages speak of the cloud preceding Israel on its journeys (Exod. 13:21); guiding it (Exod. 40:34–38); standing in front of the Tabernacle (Exod. 33:7–11). *The reason for this detailed passage containing previously stated information is not clear.*"[7]

Of Plaut's three references, only Exod. 40:34–38 relates directly to the subject matter of Num. 9:15–23. In P's Exod. 13:21, the Lord did go before the people "in a pillar of cloud by day, to guide them along the way" and a "pillar of fire by night, to give them light." But as the "pillars" that guided Israel toward Sinai, they *preceded* the Tent/Tabernacle. And it is the "setting up" that triggers the "details" of Num. 9:15–23. Finally, in Exod. 33:7–11, it is E who tells of a cloud descending on a Tent of Meeting that Moses, himself, had pitched "outside the camp." Though perhaps from a similar tradition, E's Tent was distinct and apart from P's Tent/Tabernacle.

Thus, the only "previously stated information" relevant to "this detailed passage" is that of Exod. 40:34–38. In turn, Num. 9:15–23 is meant to pick up where Exod. 40 ends. (Again, this relates to the problems of sequence first posed by Num. 7. See Comment N–8 pt. 1). R's inclusion of these "details" at this point may be explained by their role in introducing Num. 10—in which Israel will finally begin its journey from Sinai to Canaan.

In Num. 10:1–10 the Lord instructs Moses on the making and use of "two silver trumpets . . . of hammered work." Their purpose is "to summon the community and to set the divisions in motion" (10:1–2).

Note N–33: The "divisions" are the four tribal divisions of Num. 2.

Num. 10:3–7 describes the distinctive blasts to be blown for each of the following purposes: (1) to assemble the community at the entrance of the Tent of Meeting, (2) to assemble the chieftains before Moses, and (3) to set the divisions in motion. The trumpets are to be blown by Aaron's sons, "as priests." They are to be "an institution for all time throughout the ages" (10:8).

Num. 10:9–10 tells of further uses of the trumpets:

> When your are at war in your own land against an aggressor who attacks you, you shall sound short blasts on the trumpets, *that you may be remembered before the Lord your God and be delivered from your enemies.* And on your joyous occasions, your fixed festivals and new moon days, you shall sound the trumpets over your burnt offerings and your sacrifices of well-being. *They shall be a reminder of you before the Lord your God: I the Lord am your God.*

Comment N–10. On trumpets as alternatives to the ram's horn and reminders to the Lord, its God, that Israel turns to Him as its source of safety and joy

1. On the trumpets as alternatives to the ram's horn

The use of two trumpets poses a question of their relationship to the ram's horn, or shofar. We first encounter the blast and blare of the ram's horn in passages (by J and E?) that announce the Presence of God in the first theophany at Mount Sinai (Exod. 19:13, 16, 19). With regard to *rosh hashonah* (or the "first day of the seventh month"), Lev. 23:24 speaks only of a "blast" (or *teruah*) without identifying its source. But in Lev. 25:9, on the occasion of *yom hakippurim* (or the "tenth day of the seventh month"), as it occurs in the Jubilee year, the Lord commands, "You shall have the horn [i.e., the *shofar*] sounded throughout your land."

In Num. 10:2, the distinction that is intended between the ram's horn, or *shofar*, and the trumpets is confirmed in the Hebrew *chatzotzrot*, which identifies the trumpets. Since the *shofar* and *chatzotzroht* are common to the P source, a distinction is clearly intended. Their different uses may have reflected their different tonal qualities.

2. On the trumpets as reminders to the Lord, its God, that Israel looks to Him for safety and joy

Amid the perils of an enemy attack, the trumpets are to be blown so that the Israelites "may be remembered before the Lord." Amid the joys of the festivals, they are to be blown as a "reminder of you before the Lord your God." So used, the trumpets would serve much like the lamb's blood in Egypt which the Israelites were commanded to place on their doorposts and lintels as a sign of their identity. Those who failed in this way to acknowledge the Lord as their God would, like their errant predecessors in Egypt, lose the Lord's protection (Exod. 13:21–23).

Similarly, in Num. 10:9–10 the Lord, as Israel's God, instructs His people to sound their trumpets as a sign that they acknowledge Him as their source of safety and joy. Only then will He "remember" His role as their God. Note, however, that the Lord promises to save Israel from its enemies *only* when "*at war in your own land against an aggressor who attacks you.*" Will Israel, in all other wars of its own choosing, sound its trumpets in vain?

Now, "in the second year, on the twentieth day of the second month, the cloud lifted from the Tabernacle of the Pact and the Israelites set out on their journeys from the wilderness of Sinai. The cloud came to rest in the wilderness of Paran" (10:11–12).

> *Note N–34: It is now twenty days after the beginning of Numbers (cf. Num. 1:1).*

Num. 10:13–28 sets out "the Israelites' order of march, as they marched troop by troop" (10:28). The "order" includes that of the twelve non-Levitical tribes and their four divisions, as reported in Num. 2; and of the three Levitical divisions, as reported in Num. 3. The order of march, including tribes, divisions, and assignments, are all as described in Num. 2 and 3. So, too, are the names of all other tribal chieftains and their fathers, as repeated in Num. 7 from Num. 2—but with the one notable exception involving the tribe of Gad.

> *Note N–35: The stated names of the Gadite chieftain and his father are (1) "Eliasaph the son of Reuel" (2:14), (2) "Eliasaph the son of Deuel" (7:42), and (3) as in (2) (10:20). (These names follow the Hebrew text of the three verses. Might "Deuel" or "Reuel" trace back to a "typo" in the parchment? Neither Rashi nor Ramban speak to the matter. But what follows surely suggests that the "error" lies in the "R" of "Reuel" in Num. 2:14.*

In 10:29 Moses pleads with "*Hobab son of Reuel the Midianite, Moses' father-in-law*" to join the Israelites on their journey to Canaan. "We are setting out for the place of which the Lord has said, 'I will give it to you.' Come with us and we will be generous with you; for the Lord has promised to be generous to Israel." When Hobab declares his intent to return to his own native land (i.e., Midian), Moses offers an astonishing reason for his request: "Please do not leave us, *inasmuch as you know where we should camp in the wilderness* and can be our guide" (10:31).

> *Note N–36: By use of a comma after Hobab in 10:29 (see above), JPS1 means to remove any possible doubt that Hobab is indeed the son of Reuel, the Midianite. However, Reuel, the Midianite (also known as Jethro), has been identified as the father of Zipporah, Moses' wife (see Exod. 2:16–22). If the Reuels of Num. 10:29, Exod. 2:18, and Num. 2:14 are all the same, then Hobab, as Reuel's son, is a brother or half-brother to Eliasaph. Yet how could Reuel, as "priest of Midian" (Exod. 2:16), be, or have been, the father of a Gadite chieftain?*

Comment N–11. On the help that Moses sought from Hobab

How will the Lord, as Israel's God, take this request from Moses to Hobab. Was He, Himself, not to be Israel's guide? "And whenever the cloud lifted from the Tent, the Israelites would set out accordingly; *and at the spot where the cloud settled, there the Israelites would make camp.* On a sign from the Lord the Israelites broke camp, and on a sign from the Lord they made camp" (Num. 9:17–18). In the choice of camp sites, why would Moses seek to "second-guess" the Lord through Hobab?

One explanation might come from considering the "precise" role that Moses contemplates for Hobab in 10:31. In JPS1/RSV, rather than asking Hobab to help in *selecting* camp sites, Moses asks him to (1) show them how to encamp in the wilderness and (2) serve "as eyes" to the Israelites (as derived from *v'hahyeetah lahnoo l'aynahyim*). In short, in knowing the terrain, Hobab might help the Israelites to "settle safely" into the sites selected by their God.

Does Friedman's attribution of 10:29–36 to J rather than P, better explain the matter? Consider what follows.

"[The Israelites] marched from the mountain of the Lord a distance of three days. The Ark of the Covenant of the Lord traveled in front of them on that three days' journey to seek out a resting place for them; and the Lord's cloud kept above them by day, as they moved on from the camp. When the ark was to set out, Moses would say: "Advance, O Lord! May your enemies be scattered, And may your foes flee before You!" And when it halted, he would say: Return, O Lord, You who are Israel's myriads of thousands" (10:33–36).

Note N–37: If Num. 10:33–36 is indeed by J, it serves to associate J as well as P with the image of Israel being lead by the "Lord's cloud." But there are also differences between Num. 10:33–36 and Num. 9:15–23 and Exod. 40:34–38, the earlier passages on the same theme (see Comment N–9). Unlike the earlier passages, Num. 10:33–36 links the cloud to the Ark alone, with no mention of a Tabernacle. Nor does Num. 10, unlike Exod. 40:34–35, link the cloud to the Lord's actual Presence (as possibly distinguished from His "simply" using the cloud to guide the Israelites). Combined with the prudent self-reliance ascribed to Moses in seeking Hobab's help in settling into camp sites, these differences support Friedman's ascription of 10:33–36 to J.

Num. 11 tells of rapidly eroding relationships among the Israelites, the Lord, their God and Moses. It begins with their joint arrival at Taberah, following a three day trek that marked the first leg of the journey from Sinai to Canaan (cf. 10:33, 11:3). Soon after their arrival, "the people took to complaining bitterly before the Lord" (11:1). An irate Lord responds with a fire, thereby "ravaging the outskirts of the camp" (11:1). After Moses intercedes through prayer, "the fire died down" (11:2).

Egged on by the "riffraff in their midst" (perhaps from among the "mixed multitude" of Exod. 12:38), the people weep for lack of meat (11:5). As their "cravings" grow, they "remember the fish that we used to eat free in Egypt, the cucumbers, the melons, the leeks, the onions, and the garlic. Now, there is only "this manna to look to!" (11:6).

But what the Lord's manna lacked in variety, it made up with substance and sufficiency. It was like "coriander seed," with the [pale yellowish or whitish] color of "bdellium" (11:7). The people would "gather it, grind it between millstones or pound it in a mortar, boil it in a pot, and make it into cakes. It tasted like rich cream" (11:8). Each night, "when the dew fell on the camp . . . the manna would fall upon it" (11:9).

Manna alone might sustain them, but it did not meet their broader cravings. They wept openly, "every clan apart, each person at the entrance of his tent" (11:10).

Note N–38: As for meat itself, the Israelites had left Egypt with "very much livestock, both flocks and herds" (Exod. 12:38). Many would have been kept for dairying and breeding. And as the Tabernacle was but lately completed, not many would have yet been sacrificed. Yet future sacrificial requirements could take a heavy toll. While some offerings allowed offerors to consume a portion of the meat, offerings alone would hardly provide a reliable source of meat for most Israelites. But more to the point, the matter of meat, or food in general, seems more a symbol than a root cause of the peoples' distress.

Preying on them was their decision to leave the relative comfort of Egypt for a destiny that remained no more than a promise. Even the Lord was concerned that at the first sign of trouble they would choose to return to the relative security of Egypt (see Exod. 13:17–18 and Comments E–33 and E–43).

In turn, "the Lord was very angry, and Moses was distressed" (11:10). He expresses his distress in an anguished complaint to the Lord:

Why have You dealt ill with Your servant, and why have I not enjoyed Your favor, that You have laid the burden of all this people upon me? Did I conceive all this people, did I bear them, that You should say to me, "Carry them in your bosom as a nurse carries an infant," to the Land that You have promised on oath to their fathers. Where am I to get meat to give to all this people, when they whine before me and say, "Give us meat to eat!" I cannot carry all this people by myself, for it is too much for me. If You would thus deal with me, kill me rather, I beg You, and let me see no more of my wretchedness. (11:11–15)

The Lord's sympathy is for Moses alone.

Gather for Me seventy of Israel's elders of whom you have experience as elders and officers of the people, and bring them to the Tent of Meeting and let them take their place with you. I will come down and speak with you there, *and I will draw upon the spirit that is in you and put it upon them*; they shall share the burden of the people with you, and you shall not bear it alone. And say to the people: Be ready for tomorrow and you shall eat meat, for you have kept whining before the Lord and saying, "If only we had meat to eat! Indeed, we were better off in Egypt!" The Lord will give you meat and you shall eat . . . a whole month, until it comes out of your nostrils and becomes loathsome to you. For you have rejected the Lord who is among you, by whining before Him and saying, "Oh, why did we ever leave Egypt." (11:16–20)

But given the growing schism between the Lord and His people, not even the Lord's proposals for Moses to share his burdens with others could dispel his anguish. Moses was dangerously near the end of his rope.

The people who are with me number six hundred thousand men; yet You say, "I will give them enough meat to eat for a whole month." Could enough flocks and herds be slaughtered to suffice them? Or could all the fish of the sea be gathered to suffice them? (11:21–22)

Note N–39: As Abraham had questioned the Lord's powers (by giving Sarah to the Pharaoh and Abimelech and by "laughing" at the thought of a son at Sarah's age), so, too, does Moses.

The Lord responds indignantly to Moses' waning faith. "Is there a limit to the Lord's power? You shall soon see whether what I said happens to you or not" (11:23).

Moses reported the Lord's words to the people and gathered seventy elders around the Tent. "Then the Lord came down in a cloud and spoke to him: He drew upon the spirit that was in him and put it on the seventy elders. And when the spirit rested upon them they spoke in ecstasy, but did not continue" (11:24–25). Of the seventy chosen elders, Eldad and Medad had "remained in camp" (11:26).

> Note N–40: Num. 11:26, in which two elders "remained in camp," contradicts 11:24, in which Moses gathered all "seventy . . . elders" and "stationed them around the Tent." Putting the anomaly aside, what seems especially important in regard to Friedman's imputation of the passage to E is that Eldad and Medad had "remained in camp." Thus, by placing the Tent outside the camp, this passage tracks E's Exod. 33:7–11, in which "Moses would take the Tent [of Meeting] and pitch it outside the camp" (33:7).

Although physically separated from the Lord's Presence, "Eldad and Medad spoke in ecstasy [or prophesied] in the camp" (11:26). A youth ran out to tell Moses that they were "acting the prophet in the camp." On hearing this, "Joshua son of Nun, Moses' attendant from his youth, spoke up and said, 'My Lord Moses, restrain them.' " But a dispirited Moses takes no joy in his monopoly. "Are you wrought up on my account? Would that all the Lord's people were prophets, that the Lord put His spirit upon them!" (11:27–29).

Num. 11:31–32 tells of an overkill of quail covering "about a day's journey on this side and . . . on that side, all around the camp . . ." and they lay "some two cubits deep on the ground." For two days and a night the people gathered quail. But while "meat was still between their teeth, not yet chewed . . . the anger of the Lord blazed forth against the people and the Lord struck the people with a very severe plague" (11:33). The place was named "Kibroth-hattavah" because "the people who had the craving were buried there" (11:34).

> Note N–41: The number slain is not reported.

Then the people left for Hazeroth (11:35).

Comment N–12. On E's tale of a tragic descent by the People, Moses and the Lord from the heights of Sinai to the depths of despair

Among the three sources of Exodus (i.e., J, E, and P), only the Israelites of E had not witnessed the Lord's power through His plagues in Egypt. We might therefore expect that "E's Israelites" had left Egypt in less awe of His powers than the Israelites of other sources. Their possible "ignorance" of the plagues may explain why E's people now appear as the prime "kvetches" in the wilderness. (But in this the people of J and P will soon join those of E.)

As the exodus began, it was E who first spoke of God's forebodings that the people might actually prefer the security of Egypt to the hardships of the journey (see Exod. 13:17–18 and Note N–38). Later, as the pursuing Egyptians drew near, only the frightened people of E assumed imminent disaster and decried their departure from Egypt (Exod. 14:11–12). In time, they would complain of a lack of water with such vigor that Moses cried out to the Lord, "What shall I do with this people. Before long they will be stoning me." And again they decried their departure from Egypt (Exod. 17:2–7).

On arriving at the base of Sinai, however, their mercurial spirits soared as they began to sense the actual Presence of the Lord. Recall their ebullience on hearing His words through Moses (Exod. 19:2–8). Before offering specifics, the Lord asked only that they "obey Me faithfully and keep My covenant." If so, they will become His "treasured possession among all the peoples . . . a kingdom of priests and a holy nation." Enthused as they were by the promise of a unique relationship with a Lord of unusual powers (witness the water at Meribah), they shouted their answer: "All that the Lord has spoken we will do."

The Lord's revelation of His *mishpatim*, or Covenant Code, may have raised doubts among the people of E regarding their human capacity to fulfil them (Exod. 21:1–23:19). But their concerns were offset by the promised fruits of obedience and the force of the Lord's commitment to "make all your enemies turn tail before you" (Exod. 23:20–33). And so they responded twice to Moses, "All the things that the Lord has commanded we will do!" and "All that the Lord has spoken we will faithfully do!" (Exod. 24:3, 7).

That E's people led Aaron to cast an image of the Lord as a golden calf resulted from a variety of motives (Exod. 32; see also Comments E–86 and 87.) The selective mayhem that followed should have alerted E's people to the Lord's capacity for wrath (Exod. 32:21–33:6). But, later, they were surely heartened when the Lord spoke with Moses in the Tent "face to face, as one man speaks to another." For Moses, however, such memories could only add to his mounting tensions from the growing rift between the people and the Lord. Indeed, within Num. 11 alone, a distraught Moses had manifested three potentially fateful failures: (1) a failure of resolute leadership in answering the peoples' complaints (11:10–15), (2) a failure of faith in regard to the Lord's powers to provide meat (11:21–22), and (3) a failure of judgment in dismissing Joshua's fears of the erosive impact of multiple prophets on Moses' authority (11:28–29).

Still with E, we move inexorably toward the tragic events of Num. 11. They result from the intense interplay among the distinctive qualities and concerns of the three great protagonists. Following the serenity of their relations with the Lord at the Tent of Meeting, E's people are blessed with a hopeful spirit—but subject to manic-depressive volatility. In turn, a proud and wrathful Lord demands that His chosen people commit their destiny to

His judgment and power. And between E's people and their God stands Moses, torn by a profound commitment to both. In Num. 11, E permits the inevitable tragedy to unfold. But the worst now comes in Num. 12, when E's vulnerable Moses is attacked by his own brother and sister!

"When they were in Hazeroth [recall 11:35], Miriam and Aaron spoke against Moses because of the Cushite woman he had married: "He married a Cushite woman" (12:1).

> Note N–42: Moses' wife Zipporah is clearly identified as a Midianite (Exod. 2:15–22). The term "Cushite," often identified as Northeast African or Ethiopian, would seem to describe an unidentified second wife. Although not descended from Abraham and Sarah through Isaac and Jacob, the Midianites, were (presumably) the descendants of Abraham's son Midian by Keturah (Gen. 25:1–2). If so, Zipporah was of a people who, with the Israelites, claimed a common ancestor in Abraham.

In addition to attacking the true worth of Moses' credentials in having married a non-Israelite woman, Miriam and Aaron also stake their claim for joint leadership with him: "Has the Lord spoken only through Moses? Has He not spoken through us as well?" (12:2).

> Note N–43: Friedman attributes 12:1–3 to E. As yet, Aaron's claim to prophecy finds no support in previous E passages. In Exod. 15:20, however, E refers to "Miriam the prophetess, Aaron's sister."

In exonerating Moses, E now describes him as a "very humble [or meek] man, more so than any other man on earth" (12:3). Then, having "suddenly" called to Moses, Aaron, and Miriam, "Come out you three, to the Tent of Meeting," the Lord "came down in a pillar of cloud." From the entrance of the Tent, He called out "Aaron and Miriam" (12:4–5).

An irate Lord now directs His anger to Aaron and Miriam for claiming a prophetic parity with Moses. "Hear these words: When a prophet of the Lord arises among you, I make myself known to him in a vision, I speak with him in a dream. Not so with My servant Moses: he is trusted throughout My household. With him I speak mouth to mouth, plainly and not in riddles, and he beholds the likeness of the Lord. How then did you not shrink from speaking against My servant Moses!" And so, "still incensed with them, the Lord departed" (12:6–9).

> Note N–44: Here the Lord does speak directly to Aaron and Miriam, but only to remonstrate. On His speaking "mouth to mouth" with Moses, see E's Exod. 33:7–11).

As the cloud signifying the Lord's Presence withdrew from the Tent, "there was Miriam stricken with snow-white scales!" And when Aaron turned to her, he indeed saw "that she was stricken with scales" (12:10).

> *Note N–45: "Scales" come from the Hebrew tzara'at. The "snow-white scales" reminds one of the "leprous" condition of Lev. 13:9–17. For the same offense as Miriam, Aaron suffers no similar condition. And for whatever reason, the "Miriam and Aaron" of 12:1 become the "Aaron and Miriam" of 12:5 (as they are reprimanded by an angry Lord).*

To his credit, Aaron is immediately overcome with compassion for his sister and partner in sin against both the Lord and Moses, as His one true prophet. In pleading with Moses to intercede for their sister, Aaron speaks to him in a manner responsive to the Lord's "lecture." "O my lord, account not to us the sin which we have committed in our folly. Let her not be as one dead, who emerges from her mother's womb with half *his* flesh eaten away" (12:11–12). An ever-forgiving Moses promptly cries out to the Lord, "O God, pray heal her" (12:13).

The Lord is prepared to forgive her, but not with the alacrity sought by Moses. "If her father spat in her face [i.e., if he cursed her for some good reason], would she not bear her shame for seven days. Let her be shut out of camp for seven days, and then let her be readmitted" (12:14). Yet, such was the Lord's concern for Miriam, that He delayed leading the people from Hazeroth toward the "wilderness of Paran" until after the seven days when Miriam was readmitted to the camp (Num. 12:16; cf. Num. 9:17–23).

The Israelites are now encamped in the wilderness of Paran. To the north is the Negeb (or "Negev" today), the southern and least fertile portion of Canaan. Then the Lord spoke to Moses: "Send men to scout the land of Canaan, which I am giving to the Israelite people; send one man from each of the ancestral tribes, each one a *chieftain* among them" (13:1–2). Moses then "sent them out from the wilderness of Paran, all the men being *leaders* of the Israelites" (13:3).

> *Note N–46: Since the Lord would have known what the scouts were sent to learn, the expedition must have been meant to test, or hone, their own scouting skills.*

The name of each (nonlevitical) tribe and of each "man," "chieftain," or "leader" to serve as scouts are listed in 13:4–16. The tribes are listed, however, in a different order from the listings in Num. 2, in regard to their positions around the Tent (see Comment N–3). Here the order is Reuben, Simeon, Judah, Issachar, Ephraim, Benjamin, Zebulun, *Joseph (namely, the tribe of Manasseh)*, Dan, Asher, Naphtali, and Gad. Also listed are the chosen "leaders" from each tribe, together with their fathers. With the exception of Caleb, of the tribe of

Judah and Hosea (renamed Joshua by Moses), of the tribe of Ephraim, neither the sons or fathers are of particular prominence.

> Note N–47: In maintaining twelve tribes, those of Ephraim and Manasseh replace those of Levi and Joseph. Yet only Manasseh, and not Ephraim, is credited to Joseph (see Comments G–94 and 96).

Comment N–13. On the order of the tribal listing and the identity of the tribal "chieftains," or "leaders," chosen to serve as scouts

Friedman attributes Num. 13:1–16 to P, as he does all of Num. 2. There are, however, two noteworthy differences in these passages. The first involves the order of tribal listing; the second involves the tribal leaders, or chieftains, chosen for the separate purposes of Num. 2 and 13.

1. The order of tribal listing in Num. 13:4–16

As to the order of tribal listings in Num. 2, I reached the following conclusion. "In sum, both the external and internal ranking [i.e., among and within the four divisions] of the tribes reflected a balance between the factors of (1) birth order and (2) Jacob's personal evaluations of his sons, *as expressed in his final testament and blessing*" (see Gen. 49:1–27 and Comments G–98 and 99). Clearly, Num. 13:4–16 employs a different principle.

In 13:4–16, the initial listing of Reuben, Simeon, and Judah hints of a birth order principle. These were the first, second, and fourth of Jacob's sons, all born of Leah. (Given its unique status, the tribe of Levi, the third born of Jacob and Leah, is not included here.) However, that Dan, Asher, Naphtali and Gad conclude the list precludes an absolute birth order principle in that Joseph and Benjamin were the youngest of Jacob's sons, born of Rachel.

Accordingly, though birth order remains a major factor in the tribal listing, it is not the sole factor. Instead, precedence is accorded to the sons of Leah and Rachel, as Jacob's wives, over those of Zilpah and Bilhah, his concubines. Thus, the listing ends with Dan (Bilhah), Asher (Zilpah), Naphthali (Bilhah), and Gad (Zilpah). As Tevye might say, "It's no disgrace to be born of a concubine, but neither is it any great honor." But could Tevye also explain (1) why only Manasseh, and not Ephraim, is said to be from the tribe of Joseph and (2) why Ephraim, a son of Joseph, who himself was born after Zebulun, a son of Leah, is listed before Zebulun? And the same can be said of Benjamin, who is also listed before Zebulun (Gen. 30:19–24).

That the order of tribal listing in Num. 13 differs from that of Num. 2 does not suggest that both are not from the same P source. The listing in Num. 2 sought to accommodate birth order to something closer to the "general repute" of the sons of Jacob. Having no such purpose, the listing in Num.

13 reflects the normal importance of birth order, *as accommodated to the status of the mother.*

2. The identity of the "chieftains" or "leaders" of the tribes designated in Num. 13:4–16 to serve as scouts

Whether translated as "leader" or "chieftain," or in some cases as "prince," each *nasee* of P in Num. 13 is a different person than any *nasee* of P in Num. 2 and 13. The similar identification of different persons as such in Num. 13 suggests that they were chosen for their particular skills in different roles.

The displacement of the "princes" of Num. 2 by those of Num. 13 did not result from the mere passage of time. The period between the two chapters is too brief to allow for the *normal* deaths of all twelve tribal leaders. In theory, of course, the "princes" of Num. 2 could have been slain in the Lord's plague that concludes Num. 11 (11:33). But the coincidence seems too great. Another possibility is that having been chosen to serve as scouts, for which they were uniquely well suited, those chosen were given the rank of *nasee*, commensurate with their responsibilities.

Moses' instructions to the scouts covered a broad range of military and agricultural intelligence on "the Negeb" and "the hill country" to the north (13:17). "See what kind of country it is. Are the people . . . strong or weak, few or many? Is the country . . . good or bad? Are the towns . . . open or fortified? Is the soil rich or poor? Is it wooded or not? And take pains to bring back some of the fruit of the land." (Here an unknown narrator notes that "now it happened to be the season of the first ripe grapes" (13:18–20).

As stated by P in Num. 13:21, the scouts went "from the wilderness of Zin to Rehob, at Lebohamath"—thus covering a route from south of Canaan in the Negev to the vicinity of what is now Mount Herman in the far north.

Num. 13:22–24, however, describes a different route of the scouts and in greater detail. "They went up into the Negeb and came to Hebron, where lived Ahiman, Sheshai, and Talmai, the Anakites." (Here J, the story teller, permits himself another historical "aside": "Now Hebron was founded seven years before Zoan of Egypt" [13:22]). Near Hebron, they reached a place they called "the wadi Eschol [or valley of the cluster (of grapes)]." There, they cut down "a branch with a single cluster of grapes." It was so large that "it had to be borne on a carrying frame by two of them—and some pomegranates and figs."

On returning after forty days, the scouts reported to Moses and Aaron and the whole Israelite community at "Kadesh in the wilderness of Paran" (13:26). On showing them "the fruit of the land," they also told of their serious forebodings (13:26–28).

"We came to the land you sent us to; it does indeed flow with milk and

honey, and this is its fruit. *However, the people who inhabit the country are pow-*
erful, and the cities are fortified and very large; moreover, we saw the Anakites there.
Amalekites dwell in the Negeb; Hittites, Jebusites, and Amorites inhabit the hill
country; and Canaanites dwell by the Sea and along the Jordan" (13:29).

> Note N–48: *The site of the scouts' reports is given as "Kadesh in the wilder-*
> *ness of Paran" (13:26). As do many maps of the general area, R will also*
> *place Kadesh in the wilderness of Zin (Num. 33:36).*

Of all the scouts, only Caleb of the tribe of Judah speaks confidently of the
Israelites' ability to defeat their foes. "Let us by all means go up, and we shall
gain possession of it, for we shall surely overcome it" (13:30). But the other
scouts are quick to embellish the basis of their fears. "We cannot attack that
people, for it is stronger than we. . . . The country that we traversed is one that
devours its settlers. All the people we saw in it are men of great size; *we saw the*
Nephilim there—the Anakites are part of the Nephilim—and we looked like
grasshoppers to ourselves, and so we must have looked to them" (13:31). But the
narrator condemns their fears as "calumnies" (13:32).

Comment N–14. On the report of the scouts from Canaan

That only Caleb, the *Judahite*, remains confident might suggest the work of
J or P, between whom Friedman divides the whole of Num. 13. In general, the
other scouts describe the people of Canaan as "powerful" and of "great
size," whose cities were "fortified and very large." It was to these already
formidable defenders and defenses that the scouts added the Anakites.
"*Moreover*, we saw the Anakites there." Describing themselves as "grasshoppers" in the presence of the Anakites, the scouts went on to claim that the
Anakites were "part of the Nephilim"—thus raising fears of confrontations
with the superhuman powers of "divine beings" (see Gen. 6:4 and Comment
G–12).

Most notable among the wholly human tribes of Canaan (including the
Hittites, Jebusites, Amorites, and Canaanites) were the fierce Amalekites with
whom "the Lord will be at war [forever]" (see Exod. 17:8–16 and Comment
E–51).

Here, however, the Amalekites are included as part of a more "objective" effort to identify the tribes of Canaan. The battle with the Amalekites
in Exod. 17 likely comes from E. If so, neither J nor P would *necessarily* have
known of Amalekite fighting prowess, as revealed in the battle. But quite
apart from Torah authorship, the Amalekites were a people to be taken seriously. They included an impressive configuration of tribes who cut a wide
swath throughout the near east.[8]

Num. 14 first tells of the great fear and despair that the report of the scouts (other than Caleb) aroused in the people. The "whole community broke into loud cries" and "the people wept" (14:1). "All the Israelites" railed against both Moses and Aaron. "If only we had died in the land of Egypt . . . or if only we might die in this wilderness" (14:2). They wonder why the Lord should take them "to *that land* to fall by the sword." They envision their "wives and children" being "carried off" and cry out that "it would be better for us to go back to Egypt" (14:3).

The people were not the only ones to despair. "Moses and Aaron fell on their faces before all the assembled congregation of the Israelites" (14:5). "Of those who had scouted the land," however, "Joshua son of Nun and Caleb son of Jephunneh, rent their clothes and exhorted the whole Israelite community: 'The land we traversed and scouted is an exceedingly good land. *If the Lord is pleased with us* He will bring us into that land, a land that flows with milk and honey, and give it to us; only you must not rebel against the Lord. Have no fear then of the people of the country, for they are our prey: their protection has departed from them, but the Lord is with us. Have no fear of them!' " (14:6–9).

"As the whole community threatened to pelt [Caleb and Joshua] with stones, the Presence of the Lord appeared in the Tent of Meeting to all the Israelites" (14:10).

> Note N–49: *Most striking here is the despair of Moses and Aaron as compared to the stalwart confidence of Joshua and Caleb. Has the time come for younger leadership? Also noteworthy is the coupling of Joshua with Caleb in 14:6, as compared to Caleb's lone and unsupported stance in 13:30. Friedman assigns 13:30 to J and 14:6 to P.*

An unhappy Lord then speaks to Moses. "How long will this people spurn Me, and how long will they have no faith in Me despite all the signs I have performed in their midst? I will strike them with pestilence and disown them, and I will make *of you* a nation far more numerous than they" (14:11–12).

Much as he had in the wake of the golden calf, when the Lord threatened Israel's extinction, Moses again puts His knowledge of the Lord to good use with a similar argument. "When the Egyptians hear the news [of the Lord's destruction of the Israelites] . . . they will tell it to the inhabitants of that land. Now they have heard that You, O Lord, are in the midst of this people . . . that you appear in *plain sight* when your cloud rests over them. . . . If you then slay this people *to a man*, the nations who have heard Your fame will say, 'It must be because the Lord was powerless to bring that people into the land which He had promised them on oath that He slaughtered them in the wilderness' " (14:13–16).

Note N–50: As to (1) the Lord's threatened extinction of Israel, (2) His intent to make a new nation of Moses, (3) Moses' successful rhetorical appeal to the Lord's pride, and (4) the Lord's acquiesence, Friedman's J passage of Num. 14:11–20 tracks almost precisely his E passage of Exod. 32:9–14. Taking his attributions as correct, a broad tradition surely existed regarding such an episode between the Lord and Moses (see Comment E–88).

Note N–51: In Num. 14:14, from the Hebrew ahyin b'ahyin *(literally "eye to eye"), JPS2 has Moses speak of the Lord's appearance to the people in "plain sight when Your cloud rests over them." But in JPS1 and RSV his words are "face to face," the same term that both use in a literal rendering of E's* pahneem el pahneem *in Exod. 33:11. Whether J posits* ahyin b'ahyin, *or "eye to eye," as equivalent to the Lord's appearance to Abraham at Mamre, or as reflecting the Lord's appearance within the cloud is not clear. (See Comment G–29, Exod. 33:1–11, and Comments E–91 and E–92.)*

Moses now appeals to the Lord's mercy as well as His pride. "Therefore, I pray, let my Lord's forbearance be great, as You have declared, saying, 'The Lord! slow to anger and abounding in kindness; forgive iniquity and transgression; *yet not remitting all punishment....* Pardon, I pray, the iniquity of this people according to Your great kindness, as You have forgiven this people ever since Egypt" (14:17–19).

The Lord's answer in 14:20–25 is less than responsive to Moses' plea: "I pardon, as you have asked. *Nevertheless...* none of the men [who have seen my Presence and my signs in Egypt and the wilderness] and who have tried Me these many times and disobeyed Me, shall see the land that I promised on oath to their fathers.... But My servant Caleb, because he was imbued with a different spirit and remained loyal to Me—him will I bring into the land which he entered, and his offspring shall hold it as a possession. Now the Amalekites and the Canaanites occupy the valleys. Start out, then tomorrow and march into the wilderness by way of the Sea of Reeds."

Note N–52: Where is the yam soof, *or "Sea of Reeds," of Num. 14:25? The term was first used by E in Exod. 13:18 to identify the body of water encountered by the Israelites shortly after leaving Egypt. Now the term appears again in J's Num. 14:25. (More traditional translations speak of the "Red Sea.") From the* yam soof(s) *of Exodus 13:18 and 15:22a they went to Sinai and from there to the wilderness of Shur. Now in Num. 14:25, they have moved east to the wilderness of Paran, south or southwest of the Negeb and Canaan. (See Num. 10:11–12 and 12:16, ascribed in turn by Friedman to P and E.) J, however, does not yet so locate the Israelites.*

Although in Num. 14:25 the Lord directs the Israelites to march "into the wilderness by way of the Sea of Reeds," He would not likely direct them back to a body of water in the far western Sinai. Friedman in fact attributes the two earlier references to the "Sea of Reeds" to E and R, while Num. 14:25 concludes a J passage. R (or possibly J) will also refer again to yam soof in 21:4a as part of their southerly route "to skirt the land of Edom." Clearly, the yam soof of 21:4a is the Gulf of Aqaba, an arm of the Red Sea to modern Elath. Note that derech yam soof, or "by way of the Sea of Reeds" appears both in 14:25 and 21:4a.

After wandering in the vicinity for thirty-eight years, the people will return to Kadesh in the wilderness of Zin (20:1). Zin, also south of Canaan, in or near the Negev, lies northeast of Paran. Between 14:25 and 20:1, however, nothing will be said of the route of their wanderings. Nevertheless, whether the derech yam soof of 21:4a is by J or R, the yam soof of Num. 14:25 is more likely the yam soof of 21:4a than it is the "jumping off" sites of Exod. 13:18 and 15:22a. (In time, Num. 33:35–36 may provide our answer.)

Comment N–15. On who is to "see" the promised land according to Num. 14:20–25 and Joshua and the J source

Who of the generation of adults who left Egypt will live to "see" and "enter" the promised land is as yet uncertain (see Num. 14:20–25). In 14:24 it is Caleb, and only Caleb. What, then, of Moses and Aaron, whom the Lord does not except by name. Does He regard them less deserving than Caleb? Their story must yet unfold.

And what of Joshua? In 14:24 J does not except Joshua as he does Caleb. Yet in 14:30 P excepts them both. These follow the same pattern established by J in 13:30 and P in 14:6. Whether Joshua's destiny will be settled by J or P is yet to be revealed. In any case, as to Moses and Aaron, P provides no more solace than J.

Of particular interest, however, is the absence of Joshua in any Torah passage that Friedman attributes to J. Was it possible that when J wrote (c. 900 B.C.E.) nothing was yet known of Joshua (c.1300 B.C.E.)? This was Joshua, the conqueror of Canaan, whose name in time would grace the sixth book of the Hebrew Bible! Or is it possible that Joshua was a later creation known only to E, D, and P, and that the "Deuteronomic" history of the early prophets was largely fiction, created by later authors? Joshua's absence in J is inadequate in itself to make the case, but not to pose a question.

Speaking further to Moses and Aaron, the Lord again decries "the incessant muttering of the Israelites against Me" (14:26–27).

Note N–53: Possibly in part because of Aaron's presence as an auditor, Friedman attributes 14:26–39 to P.

"As I live . . . I will do to you just as you have urged Me. In this very wilderness your carcasses shall drop." Of all those recorded in the census of Israelites "over twenty" (see Num. 1), "not one shall enter the land in which I swore to settle you—save Caleb son of Jephunneh and Joshua son of Nun" (14:28–30). (See Comment N–15.)

The Lord continues to reveal how the treatment of those less than twenty years of age will differ from that of their parents. "Your children . . . will I allow to enter; they shall know the land *that you have rejected.* But your carcasses shall drop in this wilderness, while your children roam the wilderness for forty years, suffering for your faithlessness, until the last of your carcasses is down in the wilderness" (14:31–33).

The Lord then explains why the wandering must continue for forty years. "You shall bear your punishment for forty years corresponding to the number of days—forty days—that you scouted the land: a year for each day" (14:34). And why must it be a year for each day? "Thus shall you know what it means to thwart me" (14:34). Referring then to the "wicked band that has banded against Me," the Lord again tells the people that "in this very wilderness they shall die to the last man" (14:35). The narrator then observes that all the scouts other than Caleb and Joshua "died of plague, by the will of the Lord" (14:36–38).

Comment N–16. On the Lord's complaint that the Israelites had "thwarted" Him

Consider the text of 14:34 as rendered by JPS2: "Thus you shall know what it means to thwart Me." But why would P, of all sources, vest the Israelites with power to thwart the Lord. In contrast, for example, from the Hebrew *t'nuatee*, JPS1 and RSV both derive "[you shall know] *My displeasure.*" The JPS2 editors explain the change as follows: "See Luzzato, and R. Loewe, pp. 137–58 in the C. D. Winton Jubilee Volume (1968). Trad., 'My displeasure.' "[9]

Whatever else might justify JPS2's reading of *t'nuatee* as "thwart," the idea of the people thwarting the Lord in 14:34 seems well suited to the circumstances. The question it raises on the limits of divine power recalls the Lord's revelation to Moses in Exod. 12:12 that He would "mete out punishments to [or execute judgments on] all the gods of Egypt" (12:12). In Rashi's view, the resulting destruction of the idols of the Egyptian gods could "thwart" (my word) their very existence through loss of their sole abodes in the minds of the newly disillusioned Egyptians.

Could the "thwarting" of the Lord in Num. 14:34 terminate His existence in the same way that Rashi would have disbelief terminate the existence of Egypt's gods (see Comment E–34)? As the source of both verses, P would reject the thought at once as incompatible with the Lord's independent existence, apart from any need for human belief. While the existence of His "volitional" role as God of Israel could end with Israel's disbelief, His existence, and His power, as Lord of the Universe remains unaffected. For P above all, Israel might thwart the Lord as its God, but never as the Lord (see Comments L–43 and 45).

On hearing the Lord's judgment from Moses, "the people were overcome with grief" (14:38). The next morning, conceding that "we were wrong," the people declared their intent "to go up to the place that the Lord has spoken of." But Moses asks why they mean to "transgress the Lord's command" (14:41). He assures them that they "will not succeed . . . for the Lord is not in your midst" (14:42). In particular, "the Amalekites and the Canaanites will be there to face you, and you will fall by the sword, inasmuch as you have turned from the Lord and the Lord will not be with you" (14:43).

> *Note N–54: Here Moses refers to violations of two prior commands, one denying entry into Canaan to the entire adult generation that had left Egypt (14:20–23), the other telling the people to "march into the wilderness by way of the Sea of Reeds" (14:25).*

Ignoring Moses, and with neither him nor "the Lord's Ark of the Covenant" in their midst, they marched "to the crest of the hill country" (14:44). There, "the Amalekites and the Canaanites . . . came down and dealt them a shattering blow at Hormah" (14:45).

> *Note N–55: Num. 15 turns abruptly from narrative to rituals, many of which repeat or embellish earlier commands. Friedman attributes 15:1–31, not to a primary source, but to R. He attributes the balance (15:32–41) to P.*

The focus of Num. 15:1–12 is on an added meal offering to accompany "any offering by fire to the Lord from the herd or from the flock, be it burnt offering or sacrifice, in fullfillment of a vow explicitly uttered, or as a freewill offering or sacrifice, or at your fixed occasions, producing an odor pleasing to the Lord." The requirement, however, was not to become effective until "you enter the land which I am giving you to settle in" (15:2–3).

> *Note N–56: In being deferred to the "promised land," the "supplemental" meal offerings of Num. 15:1–12 differ from the Levitical offerings of Lev. 1:1–2, 2:1, 3:1; 6, 7, and 8. As to those, the Lord says nothing to delay implementation.*

In every case the added meal offering consisted of "a measure of choice flour" with a portion of "a hin of oil mixed in." Added as a "libation" was a portion of "a hin of wine." The amounts of flour, oil, and wine also varied with the value of the type of animal offered: for *sheep*—choice flour, a tenth of a measure; oil, a quarter of a hin; and wine, a quarter of a hin: for *rams*—choice flour, two-tenths of a measure; oil, a third of a hin; and wine, a third of a hin; and for *animals of "the herd"*—choice flour, three-tenths of a measure; oil, a half of a hin; and wine, a half of a hin (15:4–10).

The passage then concludes: "Thus shall be done with each ox, . . . ram, and . . . sheep or goat, as many as you offer; you shall do thus with each one, as many as there are. Every citizen, when presenting *an offering by fire of pleasing odor to the Lord*, shall do so with them" (15:11–13).

> Note N–57: Literally, *the italicized limitation would seem to exclude many, or all, of the atonement offerings of Lev. 4 and 5.*

Num. 15:14–16 deals with offerings "of pleasing odor to the Lord" by "a stranger who has taken up residence with you, or one who live among you." Why? "There shall be one law for you and the resident stranger . . . throughout the ages. *You and the stranger shall be alike before the Lord*; the same ritual and the same rule shall apply to [both]."

> Note N–58: Regarding the rights and duties of "strangers" see Lev. 17:8–10, 19:34, 24:15–22, and Comments L–42 and 57.

Like the meal offering rules of 15:2–16, those on the "first yield" of bread are not to apply until "you enter the land to which I am taking you" (15:17–21). One specific requirement is that "as the first yield of your baking, you shall set aside a loaf as a gift" (15:20). The people are then commanded to make this gift to the Lord "from the first yield of your baking, throughout the ages" (15:21).

> Note N–59: The Hebrew word for the "loaf" to be set aside is chalah, which today enjoys a quasi-ritualistic status.

Num. 15:22–31 returns to "unwitting" sins: "If you unwittingly fail to observe any one of the commandments which the Lord has declared to Moses— *anything* that the Lord has enjoined upon you through Moses—*from the day that the Lord gave the commandment* and on through the ages." Here, two types of unwitting sins are identified and subjected to separate rituals: those involving "inadvertence of the community" (15:24–26) and those involving "an individual who has sinned unwittingly" (15:27–31).

The protocols of expiation for unwitting sins involving the "inadvertence of the community" required the following offerings: "one bull . . . as a burnt offering of pleasing odor to the Lord, with its proper meal offering, and one he-goat as a sin offering" (15:24). Those for the "individual who has sinned unwittingly" required but a "she-goat in its first year as a sin offering" (15:27).

When the priest made the proper offerings "in expiation before the Lord," forgiveness was granted, to "the whole Israelite community and the stranger" alike (15:26). And so, too, with unwitting individual sins, for which "you shall have one ritual for anyone who acts in error" (15:29).

Comment N–17. On the relationship of the "unwitting" sins of Num. 15:22–31 to those of Lev. 4

The protocols of expiation for these unwitting "sins" of Num. 15 recall those of Lev. 4. In particular, the first category involving the "inadvertence of the community" (15:24–26) looks back to Lev. 4:13–21, in which "the whole community of Israel . . . has erred." The second category, involving "an individual who has sinned unwittingly," looks back to Lev. 4:27–35, in which "any person from among the populace unwittingly incurs guilt."

While the two sets of commands overlap, they also differ. Lev. 4 is limited to the unwitting commission of prohibited acts (i.e., "when a person unwillingly incurs guilt in regard to any of the Lord's commandments *about things not to be done*, and does one of them" [Lev. 4:2]). (Literally, at least, Lev. 4, does not cover affirmative commands, such as a failure to "Honor thy father and mother." Num. 15, however, covers sins of omission as well as commission (15:22–23).

As to procedures and offerings, the expiation rituals of Num. 15 differ from those for corresponding categories in Lev. 4 (cf. Num. 15:24–26 with Lev. 4:13–21, and Num. 15:27–29 with Lev. 4:27–35). In addition, Num. 15 omits the two categories of unwitting sins of an "anointed priest" and a "chieftain" (see Lev. 4:3–12, 22–26). (Comment L–10 compares the unwitting sins of Lev. 4 and 5.)

As stated in Note N–55, Friedman attributes Num. 15:1–31 to R. Noting the complete absence of the Levitical Tabernacle in Num. 15, Friedman suggests that R adapted the commands to prevailing practices during the Second (or post-exilic) Temple, dating from c. 516 B.C.E.[10]

The subject closes with a dramatic characterization and condemnation of especially spiteful violations of a Lordly command. "But the person, be he citizen or stranger, who acts *defiantly* [and] *reviles* the Lord; that person shall be cut off from among his people. Because he has spurned the word of the Lord and violated His commandment, that person shall be cut off—he bears his guilt" (15:30–31).

Num. 15:32–36 tells of a wilderness enforcement of the Lord's earlier decree of death for anyone who violated the sanctity of sabbath by work. (See Exod. 31:14–15.)

Once, in the wilderness, "the Israelites . . . came upon a man gathering wood on the sabbath day." He was brought before "Moses, Aaron, and the whole community." He was then placed in custody, *for it had not been specified what should be done to him.*" The Lord then spoke to Moses. "The man shall be put to death: the whole community shall pelt him with stones outside the camp." And so they did, "as the Lord had commanded Moses."

> Note N–60: *Having previously prescribed death for work on sabbath (Exod. 31:14–15), P now specifies at least one method.*

Num. 15:37–40 prescribes a mnemomic device. In it the Lord commands the Israelites to "make for themselves *fringes on the corner of their garments* through out the ages, let them attach a cord of blue to the fringe at each corner." Each fringe (or *tzitzit*) would serve as a memory aid: "look at it and recall all the commandments of the Lord and observe them. . . . Thus you shall be reminded to observe all My commandments and to be holy to your God."

As to the source of authority and enforcement, Israel is again reminded: "I the Lord am your God, who brought you out of the land of Egypt to be your God; I the Lord, your God" (15:41).

> Note N–61: *The fears of the people had led them to defy the Lord's command and Moses' sound counsel. Their wilfulness then brings them to a "shattering" defeat by the Amalekites and Canaanites (14:39–45). Their morale is so low as to encourage the ensuing revolts of Num. 16.*

In Num. 16, two revolts occur under four leaders. One is led by Korah, son of Izar son of Kohath son of Levi; the other by Dathan and Abiram, sons of Eliab and On, son of Peleth—descendants of Reuben. Included among them were "two hundred and fifty Israelites, chieftains of the community, men of repute" (16:2). "They combined forces against Moses *and* Aaron and said to them, 'You have gone too far! *For all the community are holy*, all of them, and the Lord is in their midst. *Why then do you raise yourself above the Lord's congregation?*" (16:3).

> Note N–62: *The revolts of the Levites under Korah against Aaron and of the Reubenites under Dathan and Abiram against Moses are separate. Here, however, the two groups combine their complaints. We might think that the two hundred fifty chieftains would have been more concerned with Moses' "governmental" role than with Aaron's priestly role. But events will show them to be a part of Korah's revolt.*

On hearing the complaint, a despairing Moses "fell on his face" (16:4). He then proposes to "Korah and his company" that they leave the matter to the Lord. "Come morning, the Lord will make known who is His and who is holy, and will grant him access to Himself; He will grant access to the one He has chosen" (16:5).

> Note N–63: Moses' words might seem to refer to his own prophetic based leadership rather than Aaron's priestly monopoly. But he goes on.

"Do this: You, Korah, and all your band, take fire pans, and tomorrow put fire in them and lay incense on them before the Lord. Then the man whom the Lord chooses, he shall be the holy one. You have gone too far, *sons of Levi*" (16:6–7).

> Note N–64: Moses speaks only to "Korah, and all your band . . . sons of Levi." Thus, P portrays the revolt against the Aaronide priesthood as Moses' first concern.

"Hear me, sons of Levi. Is it not enough for you that the God of Israel has set you apart from the community of Israel and given you access to Him, to perform the duties of the Lord's Tabernacle, and to minister to the community and serve them? Thus He has advanced you and all your fellow Levites with you; yet you seek the priesthood too! Truly it is against the Lord that you and all your company have banded together. For who is Aaron that you should rail against him" (16:8–11).

The story then turns to Dathan and Abiram. (No more is said of On, the third Reubenite.) When Moses sends for Dathan and Abiram, they reject his authority to summon them. "We will not come! Is it not enough that you brought us from a land flowing with milk and honey to have us die in the wilderness, that you would also lord it over us? Even if you had brought us to a land flowing with milk and honey, and given us possession of fields and vineyards, should you gouge out those men's eyes? We will not come" (16:12–14).

> Note N–65: Thus, the essence of Dathan's and Abiram's charge against Moses is that of "lord[ing] it over us."

As implied in his words to the Lord, an "aggrieved" Moses interprets the charges against him as those of venality and injustice (16:15). "Pay no regard to their oblation [or "offering" (*minchatam*)]. I have not taken the ass of any of them nor have I wronged any of them" (16:15).

In Num. 16:16–17 Moses speaks again to Korah of the test of firepans (see 16:5–7). "Tomorrow, you and all your company appear before the Lord, you and they and Aaron." Each is to place incense in his fire pan and bring it before the Lord, "two hundred and fifty pans." Korah and Aaron are also to bring their fire pans.

> Note N–66: Given the count of fire pans, "all your company" in 16:11 refers to the two hundred and fifty "chieftains of the community." It does not include Dathan or Abiram, the Reubenites.

At the appointed time, "each of them took his fire pan, put fire in it, laid incense on it, and took his place at the entrance of the Tent of Meeting, as did Moses and Aaron" (16:18). Also, at the entrance of the Tent, "Korah gathered the whole community against them" (16:19).

Now the Presence of a wrathful Lord "appeared to the whole community." There will be no test. He means to destroy "the whole community" at once, other than Moses and Aaron. To that end He says: "Stand back from this community that I may annihilate them in an instant!" (16:21).

> Note N–67: The Lord apparently views the community's presence as proof of their support of Korah. He makes no allowance for curiosity or concern. Thus, the first impulse of P's Lord God continues to be that of total annihilation.

Stunned by the imminence of their mass annihilation, the people seek to avert the decree. They "fall on their faces" and remind the Lord of the value of life, as He has taught them. "O God, Source of the breath of all flesh! When one man sins, will you be wrathful with the whole community?" (16:22). The Lord then repents and annuls His first impulse. He instructs Moses to tell the community to "withdraw from the abodes of Korah, Dathan, and Abiram" (16:23–24).

Then "Moses rose and went to Dathan and Abiram, the elders of Israel following them" (16:25). He speaks to the community: "Move away from the tents of these wicked men and touch nothing that belongs to them, lest you be wiped out for their sins" (16:26). And so, "they withdrew from about the abodes of Korah, Dathan and Abiram" (16:27).

> Note N–68: The appearance of Dathan and Abiram in 16:24, 25, and 27 now intrudes on the story of Korah. See Comment N–18, which considers the structure of Num. 16.

Although 16:27a speaks of the abodes of "Korah, Dathan and Abiram," in 16:27b only "Dathan and Abiram" come out to stand at the entrance of their tents, "with their wives, their children, and their little ones." And Moses tells only Dathan, Abiram, and their families how the Lord will reveal His judgment in their revolt against Moses.

"By this you shall know it was the Lord who sent me to do all these things;

that they are not of my own devising: if these men die as all men do, if their lot be the common fate of all mankind, it was not the Lord who sent me. But if the Lord brings about something unheard-of, so that the ground opens its mouth wide and swallows them up with all that belongs to them, and they go down *alive* into Sheol, you shall know that these men have spurned the Lord" (16:28–30).

> Note N–69: *Friedman attributes this passage and two earlier references to "Sheol" to J (see Comment G–83). Jacob spoke of Sheol as the destiny of all dead souls (Gen. 37:35, 42:38). In Num. 16:30, however, those who spurn the Lord's authority descend into Sheol alive.*

When He had "scarcely finished speaking . . . the ground under [Dathan and Abiram] opened its mouth and swallowed them up *with their households, all Korah's people* and all their possessions. They went down *alive* into Sheol, with all that belonged to them" (16:32–33). Fearful that "the earth might swallow us," all Israel fled at their shrieks (16:34).

> Note N–70: *Korah is not mentioned from 16:27a to 16:32b, in which "all Korah's" people are "swallowed" into the earth. Apart from his "people," Korah's own fate seems unclear.*

The Lord's final act is to "consume" by "fire" the two hundred fifty chieftains who followed Korah and came to offer incense in the fire pans (16:35).

Comment N–18. On the integration in Num. 16 of two stories of separate revolts against Moses and Aaron

What would later become Num. 16 of the Torah was shaped by R to combine separate passages by J and P into a single, integrated narrative. In the two Creation stories of P and J, R was also confronted with two distinctive stories, each with a unique perspective. To preserve the distinctive character of each, R chose to combine them through an early version of "separate but equal." The stories were told successively, first one, then the other. The full power of each was retained and their "integration" was left to posterity.

Not so, however, with Noah and the Flood. In that the complete separation of J and P was precluded by too many common elements, both of plot and characters. Accordingly, the stories were integrated into one, despite such anomalies as two sets of animals in twos and sevens.

Because Num. 16 seeks to integrate two stories of two different events, it differs from both Creation and the Flood, each of which deals with the same event. While the common theme of revolt provides a unity that justifies the format of Num. 16, the fact of different characters and objectives could also justify separate stories.

In the end, R may have concluded that the people's growing frustration and discontent could best be dramatized in a single integrated episode of revolt against all early aspects of Godly authority.

Friedman attributes Korah's Levitical revolt against Aaron, as priest, to P, and Dathan's and Abiram's Reubenite revolt against Moses to J. P's enduring concern throughout the Torah has been to validate the unique status of Aaron and his sons as the Lord's solely anointed priests. To challenge their status is to challenge the Lord. In turn, J's loyalty to the southern tribe of Judah over the northern tribe of Reuben finds expression in its disastrous revolt (see, e.g., Comment G–73).

In attributing Korah's revolt to P and the Dathan and Abiram revolt to J, Friedman attributes two important integrative verses to R: 16:24 and 27.[11]

The episode of the revolts concludes in Num. 17:1–15. Through Moses, the Lord directs Aaron's son, the priest Eleazer, to remove the newly sacred firepans "from among the charred ruins." The fire pans of "those who have sinned at the cost of their lives [i.e., the two hundred fifty community chieftains]" were to be made into "hammered sheets as plating for the altar." Eleazer did so. It was the Lord's intent that the plating serve as a "reminder to the Israelites, so that no outsider—one not of Aaron's offspring—should presume to offer incense before the Lord and suffer the fate of Korah and his band" (17:1–5).

> Note N–71: This reference to "the fate of Korah," as an individual, resolves the odd silence in 16:32 regarding Korah's personal fate.

But the peoples' discontent remained. The next day "the *whole Israelite community* railed against Moses and Aaron, saying 'You have brought death upon the Lord's people' " (17:6). As the community "gathered against" Moses and Aaron, the Presence of the Lord appeared in a cloud at the Tent of Meeting (17:7). He does not take kindly to the identification of those whom He had killed as His "people." When Aaron and Moses reach the Tent, the Lord tells them to "remove yourselves from this community, that I might annihilate them *in an instant*." Once again, they fall on their faces in despair for the fate of the people (17:8–10).

As a compassionate leader, Moses knows of despair. But rather than succumbing to it in the pending crisis, He moves at once to avert or minimize the annihilation of his people. He tells Aaron, "Take the fire pan, and put on it fire from the altar. Add incense and take it quickly to the community and make expiation for them. For wrath has gone forth from the Lord: the plague has begun" (17:11). Aaron does so. He runs to "the midst of the congregation, where the plague had begun." He then stands between the dead and the living until the plague is checked, at which point he returns to Moses at the entrance of the

Tent of Meeting. Rather than the annihilation of the "whole community," the dead numbered "fourteen thousand and seven hundred, aside from those who died on account of Korah" (17:12–15).

Comment N–19. On the courage and compassion of Moses and Aaron in averting the annihilation of the whole community

The death of fourteen thousand seven hundred Israelites attests to the seriousness of the Lord's stated intent to "annihilate [this community]" (17:10). Refusing to remove themselves, as commanded by the Lord, Moses, and Aaron (on Moses' initiative) stay with their people. Moses then contrives, and Aaron implements, an ad hoc protocol of expiation that includes none of the usual sacrifices and offerings, which time would not permit in any case. *It is a moment of high courage, in which Moses, with Aaron's help, places a priority on human life over obedience to the Lord.*

What accounts for his success over an omnipotent Lord who has already embarked on His deadly course? It is as if the Lord had anticipated some response by Moses in defense of his people. He could have completed the annihilation "in an instant." Instead, He paused—as if to give Moses time to respond, despite His command to "remove yourselves." Here, Aaron, as well as Moses, had confronted the Lord and prevailed. It was a victory of the human spirit over the Lord's destructive wrath.

> Note N–72: *Korah, for rising against Aaron, and Dathan and Abiram, for rising against Moses, suffered the Torah's more usual consequences for denying the authority of its God. Yet, in less threatening times, their questions were those that thoughtful and responsible human beings might well ask of their leaders. And even here, if they were sincere in questioning the legitimacy and quality of Moses' and Aaron's leadership, they deserved a better fate. Yet, the form and manner of their questions also suggest that sheer jealousy may have outweighed any legitimate concerns. If so, Korah, Dathan, and Abiram may have deserved their fate. But as always, there is the troubling question of their families.*

The Lord now acts to erase any doubt as to His chosen priest for all the tribes. Moses is to take "from the chieftains of their ancestral houses—one staff for each chieftain . . . *twelve staffs in all*" (17:17a) The Lord then tells Moses, "Inscribe each man's name on his staff, there being one staff for each head of an ancestral house; *also* inscribe Aaron's name on the staff of Levi" (17:17b–18).

> Note N–73: *The passage speaks of "twelve staffs in all." But what tribes do the twelve include? It might be inferred from 17b–18 that the "twelve staffs" include that of the tribe of Levi, on whose Aaron's name is to be inscribed.*

But given the tribes of Ephraim and Manasseh as "successors" of Joseph, there are already twelve tribes (and staffs), excluding the tribe of Levi (see Num. 1:10, 32–34; 7:48, 54). By reading the vau of 17:18 as "also" rather than "and" (as in JPS1/RSV), JPS2 properly seeks to emphasize the separation of Aaron's staff from the others (17:17–18).

Moses is then told to "deposit [the staffs] in the Tent of Meeting before the Pact, where I meet with you" (17:19). And now the Lord reveals His sign: "The staff of the man whom I choose shall sprout, and I will rid Myself of the incessant muttering of the Israelites against you" (17:20).

Accordingly, the chieftains gave Moses "a staff for each chieftain of an ancestral house, *twelve staffs in all; among these staffs was that of Aaron*" (17:21). As directed by the Lord, Moses placed them in the Tent.

Note N–74: While the ambiguity of "among these staffs" cannot be fully erased, the simple fact is that Aaron, as the priest of Israel, was not "chieftain" of the tribe of Levi. From the chieftains of the "secular" tribes there were "twelve staffs in all." Thus Aaron's was necessarily the thirteenth.

As directed by the Lord, Moses then "put Aaron's staff back before the Pact, as a lesson to rebels, so that their muttering against Me may cease, lest they die" (17:25–26). But now, as the people remain around the Tent, they look on it more as a site of death than of the Lord's Presence. To Moses they cry out, "Lo, we perish! We are lost, all of us lost. Everyone who so much as ventures near the Lord's Tabernacle must die. Alas, we are doomed to perish!"(17:28).

Note N–75: The line of Aaron has prevailed against all challenges. Accordingly, in Num. 18, to Aaron alone, P's Lord speaks on the duties and perquisites of both the priests and the Levites, who will assist them.

The Lord first speaks of priestly responsibilities: "*You and your sons and the ancestral house under your charge shall bear any guilt connected with the sanctuary; you and your sons alone shall bear any guilt connected with your priesthood* (Num. 18:1). You shall associate with yourself your kinsmen, the tribe of Levi, your ancestral tribe, to be attached to you and to minister to you and to your sons under your charge before the Tent of Pact . . . but they must not have any contact with the furnishings of the Shrine or with the altar, lest both they and you die" (18:2–3).

Comment N–20. On the responsibility of the priests for the conduct of the Levites within the Tabernacle

Should Levite workers actually make "contact" with the "furnishings of the Shrine or altar," both they and the priests were to die (18:3). But broader than this specific warning is the general charge of 18:1 to Aaron: "You with your sons and the ancestral house under your charge shall bear *any guilt connected with the sanctuary.*" Literally, this would seem to contradict the provisions of Num. 4:18–20. There it is said that if hapless Levite workers merely "*witness* the dismantling of the sanctuary," they, but only they, must die. The passage says nothing of the punishment of priests for "guilt connected with the sanctuary" (see Num. 4:18–20 and Comment N–5).

Lest "wrath . . . again strike the Israelites," the Lord warns Aaron not to allow "outsiders" to "intrude" into duties "connected with the Shrine and altar" (18:4–5).

> Note N–76: *This warning is limited to duties relating to the "Shrine and altar," as assigned to the Kohathites (Num. 3:31). "Outsiders," therefore, might well include the Gershonites (3:25–26) and Merarites (3:36–37) whose duties as Levites did not extend to the Shrine and altar.*

The Lord again tells Aaron that his "fellow Levites from among the Israelites . . . are assigned to you in dedication to the Lord, to do the work of the Tent of Meeting." As for Aaron and his sons (who are also under his charge), the Lord states, "I make your priesthood a service of dedication; *any outsider who encroaches shall be put to death*" (18:6–7).

Having defined the scope of priestly responsibilities, the Lord now turns to their perquisites. What they lack in secular sources of sustenance, shall be made up through sacred offerings. Thus, the Lord tells Aaron, "I hereby give you charge of My gifts, all the sacred donations of the Israelites; I grant them to you and to your sons as a perquisite, a due for all time" (18:8). From among "the holy sacrifices, the offerings by fire," Aaron and his sons are to be allotted "every meal offering, sin offering, and penalty offering of theirs" (18:9). These were "sacred donations." As such, they were "consecrated" for consumption by "males" only (18:10). However, "daughters that are with you" (i.e., unmarried "daughters" of the household), like sons, could eat of the "heave offerings of their gifts, all the wave offerings of the Israelites." Indeed, "as a due for all time; *everyone of your household* who is [ritually] clean may eat of it" (18:11).

> Note N–77: *In referring to "everyone of your household," 18:11 finally allows the wives and mothers of priestly households, who were omitted in Lev. 10:12–15, to eat of these offerings.*

Num. 18:12–19 clarifies that the "sacred donations" granted as "perquisites" to Aaron and his sons are to include "everything that has been proscribed [or devoted] in Israel." This phrase covers all entitlements of the Lord from among the "first first fruits of everything in the land," including the "first issue of the womb of every being, man or beast." Added to these entitlements, were the voluntary offerings, which might include "the best of the new oil, wine and grain."

Also included were payments for the redemption of unclean animals. While the firstborn of such animals were technically a part of the Lord's entitlement, they could not be consecrated for use in the sanctuary. The entitlement, therefore, took the form of a redemption payment. "Clean" animals within the Lord's entitlement, however, were deemed to be consecrated for use in the sanctuary. Accordingly, they were not redeemable. (The Lord specifically states: "the firstlings of cattle, sheep, or goats may not be redeemed; they are consecrated. You shall dash their blood against the altar, and turn their fat into smoke as an offering by fire for a pleasing odor to the Lord. But their meat shall be yours; it shall be yours like the breast of the wave offering and like the right thigh" (18:18).

> Note N–78: This passage generally tracks the relevant portions of Lev. 27:9–18.

In short, whether received by the Lord as entitlements or voluntary contributions, "*all the sacred gifts that the Israelites set aside for the Lord I give to you, to your sons, and to the daughters that are with you, as a due for all time*" (18:19). In return, of course, the priests would "have no territorial share among them or own any portion in their midst; I am your portion and your share among the Israelites" (18:20).

> Note N–79: These various entitlements and voluntary contributions appear both in earlier P passages and other sources. On the entitlements of the "first issue of the womb of every being, man or beast" see, for example, Gen. 4:34 (in which Abel had the prescience to bring a "firstling"); Exod. 13:2, 11–13; Exod. 22:28–29; and Num. 3:11–13. On the first fruits of agricultural produce see Exod. 23:19, Lev. 2:14–16, Lev. 19:23–25, and Lev. 23:9–17. On the wave and heave offerings of the sacrifice of well-being see Exod. 29:26–28, Lev. 7:28–36, Lev. 10:12–15, Lev. 23:17–21, Num. 6:20–25, and Num. 8:11, 13, 15. For other rules on voluntary gifts, or dedications see Lev. 27.

The Lord concludes by telling Aaron that for their " services of the Tent of Meeting," He will give the Levites "all the tithes in Israel" (18:21).

> Note N–80: On tithes, see Lev. 27 and Note L–123.

The Lord then emphasizes anew that no one else may do the work of the Levites. "Henceforth, Israelites shall not trespass on the Tent of Meeting, and thus incur guilt and die: only Levites shall perform the services" (18:22–23).

The tithes will also compensate the Levites for a different contribution to Israel that would rival their services in the Tent. Like the priests, they will own no land. Thus, their otherwise rightful share will be allotted to other tribes. As stated by the Lord: "[the Levites] shall have no territorial share among the Israelites; for it is the tithes set aside by the Israelites as a gift to the Lord that I give to the Levites as their share" (18:23–24).

As beneficiaries of the tithes of other Israelites, the Levites must in turn tithe to the Lord. Of this, the Lord once again speaks to Moses rather than Aaron (18:25–31).

"Speak to the Levites and say to them: 'When you receive from the Israelites their tithes, which I have assigned to you as your share, you shall remove from them one-tenth of the tithe as a gift to the Lord' " (18:25–26). The Levites' tithe will come from all tithes received by them, whether as "new grain from the threshing floor or the flow from the vat" (18:27). They must be brought "as a gift for the Lord to Aaron the priest." All such tithes must come from the "best portion" of the tithes received by them, "the part . . . that is to be consecrated" (18:28–29).

Once the Levites had tithed to the Lord (i.e., to the priests), the remaining nine-tenths of the tithes was theirs. "You and your households may eat it anywhere, for it is your recompense for your services in the Tent of Meeting. You will incur no guilt through [your use of the tithes], once you have removed the best part from it [for the priests]; but you must not profane the sacred donations of the Israelites, lest you die" (18:31–32).

In Num. 19, by speaking again both to Moses and Aaron, P's Lord manifests His understanding of the limits of human credulity (19:1). Neither of them could ever persuade the other that the Lord had indeed said to him alone what He is about to say to both. And so His opening words to both: "This is the ritual law that the Lord has commanded" (19:2).

> Note N–81: The particular "ritual law" is that of the red heifer (parah adumah), to be used in purifying persons who become unclean through contact with a corpse. Its rituals were sufficiently arcane to have prompted Rashi to explain the Torah's first use of the term "ritual law" (or "statute of the law") as follows: "This is the statute of the Law, Because Satan and the nations of the world taunt Israel, saying 'What is this commandment and what reason is there in it?' Therefore (Scripture) terms it a 'statute' [chukah], [implying that] it is a decree from before Me; you have no right to criticize it.' "[12] As Rashi might have added, "It is a test of faith."

"Instruct the Israelite people to bring you a red cow [or "red heifer" (JPS1/RSV)] without blemish, in which there is no defect and on which no yoke has been laid" (19:2).

Note N–82: A heifer is an uncalved cow over one year of age. Absent any significant genetic changes in bovine coloration in the past 2,500 to 3,000 years, a perfect red heifer would have been as rare then as now. That it could not have been "yoked" speaks to its never having been debased by secular use.

On receiving it Moses and Aaron must then give the heifer to "Eleazer the priest," to be taken "outside the camp" and "slaughtered in his presence" (19:3). Eleazer will then "take some of the blood with his finger and sprinkle it seven times toward the front of the Tent of Meeting" (19:4). The heifer's whole corpse is then burned, "hide, flesh and blood . . . its dung included," with the bones as well, reduced to ashes" (19:5, 9).

As the carcass burns, "the priest" is to throw "cedar wood, hyssop, and crimson stuff" into the fire (19:6). Even at this early stage of the ritual, both "the priest" and "He who performed the burning" (perhaps a Levite assistant) are declared unclean. Each participant is required to "wash his garments [and] bathe his body in water" (19:7–8). As for the priest, he "may reenter the camp, but he shall be unclean until evening" (19:7).

Note N–83: Nothing is said of whether "he who performed the burning" may also re-enter the camp on completing his ablutions, but before becoming clean with the arrival of evening (19:8).

Num. 19:9 reveals the purpose of it all. "A man who is clean shall gather up the ashes of the cow and deposit them outside the camp in a clean place, *to be kept for water of lustration [i.e., purification] for the Israelite community. It is for cleansing.*" Although required to be clean for gathering the ashes, the "man" who does so thereby becomes "unclean until evening." While he, too, must "wash his clothes," nothing is said of his personal cleansing (19:10).

As a "permanent law for the Israelites and strangers who live among you" (19:10), Num. 19:11–13 describes the cleansing role of the red heifer's ashes: "He who touches the corpse of any human being shall be unclean for seven days. He shall cleanse himself with [the "water of lustration"] on the third day and the seventh day, and then be clean." He who does not "shall not be clean" (19:12).

Note N–84: In theory, the preparatory ritual would have to be repeated often enough to maintain an adequate and constant supply of "water of lustration" for all Israel.

The punishment for not being cleansed after touching a corpse speaks to the seriousness of the offense and the importance of the ritual. Not to be so cleansed "defiles the Lord's Tabernacle," thus requiring the person to be "cut off from Israel" (19:13).

Num. 19:14–16, which begins with *zoht hatorah* ("This is the law") both overlaps and adds to the circumstances of 19:11–13: "When a person dies in a tent, whoever enters the tent and whoever is in the tent shall be unclean seven days; and every open vessel with no lid fastened down, shall be unclean. And in the open, *anyone who touches a person who was killed or who died naturally*, or human bone, or a grave, shall be unclean seven days."

In fuller detail, Num. 19:17–19 describes the use of the "water of lustration" in cleansing a person who unclean under the rules of 19:11–16. "Some of the ashes from the fire of cleansing shall be taken for the unclean person, and fresh water shall be added to them in a vessel. A person who is clean shall take hyssop, dip it in the water, and sprinkle on the tent and on all the vessels and people who were there, or on him who touched the bones or the person who was killed or died naturally or the grave" (19:17–18). "The clean person shall sprinkle it upon the unclean person on the third day and on the seventh day, thus cleansing him by the seventh day. He shall then wash his clothes and bathe in water, and at nightfall he shall be clean" (19:19).

Num. 19:20 again declares the failure to be cleansed, as required, a defilement of the Lord's sanctuary. As before, such person "shall be cut off from the congregation." The ritual then concludes by addressing the newly declared uncleanness of "he who sprinkled the water of lustration" (19:21). First, he must wash his clothes. Then "he," together with "whoever" has touched the water of lustration "shall be unclean until evening" (19:21). In addition, "whatever that unclean person touches shall be unclean; and the person who touches him shall be unclean until evening" (19:22).

Comment N–21. On the necessarily limited role of the Tent, and later the Temple, in the red heifer ritual

The law of the red heifer was declared a permanent law, both in the wilderness and in Canaan. But once dispersed in Canaan, would it be possible for the Israelites to honor the command? An answer requires the consideration of two separate aspects of the command: (1) preparing the water of lustration from the ashes of the red heifer and (2) using the water in restoring unclean persons to cleanness.

P viewed the Jerusalem Temple and its Aaronide priesthood as sole successors to the Tent and Eleazer. Thus, as envisioned by P, the production of the water of lustration through the red heifer ritual could only take place in the immediate vicinity of the Temple (19:2–10). But what of the use of the water by Israelites dispersed throughout Canaan? How could the water be made available, as needed? Cleansing with the water was required on the third and seventh days following an encounter with a corpse. Thus, for many, if not most, Israelites, it would have been impossible to gain timely access to waters in Jerusalem.

However, unlike the protocols covering the water's production, the cleansing alone involved neither *the* Tent nor its priest. The main need for those who required cleansing was access to the waters of lustration. But this in itself would present daunting logistical problems.

On arriving "at the wilderness of Zin on the first new moon," the Israelites "stayed at Kadesh" (20:1a).

> Note N–85: So "fluid" were these locations that 13:26 first places Kadesh the wilderness of Paran. (Friedman attributes 13:26 to P and 20:1a to R.) See Notes N–48 and 52.

It is then said that "Miriam died there and was buried there" (20:1b) What follows also portends the deaths of Moses and Aaron before entering Canaan.

Once more, the problem is water. "The community was without water, and they joined against Moses and Aaron. The people quarreled with Moses, saying, 'If only we had perished when our brothers perished at the instance of the Lord!' " (20:2–3). Indeed, either the people do not recall, or will not acknowledge, why they had been brought out of Egypt. " 'Why did you make us leave Egypt to come to this wretched place, a place with no grain or figs or vines or pomegranates? There is not even water to drink!' " (20:5).

At the entrance to the Tent of Meeting, where the despairing Moses and Aaron had "[fallen] on their faces," the Presence of the Lord appeared (20:6). His instructions to Moses are quite precise: "You and your brother Aaron *take the rod and* assemble the community, and before their very eyes *order the rock to yield its water.* Thus *you* shall provide water for them from the rock and provide drink for the congregation and their beasts" (20:8).

> Note N–86: In JPS2 the "you" of 20:8b appears only once, as the subject for "shall provide water" and "shall provide drink." JPS1 and RSV give added emphasis to "you" by stating it in each phrase. On the importance of "you" in describing the source of water see Comment N–22 pt. 2.

"Moses took the rod from before the Lord [i.e from its place before the Ark of the Tent (17:25)] as He had commanded him"; "Moses and Aaron assembled the congregation in front of the rock" (20:9–10). Presumably in Aaron's presence, Moses then asks the following fateful question: "Listen, you rebels, shall *we* get water for you out of this rock?" (20:10). His next act reasonably assumes their answer. "And Moses raised his hand *and struck the rock twice with his rod.*" As he did so, "out came copious water, and the community and their beasts drank" (20:11).

In the eyes and minds of the people, who had brought forth the water? The

Lord's answer is revealed in His next words to "Moses and Aaron": "*Because you did not trust Me enough to affirm My sanctity in the sight of the Israelite people, therefore you shall not lead this congregation into the land that I have given them*" (20:12). To this the narrator adds, "Those are the waters of Meribah—meaning that the Israelites quarrelled with the Lord—through which He affirmed His sanctity" (20:13).

Comment N–22. On three aspects of the "Waters of Meribah"

1. On the "Waters of Meribah" according to E and P

So similar are the details of the two stories of the waters of Meribah in Exod. 17:1–7 and Num. 20:2–13 that we must place their origins in a single, widely known tradition. But what of the distinctive uses which E and P make of the single tradition? Both occur as a miracle in the use of a rock to satisfy the water needs of the entire Israelite community. For E, however, the event occurs near Mount Horeb, most likely in the southern sector of the Sinai Peninsula. As for substance, there is never a question in E that God alone had caused water to flow from the rock.

In turn, P places Meribah near Kadesh in the wilderness of Zin, not far from the border of Edom. But here all other differences pale in importance before the question of to whom the people should feel beholden for their water. Because the Lord believes that Moses had "conspired" with Aaron to claim credit for *His* miracle, P's version becomes a morality tale of their fate. But as to the justice of their fate, two questions remain. First, did the Lord's instructions justify His chastisement of Moses and Aaron for the manner of their performance? Second, why did P cause the Lord to chastise not only Moses, but also the relatively passive Aaron, with whom P was so closely identified?

2. On the justice of the Lord's denying Moses and Aaron entry into the promised land

Ignoring the question of whether their overall "batting averages" didn't entitle Moses and Aaron to the Lord's forgiveness, with what did He charge them? In the Lord's own words: "*Because you did not trust Me enough to affirm My sanctity in the sight of the Israelite people, therefore you shall not lead this congregation into the land that I have given them.*" Or, as He might have said more directly, "You hid the truth that it was My concern for My people and My power that brought water from the rock. Instead, by wrongful use of your rod, you sought credit for yourselves."

What, then, of the evidence? First, although the Lord told Moses and Aaron to carry Aaron's rod with them as they sought to bring water from the rock (20:8), He had not told them to use it. Yet, rod in hand, and before "the very eyes of the people," they were to "order the rock to yield its water."

Amidst the tumult, Moses then struck the rock with his rod, as he *rightfully* had at Horeb before (Exod. 17:6).

In doing so, Moses could have given the impression that he himself, with the aid of Aaron's rod, had brought forth water from the rock. Adding to this impression with Aaron at his side, Moses preceded the act itself with these words: "Listen you rebels, shall *we* get water for you out of this rock?" (20:10). To whom could "we" refer other than Moses and Aaron? In sum, although merely acting as the Lord's agents, when water flowed from the rock, Moses and Aaron appeared to present themselves as its source.

What can be said in their defense? As for their striking the rod on the rock, it was an act that the Lord, Himself, had ingrained in them. Had not the rod been regularly used as a symbol of *His* power? (See, e.g. Exod. 7:10–12, 17, 19–20; 8:1–2, 12–13; 9:23; and 10:12–13.) And once before, when the Lord first brought forth waters from the rock at another Meribah, had He not told Moses to strike the rock with the rod? (Exod. 17:5–6). Given the format that Moses recalled so well, why should this effort be different? If the Lord didn't want Moses to strike the rock with the rod He had told him to carry, He had but to say so.

But what of Moses' use of *we*, with Aaron beside him, in apparent reference to the source of the water? Consider that the Lord Himself had attributed the production of the water and the provision of drink to "you" (i.e., Moses and Aaron) (20:8). (See Note N–86.) Why should Moses not identify his role, and Aaron's, in a manner fully consistent with the Lord's own identification?

But in the end, how could these subtleties ever be known to the people? All they knew was what they saw and heard. And from this the people might well conclude that Moses and Aaron were the source of the water, as confirmed by their claim. And this is what angered the Lord.

We may conclude, then, that P provides the Lord with just enough technical grounds to chastise Moses and Aaron. But equally true, the Lord had cunningly "entrapped" them.

3. On P's purpose in contriving the chastisement of Moses and Aaron

We might view P's contrived chastisement of Aaron as delayed retribution for the golden calf of Exodus 32. But as we know, Aaron's creation of the golden calf comes from E rather than P. In any case, P has clearly identified the "waters of Meribah" as the Lord's sole stated reason for denying entry into Canaan to Moses as well as Aaron. The question, then, is why does P draw on the waters of Meribah as an excuse to do so.

First, the prevalence of a tradition that denied the entry of Moses and Aaron into Canaan may have compelled P to provide an explanation. As to Moses, this tradition finds powerful attestation in the closing chapters of Deuteronomy. Particularly in Deut. 31, 32, and 34, we will find that a source other than P speaks poignantly of the death of Moses in Moab, as Israel prepares to enter Canaan. *P's purpose therefore, may have been to justify the Lord's barring Moses and Aaron from Canaan while minimizing their own fault.*

Yet Moses persists in his duties. He now seeks to invoke kinship as grounds for gaining passage through Edom. Having decided to enter Canaan from the east rather than the south, Moses sends messengers from Kadesh to the king of Edom. *"Thus says your brother Israel:* You know all the hardships that have befallen us; that our ancestors went down to Egypt, that we dwelt in Egypt a long time, and the Egyptians freed us from Egypt. Now we are in Kadesh, the town on the border of your territory. Allow us, then, to cross your country. We will not pass through fields or vineyards, and *we will not drink water from the wells.* We will follow the king's highway, turning off neither to the right nor to the left until we have crossed your territory" (20:14–17).

> Note N–87: *The term "your brother Israel" was not mere rhetoric fashioned by Moses for the occasion. Recall the opening of Gen. 36: "This the line of Esau—that is, Edom." Esau had settled in Edom (Gen. 32:4) and was known as the "ancestor," or "father" of the Edomites (Gen. 36:9). Thus, the kinship invoked by Moses was through Jacob (or Israel).*

Moses pleads to no avail. "Edom" answers him with a flat refusal and a threat to "go out against you with the sword" (20:18). But Moses continues to press his case. He promises that *"if we or our cattle drink your water, we will pay for it"* (20:19). Edom again replies, "You shall not pass through." Edom then "went out against [the Israelites] in heavy force, strongly armed" and Israel "turned away from them" (20:20–21).

Comment N–23. On the Israelites' request for passage through Edom

Any brotherly feelings that Edom's king might have harbored for the Israelites now on his doorstep would be sorely tested by the vision of thousands of wanderers on his highway. (We are not told how the decimation of the adult generation that left Egypt had affected the net count of "603,550" adult males, plus women, children, and Levites. See Num. 2:32–33 for the most recent count.) The king would also note that Moses had modified his initial promise not to drink water from wells into a promise to pay for what the people and cattle use while on "the beaten track" (20:17, 19). Moses was surely sincere in his promise to pay. But he, above all, would know the priceless value of water.

Meanwhile, Aaron's time had come. "Starting out from Kadesh, the Israelites arrived in a body at Mount Hor, "on the boundary of the land of Edom" (20:22–23).

The Lord then said to Moses and Aaron, "Let Aaron be gathered to his kin: he is not to enter the land that I have given to the Israelite people, *because you disobeyed my command about the waters of Meribah*" (20:24). Moses is to take Aaron and Eleazer on Mount Hor, where Aaron's "vestments" are to be taken from him and put on Eleazer. "There Aaron shall be gathered unto the dead" (20:25–26).

This they did "in the sight of the whole community . . . and Aaron died there on the summit of the mountain" (20:27–28). "When Moses and Eleazer came down from the mountain, the whole community knew that Aaron had breathed his last. All the house of Israel bewailed Aaron thirty days (20:28–29).

> Note N–88: That Israel bewailed Aaron for thirty days and that Eleazer suc- ceded him tells of P's effort to preserve his stature. In the end, despite their mutual reluctance, both P and P's Lord may have been compelled by the weight of human tradition to deny Aaron entry to Canaan.

Following Israel's failure to gain passage north through Edom, Num. 21:1–3 tells of a second encounter with the Canaanites at Hormah (cf. 14:39–45).

"When the Canaanite king of Arad, who dwelt in the Negeb, learned that Israel was coming by Atharim, he engaged Israel in battle and took some of them captive. Then Israel made a vow to the Lord and said, 'If you deliver this people into our hand, we will proscribe their towns.' The Lord heeded Israel's plea and delivered up the Canaanites; and they and their cities were [utterly destroyed (per JPS1/RSV)]. So that place was named Hormah" (21:1–3).

Comment N–24. On Israel's two separate encounters with the Canaanites in the south

In trying to enter Canaan from the south at Hormah—thus defying the Lord's edict that their generation would not see the promised land—Israel suffered a "shattering blow" from the Canaanites and Amalekites (14:39–45). Now, some thirty-eight years later, in another encounter at Hormah, Israel routs the Canaanites (21:1–3).

That the king of Arad had "learned" (JPS2) or "heard tell" (JPS1) or "heard" (RSV) that the Israelites would now move north through Atharim hints of pure rumor. For even after thirty-eight years, the Israelites could recall what happened when their parents tried to do much the same. Their children, now grown, would have had little taste for again testing the Lord or the Canaanite tribes at Hormah. But in sensing the Israelites' intent to obey His as yet unrevoked command, the Lord quickly comes to their defense—not to open a route to Canaan through Hormah, but to protect His people. But what of the final command of 14:25 to go "by way of the Sea of Reeds" into the wilderness and, ultimately, their final destination? Had it been fulfilled in prior wanderings? Or was it yet to be honored?

Following Aaron's death and Israel's victory at Hormah (20:22–21:23), 21:4a picks up from Edom's refusal to permit Israel to move north through its land (20:21). Thus, "[Israel] set out from Mount Hor *by the road* to the Sea of Reeds to skirt the land of Edom" (21:4a).

In Num. 21:4b–9, "the people [again] grew restive on the journey" (21:4b) "There is no bread and no water, and we have come to loathe this miserable food" (21:5). In reply, the Lord sent serpents, which bit the people. As a result, "many of the Israelites died" (21:6). They then acknowledge to Moses that they "sinned by speaking against the Lord and against you." Heeding their pleas, Moses asks the Lord "to take the away the serpents" (21:7). Rather than doing so, the Lord tells Moses to "make a *seraph* figure and mount it on a standard. And if anyone who is bitten looks at it, he shall recover." Moses then "made a copper serpent and mounted it on a standard; and when any one was bitten by a serpent, he would look at the copper serpent and recover" (21:8–9).

> *Note N–89: Now it is the "new" generation, soon to enter the promised land, that complains of its hard lot. Will the Lord now be "thwarted" by them as by their parents? See Comment N–16. (Friedman ascribes 21:4b–9 to E.)*
>
> *But why did the Lord not simply remove the serpents? Again, as with the peoples' marking their lintels with blood in Egypt to avoid the slaying of their firstborn, He seeks a sign of obedience as the condition of His protection.*

The remainder of Num. 21 tells of Israel's northward journey while "skirting" the "King's Highway" in Edom which lies to the east. The people first encamp at Oboth and then at Iye-abarim, both "in the wilderness bordering on Moab to the east" (21:10–11). Thence to the "wadi Zered" and beyond to the Arnon River, "the boundary between Moab and the Amorites" (21:12–13).

> *Note N–90: A "wadi" is a dry watercourse that "runs" only in periods of rain.*

Here a rare reference is made to an external source. "Therefore *the Book of the Wars of the Lords* speaks of '. . . Waheb in Suphah, and the wadis: the Arnon with its tributary wadis, stretched along the settled country of Ar, hugging the territory of the Moab' " (21:14–15).

> *Note N–91: If the "Book" ever existed, it was later lost.*

From the Arnon River (which flows from the mid-eastern shore of the Dead sea) they travel to Beer (meaning "well"). There the Lord arranges a salutary event for Himself and the people. He thus tells Moses, "Assemble the people that I might give them water" (21:16).

Note N–92: The event lacks the drama of the "waters of Meribah." Instead, the Lord simply brings the people to an established source of water.

The people respond to this simple kindness with a song: "Spring up O well—sing to it—/ The well which the chieftains dug,/ Which the nobles of the people started/ With maces, with their own staffs./ And from Midbar to Mattanah, and from Mattanah to Nahaliel, and from Nahaliel to Bamoth, and from Bamoth to the valley that is in the country of Moab, at the peak of Pisgah, overlooking the wasteland" (21:16–20).

Note N–93: Here the people openly extol the well as a great human achievement. Friedman attributes the passage to R, with the caveat that its origin is "difficult to identify.

Except for its locale and outcome, the scenario of Num. 21:21–25 closely follows that of 20:18–21, in which the Israelites were denied a right of passage through Edom.

"Israel now sent messengers to Sihon king of the Amorites, saying, 'Let me pass through your country. We will not turn off the fields or vineyards, and we will not drink water from the wells. We will follow the king's highway until we have crossed your territory.' " But Sihon would not let Israel pass through his territory. Instead, "He came to Jahaz and engaged Israel in battle" (21:21–23).

Here the similarities between the two episodes end. "But Israel put them to the sword, and took possession of their land, from the Arnon to the Jabbok, as far as [Az] of the Ammonites, for Az marked the boundary of the Ammonites" (21:24). Israel then "settled in all the towns of the Amorites, in Heshbon and all its dependencies" (21:25).

Note N–94: At this point, Israel's steady move to the north is briefly interrupted by a song of uncertain origin. It praises both Sihon, whom Israel had defeated, and Heshbon, which it had captured. The qualities that the song ascribes to both serve to heighten the glory of the victory.

"Now Heshbon was the city of Sihon king of the Amorites, who had fought against a former king of Moab and taken all his land from him as far as the Arnon. Therefore the bards would recite: 'Come to Heshbon, it is built firm; / Sihon's city in well founded. / For the fire went forth from Heshbon, / Flame from Sihon's city, / Consuming Ar of Moab, / The lords of Bamoth by the Arnon. / Woe to you O Moab! / You are undone, O people of Chemosh! / His sons are rendered fugitive/ And his daughters captive. / By an Amorite king, Sihon. / Yet we have cast them down utterly, / Heshbon along with Dibon; / We have wrought desolation at Nophah, / Which is hard by Medeba' " (21:26–30).

Israel completes its northward advance in Num. 21:31–35, while "skirting" the land of Edom. After Israel had "occupied the land of the Amorites," Moses "sent to spy out Jazer, and they captured its dependencies and dispossessed the Amorites who were there" (21:31–32). As they proceeded on the road to Bashan, "Og king of Bashan, with all his people, came out to Edrei to engage them in battle" (21:33). But the Lord reassures Moses. "*I give him and all his people and his land into your hand*" (21:34). Thereupon, "They defeated him and his sons and all his people, *until no remnant was left of him*, and they took possession of his country" (21:35).

> *Note N–95: The description of the victory establishes the Lord's role in it. But what is that role? Is it to demoralize Israel's foe through fear? Or to arm Israel with overwhelming self-confidence through faith? Or both?*

Num. 22–24 tells a story of Balaam and the Lord; of Balaam and Balak, king of Moab; and of Balaam and his ass.

> *Note N–96: Friedman assigns the entire three chapters to E. But the text also suggests a possible amalgam of E and J.*[13]

Having defeated the kings of the Amorites and of Bashan on its march north, Israel is now "encamped in the steppes of Moab, across the Jordan from Moab" (22:1). Moab "dreaded" the newly arrived and triumphant Israelites who stood at its borders. It was "alarmed" by their numbers (22:3). To the "elders of Midian" Moab decries the presence of "this horde" who, he says, "will lick clean all that is about us as an ox licks up the grass of the field" (22:4).

Balaam, who lives in Pethor on the Euphrates, is highly regarded as a diviner, or soothsayer. Balak, as king of Moab, decides to hire him for the purpose of cursing Israel.

> *Note N–97: By common belief, such a curse could weaken Israel to the point of assuring its defeat.*

Balak first sends messengers to Balaam at his home in Pethor, with the following invitation:

> There is a people that came out of Egypt; it hides the earth from view, and is settled next to me. Come then, put a curse on this people for me, since they are too numerous for me; *perhaps* I can thus defeat and drive them out of the land. *For I know* that he whom you bless is blessed indeed, and he whom you curse is cursed. (22:5–6)

On receiving Balak's message from "the elders of Moab and the elders of Midian," Balaam immediately reveals his dependence on the Lord's wishes. He asks the deputation to remain the night, after which he will reply "as the Lord may instruct me" (22:7–8).

> Note N–98: *The Lord to whom Balaam refers is indeed* yahweh *Himself.*

But now it is God, *elohim*, who comes to ask Balaam, "What do these people want of you?"

> Note N–99: *As with Adam and Eve, and no less Cain,* yahweh elohim *knows the answer. But as with them, He wants to hear Balaam's answer from Balaam himself.*

As the gist of Balak's message, Balaam tells God, "Here is a people that came out of Egypt and hides the earth from view. Come now and curse them for me; perhaps I can engage them in a battle and drive them off." God then tells Balaam, "Do not go with them. You must not curse that people, for they are blessed" (22:9–12).

In the morning, just as God had instructed him, Balaam tells "Balak's dignitaries" to return to their country because "the Lord will not let me go with you." On returning to Moab, they simply tell Balak that "Balaam refused to come with us," thus omitting any reference to "the Lord's" role in his refusal. (22:13–14).

> Note N–100: *In this integral passage,* elohim *and* yahweh *again appear interchangeably (see* elohim, *or "God," in 22: 9, 10, and 12;* yahweh, *or "the Lord," in 22:13).*

Balak then sends other dignitaries, "more numerous and distinguished than the first." His message is even more urgent than before. "Please do not refuse to come to me. I will reward you richly and I will do anything you ask of me. Only come and damn this people for me" (22:15–17).

In reply, Balaam assures the dignitaries that were Balak to offer "his house full of silver and gold," he would never "do anything, big or little, contrary to the command of the Lord *my* God." He invites the group to stay the night until he can find out "what else the Lord may say to me" (22:18–19).

Although Balaam had spoken of what "the Lord" might say (22:19), it is "God" who brings a message in the night: "If these men have come to invite you, you *may* go with them. But whatever I command you, that shall you do" (22:20).

On arising in the morning, Balaam "saddled his ass and departed with the Moabite dignitaries." But now "God was incensed at his going; so an angel of the Lord placed himself in his way as an adversary" (22:21–22).

Note N–101: Why is God suddenly incensed and why does He send "an angel of the Lord . . . as an adversary"? What is His concern? If Balaam were to succumb to Balak's "bribery" and utter a curse, could the Lord God of Israel not "undo" it? Or can He, too, be "thwarted" by deep-rooted traditions regarding the efficacy of personal divination? Even though such human powers could not possibly transcend His own, does the Lord God fear the impact of a general human belief that they can? In any case, He had said nothing before Balaam's departure to withdraw His permission for Balaam to go.

Num. 22:22–34 then relates a touching tale of Balaam and his ass that probes deeply into the usually unspoken relationships between human beings and the patient animals who serve them.

As Balaam rode his she-ass, along with two servants, the ass "caught sight of the angel of the Lord standing in the way, with his drawn sword in his hand." To avoid it, the ass "swerved from the road and went into the fields." Balaam then beat the ass to get it back on the road. On their return to the road, the angel "stationed himself in a lane between the vineyards, with a fence on either side." With such limited space, the ass "pressed herself against the wall and squeezed Balaam's foot against [it]. Once again, Balaam beat his faithful but unhappy ass.

Now the angel escalates the confrontation. He "stationed himself on a spot so narrow that there was no room [for the ass] to swerve left or right." At this point the ass gives up. "She lay down under Balaam." The furious Balaam once again "beat[s] the ass with his stick."

Now the Lord thought it time to open a dialogue between Balaam and his ass on the nature of their impasse. "The Lord opened the ass's mouth [as he had once opened the serpent's], and she said to Balaam, 'What have I done to you that you have beaten me these three times?' " Though exasperated, Balaam is quite prepared to discuss the problem, man to beast.

Balaam first tells the ass of his embarrassment before his servants because of his inability to control an animal. "You have made a mockery of me! If I had a sword with me, I'd kill you." In return, the faithful ass gently reminds Balaam of her past services. "Look, I am the ass you have been riding all along until this day! Have I been in the habit of doing thus to you?" Balaam was an honest man and the ass had told the truth. He could only answer, "No." The Lord then "uncovered Balaam's eyes" so that he could see what the ass had seen from the start—"the angel of the Lord standing in the way, his drawn sword in his hand." Balaam "fell on his face" before Him.

Speaking through the angel, the Lord rebukes Balaam. "Why have you beaten your ass these three times? It is I who came out as an adversary, for the errand is obnoxious to me. And when the ass saw me, she shied away because of me those three times. If she had not shied away from me you are the one I should have killed, while sparing her."

Because the Lord had not told Balaam of His change of mind regarding his departure for Moab, Balaam is stupefied. "I erred because I did not know that you were standing in my way. If you still disapprove, I will turn back" (22:34).

> Note N–102: *Although Balaam remains fully committed to the Lord's wishes, JPS1, JPS2, and RSV all read Balaam's reference to the Lord as "you" (or "thou," with a lowercase first letter). Is the lowercase a translational "conspiracy" to portray Balaam as somehow less than mindful of the Lord's sanctity?*

Balaam's willingness to abandon his visit to Balak reassures the Lord of his fidelity. But in telling Balaam to "go with the men," the angel repeats the Lord's warning to "say nothing except what I tell you" (22:35).

> Note N–103: *The Lord accepts Balaam's good intentions (22:20). Yet He insists that Balaam say nothing but His own words. Does this imply that the Lord ascribes consequences to Balaam's words beyond His own powers to modify?*

When Balak hears of Balaam's approach, he travels to a far boundary of Moab to greet him. He asks Balaam why he had not returned with the first delegation. He wonders if Balaam doubts that he can reward him adequately. In reply, Balaam's only concern is whether Balak can really accept the necessary conditions of his service. "And now that I have come to you, *have I the power to speak freely? I can utter only the word that God puts into my mouth*" (22:36–38).

Without answering, Balak brings Balaam to Kiriath-huzoth, where he "sacrificed oxen and sheep" and had them served to Balaam and the dignitaries.

> Note N–104: *Here the Torah depicts Moabite and Midianite animal "sacrifices" for food. The role of their gods, or priests, however, is not revealed.*

In the morning Balak took Balaam up to Bamoth-*baal* from which Balaam could see "a portion of the people" (i.e., the Israelites) (22:39–41).

In preparing to receive the Lord's "manifestation," Balaam asks Balak to "build me seven altars here and have seven bulls and seven rams ready here for me." Together, they "offered up a bull and a ram on each altar." Balaam then tells Balak, "Stay here beside *your offerings* while I am gone. Perhaps the Lord will grant me a manifestation, and whatever He reveals to me I will tell you." Balaam then went off alone (23:1–3).

> Note N–105: *JPS2 speaks only of "your offerings." JPS1/RSV both render the olahtechah of 23:3 more literally as "your burnt offering," the basic ritual offering of Israel, first introduced "formally" in Lev. 1.*

God "manifested Himself to Balaam," who tells Him, "I have set up *the* seven altars and offered up a bull and a ram on each altar." The Lord then "put a word" in his mouth and told him to "return to Balak and speak thus" (23:4–5).

> Note N–106: *Here there is a question of what rituals, if any, were followed by Balaam in his own sacrifices. Unlike Balak's sacrifices, Balaam's are under the Lord's aegis, from whom he hopes to receive "a manifestation." This might explain the use of "burnt offering" in 23:3. Had Moab and Midian adopted, and then adapted, Israel's practices? Or had Israel adopted and adapted theirs, and others?*

Balaam returned to Balak and "found him standing beside his [burnt] offerings, and all the Moabite dignitaries with him." Balaam then "took up his theme" by repeating the "word" that the Lord had "put" in his mouth (23:6–7).

> From Aram has Balak brought me,/ Moab's king from the hills of the East:/ Come, curse me Jacob,/ Come, tell Israel's doom!/ How can I damn whom God has not damned?/ How doom when the Lord has not doomed?/ As I see them from the mountain tops,/ Gaze on them from the heights,/ There is a people that dwells apart,/ Not reckoned among the nations./ Who can count the dust of Jacob, Number the dust-cloud of Israel?/ May I die the death of the upright,/ May my fate be like theirs! (23:7–10).

Clearly, Balak had missed the point of Balaam's earlier warning that he could say only what the Lord "reveals to me." To Balak's angry question of why he blessed Israel, Balaam replies, "I can only repeat faithfully what the Lord puts in my mouth."

> Note N–107: *Here Balaam describes the role of a true prophet of the Torah. He is neither diviner, nor soothsayer. He will neither predict, nor claim to influence events, except through the Lord's revealed will, or intent.*

But Balak remains undeterred. He eagerly urges Balaam to try again. "Come with Me," he says to Balaam, "to another place from which you can see them—and damn them for me from there." With that, he took Balaam to "Sedeh-zophim, on the summit of Pisgah." They again "built seven altars and offered a bull and a ram [at each]." Balaam then goes to seek another "manifestation" (23:11–15).

As before, "the Lord manifested Himself to Balaam and put a word in his mouth, saying, 'Return to Balak and speak thus.' " And Balaam repeated His new words to Balak (23:16).

> Up, Balak, attend,/ Give ear unto me, son of Zippor!/ God is not man to be capricious,/ Or mortal to change His mind./ Would He speak and not act,

Promise and not fulfill?/ My message was to bless:/ When He blesses, I cannot reverse it./ No harm is in sight for Jacob, No woe in view for Israel./ The Lord their God is with them,/ And their king's acclaim in their midst./ God who freed them from Egypt/ Is for them like the horns of a wild ox./ Lo, there is no augury in Jacob,/ No divining in Israel:/ Jacob is told at once,/ Yea Israel, what God has planned./ Lo, a people that rises like a lion,/ Leaps up like the king of beasts,/ Rests not till it has feasted on prey/ And drunk the blood of the slain." (23:18–24)

> Note N–108: Even as metaphor, to extol Israel's drinking "the blood of the slain" is to fly in the face of every past prohibition against the consumption of any blood. Were these indeed the Lord's words to Balaam?

On hearing Balaam repeat the words of blessing, Balak decides to avoid disaster by ending his efforts. "Don't curse them and don't bless them!" he tells Balaam. But Balaam answers that it's already too late. "Whatever the Lord says, that I must do" (23:25–26). Balak then seeks to grasp a final straw. "Come now, I will take you to another place. Perhaps God will deem it right that you damn them for me there" (23:27). So he brings Balaam to "the peak of Peor, which overlooks the wasteland" (27:28). As Balaam requests, Balak prepares the same seven altars and the same animals; and the offerings are made as before (23:29–30).

By now, however, Balaam is utterly persuaded "that it pleased God to bless Israel." Accordingly, instead of "[going] in search of omens," Balaam turned his face toward the wilderness. As he "looked up and saw Israel encamped tribe by tribe, the spirit of God came upon him" (24:1–2). "Taking up his theme," he spoke these words before Balak:

> Word of Balaam son of Beor,/ Word of the man whose eye is true,/ Word of him who hear's God's speech,/ Who beholds visions from the Almighty,/ Prostrate, but with eyes unveiled:/ How fair are your tents, O Jacob,/ Your dwellings, O Israel!/ Like palm graves that stretch out,/ Like gardens beside a river,/ Like aloes planted by the Lord,/ Like cedars beside the water;/ Their boughs drip with moisture,/ Their roots have abundant water./ Their king shall rise above Agag,/ Their kingdom shall be exalted./ God who freed them from Egypt/ Is for them like the horns of the wild ox./ They shall devour enemy nations,/ Crush their bones,/ And smash their arrows./ They crouch, they lie down like a lion,/ Like the king of beasts; who dare rouse them?/ Blessed are they who bless you,/ Accursed they who curse you! (24:3–9)

Balak is "enraged at Balaam." Striking his hands together, he berates Balaam with a complaint that seems fair enough on its face. "I called you to damn my enemies, and instead you have blessed them these three times! Back with you to your own place! I was going to reward you richly, but the Lord has denied you the reward" (24:10–11).

Balaam then reminds Balak of how he had tried to alert him to the limitations of his own powers. "I even told the messengers you sent to me, 'Though Balak were to give me his house of silver and gold, I could not of my own accord do anything good or bad contrary to the Lord's commmand. What the Lord says, that must I say' " (24:12–13).

As Balaam prepares to leave, he tells Balak of one more prophecy. He calls it a prophecy of "what this people will do to your people in days to come," but its scope extends beyond the affairs of Israel and Moab alone.

> Word of Balaam son of Beor,/ Word of the man whose eye is true,/ Word of him who hears God's speech,/ Who obtains knowledge from the Most High,/ And beholds visions from the Almighty,/ Prostrate, but with eyes unveiled:/ What I see for them is not yet,/ What I behold will not be soon:/ A star rises from Jacob,/ A meteor comes forth from Israel;/ It smashes the brow of Moab,/ The foundation of all children of Seth./ Edom becomes a possession,/ Yea, Seir a possession of its enemies;/ But Israel is triumphant./ A victor issues from Jacob/ To wipe out what is left of Ir./ He saw Amalek and, taking up his theme, he said:/ A leading nation is Amalek;/ But its fate is to perish forever./ He saw the Kenites and, taking up his theme, he said:/ Though your abode be secure,/ And your nest be set among cliffs,/ Yet shall Kain be consumed,/ When Asshur takes you captive,/ He took up his theme and said:/ Alas, who can survive except God has willed it!/Ships come from the quarter of Kittim;/ They subject Asshur, subject Eber./ They, too, shall perish forever. (24:15–24)

"Then Balaam set out on his journey back home, and Balak also went his way" (24:25).

> *Note N–109: In general, the prophecy speaks of future Israelite triumphs over a variety of neighboring lands and tribes. These include Moab itself, Edom and the fearsome Amalekites. However, when speaking to Balak of "when Asshur takes you captive," Balaam adds, "Alas, who can survive except God has willed it!" As a lament, this prophecy might refer to Assyria's growing encroachments during the ninth and eighth centuries B.C.E., leading to the conquest of the northern kingdom of Israel in 722 B.C.E. E in particular may have known of the early stages of this developing doom.*

Comment N–25. On the Balaam of Num. 22–24 as a "righteous non-Israelite," with an addendum on Balak

Plaut correctly summarizes the traditional "Jewish and Christian" view of Balaam "as a sorcerer, a man who loved money more than truth and who ended up in hell." (He notes that "the rabbis interpreted 'home' [or 'place'] in Num. 24:25 . . . to mean hell, which was 'home' to him, 'his place.' ") Plaut also correctly observes that "the reasons for this perjorative judgment are found not so much in the 'Book of Balaam' (Num. 22:2–24:25) as in later passages."[14] In particular, Num. 31:8 and 16 contain two terse charges of villainy against Balaam that lack any supporting narrative. In turn, Deut. 23:4–6 includes a curt summary of the Balaam story of Num. 22–24 that is totally at odds with its substance. Balaam, himself, never appears "in person" after Num. 22–24. (For an overview of Balaam in Numbers see Comment N–31.)

In judging the righteousness of Balaam in Num. 22–24, however, we must judge him as the Torah would judge any Israelite. But what can we yet say of the Torah's fundamental standard of righteousness? I would describe it as the disciplined subordination of all personal preferences to the revealed will of the Lord. Its attainment lies in a commitment to know the Lord's will and in a resolve to conform to it. By this standard, who can doubt the righteousness of the Balaam of Num. 22–24?

Our test is not in what others may say of him "behind his back," but in what we "know" of him from the point at which he first receives messengers from Balak, king of Moab. Balak regards Balaam's curse on Israel as Moab's surest defense against this sudden new threat (22:3–6). Indeed, Balak seems assured that Balaam's curse would transcend the power of the Lord, as Israel's God.

Although Balak has not yet offered any particular reward, Balaam knows that compliance could bring him riches. But Balaam's answer to Balak subordinates any thought of reward to a more compelling concern. His only thought is to say and do as the Lord says. "I shall reply to you as the Lord may instruct me" (22:8). Thus, when the Lord tells Balaam not to go to Balak because the Israelites are blessed (22:12), he accepts His command without question. He tells the deputation to return home, "for the Lord will not let me go with you" (22:13).

Balak sends a second deputation to Balaam. It comes with an explicit promise of rich rewards and the grant of "anything you ask of me" (22:17). But Balaam assures them that riches are subordinate to his primary concern. Under no circumstances could he "do anything, big or little, contrary to the command of the Lord my God" (22:18).

When God comes to him in the night, Balaam asks nothing of Him; but God, on His own initiative, tells Balaam that he "may go with them" (22:20). While God does not command Balaam to go, He implies a purpose in granting permission to go. Thus, His words, "But whatever I command you, that you shall do" (22:20). Balaam departs in the morning, intent on obeying God's commands. As Balaam leaves, it hardly seems likely that even a quixotic God would become "incensed at his going" (22:22).

Following the episode of the Lord's "adversary" angel and the talking ass, the angel reveals his presence to Balaam together with the Lord's advice that "the errand is obnoxious to me" (22:32). Balaam apologizes for his ignorance of the angel's presence and readily accepts the fact that the Lord had changed His mind. He assures the Lord, through the angel, that "if you still disapprove, I will turn back" (22:34). In reply, the Lord withdraws His objection. Beyond giving Balaam mere permission to go with the men (as in 22:20), the Lord orders him to go (22:35).

Thereafter, Balaam sacrifices to the Lord through the rituals of burnt offerings. He also delivers four blessings on Israel, two in the Lord's precise words and two in his own words, all fully in keeping with the Lord's intent. In doing so, he forfeits the rich rewards offered by Balak, whose rage he must also endure (24:10–13).

Thus, the Balaam of Num. 22–24 proves to be a non-Israelite on whom the Lord can totally rely as a prophet committed to the fulfillment of His purposes. Indeed, before Balaam himself, he identifies the Lord as *my* God (22:18). There are no riches that Balaam will not sacrifice to fulfil the Lord's will. If Balaam is not righteous by Torah standards, who but a Moses could ever hope to be so? (That Balaam all too quickly judged, rebuked, and struck his ass confirms his basic humanity as a person prey to great pressures.)

> *Note N–110: As an enemy of Israel, Balak, by Torah standards, represented the antithesis of righteousness. But we must avoid a precipitous rush to judgment. Balak is responsible for his kingdom and its people. A huge array of Israelites have suddenly appeared from nowhere. They have subdued neighboring tribes and kingdoms. Balak knows little of them other than their fighting prowess. His task is to protect his kingdom and his people by any means available.* In that the curse of a skilled diviner on a foe was thought to be a powerful defense, Balak would have been derelict not to arrange for its use. *To have sought the help of a diviner such as Balaam was prudent rather than perfidious. Balak's error, if any, was in picking an honest man.*

Num. 25:1–5 recounts how "the people" were seduced by Moabite harlots into the worship of heathen gods. Num. 25:6–18 tells of a fatally egregious act between an Israelite man and a Midianite woman.

The Moabite harlotry is described in 25:1–3: "While Israel was staying at Sittim, the people profaned themselves by whoring with the Moabite women, who invited *the people* to the sacrifices for their god. The people partook of them and worshiped that god. Thus *Israel* attached itself to Baal-peor, and the Lord was incensed with Israel." The Lord then directs Moses to have "the ringleaders . . . publicly impaled before the Lord, so that [His] wrath may turn away from Israel" (25:4). In turn, Moses orders Israel's officials to "slay those of his men who attached themselves to Baal-peor" (25:5).

> *Note N–111: Consistent with Friedman's attribution of both Num. 25:1–5 and Exod. 34:16 to J, they are closely related. Exod. 34:16 warns against (but does not prohibit) marriage with "inhabitants of the land." The danger is that*

"their daughters will lust after their gods and will cause your sons to lust after their gods." As we know, however, Moses himself had fathered two sons by a Midianite wife. And though sons of Joseph by birth and Jacob by adoption, Ephraim and Manasseh were also born of an Egyptian mother. By implication, the Lord had considered these notable exceptions to be justified by time or circumstances. Nevertheless, the cogency of J's warning in Exod. 34:16 against marriage with the people of Canaan is dramatically affirmed in Num. 25:1–5. Whether through marriage or harlotry, the lure of sexuality can lead to apostasy. As yet, however, given Moses' precise directive to "Israel's officials," it appears that relations between Israelite men and non-Israelite women were not sins as such. He does not order them to slay all who engaged in harlotry—only those "who attached themselves to Baal-peor" (25:5). In this, however, Moses seems to have ordered the death of more offenders than did the Lord Himself. In Num. 25:4 the Lord speaks only of "publicly impaling the ringleaders" (JPS2), or "hanging the chiefs" (JPS1/RSV). Yet Moses would order the death of all who "attached themselves to Baal-Peor."

Num. 25:6–18 then turns to P's more vivid, but more focused, story of two miscreants and a priestly hero.

"Just then one of the Israelites came and brought a Midianite woman over to his companions, in the sight of Moses and of *the whole Israelite community* who were weeping at the entrance of the Tent of Meeting" (25:6). This was seen by "Phinehas, son of Eleazar son of Aaron the priest." He took a spear at once and "followed the Israelite into the chamber." There he "stabbed both of them, the Israelite and the woman, through the belly. Then the plague against the Israelites was checked. Those who died from the plague numbered twenty-four thousand" (25:7–9).

Note N–112: *When had this "silent" plague begun? Also, Rashi suggests that the* kavatah *of 25:8 denotes not the "belly" of each miscreant, as often appears, but the male and female genitalia.*[15]

For his immediate and decisive response, Phinehas receives high praise from the Lord, as expressed to Moses. "Phinehas, son of Eleazar son of Aaron the priest, has turned back My wrath from the Israelites by displaying among them his passion for Me, so that I did not wipe out the Israelite people in My passion" (25:10–11). Accordingly, the Lord tells Moses of His reward to Phinehas. "Say, therefore, 'I grant him My pact of friendship. It shall be for him and his descendants after him a pact of priesthood for all time, because he took impassioned action for his God, thus making expiation for the Israelites' " (25:12–13).

Note N–113: *That the "descendants" of Phinehas, a grandson of Aaron and a son of Eleazer, should be reanointed through this single event seems "gra-*

tuitous." It would enable P, however, to reaffirm the Lord's anointment of "Aaron and his sons" as His priests.

Num. 25:14–15 identifies the offending couple slain by Phinehas. They were "Zimri son of Salu, chieftain of a Simeonite ancestral house" and "Cozbi, daughter of Zur," a "tribal head of an ancestral house in Midian."

The Lord then directs Moses to "assail the Midianites and defeat them" (25:16). As to why He includes *all* Midianites, the Lord adds, "for they assailed you by the trickery they practiced against you—because of the affair at Peor *and* because of the affair of their kinswoman Cozbi, daughter of the Midianite chieftain, who was killed at the time of the plague on account of Peor" (25:17–18).

Through the tumult of Num. 25, as through the preceding story of Balaam, the Israelites remained encamped "on the steppes of Moab, at the Jordan near Jericho" (cf. 26:3 and 22:1). Num. 26 tells of a further census meant to replicate the earlier census of Num. 1 in the wilderness of Sinai. Thus, "the Lord said to Moses and to Eleazar son of Aaron the priest, 'Take a census of the whole Israelite community from the age of twenty years up, by their ancestral houses, all Israelites able to bear arms'" (26:1–2; cf., Num. 1:1–3).

Moses and Eleazar then "gave instructions about them, namely, those from twenty years up, as the Lord commanded Moses" (26:3–4).

Note N–114: The counts of "ancestral houses" in Num. 26 and 1 appear below. As to being "able to bear arms," see Note N–2.

Ancestral House	Num. 26 Census	Num. 1 Census
Reuben	43,730	46,500
Simeon	22,200	59,300
Gad	40,500	45,650
Judah	76,500	74,600
Issachar	64,300	54,400
Zebulun	60,500	57,400
Manasseh	52,700	32,200
Ephraim	32,500	40,500
Benjamin	45,600	35,400
Dan	64,400	62,700
Asher	53,400	41,500
Naphtali	45,400	53,400
Total	601,730	603,550

Comment N–26. On the ability of Israel to sustain its numbers during some thirty-nine years in the wilderness

We should again recall that the totals in the table above compare to "about six hundred thousand men on foot, aside from children" who left Egypt (Exod. 12:37). After a year and two months it remained the same (see Comment N–1 and Num. 1:1). Some thirty-nine years have elapsed since Num. 1. What might have been a more normal relationship between births and deaths in this period has been skewed by four separate intervening plagues and one mass-killing that the Torah does not characterize as a plague. The plagues were reported in (1) 11:33, (2) 14:36–38, (3) 17:12–15, and (4) 25:7–9. The additional "mass-killing" following the revolts of Korah against Aaron and Dathan and Abiram against Moses are reported in 16:27–35, as modified in 26:6–9. (Recall also that a comparison of the Num. 1 census to the number of adult males departing Egypt was also skewed, following the golden calf, by the death of 3,000 in Exod. 32:25–28 and the plague of Exod. 32:35.)

Plague (1) is described as a "very great plague," but with no "supporting" numbers.

The victims of plague (2) fell within a limited class. From among the twelve scouts Moses had sent to scout Canaan (13:4–15), the victims were limited to "those who came back and caused the whole community to mutter against him [Moses] by spreading calumnies about the land." These were all of the scouts other than Joshua and Caleb (14:38). Thus, the total slain in "plague" (2) was a modest ten.

Due to the quick action of Moses and Aaron, plague (3) resulted in the death of only 14,700, "aside from those who died on account of Korah" (Num. 17:8–13).

Plague (4) resulted in the death of 24,000 Israelites.

As for those who died in the mass-killing "on account of Korah," the numbers are not known. The class itself is also blurred by a discrepancy between 16:32 and 26:11 as to Korah's children. Apart from the possible exclusion of Korah's sons, those who died were "Dathan and Abiram," together with "their wives, their children and their little ones"; "all Korah's people"; and the "two hundred fifty [chieftains]" (16:1–2, 35). The total of the two families of Dathan and Abiram, all of "Korah's people," and the two hundred fifty chieftains would not likely exceed a total of three hundred fifty persons. If so, in all, the number of "unnatural" deaths (i.e., those slain by the Lord) would not have exceeded 39,210—but for the unknown numbers of the first "very severe plague of 11:33."

As shown in the total tribal count above, the thirty-nine intervening years between the two censuses resulted in a net decline of 1,820 males "from twenty years up." The impact of the plagues on the count cannot be determined because of (1) uncertainty as to the total number slain; (2) uncertainty as to the age distribution of the slain (i.e., whether they would have been more or less than twenty at the time of the second census), and (3) uncertainty as to the number of females slain, of whatever age (if any). However many may have died at the Lord's hands, the figures suggest that despite His own actions, and other wilderness hardships, Israel had maintained its population. (To offset His plagues, the Torah attributes Israel's collective salvation to the manna and water provided by its God.)

The total net reduction of males over twenty years from 603,550 to 601,730 is but 1 percent. Variances among the tribes, however, are considerably more. In the order of their listing, those with increases and their percentages are Judah, +3 percent; Issachar, +18 percent; Zebulun, +5 percent; Manasseh, +64 percent; Benjamin, +29 percent; Dan, +3 percent and Asher, +29 percent. Those with decreases and their percentages are Reuben, –6 percent; Simeon, –63 percent; Gad, –20 percent; Ephraim, –20 percent; and Naphtali, –15 percent.

Manasseh's 64 percent increase and Simeon's 63 percent decrease are most notable. Smaller, but significant, are Benjamin's and Asher's 29 percent increases and Gad and Ephraim's 20 percent decreases. Nothing is said explicitly to explain the various changes. Simeon's decrease might be thought to reflect his relatively low repute. But if relative moral worth is a factor, why did Manasseh in particular grow so? Also, what explains the large decrease in the tribe of Ephraim, Joseph's other son, and the minimal increase in the tribe of the admirable Judah?

> Note N–115: The listed order of tribes in Num. 26 is as it appears in the table above. A notable feature is the "elevation" of Gad to third in order, ahead of Judah (cf., e.g., the tribal listing of Num. 13:4–15, in which Gad appears last). Tribal listings are discussed in Comment N–13. As he does previous tribal listings, Friedman ascribes Num. 26 to P (except for 26:9–11 on Korah's sons).
>
> Listed together with each of the twelve (non-Levitical) tribes are various tribal clans, named for sons and (or) other male descendants of the tribal founder. The rarity of a daughter's identification occurs twice in these listings. Having been singled out for identification as Asher's daughter among the otherwise unnamed granddaughters of Jacob en route to Egypt (Gen. 46:17), Serah (though long dead) is similarly singled out in Num. 26:46. Also named are five daughters of Zelophehad, of the tribe of Manasseh (26:33). In Num. 27 we learn of their unique plight and plea.

The Lord then states the purpose of the tribal census. "Among these shall the land be apportioned as shares, according to the listed names: with larger groups increase the share, with smaller groups reduce the share. *Each is to be assigned its share according to its enrollment.* The land, moreover, is to be apportioned by lot; and the allotment shall be made according to the listings of their ancestral tribes. Each portion shall be assigned by lot, whether for larger or smaller groups" (26:52–56).

> *Note N–116: The repetition of this basic intertribal land allocation formula attests to its importance. In essence, it would seem, the area entitlement of each tribe will reflect the number of males twenty years and up, able to bear arms. The general territorial situs of each tribe in Canaan will be settled peaceably by lot, with the particular boundaries to be adjusted for size.*

Num. 26:57–62 describes "the enrollment of the Levites by their clan." The clan listings begin with the same three major clans of Gershon, Kohath and Merari, the sons of Levi (see Num. 2:14–20). Particular note is made of the lineage of Moses, Aaron, and Miriam, as the sons and daughter of Amram and Jochebed. Amram is again identified as a son of Kohath and a grandson of Levi and Jochebed as a daughter of Levi—thus confirming their dual relationship as husband and wife and nephew and aunt (see Exod. 6:14–25).

The total of Levite males "from a month up" (as called for in Num. 3:15) was 23,000, as compared to the 22,000 reported in Num. 3:39 (but see Comment N–4).

Num. 26:63–65 then provides a summation. "These are the persons enrolled by Moses and Eleazar the priest who registered the Israelites on the steppes of Moab, at the Jordan near Jericho. *Among these there was not one of those enrolled by Moses and Aaron the priest when they recorded the Israelites in the wilderness of Sinai* [i.e., in the census of Num. 1]. For the Lord had said of them, 'They shall die in the wilderness.' *Not one of them survived, except Caleb son of Jephunneh and Joshua son of Nun.*"

In Num. 27:1–8, on the initiative of the five daughters of Zelophehad, the status of women is suddenly enhanced by a change in the law of inheritance. Zelophehad's daughters were Mahlah, *Noah*, Hoglah, Milcah, and Tirzah. As Manassites, like their father, they were in fact the great great great granddaughters of Joseph and the great great granddaughters of Manasseh (27:1). The story begins with a petition to "Moses, Eleazar the priest, the chieftains, and the whole assembly at the Tent of Meeting" (27:2).

> Our father died in the wilderness. He was not one of the faction, Korah's faction, which banded together against the Lord, but died for his own sin and he has left no sons. Let not our father's name be lost to his clan just because he had no son! Give us a holding among our father's kinsmen! (27:3–4)

Moses brought the case to the Lord, Who declared their plea to be "just." He thus instructed Moses to "give them a hereditary holding among their father's kinsmen: transfer their father's share to them" (27:5–7).

Note N–117: The daughters' plea is well devised. First, they base it on the need to protect their father's name. Second, they separate their father from Korah, for as Korah's follower, both his "name" and his patrimony would have been forfeit (see Num. 16 and Comment N–18). In having died for "his own sin," their father had shared the common fate of all Israelite adults who were to die before entering the promised land. Whatever Israel's collective sin, P's Lord had no intent to forfeit the "names" and patrimonies of an entire generation.

The Lord then declared this new law of inheritance.

If a man dies without leaving a son, you shall transfer his property to his daughter. If he has no daughter, you shall assign his property to his brothers. If he has no brothers, you shall assign his property to his father's brothers. If his father had no brothers, you shall assign his property to his nearest relative in his own clan, and *he* shall inherit it. (27:8–11)

Comment N–27. On daughters as heirs after Num. 27:1–11

However "progressive" the new law, any hope of daughters to keep their father's patrimony in *his* family would be defeated by their own marriages. Their property would then accrue to their husbands, from whom they could not reinherit. Should a daughter have a son (or sons), what had been once been *her father's patrimony* would pass to him (or them) as her husband's patrimony. Only if *sisters* could qualify as "nearest relatives," and thus be eligible to inherit from brothers lacking other heirs, could they regain their father's patrimony. But at least in the absence of a brother, a daughter could take directly from her own father.

The new inheritance law of 27:8–11 does not explicitly deal with the property of an unmarried daughter who, having inherited her father's patrimony, remains unmarried. Presumably, it would pass under the same rules as for a childless son. But consider the pre-marital dilemma faced by a daughter who, but for her brother, was the only living child of an elderly father. Should she marry, only to be preceded in death by her sickly brother, her father's patrimony would pass through her to her husband. But what if she wished, rather than to marry, to keep her father's patrimony in the family; *but, yet, were she to lose her inheritance to her brother, she would prefer to marry*? For such a daughter, a decision to marry was a bit of a gamble. But she might find comfort in knowing that the decision in any case was not likely hers.

In Num. 27:12–14 the Lord begins to fulfil His earlier decree that will bar Moses from entering Canaan. He thus tells Moses, " 'Ascend these heights of Abarim and view the land that I have given to the Israelite people. When you have seen it, you too shall be gathered to your kin, just as your brother Aaron was. For, in the wilderness of Zin, when the community was contentious, you disobeyed My command to uphold My sanctity in their sight by means of the water.' Those are the Waters of Meribath-kadesh, in the wilderness of Zin" (27:12–14).

Being who he was, Moses does not succumb to personal disappointment. He urges the need for a new leader to replace him once he has gone. "Let the Lord, Source of the breath of all flesh, appoint someone over the community . . . so that the Lord's community may not be like sheep that have no shepherd" (27:15–17).

And the Lord replied, "Single out Joshua son of Nun, an inspired man, and lay your hand upon him. Have him stand before Eleazar the priest and before the whole community, and commission him in their sight. Invest him with some of your authority, so that the whole Israelite community may obey. *But he shall present himself to Eleazar the priest, who shall on his behalf seek the decision of the Urim before the Lord.* By such instruction they shall go out and . . . come in, he and all the Israelites" (27:18–21).

Then "Moses did as the Lord commanded him" (27:22–23).

Comment N–28. On Joshua as the successor to Moses: an initial view

The Lord tells Moses to "invest [Joshua] with *some of* your authority" (27:20). The apparent aim is to give Joshua the experience of shared authority with Moses. Not until Moses dies, however, will Joshua "replace" him.

But even then will Joshua approach the stature of Moses? The question arises because of the need for P's Joshua to "process" inquiries to the Lord through Eleazar, who will then seek answers "of the Urim before the Lord." Does Joshua's need for Urim imply that he, unlike Moses, will not speak directly with the Lord? (See Exod. 28:30 on the use of Urim and Thummin in construing God's will.) *Yet, while P, ever eager to expand the role of the Aaronide priests, would "relegate" Joshua to Eleazer's "intermediation," in D's post-Torah book of Joshua, the Lord will speak directly to him* (see Josh. 1:1).

Num. 28 and 29 together provide a comprehensive list of offerings to be rendered at what would seem to include every appointed time of the year. As stated, "the Lord spoke to Moses saying: Command the Israelite people and say to them: Be punctilious in presenting to Me at stated times [i.e., *b'mohahdoh*] the offerings of food due Me, as offerings of pleasing odor to the Lord" (28:1–2).

> *Note N–118: The passage is reminiscent of Lev. 23 in which "the Lord spoke to Moses, saying: Speak to the Israelite people and say to them: These are my fixed times, the fixed times of the Lord which you shall proclaim as sacred occasions" (Lev. 23:1–2).*

What follows is a summary of these "stated times" and their requirements, including the "offerings by fire."

A. Each Day (28:3–8):

1. A burnt offering of "two yearling lambs without blemish" (i.e., one each in the morning and at twilight, "a regular burnt offering instituted at Mount Sinai—an offering by fire of pleasing odor to the Lord")
2. With each burnt offering, a meal offering of "choice flour" and "beaten oil"
3. With each set of burnt/meal offerings, a libation "to be poured *in the sacred precinct* [or "holy place" (*bahkodesh*)] as an offering of fermented drink to the Lord"

B. Each Sabbath (28:9–10):

1. A burnt offering of "two yearling lambs without blemish, . . . in addition to the regular burnt offering and its libation"
2. One double-sized meal offering (i.e., "two-tenths," rather than the daily "one-tenth," of a measure of "choice" flour)
3. A "proper libation" (as for each day)

C. Each New Moon (Rosh Chodesh) (28:11–15):

1. A burnt offering of "two bulls of the herd, one ram, seven yearling lambs, without blemish"
2. A meal offering for each animal offering (ten in all), with varying measures of choice flour and oil, as determined by the type of animal that it accompanies
3. A libation of wine for each animal offering, also varied in amount for each type of animal
4. A sin offering of one goat, "in addition to the regular burnt offering and its libation"

   Note N–119: *Were offerings, including daily offerings, meant to be cumulative on coincidental "stated times"?*

D. Passover (beginning on the evening of the fourteenth day of the first month, a seven day festival) (28:16–25):

1. On the fourteenth day of the first month, "a passover sacrifice to the Lord" (or "the Lord's passover," from *pesach lahyahweh*) (28:16)

2. On the fifteenth day of the first month (the first full day of seven days), "a festival" and "a sacred occasion," on which occupational work is forbidden

> Note N–120: In Num. 28:17 the single word chag is used to denominate the "festival" or "feast" of the fifteenth day of the first month. Lev. 23:6 explicitly assigns this day to the Lord as chag hahmatzot layahweh, the "Lord's Feast of Unleavened Bread."

3. Unleavened bread is eaten for seven days
4. On each of seven days, the following offerings:
   a. A "burnt offering to the Lord" of two bulls, one ram, and seven yearling lambs, all without blemish
   b. A meal offering for each animal offering (again ten in all), with varying measures of choice flour and oil, as determined by the type of animal that it accompanies
   c. A goat for a sin offering to make expiation
   d. Together with their libations, offerings (a) through (c) are to be made "in addition to the morning portion of the regular burnt offering"
   e. like the first full day of Passover, the seventh and final day is declared a "sacred occasion," on which occupational work is forbidden

E. Feast of Weeks (a spring harvest festival on the day of "the first fruits . . . when you bring an offering of new grain to the Lord," known today as shavuot) (28:26–30).

1. It is a sacred occasion, on which occupational work is forbidden
2. A burnt offering (of the usual pleasing odor to the Lord) of two bulls, one ram, and seven yearling lambs, without blemish
3. A meal offering for each animal offering (again ten in all), with varying measures of choice flour and oil, as determined by the type of animal which it accompanies
4. "One goat for expiation in your behalf"
5. These offerings, together with their libations "are in addition to the regular burnt offering and its meal offering" (see Note N–119)

F. The First Day of the Seventh Month (not named here or in Lev. 23:24, but now known as rosh hashonah) (29:1–6):

1. The day is declared a "sacred occasion," on which occupational work is forbidden, and to be observed as a day "when the horn is sounded"

2. A burnt offering (also of pleasing odor to the Lord) of two bulls, one ram, and seven yearling lambs, without blemish
3. A meal offering for each animal offering (again ten in all), with varying measures of choice flour and oil, as determined by the type of animal that it accompanies
4. A goat for a sin offering to make expiation
5. Together with their libations, these offerings are "in addition to the burnt offering of the new moon with its meal offering and the regular burnt offering with its meal offering" (see Note N–119)

G. The Tenth Day of the Seventh Month (the Day of Atonement, or *yom hakip-purim*) (29:7–11):

1. Like the first day of the seventh month, this tenth day is also declared a "sacred occasion;" but in addition it is a day of "self-denial" and one on which *all* work, in addition to *occupational* work, is forbidden
2 and 3. The same offerings as in F (2) and (3)
4. "One goat for a sin offering, *in addition* to the sin offering of expiation and the regular burnt offering with its meal offering, each with its libation"

> Note N–121: The difference between the two "sin offerings" of (4) is not immediately apparent. The one "in expiation" may relate to the priestly ritual of the "people's goat of sin offering" (see Lev. 16:15–17). As to the requirement of "self-denial," nothing is said regarding its details. It would later be construed to include a fast. At the time, however, absent an explicit requirement, a fast would seem to have been precluded, at least for officiating priests, by the ritually required consumption of offerings and libations.

H. The Fifteenth Day of the Seventh Month (the first day of the seven-day Feast of Booths [i.e., *sukot*] (29:12–34):

1. This first day is declared a "sacred occasion," on which occupational work is forbidden
2. A burnt offering (also of pleasing odor to the Lord) of thirteen bulls, two rams, and fourteen yearling lambs, without blemish
3. A meal offering for each animal offering (twenty-nine in all), with varying measures of choice flour and oil, as determined by the type of animal that it accompanies
4. A goat for a sin offering to make expiation—"in addition to the regular burnt offering, its meal offering and libation"

Note N–122: The offerings of the second through the seventh days are the same as those of the first day, with one exception. That is, on each succeeding day the number of bulls for a burnt offering is reduced by one. Thus, on the seventh day, only seven bulls are offered.

I. The Eighth Day Following the First Day of the Festival of Booths (or *shemini atzeret*) (29:35–39):

Note N–123: As indicated, the Festival of Booths, or sukot, as such, continues only through seven days. However, the eighth day following the fifteenth day of the seventh month is declared a day of "solemn gathering." The Hebrew, shemini atzeret, derives from bahyom hahshemini (on the eighth day), and atzeret (solemn gathering); thus, the solemn gathering of the eighth day.

1. A day of solemn gathering on which occupational work is forbidden
2. A burnt offering (of pleasing odor, etc.) of one bull, one ram, and seven yearling lambs without blemish
3. A meal offering for each animal offering (nine in all), with varying measures of choice flour and oil, as determined by the type of animal that it accompanies
4. A goat for a sin offering to make expiation—"in addition to the regular burnt offering, its meal offering and libation"

All the preceding requirements for the "stated times" of Num. 28 and 29 are then declared to be "in addition to your votive and freewill offerings, be they burnt offerings, libations, or offerings of well-being" (29:39).

Note N–124: JPS2's "stated times" of Num. 28 and 29 closely track, but also vary from, the "fixed times" of Lev. 23. Only three of the "stated," or "fixed," times are not common to both. These are the waving of the omer (only in Lev. 23:9–14), the daily offerings (only in Num. 28:3–8), and the monthly new moon offerings (only in Num. 28:11–15). In Lev. 23 no particular offerings are prescribed for most "fixed times," including, for example, the sabbath, passover, rosh hashonah, yom hakippurim, and sukot. A major purpose of Num. 28 and 29 is to set out prescribed offerings and rests for every occasion. Where particular offerings are designated in Lev. 23, they may differ from those of Num. 28 and 29, as in the case of shavuot (the Feast of Weeks). The need in Lev. 23:42–43 for all Israel to "live in booths" for the seven days of sukot is not repeated in Num. 29.

The main focus of Num. 30 is on "a *vow* to the Lord" or "an *oath* imposing an obligation on [oneself]." The core principle is stated in the rule governing "a man."

Thus, "if a *man* makes a vow to the Lord or takes an oath imposing an obligation on himself, *he shall not break his pledge; he must carry out all that has crossed his lips.*"

As to vows and oaths, the word "man" included a "woman." But to balance the sanctity of vows and oaths with the subordinate state of wives and unmarried daughters, their vows and oaths were subject to the following conditions:

1. As to an unmarried "woman" *"still in her father's household by reason of her youth"* (30:3–6).

   Note N–125: *The reference to a "woman" who remains unmarried "by reason of her youth" seems to imply an age of responsibility for unmarried women? If so, the Torah does not reveal it.*

   a. Should she make "a vow to the Lord" or assume an obligation by oath, *of which her father learns* and to which he offers no objection, the vow or obligation "shall stand."
   b. Should the father restrain her "on the day he finds out," her vow and oath is annulled and "the Lord will forgive her, since her father restrained her."

2. As to an unmarried "woman" who marries "while her vow or the commitment to which she bound herself is still in force" (30:7–9).

   a. Should the husband learn of it and offer no objection *"on the day he finds out,"* her vow and obligation shall stand.
   b. Should he restrain her "on the day that he learns of it, he thereby annuls her vow which was in force . . . and the Lord will forgive her."

   Note N–126: *Until the husband learns of and annuls a vow or oath not previously annulled by his wife's father, it remains "in force." Only on learning of it may the husband apply his own judgment to his wife's premarital vow or oath—as to its propriety or how it might affect him. Could a married woman (or an unmarried daughter) affirmatively seek to annul an inconvenient vow by informing her husband (or father) of it, with a plea that he "restrain" her?*

3. As to a widow or a divorced woman (30:10). "The vow of a widow or divorced woman, however, whatever she has imposed on herself, shall be binding upon her."

   Note N–127: *So stated, the vow or oath survives a remarriage, even if the husband should learn of it. She has made it while in an apparent state of emancipation.*

4. As to a married woman who first makes a "*vow*" or "*oath*" "while in her husband's household" (30:11–16).

 a. Should her husband learn of it, but not object to it on the same day ("thus failing to restrain her"), "all her vows . . . and . . . self-imposed obligations shall stand."

 b. "But if her husband does annul them on the day he finds out, then nothing that has crossed her lips shall stand. . . . Her husband has annulled them, and the Lord will forgive her." In general, "every vow and every sworn obligation of self-denial may be upheld by her husband or annulled by her husband." But should he first annul them "*after* the day he finds out, *he shall bear her guilt.*"

Note N–128: That her husband "shall bear her guilt" confirms what has been already been stated in regard to a woman of "responsible" age. A vow or oath not annulled by her father or husband creates "a guilt that she must bear." It is especially noteworthy, however, that the woman is not obliged to tell her father or husband of her vow. This serves to minimize the chances for annulling vows or oaths. It thus effects a balance between the principles of male dominance and the general sanctity of vows.

Comment N–29. On the oaths of Lev. 5:4 and the vows and oaths of Num. 30

Clearly, the "oaths" of Lev. 5:4 and Num. 30 are related—but to what extent? For one thing, Lev. 5:4 speaks only of an "oath" (*sh'vuhah*), while Num. 30 speaks both of a "vow" (*nehdehr*) and an "oath" (*sh'vuhah*). Thus, "if a man *makes a vow* to the Lord *or takes an oath imposing an obligation on himself*, he shall not break his pledge; he must carry out all that has crossed his lips" (30:3). In that the "vows" and "oaths" of Num. 30 both "cross the lips" of those who make them, they share the same degree of solemnity. Accordingly, the phrase "imposing an obligation on himself" should be read to modify both. If any technical distinction between the two terms is intended, the text does not reveal it. Nor is any reason given to distinguish between the *sh'vuhah*(s) of Lev. 5 and Num. 30.

But one further point can be made in regard to Lev. 5:4. Unlike the general rule of Num. 30 that men and women must honor vows and oaths, the particular sin of Lev. 5:4 seems to focus on the failure to recall an oath, once made. However, if recalled in time for the oath to be honored, there would seem to be no reason to declare a sin. As one possibility, therefore, I suggest that the sin of Lev. 5:4 was incurred only when the oath was recalled too late to be honored. But if recalled in time to be honored, it would seem to fall within Num. 30.

Num. 31 now picks up from the close of Num. 25. There, "the Lord spoke to Moses, saying, 'Assail the Midianites and defeat them—for they assailed you by the trickery they practiced against you—*because of the affair at Peor* and because of the affair of their kinswoman Cozbi, daughter of the Midianite chieftain, who was killed at the time of the plague on account of Peor" (25:16–18). Num. 31:1–2 then confirms the Lord's grim pronouncement in Num. 27:12–14: "*Avenge the Israelite people on the Midianites*: then you shall be gathered to your kin."

Preparations for the battle that follows, the battle itself, and its initial consequences are described in Num. 31:3–12. Moses first tells the people of an imminent campaign "to wreak the Lord's vengeance on Midian." It will require a thousand men from each of Israel's twelve tribes. In due course he sends them forth "with Phinehas son of Eleazar serving as priest on the campaign, equipped with the sacred utensils and the trumpets for sounding the blasts."

So it was that Israel "took the field against Midian, as the Lord had commanded Moses, *and slew every male*. Along with their other victims, they slew the kings of Midian: Evi, Rekem, Zur, Hur, and Reba, the five kings of Midian. *They also put Balaam son of Beor to the sword*" (31:8). (On P's "deconstruction" of the Balaam of J and E, see Comment N–31.)

As spoils of war, "the Israelites took the women and children of the Midianites captive, and seized as booty all their beasts, all their herds, and all their wealth." They also burnt down "all the towns in which they were settled, and their encampments." The troops then brought "the captives, the booty, and the spoil to Moses, Eleazar the priest, and the whole Israelite community, at the camp in the steppes of Moab, at the Jordan near Jericho."

Notwithstanding the enormity of their victory and their spoils, "Moses became angry with the commanders of the army, the officers of thousands and the officers of hundreds, who had come back from the military campaign" (31:14). Why is he angry? In his words: "You have spared every female! Yet they are the very ones who, *at the bidding of Balaam*, induced the Israelites to trespass against the Lord in the matter of Peor, so that the Lord's community was struck by the plague. *Now, therefore, slay every male among the children, and slay also every woman who has known a man carnally; but spare every young woman who has not had carnal relations with a man*" (31:15–18).

> Note N–129: Rather than "spare every young woman," JPS1/RSV derive from hachahyu lahchem "keep [such young women] alive for yourselves" (31:18).

Comment N–30. On Moses and the annihilation of the Midianites

To be sure of fulfilling the Lord's terse command to "*avenge the Israelite people on the Midianites*, Moses felt compelled to cast a wide net. In order to slay every woman who might possibly have seduced an Israelite man,

Moses "plays safe" by ordering the death of "every woman who has known man by lying with him." *With the added slaying of every male child, all the Midianites of Num. 31 would have been annihilated, but for captive virgin females.* Did the slain include Zipporah, the wife of Moses, his two sons Gershom and Eliezer, and (if still alive) his father-in-law, Jethro? Given the future presence of Midianites elsewhere, their annihilation in Num. 31 must have been limited to clans within the immediate area. (Yet we are told of the killing, not merely of "five of the kings of Midian," but rather of "*the* five kings of Midian" [31:8].)

To give Moses his due, we might view his anger with the military commanders as an expression of his anguish in having to express the Lord's intent in such explicit terms. Indeed, not even the military commanders could contemplate such severity. But even as myth rather than history, or as fiction rather than fact, it is painful to hear such words from Moses. Thus, there might be comfort in the thought that having reached "the steppes of Moab, at the Jordan near Jericho," Moses could find solace in knowing that death would free him of the endless anguish of fulfilling the Lord's will. If so, he would be quite ready to be "gathered *to [his] kin*" (31:2).

Comment N–31. On P's "deconstruction" of Balaam

From what we know of Balaam through Num. 22–24, we might view his execution in 31:8, and the reason for it in 31:16, as a tragic case of mistaken identity (see Comment N–25). But if P could so debase Moses' humanity, why should Balaam be immune from P's zeal?

As first revealed by E in Num. 22–24, Balaam was a faithful prophet of the Lord God of Israel. Now in Num. 31, absent any supporting narrative, P has him slain for having effected, through the women of Midian, the mass seduction of Israelite men into the worship of Baal.

That Balaam figured prominently in the traditions of Israel seems clear from his prominence in the Torah. Among the "postmythic" non-Israelites of the Torah, only Balaam provides a human focus for what would later become three full chapters of the Torah. And in them E (and perhaps J as well) draws a clear portrait of an honest and faithful non-Israelite prophet of the Lord (see Comment N–25).

Whether E's story accurately follows every element of a traditional story of Balaam, we do not know. But we may presume that its coherent and compelling details catch the essence of his character in earlier traditions of Israel. Yet, on one brief report of his having induced Israelites to worship Baal-Peor, this same Balaam, who blessed, and who would not for any reward curse, Israel, is revealed as a foe.

Deuteronomy will offer further evidence of a priestly reluctance to view Balaam as a righteous non-Israelite. There, it will be said that "the Lord your

God turned [Balaam's] curse into a blessing for you" (Deut. 23:5–6). While this statement turns E's detailed treatment of Balaam on its head, it at least places him in the context of Num. 22–24. In contrast, Balaam's presence in Midian seems contrary to the Torah's assertion that from Moab, Balaam "set out on his journey back home" (Num. 24:25) to "Pethor, *which is by the Euphrates*, in the land of his kinfolk" (22:5). Instead, to make mischief for Israel, did he truly tarry with the Midianites? For its own purpose, P would have it so.

Ironically, the P source stands as a friend to the "stranger." It professes to respect the common humanity of all persons who would live in peace with Israel and Israelites (Lev. 19:33:34). Indeed, the needy "stranger" is a proper object for charity (Lev. 19:9–10, 23:22). What, then, makes Balaam so hateful to P? What prompts P to reverse Balaam's role as an inspired agent of Israel's God into a calculating agent of Baal-Peor? Simply put, as a righteous non-Israelite prophet on whom E's God relies for help, Balaam would be perceived by P as a threat to the unique post-Moses role of the Aaronide priesthood as agents of its God.

Following the battle, for their own purification and that of the people, Moses directs the Israelite army and its captives to remain outside the camp for seven days. In the interim, "every one among you or among your captives who has slain a person or touched a corpse shall clean *himself* on the third and seventh days." They must also "cleanse every cloth, every article of skin, everything made of goats' hair, and every object of wood" (31:19–20).

> Note N–130: *The only captives were female virgins, some of whom in grief may have touched the corpse of a parent. To include them as "himself" could be misleading (31:15–18). JPS1/RSV avoid the problem by use of "whoever" and "yourselves."*

Eleazar then reviews the purification rituals "that the Lord has enjoined upon Moses." In essence, "any article that can withstand fire" must be passed through fire and cleansed with the "water of lustration" (as to which, see Num. 19:9). Burnable materials need only be passed through water. "On the seventh day you shall wash your clothes and be clean, and after that you may enter camp" (31:21–24).

In Num. 31:25–30 the Lord calls for an inventory and for the subsequent division of "the booty that was captured, man and beast." The inventory is to be taken by "you [i.e., Moses] and Eleazar the priest and the family heads of the community." It will then be divided "equally between the combatants who engaged in the campaign and the rest of the community." From both of these half shares of "persons, oxen, asses, and sheep" Moses was to "exact a levy for the Lord." The levy on "warriors who engaged in the campaign" would be "one item in five hundred"; on "the other Israelites, . . . one in every fifty." The total levy of "human beings as well as cattle, asses, and sheep—all the animals" would go to "to the Levites, who attend to the duties of the Lord's Tabernacle."

Num. 31:31–47 records the inventory count and its distribution among (1) "those who had engaged in the campaign"; (2) "the other Israelites"; and (3) "the Levites, who attended to the Lord's Tabernacle." The total booty, "other than the spoil that the troops had plundered," came to 675,000 sheep, 72,000 head of cattle, 61,000 asses, and "a total of *32,000 human beings, namely, the women who had not had carnal relations*" (31:35). Less the Lord's two levies of one in fifty and one in five hundred, the totals were equally divided between the army and all other Israelites. From both sources the Lord's levy would be 7,425 sheep, 792 cattle, 671 asses, and 352 women.

> *Note N–131: The amounts of the Lord's levy on the army's share, being one-tenth the amount of the levy on the "peoples" share, are set out in 31:36–41. The amounts of the Lord's ten-fold levy on "other Israelites" are left to the reader's calculation. Not reported, however, are the allocation principles governing the one-half of the booty given to "the other Israelites." This group included some 588,000 adult males as compared to the 12,000 in the army. Available for allocation among them were 337,500 sheep, 36,000 cattle, 30,500 asses, and 16,000 women. The Torah (wisely?) leaves all further allocations to communal discretion.*

Num. 31:48–54 tells of an expression of gratitude to the Lord from "the commanders of the troop divisions, the officers of thousands and the officers of hundreds." They explain it to Moses. "Your servants have made a check of the warriors in our charge, and *not one of us is missing*. So we have brought as an offering to the Lord such articles of gold as each of us came upon: armlets, bracelets, signet rings, earrings, and pendants, *that expiation may be made for our persons before the Lord*" (31:49–50).

Moses and Eleazar accept the gold as "a contribution to the Lord" (i.e., in support of the Tent, the priests and Levites). It totalled 16,750 shekels. "But in the ranks everyone kept his booty for himself." Moses and Eleazar then brought the gold to the Tent of Meeting, "as a reminder in behalf of the Israelites before the Lord."

Comment N–32. On the officers' felt need to atone

The officers express a need for "expiation" (JPS1 and RSV render *l'chahpayr ahl naphshohtaynu* in 31:50 as "to make atonement for our souls [or ourselves]"). But given the circumstances, why must they atone and seek expiation? Should they not have rejoiced in a job well done? Or had the slaughter of every Midianite, but for female virgins, touched their consciences? Or was it just the reverse? Were they in fact guilt-stricken by not having sensed the need to do so initially? Others might deplore the mayhem, but not P, the most zealous guardian of the Lord's sanctity and authority. (Rashi realistically ignores the slaughter as grounds for penitence. He suggests that their remorse arose from thoughts rather than deeds, i.e., their "impure thoughts of the heart toward the daughters of Midian."[16])

The focus of Num. 32 is on tribal locations and land allotments. It may presage future tensions in Israel between national and tribal identities and loyalties.

> *Note N–132: Recall that in Num. 26:52–56 the Lord instructs Moses on the principles of land apportionment in Canaan among the tribes. Tribal portions are to reflect tribal populations (or, more precisely, "enrollments" of males twenty years and over). The general location of each tribal territory will be determined by lot. As of Num. 32, the enrollments are known from the census of Num. 26, but general tribal locations are not yet fixed. What seems "fixed" for the moment, however, is the Lord's intent for all tribes to settle within the land promised to Abraham. In finally defining that land for Abraham, the Lord refers to "all the land of Canaan." Canaan alone, therefore, will be Israel's "everlasting possession" (Gen. 17:8). But now, as the time approaches for Israel's entry into Canaan, the tribes of Reuben and Gad propose to settle on certain lands outside Canaan.*

In essence, the tribes of Reuben and Gad, the owners of many cattle, seek permission to settle in the "cattle country" of "Jazer and Gilead," *east* of the Jordan River. They ask this of "Moses, Eleazer the priest, and chieftains of the community" (32:1–2). They would keep the land as "a holding," in lieu of crossing the Jordan (32:4–5).

Moses, however, is more concerned with the peoples' unity and determination in fulfilling the Lord's plan than with maximizing cattle output. He sees a variety of problems impacting on (1) Israel's military capacity to conquer all Canaan and (2) its general morale.

First, who will replace the troops of the two tribes? "Are your brothers to go to war while you stay here?" (32:6).

Second, how will other tribes interpret the reluctance of Reuben and Gad to cross over into the promised land? Will they attribute it to a fear of defeat? Moses then recalls the disastrous events in the wilderness through which Israel's morale was shattered by scouts who spread "calumnies about the land" (see Num. 12). He reminds the two tribes of the consequential "forty years" of wandering before Israel could enter Canaan, during which, but for Caleb and Joshua, "the whole generation died" (32:10–13). Moses then envisions the possible disaster of the Lord's similar response against a new and divided generation. "And now you, a breed of sinful men, have replaced your fathers, to add still further to the wrath against Israel. If you turn away from Him and He abandons them once more in the wilderness, you will bring a calamity upon all this people" (32:14–15).

Comment N–33. On the irony of the Waters of Meribah, the Midianites, and Gilead

1. At P's Meribah of Num. 20:2–13, Moses struck the rock with his rod without (in this second similar episode) having being told to do so (cf. E's "Meribah" of Exod. 17:2–7). Thus, by seeming to participate in supplying the water and thereby denying the Lord as its sole source, Moses (and Aaron) are to be punished for demeaning His sanctity. Neither of them "shall lead this congregation into the land that I have given them" (see Comment N–22).

2. Following the apostasy of many Israelite men with Midianite women, the Lord tells Moses to "avenge the Israelite people on the Midianites: then you shall be gathered to your kin" (31:1–2). *Lacking further instructions*, Moses must himself decide which Midianites must die and who may live. Thus, when the troops return, he sends them back at once with orders to slay all nonvirgin females and male children (31:14–18).

3. Knowing of the Lord's plan for all of Israel to settle in Canaan, Moses will nevertheless negotiate terms under which the tribes of Reuben and Gad may settle east of the Jordan. (Having begun at 32:2, the negotiations and their rather convoluted consequences continue through 32:42.)

4. By silent acquiescence and confirmatory acts, the Lord affirms the initiatives of Moses in (2) and (3).

And yet, in having failed to affirm the Lord's sanctity through faulty reliance on an earlier command, Moses must die before leading his people into Canaan. But even in denying Moses this well-earned culmination of his brilliant leadership, the Lord turns twice more to his leadership to resolve two matters of utmost moral and national importance. The first involves life or death for an entire people (other than virgin females); the second involves Israel's sense of nationhood within Canaan itself.

As for the first, we must deplore the need felt by Moses to rebuke the leniency of his military commanders for failing at first to kill the male children and nonvirgin females of the Midianites. But in doing so, Moses spoke not for himself, but for what he "knew" of the mind of Israel's Lord God. And for the same reason Moses was quite ready to negotiate the petition of the Reubenites and Gadites to remain in Gilead. After forty years with the Lord, P's Moses had come to understand His mind in every way but one. As reflected in the waters of Meribah, and in its results that would forever perplex his descendants, Moses could never fully grasp the full extent of the Lord's pride in His sanctity.

The Reubenites and Gadites assure Moses of their good intentions. After providing "*sheepfolds for our flocks and towns for our children*" they will join the other tribes in the conquest of Canaan (32:16). Indeed, they promise to "*hasten as shock-troops* in the van of the Israelites until we have established them in their home" (32:17). Moreover, they will not return to their homes "until every one of the Israelites is in possession of his portion" (32:18). Finally, they disclaim all rights to land in Canaan (i.e., in "territory beyond the Jordan") (32:19).

Moses agrees at once. "If . . . every shock-fighter among you crosses the Jordan, at the instance of the Lord, *until He has dispossessed His enemies before Him, and the land has been subdued, at the instance of the Lord*, and then you return—you shall be clear before the Lord and before Israel; and this land shall be your holding under the Lord. But if you do not do so, you will have sinned against the Lord; and know that your sin will overtake you. *Build towns for your children and sheepfolds for your flocks*, but do what you have promised" (32:20–24).

In reply, the Gadites and Reubenites assure Moses that, as his "servants," they will fulfil all his commands (32:25–27). Moses then explains the unique situation of the two tribes to "Eleazar the priest, Joshua son of Nun, and the family heads of the Israelites" (32:28).

JPS2 describes the condition under which Reuben and Gad could remain in Gilead as follows: If "every *shock-fighter*" of Gad and Reuben crosses the Jordan to do battle, and Canaan is subdued, "you [Joshua and Eleazer] shall give them the land of Gilead as a holding. But if they do not cross over with you *as shock-troops*, they shall receive holdings among you in the land of Canaan" (32:29–30).

> *Note N–133: In Num. 32:29–30 JPS2 conditions the grant of Gilead to Gad and Reuben on their serving as "shock-troops" who lead the invasion of Canaan. However, JPS1/RSV would require less—only that they "pass with you over the Jordan" and, together with the other tribes, "subdue" the land. Further, "if they will not pass over with you armed, they shall have possessions among you in the land of Canaan." The difference is in the meaning of chalutz.*

The tribes agree. "Whatever the Lord has spoken concerning your servants, that we will do. We ourselves will cross over as shock-troops [*chalutzim*], at the instance of the Lord, into the land of Canaan; and we shall keep our hereditary holding across the Jordan" (32:31–32).

> *Note N–134: The tribes ascribe Moses' decision to the Lord.*

But now it appears that yet another tribe would also stay in Gilead (32:33–42)!

"So Moses *assigned* to them—to the Gadites, the Reubenites, *and the half-*

tribe of Manasseh son of Joseph—territories of their surrounding towns." The division of lands east of the Jordan among the two and one-half tribes are then described in Num. 32:34–42. Towns rebuilt and occupied by the tribes of Gad and Reuben are set out in 32:34–36 and 37–38, respectively. Most notable, given the earlier text, are the lands of Manasseh in regard to Gilead (32:39–42). *"The descendants of Machir son of Manasseh went to Gilead and captured it*, dispossessing the Amorites who were there; *so Moses gave Gilead to Machir son of Manasseh*, and he settled there" (32:39–40).

Comment N–34. On Num. 32—one history from two sources

We know of "Gilead" as a son of Machir and grandson of Manasseh (Num. 26:29, 27:1). How did the tribes of Reuben and Gad come to know the land of Gilead, as such, even "before" its capture by Manasseh? (See 32:1, 25–30, and 33–42.) No less of a puzzle is the ultimate assignment of Gilead to Manasseh (32:40), despite its earlier conditional assignment to Reuben and Gad by Moses (32:28–30). And why are they now content to cede their coveted cattle region of Gilead to Manasseh in return for the kingdoms of Sihon and Og (32:33)?

Num. 32 must be read and interpreted as R's amalgam of more than one source. Friedman observes that "this chapter appears to contain elements of J and P. Precise identification by verses in difficult."[17] He surely has a point.

We might also take note that in JPS2's 32:33 Moses is said to have "assigned" the "kingdom of Sihon king of the Amorites and the kingdom of Og king of Bashan" to the two and one-half tribes of Gad, Reuben, and Manasseh. Num. 32:39–40 then states that Moses "gave" Gilead to Manasseh. One might assume a different status between lands "given" and "assigned." Both, however, are from *vahyitayn moshe* ("and Moses gave"). However, if all land allotments east of the Jordan are assumed to have been conditional, the use of "assigned" might better suggest their tentative status.

As Israel prepares to invade Canaan from the plains of Moab across the Jordan near Jericho, the Torah pauses to "recapitulate" the past forty-year journey from Egypt.

Num. 33 opens as follows: "These were the marches of the Israelites who started out from the land of Egypt, troop by troop, in the charge of Moses and Aaron. Moses recorded the starting points of the various marches as directed by the Lord. As for their first starting point: "They set out from Rameses in the first month, on the fifteenth day of the first month. It was on the morrow of the passover offering that the Israelites started out boldly, in plain view of all the Egyptians. The Egyptians meanwhile were burying those among them whom the Lord had struck down, every firstborn—whereby the Lord executed judgment on their gods" (33:1–4).

Note N–135: Num. 33:5–39 reflects R's effort to "integrate" the course of Israel's forty-year passage from Rameses, in Egypt, to the plains of Moab. Given the ambiguities, gaps and contradictions among the primary sources, as well as a the "blank" period of some thirty-eight years in the wilderness, R's effort involves more than a recapitulation. Its inclusion of sites and routes not yet identified might even suggest the presence of traditions not previously recorded.

Seemingly absent is a discernible basis for R's inclusion or exclusion of particular events. Among those not mentioned are the parting of the Sea, the Lord's provision of manna, the theophanies and revelations at Sinai, the construction of the Tent/Tabernacle, and the apostasies of Baal-Peor and their consequences. Indeed, the only noted events are the lack of water at Rephidim, the death of Aaron on Mount Hor (33:38–39), and the simple observation that "the Canaanite, king of Arad, who dwelt in the Negeb . . . learned of the coming of the Israelites" (33:40). However, of particular interest in R's account of routes taken during the thirty-eight years of wandering is a previously unrecorded movement to Ezion-geber, at the Gulf of Aqaba, followed by Israel's final return to Kadesh (33:35–37).

Although the Torah offers no explicit foundation for portions of R's itinerary, it does bring Israel's forty years of wandering to a close on "the plains of Moab" (subject only to D's further recapitulation in Deut. 1–3).

Num. 33:52–56 contains the Lord's instructions to Moses in "the steppes of Moab, at the Jordan near Jericho," as to the duties of the "Israelite people" in Canaan (33:50–51). On crossing the Jordan, they are to "dispossess all the inhabitants of the land; . . . destroy all their figured objects [and] molten images, and . . . demolish all their cult places." Once they have purified the land by destroying all physical vestiges of idolatry, they are directed by the Lord to "take possession of the land and settle in it, for I have given you the land to possess it" (33:52–53).

Num. 33:54 repeats the land apportionment principles of Num. 26:52–56. Num. 33 then closes with the Lord's somber warning of 33:55–56: "But if you do not dispossess the inhabitants of the land, those whom you allow to remain shall be stings in your eyes and thorns in your sides, and they shall harass you in the land in which you live; *so that I will do to you what I planned to do to them.*"

Note N–136: The warning against allowing any previous inhabitants "to remain" carries the same sense of urgency as the command to destroy all physical vestiges of idolatry in Canaan (33:51–52). Idolators, as well as the paraphernalia of idolatry, must be expunged from the land. If this is the intent of this putative P passage, it contradicts the gradual process of removal described by the Lord in the E passage of Exod. 23:29–30: "I will not drive [the Canaanite tribes] out before you in a single year, lest the land become desolate and the wild beasts multiply to your hurt. I will drive them out before you little by little, until you have increased and possess the land."

So that the "Israelite people" may know, the Lord speaks to Moses of "the land that shall fall to you as your portion, the land of Canaan with its various boundaries" (Num. 34:1–2). In turn, He describes the "southern sector" (or "side") (34:3–5); the western boundary (34:6); the northern boundary (3:7–9) and the eastern boundary (34:10–12). Of these, of course, the most easily visualized is the "Great Sea" on the west (i.e., the Mediterranean). For most readers today, any useful visualization of the other boundaries, as they appear in Num. 34, requires a map.[18]

The southern boundary begins at the southern shore of the Dead Sea and moves southwestward in a "gentle" ark through the wilderness of Zin, just south of Kadesh-barnea, thence northwestward to the southern shore of the Great Sea at the "Wadi," or "Brook," of Egypt. (This is probably the "river of Egypt" in Gen. 15:18. Also see Comment G–22.) In modern terms, the line lies well south of the city of Gaza and includes all, or much of, the "Gaza strip." But being well north of the Gulf of Aqaba/Elath, it excludes a large portion of what is now southern Israel.

As described, the northern boundary, running from the Great Sea through Mount Hor (in the north) to Hazar-enan through Lebo-hamath, lies well to the north of Damascus in Syria. (There is a significant consensus among scholars that this boundary generally corresponds to the northern boundary of Egypt's earlier province of Canaan. More important to its presence in the Torah, however, is the northern boundary established for a time in the reign of David. Like the "idealized" boundaries of Gen. 15:18 ("from the river of Egypt, to the great river, the river Euphrates"), the similar boundary of Num. 34:7–9 likely comes from the same post-Davidic period (again see Comment G–22). (Genesis also includes other, if less precise, descriptions of the land promised to Abraham's descendants. See Comments G–20 and 24.)

Most problematic is the the eastern boundary. First moving southward from Hazar-enan, it then turns eastward to what the Torah designates as the Sea of Chinnereth (Lake Kinneret or Tiberias today and formerly the Sea of Galilee). Since Hazer-enan lies roughly as far east of Damascus as Damascus lies east of the Mediterranean, a large portion of Syria (as well as Lebanon) falls within the Canaan of Num. 34. From the Sea of Chinnereth south to the Dead Sea, the Jordan River constitutes the eastern boundary.

In Num. 34:13–15 Moses characterizes the land within these boundaries as "the land you are to receive by lot as your hereditary portion, *which the Lord has commanded* to be given to the nine and a half tribes" (34:13). To this he adds that the "Reubenite tribe ... the Gadite tribe ... and the half-tribe of Manasseh" have already received their portions "across the Jordan, opposite Jericho, on the east, the orient side" (34:14–15).

> Note N–137: Moses does not explicitly attribute his land allotments east of the Jordan to the Lord. (See Comments N–33 and 34.)

In Num. 34:16–28 the Lord tells Moses "the names of the men through whom the land *shall be apportioned for you*" (34:17). Once the Lord has named the men, their roles are repeated: "It was these whom the Lord designated to allot portions to the Israelites in the land of Canaan" (34:29).

> *Note N–138: The text is vague on the men's duties. Although Friedman attributes both allotment passages of Num. 26:55–56 and 34:17 and 29 to P, a possible difference in the manner of apportioning (by men in Num. 34 and by lot in Num. 26) might suggest a conflict. Rashi, however, in summarizing the men's duties of 34:17 and 29, states that "they shall cause you to take possession of it according to its divisions."[19] He thus suggests a distinction between the method of allotting lands (by lot) and the implementation of the method (by men).*

As members of the group, the Lord first names "Eleazar the priest and Joshua son of Nun" (34:17).

> *Note N–139: To represent the interests of all Israel, Joshua, the future successor to Moses (Num. 27:18–20), and Eleazar, as high priest, will lead the group.*

In addition, the Lord names a representative from each tribe (34:18–28). Except for Caleb from the tribe of Judah (see Num. 14:29–30), the tribal leaders are of less interest here than the tribes.

Of the twelve non-Levitical tribes of Israel (i.e., counting the half-tribes of Manasseh and Ephraim as one each), only ten are named. Excluded are the tribes of Reuben and Gad. *Among those named is the tribe of Manasseh.*

> *Note N–140: Given their prior arrangements with Moses for lands east of the Jordan River, the exclusion of Reuben and Gad is fully warranted. They had no rightful role in the allotment of tribal territories in Canaan itself. Why, then, is the tribe of Manasseh given a voice? As stated in Num. 32:40, "so Moses gave Gilead [being east of the Jordan River] to Machir son of Manasseh, and he settled there." Moreover, Moses confirms this assignment in Num. 34:14–15.*
>
> *Did the author of 34:18–28 not know of 32:33–42 and 34:14–15. Surely the "logic" that bars Reuben and Gad from any role in allotting lands west of the Jordan applies no less to the Manasseh. If it were not for Num. 34:14–15, we could attribute the confusion regarding Manasseh to the composite authorship of Num. 32 (most likely as between P [32:1–32] and J [32:33–42]). Recall here Friedman's conclusion that Num. 32 "appears to contain elements of J and P. Precise identification by verses is difficult."*

Complicating the matter, however, Friedman attributes the whole of Num. 34 to P, including the assignment of land east of the Jordan to Manasseh (34:14–15).

Why then does P's Lord in 34:23 involve the tribe of Manasseh in apportioning the lands of Canaan among the tribes? Either Manasseh is also to have land in Canaan (which seems unlikely from the text of 34:14:15), or, contrary to Friedman, the author of 34:14–15 was not the author of 34:23. This possibility finds support in the fact that it is "Moses" who locates the Manassites east of the Jordan in 34:14–15, while it is "the Lord" who involves them in apportioning lands in Canaan (34:23).

Num. 35:1–9 addresses the practical problems created by the following provisions of Num. 18:23–24 regarding the allocation of lands to the Levites. "But they shall have no territorial share among the Israelites; for it is the tithes set aside by the Israelites as a gift to the Lord that I give to the Levites as their share. Therefore I have said concerning them: They shall have no territorial share among the Israelites."

Note N–141: The tithing system in support of the priests and their duties is described Num. 18.

The first question is where will the Levites live when all lands are apportioned among non-Levitical tribes. This is the subject of Num. 35, as Israel remains encamped "in the plains [or steppes] of Moab at the Jordan near Jericho."

Out of their own respective holdings, the various tribes are to "assign . . . towns for the Levites to dwell in," together with "pasture land around their towns" (35:2). "The towns shall be theirs to dwell in, and the pasture shall be for cattle they own [through tithing] and all their other beasts" (35:3).

The next two verses suggest an anomaly. "The town pasture that you are to assign to the Levites shall extend a thousand cubits outside the town wall all around. You shall measure off two thousand cubits outside the town on the east side, two thousand on the south side, two thousand on the west side, and two thousand on the north side, with the town in the center. That shall be the pasture for their towns" (35:4–5).

Note N–142: Do the two thousand cubits of 35:5 supercede the one thousand cubits of 35:4. To resolve the point, Rashi suggests that of the two thousand cubits, the "inner one thousand" was to serve as "open land" (or grazing), while the "outer one thousand" would be used "for fields and vineyards" (or growing).[20] If so, why are the one thousand and two thousand cubit allotments both described as "pasture," or "open land" (i.e., migr'shay hehahrim, *35:4–5)? Rambam's attentive analysis should hold a special fascination for mathematicians.*[21]

Num. 35:6–8 deals further with the Levitical cities previously described as "towns for Levites to dwell in" from among "the holdings apportioned to the [non-Levitical tribes]" (35:2). In all, there are to be forty-eight such cities, including "the six cities of refuge which you are to set aside for a manslayer to flee to."

> *Note N–143: The need for such sites of refuge was first signaled in E's mishpat of Exod. 21:13 in regard to unintentional killings (see Comment E–68 and Num. 35:9–15).*

The provision of Levitical cities would be shared fairly among the tribes. "In setting aside towns from the holding of the Israelites, take more from the larger groups and less from the smaller, so that each assigns towns to the Levites in proportion to the share it receives" (35:8).

Num. 35:9–15 covers instructions regarding the six Levitical cities of refuge of 35:6. They are to serve "as cities of refuge to which a manslayer who has killed a person unintentionally may flee." More specifically, "the cities shall serve you as a refuge from the avenger, so that the manslayer may not die *unless he has stood trial before the assembly*" (35:12). But for the placement of three such cities on both sides of the Jordan, Num. 35:13–15 largely repeats earlier verses. Num. 35:15 also clarifies the class entitled to refuge: "These six cities shall serve the Israelites *and the resident aliens among them*, so that *anyone* who kills a person unintentionally may flee there."

> *Note N–144: Are the Levites to have no duties other than administering the law of refuge?*

Num. 35:16–24 deals with the determination of intent, or its absence. Thus, "any one . . . who strikes another with an iron object so that death results is a murderer; the murderer must be put to death" (35:16). "If he struck him with a stone tool [or, "similarly," with a "wooden tool"] that could cause death, and death resulted, he is a murderer; the murderer must be put to death" (35:17–18). To the foregoing is added the following perplexing command: "The blood-avenger himself shall put the murderer to death; it is he who shall put him to death *upon encounter*" (35:19). "So, too, if he pushed him in hate or hurled something at him on purpose and death resulted, or if he struck him with his hand in enmity and death resulted, the assailant shall be put to death, he is a murderer. *The blood-avenger shall put the murderer to death upon encounter*" (35:20–21).

To prove a lack of intent to kill, the emphasis is on motivation. "But if he

pushed him without malice aforethought or hurled any object at him unintentionally, or inadvertently dropped upon him any deadly object *of stone*, and
death resulted—though he was not an enemy of his and did not seek his harm—
in such cases the assembly shall decide between the slayer and the blood-avenger"
(35:22–24).

Num. 35:25–29 sets out the jurisdiction of the assembly and various rules
pertaining to the cities of refuge. First, "the assembly shall protect the manslayer
from the blood-avenger, and the assembly shall restore him to the city of refuge
to which he fled, *and there he must remain until the death of the high priest who was
anointed with the sacred oil*" (35:25). On leaving "the limits of the city of refuge"
before the death of the high priest (as of the time of trial?), the innocent
manslayer was at peril. Should the blood-avenger find and kill him beyond the
city limits, "there is no blood guilt on his account." Only "after the death of the
high priest" may the innocent manslayer "return to his land holding" (35:26–28).

Literally, Num. 35:30 served as a limit on the right of a "blood-avenger" to
"put the murderer to death *upon encounter*" (35:19). Thus, "if *anyone* kills a
person, the manslayer may be executed only on the evidence of witnesses; the
testimony of a single witness against a person shall not suffice for a sentence of
death" (35:30).

Num. 35:31–32 prohibits the use of "ransoms" (i.e., monetary substitutes for
prescribed punishments) in two cases: (1) by an intentional killer to avert a punishment of death (35:31) and (2) by an otherwise innocent manslayer to buy
"early parole" from a city of refuge (i.e., prior to the high priest's death) (35:32).

Num. 35 concludes with a homily on the shedding of blood as a defilement
of both the land and the Lord. "You shall not pollute the land in which you live;
for blood pollutes the land, and the land can have no expiation for blood that is
shed on it, except by the blood of him who shed it. You shall not defile the land
in which you live, *in which I Myself abide for I the Lord abide among the Israelite
people*" (35:33–34).

Comment N–35. On several aspects of the rules governing intentional and unintentional killings

1. On defining intent

In determining intent, a defendant's state of mind and the nature of his act
are *theoretically* independent factors. In practice, however, the nature of the
act will sometimes speak to the matter of intent. In Num. 35:16–18 the point
is carried to the extreme. With no apparent exception, a person who kills by
striking another person with an "iron object," a "stone tool," or "wooden
tool" is declared "a murderer" who "must be put to death." How the object
came to be used would seem irrelevant. As to intent, its use is declared conclusive. In time, it, too, like the rule of *lex talionis*, would have to be modified.

But here a possible modification soon follows in Num. 35:20–21 with the introduction of motivation, apart from method, as a measure of intent. Thus, rather than determining intent by the act itself (as in 35:16–18), the test of 35:20–21 is whether *any* act resulting in death was done with "hate," "on purpose," or "in enmity." If so, with no exception, the actor is declared a murderer and subject to death. It is implied, however, that a killing effected without "hate," "actual intent," or "enmity" is an innocent act. But even if by means of an "iron object," or a "stone" or "wooden" tool? The path to justice has ever been strewn with such ambiguities.

How these rules, and their combined ambiguities, might affect pleas of self defense, or mental incapacity, must be considered elsewhere.

2. On jurisdictional problems under Num. 35:16–34 in determining of guilt or innocence

Consider the following provisions:

1. "The blood-avenger shall put the murderer to death *upon encounter*" (35:21). (To the same effect see 35:19.)
2. "In such cases [in which the defense is a lack of intent] the assembly [of the city of refuge] shall decide between the slayer and the blood-avenger" (35:24).
3. "If anyone kills a person, the manslayer may be executed only on the evidence of witnesses: the testimony of a single witness against a person shall not suffice for a sentence of death" (35:30).

What needs clarification is whether the provisions of (1) give license to an irate "blood-avenger" to slay the "murderer" *upon encounter*. This, of course, depends in part on the meaning of "murderer," rather than "manslayer." In theory, a fleeing "manslayer" becomes a "murderer" only by the judgment of the assembly of the city of refuge. There is also a question of whether the need for two witnesses applies to the manslayer's intent as well as to his actual identity as such.

These and related questions are amenable to legal analysis. But we had best leave the task to another venue—together with the fate of a distraught "blood-avenger" who mistakenly, but in good faith, kills the wrong person.

3. On the requirement of the innocent killer to remain in the city of refuge until the death of the high priest

The exonerated killer was required to remain in the city of refuge until the death of the current high priest. On leaving prematurely he was fair prey for a "guiltless" killing by the blood-avenger. Why was the innocent killer required to await the death of the high priest before departing the city of refuge? This could relate to the central role of the "anointed priest" in the rituals of atonement for the "unwitting" sins of Lev. 4. Of all the "unwitting" sins for which expiation through atonement was allowed, surely to kill was the most egregious. Perhaps it was thought that the priest's atonement for an unintentional killing committed during his tenure would continue until his death. It might then follow that the killer could not resume a normal life until the priest's atonement had ended.

4. On the relationship of Num. 35 to Exod. 21:13

Num. 35 sets out P's more detailed development of the laws of intentional and unintentional killings and of the role of Levitical cities of refuge in their implementation. However, the earliest foundation for P's laws appears in E's *mishpatim* of Exod. 21:12–13: "He who fatally strikes a man shall be put to death. If he did not do it by design, but it came about by an act of God, I will assign you a place to which you can flee" (Exod. 21:12–13). In dealing with "intent" (or "design") in Num. 35, P omits E's fascinating concept of "an act of God" (see Comment E–68). But through its "cities of refuge" P does meet E's unfulfilled need for "a place to which you can flee."

Num. 36, the last chapter of the Book of Numbers, returns to the unfinished business of Num. 27:1–8. It was there that the Lord allowed the five brotherless daughters of Zelophehad to inherit directly from their father, to the exclusion of other male relatives. In order to maintain the integrity of family and clan property, a broad new principle of inheritance was thus established. "If a man dies without leaving a son, you shall transfer his property to his daughter(s)" (27:8).

As discussed in Comment N–27 the new law, in itself, could not prevent the transfer of the family's estate to daughter's husband—of whatever tribe. In Num. 36:3, the daughters give voice to this deficiency as a tribal issue. "Now, if [we] marry persons from another Israelite tribe, [our] share will be cut off from our ancestral portion and be added to the portion of the tribe into which [we] marry; thus our allotted portion will be diminished."

"At the Lord's bidding," Moses announces a new command to resolve the problem (27:5):

> This is what the Lord has commanded concerning the daughters of Zelophehad: They may marry anyone they wish, *provided they marry into a clan of their father's tribe*. No inheritance of the Israelites may pass over from one tribe to another, but the Israelites must remain bound each to his ancestral portion of the tribe. Every daughter among the Israelite tribes who inherits a share must marry someone from a clan of her father's tribe, in order that every Israelite may keep his ancestral share. Thus no inheritance shall pass over from

one tribe to another, but the Israelite tribes shall remain bound each to its portion." (27:6–9)

And so the five daughters of Zelophehad, these being Mahlah, Torzah, Hoglah, Milcah, and Noah, "did as the Lord had commanded Moses." They married "sons of their uncles [i.e., their first cousins] . . . descendants of Manasseh son of Joseph." And accordingly, "their shares remained in the tribe of their father's clan (36:10–12).

> Note N–145: The command did not bar intertribal marriages, except as necessary to keep a daughter's inherited tribal assets within the tribe. However, the very purpose and effect of the constraint might deter "brotherless" daughters of a living father from marrying outside the tribe, pending the possible birth of a brother before their father's death.

Numbers then concludes with a final summation by the unknown, but ubiquitous, narrator of the Torah. "These are the commandments and regulations that the Lord enjoined upon the Israelites through Moses, on the steppes of Moab, at the Jordan near Jericho" (36:13).

CONCLUSION: ON ISRAEL AS A NATION OF TRIBES AND PEOPLE—WITH THOUGHTS OF BALAAM AND MOSES

Forty years of shared experience, from Egypt to "the steppes of Moab," has forged the Israelites of Egypt into the nation of Israel. It is as much a nation of tribes, however, as of people. From the opening tribal census in Numbers to its closing restraints on intertribal marriages, the constant effort has been to preserve tribal identities and the integrity of tribal properties. It will culminate in the allotment of specific lands to separate tribes.

Like the federalism of the United States Constitution, the tribalism of Israel served more to divide than to unify the nation. Yet, like federalism, the tribalism of Israel was a source of strength in the nation's development. Given the limits of transportation and communication, tribal and clan affiliations were essential as a source of social cohesion through common ancestry, kinship and traditions.

Yet, to maximize tribal identity through the total prohibition of intertribal marriages could seriously impair the continuing growth and strength of Israel as a nation of people. Such restrictions would have reinforced tribal parochialism and perhaps even reduced the number of births. Whether as a collectivity of tribes or as a single people, Israel was surrounded by foes, both actual and potential. In the circumstances, Israel could ill afford to discourage potentially fruitful unions that otherwise met its moral tenets.

As a unifying force to generate a sense of nationhood amidst its basic trib-alism, the Torah's authors created the Being of the Lord, its God. Through the projected power and sanctity of His Being, Israel would develop a common code of (1) moral and ethical standards, (2) civil and criminal laws, (3) cultic prac-tices, and (4) rituals of obeisance.

On one central aspect of the Lord's role in unifying Israel, however, the Torah was at odds with itself. This was on Israel's need to claim the Lord as its God alone. Would Israel's pride and sense of nationhood suffer from the knowl-edge that the Lord, as its God, might turn to "alien" prophets to fulfil His pur-poses—even in support of Israel itself? Would such occurrences subvert the role of the very priests who had been ordained as guardians of their God's sanctity?

The issue reaches a climax with Balaam. Unlike E (and possibly J) in Num. 22–24, P saw Balaam as a threat to Israel's unifying self-image as *the* one people under *its* One God. To eradicate such subversion, P felt compelled to reshape Balaam to its image of a scheming false prophet.

But P's consequential deconstruction of Balaam would prove a defining episode in the traditions of Judaism. It addresses the difference between (1) a view of the Torah's God as a Universal Being whose role as God is to be shared in time with all humanity and (2) a view of a Him as Lord of the Universe, but as Israel's God alone, and as such, the core of its self-identity. Among the monotheistic religions rooted in the Torah, however, this tension is hardly unique to Judaism. The omnipotence of a people's God is not easily shared with others.

5.

DEUTERONOMY

INTRODUCTION

The closing chapters of Numbers repeatedly place the Israelites "on the steppes of Moab, at the Jordan near Jericho" (Num. 22:1; 26:3, 63; 31:12; 33:50; 35:1; 36:13). Thus, the opening words of Deut. 1:1 alert a reader to the presence of a new source: "These are the words that Moses addressed to all Israel *on the other side of the Jordan.*"

In Num. 27:12–23 the Lord directed Moses to prepare for death and to provide for Joshua's succession. But both were delayed by the intervening events and recapitulations of Num. 28–35. And now in Deuteronomy, the death of Moses is again deferred to its conclusion, to allow for D's version of past laws and events, including the earlier Code of Law of Deut. 12–26. The period covered is from the revelations at Sinai/Horeb to the present (i.e., "on the other side of the Jordan"). Although the Lord, as Israel's God, and his laws and rules remain at the center of the text, He Himself "appears" only briefly in the closing chapters, mainly to prepare Moses for his imminent death.

> Note D–1: *Modern scholars identify "D," the Deuteronomist, as the source of Deuteronomy (as well as much of Joshua through 2 Kings). However, Deuteronomy itself, including an earlier Code of Law dating back perhaps to the mid-eighth century* B.C.E., *was reputed to have been "found" in the Temple by the high priest Hilkiah in 622* B.C.E., *in the reign of King Josiah (see 2 Kings 22:8–13).*
>
> *As a testament to the breadth of Israel's traditions, much of Deuteronomy repeats, or approximates, many of the laws, events, and Godly attributes encountered in J, E, and P. Yet its broad perspective is markedly distinctive.*

The discourses of Moses beginning at Deut. 1:6 are preceded by the brief homiletic narration of 1:1–5. It compares a journey that *was* with one that *might have been.* "Through the wilderness in the Arabah near Suph, between Paran and Tophel, Laban, Hazeroth, and Di-zahab, *it is eleven days from Horeb [Sinai] to Kadesh-Barnea* by the Mount Seir Route.—*It was in the fortieth year, on the first day of the eleventh month, that Moses addressed the Israelites* in accordance with the instructions that the Lord had given him for them (1:3b), after He had defeated [Sihon, king of the Amorites at Heshbon and Og, king of Bashan]" (1:1b–4).

> Note D–2: *The route from Horeb to Kadesh-Barnea by the named locations is difficult to follow (1:1–2). But irony permeates the passage. Had Israel but trusted the Lord for victory (Num. 14:26–35), it would have reached Kadesh from Horeb in just eleven days, thus avoiding the interim death of a generation in thirty-nine years of wandering. (The victories over Sihon and Og in 1:4 are first reported during Num. 21:21–31 and 21:33–35. They occur, however, not in thirty-eight years of wandering, but in the more purposeful final journey from Kadesh to Moab.) (See Num. 20:14–22:1.)*

And so, "*on the other side of the Jordan, in the land of Moab,* Moses undertook to expound this teaching" (1:5).

> Note D–3: *Moses' review of routes and events leading from Mount Horeb to Moab (1:6–3:29) will cover three major stages. These are from (1) Horeb through Hazeroth to the defeat at Hormah in (or near) the wilderness of Paran/ Zin; (2) thirty-eight years of wandering that concludes with a final return to Kadesh in Num. 20 (unrecorded but for R's reconstruction in Num. 33), and (3) from Kadesh to where Israel is now encamped in Moab, east of the Jordan.*

Deut. 1:6–8 is remarkable for its description of the land "that the Lord swore to your fathers, Abraham, Isaac and Jacob, to give to them and their offspring after them" (1:8). It would include not only Canaan, but in all, the surrounding "hill country of the Amorites [largely in Canaan] and to all their neighbors in the Arabah, the hill country, the Shephelah, the Negeb, the seacoast, the land of the Canaanites, and the Lebanon, as far as the Great River, the River Euphrates (cf. Comments G–20, 22, and 24). Moses tells the people that the land has been placed "at your disposal," and so to "Go, take possession" (1:7–8).

In Deut. 1:9–18 Moses reveals his early doubts of his ability "to bear the burden of you by myself" (1:9). As God continued to multiply Israel (to the point that it was now "as numerous as the stars in the sky"), he asked himself, "How can I bear unaided the trouble of you, and the burden, and the bickering!" (1:10–12). Thus, with the people's approval, he took "tribal leaders, wise and experienced men, and appointed them heads over you: chiefs of thousands . . . hundreds . . . fifties and . . . tens" (1:13–15).

He next recalls his charge to the judges. "Hear out your fellow men, and decide justly between any man and a fellow Israelite *or a stranger*." Partiality between "high and low alike" was forbidden. Nor should a judge fear any man, "for judgment is God's." Moses also explains that his need to delegate the resolution of disputes to judges did not portend his withdrawal from the administration of justice. "And any matter that is too difficult for you, you bring it to me and I will hear it" (1:16–17).

In Deut. 1:19–21, Moses recalls the hard trek through the "great and terrible wilderness" from Horeb to Kadesh-Barnea. There Moses told the people they had reached "the hill country of the Amorites which the Lord our God is giving us" (1:20). Since He had placed the land "at your disposal," they must now "go up, take possession, as the Lord, the God of your fathers, promised you. Fear not and be not dismayed" (1:21).

Moses then recounts the essence of Num. 13:1–14:45, but with differences that confirm the work of a source other than J or P (as Friedman's putative authors of Num. 13:1–14:45) (1:22–45). Both versions begin with a decision to send a man from each tribe to scout Canaan. Both end with the defeat of the Israelites at Hormah. But critical variations in the two versions preclude any credible accomodation.

In Num. 13:2 the Lord tells Moses to send men to scout Canaan. In Deut. 1:22–23 Moses recalls that it was "all of you" who "came to me" to urge that men be sent to scout the land. In reply, Moses says, "I approved." Thus, to the contrary of Numbers, Deuteronomy tells us that the scouting mission that eventually doomed Israel to wander in the wilderness was initiated by the people rather than the Lord. But more akin to Num. 13, D's version includes the scouts' reports of "a good land that the Lord our God is giving us" (1:25) and of "a people stronger and taller than we, large cities with walls sky-high, and even Anakites" (cf. Deut. 1:25–28 and Num. 13:27–28).

What D oddly echoes, however, is the confusion in Num. 13 on whether Joshua and Caleb, or Caleb alone, will enter Canaan. Compare (1) "none except Caleb . . . shall see it and to him and his descendants will I give the land" (1:36) and (2) "Joshua son of Nun, who attends you, he shall enter it" (1:38). (See Comment N–15.)

> *Note D–4: Plaut correctly cites the different explanations given for the entry of each: that is, Caleb, for his loyalty to the Lord and Joshua, as Moses' successor.[1] However, in naming Joshua as successor to Moses, the Lord would surely have accepted nothing less than total loyalty. In any case, the texts of 1:36 and 1:38 are literally at odds. (However, the internal variance in Deuteronomy between 1:36 and 1:38 will soon be overshadowed by the external variance between Deut. 1:37 and Num. 27:12–14.)*

As in Numbers, the people's fear of the powerful Anakites proves greater than their confidence in the Lord's protective powers. They refuse to enter Canaan from the south. Indeed, they bitterly charge the Lord with hatred against them. From their fear-drenched imaginations emerges a plot by the Lord "to hand us over to the Amorites to wipe us out" (1:26–28). Being so dominated by fear, they reject every effort by Moses to renew their trust in the power and purposes of the Lord, their God (1:29–33).

Speaking now of these matters, Moses tells the people, "*Because of you the Lord was incensed with me too, and He said: 'You shall not enter it either'*" (1:37).

> Note D–5: *The portentous episode of the Waters of Meribah occurs in Num. 20 after Israel's final arrival at Kadesh, following thirty-eight years of wandering. In Deuteronomy, the Lord's decision to bar Moses from Canaan reflects His general anger over the events of Num. 13 and 14, thirty-eight years earlier, that led to the interim wandering.*

Moses then recalls how the people, through remorse, rashly resolve to attack the Canaanites from the south. But having already commanded the entire generation (but for Caleb and Joshua) to die before entering Canaan (1:35), the Lord cautions them that without His support their scheme is hopeless (1:42). Deut. 1 then concludes with Moses' sad reminder that "the Amorites . . . came out against you like so many bees and chased you, and they crushed you at Hormah in Seir." And so "you wept, but the Lord would not heed your cry" (1:44–45).

> Note D–6: *By using "you" throughout this discourse, Moses attributes the conduct of their parents to the present generation whom he addresses. In this way, D portrays a continuity in Israel's peoplehood over time.*

Comment D–1. On yet another reason for barring Moses from Canaan

It must have been a compelling tradition indeed that precluded the entry of Moses into Canaan. Nevertheless, balance was essential. The Lord would need good reason to deny Moses his rightful expectation; and though sufficient to warrant such treatment, His reason could not demean the essential character of Moses.

As suggested in Comment N–22, P was able to contrive such a balance through the Waters of Meribah. Although the Lord condemned Moses for having demeaned His sanctity, Moses' guilt was softened by the clear impression of an "unwitting" sin. D, however, reaches a different balance. There is no insult to the Lord's sanctity, "unwitting" or not. Instead, the failing is of one human leadership—in this case, a failure to persuade the people to overcome their fears of fulfilling the Lord's command to enter Canaan from the south. In having failed to avert the very conduct that led to thirty-eight years of wandering in the wilderness, Moses, as its leader, had egregiously failed Israel. Yet it was a failure that other human beings could, more easily than a wrathful God, understand and forgive.

Having concluded his recall of the defeat at Hormah in Deut. 1:45 (cf. Num. 14:45), Moses then speaks of having *"remained in Kadesh all that long time," after which* "we marched back into the wilderness, toward the Sea of Reeds, as the Lord had spoken to me, and skirted the hill country of Seir [or Edom] for a long time" (1:46–2:1).

> *Note D–7: Moses' brief mention of having* "remained in Kadesh all that long time" *is D's first reference to the thirty-eight years of wandering in the wilderness. This is contradicted, however, in 2:14 in which the thirty-eight years of wandering is said to have occurred* "in travel *from Kadesh [to] the Wadi Zered." Apart from R's largely* "undocumented" *itinerary in Num. 33, neither Numbers nor Moses reveals any details of the prolonged wandering that began and ended at Kadesh.*

The events of the first episode at Edom on Israel's passage from Kadesh to Moab recall its earlier counterpart in Num. 20:14–21 (2:2–7). But now, as Israel crosses through Edom, we encounter a remarkably different scenario.

As related by Moses, the Lord eventually told him, "You have been skirting the hill country long enough; now turn north" (2:2). *Moses is to tell his people that they will be passing through* "the territory of your kinsmen, the descendants of Esau, who live in Seir." But in passing through, the Israelites are warned "not to start a fight with them." And why not? Because, in essence, Israel will gain nothing by a victory. Moses thus quotes the Lord: "I will not give you of their land so much as a foot can tread on; I have given the hill country of Seir as a possession to Esau." Accordingly, "What food you eat you shall obtain from them for money" and so, too, with "the water you drink" (2:3–6). As to how Israel will pay the Edomites for food and water, Moses observes that "the Lord your God has blessed you in all your undertakings. He has watched over your wanderings and . . . has been with you *these past forty years*: you have lacked nothing" (2:7).

> *Note D–8: In Num. 20:14–21 the Edomite king denies entry to Israel. In Deut. 2:4–7 the Lord Himself provides for Israel's passage through the country. Thus, D uses the Lord in the mid to late seventh century to project a far more friendly view of the Edomite descendants of Esau than did J, about two centuries earlier. But much had changed since the demise of the Davidic and Solomonic empires of the earlier era. By c. 650–622* B.C.E.*, the United*

Monarchy had split into the separate kingdoms of Judah and Israel (c. 922 B.C.E.), followed by Assyria's conquest of Israel (c. 722).

On leaving their "kinsmen, the descendants of Esau," the Israelites turned away from "Elath and Ezion-geber" toward "the wilderness of Moab." Moses then recalled the Lord's words regarding another people. "Do not harass the Moabites or engage them in war, For I will not give you any of their land as a possession; I have given Ar as a possession to the descendants of Lot" (2:8–9).

> Note D–9: Is it possible that the Moabites so favored by D are the same Moabites ruled by King Balak, who had sought to curse Israel through Balaam (Num. 22–24)? Are D's Moabites the same Moabites of Num. 25, whose women enticed Israelite men into the worship of Baal? Or, as in the case of Edom, might we attribute this tidal change in relationships to the circumstances of D's times?

In Deut. 2:10–11 Moses "pauses" to tell of the Emim who, before Lot, occupied the area of Ar in Moab. They were a "great and numerous" people and as "tall as the Anakites" (see Num. 13:33). He also tells of the Horites who had inhabited "Seir" (or Edom) until Esau's descendants "dispossessed them . . . *just as Israel did in the land they were to possess*" (2:12).

> Note D–10: Here Moses speaks of Israel's conquest of Canaan as an accomplished fact.

"Up now! Cross the wadi [a semidry watercourse] Zered! So we crossed [it]. *The time that we spent in travel in Kadesh-barnea until we crossed the wadi Zered was thirty-eight years*, until that whole generation of warriors had perished from the camp, as the Lord had sworn concerning them. Indeed, the hand of the Lord struck them, to root them out from the camp to the last man. "When all the *warriors* among the people had died off, the Lord spoke to me saying: 'You are now passing through the territory of Moab, *through Ar*'" (2:13–18).

As Israel came "close to the Ammonites" in the territory of Moab, through Ar," Moses recalls another warning from the Lord. "Do not harass them or start a fight with them. For . . . I have given [the land] as a possession to the descendants of Lot" (2:18–19).

> Note D–11: This warning complements the earlier warning of 2:9. Recall that the other son of Lot, born of his younger daughter, was Ben-ammi, the "father of the Ammonites today" (Gen. 19:38).

As in Deut. 2:10–11, 2:20–23 cites cases of the displacement of one people by another in other lands. Thus, from land later given to the Ammonites, the Lord first "wiped out" the Rephaim, a people "as great and as tall as the Anakites" (2:20–22). However, as to the Avvim who dwelled in the villages near Gaza, it was the Caphtorim, themselves, "who came from Crete" and who "wiped them out and settled in their place" (2:23).

> *Note D–12: Moses must cite these varied and widespread examples of population displacements as morale builders.*

In Deut. 2:24 Moses returns to the theme of his principal discourse. "Up! Set set out across the wadi Arnon!" (20:24a). Then follows D's version of Israel's victory over "Sihon king of the Amorites, who lived in Heshbon" (2:24b–37).

The "events" of 2:24b–37 should be compared to the simpler account of Israel's victory over Sihon in Num. 21:24. "But Israel put them to the sword, and took possession of their land." Num. 21:21–25 makes no reference to Israel's Lord God. In contrast, consider the following several excerpts from D's version.

1. "But the king of Heshbon would not let us pass through, *because the Lord had stiffened his will and hardened his heart*—in order to deliver them into your power, as is now the case. And the Lord said to me: See, I begin by placing Sihon and his land at your disposal. Begin the occupation; take possession of his land" (2:30–31).

> *Note D–13: As to the king's free will in the matter, compare the "hardening of hearts" and the "stiffening of wills" by D's Lord to Comments E–21, 22, and 30–32 and related text. Here D seems closer to P than to J.*

2. "And the Lord our God delivered him to us and we defeated him and his sons and all his men" (2:33).

3. "Not a city was too mighty for us; the Lord our God delivered everything to us" (2:36).

> *Note D–14: The details of the "division of labor" between the Lord and the people in achieving the victory remain obscure. But the message does not. D, in contrast to J, focuses on the Lord, to the virtual exclusion of the people, as the source of Israel's victory over Sihon.*

One other striking embellishment of J's version by D is found in 2:33. In J's defeat of Sihon, Israel simply "put them to the sword, and took possession of the land" (Num. 21:24). But for D there was more to be done (or at least more to be made explicit). And so "we doomed every town—men, women and children—leaving no survivor" (2:34).

Comment D–2A. On the effect of time and circumstances on Israel's military ethos and the role of its Lord God in battle—a speculation

As stated, the role of J's Lord in Israel's triumph over Sihon was incidental at most—limited perhaps to the value of His Presence on Israel's morale. Conversely, as to the same battle, D leaves no doubt that the Lord alone had gained the day.

A reader might be inclined to attribute the differences to the distinctive views of J and D regarding God and humankind. But to do so might overlook important external factors of time and circumstances. J wrote mainly, or entirely, during the era of the United Monarchy, most likely during the latter period of David's reign and over much of Solomon's. It was an era in which Israel faced no serious threat of destruction. It was a *relatively* "quiet" time (if any there ever was) when Israel might relax at least slightly to contemplate its accomplishments. And it was a time when the virtual genocide of Israel's foes, so often associated with the Lord's will, might have seemed less necessary as a source of morale.

In contrast, D1 wrote in the late seventh and early sixth centuries, following Assyria's conquest of the northern kingdom of Israel, c. 722 B.C.E., and amid the growing threat of Babylon as well. In the circumstances, Israel could hardly look with confidence to its earthly resources as the sole source of salvation. Would it not help morale to "recall" the Lord's role in Israel's past battles?

But such speculations will be put to test at once in the J and D versions of Israel's victory over "Og king of Bashan." These are found in Num. 21:33–35 and Deut. 3:1–7.

The words in Hebrew of D's Lord to Moses in Deut. 3:2 are identical to those of J's Lord in Num. 21:34: "But the Lord said to me: *Do not fear him, for I am delivering him and all his men and his country into your power, and you will do to him as you did to Sihon king of the Amorites, who lived in Heshbon.*" But despite these identical words, in comparing J's Num. 21:35 and D's Deut. 3:3 we encounter a distinction consistent with those discussed in Comment D–2A. Thus, in J's view it is the people who finally triumph. "*They* [i.e., *the Israelites*] defeated him and his sons and all his people, until no remnant was left him; and they took possession of his country." For D, however, the Lord had authored a triumph in which the Israelites were but dutiful actors. "*So the Lord our God also delivered into our power Og king of Bashan,* with all his men, and we dealt them such a blow that no survivor was left."

For J, the victory over Og is now complete. For D, however, there remains a need to maximize its potential.

There was not a town that we did not take from them: sixty towns . . . all those towns were fortified with high walls, gates and bars—apart from a great number of unwalled towns. We doomed them as we had done in the case of Sihon king of Heshbon; *we doomed every town—men, women, and children—and retained as booty all the cattle and spoil of the towns.* (3:4–6)

Comment D–2B. On the speculations of Comment D–2A after Og

Unless effected later by R, the identity in the Hebrew text of Deut. 3:2 and Num. 21:34 suggests the presence of a controlling tradition by which both J and D felt bound. However, their varied identifications of the source of victory (as between D's "the Lord our God" and J's "They") tends to support the speculations of Comment D–2A. So, too, does Deut. 3:4–6, D's highly dramatic addendum to J's story of Og. To the same effect, in 3:11 D will uniquely identify Og as the last of the Rephaim, a people "as great and as tall as the Anakites" (2:20–22).

As a result of its preceding victories, Israel occupies territory "from the wadi Arnon to Mount Hermon [in south Lebanon]" in "the country across the Jordan" and "all the towns of the Tableland ["steppes"] and the whole of Gilead and Bashan" (3:8–10). D's account of Israel's victories then closes with an unusual historical "footnote": "Only Og king of Bashan was left of the remaining Rephaim," whose ranks included the giant Anakites and Emim (2:10). "*His bedstead, an iron bedstead,* is now in Rabbah of the Ammonites, it is nine cubits long and four cubits wide, by the standard cubit!" (3:11).

> Note D–15: *Although these words appear to be spoken by Moses after Og's defeat, "now" can only mean in the author's time. More important, since a cubit was about eighteen inches, the bedstead was about thirteen feet long. This would have suitably bedded a king of eleven to twelve feet in height— clearly a foe to be held in awe.*

In Deut. 3:12–16 Moses briefly recalls the assignments of lands east of the Jordan to the tribes of Reuben and Gad and the half-tribe of Manasseh (Num. 32). To the Reubenites and Gadites Moses assigned "The part from Aroer along the wadi Arnon, with part of the hill country of Gilead and its towns" (3:12). To the half-tribe of Manasseh he assigned "the rest of Gilead, and all of Bashan under Og's rule—the whole Argob district, all that part of Bashan which is called Rephaim country" (3:13).

The relative clarity of these assignments (apart from their novelty) is then complicated by the assignments of 3:14–16 in which (1) the Manassite clan of Jair received "the whole Argob district (that is Bashan) as far as the boundaries of the Geshurites and the Maacathites, and named it after himself—Havvoth-jair—*as is still the case*" (3:14); (2) the Manassite clan of Machir received "Gilead" (with no stated exception of any part); and (3) the Reubenites and

Gadites received "the part from Gilead down to the wadi Arnon, the middle of the wadi being the boundary, and up to the wadi Jabbock, the boundary of the Ammonites" (3:16).

> Note D–16: As for the boundary delineations of 3:12–16, Moses speaks of having assigned the lands himself, with no participation by the Lord. This conforms to procedures of Num. 32 (see Comment N–34). Also, the assignments in 3:12 and 3:16 of parts of "Gilead" to Reuben and Gad contradict 3:15, in which Gilead, without exception, is assigned to the Manassite descendants of Machir. Adding to the confusion are varied assignments of land in 3:13–15 to what seem to be separate components of the Manassites.

Deut. 3:17 concludes the identification of the lands taken by Israel east of the Jordan. Thus, "[we also seized] the Arabah, from the foot of the slopes of Pisgah on the east, to the edge of the Jordan, and from Chinnereth down to the sea of the Arabah, the Dead Sea."

Deut. 3:18–20 states the conditions under which Reuben, Gad, and Man-asseh may settle in the lands assigned to them east of the Jordan. "You must go as shocktroops, warriors all, at the head of your Israelite kinsmen." However, wives, children, and livestock were to remain in these lands during the course of the battle for Canaan. The fighting men of the tribes could then return to their holdings once "your kinsmen . . . have taken possession of the land that the Lord your God is giving them beyond the Jordan."

> Note D–17: D's conditions say nothing of the consequences for the "favored" tribes should they not fulfil their conditions. Minimally, we may assume that their lands east of the Jordan would be forfeit. But would they be punished further for failing to "go as shocktroops . . . at the head of your . . . kinsmen?" Would they be denied other lands in Canaan? (Cf. Comment N–34, Note N–133.)

In Deut. 3:21–22, D gives new emphasis to the Lord's role in Israel's coming victories. As Moses states in his charge to Joshua, "You have seen with your own eyes all that the Lord your God has done to these two kings; so shall the Lord do to all the kingdoms into which you shall cross over. Do not fear them, for it is the Lord your God who will battle for you." (Cf. Comments D–2A and B.)

Deut. 3 closes with Moses telling the people of his pleas to a remote and pitiless Lord regarding his entry into Canaan. "I pleaded with the Lord at that time, saying, 'O Lord God, You who let Your servant see the first works of Your greatness and Your mighty hand, You whose powerful deeds no god in heaven or on earth can equal! Let me, I pray, cross over and see the good land on the other side of the Jordan. . . .' But the Lord was wrathful with me on your account and would not listen to me. The Lord said to me: 'Enough! Never speak to me of this matter again. Go up to the summit of Pisgah and gaze about. . . . Look at it well for you shall not cross the Jordan. Give Joshua his instructions, and imbue him with strength and courage, for *he* shall go across at the head of this people and *he* shall allot to them the land that you may only see' " (3:23–28). Meanwhile Moses and the people stayed on in the valley near Beth-Peor (3:39).

Comment D–3. On the dispensability of Moses to an ungracious Lord

Clearly, the Torah's God is bound by tradition to deny Moses entry into the promised land (see Comments N–22, D–1). Nor can Moses' exemplary leadership, utter loyalty, incredible patience, innate compassion and quick wits effect a change of fate. But granted so, did tradition also compel the Lord to treat Moses as a personal pariah, with no claim, even in the face of personal tragedy, to kindness or compassion from his God. If so, and no less as to D than P, to what purpose? Must Moses be "sacrificed" so that all Israel could know that no human being should be honored for great deeds whose true source lies in the Lord's power and will. As such, it would be a depressing view of the worth of humanity. But must it be a final view?

> *Note D–18: Through the words of Moses himself, D suggests the pervasiveness of monolatry in seventh century* B.C.E. *(i.e., a belief that gods other than Israel's Lord God exist). "You whose powerful deeds no god in heaven or on earth can equal!" (Deut. 3:24). (Cf. Exod. 19:3: "You shall have no other gods before me"; see also Comment E–55.)*

Deut. 4:1–40 consists largely of an extended rationale and plea by Moses for total obedience.

In Deut. 4:1–14 Moses offers an introductory homily on the need to "give heed to the laws [*chukim*] and rules [*mishpatim*] which I am instructing you to observe, so that you may live to enter and occupy the land that the Lord, the god of your fathers, is giving you" (4:1).

> *Note D–19: Among JPS1, RSV, and JPS2, only JPS2 refers to "god" rather than "God" (cf. Note G–42). If it is but a "typo," I have only empathetic compassion.*

> *Note D–20: JPS1/RSV refer to the "laws" and "rules" of JPS2 as "statutes" and "ordinances." But the basic import lies in the Hebrew* chukim *and* mishpatim. *That two distinct classes of commands are intended seems clear, but the nature of the distinction is less so. Did D (and the tradition on which D drew) mean to distinguish between religious law and civil law, that is,*

between obligations to the Lord and to other human beings? At this point we might recall Rashi's view of the mishpatim *as derivations from the theology and moral precepts of the Ten Commandments. From this perspective, are the two orders of commands meant to be viewed as less mutable "laws" and more mutable "rules"? (See Comment E–75.)*

The following precis covers the gist of Moses' opening words on the nature and need for obedience to the "laws" (or "statutes," "rules," or "ordinances"; Deut. 1–8):

Observance of "laws and rules" constitutes the condition on which Israel "may live to enter and occupy the [promised] land (4:1).

"You shall not add anything to what I command you or take anything away from it" (4:2).

Note D–21: But for the essential fiction of the "oral law," would this command not preclude much Talmudic interpretation? (See pp. 35–36.)

Israel must be ever mindful of what "you saw" the Lord do "in the matter of Baal-Peor," including the death of "every person" who followed Baal-Peor, while those "who held fast to the Lord, are all alive today" (4:3–4).

The laws and rules were promulgated "for you to abide by in the land which you are about to invade and conquer" (4:5). They are of such quality that your faithful observance will prove your wisdom and discernment to others, thus leading them to say, "Surely, that great nation is a wise and discerning people" (4:6).

But while other peoples will praise Israel for its laws and rules, Israel will know that their source is the Lord, their God. "For what great nation is there that has a god so close at hand as is the Lord our God whenever we call upon Him? Or what great nation has laws and rules as perfect as all this Teaching that I set before you this day" (4:7–8).

Moses then turns to the covenant at Mount Horeb. He admonishes the people to "take utmost care" not to forget what "you saw with your own eyes" and make known all you have seen "to your children and their children" (4:9). Moses urges them to recall in particular the day they stood before the Lord at Horeb, when the Lord said, "Gather the people to Me . . . that they might hear My words in order to revere Me all their days and so teach their children; and you stood at the foot of the mountain which was ablaze with flames to the very skies" (4:10–11).

Moses recalls that when the Lord spoke from out of the fire, "you . . . perceived no shape—nothing but a voice" that declared the covenant of the Ten Commandments which He then inscribed "on two tablets of stone" (4:12–13).

Note D–22: Here D combines two separate P episodes: (1) the Lord's spoken revelation of the Ten Commandments amid fire and smoke from Horeb (Exod. 19:14–20:18) and (2) His own inscription of the "words" on the two tablets (Exod. 31:18). This also differs from J's version in which the Lord directs Moses to inscribe the words on the tablets (Exod. 34:27–28). (See Comments E–94 and 96.)

In Deut. 4:15–31 Moses expands on his words of 4:12. "The Lord spoke to you out of the fire [at Horeb]; *you heard the sound of words but perceived no shape— nothing but a voice.*" Though Moses does not cite the Second Commandment as text for the sermon that follows, his words are clearly inspired by a portion of its provisions: "You shall not make for yourself a sculptured image, or any likeness of what is in the heavens above, or on the earth below, or in the waters under the earth. You shall not bow down to them or serve them" (Exod. 20:4–5a).

And so Moses continues: "For your own sake, therefore, be most careful . . . not to act wickedly and make for yourselves a sculptured image in any likeness, whatever: the form of a man or a woman, the form of any beast on earth, the form of any winged bird that flies in the sky, the form of anything that creeps on the ground, the form of any fish that is in the waters below the earth" (4:15–18).

Note D–23: Unlike the Second Commandments of Exod. 20:4–5a and Deut. 5:7–10, Deut. 4:15–18 prohibits the making but not the worship of images. It assumes, as may have been the case, that idols and images were generally "made" to portray the reality of other gods. As for Israel's God (with the likely exception of my surmise regarding E), the use of an idol or image was viewed as a blasphemous attempt to portray the unportrayable. (For my thoughts on E's exception, see Comments E–86 through 90.)

Moses then turns from man-made idols and images to the great inanimate objects of the Lord's natural order. "And when you look up to the sky and behold the sun and the moon and the stars, the whole heavenly host, you must not be lured into bowing down to them or serving them. *These the Lord allotted to the other peoples everywhere under heaven;* but you the Lord took and brought out of Egypt, that iron blast furnace, to be His very own people, as is now the case" (4:19–20).

Comment D–4. On the Lord's distinction between the making of images by non-Israelites and their worship of objects within His natural order

In 4:19 the Lord gives express permission for non-Israelites to worship the heavenly objects of His natural order. In effect, since He was not to be a God to the non-Israelites, He would at least allow them to worship the more awesome objects of His own natural order. (As to making images, however, His disapproval is implied by His silence.)

The point may be that D, in particular, regarded the feeling and expression of reverence as worthy human qualities. Thus, even if the Lord were to serve only Israel as its God, it should still be open to others to show reverence for His natural order.

In Deut. 4:21–22 a more resigned and less distraught Moses wistfully repeats the Lord's determination that "I should not cross the Jordan and enter the good land that the Lord your God is giving you as a heritage" (cf. Deut. 3:23–28 and Comment D–3). Deut. 4:23 identifies as a covenantal obligation the ban against making "for yourselves a sculptured image in any likeness." It is followed by the reminder that "the Lord your God is a consuming fire, an impassioned God" (4:24).

That the Israelites of D's era must have been deeply drawn to the making and worship of images is reflected in D's reluctance to let the matter rest: "Should you [and your descendants] act wickedly and make for yourselves a sculptured image in any likeness, causing the Lord your God displeasure and vexation, I call heaven and earth this day to witness against you that you shall soon perish from the land [and] shall be utterly wiped out. The Lord will scatter you among the peoples, and only a scant few of you shall be left among the nations to which the Lord will drive you. There you will serve man-made gods of wood and stone, that cannot see or hear or eat or smell" (4:25–28).

> Note D–24: To speak of gods "that cannot see or hear or eat or smell" recalls the evocations by J, E, and P of a greater God with all of these capacities— and who could talk as well (see Comments G–29, E–78, E–91, and L–50).

But now the vision of the "Lord your God" changes. To "find Him" requires "only [that] you seek Him with all your heart and soul" (4:29). "For the Lord your God is a compassionate God; He will not fail you nor will He let you perish; He will not forget the covenant which He made on oath with your fathers" (4:31).

Comment D–5. On "wrath," "compassion," and "reflection" in the Lord, God of Israel

In Deut. 3:26, D's Moses characterizes the Lord as "wrathful with me on your account," as a result of which he must die before entering Canaan. But in Deut. 4:31, D's Moses speaks of "the Lord your God" as a "compassionate God" (much as the Lord had characterized Himself at the close of Exodus). The wide emotional range of Israel's Lord, God is especially evident in the blessings and curses of Lev. 26.

But the quality not yet evident in His direct relations with humankind is that of thoughtful reflection. Apart from the rare occasion of an affirmative response to the patient rectitude of Abraham or the practical wisdom of Moses, emotion rather than reflection is His trademark. (As to these "rarities," see Gen. 18:16–33 and Comment G–28, and also Exod. 32:7–14 and Comment E–88.)

As Moses continues to extol the unique attributes of Israel's Lord God, his words reveal a tension between the ideal of monotheism and the reality of monolatry (4:32–40).

What are these unique attributes? Although expressed by Moses through rhetorical questions, they are in essence:

1. Ever since "God created man on earth," nothing "as grand as this" has ever happened (4:32).
2. No other people have "heard the voice *of a god* speaking out of a fire, *as you have*, and survived" (4:33).
3. "Or has any god ventured to go and take for himself one nation from the midst of another by prodigious acts, by signs and portents, by war, by a mighty and outstretched arm and awesome power, as the Lord God did for you in Egypt before your very eyes?" (4:34).

   Note D–25: Here JPS2's use of lowercase "god," for elohim *is clearly not a "typo" (see Note D–19). I make the point because of JPS1's contrary reading of* elohim *as "God." As reflected in JPS2 and RSV, however, D's purpose here is to distinguish Israel's God from all other gods. This is reflected in the use of* yahweh *to identify "Lord God" at the conclusion of the verse.*

4. "It has been clearly demonstrated to you that the Lord alone is God; there is none beside him" (4:35).

   Note D–26: The first clause of 4:35 can be read as a flat assertion of monotheism, but the ambiguity of "there is none beside him" (i.e., "equal to" or "other than") remains. (See Comment E–55. But to the contrary, see item 7, which follows.)

5. "From the heavens He let you hear His voice to discipline you; on earth He let you see His great fire [from which] you heard His words" (4:36).
6. "And because He loved your fathers, He chose their offspring after them; He, Himself, in His great might, lead you out of Egypt, to drive from your path nations greater and more populous than you, to take you into their land and give it to you as a heritage, *as is still the case*" (4:37–38).

Note D–27: Here D speaks directly to his own generation of the Lord's love and power.

7. "Know therefore this day and keep in mind that the Lord alone is God in heaven above and on earth below; there is no other" (4:39).
8. "Observe His laws and commandments, which I enjoin upon you this day, that it may go well with you and your children after you, and that you may long remain in the land that the Lord your God is giving you for all time" (4:40).

Deut. 4:41–43 deals with a matter left open in Num. 35:13–15 involving three cities of "refuge" to be located "east of the Jordan" (there being six in all). (See Comment N–35.) Moses now sets aside "Bezer, in the wilderness in the Tableland, belonging to the Reubenites; Ramoth, in Gilead, belonging to the Gadites; and Golan, in Bashan, belonging to the Manassites."

Note D–28: Just as the tribal land assignments east of the Jordan varied between P and J, so do D's seem to vary from both (cf. Num. 32:1–32, 32:33–42, 33:13–15, 33:16–23, Comment N–34, and Note N–140).

Deut. 4:44–49 introduces Moses' second discourse. A narrator states its purpose in 4:44–45: "This is the Teaching that Moses set before the Israelites; these are the exhortations, laws and rules that Moses addressed to the people of Israel, after they had left Egypt." Deut. 4:46 describes the site of his discourse as "beyond the Jordan, in the valley at Beth Peor, in the land of the Sihon king of the Amorites, who dwelt in Heshbon, whom Moses and the Israelites defeated after they had left Egypt." Deut. 4:47–49 then summarizes the more recent events east of the Jordan that brought Israel to its present location. (Its northward passage from Edom through Moab and beyond is described in Deut. 2 and 3.)

In Deut. 5:1–5 Moses introduces his second discourse. On summoning "all the Israelites" to come within earshot (as space and numbers might allow?), he declares, "Hear, O Israel, the laws and rules that I proclaim to you this day! Study them and observe them carefully!" (5:1). He then describes a scene at Horeb that recalls Exod. 19:3–25 preceding the Lord's revelation of the Ten Commandments in Exod. 20:1–14: "The Lord our God made a covenant with us at Horeb. It was not with our fathers that the Lord made this covenant, but with us the living, every one of us who is here today. Face to face the Lord spoke to you on the mountain out of the fire—*I stood between the Lord and you at that time to convey the Lord's words to you,* for you were afraid of the fire and did not go up the mountain" (5:2–5).

Moses then restates the Ten Commandments as first revealed in Exod. 20:2–14.

The *First Commandment* (5:6) follows the precise Hebrew text of Exod. 20:2. (For the previous discussion of the First Commandment, see Comment E–54.)

The *Second Commandment* (5:7–10) differs from the original Hebrew text of Exod. 20:3–6 in only four words. As reflected in all translations, the differences are totally lacking in substance. (On the Second Commandment see Comments E–54 and 55.)

> Note D–29: *In general, I will ignore nonsubstantive changes in the Hebrew texts. Cumulatively, however, such changes may be of interest for possible insights into editorial processes or the transmission of traditions.*

The *Third Commandment* (5:11) follows precisely that of Exod. 2:7. (On the Third Commandment, see Comment E–56.)

The *Fourth, or Sabbath, Commandment* of Deuteronomy has achieved a special prominence for reason of its distinctive rationale, as compared to that of the Exodus Commandment.

> Note D–30: *Major changes from Exod. 20:8–11 are in italics.*

"*Observe* the sabbath day and keep it holy, *as the Lord God has commanded you*. Six days shall you labor and do all your work, but the seventh day is a sabbath of the Lord your God: you shall not do any work—you, your son or your daughter, your male or female slave, your ox or your ass, or any of your cattle, or the stranger in your settlements, *so that your male and female slave may rest as you do*. *Remember that you were a slave in the land of Egypt and the Lord your God freed you from there with a mighty hand and an outstretched arm; therefore the Lord your God has commanded you to observe the sabbath day*" (5:12–15).

> Note D–31: *The opening "Observe" of the Deuteronomic command replaces "Remember" of the Exodus command. The relative passivity of "remembering," as a state of mind, is often compared to the more affirmative conduct implied by the process of "observing" (in the sense of "fulfilling"). Accordingly, many commentators find a purpose in the distinction.[2] However, the ultimate and fundamental command in both versions is to "keep [the sabbath] holy." This underlying "common denominator" tends to erode the significance of any differences between the "introductory" imperatives. To "keep it holy," as intended by the Torah, involves a twofold obligation: to refrain from doing what is prohibited and to do all that is required. To do both is to "remember" and "observe."*

Comment D–6. On the different rationales for the Sabbath Commandments of Exodus and Deuteronomy

Apart from the revelations of the laws and rules at Sinai/Horeb, the Torah regards Creation and the Exodus from Egypt as its central defining events. Either one would suffice as a compelling rhetorical foundation for the Sabbath Commandment.

Of the Creation rationale, little more need be said. As the Torah's God rested on the seventh day to consider the future of His Creation, so should all Israel rest from the week's toil to consider its own higher human purposes. As for the Exodus rationale, the hard lesson of Egypt was that neither Israel nor humanity in general can live by work alone. Beyond gaining one's sustenance, and perhaps more, the human spirit requires repose to consider human purposes other than material needs.

The effect of two formal Sabbath rationales, when either would suffice, is to endow the Sabbath with a stature independent of the other. Indeed, the point was made by J and E long before P in Exodus or D in Deuteronomy. Consider E's simple sabbath *mishpat* of Exod. 23:12: "Six days shall you do your work, but on the seventh day you shall cease from labor, in order that your ox and your ass may rest, and that your bondman and the stranger may be refreshed." And before E, J had written of an even simpler sabbath command. "Six days shall you work, but on the seventh day you shall cease from labor; you shall cease from labor even at plowing time and harvest time" (Exod. 34:21). *J and E thus left it to their successors, P and D, to "reinforce" the Sabbath command by associating it with the Torah's defining events.*

Thus, the concept of a sabbath rest from daily work appears to have taken early root in Israel's traditions. That it developed from a recognition of the need for rest from daily toil lies at the essence of its spirituality. Without a time for rest and repose, the mind is hard pressed to consider a human potential beyond daily toil. Rest alone cannot inspire the human mind to consider that potential. But time for thought may well be a condition of such consideration.

The Fifth Commandment ("Honor thy father and mother"), *the Sixth Commandment* (not to "murder"), *the Seventh Commandment* (not to commit "adultery"), *the Eighth Commandment* (not to "steal"), and *the Ninth Commandment* (not to "bear false witness") are substantively the same as in Exodus. For comments on the Exodus commands, see Comments E–58 through 62, respectively (5:16–17).

JPS2 renders *the Tenth Commandment* of Deut. 5:18 as follows: "You shall not covet your neighbor's wife. You shall not crave your neighbor's house, or his field, or his male or female slave, or his ox, or his ass, or anything that is your neighbor's."

Note D–32: As such, Deut. 5:18 differs from Exod. 20:14 by reversing the order of the neighbor's wife and house. By placing a period after "wife" rather than the more usual semicolon, JPS2 strengthens the priority that D may have meant to assign to the prohibition of coveting a neighbor's wife. (JPS1/RSV use semicolons with the effect of more nearly equalizing the import of the ban on the various coveted objects.) (See Comments E–54 pt. 2 final par., and E–63.)

Just as Deut. 4:10–14 recalls the scene at Horeb before the Lord's direct revelation of the Ten Commandments (Exod. 19:16–25), so, too, does Deut. 5:19–24 recall the scene that immediately follows (Exod. 20:15–18). Most notably, both passages speak of the people's fear of remaining in the Lord's direct Presence—or if not his Presence, as such, then of its accompanying signs and manifestations. Thus, they plead with Moses to receive the Lord's remaining words himself, for transmittal to them.

> The Lord our God has just shown us His majestic Presence, and we have heard His voice out of the fire; we have seen this day that man may live though God has spoken to them. Let us not die, then, for this fearsome fire will consume us; if we hear the voice of the Lord any longer we shall die.... *You go closer and hear all the Lord says, and then tell us everything that the Lord our God tells you, and we will willingly do it.* (5:20–24)

In Deut. 5:25–28 Moses recalls the Lord's acceptance (at Horeb) of the people's plea that he serve as their ears in the Lord's revelations of His laws, rules, and commands. He tells Moses, "They did well to speak thus" (5:25). But His primary focus is on their avowal of obedience of all that is revealed. "May they always be of such mind, to revere Me and follow *all* My commandments, that it may go well with them and with their children forever!" (5:26).

Note D–33: In 5:19–24, as in 4:10–14, the Lord at Mount Horeb reveals no more than the Ten Commandments directly to the people. Whether at the people's wish (as recalled in 5:19–24), or as the Lord's own insight (as suggested in 4:13–14), all that follows is transmitted through Moses. From Exod. 20:15–19, following the Sinaitic revelation of the Ten Commandments, we know P and D to have been in full accord. The overwhelming, indeed the debilitating, source of fear and awe attributed to the Lord in direct revelations to the people renders a prophet such as Moses indispensable to any relationship between early Israel and the Torah's God.

Having had Moses direct the people to return to their tents (5:28), He bade Moses to "*remain here with Me, and I will give you the whole Instruction—the law and the rules*—which you shall impart to them, for them to observe in the land that I am giving them to possess" (5:28).

Note D–34: This single Deuteronomic version of the Lord's revelation at Horeb avoids the complications of the varied versions of Exodus (see Comments E–96 and 100). Further reference, however, to a second set of "two tablets" is found in 9:8–10:5, in the context of the "molten calf." (See Notes D–44 through 48.)

And so Moses concludes his summary of the Lord's revelation of the Ten commandments. "Be careful, then, to do as the Lord your God has commanded you. Do not turn aside to the right or to the left: follow only the path that the Lord your God has enjoined upon you, so that you may thrive and that it may go well with you, and that you may long endure in the land you are to occupy" (5:29–30).

In Deut. 6 we first encounter Israel's great *shema*, the Deuteronomist's brilliant encapsulation of the First and Second Commandment (6:4). The introductory words of Deut. 6:1–3 continue the theme of Deut. 5:25–30; that is, that Israel's obedience to the Lord's commandments is both the source and condition of its well-being. They are to observe "*all* His laws and commandments . . . to the end that you may long endure" (6:2). And then the *shema* itself: "Hear, O Israel! the Lord is our God, the Lord alone" (*Shema, yisrael! adonai elohainu, adonai echad* [6:4]); And thus, "you shall love the Lord your God with all your heart and with all your soul and with all your might" (6:5).

Note D–35: As previously noted, adonai *is the spoken form of* yahweh.

D viewed these pronouncements to be of such importance as to require the following unique and constant reminders:

Take to heart these instructions with which I charge you this day. Impress them upon your children. Recite them when you stay at home and when you are away, when you lie down and when you get up. Bind them as a sign on your hand and let them serve as a symbol on your forehead; inscribe them on the doorposts of your house and on your gates. (6:6–9)

Note D–36: Strictly observant Jews fulfil the final commands of Deut. 6:8–9 by twice daily recitations of the shema, *the "laying" of tefillin on hand and forehead and the fixing of* mezuzim *on doorposts, with the* shema *enclosed.*

Comment D–7. On the attributes of the Lord, God of Israel, as reflected in varying translations of the *shema*

Translations of the *shema* vary—mainly in two respects. First, by either omitting (RSV and JPS1) or including (JPS2) the unexpressed Hebrew "is" in the second clause. Thus, absent the "is," JPS2's version (quoted above) would be:

"HEAR, O ISRAEL! THE LORD OUR GOD, THE LORD ALONE" (6:4). While both forms acknowledge the Lord as Israel's God, the absence of "is" tends to minimize any functional distinction between the Lord as Lord, and the Lord as Israel's God (see Comments L–43 and 45). Conversely, the use of "is" tends to suggest a functional distinction.

Also bearing on this issue are the varied translations of the final word, *echad*, the principal meaning of which is "one." But in itself, "one" can suggest either the Lord's internal *unity* (or *singleness*) or His *uniqueness* (or *singularity*). Or it can express both. By reading *echad* as "alone" *and* inserting the "is," JPS2 emphasizes the uniqueness of the Lord. (But the nature of His singularity also requires explanation. Is it that He *alone* is Israel's God? Or that, as God, He serves Israel *alone*? Or is it that He *alone* possesses His Lordly powers and other attributes? Or does the *shema* serve to affirm all three?

Most expressive of "singleness" is RSV's "The Lord our God is one Lord." Consistent with its exclusion of JPS2's "is" (i.e., between "Lord" and "Our God"), RSV projects a primary perception of the Lord's "internal" unity. In between is JPS1, which emphasizes the ambiguity of "one"—that is, "The Lord our God, the Lord is one." This would seem to effect the closest balance between the unity and the uniqueness of the Lord, as Israel's God.

Such translational nuances may be of use in analyzing the *meaning* of the words of the *shema*, but the first of the three homilies that follow it addresses its *broader purpose*.

> When the Lord your God brings you into the land which he swore to your fathers . . . to give you—great and flourishing cities which you did not build, houses full of all good things which you did not fill, hewn cisterns which you did not hew, vineyards and olive groves which you did not plant—and you eat your fill, take heed that you do not forget the Lord who freed you from the land of Egypt, the house of bondage. *Revere only the Lord your God and worship Him alone, and swear only by His name. Do not follow other gods, any gods of the peoples about you*—for the Lord your God is an impassioned God—lest [His] anger blaze forth against you and He wipe you off the face of the earth." (6:10–15)

Comment D–8. On the *shema* and monotheism in the Torah

Characteristically, the homily is divided into three parts. First, the Lord, as Israel's God, will bring Israel great blessings in the promised land, for which Israel must be eternally grateful to Him (Deut. 6:10–12). Then, by invoking the essence of the Second Commandment, the passage specifies the nature of Israel's reciprocal obligations. Israelites must never worship or "revere" any gods other than the Lord, its God. (6:13a). And because among all gods, only the Lord, God of Israel was the source of truth, Israelites, in swearing oaths, could invoke only His "name," or Being, to affirm its truth or sincerity.

Note D–37: The risk in invoking the Lord's name at all, of course, was in a possible violation of the Third Commandment (see Comment E–56).

Finally, in all these respects, should Israel not adhere to the Lord, its God, alone, His anger, "will blaze forth" and He will "wipe you off the face of the earth" (6:15).

Comment D–9. On "fear" and "reverence" of and for the Lord

Contrary to RSV/JPS1, JPS2 renders the *yod/resh/aleph* root in 6:13 as "revere" rather than "fear." (To the same effect see 5:26, 6:2, and 6:24. Here the actual verb form is *teerah*.) However, given the general acceptance of "revere" as a meaning for this verb root, my problem *in 6:13* is more with contextual consistency than lexicology.

In 6:15 itself Moses surely looks to fear rather than reverence as the human emotion on which the Lord relies to gain Israel's obedience. Consider his words in describing the Lord's response should Israel fail to "worship Him alone," or should it "follow other gods" as well (6:13–14): "for the Lord your God in your midst is an impassioned God—lest the anger of the Lord your God blaze forth against you and He wipe you off the face of the earth" (6:15). While the Torah seeks Israel's reverence for its God, reverence will be best inspired by the blessings of obedience (as in 6:3). Given the unpredictable wrath of the Torah's God, Moses himself views fear as the surest impetus to obedience. As he seems to say from hard experience, fear leads to obedience, obedience leads to blessings and blessings lead to reverence. Thus, we, too, might conclude that the foundation, though not the sole source, of Israel's desired relationship with *yahweh* is fear. (See Comment D–16.)

At the heart of the second homily (6:16–19) is its relationship to the standard of conduct of 6:1–2. There the relatively simple need was to observe "*all* [the Lord's] laws and commandments." But now in 6:18 Israel's obligation is to "do what is *right and good in the sight of the Lord,* that it may go well with you and that you may be able to occupy the good land which the Lord your God promised on oath to your fathers."

Comment D–10. On the standards of conduct of Deut. 6:1–2 and 6:18

Does D consider that obedience to the Lord God's laws and commandments constitutes all that is "right and good *in the sight of the Lord*"? Perhaps so. Yet, the reference to "right and good" hints of deviations from the letter of the law not unlike the later relationship between law and equity in English based jurisprudence. And so it was intrepreted by the Rabbis.[3] In general, equity serves to ease any unduly harsh consequences of the law by recourse to overriding principles of fairness.

In this regard, two interpretations of "right and good" are possible. Either "right" alludes to "law and rules" and "good" alludes to "equity"; or together, they constitute equitable exceptions to the letter of the law. Either view is plausible, but neither sheds light on what might be "right" or "good," "*in the sight of the Lord*." Indeed, Deut. 6:18 can be read as D's, and the Torah's, concession that not all "right and good" is found in His laws and rules. But this creates the problem of how Israel is to learn what is "right and good" *in His sight* other than by what He has revealed in His "laws and rules." What fate awaits the judge who errs "*in the Lord's sight*" by "suspending" an applicable law or rule in order to achieve his own view of what is "right and good?"

Given the Lord's insistence that Israel obey *all* His laws and rules, I conclude that the "right and good" of 6:18 creates no exceptions to the "laws and rules" of 6:1–2. Instead, Deut. 6:18 is meant as a "canon" of interpretation. In essence, it requires that laws and rules, *within their reasonable meanings*, be interpreted and applied toward the goal of fairness. As Rashi states the matter: "That which is right and good: This (refers to) compromise *inside the line of law*."[4]

The third and final homily is in Deut. 6:20–24.

When, *in time to come* . . . your son asks you, "What mean the exhortations, laws and rules which the Lord our God has enjoined upon you?" you shall [answer], "We were slaves to Pharaoh in Egypt and the Lord freed us from Egypt with a mighty hand. [He] wrought before our eyes marvelous and destructive signs and portents . . . and He freed us from there, that he might take us and give us the land that He had promised on oath to our fathers. Then the Lord commanded us to observe all these laws . . . for our lasting good and survival, *as is now the case*. It will be therefore to our merit before the Lord our God to observe faithfully this whole Instruction, as He has commanded us.

Comment D–11. On the means by which Israel's faithful observance of "all these laws" will bring about its "lasting good and survival"

In what way does Moses imply that Israel's faithful observance of "all these laws" will bring about its "lasting good and survival?" Will its blessings derive from the inherent social value of its laws in the development of a people and its culture? Or from the ministrations of the Lord, their God as the fruits of obedience?

Beyond doubt, many of the laws and rules of the Torah's God would contribute to the well-being of Israel, and all humanity. Yet nothing in 6:20–24 itself looks to their substance as the principal assurance of Israel's well-being. As declared by Moses, Israel's ultimate reward for obedience to "this whole instruction" will derive from "our *merit before the Lord our God*."

Deut. 7 opens with Moses' reminder of the Lord's unsparing condemnation of the seven named tribes who currently occupy Canaan and, accordingly, His commands on how the Israelites should deal with them (7:1–5). The named tribes are the "Hittites, Girgashites, Amorites, Canaanites, Perizzites, Hivites, and Jebusites, seven nations much larger than you" (7:1).

> Note D–38: Reappearing for the first time since the J passages of Gen. 10:16 and 15:21 the Girgashites, are now added to the most common listing of six Canaanite tribes (see Exod. 3:8, 3:17, 23:23, 33.2, 34:11, Deut. 20:17). Friedman basically links the Exodus listings with J and E, while Deut. 20:17, as part of the Deuteronomic Code of Law (Deut. 12–26), derives from the earlier northern Shiloh priests. But the point here is the oddity that only J and D ever mention the Girgashites. Unique to J, as well, are the Kenites, Kenizzites, and Kadmonites of Gen. 15:19.

Moses then recalls how Israel is to deal with the inhabitants of Canaan. They must doom them to destruction, grant no terms and give them no quarter (7:2). They may not intermarry with them, lest they "turn your children away from Me to worship other gods."

> Note D–39: Cf. J's similar admonition in Exod. 34:16. See also Num. 25:1–5 and Note N–111.

Should Israelites through intermarriage turn to "worship other gods," then "the Lord's anger will [again] blaze forth." He will "promptly wipe you out" (7:3–4). It will be Israel's duty to "tear down their altars, smash their pillars, cut down their sacred posts, and consign their images to fire" (7:5).

In Deut. 7:6–8 Moses seeks to ease what might have been the people's growing sense of terror. Thus, "of all the peoples on earth the Lord chose you to be His treasured people" (7:6). And "it was because the Lord loved you and kept the oath He made to your fathers that [He] freed you with a mighty hand and rescued you from the house of bondage, from the power of Pharaoh king of Egypt" (7:8).

In Deut. 7:9–11 Moses contrasts the bliss of obedience with the heavy wage of disobedience by recalling the Lord's emotional polarities. On the one hand, "Only the Lord your God is God . . . who keeps His gracious covenant to the thousandth generation of those who love Him and keep His commandments." But, on the other, "who instantly requites with destruction those who reject Him—never slow . . . but requiting them instantly." Thus, Israel must "observe faithfully the Instruction—the laws and rules—with which I charge you today" (7:11).

Note D–40: Through punctuation, JPS2 uniquely identifies the "laws and rules" as the two components of the "Instruction." The three Hebrew terms are mitzvah, chukim, *and* mishpatim.

To clarify the generality of the blessings of obedience in 7:9, Moses details the fecundity and health that will be Israel's for "faithfully observing" the "rules" (*mishpatim*) (7:12–15). In sum, the "Lord your God" will "love and bless and multiply you"; "bless the issue of your womb and the produce of your soil [including new grain and wine and oil and the calves and the lambs]"; assure that there will be "no sterile male or female among you or among your livestock"; "ward off from you all sickness," including the "dreadful diseases of Egypt." These, however, He "will inflict upon all your enemies."

With much emphatic repetition, the balance of Deut. 7 deals with the respective roles of the Israelites and the Lord, their God in the coming conquest of Canaan (7:16–26).

Israel's first charge is to "destroy all the peoples that the Lord your God delivers to you, showing them no pity" (7:16). A more benign expression of 6:14–15 then follows: "And you shall not worship their gods, for that would be a snare to you."

Deut. 7:17–24 emphasizes the Lord's dominant role in "delivering" the Canaanite tribes to Israel. Israel need "have no fear of them." Rather, it should bear in mind "what the Lord did to Pharaoh and all the Egyptians" (7:18). Moses speaks of "the wondrous acts that you saw with your own eyes" including "the signs and portents, the mighty hand, and the outstretched arm by which the Lord your God liberated you" (7:19). So will He do "to all the peoples you now fear." He will "send a plague against them, until those who are left in hiding perish before you" (7:20).

Comment D–12. On the Torah's "manipulation" of its God

Why should the Lord, God of Israel continue to harbor such unseemly passions for the utter destruction of entire peoples? Why should He be so hateful to those whom *He* has not chosen to serve as God? And if their worship of other gods and attendant practices do require chastisement, can this omnipotent Creator of all humanity not devise a response short of total destruction? In truth, He cannot. Having been created to fulfil human purposes, the Lord, God of Israel, has no choice. He is a servant of his creators, who, primarily, are creating a people and a nation.

In Deut. 7:22 Moses describes the conquest of Canaan in terms that belie the verses that precede and follow it: "*The Lord your God will dislodge those people before you little by little; you will not be able to put an end to them at once, else the wild beasts would multiply to your hurt*" (cf. Exod. 23:29–30). Like 7:20–21 before it, however, 7:23–24, which follows, is not much given to gradualism. "The Lord your God will deliver them up to you, throwing them into utter panic until they are wiped out, He will deliver their kings into your hand; . . . no man shall stand up to you until you have wiped them out" (7:23–24).

> Note D–41: The persistence of a tradition regarding Israel's gradual occupation of Canaan may explain D's inclusion of 7:22 (as well as E's earlier inclusion of Exod. 23:29–30). In 7:20–21 and 23–24, however, D offers assurance that the Lord's needful prudence in 7:22 implied no lessening in the intensity and ferocity of His intent to destroy the existing inhabitants of Canaan.

Deut. 7:25–26 concludes with a final charge to Israel to pile the gods of Canaan on the junkheap of history. "You shall consign the images of their gods to the fire." Nor could the people keep "the silver and the gold on them" lest they be "ensnared." No "abhorrent thing" could be brought in one's house "for it is proscribed."

In Deut. 8 Moses continues on the need for obedience as the source Israel's well-being. "You shall faithfully observe all the Instruction that I enjoin upon you today, *that you may thrive and increase and be able to occupy the land which the Lord promised on oath to your fathers.* But as a prelude to the blessings of the "good land" that lies across the Jordan, Moses recalls the hardships by which the people were tested for forty years in the wilderness—all with the aim of determining "what was in your hearts; whether you would keep His commandments or not" (8:2).

In response to the hunger (to which "*He* subjected you"), the Lord then "gave you manna . . . in order to teach you that *man does not live on bread alone, but that man may live on anything that the Lord decrees*" (8:3).

Comment D–13. On "Man does not live on bread alone"

As stated by Moses in JPS2, the Lord provided manna so that Israel should know "that man does not live *on* bread alone, but that man may live *on* anything that the Lord decrees" (8:3). RSV, however (and JPS1 in essence), states that "man does not live *by* bread alone, but that man lives *by everything that proceeds out of the mouth of the Lord*" (*key ahl kol mohzah phee yahweh*). Is the much noted aphorism meant to state a gastronomic or a spiritual truth?

Ramban reads Deut. 8:3 to reflect the Lord's intent "to inform them that it is He Who *preserves* man with whatever He decrees, and if so *observe His commandments, and live.*"[5] In essence, the Lord God will sustain those who obey Him, not necessarily by bread, but by whatever means He might choose. Here there are elements of both gastronomy and spirituality.

RSV/JPS1 seem to strive toward the latter. To live "by," rather than "on," bread alone, tends to view "bread" as a broader metaphor for *materialism*, or material well-being, rather than food alone. Conversely, to live "on" bread alone is more suggestive of "bread" as food.

Both RSV/JPS1 and JPS2 remain consistent with their respective initial uses of "by" and "on." When RSV/JPS1 speak of "everything that proceeds out of the mouth of the Lord" they evoke a sense of all of His "words"— including His "Ten Words." As such, His "words" suggest an intended enrichment of the human spirit. Conversely, JPS2's use of the "Lord's decrees" seems more directed to individual topical "decrees," such as His decision that Israel should subsist on manna in the absence of bread.

In the choice between bread as a gastronomic or a spiritual metaphor, JPS2 is on sound grounds in emphasizing the former. Literally, it was physical and not spiritual hunger that necessitated the Lord's immediate provision of manna. Beyond doubt, however, the Torah intended spiritual consequences from the manna. Its "price" would be paid in grateful obedience to its provider. And by the Torah's standards, obedience to its God was the ultimate expression of spirituality. RSV/JPS1 is, therefore, on equally sound grounds. Thus, to paraphrase Ramban again, the intent of the *entire aphorism* of Deut. 8:3 is that the Lord, God of Israel, by means of His own choosing, will meet all needs of the obedient, whether they be of body or spirit.

Deut. 8:4 goes on to remind this surviving generation of other miracles by which the Lord, its God, sustained it through forty years in the wilderness. Their clothes "did not wear out" nor did their "feet swell." To this Moses adds an ironic commentary on the plagues visited by the Lord on the Israelites in the wilderness, and His many threats of extinction should they worship other gods: "Bear in mind that the Lord disciplines you just as a man disciplines his son" (8:5). Thus, they must "keep [His] commandments; walk in His ways and *revere* Him" (8:6).

> *Note D–42: JPS1/RSV both use "fear" rather than "revere." On the matter "fear" and "revere" see Comments G–40, E–64, D–9, and D–16.*

In Deut. 8:7–10 Moses extols the blessings of the "good land" to which "the Lord your God is bringing you." It is a land "with streams and springs and fountains issuing from plain and hill"; a land of "wheat and barley, of vines, figs, and pomegranates"; a land "of olive trees and honey"; a land "where you may eat food without stint, where you will lack nothing"; a land "whose rocks and iron are from hills you can mine copper." And for all this, Moses tells them, "When you have eaten your fill, give thanks to the Lord your God for the good land He has given you."

> *Note D–43: And thus the ritual of postmeal "grace?"*

Deut. 8:11–18 then expands on "the bread" of 8:3. Beyond providing Israel's basic sustenance, its Lord God will bless it with material well-being far beyond the need for mere survival. But seeing danger in such bliss, Moses sounds a warning:

> Take care lest you forget the Lord your God and fail to keep His command-ments, His rules and His laws. . . . [When you have eaten your fill and live in fine houses and when your herds and flocks and silver and gold and everything you own has prospered] beware lest your heart grow haughty and you forget the Lord your God [Who, since freeing you from bondage, has preserved you from countless dangers in the great and terrible wilderness] to test you by hardships only to benefit you in the end." (8:11–16)

However, it is not wealth itself that the Lord will provide, but rather the "power" to create wealth. This leads to Moses' fear that the people will fail to credit the Lord with their success; that they will claim, "My own power and the might of my own hand have won this wealth for me" (8:17). In anticipation of such self-pride, he warns the people, "Remember that it is the Lord your God *Who gives you the power to get wealth*, in fulfillment [of His covenant with your fathers], as is still the case" (8:18).

Comment D–14. On why the Lord would give manna to Israel in the wilderness but only the *"power* to get wealth" in the promised land

In the absence of "bread" in the wilderness, it would have been of little use for the Lord to give the Israelites "the power to get other food." In the wilderness, human "power" alone could not have provided enough food to meet their needs. Accordingly, the Lord, their God is said to give them food directly—in the form of manna. *By the logic of the Torah*, He did so because (1) their survival was at stake and (2) their obedience was as yet untested. Only a God-sent "miracle" could save the people; and the Lord responded.

Conversely, Israel's acquisition of wealth in the promised land was not a condition of survival but the basis for a better life. Thus, only by instilling obedience to His laws and rules would the Lord have thereby enabled a new generation to acquire "the power to get wealth."

Another warning against the worship of other gods then follows: "If you forget the Lord your God and follow other gods . . . I warn you this day that you shall cer-tainly perish; like the nations that the Lord will cause to perish before you, so you shall perish—because you did not heed the Lord your God" (8:19–20).

In Deut. 9 Moses seeks to disabuse the Israelites of any thought that they deserve the promised land. He begins, however, by reminding them of both the challenge they face in conquering Canaan *and* the Lord's promise of success. Their foes are "greater and more populous" and their "great cities" have "walls sky-high" (9:1). Worse yet, Israel will face the "great and tall" Anakites, of whom they have heard it said, "Who can stand up to the children of Anak?" (9:2). But the Lord will "wipe them out" with a "devouring fire," so that "you may quickly dispossess and destroy them, *as the Lord has promised you*" (9:3).

But when the Lord their God clears their path, the Israelites are not to say, "[He] has enabled me to occupy this land because of my virtues" (9:4). In sum, "it is not because of your virtues and your rectitude that you will be able to occupy their country, but because of the wickedness of those nations that the Lord is dispossessing them before you, and in order to fulfill the oath that the Lord made to your fathers, Abraham, Isaac and Jacob" (9:5).

Moses then raises the tone of his criticism: "Know, then, that it is not for any virtue of yours that the Lord your God is giving you this good land to occupy, for you are a stiff necked people" (9:6). Moreover, you have "provoked the Lord your God to anger" and have continued "defiant toward [Him]" (9:7).

In Deut. 9:8–21 Moses speaks of Israel's greatest failing—the apostasy of the "molten calf" (but see Comments E–86 through 90). He first tells of ascending the mountain "to receive the tablets of stone inscribed by the finger of God," during which, for forty days and nights, he "[ate] no bread and [drank] no water" (9:9). There the Lord gave him "the two tablets of stone inscribed by the finger of God," exactly as He first spoke them "out of the fire on the day of the Assembly" (9:10). (See Exod. 31:18, Exod. 19:9–20:18, and Comment E–85).

Moses then relates the entire episode (9:11–21). In essence, having received "the two tablets of stone, the Tablets of the Covenant," Moses is told by the Lord of wickedness of the people "whom *you* brought out of Egypt." They had made themselves a "molten image" (9:11–12). In condemning them as "stiffnecked," the Lord tells Moses, "*Let me alone* [spare me arguments] and I will destroy them . . . and make *you* a nation far more numerous than they" (9:13–14).

On descending the mountain with "the two Tablets of the Covenant" in his hands, Moses saw the "molten calf" for himself. He immediately "flung away" the tablets, "smashing them before your eyes" (9:15–17).

Moses further recalls how he "threw [himself] down before the Lord" and went without bread or water for yet another forty days and nights. His fear was that the Lord's "fierce anger" would move Him "to wipe you out" (9:18–19). To this he adds, "Moreover the Lord was angry enough with Aaron to have destroyed him, so I also interceded for Aaron at that time" (9:20).

> *Note D–44: In Exodus, on first encountering Aaron, Moses rebukes him (32:21–24). In contrast, the Lord never singles Aaron out for opprobrium. Did E and D differ as to Aaron's guilt before the Lord? (See Comment E–87.)*

Moses concludes the episode of the "molten calf" by recounting how he put the calf "to the fire" and broke it and ground it "until it was as fine as dust." He then threw it all "into the [mountain] brook" (9:21).

Note D–45: In Exod. 32:20 Moses "makes" the Israelites drink the "powder" filled water.

Having reminded the remaining generation of the apostasy of the "molten calf" at Horeb, Moses recalls other lesser, but still serious, occasions, on which the people were "defiant toward the Lord" (9:24.) These were at (1) Taberah (Num. 11:1–3), (2) Massah (Exod. 17:1–7), (3) Kibroth-hattaavah (Num. 11:4–35), and (4) Kadesh-barnea (Num. 13 and 14). (See Deut. 9:22–23.)

Note D–46: At Kadish-barnea, following the report of the scouts, the Israelites became so fearful of invading Canaan as to mutter a preference for dying in the wilderness or returning to Egypt. In near open revolt, they would have pelted Moses and Aaron with stones, but for the sudden Presence of the Lord (Num. 13:30–14:10). It was here the Lord vowed to grant their rash preference through forty years of wandering in the wilderness (Num. 14:26–35). Following Deut. 9:22–23, however, Moses says nothing of the forty years of wandering and the death of an entire generation. Instead he speaks again of the Lord's wrath following the golden calf.

Moses now alludes to "forty days and nights" that he "lay prostrate" before the Lord because He was determined to "destroy you" (9:25).

Note D–47: Exod. 32 says nothing, however, of Moses lying prostrate before the Lord for forty days and forty nights in penance for the people.

In 9:26–29, D largely repeats Moses' plea of Exod. 32:11–14 that led to the Lord's renunciation of "the punishment He had planned"

O Lord God, do not annihilate Your very own people, whom you redeemed in Your majesty and whom you freed from Egypt with a mighty hand. [Think of] Abraham, Isaac and Jacob, and pay no heed to the stubborness of the people, its wickedness and its sinfulness. *Else the country from which You freed us will say, "It was because the Lord was powerless to bring them into the land He had promised them, and because He hated them, that He brought them out to have them die in the wilderness."* Yet they are your very own people, whom you freed." (9:26–29)

In Deut. 10:1–5 Moses offers a brief reprise of Exod. 34. Moses recalls his preparing a second set of stone tablets "like the first" (which he had smashed on seeing the "molten calf" and related activities). He also recalls that "the Lord inscribed on the tablets the same text as on the first, the Ten Commandments."

Note D–48: In Exod. 34:27–28, at the Lord's direction, it is Moses who "writes down" the Commandments.

Moses then took these down from the mountain and deposited them "in the ark that I had made, *where they still are as the Lord had commanded me*" (10:1–5).

> *Note D–49: The ark of which Moses speaks of having made is foreign to Exod. 34. The permanent ark as a repository of the tablets had not yet been constructed (Exod. 35:10–19).* That Moses speaks of their deposit in the ark suggests that D knew of the general tradition of an ark, but not of its later embellishments by P *(Exod. 35–40).*

In Deut. 10:6–7 the Israelites march from Beeroth-bene-jaakan to Moserah, Gudgod, and Jotbath (cf. Num. 33). In 10:6, Moses also tells of Aaron's death at Moserah, where "Eleazar became priest in his stead" (see Num. 20:22–26).

> *Note D–50: P and D refer differently to the site of Aaron's death as Mount Hor and Moserah.*

Following Aaron's death D moves the Israelites on to Gudgod and Jotbath (10:7). Deut. 10:8 then states: "*At that time* the Lord set aside the tribe of Levi to carry the Ark of the Lord's Covenant."

> *Note D–51: Contrary to Num. 20:23–29, D's chronology would fix Aaron's death before the Lord placed the Levites "in charge of the Tabernacle of the Pact" (Num. 1:47–53). D's timing of these events foretells the fundamental differences between Deuteronomy and the P portions of Exodus, Leviticus, and Numbers relating to the Aaronide priesthood and the Temple.*

Moses, however, remains transfixed on his second stay on the mountain, during which the Lord's wrath over the calf finally abates. "I stayed on the mountain, as I did the first time, forty days and forty nights, and the Lord heeded me once again: the Lord agreed not to destroy you." So it was, in effect, that the Lord told him to move on " at the head of people," that they might . . . occupy the land that I swore to their fathers to give them" (10:10–11).

Moses then poses a question with which he means to touch the core of Israel's hopes and fears: "And now, O Israel, what does the Lord your God demand of you?" (10:12a).

And so he replies, "Only this: to revere [or "fear"] the Lord your God, to walk only in His paths, to love Him, and to serve [Him] with all your heart and soul, keeping [His] commandments and laws, which I enjoin upon you today, for your good" (10:13).

> *Note D–52: On "fear" or "revere," see Comment D–9. Having made my point, I will now use "fear" rather than "revere" for the yod/resh/aleph root.*

Moses then reminds them, although "the heavens . . . the earth, and all that is on it . . . belong to the Lord your God," "Yet it was to your fathers that the Lord was drawn in His love for them, so that He chose you, their lineal descendants" (10:14–15). "Cut away . . . the thickening about your hearts and stiffen your necks no more" (10:16).

> Note D–53: The reference to "hearts" is from oomaltem ayt ahrlat l'vav'chem, more traditionally rendered as "Circumcise therefore the foreskin of your heart" (JPS1/RSV).

Moses then speaks of the Lord God's power, justice and compassion. He is "God Supreme and Lord Supreme, the great, the mighty, and the awesome God, who shows no favor and takes no bribe, but upholds the cause of the fatherless and the widow, and befriends the stranger, providing him with food and clothing—You too must befriend the stranger, for you were strangers in the land of Egypt" (10:17–19).

Deut. 10:20 repeats the essence of how Israel must relate to the Lord, its God. "You must fear [Him]: only Him shall you worship, to Him you shall hold fast, and by His name you shall swear." He is your glory and He is your God, who wrought for you these marvelous, awesome deeds that you saw with your own eyes."

Deut. 10 concludes by recalling the acme of the Lord's "marvelous, awesome" deeds. "Your ancestors went down to Egypt seventy persons in all: and now the Lord your God has made you as numerous as the stars of heaven" (10:22).

> Note D–54: As to the "seventy persons in all" in Jacob's party, see Comments G–89A and B.

In Deut. 11:1, Moses sums up his answer to the central question of 10:12a (that is, "What does the Lord demand of you?). "Love, therefore the Lord your God, and always keep His charge, His laws, His rules, and His commandments."

> Note D–55: As a state of mind and spirit, love can neither be commanded nor compelled by threat of punishment. But it can develop from gratitude for past blessings and the expectation of future blessings. One purpose of Deut. 11 is to inspire a love born freely of gratitude.

To justify the claim of Israel's Lord God to its love, Moses first recalls certain defining events of the Exodus, as experienced and witnessed not by "your children" (11:2), but by "you who saw with your own eyes all the marvelous deeds that the Lord performed" (11:7).

In speaking of the Lord's role as Israel's God and Protector, Moses attributes these events to "His majesty, His mighty hand, His outstretched arm" (11:2).

They include (11:2–4): (1) "the signs and deeds that He performed in Egypt against Pharaoh king of Egypt and all his land"; (2) "what He did to Egypt's army, its horses and chariots"; and (3) "how [He] rolled back . . . the Sea of Reeds when they were pursuing you, thus destroying them once and for all."

While Moses means to focus on what the Lord "did *for* you in the wilderness," he also recalls an act of severe chastisement. It is what "[The Lord] did to Dathan and Abiram, sons of Eliab son of Reuben . . . when the earth opened her mouth and swallowed them, along with their households, their tents, and every living thing in their train, from amidst all Israel" (11:6).

Comment D–15. On the the fate of Dathan and Abiram as a reason for Israel's gratitude

In the context of 11:2–7, why does D include the fate of Dathan and Abiram among "all the marvelous deeds that the Lord performed"? Why was their annihilation an act for which the people should be grateful?

As told in Num. 16, the story includes Korah as a third rebel. His absence in Deut. 11 might be explained by P's authorship of Korah and J's of Dathan and Abiram. Thus, P or R may have later combined the two stories. But more to the point, the fact of a rebellion led the Lord to direct Moses and Aaron to "Stand back from this community that I may annihilate them in an instant." Moses and Aaron then "fell on their faces" to plead: "When one man sins, will you be wrathful with the whole community?" To which the Lord (perhaps recalling Abraham) replied to Moses: "Speak to the community and say: Withdraw from about the abodes of Korah, Dathan, and Abriham" (Num. 16:16–23). Experience tells us, therefore, that the basis for gratitude in this story could be the Lord's decision to distinguish between the guilty and the innocent. That He pauses to reflect in such cases was always an occasion for gratitude.

Deut. 11:8–9 again evokes a major theme of the Torah. "Keep, therefore, all the Instruction that I [Moses] enjoin upon you today, *so that you may have the strength to invade and occupy the land* which you are about to cross into and occupy, *and that you may long endure upon the soil* which the Lord swore to your fathers . . . and . . . their descendants."

> Note D–56: As in Comment D–11, the issue is how Israel's obedience to the "Instruction" is meant to serve as a source of strength? Will it emerge from the intrinsic qualities of the "Instruction" or from the Lord's beneficient response to obedience?

In Deut. 11:9b–12 Moses compares Egypt with Canaan, "a land flowing with milk and honey." It is a difference between a land that "had to be watered with your own labors" and "a land of hills and valleys" that "soaks up its waters from the rains of heaven." And just as the Lord chose Israel, among all peoples, so did He choose Canaan as "a land which [He] looks after, on which [He] always keeps His eye, from year's beginnings to year's end."

In Deut. 11:13–17 Moses tells how the Lord will respond to Israel's obedience, or lack thereof, through manipulation of His natural order.

> If then, you obey the commandments that I enjoin upon you this day, loving the Lord your God and serving Him with all your heart and soul, I will grant the rain for your land in season, the early rain and the late. . . . I will also provide grass in the fields for your cattle—and thus you shall eat your fill. Take care not to be lured away to serve other gods and bow to them. For the Lord's anger will flare up against you, and He will shut up the skies so that there will be no rain and the ground will not yield its produce; and you will soon perish from the good land the Lord is giving you.

> *Note D–57: In 11:14 and 15, Moses is said to tell the people that as the fruits of obedience "I" will "grant the rain" and "I" will "provide grass." In that these were rewards that only the Lord could assure, Moses would seem to have done it again in the matter of water. Has he not demeaned the Lord's sanctity in the same way the Lord had perceived him to do by striking his rod on the rock at Meribah? (See Comment N–22.) As we are told in 1:37, however, D's Lord has already barred Moses from entering Canaan for his failure of leadership on first arriving at Kadesh-barnea (see Deut. 1:19–37 and Comment D–1).*

> *That Moses was spared added publishment for this stark transgression may have reflected D's belief that no further punishment could exceed the enormity of his having been denied entry into Canaan. But punishment aside, 11:14–15 may also imply that after some forty stressful years as the Lord's prophet to Israel, even Moses at times could become confused to the point of merging their separate identities.*

Comment D–16. On stark fear, reverential fear and love as foundations for Israel's obedience to its Lord God

As observed in Note D–55 in regard to 11:1, "As a state of mind and spirit, love can neither be commanded nor compelled by threat of punishment." But once absorbed into the mind and spirit, love provides a powerful impetus to obedience. Thus far, Deut. 11 speaks of love rather than fear as a source of Israel's obedience. However, in recalling the specter of apostasy, D resorts to the Torah's primary impetus to obedience, namely fear (see Comment D–9).

In general, the power and wrath of the Torah's God is intended, above all, to inspire a stark and uncomplicated fear of certain, and often immediate, punishment. Beyond this basic primordial fear, however, is the fear which the sacrifice of Isaac was meant to test in Abraham. It is a reverential and awesome fear born from a sense of the sanctity of a Being whose power enables him to fulfil all of His purposes (see Comments G–39, 40, and 41.) Stark fear, of course, spawns no more than a coerced obedience. To coercion alone reverential fear adds an element of free choice. As a source of obedience through free choice alone, however, reverential fear must still overcome doubts arising from inner conflict. For a love that transcends all doubt, however, the Torah invokes the support of abiding gratitude. Yet, ironically enough, the Torah offers no basis for gratitude without the obedience that it seeks to foster through fear.

So that Israel's duties and the power of its Lord God to punish and reward are never forgotten, Moses commands every Israelite to "bind *them* as a sign on your hand and . . . as a symbol on your forehead, and teach *them* to your children—reciting them when you stay at home and when you are away, when you lie down and when you get up; and inscribe *them* on the doorposts of your house and on your gates." All this, so that "you and your children may endure in the land that the Lord swore to your fathers . . . as long as there is a heaven over the earth" (11:18–21).

> *Note D–58: These verses augment the ritual reminders of Deut. 6:8–9.*

In Deut. 11:22–25 Moses speaks to Israel of the salutary consequences of "faithfully [keeping] all this Instruction that I command you, loving the Lord your God, walking in all His ways, and holding fast to them" (11:22).

> *Note D–59: On the possible meaning of "walking in all His ways" see Comment D–35.*

And what were the promised results? (1) The Lord will dislodge nations before you "nations greater and more numerous than you" (11:23). (2) Israel's territory shall extend "from the wilderness to the Lebanon and from the River—the Euphrates—to the Western Sea" (11:24). (3) "No man shall stand up to you: the Lord your God will put the dread and fear of you over the whole land . . . as He promised you" (11:25).

The final verses of Deut. 11 (i.e., 26–32) can be read either as (1) a conclusion to Deut. 11, (2) an introduction to the Code of Law in Deut. 12–26, or (3) as a partial introduction to Deut. 27, following the Code of Law.

Deut. 11:26–28 tells again of Israel's choice of a blessing or curse. Needless to say, "blessing" will come from obedience and "curse," from disobedience—particularly should Israel "follow other gods, whom you have not experienced" (11:28). On Israel's entry into Canaan, the blessing is to be "pronounced at"

484

Mount Gerizim and the curse at Mount Ebal. "Both are on the other side of the Jordan . . . in the land of the Cananites . . . near Gilgal, by the terebinths of Moreb" (11:29–30).

The final admonition of 11:31–32 is that Israel, having occupied and settled in Canaan, "take care to observe all the laws and rules that I have set before you this day." These words precede the Deuteronomic Code of Law that follows (Deut. 12–26). However, the previous mention in Deut. 11:26–30 of the "blessing at Mount Gerizim" and the "curse at Mount Ebal" serves even more effectively to introduce the subject matter of Deut. 27. It is possible, therefore, that when an editorial decision was made to interject the older Code of Law, the intended introduction to Deut. 27 was disconnected from its intended subject.

And so begins the Deuteronomic Code of Law. "These are the laws and rules you must carefully observe in the land that the Lord, God of your fathers, is giving you to possess *as long as you live on earth*" (12:1).

Note D–60: For another view of "immutability," see Comment E–75.

Note D–61: Friedman attributes Deut.12:1–26:15, not to a Deuteronomic historian (D1 or D2), but simply to "Other." In his text, however, he persuasively identifies "Other" as the levitical priests of Shiloh, who wrote before the Assyrian conquest and the extinction of Israel in c. 722 B.C.E. While committed to a central sanctuary, their situs was Shiloh, rather than Jerusalem. This explains the total absence of the Aaronide priesthood in the Deuteronomic Code of Law.[6] *(See Note D–73 and Comment D–17.)*

Another aspect of the Code of Law is the absence of Moses throughout—from Deut. 12:1 through 26. Not until Deut. 27:1 is his presence again acknowledged. By failing to identify any narrator, the Code of Law permits a reader to assume, without textual verification, that it is Moses who speaks.

Deut. 12 aims to abolish the widespread practices implied in E's earlier praise of decentralized sacrifices and worship. It's purpose, therefore, may be best understood by a reminder of Exod. 20:21.

Make for Me an altar of earth and sacrifice on it your burnt offerings and your sacrifices of well-being, your sheep and your oxen; *in every place where I cause My name to be mentioned* I will come and bless you.

It is in relation to Exod. 20:21 that we should consider the Code's firm rejection of the decentralized sacrifices and worship. But even as Israel looks to fulfil its own ritual obligations, it must deal no less with the heathen practices of the Canaanites.

You must destroy all the sites at which [the nations of Canaan] worshiped their gods, whether on lofty mountains and on hills or under any luxuriant tree. Tear down their altars, smash their pillars . . . cut down the images of their gods. (12:2–3)

But where, then, may Israel worship its own Lord God? As stated in 12:4–12:

Look only to the site that the Lord your God will choose amidst all your tribes as His habitation. . . . There you are to go, . . . to bring your burnt offerings and other sacrifices, your tithes and contributions, your votive and freewill offerings, and the firstlings of your herds and flocks. [There, you and your households] shall feast before the Lord your God.

You shall not act at all as we now act here, every man as he pleases, because you have not yet come to the allotted haven that the Lord your God is giving you. When you cross the Jordan and settle in the land . . . and you live in security, then you must bring everything that I command you to the site where the Lord your God will choose to establish His name: [i.e., burnt offerings and other sacrifices, tithes and contributions, and all votive offerings]. And there you shall rejoice before the Lord your God with [your children, slaves, and the Levite of your settlement].

Comment D–17. On the central sanctuary of Deuteronomy

In Deut. 12:11 the place for sacrifices will be "at *the* site where the Lord your God will choose to establish His name." It is the antithesis of conducting sacrifices "*in every place* where I cause my name to be mentioned" (as E would have it) (Exod. 20:21). But no less significant than this priestly reformation of E is the distinction between the Code of the priests of Shiloh and P.

Consider once more these words of 12:8–9: "You shall not act at all as we now act here, every man as he pleases, because you have not yet come to the allotted haven that the Lord your God is giving you." Only after entering Canaan must the Israelites "bring everything that I command to the site where the Lord your God will choose to establish His name" (12:10–11).

Clearly, the levitical authors of the Code of Law in Shiloh knew nothing of the P tradition, which had required centralized sacrifices at the Tent and Tabernacle from the time of Sinai onward. (Or if they did know of it, they totally rejected it.) The priests of Shiloh would not begin their sacrificial rituals until the Lord had chosen a site in Canaan itself. And even then, it would be not a site at which the Lord would dwell among them, but only where He would "establish His name" (cf. Exod. 25:8.).

Indeed, the Tent and Tabernacle of Exodus, Leviticus, and Numbers are totally ignored throughout Deuteronomy. A Tent of Meeting in Deuteronomy will appear only in 31:14–15. Its obvious forerunner, however, is E's Tent of Meeting in Exod. 33:7–11. A Tabernacle is never mentioned.

Deut. 12:13–14 deals further with the centralization of sacrifices at the single site to be chosen by the Lord.

> Take care not to sacrifice your burnt offerings in any place you like, *but only in the place which the Lord will choose in one of your tribal territories.* There you shall sacrifice your burnt offerings and there you shall observe all that I enjoin upon you.

Apart from sacrificial slaughtering, however, Deut. 12:15–16 explicitly allows the "decentralized" slaughter of "edible" animals for food. "But whenever you desire, you may slaughter and eat meat in any of your settlements." A person could eat of all permitted animals, included those not suitable for sacrifice (such as the "gazelle and deer"; 12:15). But as for blood, "you must not partake of [it]; you shall pour it out on the ground like water" (12:16).

Deut. 12:17–27 distinguishes the animal related rituals to be fulfilled at the central sanctuary from those which were suitable to "your settlements."

> *Note D–62: For the eighth century* B.C.E. *authors of the Code of Law the situs of the "central sanctuary" was Shiloh. By c. 622* B.C.E., *of course, it was in Jerusalem, where the main text of Deuteronomy was supposedly "discovered."*

Among the rituals limited to the central sanctuary were those involving "tithes [whether of grains, other produce or firstlings of sacrificial animals], votive [and] freewill offerings, or . . . contributions." Only there (i.e., "not . . . in your settlements") were the tithes to be consumed by offerors, their families, their slaves and "the Levites in your settlements" (12:17–18). To underscore participation in the tithes by "the Levites in your settlements," the people were admonished "not to neglect the Levite as long as you live in your land" (12:19).

Deut. 12:20–22 turns again to the slaughter of animals for food and the consumption of meat. Once in Canaan, Moses explained, "you may eat meat *whenever you wish*" (12:20). Moreover, where the central sanctuary is "too far, . . . you may slaughter any of the cattle or sheep that the Lord gives you, as I have instructed you; and you may eat to your heart's content" (12:21). Thus, though "eligible" to be sacrificed, animals from the herd or flock could be eaten "as the gazelle and deer are eaten: the [ritually] unclean . . . together with the clean" (12:22).

Deut. 12:23–26 again prohibits the consumption of blood, together with a rationale: "for the blood is the life, and you must not consume the life with the flesh" (12:23). Accordingly, "you must pour it out on the ground like water" (12:24). In describing the consequences of disobedience, the priests of Shiloh, while decisive, are more benign and less menacing than P will prove to be. Thus, "you must not partake of it, in order that it may go well with you and with your descendants to come, for you will be doing what is right in the sight of the Lord" (12:25).

Deut. 12:26–27 returns to the central sanctuary as the required site of "sacred and votive offerings" (12:26) including "your burnt offerings" and "other sacrifices." In the case of non-consumed burnt offerings, "both the flesh and the blood" were to be offered "on the altar." As for consumable sacrifices, "the blood shall be poured out on the altar . . . and you shall eat the flesh" (12:27). Deut. 12:28 offers a homiletic command, or reminder, to "heed all of these command- ments which I enjoin upon you." And as in 12:25, "it will go well with you and with your descendants after you forever, *for you will be doing what is right and good in the sight of the Lord your God*" (12:28).

> Note D–63: *The conclusion of Comment D–10, that D intends an identity between "right and good" and obedience to all "commandments," or "laws and rules," finds near decisive support in 12:28. Literally, "to heed all of these commandments" is to do "what is right and good" (see Note D–64).*

Deut. 12 closes with a warning against the gods of Canaan. (12:29–31). It calls for Israelites not only to scorn such gods, but to remain ignorant of them. And this, even after "they have been wiped out before you" (12:29–30a). Thus, "*do not inquire about their gods*, saying, 'How *did* those nations worship their gods? I too will follow those practices" (12:30b).

Deut. 12:31 then speaks to the purpose and value of this mandate of igno- rance. "You shall not act thus *toward* the Lord your God, for they perform for their gods every abhorrent act that the Lord detests; they even offer up their sons and daughters in fire to their gods."

Comment D–18. On a textual intimation of the Torah's God as Israel's conscience

The focus of Deut. 12:31 is less on the sin of apostasy itself than on the "abhorrent act" of child sacrifice to which it might lead. For an Israelite to sacrifice children as a part of their worship of other gods was to plummet to the depths of human depravity. JPS1/RSV both read *lahyahweh* as "to the Lord your God." ("You shall not act thus *to* the Lord your God.")

That the evil of child sacrifice is done *to* rather than *against* Israel's God speaks of conduct even more degraded than apostasy itself. *The deed tran- scends His pride.* His wrath is converted to sadness. True, His sanctity has been dishonored, but more important, His soul has been wounded. Accordingly, that this "abhorrent act" is done *to*, rather than *against*, the Torah's God is to elevate Him from His role as Israel's omnipotent Lord to that of its con- science. By subordinating His sanctity to His compassion, the priests of Shiloh honor Him and themselves. (JPS2 is correct, but less direct, in reading the *lah* of *lahyahweh* as "toward" rather than "to" the Lord.)

While Deut. 12:1 emphasizes the permanence of the "laws and rules," Deut. 13:1 now emphasizes their precision. Thus, "Be careful to observe only that which I enjoin upon you; *neither add to it nor take away from it*."

> Note D–64: *Deut. 13:1 explicitly confirms the conclusion that "right and good" is to serve as a standard for interpreting "laws and rules" rather than as a source of "extralegal" standards of fairness (see Comment D–10 and Note D–63).*

Deut. 13:2–6 addresses the particular lure to other gods of the "prophet" or "dream-diviner" who gives "a sign or portent" while inveighing, "Let us follow and worship another God" (13:2–3). Even if the sign or portent "comes true," his words must not be heeded. *That it does come true is only because "the Lord your God is testing you to see whether you love [Him] with all your heart and soul"* (13:4). In essence, the Lord, and only the Lord, is to be followed, revered, obeyed, heeded, and adhered to (13:5). As for the fate of the false prophet, "he shall be put to death; for he urged disloyalty to the Lord your God. . . . Thus will you sweep out evil from your midst" (13:6).

> Note D–65: *How are the people to identify false prophets if, to test the people, the Lord causes their predictions to "come true?" See Deut. 18:19–22 and Comment D–25.*

Deut. 13:7–12 deals with tempters toward other gods among one's own family and friends. Specifically, "your brother, your own mother's son [i.e., a half-brother], or your son or daughter, or the wife of your bosom, or your closest friend" (13:7).

The concern here is the lure of novelty for the sake of novelty, as to which family members or friends might prove especially influential. Thus, they may say, " 'Come let us worship other gods'—whom neither you nor your fathers have experienced—from among the gods of the peoples around you, either near to you or distant, anywhere from one end of the earth to the other" (13:8).

> Note D–66: *That parents are not identified as such may signify the Torah's presumptive respect for their status rather than absolution for their acts.*

Without regard to personal feelings, such enticers must be shown "no pity or compassion." Instead, "let your hand be the first against him [or her] to put him to death, and the hand of the rest of the people thereafter. Stone him to death, for he sought to make you stray from the Lord your God . . . *Thus all Israel will hear and be afraid, and such evil things will not be done again in your midst*" (13:9–12).

Deut. 13:13–19 returns yet again to the central concern of apostasy, in this case "among the towns that the Lord your God is giving you to dwell in." With the required extirpation of an entire town in mind, should "you hear it said . . . that some scoundrels among you have gone and subverted the inhabitants of their town [with pleas to worship other gods], *you shall investigate and inquire and interrogate thoroughly*" (13:13–15). Should the rumor prove true, both the "inhabitants of that town . . . and its cattle" were to be "put to the sword." Having been "doomed," the entire town and "all its spoil" was to be burnt. It would then remain "an everlasting ruin, never to be rebuilt" (13:16–17).

Nor could the Lord's human avengers seek gain from their efforts. "Let nothing that has been doomed stick to your hand, *in order that the Lord may turn from His blazing anger and show you compassion*, and in His compassion increase you as He promised your fathers on oath" (13:18).

> *Note D–67: Here the priests of Shiloh are seen to embrace the principle of communal responsibility. That "some scoundrels" have "subverted the inhabitants of their town" suggests a breadth of guilt that touches the entire adult population. But even if this were a kind of Sodom and Gomorrah stained by apostasy rather than sexual deviance, what of the town's innocent children? As in the Flood and at Sodom, has the conduct of their parents condemned them to death?*

Deut. 13:19 again suggests the identity between "doing what is right" and total obedience (see Comment D–10 and Note D–63). The words of 13:18 are followed by: "For you will be heeding the Lord your God, obeying all His commandments which I join upon you this day, doing what is right in the sight of the Lord your God" (13:19).

Deut. 14 largely duplicates (or, more likely, anticipates) a variety of Levitical laws. In declaring the Israelites to be "children of," and "consecrated to, the Lord your God," Deut. 14:1–2 commands that "you shall not gash yourselves or shave the front of your heads because of the dead."

> *Note D–68: As he did in regard to Lev. 19:27–28, Rashi views the "gashes" as "a custom of the Amorites."*[7]

Deut. 14:3–21 largely replicates the dietary laws of Leviticus. As in Lev. 11, Deut. 14:3–8 begins with land animals. The general test of ritual edibility, as in Lev. 11:2–8, was that an animal have "true hoofs which are cleft in two" and that it "brings up the cud" (14:6). Also, the camel, hare, daman and swine are explicitly excluded to avoid possible confusion from their possession of one of the two qualifying characteristics. Included among the ritually edible animals were nondomesticated animals that, though "edible," were excluded from the class of sacrificial animals. These were the deer, gazelle, roebuck, *wild* goat, ibex, antelope, and *mountain* sheep. As to "abhorrent," or nonedible, animals, "you shall not eat of their flesh or touch their carcasses" (14:8).

Deut. 14:9–10, like Lev. 11:9–12, covers "all that live in the water." And as in Leviticus, "you may eat anything that has fins and scales" (14:9). All else cannot be eaten because "it is unclean for you."

> *Note D–69: Though the actual commands are identical, their styles are distinctive. Deuteronomy simply states the command, while Leviticus 11:11–12 embellishes it by condemning all other denizens of the water, not once or twice, but three times, as abominable (or "detestable").*

As in Lev. 11:13–19, Deut. 14:11–18 identifies ritually edible birds by naming those that did *not* qualify. Thus, all unnamed birds were edible. The birds named in both are identical: "the eagle, the vulture and the black vulture; the kite, falcons of every variety; all varieties of ravens; the ostrich, the nighthawk, the sea gull; hawks of every variety; the little owl, the cormorant and the great owl; the white owl, the pelican and the bustard; the stork; herons of every variety; the hoopoe, and the bat."

> *Note D–70: As first noted in regard to the Levitical listing, ornithology was not yet a science, thus accounting for the inclusion of the mammalian bat as a bird (see Note L–25). Of greater interest, however, is the identity of the birds. Did R effect an identity between (what became) Leviticus and Deuteronomy? Or were both drawn from a common and precise tradition?*

As to "winged swarming things," Deuteronomy and Leviticus differ. Of these, as stated in Deut. 14:19–20, "all winged swarming things are unclean for you: they may not be eaten. You may eat only clean winged creatures."

> *Note D–71: Thus, of all "winged creatures," only the "nonswarming" were "clean." Yet nothing is said to distinguish one type from the other. Perhaps observation alone was enough to support indisputable distinctions.*

The dietary laws conclude as follows: "You shall not eat anything that has died a natural death; give it to the stranger in your community to eat, or you may sell it to the foreigner. For you are a people consecrated to your God. You shall not boil a kid in its mother's milk" (14:21).

> *Note D–72: That meat from a nonslaughtered animal could be given to neighbors presumably implies that it was prohibited to Israelites for cultic rather than hygienic reasons. In the case of an obviously diseased animal,*

hygienic concerns might prevail. But for that matter, the law made no distinction between healthy and diseased animals among those that were slaughtered, and thus edible. But here the law was rudimentary at most.

Unlike those of Exod. 23:19 and 34:26, this third and final appearance of the ban on "[boiling] a kid in its mother's milk" does appear in a dietary context. However, on the point of its being more related to apostasy than diet, see pp. 35–36.

From dietary matters Deut. 14:22–26 returns to tithes. The basic command is in 14:22–23 (cf. 12:17–19).

You shall set aside every year a tenth part of all the yield of your sowing that is brought from the field. You shall consume the tithes of your new grain and wine and oil, and the firstlings of your herds and flocks, *in the presence of the Lord your God* in the place where He will choose to establish His name, so that you may learn to revere [Him] forever.

Comment D–19. On P's central sanctuary and that of the Levitical priests of Shiloh: an introduction to their irreconcilable differences

Among our three translations, the phrase *"in the presence of the Lord your God"* appears in only JPS2. From it, in the wake of Exodus and Leviticus, a reader might conclude that D, like P, views the sanctuary as the place that the Lord "might dwell among them" (Exod. 28:5). Similarly, RSV renders *liphnay yahweh elohechah* (as does JPS1 almost identically) as "before the Lord, your God."

As used in this Code of Law, however, the phrase "where He will choose to establish His name" is the poetic equivalent of the place on which the Lord bestows His official imprimatur. In all of Deuteronomy there is nothing that remotely approaches P's emphasis on the sanctuary as the Lord's abode with Israel (see Exod. 25:8, 29:45–46, 40:30–38; Lev. 9:5–6, 23–24). (See Comment D–25.)

Deut. 14:24–26, however, offers an alternative to the "centralization" command of 12:17–18 in regard to tithes.

Should the distance be too great for you [or the tithes of your produce to bountiful to transport], . . . *you may convert them into money.* Wrap up the money and take it with you to the place that the Lord your God has chosen, *and spend the money on anything you want*—cattle, sheep, wine, *or other intoxicant*, or anything you may desire. And you shall feast there, in the presence of the Lord your God, and rejoice in your household.

Note D–73: As authors of the Deuteronomic Code of Law, the pre–722 B.C.E. levitical priests of Shiloh would have written of the centralization of *rituals in Shiloh itself. But Friedman persuasively makes the case that it was only after the destruction of the Northern Monarchy that D incorporated the earlier "Shiloh" Code into what would become Deuteronomy (see Note D–61). It is ironic, therefore, that when finally compiled in c. 622 B.C.E., their Code of Law came to be identified with Jerusalem rather than Shiloh.*

Deut. 14 concludes by directing a different disposition every third year for the tithes of 14:22–26:

> But do not neglect the Levite in your community, for he has no hereditary portion as you have. Every third year you shall bring out the full tithe of your yield of that year, but leave it within your settlements. Then the Levite . . . and the stranger, the fatherless, and the widow in your settlements shall come and eat their fill, so that the Lord your God may bless you in all the enterprises you undertake. (14:27–29)

Comment D–20. On two methods of Torah interpretation: herein on "reconciling" the tithing commands of Lev. 27:30–33/Num. 18:21–24 and Deut. 14:22–29

In essence, Lev. 27:30–33 requires annual tithes from all agricultural produce. P then allocates the tithes in Num. 18:21–24. Every year "all the tithes" must be transferred "to the Levites . . . as their share in return for the services that they perform, the services of the Tent of Meeting." The tithes are in lieu of any "territorial share among the Israelites." To the contrary, in two of every three years the Deuteronomic tithes are for use, as directed, by the producing household. Only in each third year do all tithes accrue to the Levites and others in need. How can the obvious conflict be reconciled, if at all?

Consider first the views of Rabbi J. R. Hertz, a distinguished twentieth-century traditionalist who seeks consistency in these seemingly contradictory revelations from a faultless Being. As to the first- and second-year tithes of Deut. 14:22–26, he states, "This tenth is the so-called 'second tithe,' as contrasted with the tithe of the produce that was to be given for the maintenance of the Levites. Num. XVIII, 26f."[8] As to the third-year tithe of 14:28–29, he states, "This was due in the third and sixth year of the Sabbatical period instead of the second tithe, which, or its equivalent in money, had to be consumed in Jerusalem. In those years, what would have been the Second Tithe is to be retained at home for the poor to consume."[9]

Conversely, in approaching the Torah as the creation of human authors, who wrote at different times from different perspectives, *The Anchor Bible Dictionary* accepts the contradictions:

> These differences reflect the sociological viewpoints of D and P. D is a "popular" writing concerned with the whole of Israelite society: it could not easily

ignore the plight of the poor. P, however, was more concerned with the status of the priestly class and less with that of the masses.[10]

> *Note D–74: Here* The Anchor Bible Dictionary, *unlike Friedman, associates Deut. 14:22–29 with D rather than the earlier levitical priests of Shiloh.*

The relative credibility of these two approaches to Torah interpretation will depend largely on a reader's basic beliefs. Note, however, that to reconcile Leviticus/Numbers with Deuteronomy the traditionalist commentator must read the tithe of 14:22–29 as a "second" tithe. However, as "scripture" that supports the central point of *The Anchor Bible Dictionary*, I would cite the verse that opens Deuteronomy's Code of Law: "These are the laws and rules which you must carefully observe in the land that the Lord God of your fathers, is giving you to possess" (12:1). This is by authors who knew little, if anything, of P's precise rules of Leviticus and Numbers. What they wrote was meant to be self-contained and complete.

Deut. 15 opens with a command even more novel to the Torah than the tithing commands of Deut. 12 and 14. Unlike the Fiftieth Jubilee year debt remission of Lev. 25, Deut. 15 requires that "every seventh year you shall practice remission of debts" (15:1). To that end, "every creditor shall remit the due that he claims from his neighbor; he shall not dun his neighbor or kinsman, for the remission proclaimed is of the Lord" (15:2).

Here, however, Deuteronomy ignores the Levitical law that "the stranger that resides with you shall be to you as one of your citizens" (Lev. 19:34). Thus, "you may dun the foreigner; but you must remit everything that is due from your kinsmen" (Deut. 15:3).

> *Note D–75: Deuteronomy is not alone in departing from the principle of Lev. 19:34. Thus, E's God prohibited interest on loans only "if you lend money to My people" (see Exod. 22:24 and Comment E–73). Leviticus similarly distinguishes between needy "Israelite brothers" who cannot repay their debts and "resident aliens" acquired as slaves (see Lev. 25:39–46 and Comment L–57).*

The text next describes a conditional prosperity:

There shall be no needy among you—since the Lord your God will bless you in the land [He] is giving you as a hereditary portion—if only you heed [Him] and take care to keep all the Instruction that I enjoin on you this day. For [He] will bless you as He has promised you: you will extend loans to many nations, but require none yourself; you will dominate many nations but they will not dominate you. (15:4–6)

But he is quick to acknowledge the difficulty of the condition and the results of failure:

> If, however, there is a needy person among you, one of your kinsmen . . . do not harden your heart and shut your hand against [him]. Rather, *you must* open your hand and lend him sufficient for whatever he needs. [Avoid] the base thought, "The seventh year, the year of remission, is approaching," so that you are mean to your needy kinsman and give him nothing. He will cry out to the Lord . . . and you will incur guilt. Give to him readily and have no regrets . . . for in return the Lord your God will bless you in all your efforts. . . . *For there will never cease to be needy ones in your land*, which is why I *command* you: open your hand to the poor and needy kinsman in your land. (Deut. 15:7–11)

> *Note D–76: A required loan to a poor credit risk with automatic debt remission in the seventh year will most often prove to be a compulsory "gift." To protect the loan, as a loan, the lender might impose an early maturity date. However, to permit "lenders" to do so would defeat the charitable purpose of the financial arrangement.*
> *But what if the financial status of a needy borrower has nicely improved by the time of remission in the seventh year? Here indeed is a test for whether a standard of "right and good" can only serve to interpret the law (see Comment D–10 and Notes D–63 and 64). In terms of "right and good," if not of law, should the "charitable loan" not be repaid? Or would enforceable repayment defeat the purposes of the seventh-year debt remission by subordinating its simplicity to contentious litigation?*

Deut. 15:12–18 deals with the status and treatment of an indentured "fellow Hebrew, man or woman" (15:12).

> *Note D–77: This is a rare post-Exodus reference to a "Hebrew man" or a "Hebrew woman" (hahivree and hahivreeah). It recalls the "Hebrew slave/servant" of E's mishpatim, Exod. 21:2–11, which Deut. 15:12–18 tracks closely, but not precisely.*

To begin, every "Hebrew, man or woman," who is "sold to you . . . shall serve you six years" and shall be set free in the seventh (15:12).

> *Note D–78: Exod. 21:2 does not explicitly mention a "woman."*

Nor can "he" be let go "empty-handed." The master must furnish a departing indentured servant "out of the flock, threshing floor and vat" (15:14). He must remember that "you were slaves in the land of Egypt and the Lord your God redeemed you" (15:15).

But if the servant prefers to remain because "he loves you and your household and is happy with you," the master must "take an awl and put it through his ear into the door, and he shall become your slave in perpetuity." Do the same with your female slave" (15:16–17).

> Note D–79: *As an alternative to the painful ordeal required as the "price" for a lifetime of slavery, many Israelites who would otherwise face it might well opt for freedom.*

In E's "forerunner" of this passage (Exod. 21:2–11), a woman sold by her father "as a slave" was "not freed [in the seventh year] as male slaves are" (Exod. 21:7). She remained a slave instead, subject to the terms of Exod. 21:8–11. An equally striking difference from previously stated (but later) Levitical law is the concept of slavery "in perpetuity" (or "forever," JPS1/RSV). This contradicts the Levitical requirement that all *Israelite* slaves be freed every fiftieth, or jubilee, year (Lev. 25:39–40, 45–46).

Deut. 15:18a offers solace to the master of a slave who chooses to be freed in the seventh year: "When you do set him free, do not feel aggrieved; for in six years he has given you double the service of a hired man."

> Note D–80: *Such solace might look to the master's past benefits from having had a slave in the household who was "on call" at all times. However, if the gain was of double services in the past, the loss would be of double services in the future. Thus, his true solace would come from 15:18b: "Moreover the Lord your God will bless you in all you do."*

Deut. 15 closes on the subject of consecrating "all male firstlings" of the "herd and . . . flock" to the Lord your God. (15:19–23; cf. Exod. 34:19–20, Lev. 27:26–27, Num. 18:15–18). First, "male firstlings" could not be used for work or other personal gain. Thus, "you must not work your firstling ox or shear your firstling sheep" (15:19b). Instead, its owner and his household were to eat such animals "annually before the Lord your God in the place that the Lord will choose."

While the priority was for the "male firstling" to be offered in sacrifice and eaten at the central sanctuary, 15:21 goes on to prohibit all sanctuary sacrifices of any animal with any manner of "ill blemish" (JPS1/RSV) or "serious defect" (JPS2). Animals with blemishes, or defects, were to be eaten in "your settlements," by "the unclean . . . no less than the clean, just like the gazelle or deer." But wherever the point of consumption, there is the admonishment, as always "not to partake of its blood," but to "pour it out on the ground like water."

> Note D–81: *In essence, defective "male firstlings" could be eaten like any other edible, but ritually impure, animal. "Male firstlings" are also the sub-*

ject of Exod. 11:11–15 and 34:19–20, Lev. 27:26–27, and Num. 18:15–18. The subject treatment here, however, is quite distinctive.

Note D–82: Among the holy days of Israel, Deut. 16 includes only Passover and the harvest festivals of Shavuot and Sukot. The Sabbath, of course, has been the subject of the Fourth Commandment (see Deut. 5:12–15 and Comment D–6). That the holy days of Deuteronomy exclude the New Year (rosh hashonah), the Day of Atonement (yom hakippurim) and others is discussed in Comment D–21.

Deut. 16:1–8 sets Passover on an unstated date in Abib. It looks first to the passover sacrifice "from the flock or herd" to be offered at the central sanctuary (16:1–2).

Note D–83: The beginning of Passover is fixed elsewhere on the fourteenth day of the first month (see P's Exod 12:6 and Lev. 23:5 and R's Num. 28:16). A sacrifice from the "herd" contradicts Exod. 12:3–5, which is limited to a male lamb or goat, and Exod. 12:16–26, to only a lamb. Far more elaborate are the passover sacrifices of Num. 28:16–25.

Nothing "leavened" could be eaten with the sacrificial animal. Further, to remember "*your* departure from Egypt" (denoting a people united in time as well as proximity), "for seven days thereafter you shall eat unleavened bread, the bread of distress." Indeed, "for seven days no leaven shall be found with you in all your territory." Finally, no flesh of an animal sacrificed on the first night could "be left until morning" (16:3–4).

Deut. 16:5–7 restates the need to slaughter the Passover sacrifice at the central sanctuary: "There alone shall you slaughter the passover sacrifice, in the evening, at the sundown." And there, as well, it was to be cooked and eaten. However, the visit was only "overnight," so that "in the morning you may start back on your journey home." Thereafter, "after eating unleavened bread six days, you shall hold a solemn gathering for the Lord your God on the seventh day: you shall do no work" (16:8).

Elsewhere, the first day was a "sacred occasion" on which "occupational work" was prohibited (Lev. 23:7, Num. 28:18). Here, however, permission is given to travel home on the first full day of the seven-day period—which is not declared a "sacred occasion." Technically, the journey home in itself might not have violated the limitations of a "sacred occasion" on which *only* "occupational work" was prohibited. More likely, however, the author(s) of Deut. 16 did not yet recognize the first day of Passover as a "sacred occasion." Why else would 16:1–8 name only the seventh day as a "solemn gathering" while allowing travel on the first?

Deut. 16:9–12 commands the Feast of Weeks, or *shavuot*, which was to begin following a "count" of "seven weeks when the sickle is first put to the standing grain" (16:9).

> Note D–84: *Lev. 23:11 and 15 count the Feast from "the day after the sabbath" (later reckoned as the second day of passover; see Note L–98). E, J, and R state no specific day (Exod. 23:16, 34:22; Num. 28:26–30).*

The spring harvest festival of *shavuot* required a proportional "freewill contribution" (i.e., "according as the Lord your God has blessed you" [16:10]). "You" shall "rejoice before [Him] with your [children], [slaves], the Levites in your communities, and the stranger, the fatherless, and the widow in your midst, *at the [central sanctuary]*" (16:11). Like Passover itself, the Feast was an occasion to recall Egypt: "Bear in mind that you were slaves in Egypt, and take care to obey these laws" (16:12).

Deut. 16:13–15 concludes the three annual festivals at the central sanctuary with the fall harvest, the Feast of Booths (*chag hasukot*):

> After the ingathering from your threshing floor and your vat, you shall hold the Feast of Booths for seven days. You shall rejoice in your festival, with your [children], [slaves], the Levite, the stranger, the fatherless, and the widow in your communities. You shall hold festival for the Lord your God seven days, *in the place that the Lord shall choose*; for [He] will bless all your crops and all your undertakings, and you shall have nothing but joy."

> Note D–85: *As with shavuot, no date is fixed for sukot. Will they be determined by the time of harvest? If so, might they differ among the agricultural areas? Also, nothing is said of the rituals at the central sanctuary (cf. Exod. 23:16–17, 34:22–23; Lev. 23:33–43; Num. 29:12–34).*
>
> *Note also that the Lord's harvest blessings are said to be unconditional. Does the Lord, therefore, mean to guarantee an annual harvest worthy of celebration? In years of drought or other adverse conditions, what are the people to believe? That He lacks power to honor His promise? Or, that like all of His blessings, those of the harvest will reflect their degree of obedience?*

Deut. 16:16–17 contains a summary reference to the Feasts of Unleavened Bread, of Weeks and of Booths, at which "all your males (*chal-tz'churchah*) shall appear before the Lord your God in [the central sanctuary]." Added to this duty is a reminder of gratitude to "the Lord Your God." No one was to appear before Him "empty-handed"—but "each with his own gift, according to the blessing that the Lord has bestowed upon you" (16:16–17; see also 16:10).

Note D–86: In that the "gifts" were "according to the blessing that the Lord has bestowed upon you," they would presumably include money, or other nonagricultural assets from any "males" not engaged in farming.

Comment D–21. On the evolution and progressive embellishment of the holidays and festivals of Israel

From Friedman's attributions of verses to sources, and from their generally accepted chronological relationships, it is possible to trace a steady evolution of the Torah's holidays and festivals from the earliest (J's Exod. 34:18 and 22), to the next earliest (E's Exod. 12:24–27 and 13:3–10 as to Passover only and Exod. 23:14–17); then to the levitical priests of Shiloh (as incorporated by D into what became Deut. 16); then to P (i.e., Lev. 16 for the Day of Atonement, or *yom hakippurim*, only and Lev. 23 as to all "fixed times"), and lastly to R (Num. 28 and 29).

As to every holiday and festival there is a consistent pattern of increasing complexity in regard to the time of and manner observance. To sense the polarities in this steady evolution, compare J's *combined* two verse treatment of the Festival of Weeks (*shavuot*), the Festival of Ingathering (or Booths, i.e., *sukot*), and Passover with R's corresponding passages in Num. 28:26–29, 29:12–38, and 28:16–25. To similar effect compare P's Lev. 23 with R's Num. 28 and 29.

Consider as well (1) that neither J, E nor D ever mention *rosh hashonah* and *yom hakippurim*; (2) that apart from the sabbath, neither J nor E associate any degree of rest with the three festivals known to them; and (3) D forbids occupational work only on the seventh day of Passover while P and R designate both the first and seventh.

Like the three festivals of Deut. 16, the Sabbath was known to every source. But neither J nor E give any reason other than the basic value of periodic rest (as to J and E see Exod. 34:21 and 23:12). The Fourth Commandment of Deuteronomy also evokes the need for rest, as commanded by the Lord God who freed Israel from Egypt (Deut. 16:12–15). However, only P's Sabbath relates to the cycle of Creation (Exod. 20:8–11).

In all, a steady growth in numbers and ritualistic complexity tells of a continuing process of evolution in Israel's holidays and festivals from c. 950 to c. 450 B.C.E.

Deut. 16 closes on a different subject more closely related to that of Deut. 17. Deut. 16:18–22 first calls for the appointment of "magistrates and officials for your tribes" whose duty will be to "govern the people with due justice" (*mishpat tzedek*) (16:18). Unfairness, partiality, and bribes were forbidden. The latter was said to "blind the eyes of the discerning and upset the plea of the just." In sum, "justice, justice shall you pursue, that you may thrive and occupy the land" (16:19–20).

Following this eloquent and compelling charge to human judges, Deut. 16 returns to the sanctity of Israel's Lord God with a repeated warning against one particular practice of (an)other religion(s): "You shall not set up a sacred post—any kind of pole beside the altar of the Lord your God that you may make—or erect a stone pillar; for such the Lord your God detests" (16:21–22). (Cf. 7:5.)

Deut. 17:1 returns to the subject of duties owed to the Lord, as Israel's God. Similar to the perfection required for "firstlings" consecrated to Him (15:21), a sacrificial "ox or sheep" was to be without "serious defect."

Deut. 17:2–7 then returns to the theme of judicial administration. Thus, "if there is found among *you* [in Canaan] a man or woman who has affronted the Lord your God and transgressed His covenant—turning to the worship of other gods and bowing down to them, to the sun or the moon or any of the heavenly host, something I never commanded—and you [have heard of it] then *you* shall make a thorough inquiry." If it is proved, "an abhorrent thing was perpetrated in Israel" (17:2–4). Thus, "*you* shall take the man or woman who did that wicked thing out to the public place, and you shall stone them, *man or woman*, to death" (17:5). However, "a person shall be put to death only on the testimony of two or more witnesses; *he must not be put to death on the testimony of a single witness*" (17:6). The witnesses should be "the first against him to put him to death," and then "the hands of the rest of the people." In this way "you will sweep evil from your midst" (17:7).

Comment D–22. On the proof and punishment of apostasy in Deut. 17:2–7

Overall, the passage seeks to balance a compelling need to punish apostates with a compelling need to establish their guilt beyond reasonable doubt. Technically, however, that two or more witnesses are required to punish an offender *by death* does not *in itself* establish that two witness are needed for conviction. It is conceivable, therefore, that the credible evidence of but one witness could support a conviction for apostasy with a punishment less than death. But conviction alone would depend on whether the sin of apostasy would ever permit a punishment less than death.

No less important than the standard for proving guilt is the process by which the standard is applied. The levitical priests of Shiloh were wise to relieve the impulsive Lord, God of Israel from the need to judge this egregious alleged assault on His sanctity. By vesting jurisdiction in human judges charged with the duty of pursuing "justice, justice," they freed the Lord from the emotional pressure of vindicating His sanctity.

Deut. 17:8–13 establishes the "levitical priests" of the central sanctuary, or "the magistrate in charge at the time," as Israel's only, and thus highest, appellate court.

Note D–87: The reference is to the "levitical priests" (hahkohahnim hahlviyim) (JPS2/RSV), or "the priests the Levites" (JPS1). Totally absent are Aaron and his sons, who, through P, had been variously ordained, consecrated and anointed to "have priesthood as their right for all time" (Exod. 29:9). (In general, see Exod. 29 and Lev. 8 and 9.) Thus the continuing irony that in writing of their central sanctuary in Israel, the "levitical priests of Shiloh" would seemingly legitimize P's central sanctuary in Jerusalem (i.e., Judah). (See Comment D–19 and related text.)

Unlike the Supreme Court of the United States in regard to most appeals, the "Court" of the central sanctuary could not decline to review an appeal. Nor were litigants entitled to bring appeals. Instead, "If [any case, civil or criminal] is too baffling for *you* to decide ["you" being the "tribal magistrates and officials," or "trial courts"] . . . you shall promptly repair to the [central sanctuary]" (17:8). Only then would the "levitical priests," or "the magistrate in charge at the time," acquire juridiction.

Note D–88: How cases were allotted to one or the other is not indicated.

The processes of human justice decreed by the Lord, as Israel's God, then became an aspect of his sanctity.

When they have announced to you the verdict in the case [in matters of "homicide, civil law, or assault"] you shall carry [it] out . . . observing scrupulously all their instructions to you. You shall act in accordance with the instructions given you and the ruling handed down to you; you must not deviate from the verdict . . . either to the right or to the left. Should a man act presumptuously and disregard the priest . . . or the magistrate, *that man shall die.* Thus you will sweep out evil from Israel; all the people will hear and be afraid and will not act presumptuously again. (Deut. 17:9b–13)

Note D–89: The penalty of death for violating any court decree, even in civil matters (17:8), seems harsh. But it might seem less so in the social context of an ingrained belief that the decree of a human court was the judgment of Israel's Lord God, Himself.

Deut. 17:14 turn to the governance of Israel in the promised land with a question. What if it is said, "I will set a king over me, as do all the nations about me"? To this came the reply:

You shall be free to set a king over yourself, *one chosen by the Lord your God. Be sure to set as king over yourself one of your own people, you must not set a foreigner over you, one who is not your kinsman.* Moreover, he shall not keep many horses or send people back to Egypt to add to his horses, since the Lord has warned you, "You must not go back that way again." And he shall not have many wives, lest his heart go astray; nor shall he amass gold and silver to excess." (18:15–17)

Comment D–23. On Deut. 17:14–17 and the protocols and politics of choosing a king

This brief litany of qualities to be shunned in a king might be best understood as a condemnation of Solomon by the levitical priests of Shiloh. Surely they would have been among the least of his admirers. Apart from the excesses that the passage recalls, was it not Solomon who had built the great Temple in Jerusalem, the capital of Judah?

As for wives, such were Solomon's many unions in marriage, or other relationships, that 1 Kings 11:3–4 takes note of "seven hundred wives, princesses, and three hundred concubines, and . . . his wives turned away his heart after other gods and his heart was not whole with the Lord his God." Among his wives were Moabites, Ammonites, and numerous other adjoining nations and tribes.[11]

The passage also describes a confusing division of power. Although Israel's king will be "chosen by the Lord your God," yet "you [i.e., Israel] must not set a foreigner over you." Rashi ignores the conundrum of why, *if the Lord is to choose a king* (see 17:15), Israel should be forbidden to name a "foreigner."[12] Ramban addresses the problem, but to no real avail.[13] Even if the Lord's "choice" was but to "veto" Israel's choice, the injunction would serve no purpose, *except* to put Israel on notice that the Lord would "veto" all foreigners. His "veto," in effect, could be taken as a "constitutional" limitation on Israel's own choice.

"When seated on his royal throne," a future king must have with him a copy of "this Teaching [*hahtorah hahzeh*] written for him on a scroll by the levitical priests." It must "remain with him" so that he may "read in it all his life, so that he may learn to revere the Lord, his God, to observe faithfully every word of this Teaching [*hatorah hahzeh*] as well as these laws" (17:18–19).

Deut. 17 closes with a statement of the beneficent consequences of diligent kingly attention to *hatorah hahzeh*.

Thus [the king] will not act haughtily toward his fellows or deviate from the Instruction to the right or to the left, to the end that he *and his descendants* may reign long in the midst of Israel. (17:20)

> *Note D–90: The priests of Shiloh, as authors of the Deuteronomic Code of Law, knew nothing of an entire Torah. Thus, their use of* hatorah hazeh *must refer to* their own *"Teaching," as embodied in their Code of Law. Only as spoken by R could* hahtorah hahzeh *refer to the entire Torah.*

Deut. 18:1–8 deals with the role and support of the Levites. With minor omissions it reads as follows:

> *The levitical priests, the whole tribe of Levi*, shall have no territorial portion with Israel. They shall live only off the Lord's offerings by fire as their portion, and shall have no portion among their brother tribes; the Lord is their portion. . . .
>
> This then shall be the priests' due from the people: Everyone who offers a sacrifice, whether an ox or a sheep, must give the shoulder, the cheeks and the stomach to the priest. You shall also give him the first fruits of your new grain and wine and oil, and the first shearing of your sheep. For the Lord your God has chosen him and his descendants . . . to be in attendance for service in the name of the Lord for all time.
>
> If a Levite would go, from any of the settlements throughout Israel where he has been residing, to the [central sanctuary], he may do so whenever he pleases. *He may serve in the name of the Lord his God like all his fellow Levites who are there in attendance before the Lord.* They shall receive equal shares of the dues, without regard to personal gifts or patrimonies. (18:1–8)

Comment D–24. On the singular Deuteronomic priesthood of all adult male Levites

To better understand 18:1–8 it is useful to recall D's explanation, as compared to the Shiloh Code of Law, of why the Levites would lack a tribal portion. As stated in 10:8–9, "the Lord set apart *the tribe of Levi* to carry the Ark of the Lord's Covenant, to stand in attendance upon the Lord, *and to bless in His name*, as is still the case. That is why the Levites have received no hereditary portion along with their kinsman: the Lord is their portion." In vesting, without exception, the "tribe of Levi" with authority "to bless in [the Lord's] name," D underscores the identity in 18:1 between "*the levitical priests*" and "*the whole tribe of Levi*." Together, therefore, the authors of Deuteronomy create a priesthood utterly at odds with the anointed Aaronide priesthood of P that permeates the preceding three Books (see Comment D–19).

Critical to the issue is the meaning in 18:1 of the Hebrew "*loh yihyeh lahkohanim hahlviyim kol shayvet layvi*, which JPS2 renders as "the levitical priests, *the whole tribe of Levi*." RSV's insertion of "that is" between the two phrases only reinforces their identity. A troubled JPS1, however, seeks to salvage as much as possible of P's separation of the Aaronide priesthood from all other levites. By using "even" for "that is," JPS1 hints of the separate identities of "the levitical priests" and "the whole tribe of Levi" (that is, "The priests the Levites, even all the tribe of Levi"). In the total context of 18:1–8, however, JPS1 wafts a hint that bears no substance.

Included in "the Lord's offerings by fire" in support of "the levitical priests, the whole tribe of Levi," and as the "priests' due from the people," were (1) "the shoulder, the cheeks and the stomach" of all sacrificial animal, and (2) the first fruits of your new grain and wine and oil, and the first shearing of your sheep." This will support "him [Levi] and his descendants [the Levites]" whom the Lord has chosen "to be in attendance for service in [His] name for all time" (18:3–5).

The "the shoulder, the cheeks and the stomach" are similar in purpose to P's allotments of animal parts to the Aaronide priests. P's rites, however, involve a variety of distinctive offerings (including for example, the sacrifice of well-being in which the "breast of the wave offering and the thigh of the heave offering were priestly emoluments)." *The entitlement of the "levitical priests of Shiloh" to a standard "shoulder, cheek and stomach" for all offerings indicates a sacrificial system far simpler than what P would later develop.*

In themselves, these comparisons of priestly entitlements hardly prove the common priesthood of all Levites in Deuteronomy. But they do add to the general distinctiveness of the Deuteronomic priesthood. Far more decisive on the matter of a common priesthood, however, is the open invitation of 18:6–7 for every (adult male) Levite to come from outlying settlements to the central sanctuary "to serve in the name of the Lord his God like all his fellow Levites who are there in attendance before the Lord."

Moreover, it is a nonhierarchical priesthood. Nothing distinguishes any one levitical priest from all "his fellow Levites." All are "in attendance before the Lord," doing the priestly work of the central sanctuary. And every one, without distinction, shares alike in all that is "due" to the priests. Nor can their shares be reduced by the receipt of other gifts or by patrimony they might inherit.

The point can be made, however, that the Code of Law contemplates two separate support systems for the Levites—one for the priests and one for all others. This results from the three-year cycle of tithal support for "the Levite in your community" (14:27–29) and the separate support for "the levitical priests" of 18:1–8. But given the freedom of Levites to move at will between their settlements and the central sanctuary, the fact of two support systems is consistent with a common priesthood. The choice between the two is for each levite to make as he wishes. But if the entire tribe of Levi were to serve as priests, what of their anointment and ordination? What equivalent "legitimization" was there to the solemn rites of Exod. 29 and Lev. 8 and 9 by which P ordained the Aaronide priests?

Even preceding the Code of Law of the Shiloh priests in Deut. 12–26, D had already declared that *"at that time the Lord set apart the tribe of Levi* to carry the Ark of the Lord's Covenant, to stand in attendance upon the Lord, *and to bless in His name*, as is still the case" (10:8–9). "At that time" (as it appears in 10:7) was just after a brief mention of Aaron's death and of the temporary succession of Eleazer pending implementation of the priestly arrangements announced in 10:8–9. As for these, unlike P, D needed no ceremonies. It was enough that the Lord had declared His will. Thus, the eventual consequences of 10:8–9 are described in 18:1–8. Neither Eleazer nor his name is mentioned again in Deuteronomy. In 32:50, brief mention is again made of Aaron's death and burial. Here, however, they occur on Mount Hor rather than at Moserah. (Cf. Num. 20 and Deut. 10:3. Friedman logically ascribes 32:48–52 to P and R.)

Deut. 18:9–14 warns against imitating "the abhorrent practices of those nations" that "the Lord your God is giving you." First among them was to "consign a son or daughter to the fire" (18:10). (See Comments L–24 and L–44.) In addition were the "abhorrent practices" of attempting to predict the future other than through the Lord, Himself. Thus, "let no one be found among you . . . who *is* an augur, soothsayer, diviner, a sorcerer, one who cast spells, or who consult ghosts or familiar spirits, or one who inquires of the dead" (18:10–11). It was because of these things "that the Lord your God is dispossessing [the nations of Canaan] before you" (18:12). Accordingly, "you must be wholehearted with the Lord your God. Those nations that you are about to dispossess do indeed resort to soothsayers and augurs; to you, however, the Lord your God has not assigned the like" (18:13–14).

> Note D–91: Not clear from the translations is whether 18:10–11 means to prohibit only the practitioners of these arts, or their "patrons" as well. JPS2 limits the prohibition to one who "is" an augur, diviner, and so on, while JPS1 includes anyone who "uses divination." In condemning one who "practices" divination, RSV may be closer to JPS2.
>
> Whether the Lord chooses to reveal it or not, the desire to know something of the future is an irrepressible component of human nature. That the Torah speaks of the inscrutability of its God only whets a natural desire to know His plans. It is not the desire to know the future that should be condemned. The Torah's miscreants, instead, are the fraudulent practitioners of the cultic and mystic arts. They seek to profit from the curiosity of others by claims of knowledge they do not possess. The sin is not in natural curiosity but in its exploitation.
>
> We might also note, without pursuing its significance, the absence in this particular context of any reference to P's "Urim and Thummin."

Now with a focus on prophets, Deut. 18:15–22 continues the theme of how the Lord, God of Israel, manifests His will or reveals the future. Unlike diviners, augurs, soothsayers, and sorcerers, the true prophet reveals the future only by the words of the Lord. But the common challenge to every source is to separate the true prophet from the pretender.

The passage opens with commentary on the foundation of "true" prophecy:

The Lord your God will raise up for you a prophet from among your own people, like myself; him you shall heed. This is just what you asked of the Lord your God *at Horeb* . . . saying, "Let me not hear the voice of the Lord my God any longer or see this wondrous fire any more, lest I die." Whereupon the Lord said to me, "They have done well in speaking thus, I will raise up a prophet for them from among their own people, like yourself: I will put My words in His mouth and he will speak to them all that I command him; and if anybody fails to heed the words that he speaks in my Name, I Myself will call him to account." (18:15–19)

> *Note D–92: Here in their Code of Law, the priests of Shiloh recall the first revelation of the Ten Commandments, much as D had done in 5:20–24, but a century or more later (cf. Deut. 18:15–19 and 5:19–28; see Note D–33). Note also, that while Moses is not named as the Code's narrator, the "me" of "Whereupon the Lord said to me," can only be Moses.*

Deut. 18:20–22 goes on to distinguish between prophets, true and false.

But any prophet who presumes to speak in My name an oracle which I did not command him to utter, or who speaks in the name of other gods—that prophet shall die. And should you ask yourselves, "How can we know that the oracle was not spoken by the Lord"—if the prophet speaks in the name of the Lord and the oracle does not come true, that oracle was not spoken by the Lord; the prophet had uttered it presumptuously; do not stand in dread of him.

Comment D–25. On prophets, true and false

Without the human intercession of a prophet, how could the will of the Torah's God become credibly known to His people? Unlike the quality of obedience to His revealed will that is to be forged in faith, "knowledge" of His will requires authoritative revelation. Accordingly, Moses, as prophet of the Torah's God to Israel, is no less necessary to its purposes than its God Himself. Indeed, could institutional monotheism exist under any circumstances without *some* means of authoritative "revelation"?

Accordingly, "accredited" revelation and interpretation (including the "oral law" of the Talmud in both cases) have long provided monotheism with structure and substance. And those who are doctrinally "accredited" to serve in these prophetic roles enjoy a strong presumption of compliance with the Third Commandment. That is, in revealing and interpreting God's will, they are presumed to swear truly, rather than falsely, by His name (see Comment E–56).

On whether the same could be said of a "nonaccredited" prophet, the Torah is of two minds. Thus, the same Balaam whom E portrays as an honest prophet of God's words is villified by P for inducing Israelite males to the worship of Baal (see Comments N–25 and 31).

An epilogue on the "false prophets" of 18:19–22

The single stated test for distinguishing between true and false prophets involves the revelation of future events. Thus, a false prophet is one whose prophecy of the future "does not come true" (18:22). Apart from the time that might be needed to test the truth of many prophecies, the test says nothing of nonprovable Godly decrees and commands. Thus, what test must be met by a prophet who proclaims God's "repeal" of the Ten Commandments?

> Note D–93: Deut. 19:1–13 returns to the matter of levitical cities of refuge for unintentional slayers. E first wrote of such a city as "a place to which he can flee" (Exod. 21:13). (See Comment E–68.) In Num. 35:6 and 12–15, P writes of "six cities of refuge" among the forty-eight assigned to the Levites, "to which a manslayer who has killed a person unintentionally may flee." In Deut. 4:41–43 D would have Moses "set aside three cities on the east side of the Jordan, to which "a manslayer could escape, one who unwittingly slew a fellow man without having been hostile to him in the past." But now the "levitical priests of Shiloh" deal as well with such cities of refuge within Canaan itself.

"When [you have dispossessed the nations of the promised land that the Lord your God is giving you and are are settled in their towns and homes], you shall set aside three cities in the land." You shall survey the distances, and divide into three parts the territory of the country . . . so that any manslayer may have a place to flee to—[but only] one who has killed another unwittingly, without having been his enemy in the past. For instance, a man goes with his neighbor into a grove to cut wood; as his hand swings the axe to cut down a tree, the axhead flies off the handle and strikes the other so that he dies. That man shall flee to one of these cities and live.

Otherwise, when the distance is great, the blood-avenger, pursuing the manslayer in hot anger, may overtake him and kill him; yet he did not incur the death penalty, since he had never been the other's enemy. That is why I command you to set aside these three cities.

And when the Lord your God enlarges your territory, as he swore to your fathers, and gives you all the land that He promised to your fathers—if you faithfully observe all this Instruction which I enjoin upon you this day, to love the Lord your God and to walk in His ways at all times—then you shall add three more towns to those three (19:9). Thus blood of the innocent will not be shed, bringing bloodguilt upon you in the land that the Lord your God is allotting to you." (19:1–10)

> Note D–94: As noted above, in 4:41–43, written after the chronologically earlier Code of Law, D has Moses "set aside three cities [of refuge] on the east side of the Jordan." By the terms of Deut. 11:22–25, however, Israel's re-

ceipt of any land, whether within Canaan or beyond, will be conditioned on its fidelity to the Lord.

Conversely, while D makes no distinction in 11:22–25 between lands within and beyond Canaan, the earlier Code of law does (cf. 19:1–3, 8–10). In regard to Israel's occupation of lands beyond Canaan, JPS2 reads the Hebrew im of 19:8 as "when" rather than "if." "When," however, is not the language of condition. It assumes that the event in question will occur. Here JPS2 can find justification in the language of 19:8 which refers to the Lord's expansion of Israel beyond the land of Canaan as a binding promise in itself. Thus, ignoring matters of time and authorship, it would be to the ultimate use of the three designated cities as actual places of refuge that the condition of "faithful observance" in 19:9 would apply. Conversely, by their use of the conditional "if" in 19:8, JPS1/RSV seem to regard Israel's occupation of lands beyond Canaan not as a promise, but as conditioned on "faithful observance."

Whatever the translational ambiguities in this passage, it is predicated on the past glories of the Davidic era, when a single Kingdom, still united, did indeed reach the Euphrates (see Deut. 11:24). And what were glories from the distant past to D, were recent, if not existing glories, to J (see Comment G–22 and Gen. 15:18).

Note D–95: Deut. 19:10 also tells of the communal purpose of the levitical cities. A worthy community protects the rights of its members to justice. In failing to prevent the spilling of an innocent manslayer's blood, a community would share the blood guilt of the wrongful avenger. Thus, in addition to protecting the innocent, the levitical cities served to shield the community from the guilt of failing to do so.

Deut. 19:11–13 then cautions that the need to protect the innocent did not lessen the need to punish the guilty.

If, however, a man who is his neighbor's enemy lies in wait for him and sets upon him and strikes him a fatal blow and then flees to one of these towns, the elders of his town shall have him brought back from there and shall hand him over to the blood-avenger to be put to death; you must show him no pity. Thus will you purge Israel of the blood of the innocent; and it shall go well with you."

Note D–96: This "duty of return" should have effectively discouraged the guilty from defiling the purpose of the cities of refuge.

Deut. 19:14 prohibits the theft of land by removing landmarks. It is less than precise, however, regarding the landmarks it covers. Thus, "you shall not remove your neighbor's landmarks, *set up by previous generations,* in the property that will be allotted to you in the land that the Lord your God is giving you to possess."

Comment D–26. On the different "time frames" of the Torah itself and of its authors as implied in Deut. 19:14

The Code of Law opens as follows: "These are the rules and laws which you must carefully observe in the land that the Lord God . . . is giving you to possess, as long as you live on earth" (12:1). Does this commit Israel to maintain all landmarks, as evidence of ownership, that existed as of the time of their conquest of Canaan? If not, then who are the "previous generations" of 19:14?

Logically, they could only be earlier generations of Israelites who first posted the landmarks prior to the effectiveness of the law. Deut. 12:1, however, calls on Israel to observe the entire Code of Law from the time it occupies the promised land. Yet, as to 19:14, observance would have had to await the establishment of the landmarks to which the prohibition applied. These would have been landmarks established by Israel itself. And as to these, there could be no landmarks "set up by previous generations" until the third generation at the earliest. Thus, the "you" of 19:14 whom the levitical priests of Shiloh addressed in regard to landmarks, could not have been the "you" of 12:1. If not, were they the landmarks of previous inhabitants?

Deut. 19:15–21 deals with issues of proof in the administration of justice. The first involves the number of witnesses needed to prove a charge. Thus, "a single witness may not validate against a person any guilt or blame for any offense that may be committed; a case can be valid only on the testimony of two witnesses or more" (19:15). (RSV/JPS1 are to the same effect as JPS2.)

Comment D–27. On various aspects of the general requirement of "two witnesses or more"

In Deut. 17:6 a "two witness" requirement is applied to the sin of apostasy. But there the need applies literally only to the penalty of death, not the finding of guilt. ("A person shall be put to death only on the testimony of two or more witnesses; *he must not be put to death on the testimony of a single witness.*") As implied in Comment D–22, this allows for two possibilities regarding proof in capital crimes. The first is that punishment based on "proof" of guilt by only one witness must be something short of death. The second is that since death is the required punishment for certain crimes the underlying finding of guilt must be supported by "the testimony of two or more witnesses."

The broad requirement of 19:15 for "two witnesses or more" as the basis for finding "guilt or blame for any offense" clearly supports the second alternative. Yet P has posed the same question in Num. 35:30. Thus, "if anyone kills a person, *the manslayer may be executed* only on the evidence of witnesses; *the testimony of a single witness against a person shall not suffice for a sentence of death.*" Here, as in Deut. 17:6, the requirement of two or more witnesses arguably applies to the punishment of death alone and not to the finding of guilt. This again poses the possibility that a slayer found guilty on the testimony of only one witness could be punished by lesser means than death. In any case, neither possibility addresses the issue of a confession by a conscience-stricken murderer, absent the support of any witnesses. Could a sworn confession alone, absent witnesses, sustain a finding of guilt? If so, could it support the death penalty as well?

Deut. 19:16–21 deals with false testimony given, not honestly through error, but "maliciously" (19:16). With malice as its gist, the offense does not cover perjury to protect one's self, but only lies meant to harm another.

To resolve charges of malicious defamation, the following procedures were prescribed:

1. The two parties were required to "appear before the Lord; before the priests or magistrates in authority," who then made a "thorough investigation" (19:17–18a).
2. Where the accused is found to have "testified falsely against his fellow man," he must suffer any loss or punishment "*he schemed to do to his fellow*" (19:18b–19a).

Here again, rather than to compensate the victim, the prime purpose is to deter others from same conduct. "Thus you will sweep out evil from your midst; others will hear and be afraid, and such evil things will not be done. . . . Nor must you show pity: *life for life, eye for eye, tooth for tooth, hand for hand, foot for foot*" (19:19b–21).

Comment D–28. On some final thoughts on the final appearance of *lex talionis* in the Torah

The early rabbis, followed by Rashi and Ramban, eased the maxim of *lex talionis*—"life for life, eye for eye, tooth for tooth, hand for hand, foot for foot, burn for burn, bruise for bruise"—to a more benign remedy of restitution. In the Torah, however, E's well-drawn exception of a pregnant woman whose prime loss is the fetus she bears manifests an intent to apply the rule to physical injuries whenever feasible (see, Comment E–70).

To similar effect is Lev. 24:17–20. There, if a "man," or "anyone," "kills" or "maims" another person, "the injury he has inflicted on another shall be inflicted on him—life for life . . . fracture for fracture, eye for eye, tooth for tooth." But here again, there is a necessary exception to the principle, though less compelling than a miscarriage. The exception here involves the death of a beast. Thus: "He who kills a beast shall make restitution for it [*rather than requiring the death of his own beast*]; but he who kills a human being shall be put to death" (Lev. 24:21).

Deut. 19:16–21 is of added interest in its application of *lex talionis* to other than physical harm. Thus, the punishment for maliciously harmful false testimony is that "*you shall do to him as he schemed to do to his fellow.*" The role of *lex talionis* as a deterrent is then proclaimed: "Thus you will sweep out evil from your midst; others will hear and be afraid" (19:19–20).

As the Israelites prepare to cross the Jordan into Canaan, Deut. 20 prescribes the rules of the war to come. Deut. 20:1–4 begins with the role of "the Lord your God" in creating and sustaining the army's morale.

> *When you take the field against your enemies*, and see horses and chariots—forces larger than yours—have no fear of them—for the Lord your God who brought you from the land of Egypt is with you. Before you join battle, the priest shall come forward and address the troops [saying] "Hear, O Israel! You are about to join battle with your enemy. Let not your courage falter. [Have neither fear, panic nor dread.] For it is the Lord your God *who marches with you to do battle for you* . . . to bring you victory.

Following the priest, civil officials addressed the troops on the matter of personal exemptions from the coming battle and the reasons for them (Deut. 20:5–9). These were:

1. Exemption: "anyone who has built a new house but has not dedicated it."
   Reason: "lest he die in battle and another dedicate it."

2. Exemption: "anyone who has planted a vineyard but has never harvested it."
   Reason: "lest he die in battle and another initiate it."

3. Exemption: "anyone who has paid the bride-price for a wife, but has not yet married her."
   Reason: "lest he die in battle and another marry her."

4. Exemption: "anyone afraid and disheartened."
   Reason: "lest the courage of his comrades flag like his."

Comment D–29. On the military service exemptions of Deut. 20:5–9

The common element in the exemptions of categories (1) to (3) is the "draftee's" prior expenditure of labor or money without having realized the benefits. But aside from his own personal loss, the subject matters of the exemptions also involved three of Israel's most compelling social values: (1) the home as the foundation of a family, (2) agricultural production as the source of food that sustains life, and (3) marriage as the source of reproduction. In addition to these personal and social considerations, there was also a matter of military morale. Would "draftees" of low morale corrupt their fellow soldiers and undermine general morale?

It is difficult to gauge the relative importance of the social, military, or personal concerns in the establishment of the three exemptions. All three categories, however, utilize the same decisional standard: "Let him go back to his home," with its literal implication that the soldier is free to go or to stay. The priority, therefore, lies in personal interests, as determined by each potential exemptee for himself. Only if the social interests of (1) to (3) (above) were to take precedence over personal interests, would it be necessary to mandate the exemptions.

But consider how this same standard would effect the military interests addressed in category (4). Here, the immediate concern was the potential threat to general morale by the presence of "fearful" and "disheartened" soldiers. Thus, the case for mandatory exemptions was much stronger.

The unique problem in (4), however, was the lack of an objective standard by which to ascertain "true" fear. What of the malingerer who feigned fear to avoid service for other reasons? And what of a truly timorous draftee who, while feigning a false bravado, would flee at first sight of the enemy, to the debilitating dismay of his comrades? Nevertheless, whether because of, or despite, these unique problems of self-classification, under category (4) each "draftee" was free to decide for himself.

In every case, therefore, the rules favor personal interests and discretion over communal interests and concerns (whether broadly social or specifically military). However well-founded or not, the rules could work only for a people confident in its communal strength and personal integrity.

If the rules governing exemptions seem beneficent in the circumstances, the rules governing conquests were not. In fact, however, there were two separate sets of rules. The first, as clarified in 20:15, were for "all towns that lie very far from you; towns that do not belong to nations hereabout." These are the subject of 20:10–14.

In essence, on approaching such a town, it was to be offered "terms of peace" (20:10). Should it capitulate peaceably, "all the people present there shall serve you at forced labor" (20:11). If the town instead chooses to do battle, "you shall lay siege to it; and when the Lord your God delivers it into your hand, you shall put all its males to the sword" (20:13). All else was booty and spoils. "You may, however, take as your booty the women, the children, and the livestock, and everything in the town—all its spoil—and enjoy the use of the spoil of your enemy which the Lord your God gives you" (20:14).

The harshness of the rules governing "towns that do not belong to nations hereabout" quickly pales in light of those governing "the towns . . . which the Lord your God is giving you as a heritage." Here the rule is simplicity itself: "you shall not let a soul remain alive [i.e., even though they surrender without a fight]" (20:16). Instead, "you must proscribe them [or "utterly destroy them" (RSV/JPS1)], the Hittites and the Amorites, the Canaanites and the Perrizzites, the Hivites and the Jebusites—as the Lord has commanded you, lest they lead you into doing all the abhorrent things that they have done for their gods and you stand guilty before the Lord your God" (20:17–18).

> Note D–97: As Plaut observes, "the Girgashites, mentioned in Deut. 7:1, are not listed here. Tradition explained the omission by speculating that this people had meanwhile, in anticipation of Israel's invasion, migrated to Africa" (citing Leviticus Rabbah, 17:6).[14] But we might again note that Friedman ascribes Deut. 7:1 to the later D source, just preceding King Josiah in Jerusalem, and Deut. 20 to the earlier Code of Law by the northern "levitical priests of Shiloh" (see Note D–61). Here it seems significant that Deut. 20:17–18 includes the same six tribes named by E in Exod. 23:23–24. Thus, the "northern" traditions may not have known of the Girgashites. (See also Note D–38.)

The rules of war conclude with a warning against the pointless destruction of plant life, and especially trees (20:19–20). Thus, "when in your war against a city you have to besiege it a long time in order to capture it, you must not destroy its trees, wielding the axe against them. You may eat of them, but you must not cut them down. Are trees of the field human to withdraw before you into the besieged city?" (20:19a, b). However, trees "which you know do not yield food may be destroyed, you may cut them down for constructing siegeworks against the city that is waging war on you, until it has been reduced" (20:20). (Given all else, there was a certain irony in describing a city under siege by Israel as one that is "waging war" on it.)

However arcane its procedures, Deut. 21:1–9 speaks to Israel's communal responsibility (in times of peace) for the preservation of human life. The procedures are invoked when "someone slain is found lying in the open, the identity of the slayer not being known" (21:1). By measuring distances "from the corpse to the nearby towns," the "elders and magistrates" determine the closest community. On it the duty falls to fulfil the atonement and redemptive rituals for all Israel. In essence, the elders of the town "take a heifer that has never been worked" into a "rugged" (or "uncultivated") wadi (or valley), and there break its neck (21:2–4). Then "the priests, the sons of Levi, shall come forward."

Note D–98: The priests are then identified as those chosen by the Lord "to minister to Him," and to adjudicate every type of case, with an emphasis on "assaults." The passage is not clear on whether it refers to community priests or to a judicial role of the priests at the central sanctuary (see 17:8–11).

Despite the priestly presence, the remaining rituals of atonement and redemption for the death of a person slain near their town are performed by "all the elders of the town nearest the corpse." They first "wash their hands over the heifer whose neck was broken in the wadi" (21:6). They then declare, "Our hands did not shed this blood, nor did our eyes see it done. *Absolve, O Lord, Your people Israel whom you redeemed, and do not let guilt for the blood of the innocent remain among Your people Israel.*" Through this "they will be absolved of blood-guilt" (21:7–8), and "you will remove from your midst guilt for the blood of the innocent, for you will be doing what is right in the sight of the Lord" (21:9).

Comment D–30. On Israel's collective responsibility for slayings by unknown slayers

The procedures of Deut. 21:1–9 apply only when "someone" appears to have been "slain" and the slayer is unknown. (Absent any procedure for deciding whether the death was by slaying, the matter seems to be left to a general consensus.) It then falls to the community nearest to the corpse to seek forgiveness for all Israel, so that it need not assume the onus of communal "bloodguilt."

The rituals will remind Israel of its communal duty to eliminate of the wilful and wrongful taking of life. Until then, when slayings by unknown assailants occur, all Israel must assume the guilt and the town nearest to the event must atone and seek redemption for all Israel—whoever the victim.

Deut. 21:10–14 applies to "When you take the field against your enemies, and the Lord your God delivers them into your power and you take some of them captive, and you see among the captives a beautiful woman and you desire her and would take her to wife" (21:10–11).

Note D–99: These provisions are presumably subject to the rules of war in Deut. 20:10–18, which distinguish between victories within Canaan itself and in other more remote localities. Recall that in victories over "nations hearabout," not "a soul" was to "remain alive" (20:16). Accordingly, 21: 10–14 applies only to "towns that lie very far from you" (20:15), from which, after a battle, women and children could be taken as booty (20:14), while all males were put to the sword (20:13).

But the captor could not immediately "possess" her as wife. By attention to her hair, nails and clothing, her appearance must first be adapted to Israelite standards (21:12–13a). Then, after "a month's time in [her captor's] house lamenting her father and mother," the captor could "come to her and possess her" as his wife (21:13b). But should he "no longer want her," he must "release her outright." She then had the status not of a slave but of a discarded wife: "You must not sell her for money; since you had your will of her, you must not enslave her" (21:14).

> Note D–100: *The captive woman taken as wife at least enjoyed a status above that of a transferable chattel. As implied in 21:14, the limitation of a captor-husband's ability to sell his abandoned captive-wife was a "price" to be paid for his transient pleasure with a non-Israelite woman.*

The arena of conflict in Deut. 21:15–17 turns from battlefield to home. Although it recalls the plight Leah, as the "unloved" wife of Jacob, its direct concern is for sons. Thus, "if a man has two wives, one loved and the other unloved, and both . . . have borne him sons, but the firstborn is the son of the unloved one," he is forbidden to play favorites between them, as he might among his wives. "Instead, he must accept the firstborn, the son of the unloved one, and allot to him a double portion of all he possesses; *since he is the firstborn of his vigor, the birthright is his due* (21:16–17).

> Note D–101: *If a birthright was truly the "due" (or "right") of a firstborn son, its transfer to another son should at least require his consent. Yet Deut. 21:15–17 only bars transfers by a father motivated by favoritism to a particular wife. Could a father, for other reasons, transfer a birthright? Given the quasisacred basis for the firstborn's birthright ("since he is the firstborn of his vigor"), we might expect a broader constraint. (Since a "firstborn" status was limited to sons, was the conception of daughters not thought to require "vigor"?)*
>
> *As precedent for a father's denial of the birthright of a firstborn son, Plaut cites Jacob's disavowal of Reuben (Gen. 49:3–4).[15] Here, of course, Reuben's dalliance with Bilhah (Gen. 35:22) may have been sufficiently egregious to constitute his waiver of his birthright. In the matter of other birthright transfers in the Torah, see Comments G–47, 48, 51, and 52 (as to Esau/Jacob), and Gen. 94 and 96 (as to Manasseh/Epraim).*
>
> *The most likely impetus for the rule of 21:15–17 was the beguiling influence of younger mothers of later sons.*

Deut. 21:18–21 deals with the problem of "a wayward and defiant son who does not heed his father or mother and does not heed them even after they discipline him" (21:18).

> Note D–102: *The maximum age of the "defiant son" is presumably twenty. The passage does not explicitly cover daughters.*

Such conduct is viewed as a repudiation of parental authority, whether a father's, a mother's or both. In such case both parents ("father *and* mother") "*shall* take hold of him and bring him out to the the the elders of the town at the public place of his community" (21:19).

The parents must then state their complaint to the elders: "This son of ours is disloyal and defiant; he does not heed us. He is a glutton and a drunkard" (21:20).

Thereupon, *without further inquiry*, "the men of his town shall stone him to death" (21:21). And this was to "sweep out evil from your midst: all Israel will hear and be afraid."

Comment D–31. On "parental authority" and "due process" in Deut. 21:8–12

For many, this law will be the most troubling of all laws in the Torah. Its appearance anywhere would be startling, and its belated initial appearance in Deuteronomy is even more so. Sincere and well-meaning defenders of both the substance and methods of enforcing the laws of the Torah's God too often feel compelled to rationalize the law's purpose and ease the law's impact. As they did with the law of *lex talionis* (see Comments E–70 and D–28), so do they here. As an example, Chief Rabbi Hertz cites "the rabbis" for the assertion "that this law was never once carried out." He also observes that, "by the regulations with which the infliction of the death penalty was in this case surrounded, it could not be carried out." He thus views it, not as a law to be obeyed, but as a "warning" against "the heinous crime of disobedience to parents."[16]

The Torah, of course, is replete with warnings on the consequences of disobeying laws. This makes it all the more important not to misread a law as a *mere* warning. For the Torah to issue warnings in the form of laws that are not meant to be obeyed could only undermine the sanctity and purpose of its laws, as such. No responsible author of the Torah would undertake to erode the sanctity of its God by promulgating laws that were to be honored in the breach. If some were meant to be ignored, why not others? But if the law of 21:8–12 was indeed a "dead-letter," we must ask why.

Literally, the law exposed the parents to risks no less than those of a son whose disobedience was sufficiently defiant to fall within the law. At that point the law provided that "they *shall* take hold of him and bring him to the elders of his town" (21:19). They must then denounce him to the elders as "disloyal and defiant" and as "a glutton and drunkard." In effect, by any reasonable standard of judgment, and the Lord's above all, he was considered to be "irredeemable." And should his parents fail in their duty, they would *seemingly* be no less guilty than their son.

That the parents were required to bring the son to the "elders of the town" for death by public stoning served two purposes. It marked his defiance as an offense against his community and not merely his parents, and it relieved them of the added parental anguish of actually slaying their son.

So great a threat to the community was the son's defiance perceived to be that no further procedural barriers were interposed to delay his proper fate. Thus, the joint denunciation by his parents was deemed sufficient in itself to warrant his immediate execution by stoning. No further proof was required or permitted.

Taken together, these provisions place parents and minor sons (or those old enough to know better) in a relationship much like that between Israel and the Lord, its God. Its effect was to establish the son's parents *in loco parentis* for the Lord, as Israel's God, and the *ultimate* parent of every Israelite. Thus, the parents alone were vested with authority to determine whether their son shall live or die. Only when his conduct become so defiant as to mark him as "irredeemable" were they directed to effect his death through the community. And yet, like the Lord God Himself, they retained sole discretion to determine when, if ever, his defiance was indeed "irredeemable." *Only by their judgment could their son be deemed "irredeemable."*

Whatever their difficulties of proof, the early rabbis cited by Rabbi Hertz were likely correct in viewing 21:12–18 as "dead letter." But if so, it was not because the law was not meant to be enforced, within the sound discretion of parents. Rather it was that parents, standing in place of the Torah's God, chose in every case to allow their son to reach adulthood, and so to be judged by Him.

Prompted perhaps by what precedes it, Deut. 21:22–23 deals with a the disposition of corpses:

> If a man is guilty of a capital offense and is put to death, and you impale him on a stake, you must not let his corpse remain on the stake overnight, but must bury him the same day. For an impaled body is an affront to God: you shall not defile the land that the Lord is giving you to possess.

In Deut. 22:1–4, the levitical priests of Shiloh, like E, their earlier northern cousin, show a keen respect for property rights (cf. Exod. 23:4–5). Thus, on seeing "your fellow's ox or sheep gone astray," it is your duty not to ignore it, but to "take it back to [him]" (22:1). Should you not know its owner, it becomes your duty to keep it at home, "until your fellow claims it" (22:2). And so shall you do "with his ass . . . his garment; and . . . anything that your fellow loses and you find" (22:3). Further, if you see his "ass or ox fallen on the road . . . you must help him raise it" (22:4).

Note D–103: Perhaps in assuming that an Israelite would willingly extend such aid to a friend, E limits its command to "your enemy's" animal (Exod. 23:4–5).

Deut. 22:5 seeks to restrain social modifications in the Lord's natural order. Thus, "a woman must not put on a man's apparel, nor shall a man wear woman's clothing; for whoever does these things is abhorrent to [Him]."

Deut. 22:6–7 prescribes conduct on finding "a bird's nest" at which there is "the mother" and her "fledgings or eggs." The finder must "let the mother go, and take only the young, in order that you may fare well and have a long life" (22:7).

Note D–104: The broad theme of the passage is more easily understood than its details. Why, in every case, may the "fledglings" be taken, but never the mother? As an actual mother, is the mother bird deemed more worthy of freedom? Or, more likely, is the aim to avoid leaving other helpless fledglings without any means of sustenance.

Apart from imposing "bloodguilt" on a house, Deut. 22:8 reads like a forerunner of a modern municipal housing code. "When you build a new house, you shall make a parapet for your roof so that you do not bring bloodguilt on your house if anyone should fall from it."

Note D–105: By analogy, would the "bloodguilt" on the house require its destruction?

Deut. 22:9–11 speaks to the sanctity of nonsexual aspects of the natural order. It thus prohibits: (1) the sowing of two different seeds in a single vineyard and the use of the yield, should such mixing occur; (2) plowing "with an ox and an ass together"; and (3) the wearing of a cloth that combines "wool and linen."

Note D–106: To the same general effect see Lev. 19:19. Rather than addressing the problems of an ass when joined with an ox in plowing, Lev. 19:19 prohibits the mating of a cow with any "different kind." In addition, the prohibition of wearing a cloth of "wool and linen" in Deut. 22:12 is expanded in Lev. 19:19 to any "mixture of two materials."

Citing Exod. 28:15, Plaut observes: "Since priests . . . had to wear garments made of wool or linen, this law may be seen to aim at separating the holy from the profane."[17] Exod. 28:15 calls only for linen with no mention of wool. Thus, their joint use in such garments is implicitly banned. In any case, would the priests of Shiloh concern themselves with the garb of P's Aaronide priests of Jerusalem?

Continuing the subject of garments, Deut. 22:12 requires "tassels on the four corners of the garment with which you cover yourself."

> Note D–107: In P's Num. 15:38 the tassels, or fringes, are named tzitzit. Here they are g'dilim. Again we observe the evolution of a common tradition.

Deut. 22:13–21 portrays the importance of premarital female virginity in the determination of marital rights.

Suppose a man (for whatever reason) "takes an aversion to his wife." To be rid of her, he challenges her premarital virginity: "I married this woman, but when I approached her, I found that she was not a virgin" (22:13–14).

> Note D–108: Although he discovered the condition on first "approaching her," no time limit is stated for making the charge. But the use of na'ahrah (i.e., "girl," "damsel," or "young woman"), as of the time of the husband's initial charge, may imply such a limit (22:15).

The charge alone places the burden on the wife's parents to "produce the evidence of the girl's virginity before the elders of the town at the gate." Following the father's denial of the charge, he may offer conclusive evidence of his "daughter's virginity" by "spread[ing] out the cloth before the elders of the town" (22:16–17).

On seeing the evidence of the cloth, "the elders of that town shall then take the man and flog him" (22:18). For his slander, the husband must also pay "a hundred [shekels] of silver" to the girl's father; furthermore, "he shall never have the right to divorce her" (22:19).

Without reference to any evidence other than the "cloth" itself, the converse is then stated: "But if the charge proves true, . . . then the girl shall be brought out to the entrance of her father's house, and the men of the town shall stone her to death." And why death? "For she did a shameful thing in Israel, committing fornication while under her father's authority. Thus shall you sweep away evil from your midst" (22:20–21).

Comment D–32. On proofs and punishments relating to a husband's charge of a wife's premarital sexual relations

Recall the charge of Deut. 19:18b–19a: "If the man who testified is a false witness, if he has testified falsely against his fellow man, you shall do to him as he schemed to do to his fellow." Were it applied here, the husband who falsely accuses his wife of premarital unchastity would be stoned to death. Instead, he is flogged, fined, and "fated" to live with his wife so long as either might live. Why the difference? Prevailing social standards may have required special protection for a husband's right to raise the issue.

Although the "cloth" is not otherwise identified, we may assume it to have been the sheet on the nuptial bed. The presence or absence of blood on the "cloth" would stand as proof of the wife's premarital virginity. But to present such proof, assuming it favored the wife, the parents would have had to possess the "cloth." Was it a regular practice for a wife's parents to hold the nuptial cloth—whether exculpatory or not? In any case, might the husband not have known what the cloth would reveal? If so, given the consequences (though not fatal), would a husband ever make a charge he knew to be false? Left unanswered, however, is whether the cloth was meant as the sole source of proof or as a symbol of a need for proof. If the former, what protocols would assure its availability? If the latter, how else might "guilt" or "innocence" be proved?

Of wider import, however, is the affirmation in 22:21 of the death penalty for nonadulterous sexual relations by a young woman "while under her father's authority." For one thing, her loss of virginity might prevent the father from realizing his "bride" price, in whole or in part.

Deut. 22:22–27 defines and prescribes penalties for conduct constituting adultery under the Seventh Commandment, of which 22:22 presents the simplest case: "If a man *is found* lying with another man's wife, both of them . . . shall die.

> Note D–109: *The means of death are not stated. And while the Seventh Commandment condemns adultery, however proved, 22:22 may imply a need of proof by witnesses to the act.*

Deut. 22:23–24 deals with consensual relations between "a virgin *engaged* to a man" and another man "who comes upon her *in town* and lies with her." Her consent is implied "because she did not cry for help in the town." His sin was "because he violated his neighbor's *wife*." Both were stoned to death "at the gate of that town."

> Note D–110: *By equating the contract to marry with marriage itself, the law extends the act of adultery to a virgin's premarital status. That it applies only to a virgin suggests that her prior "despoliation," whether by consent or rape, had greatly lessened her value as a wife. Moreover, even if she were not "under contract," her death would be required under 22:22.*

Deut. 22:25–27 deals with nonconsensual relations between a man who "comes upon the engaged girl in the open country, and . . . lies with her by force." Here, "only the man . . . shall die," for though the "engaged girl . . . cried for help, there was no one to save her."

Deut. 22:28–29 deals with "a man" who "comes upon *a virgin who is not engaged* and he seizes her and lies with her, and they are discovered." In such case "the man . . . shall pay the girl's father fifty [shekels of] silver, and she shall be his wife." Further, "because he violated her, he can never have the right to divorce her."

> Note D–111: *In regard to similar circumstances in Exod. 22:16, E allows the father to decide whether the couple may marry. In either case, the man must pay the standard bride price of an unstated amount. Here, however, a specific bride price is required and, with no stated right of the father to object, "she shall be his wife." It is possible, therefore, that the father's right to prevent the marriage had been superceded by an overriding social purpose of reducing the number of unmarried nonvirgins.*
>
> *But what of nonconsensual relations between a man, whether married or not, and a nonengaged nonvirgin woman? While the man's act was rape, no punishment, if any, is prescribed for the rape of a nonvirgin. Perhaps the physical abuse itself would be considered an assault. If not, did an unmarried nonvirgin, in effect, become "fair game?" Could this possibly have been a woman's price for a loss of virginity before marriage—even by rape?*

As stated in Deut. 23:1 by JPS2, "no man shall marry his father's former wife." As stated by JPS1/RSV, "a man shall not take his father's wife."

> Note D–112: *The Hebrew command of 23:1 is the same as that of Lev. 18:8, which JPS2, JPS1, and RSV all render as "your father's wife." In 23:1, JPS2 fittingly adds "former" to wife. A son could hardly purport to marry his father's "present" wife. No Torah source exempts polyandry from the law of adultery; under any circumstances, sexual relations with a father's wife would in itself be adulterous. The logic of 23:1, therefore, supports the addition of "former," as it would have in Lev. 18:8 (see Note L–41).*

Deut. 23:2 sets out a single physical impediment to "[admission] into the congregation of the Lord": "one whose testes are crushed or whose member is cut off."

> Note D–113: *Without explicitly declaring the fact to be the basis of the disqualification, Rashi observes that the eunuch "cannot beget offspring."*[18]

To this single physical impediment, Deut. 23:3 adds one of birth—not as a foreigner, however, but as an Israelite: "No one misbegotten shall be admitted into the congregation of the Lord; none of his descendants, even in the tenth generation."

Note D–114: Rather than "misbegotten," JPS1/RSV render the Hebrew momzayr more "classically" as bastard. However, as likely intended, "misbegotten" serves to identify a "bastard" as the offspring of any prohibited relationship.

Deut. 23:4–9 deals with "admission to the congregation of the Lord" by specific nationalities. To be excluded were all Ammonites and Moabites, "because they did not meet you with food and water on your journey after you left Egypt, and because they [i.e., the Moabites] hired Balaam son of Beor, from Pethor of Aram-naharaim, to curse you" (23:4–5). To this is added an "editorial" comment on Balaam himself: "But the Lord your God refused to heed Balaam; instead the Lord your God turned the curse into a blessing for you, for the Lord your God loves you" (23:7). And thus, "you shall never concern yourself with their welfare or benefit as long as you live" (23:7).

Note D–115: The northern levitical priests of Shiloh share P's reluctance to acknowledge the integrity of a non-Israelite prophet. Yet they avoid P's total "deconstruction" of Balaam (see Num. 22–24 and Comments N–25 and 31). Also of interest are the strikingly different views of the Ammonites held by D and the Shiloh priests, as authors of the Code of Law (cf. Deut. 2:19).

Deut. 23:8–9 concludes the passage on a positive note: "You shall not abhor an Edomite, for he is your kinsman. You shall not abhor an Egyptian, for you were a stranger in his land. Children born to them may be admitted into the congregation of the Lord in the third generation."

Note D–116: Why were the Edomites and Egyptians so favored? Were centuries of forced labor in Egypt to be so easily forgotten and forgiven after a mere forty years? Egypt, however, must be considered from the vantage point of mid-eighth century B.C.E., rather than the thirteenth. At the time Assyria presented a common threat both to Egypt and the Kingdom of Israel (leading to its fall in c. 722 B.C.E.). More generally as to Edom, see Note D–8.

Included in the breadth of human conduct encompassed in the Code of Holiness, is that of sanitation during war (Deut. 23:10–15).

To begin, "When you go out as a troop against your enemies, be on your guard against anything untoward."

Note D–117: By reading mikol davar rah in 23:10 as "from every evil thing," rather than "untoward," JPS1/RSV ascribe a more pungent quality to the setting that follows.

If anyone among you has been rendered unclean by a nocturnal emission, he must leave the camp, and he must not reenter the camp. [After bathing in water toward evening], at sundown he may reenter the camp. Further, there shall be an area for you outside the camp where you may relieve yourself. With your gear you shall have a spike, and when you have squatted you shall dig a hole with it and cover up your excrement. Since the Lord your God moves about in your camp to protect you and to deliver your enemies to you, let your camp be holy; let Him not find anything unseemly among you and turn away from you.

> Note D–118: *The passage addresses both ritual cleanliness involving semen, the sacred fluid of life, and basic physical cleanliness, involving the elimination of bodily waste and the prevention of disease. (As to nocturnal emissions, cf. Lev. 15:16–17.)*
>
> *Divine sanctity is more normally associated with the human spirit than with the disposition of human bodily wastes. Yet in its way, the disposition of bodily waste can be as important to human well-being as other more inspiring precepts of human conduct. By associating such lowly bodily functions with the sanctity of its God, the Torah uses Him to encourage basic sanitation practices that might otherwise be viewed with indifference.*

A deceptively simple rule follows in regard to the treatment of escaped slaves: "You shall not turn over to his master a slave who seeks refuge with you from his master. He shall live with you in any place he may choose among the settlements in your midst, wherever he pleases; you must not ill-treat him" (Deut. 23:16–17).

> Note D–119: *To what slaves does the passage refer? Only those of Israelite masters (whether indentured servants or "alien" slaves as well)? (See Exod. 21:2–11, Lev. 25:35–46, and Comments E–66 and L–57.) Rambam views the passage as related to the subject of Deut. 23:10–15: "When you go out as a troop against your enemies." He concludes that a slave who escapes from the worship of idols in other lands should be freed in Israel.*[19] *The application of the rule to indentured servants or slaves of Israelite masters would have greatly weakened this well-established and spiritually "sanctified" institution.*

As for cultic prostitution (Deut. 23:18–19):

No Israelite woman shall be a cult prostitute, nor shall any Israelite man be a cult prostitute. You shall not bring the fee of a whore or the pay of a dog into the house of the Lord your God in fulfillment of any vow, for both are abhorrent to [Him]. (23:18–19)

Comment D–33. On "cult prostitutes, whores, and dogs"

Logically, if cult prostitution is banned altogether, as stated in 23:18, there would be no "fee of a whore" or "pay of a dog" to be brought into "the house of the Lord . . . ," as stated in 23:19. Accordingly, 23:19 is not meant as a superfluous ban on the proceeds of a prohibited activity. Instead, it is a rhetorical declamation against befouling the central sanctuary with the proceeds of such a sin. Thus, the two verses might be paraphrased as follows: "Cult prostitution is hereby banned. Why? Because better should the house of the Lord forgo the offerings of such whores and dogs than to be afflicted by their presence."

Of added interest, however, is the failure to prohibit noncultic prostitution. Except in the form of sodomy (Lev.18:22, 20:13), nothing in the Torah prohibits noncultic male and female prostitutes from serving as such. That the Torah views prostitution as depraved we know from Lev. 21:9, which requires the death of any daughter of a priest (of Aaron's line) who turns to harlotry. The general disrepute of harlotry is also expressed in Lev. 19:29, which forbids a father to force a daughter into prostitution. Nowhere, however, does the Torah actually prohibit voluntary noncultic prostitution that does not involve sodomy. Indeed, the story of Tamar and Judah reveals not only its prevalence, but of how it was artfully used for a redemptive purpose. That the Torah's authors did not prohibit prostitution reflects the realities of their time. To lessen such realities was among their purposes.

In much the same manner as E (Exod. 22:24) and P (Lev. 25:35–37), Deut. 23:20–21 prohibits the exaction of interest in any form on loans to other Israelites. In effect, any arrangement that reduces the full value of the loan to the "borrower" is prohibited. Conversely, however, "you may deduct interest from loans to foreigners."

> Note D–120: The distinction between interest on loans as to Israelites and foreigners may say more of the different purposes of the loans than of the borrowers. Loans to other Israelites were largely extended as acts of charity. In contrast, loans to foreigners were more likely for commercial purposes (see Comment E–73 on interest free loans).

Deut. 23:22–24 addresses the particular sanctity of "a vow to the Lord your God." Because He "will require it of you" in any case, "do not put off fulfilling it." This is followed by a reminder that all vows are voluntary: "you incur no guilt if you refrain from vowing." But having assumed responsibility, "you must fulfil what has crossed your lips and perform what you have voluntarily vowed to the Lord your God."

Note D–121: To the same effect, see Num. 30:3. Respect for one's own integrity allows for only worthy and fulfillable vows.

Deut. 23:25–26 creates a limited right to the use of a neighbor's property. On entering his vineyard, "you may eat your fill of the grapes, *as many as you want*; but you must not put any in your vessel." And "when you find yourself amid [his] standing grain, you may pluck ears with your hand; but you must not put a sickle to [his] grain."

Note D–122: The "right," as described, could convert a private farm into a public cafeteria. Its exercise by one person might cause no great loss to the farmer. But its exercise by every passer-by with an urge to eat someone else's food could strip a farmer bare. Absent a total communal limit, therefore, the limit on each individual was meaningless. Under such laws, only a cohesive community imbued with a deep concern for its general welfare could leave farmers with enough motivation to remain farmers.

In its likely concern for the stability of marriages, Deut. 24:1–4 first reveals the precarious status of wives. Thus, when a wife "fails to please [her husband] because he finds something obnoxious about her," he may then write her a "bill of divorcement" and send her away (24:1). Should she marry another man who either divorces her in like manner or who dies, "then the first husband who divorced her shall not take her to wife again, since she has been defiled—for that would be abhorrent to the Lord" (24:2–4).

Note D–123: As stated here, the one catch-all ground for divorce was that the husband "finds something obnoxious [ehrvaht dahvar] about her." Although JPS1 refers to "some unseemly thing" and RSV to "some indecency," such variations in the standard leave the process unchanged. It is the husband's judgment, or wish, alone that enables him to "write her a bill of divorcement."

So much for the divorce. Deut. 24:1 adds little to what we already know of the status of wives in the cultural setting of the Torah. But why the flat prohibition of remarriage following such a termination of the wife's second marriage? Can a first husband's rash judgment never be corrected? Can the children who remain with the father not be reunited with their mother? Why must the law deny the potential benefits of a reunited family?

What might be unclear to us, however, was clearly evident to Ramban, given the Torah's characterization of the wife as "defiled." Ramban viewed the purpose of the rule as a prohibition of wife-swapping. Thus, "the reason for this prohibition is so that people should not exchange their wives with one another: he would be able to write her a bill of divorce at night, and in the morning she will return to him."[20]

The "one-night dalliance" cited by Ramban in support of a broad prohibition against all such remarriages may have been a concern at the time. But was it so pervasive or concern as to warrant a conclusive presumption that every such second marriage was meant to avoid the adultery of a "temporary fling"? Here the levitical priests of Shiloh swept with a broom every bit as broad as that wielded by the P source.

Deut. 24:5 seems an addendum to 20:7, in which, "lest he die," a military service exemption with no stated limit is given to a man "who has paid the bride-price." Here, however, a limited one-year exemption is given to a man who "has taken a bride." It is "for the sake of his household, to give happiness to the woman he has married."

Note D–124: Should the soldier of 20:7 who paid the "bride-price" then get married, his exemption, thus far subject to no stated limit, would presumably terminate in a year. Was this a possible disincentive to proceed with the marriage?

In the spirit of E's *mishpat* regarding pledges for loans (Exod. 22:25–26), Deut. 24:6 prohibits the taking "in pawn" of a "handmill" or an "upper millstone." Because of their use in grinding grain for bread, "that would be taking someone's life in pawn" (cf. Comment E–73).

Deut. 24:7 is of interest in its limitation to Israelites. "If a man is found to have kidnaped *a fellow Israelite*, enslaving him or selling him, that kidnapper shall die; thus shall you sweep evil from your midst."

Note D–125: Does 24:7 impliedly allow such abuse of an "alien," or "stranger," to be ignored? (On various aspects of corresponding Levitical rules, see Comment L–57.)

Deut. 24:8–9 reads as a forerunner to the laws of *tzara'at* in Lev. 13 and 14: "In cases of a skin affection be most careful to do exactly as the levitical priests instruct you. Take care to do what I have commanded them. Remember what the Lord your God did to Miriam on the journey after you left Egypt."

Note D–126: Deut. 24:8 identifies the condition as b'negah hatzara'at. (On the nomenclature of Leviticus, see Note L–32.) The reference to Miriam in 24:9 places the origins of Deut. 24:8–9 in Num. 12:1–16, which tells of Miriam's affliction with "snow-white scales" (12:10). Friedman persuasively attributes Num. 12:1–16 to E.[21] But by now the independence of Deuteronomy from Leviticus and Numbers is no novelty.

Deut. 24:10–13 returns to the theme of 24:6 regarding limits on the pledges of property as security for loans. The concern of Deut. 24:10–11 is for the dignity of the borrower and the sanctity of his home. Accordingly, having made a loan, a lender "must not enter [the borrower's] house to seize his pledge." Instead, he "must remain outside, while [the borrower] brings the pledge out."

Deut. 24:12–13 draws on the tradition of E's *mishpat* of Exod. 22:25–26. Thus, "if he is a needy man, you shall not go to sleep in his pledge; you must return the pledge to him at sundown, that he may sleep in his cloth and bless you; it will be to your merit before the Lord your God."

> *Note D–127: E does not distinguish between "needy" and other borrowers. Does the specification of "needy" here denote the expanded role of lending beyond its basic "charitable" origins in the interim between E and D?*

Departing from the "model" of Deut. 24:7, Deut. 24:14–15 again evinces equal concern for Israelites and strangers. Thus, "you shall not abuse a needy and destitute laborer, whether a fellow countryman or a stranger. . . . You must pay him his wages on the same day, before the sun sets, for he is needy and urgently depends on it; else he will cry out to the Lord against you and you will incur guilt."

> *Note D–128: The inclusion of "stranger" here only adds to the puzzle of why kidnapped "strangers" sold into slavery were not accorded the same protection as Israelites (cf. 24:7 and see Note D–125). This earlier rule of Deut. 24:14–15 is briefly restated in Lev. 19:13.*

Deut. 24:16 prescribes an ethically compelling standard of individual punishment that defies the "plague-ridden" standard of collective punishment that the Torah regularly ascribes to its God. "Parents shall not be put to death for children, nor children be put to death for parents: a person shall be put to death only for his own crime."

> *Note D–129: Alas, the rule comes too late for the children of the Flood and of Sodom, and for the newly firstborn of Egypt.*

Deut. 24:17–18 yet again invokes the experience of slavery in Egypt to kindle compassion for the unfortunate and disadvantaged. "You shall not subserve the rights of the stranger or the fatherless; you shall not take a widow's garment in pawn. *Remember that you were a slave in Egypt* and that the Lord your God redeemed you from there; *therefore I do enjoin you to observe this commandment.*"

> *Note D–130: Earlier references in Deuteronomy to the "stranger," the "fatherless" and the "widow," as metaphors for the disadvantaged, are found in 10:18, 14:29, and 16:11.*

Deut. 24:19 provides a "post harvest" addendum to the generous, if not the self-defeating, provisions of 23:25–26 (see Note D–122). "When you reap the harvest in your field and overlook a sheaf in the field, do not *turn back* to get it; it shall go to stranger, the fatherless, and the widow."

Deut. 24:20–22 continues the theme by applying the rule governing grain to the fruits of the tree and vine. "When you beat down the fruit of your olive trees, do not go over them again; that shall go to the stranger, the fatherless and the widow. When you gather the grapes of your vineyard, do not pick it over again; that shall go to the stranger, the fatherless and the widow." And again, as the moral impetus "to observe the commandment," one must remember "you were a slave in the land of Egypt."

Deut. 25 opens with a reminder of the essential dignity of every human being, even when being punished. It does so by telling of two men who "go to law" to settle a dispute. One is found "in the wrong." If he is to be punished by flogging, "the magistrate" shall see to the administration of "lashes in his presence, by count, as his guilt warrants." But there are limits: "He may be given up to forty lashes, but not more, lest being flogged further, to excess, your brother be degraded before your eyes" (25:1–3).

To concern for the dignity and self-respect of human beings, Deut. 25:4 adds concern for the welfare of animals— particularly of those for whom one is directly responsible. The simple example covers a multitude of scenarios. "You shall not muzzle an ox while it is threshing."

> Note D–131: *To deny a working animal access to grain that lies strewn around it is to ignore its existence as a feeling and sentient creature. It is an unworthy act of cruelty.*

Deut. 25:5–10 brings forward the law of levirate marriage from c. 950 to 900 B.C.E., as first recorded in J's story of Tamar and Judah, to c. 750 B.C.E. Given J's main focus in Gen. 38 on the drama of two human beings, his treatment of the legal details leaves much to speculation. However, from the details of 24:5–10, as quoted below, we detect a clear evolution toward a loosening of the obligation.

> When brothers dwell together and one of them dies and leaves no son, the wife of the deceased shall not be married to a stranger, outside the family. Her husband's brother shall unite with her; take her as his wife and perform the levir's duty. The first son that she bears shall be accounted to the dead brother, that his name not be blotted out in Israel. But if the man does not want to marry his brother's widow, [she] shall appear before the elders in the gate and declare, "My husband's brother refuses to establish a name in Israel for his brother; he will not perform the duty of a levir." The elders of his town shall then summon him and talk to him. If he insists, saying, "I do not want to marry her," the

brother's widow shall go up to him in the presence of the elders, pull the sandal off his foot, spit in his face and [declare]: "Thus shall be done to the man who will not build up his brother's house! And he shall go in Israel by the name of "the family of the unsandaled one.""

Comment D–34. On the evolution of levirate marriages from Gen. 38 to Deut. 25:5–10 and on to Lev. 20:21.

The text tells us that between J's story of Tamar and Judah (Gen. 38) and the mid-seventh century B.C.E. the levirate obligation had been limited in two important respects. As to scope, the passage repeatedly speaks of only one brother on whom the obligation falls. Clearly, this is a major contraction from the successive responsibilities of every brother (in birth order) and, if need be, the father (see Gen. 38 and Comments G–75 and 76). Ramban accepts a still later Talmudic view that limited the obligation on "the [eldest] surviving brother."[22]

The second limitation relates to enforcement. Here Deuteronomy renders the obligation totally unenforceable, except for any shame the eldest brother might feel in refusing to honor it. Thus, the "obligation" had now evolved from a legal to a moral obligation, at most.

A third possible contraction is in the reference to "When brothers dwell together." What does "together" mean? The same household, town, or country? Rashi reads it, however, as related to time rather than location: "i.e., they dwelt at the same time in the world."[23] If so, it would be an obligor-brother's duty to repair to the widow's home on hearing of the death. "Togetherness" in time, therefore, could pose problems of communications and travel.

In Leviticus the original "obligation" evolves further from an option to an anathema—at least within the Torah. Thus, the rule and punishment of Lev. 20:21: "If a man [without exception] marries the wife of his brother it is an indecency; . . . they shall remain childless." (This follows the same initial prohibition of Lev. 18:16. As to the logic of applying the ban to the brother's *widow*, see Notes L–82 and D–112.) *That P then tailors a punishment to "remain childless" for this offense reveals a specific intent to "bury" a practice that had been wholly, or largely, abandoned.*

In regard to efforts by faithful wives to aid embattled husbands, Deut. 25:11–12 opts for public propriety and female gentility. Thus, "if two men . . . fight, and the wife of one comes up to save her husband from his antagonist and puts out her hand and seizes him by his genitals, you shall cut off her hand, show no pity."

> Note D–132: *That the proscribed act might have been reasonably intended to save the husband's life from a treacherous foe would not seem to excuse it.*

This is an odd priority that would bar a wife, in the name of propriety, from a useful defense of her husband against possible death.

In the name of "the Lord your God" to whom "dishonesty" is "abhorrent," Deut. 25:13–16 demands honesty in commercial dealings. "You shall not have in your pouch alternate weights [for a balancing scale], larger and smaller. You shall not have in your house alternate measures, a larger and a smaller. You must have completely honest weights and completely honest measures" (cf. Lev. 19:35).

Deut. 25:17–19 marks the final appearance in the Torah of the tribe of Amalek. "Remember what Amalek did to you on your journey, after you left Egypt—undeterred by fear of God, he surprised you on the march, when you were famished and weary and cut down all the stragglers in your rear" (25:17–18). Therefore, [after the Lord assures your safety from your enemies in Canaan], you shall blot out the memory of Amalek from under heaven. Do not forget!" (25:19).

> *Note D–133: In the first encounter with Amalek in Exod. 17:8–16 the Lord expressed His similar resolve to Moses: "I utterly block out the memory of Amalek from under heaven." From this Moses understood that "the Lord will be at war with Amalek throughout the ages." The Exodus passage, however, says nothing of "famished and weary" Israelites whose "stragglers" were easy game for the Amalekites. However, the Amalekites were also prominent in Num. 14:25. It is their presence with the Canaanites that prompts the Lord to direct the Israelites not to enter Canaan from the south. When they disobeyed him, the two tribes routed them with a "shattering blow at Hormah" (Num. 14:39–45).*
>
> *D's embellishments exemplify the role of myths and legends in justifying and perpetuating ethnic enmities. Indeed, more than just a tribal foe, Amalek becomes a metaphor for evil itself, as Israel's eternal foe.*

Deut. 26 concludes the Deuteronomic Code of Law (Deut. 12–26). Its opening portion prescribes an annual offering of the "first fruits" at the central sanctuary (26:1–11).

As with the festivals of Deut. 12 and 16, the focus of Deut. 26:1–11 is on the central sanctuary. The protocols required every family head (at least in the northern kingdom of Israel, as contemplated by the priests of Shiloh) to "take some of the first fruit of the soil . . . put it in a basket and go to where the Lord your God will choose to establish His name" (i.e., the central sanctuary)." Each was to go to the priest in charge and say, "I acknowledge this day before the Lord your God that I have entered the land which the Lord swore to our fathers to give us" (26:3).

When the priest had taken the basket and placed it by the altar, the offeror, in explaining his offering, would recite this brief history of Israel, as a people:

> My father was a fugitive Aramean. He went down to Egypt with meager numbers and sojourned there; but there he became a great and very populous nation. The Egyptians dealt harshly with us and oppressed us; they imposed heavy labor on us. We cried to the Lord, the God of our fathers, and the Lord heard our plea and saw our plight, our misery and our oppression. [He] freed us from Egypt by a mighty hand . . . and by signs and portents. He brought us to this place and gave us this land, a land flowing with milk and honey. Wherefore I now bring the first fruits of the soil which You, O Lord, have given me. (26:5–10a)

> *Note D–134: The "father" was likely Jacob, a fugitive, first from Esau, then from Laban and finally from the famine in Canaan, from where, "with meager numbers" he went to Egypt.*

After concluding the formalities with a low bow to the Lord (26:10b), the offeror could then enter into the final festivities. "And you shall enjoy, together with the Levite and the stranger in your midst, all the bounty that the Lord your God has bestowed upon you and your household" (26:11).

Together, the passages of 26:1–11 and 12–15 supplement the previous passages of 14:28–29 and 16:9–12 relating to the triennial tithing provisions and attendant rituals. On the completion of the basic tithing requirement (i.e., for "the Levite, the stranger, the fatherless, and the widow, that they may eat their fill in your settlement"), this declaration "before the Lord your God" was made:

> I have cleared out the consecrated portion from the house; and I have given it [to those named above], just as You have commanded me; I have neither transgressed nor neglected any of your commandments: I have not eaten of it while in mourning; I have not cleared out any of it while I was unclean, and I have not deposited any of it with the dead. I have obeyed the Lord my God; I have done just as You commanded me. Look down from Your holy abode, from heaven, and bless your people Israel and the soil You have given us, a land flowing with wilk and honey, as You swore to our fathers. (26:13b–15)

> *Note D–135: With its focus on total obedience to the tithing duty, and to all related laws, the declaration takes on a metaphoric aura that extends to all Godly commands. It closes with a prayer for Godly reciprocity.*

The entire Code of Law then concludes with a statement of the mutual obligations and commitments of Israel and the Lord, its God. Together, they are a covenant (26:16–19).

Israel's obligation is described as follows:

The Lord your God commands you this day to observe these laws and rules; observe them faithfully with all your heart and soul. You have affirmed this day that the Lord is your God, that you will walk in His ways, that you will observe his laws and commandments and rules, and that you will obey him. (26:16–17)

The Lord's promise, as Israel's God, is then set out:

And the Lord has affirmed this day that you are, as He promised you, His treasured people which shall observe all His commandments, and that He will set you, in fame and renown and glory, high above all the nations He has made; and that you shall be, as He promised, a holy people to the Lord your God. (26:18–19)

Comment D–35. On the charge to "walk in His ways"

But for one major exception to be noted, the phrase "walking in the way of the Lord" (26:17), is distinctly Deuteronomic (see also 8:6, 10:12, 11:22, 19:9, 28:9 and 30:16). In the context of 26:16–19, in particular, its appearance invites three questions. First, is it meant as a summary expression for obedience to the "laws and commandments and rules" of the Lord, God of Israel, or as a separate obligation? Second, if the latter, is it also a separate covenantal condition? Third, if it is a separate duty or condition, what more does it require of Israel?

Read literally, Deut. 26:16–19, in itself, would seem to offer clear answers to the first two questions and at least an intimation of an answer to the third. Note that the statement of Israel's obligations (26:16–17) consists of four components: (1) "that the Lord is your God who commands faithful obedience to all His laws and rules," (2) "that you will walk in His ways," (3) "that you will observe his laws and commandments and rules," and (4) "that you will obey him" (23:16–17).

However, the Lord's reciprocal commitments in Deut. 26:18–19 notably exclude (2) "that you will walk in His ways." It refers only to "a treasured people which shall observe all His commandments." In essence, therefore, the condition is construed in 26:17–19 as one of faithful obedience to all *general* "laws, rules and commandments" (as in [1] and [3] and to all other commands [as in (4)]).

The literal effect of the absence of (2) in 26:18–19 is to eliminate it as a condition to the Lord's maintaining His covenant. As such, to "walk in His ways" connotes a moral undertaking to emulate His Being insofar as "humanly" possible. It is a commitment to strive for the right in all matters, whether or not the subject of a covenantal command.

None of the other Deuteronomic uses of "walking in the way of the Lord" establish an identity between "obedience to the Lords commands" and "walking in His ways." However, in four cases (11:22–23, 19:9, 28:9, and

30:16), favorable actions by the Lord are conditioned both on obedience and "walking in His ways." None, however, threatens a curse for failing to "walk in His ways." None appears as a condition for avoiding a curse. Only in 19:9 is a specific loss implied from a failure to "walk in His ways." It is not a breach of the covenant, however, but only the loss of three added cities of refuge.

The phrase also appears in Genesis 17:1 in which P's El Shaddai tells Abram (soon to be Abraham): "Walk in My ways and be blameless." Consistent with its basic use in Deuteronomy, P's use of the phrase is predictive rather than conditional. In effect, El Shaddai tells Abram, "I am blameless. And by walking in my ways, you too can be blameless." As a covenantal condition, however, El Shaddai requires only circumcision (Gen. 17:9–14). In effect, while "blamelessness," like "walking in the way of the Lord," was a worthy goal, it was even less enforceable as a covenantal condition. Much like Deuteronomy's Lord God in regard to Israel's "walking in His ways," P's El Shaddai knew the futility of conditioning His covenant on Israel's ability to achieve "blamelessness." But as to greater rewards, the importance of "walking in His ways" could not be ignored.

> Note D–136: With the Code of Law completed, Deut. 27 now picks up from Deut. 11:26–31 in regard to the "blessing at Mount Gerizim" and the "curse at Mount Ebal"—both "on the other side of the Jordan."

Deut. 27 opens with the acknowledged return of Moses. Together with its "elders," he charges Israel to "observe all the Instruction that I enjoin upon you this day" (27:1).

It is to be fulfilled "as soon as you have crossed the Jordan into the land that the Lord your God is giving you" (27:2). The Instruction then begins (27:1–8):

1. "Set up large stones [on Mount Ebal], coat them with plaster" (27:2–4) and "inscribe on them every word of this Teaching most distinctly" (27:8).
2. "Build an altar to the Lord your God of unhewn stones," untouched by any iron tool, on which "You shall offer burnt offerings to the Lord your God, and you shall sacrifice . . . offerings of well-being and eat them, rejoicing before the Lord your God" (27:5–7).

> Note D–137: To avoid violating Deut. 12:4–12 in regard to the central sanctuary, this altar would serve as a temporary ceremonial site to mark Israel's entry into Canaan.

Comment D–36A. On the meaning of "this Teaching," or this "law," in Deut. 27:3 and 8

What are "all the words of this Teaching" that are to be inscribed on the "large stones." The choice here is between the "Teaching" of the entire Torah and that of Deuteronomy itself. As it appears both in 27:3 and 27:8, the relevant Hebrew phrase is *et kol divrai hatorah hazoht*, which JPS2 and JPS1/RSV render, respectively, as "Teaching" and "law." None, however, identify it as the Torah we know today. And because the Torah as we know it, did not yet exist, they are correct. (As its completion neared, only R *might* have thought to read *hatorah* as "The" Torah. See my introduction, pp. 29–30, and Comment E–79.)

Rashi does not address the issue. Ramban, however, expresses doubt about earlier suggestions that the *hatorah* of these verses included the entire five books of Moses. "It is likely that either these stones were huge, or it was a miraculous event" (otherwise it would have been impossible to inscribe so much on a few stone tablets)."[24]

For the recitation of curses (27:9–26) and blessings (28:1–69), the "elders of Israel" are replaced by the "levitical priests" in speaking with Moses to the people. They begin with this importunity and declaration: "Silence! Hear, O Israel! *Today you have become the people of the Lord your God.*"

> Note D–138: This opening assertion might seem to belie the entire covenantal experience through which Israel had already "become the people of the Lord." The reference here, however, may be to such Deuteronomic passages as 6:1 and 12:1, in which the effectiveness of the "laws and rules" is deferred until Israel's entry into Canaan. This could well be the meaning of 27:10, which follows: "Heed the Lord your God and observe His commandments and His laws, which I enjoin upon you this day."

Deut. 27:12–14 sets the scene for the recital of curses and blessings *after crossing the Jordan*. "Simeon, Levi, Judah, Issachar, Joseph and Benjamin" will stand on Mount Gerizim "when the blessing for the people is spoken." For the curse, "Reuben, Gad, Asher, Zebulun, Dan and Naphtali" will stand on Mount Ebal. The Levites would then "proclaim [the curses of 27:15–26] in a loud voice to all the men of Israel" (even as they apparently remain on Mount Gerizim to hear the blessings).

> Note D–139: The identification of each tribe by patriarchal name alone raises a question of tribal representation. Was it to be by the current tribal chieftain, the tribal "elders" or the entire male membership or the entire tribe? Whatever the case, the tribal placements would seem to reflect certain

THE TORAH AND ITS GOD

534

protocols of "precedence." Note first, however, that the twelve tribes include those of Joseph and Levi, but exclude the sometimes half and sometimes full tribes of Ephraim and Manasseh. To hear the blessings on Mount Gerizim, the author chooses four of the six sons of Leah (Simeon, Levi, Judah, Issachar) and the two sons of Rachel (Joseph and Benjamin). To have placed all six sons of Jacob's wife Leah on Mount Gerizim would have "relegated" the two sons of Jacob's wife Rachel to the curses on Mount Ebal. Instead, Reuben and Zebulun, the two other sons of Leah, are placed with the four sons of Jacob's concubines amid the curses. That Reuben should be so "denigrated" may relate back to Bilhah (Gen. 35:22). (This would imply that D knew the tradition of Reuben's sin.) Finally, Zebulun took his place as Leah's youngest son (Gen. 30:19–20).

Deut. 27:15–26 then describes the "cursable" conduct of individual persons that will evoke God's curses. Following the recitation of each type of "cursable" conduct, "all the people" are commanded to say "Amen."

Thus, "Cursed be":

15. The man who makes a "sculptured or molten image;
16. He who insults his father or mother;
17. He who moves his neighbors landmark;
18. He who misdirects a blind person;
19. He who subverts the rights of the stranger, the fatherless, and the widow;
20. He who lies with his father's wife;
21. He who lies with any beast;
22. He who lies with his sister, whether daughter of his father or of his mother (or half-sister too);
23. He who lies with his mother-in-law;
24. He who strikes down his neighbor in secret;
25. He who accepts a bribe in the case of the murder of an innocent person;
26. He who will not uphold the terms of this Teaching and observe them.

Comment D–36B. On the meaning of "this Teaching," or this "law," in Deut. 27:26

The basic choice is between the entire "Teaching," or "law," of Deuteronomy or the particular "Teaching," or "law," of 27:15–26 (see Comment D–36A on why I exclude the entire Torah as a possible choice). Given its placement and context, and for the additional reasons set out below in Comment D–37, I conclude that the antecedent for the "teaching" or "laws" of 27:26 is the prohibited and "cursable" conduct of 27:15–26. But unlike the curses of Lev. 26 and Deut. 28, which portray the fruits of collective disobedience in horrendous detail, the curses that are to follow the "cursable" individual conduct of Deut. 27:15–25 are never identified.

Comment D-37. On the separate origins of Deut. 27:11–26 and Deut. 28

Deut. 27:15–26 and 28:15–68 both deal with curses. Yet the substance of these passages are so different as to suggest their separate origins. Consider these points.

1. Deut. 27:15–26 sets out the curses to be proclaimed by "the Levites . . . in a loud voice to all the men of Israel," but only "after you have crossed the Jordan" (27:12–14). To hear the blessings and curses, six of the tribes, or their representatives, are located on Mount Gerizim (the site of blessings) and Mount Ebal (the site of curses). In turn, the blessings and curses of Deut. 28, which include no reference to the Levites or Mount Gerizim or Ebal, appear to be rendered by Moses alone "in the land of Moab" *before* crossing of the Jordan (see 28:69).

2. But for the generality of 27:26, the twelve grounds for the curse(s) of Deut. 27 involve highly specific conduct. Nor, as noted above, does Deut. 27 describe the nature of the curses to result for the "cursable" conduct of 27:15–26 (although in most, if not all cases, death would seem most likely). However, curses are imposed only on "he" and never collectively on all Israel (cf. Deut. 28:15–68).

3. Contrary to the specific "cursable" conduct of Deut. 27:15–26, the sole standard of conduct in determining the visitation of blessings or curses in Deut. 28 is, of necessity, very broad. Both curses and blessings derive from the one basic standard of "faithful observance to all of the Lord's command-ments" (see 28:1, 13 regarding blessings; 28:15 regarding curses) Moreover, unlike the curses of 27:15–26, the blessings and curses of Deut. 28 affect all Israel alike.

Also, being subject to the common conditions of 28:1, 13, and 15, the blessings of Deut. 28:1–14 and curses of Deut. 28:15–68 are bound to each other alone, with no ties to Deut. 27. And in that (1) the curses of 27:15–26 have no offsetting blessings and (2) that they have no role in Deut. 28, the undisclosed blessings of 27:12 serve no purpose. It seems possible, therefore, that R has again honored two versions of one event, whatever the anomalies.

Comment D-38. On the collective blessings and curses of the Torah

1. Introduction

Blessings and curses are customarily the Torah's rewards and punishments for collective, rather than individual, conduct. When judged worthy (i.e., obe-dient) as a people, Israel will be blessed *as a people*. And when judged unworthy as a people, it will be cursed *as a people*. The rewards of a worthy individual, however, will come from the knowledge of God's approval (i.e., a good conscience) and the natural benefits of a life well lived. Blessings though they are, they are not named as such. Similarly, rather than being plagued with curses, the unworthy individual will be subject to specific punishments suited to the offense.

2. The "triggers" for blessings and curses in Deut. 28 and Lev. 26

Both the substance and the reasons for the blessings and curses of Lev. 26 and Deut. 28 have much in common.

As to blessings, the required level of obedience is essentially the same in both. In Lev. 26:3, the condition for blessings is that "you follow My laws and faithfully observe My commandments"; and in Deut. 28:1, that "you obey the Lord your God, to observe faithfully all His commandments which I enjoin upon you this day" (28:1).

Added to 28:1 is the second, but similar, standard of obedience in 28:2: "if you will but heed [My] word." To these and similar requirements of *obedience*, Deut. 28:9 adds words of *emulation*: "if you keep the commandments of the Lord your God *and walk in His ways*" (28:9). And to these, 28:14 adds a tone of firmness: "if only you . . . *do not deviate to the right or to the left from any of the commandments* . . . that I enjoin upon you this day and turn to the worship of other gods."

Here the use of "walk in his ways" as a condition of being "His holy people" might require me to modify my earlier conclusion in Comment D–35: i.e., that "walk in his ways" was intended as a source of added blessings and not of curses or a convenantal termination should Israel fail to "walk in his ways." The "technical" question is whether the loss of status as "His holy people" necessarily implies a complete covenantal termination. From a broad Torah perspective, we might assume such an equivalency. In Deuteronomy, however, the question must be addressed in its own context. This is considered in Comment D–35.

As to the curses, Deut 28:15 typically speaks of a failure to obey "all His commandments and laws which I enjoin upon you this day." (To similar effect see 28:45.) But here we might take special note of Deut. 28:47 as a source of curses: "Because you would not serve the Lord your God in joy and gladness over the abundance of everything." Thus, in return for His "good works," Israel's Lord God demands no less than joyful appreciation.

Similar standards (other than those of 28:47) are found in Lev. 26:14–15, 18, 21, 23, and 27. However, the latter three verses add the offense that "you [Israel] remain hostile to me." Such hostility, presumably, was reflected in disobedience.

Also on the theme of obedience, Deut. 28:58 promises plagues for Israel's failure to "observe faithfully all of the terms of *this Teaching* that are written in *this book*, to reverence this honored and awesome Name, the Lord, your

God." (For the view that "this Teaching" and "this book" refer to Deuteronomy only, see Comments D–36A and B.)

3. A brief comparison of the blessings and curses of Deut. 28 and Lev. 26

With minor variations, the blessings of both carry promises of agricultural and reproductive fertility and abundance; general peace and safety, with assured victory over foes reckless enough to attack Israel; general bliss and prosperity; and God's protective favor and Presence (Deut. 28:1–14, Lev. 26:1–13).

The escalating curses of Lev. 26:14–38, together with the redemptive provisions of 26:39–45, marking the return of exiles from Babylonia to Judah, are summarized in the text preceding Comment L–58. Friedman attributes the curses, to P and the later concluding redemptive provisions to R.

To retain the full "flavor" of the Levitical curses in a summary is difficult enough. To attempt to do so with the Deuteronomic curses is pointless. The reader is thus urged to absorb the "flavor" directly through a reading of Deut. 28:15–68. What warrants emphasis, however, is the culminating poetic horror and irony of the curses.

As to horror, consider the ultimate "success" of the curses in totally eviscerating the human spirit:

> And when you are shut up in all your towns throughout your land . . . you shall eat your own issue, the flesh of your sons and daughters that the Lord your God has given you, because of the desperate straits to which your enemy shall reduce you. He who is most tender and fastidious among you shall be too mean to the wife of his bosom and the children he has spared to share with any of them the flesh of the children he eats, because he has nothing else left as a result of the desperate straits to which your enemy shall reduce you in all your towns. And she who is most tender and dainty among you, so tender and dainty that she would never venture to set a foot on the ground, shall begrudge the husband of her bosom, and her son and her daughter, the afterbirth that issues from between her legs and the babies she bears, she shall eat them secretly, because of utter want, in the desperate straits to which your enemy shall reduce you in your towns. (28:52b–57)

As to irony, consider the ultimate futility of Israel's having been delivered from Egypt:

> The life you face shall be precarious; you shall be in terror, night and day, with no assurance of survival. In the morning you shall say, "If only it were evening!" and in the evening you shall say "If only it were morning!"—because of what your heart shall dread and your eyes shall see. The Lord will send you back to Egypt in galleys, by a route which I told you should not see again. There you

shall offer yourselves to your enemies as male and female slaves, but none will buy. (28:66–68)

Thus, Israel will even be frustrated in its efforts to return to the comforts of slavery in Egypt.

Just as Friedman identifies the final verses of Lev. 26 with the "real" events of Israel's return from Babylonian captivity, so are certain passages of Deut. 28 associated with contemporaneous events. Friedman identifies them as 28:36–37 and 63–68.

The Lord will drive you, and the king you have set over you, to a nation unknown to you or your fathers, where you shall serve other gods, of wood and stone. You shall be a consternation, a proverb, and a byword among all the peoples to which the Lord will drive you. (28:36–37)

You shall be torn from the land which you are about to invade and occupy." The Lord will scatter you among all the peoples from one end of the earth to the other, and there you shall serve other gods, wood and stone, whom neither you nor your ancestors have experienced. (28:63b–64)

Friedman attributes these "later" portions of Deut. 28 to D2, whom he distinguishes from D1, not by person, but by time. He considers both to be Jeremiah, writing earlier, before the death of King Josiah in 609 B.C.E.; and later, after the Babylonian exile of 587 B.C.E.[25]

Other authorities also identify 28:36–37 and portions of 28:47–68 with the Assyrian disasters in the north of c. 722 B.C.E. and/or in the south of c. 586–536 B.C.E.[26]

As previously noted, the curses of Lev. 26 lead into the final redemptive and remissive provisions of 26:39–46, which Friedman attributes to R—the final redactor whose work followed Israel's return from exile c. 537 B.C.E. If so, we must wonder at R's failure to provide a similar addendum to the curses of Deut. 28, whose allusions to the Babylonian exile are even more explicit.

4. On the common purpose of the blessings and curses of Deut. 28 and Lev. 26

Together, these similar treatments of a common theme attest to the pervasive strength in the Torah of the principle of collective responsibility. And well before P or D, the principle was first expressed by E, though in simpler form and through the more benign psychological impact of blessings alone (Exod. 23:20–31).

The principle of collective responsibility may also provide the moral underpinnings for the Great Flood and the repeated plagues that Israel's Lord God visits on the innocent and guilty alike. If so, they, too, promulgate the Torah's message that an indivdual's communal responsibility does not end with the avoidance of prohibited conduct. Instead, each Israelite is implicitly charged with a duty to work with his "neighbors" in maintaining the moral integrity of Israel as a people. For should Israel's collective moral worth fall below an undefined level acceptable to its Lord God, then collective disaster will displace the role of individual punishments. *However troubling it may, the Torah, nevertheless elevates collective responsibility to a level that transcends individual justice itself.* If justification can be found, it lies in the Torah's purpose of unifying a people and creating a nation. (For a social calculus of the collective blessings and curses of Deut. 28 and Lev. 26, see Comment L–59.)

> *Note D–140: Together, Deut. 29 and 30 constitute the final formal discourse of Moses to the people. Its treatment of a cycle of collective sin, collective punishment and collective forgiveness and redemption is perhaps the most powerful statement of this theme in all the Torah.* In relation to the preceding curses of Deut. 28, it also serves as a Deuteronomic equivalent to the redemptive provisions of Lev. 26:39–45. *It was the purpose of both to give heart and resolve to a people in exile whose country had been devastated by the might of Babylonia.*

And so, at the outset of Deut. 29 and 30, "Moses summoned all Israel and said to them."

He first observes that in Egypt, "You" witnessed "with your own eyes" the "wondrous feats" and "prodigous signs and marvels" that the Lord had wrought against Pharoah. "Yet," he adds, "to this day the Lord has not given you a mind to understand or eyes to see or ears to hear" (29:1b–3).

> *Note D–141: In referring to "You," Moses speaks of the people of Israel as an unbroken continuum. The generation that had witnessed the "signs and marvels . . . wrought against Pharaoh" had since died in the wilderness.*

Moses then continues to speak the Lord's words. "I led you through the wilderness forty years; the clothes on your back did not wear out, nor did the sandals on your feet; you had no bread to eat and no wine or other liquor to drink—that you might know that I am the Lord your God" (29:4–5).

He also recalls the defeat of "Sihon king of Heshbon and Og king of Bashan," who had come out to give battle. In turn their lands were given to "the Reubenites, the Gadites and the half tribe of Manasseh as their heritage" (29:6–7).

> *Note D–142: The (interspersed) J and P versions of these land allotments are in Num. 32. As to these, see Comment N–34.*

But now, to sanctify Israel's entry into Canaan, Israel and its Lord God must confirm their covenant. Neither the covenant at Horeb nor Abraham's covenant more than five hundred years earlier can suffice to sanctify the imminent fulfillment of the Lord's promise to Abraham (see Deut. 4:12–13, 4:31, and 5:1–15, esp. 5:3). Thus, Moses must now prepare Israel for the renewal of its covenant.

"You stand this day, all of you, before the Lord your God—your tribal heads, your elders and your officials, all the men of Israel" (29:9). But as the passage reveals, "all the men of Israel" now signifies "all Israel," and even more. Added to the men as parties to the covenant were "your children, your wives, *even the stranger within your camp*, from woodchoppper to water drawer" (29:9–10). They are all gathered together

> to enter into this covenant of the Lord your God, which [He] is concluding with you this day; . . . to the end that He may establish you this day as his people *and be your God*, as He promised you and as He swore to your fathers Abraham, Isaac and Jacob. I make this covenant . . . not with you alone, but both with those who are standing with us this day before the Lord our God and with those who are not with us this day. (29:11–14)

> Note D–143: *Most striking is the unconditional inclusion in the covenant of "even the stranger within your camp." These were likely meant to be the children and descendants of the "mixed multitude" of Exod. 12:38 who departed with the Israelites from Egypt. If so, by implication, those who remained with Israel, having shared its experiences over forty years, were now deemed worthy of entering into the covenant.*

Deut. 29:15–19 then turns to the single greatest threat to the permanence of the covenant. Moses reminds the people that in Egypt, and other nations they had come to know, "you have seen detestable things and the fetishes of wood and stone, silver and gold, that they keep" (29:15–16). He then speculates that there may be "some man or woman, or some [entire] clan or tribe, whose heart is even now turning away from the Lord our God, to go and worship gods of those nations" (29:17). If so, such apostates might mistakenly view the warmth of the renewed covenant in itself as a measure of tolerance for following other gods: "When such a one hears the words of [this sworn covenant], he may fancy himself immune, thinking, 'I shall be safe, though I follow my own wilful heart'—to the utter ruin of moist and dry alike" (29:18).

> Note D–144: *Here Moses would seem to be warning the people against taking the warmth of covenantal expression as a sign of God's leniency in the wake of apostasy. Also, as a true merism in this case, "moist and dry" means everything. But why the ruin of everything? Moses answers the question as follows.*

"The Lord will never forgive him. Rather will [His] anger and passion rage against that man, till every sanction recorded in this book comes down on him, and the Lord blots out his name from under heaven" (29:19). And in the case of a blasphemous tribe, "the Lord will single them out from all the tribes of Israel for misfortune, in accordance with all the sanctions of the covenant recorded in this book of Teaching" (29:20).

Now consider the following powerful (but herein edited) portrayal of what is widely regarded as a contemporary reference to Babylonia's harsh conquest of Judah in 587 B.C.E. and Israel's ensuing fifty year exile (29:21–27). As such, it stands with the curses of Lev. 26 and Deut. 28 as a dramatic warning of the fruits of disobedience.

> Note D–145: As it is clearly among the final portions of Deuteronomy to have been written, Friedman attributes the passage to D2.

And later generations will . . . see the plagues and diseases that the Lord has inflicted upon the land, all its soil devastated by sulfur and salt, beyond sowing and producing, no grass growing in it, just like the upheaval of Sodom and Gomorrah, Admah and Zeboim, which the Lord overthrew in His fierce anger—all nations will ask, "Why did the Lord do this to the land? Wherefore that awful wrath?" They will be told, "Because they forsook the covenant that the Lord, God of their fathers, made with them when He freed them from the land of Egypt; and they turned to the service of other gods and worshiped them, gods whom they had not experienced and whom He had not allotted to them. So the Lord . . . brought upon [the land] all the curses recorded in this book. The Lord uprooted them from their soil in anger, fury, and great wrath, and cast them into another land, *as is still the case.* (29:21–27)

> Note D–146: It is not clear whether the covenant of 29:24 ("that the Lord, God . . . made with them when He freed them from Egypt") refers to the Horeb covenant or the pending renewal covenant of 29:13–14.
>
> The inclusion in 29:27 of "as is still the case," in regard to the exile, offers the most poignant evidence of the Torah's "contemporary" focus when written. (See Gen. 23:19, 26:33, 32:33, 35:19, 35:27; see also Comments G–63 and 94 pt. 1 and Notes G–33 and 47).

Deut. 29 closes with a homiletic division of labor between Israel's Lord God and the people themselves. "Concealed acts concern the Lord our God; but with overt acts it is for us and our children ever to apply all the provisions of this Teaching" (29:28).

> Note D–147: As a conclusion to the preceding passage, 29:28 can be read to declare a need to prevent future disaster by the strict enforcement of the

> "Teaching" against every Israelite. Where the "sin and sinner" are known, the matter must be rectified through human justice. Only where either remains concealed, and thus known only to the Lord God, is it His responsibility to enforce His authority. As Rashi put the matter, "but the things that are revealed belong to us and our children, to remove evil from among us, and if we do not execute justice in their case, the many will be punished."[27]

As to the impact of the Babylonian conquest and exile on Israel's morale, Deut. 30:1–10 serves the same role in Deuteronomy as Lev. 26:39–45 serves in Leviticus (see Note D–140). In effect, Israel's sins will have finally brought on disaster; but however great its despair, through repentance, the covenant, with all its of blessings, may yet be restored.

> When all these things befall you—the blessing and the curses which I have set before you—and you take them to heart among the various nations to which the Lord your God has banished you, and you return to [Him], and . . . heed His command with all your heart and soul . . . then [He] will restore your fortunes and take you back with love. He will bring you together again from all the peoples where [He] has scattered you. Even if you are outcasts from the end of the world . . . from there He will fetch you. And [He] will bring you to the land which your fathers occupied, and you shall occupy it; and He will make you more prosperous and more numerous than your fathers."
> *Then [He] will open your heart and the heart of your offspring* to love [Him]with all your heart and soul so that you may live. [He] will inflict all those curses on your enemies and foes. . . . You, however, will again heed the Lord and obey all His commandments." And [He] will grant you abounding prosperity inall your undertakings. . . . For the Lord will again delight in your well-being . . . since you will be heeding [Him] and keeping His commandments and laws . . . once you return to [Him] with all your heart and soul.

> Note D–148: Comment D–39 discusses this passage in relation to human free will in the Torah.

Moses now entreats the people to consider the essential ease of comprehending and obeying the "commandment" (JPS1/RSV) or "Instruction" (JPS2) (from hamitzvah hazeh), which he enjoins on Israel this day (Deut. 30:11–14). It is neither "too baffling for you," nor "beyond reach" (30:11).

The eloquence of the man who once required his brother to speak for him (Exod. 4:10–17) then reaches new heights (30:12–14).

> Note D–149: Moses' words are indeed worthy of a Jeremiah, to whom Friedman and others attribute them (see Comment D–38 pt. 3).

It is not in the heavens, that you should say, "Who among us can go up to the heavens and get it for us and impart it to us, that we may observe it?" Neither is it beyond the sea that you should say, "Who among us can cross to the other side of the sea and get it for us and impart it to us, that we may observe it?" No the thing is very close to you in your mouth and in your heart, to observe it.

With continuing eloquence Moses, closes his third and final discourse by summarizing Israel's choices:

> See, I set before you this day life and prosperity, death and adversity. For I command you this day, to love the Lord your God, to walk in His ways, and to keep [all His laws and commands], that you may thrive and increase, and [be blessed] in the land you are about to invade and occupy. But if your heart turns away and you . . . are lured into the worship and service of other gods . . . you shall certainly perish. . . . I call on heaven and earth to witness against you this day: I have put before you life and death, blessing and curse. *Choose life*—if you and your offspring would live—by loving the Lord your God, heeding His commands, and holding fast to Him. [Thus] you shall have life and shall long endure upon the soil that the Lord your God swore to Abraham, Isaac and Jacob to give to them. (30:15–20)

Comment D–39. On a humanist view of human free will in the Torah from the further perspective of Deut. 30

Previous discussions of human free will in the Torah, as derived from the J and P sources, are found in Comments G–8, 9; E–15, 21, 22, 29 pt. 2, 30, 31, and 32. The Comments in Genesis relate to the mythological origins of human free will in J's story of Adam and Eve and the tree of knowledge of good and bad (Gen. 2:15–3:24). The Comments on P and J passages in Exodus relate to the nature of the Lord God's manipulation of the hearts of Pharoah and his people. The central issue addressed in the Exodus Comments is the intended nature of the manipulation. As the Comments reveal, the choice was between (1) the Lord God's actual displacement of Pharoah's contrary will by His own and (2) His manipulation of external events, knowing how Pharoah would respond through the operation of his own will.

As to the eagerness of Egyptians to cede their most valuable possessions to the Israelites, I concluded that their willingness to do so emanated freely from their respect for a people whose God possessed such powers. That is to say, they had reacted to external events through their own free will (see Comment E–31, final par.). As to Pharoah's "hardened" heart, I noted a consistent difference between J and P as proponents, respectively, of (1) independent human free will and (2) the Lord God's power to supercede human free will through "internal" intrusion. After resifting of the "evidence," I reached the following "nonconclusion": "Whether, or how, the tensions between J and P/R are ever resolved must remain a matter of central interest in any humanistic approach to the Torah." But now, having experienced the interplay throughout the Torah between Israel and the Lord, its God, I finally sense the triumph of J.

Consider the following verses: "I have put before you life and death, blessing and curse. *Choose life*—if you and your offspring would live" (30:19). Given the Torah's dire consequences from making the wrong choice, this would seem to be less than a free choice. But metaphorically, it is the choice that human beings face each day in weighing their transient pleasures against the long-term worth of their lives on earth. How often do we understand the cumulative harm of too many wrong choices, yet how often do we freely make them?

That "the Lord your God will open up your heart" then completes the Torah's great metaphor of human free will. It tells us that our own conscience can direct our free will in revaluing our priorities and in guiding our future choices by a resolve to attain our highest human worth.

In Deut. 31:1–8 Moses prepares the Israelites for his own pending death and Joshua's succession to his role.

> Moses went and spoke these things to all Israel. He said to them: I am now one hundred and twenty years old, I can no longer be active. Moreover the Lord has said to me, "You shall not go across yonder Jordan." [He] Himself will cross over at your head; and He will wipe out those nations from your path and you shall dispossess them.—Joshua is the one who shall cross at your head, as the Lord has spoken."
> The Lord will [wipe them out as He did the countries of Sihon and Og]. The Lord will deliver them up to you, and you shall deal with them in full accordance with the Instruction that I have enjoined upon you. Be strong and resolute . . . the Lord your God . . . will not fail or forsake you. (31:1–6)

> *Note D–150: Recall that Moses had not easily acquiesced in the Lord's decision to deny him entry to Canaan (see Deut. 3:23–29, in which Moses tells the people of the Lord's "wrathful" rejection of his prayer to "cross over and see the good land on the other side of the Jordan"). Among the most immediate of the "Instructions" would be those of Deut. 7:1–5. There the Israelites are forbidden to intermarry with the nations of Canaan. They are further commanded to destroy all vestiges of the worship of other gods and to "doom [those nations] to destruction."*

In Deut. 31:7–8 Moses speaks directly to Joshua "in the sight of all Israel." As he had sought to infuse the people with complete confidence in their mission, so, too, does he now seek to strengthen Joshua's resolve. "Be bold and resolute for it is you who shall go with the people into the land . . . and . . . who shall apportion it to them. And the Lord Himself will go before you. . . . He will not fail or forsake you. Fear not and be not dismayed."

> Note D–151: In speaking to Joshua, Moses may have recalled his own doubts of his ability to free Israel from the yoke of Pharoah and then to lead it to the border of Canaan (Exod. 4). (For this, however, he would have had to return to his origins in J and E.)

Thereafter, "Moses wrote down this Teaching and gave it to the priests, sons of Levi, who carried the Ark of the Lord's Covenant, and to all the elders of Israel" (31:9).

> Note D–152: That "this Teaching" continues to refer to that of Deuteronomy alone is evident in the reference to "the priests, sons of Levi." Still absent from Deuteronomy's Code of Law are the Aaronide priests of Exodus and Leviticus, that is, "the sons of Aaron" (see Comment D–24 and Notes D–51 and 61).

In Deut. 31:10–13, Moses gives new emphasis to the importance of the people's direct knowledge of the Teaching:

Every seventh year, the year set for remission, at the Feast of Booth, when all Israel comes to appear before the Lord your God in the place which He will choose, you shall read this Teaching aloud in the presence of all Israel. (31:10–11)

Not only are "men, women and children" to attend, but also the "strangers in your communities," so that all "may hear and learn to revere the Lord your God and to observe faithfully *every word* of this Teaching." Their children, too, who have not had the experience, shall hear and learn to revere the Lord your God" (31:12–13). (On debt remission in Deuteronomy, see 15:1–3.)

> Note D–153: Consistent with the Deuteronomic view of a wider and more accessible priesthood of all Levites is the present emphasis on "every word" of the "Teaching" as the heritage of all Israel. Whatever the priests should know, the people should know. Nevertheless, this particular device for bringing the Teaching to the people is at most symbolic. While formal rituals of token compliance may have been instituted, they could hardly have included the futile self-defeating literal requirements of the command. But as a metaphor for emphasizing the importance of "universal" personal knowledge, the "reading" serves its purpose well.

Now, as instructed by the Lord, "Moses and Joshua went and presented themselves at the Tent of Meeting." The Lord then "appeared in the Tent, in a pillar of cloud, the pillar of cloud having come to rest at the entrance of the tent" (31:14–15).

> *Note D–154: Compare these references to the Tent of Meeting with Exod. 33:7–11. They come straight from the tradition of E, to whom the much later Tabernacle would have been an anathema. This passage, like the general absence of the Aaronide priesthood, provides added evidence of the "northern" orientation of much of Deuteronomy.*

In Deut. 31:16–18 the Lord tells Moses of Israel's fate following his death.

> You are soon to lie with your fathers. The people will *thereupon* go astray after the alien gods in their midst . . . they will forsake Me and break My covenant. . . . Then My anger will flare up against them, and I will abandon them and hide My countenance from them. They shall be ready prey; and many evils and troubles shall befall them. And they shall say . . . "Surely it is because our God is not in our midst. . . ." Yet I will keep My countenance hidden on that day, because of all the evil they have done in turning to other gods.

> *Note D–155: The Lord's own certainty of "evils and troubles" may have come from prescience, but the author's knowledge more likely came from experience. What could account for Israel's earlier fall to the Assyrians and the later conquest of Judah by Babylon? A basic "Teaching" of the entire Torah is that Israel's fate rests within itself, and that the fruit of disobedience is disaster. Consider, then, the irony in the Lord's attribution of the coming disaster to the death and absence of Moses—a death which He Himself has contrived. As JPS2 puts the matter, it is only when Moses has left them that the people will "thereupon" go astray (31:16). RSV and (to a lesser degree) JPS1 also suggest causality between the events.*

The Lord then tells Moses what he must yet do before dying to deal with Israel's pending apostasy (31:19–22).

> Therefore *write down this poem* and teach it to the people . . . that [it] may be My witness against [them]. When I bring them into the land flowing with milk and honey . . . and they eat their fill and grow fat and turn to other gods to serve them, spurning Me and breaking My covenant, and the many evils and troubles befall them—then this poem shall confront them as a witness. . . . For I know what plans they are devising now, before I bring them into the land that I promised on oath. That day, Moses wrote down this poem and taught it to the Israelites.

Comment D–40A. On the possible author of the "Song of Moses," as revealed in Deut. 31:16–22

To whom do these verses mean to assign authorship of Moses' recitation. And is it to be a "poem" or a "song"? The relevant Hebrew text of 31:19 is *v'ahtah kitvoo lahchem eht hahsherah hahzoht*. In having Moses "*write down this poem*" JPS2 envisions the recordation of a precomposed poem rather than the authorship of a new poem. JPS1 can also be read to suggest the Lord as author (although of a "song" rather than a poem): "Now therefore write ye *this* song *for you*." While JPS1's use of "this" also seems to refer to a pre-composed song, the absence of "down" leaves open the possibility of an inspired "inner" revelation. In effect, RSV repeats JPS1: "Now therefore write this song."

As quoted above, JPS2 also reads 31:22 to the effect that "Moses wrote *down* this poem and taught it to the Israelites." By omitting "down" in 31:22 as well as 31:19, JPS1/RSV add a bit uncertainty regarding their intent to ascribe the poem to the Lord, rather than to Moses. (The Hebrew of 31:22 is *vah yichtov moshe ayt-hasheerah hazoht*.) Nevertheless, whether by direct revelation or inspiration, the author would seem to present the poem, or song, as the Lord's handiwork.

It would seem from JPS2's rendering of Deut. 31:23 that the Lord now speaks directly to Joshua to reinforce Moses' earlier words of assurance in 31:7–8: "And He charged Joshua son of Nun: Be strong and resolute: for you shall bring the Israelites into the land which I promised them on oath, and I will be with you."

> Note D–156: *JPS1 states "And he [clearly Moses] gave Joshua the son of Nun a charge." To the contrary, RSV reads "And the Lord commissioned Joshua . . . and said." The differences highlight the frequent difficulties encountered in identifying the speaker in these later chapters. Rashi observes that "[this verse] refers back to the Divine Presence (v.14)"[28] The words are from* vahy'tzahn et-y'hohshuah bin-nun.

Deut. 31:24–26 picks up from 31:9, in which Moses "wrote down this Teaching and gave it to the priests, the sons of Levi, who carried the Ark of the Lord's Covenant." Moses now charges the Levites to "take this book of Teaching and place it in the Ark of the Covenant . . . and let it remain there as a witness against you."

With no transition to signal a change, Moses now speaks to all the people in Deut. 31:27–29. His words are meant to prepare them for the poem, or song, that follows as "[the Lord's] witness against the people of Israel" (see 31:19).

Well I know how defiant and stiffnecked you are: even now, while I am alive and in your midst . . . how much more, then, when I am dead! Gather to me all the elders of your tribes and your officials, that I may speak all these words to them and that I may call heaven and earth to witness against them. For I know that when I am dead, you will act wickedly and turn away from the path which I enjoined upon you, and in time misfortune will befall you [for having angered the Lord].

> Note D–157: *Whether Moses speaks from anger or despair is not clear. The Lord has told him that his loss through death will bring "evils and troubles" to the people. Would his continuing leadership have averted the pending disaster? If so, why must He die now—and for so poor a reason? (See Comments N–22 and D–1.)*

"Then Moses recited the words of this poem to the very end, in the hearing of [all] Israel" (31:30).

> Note D–158: *The song, or poem, itself (32:1–43) is too long to set out verbatim. Yet, its rich poetic allusions (like those of the blessings and, even more so, the curses) should be savored in a reading. To provide a flavor of its poetry (whose richness is soon exceeded by the verses that follow), I quote the initial verses:*

Give ear, O heavens, let me speak;/ Let the earth hear the words I utter!/ May my discourse come down as the rain,/ My speech distill as the dew,/ Like showers on young growth,/ Like droplets on the grass./ For the name of the Lord I proclaim; give glory to our God!" (32:1–3)

Verses 4–6 tell of the perfection of God, "the Rock," and the baseness of Israel. He is presented as "perfect," "just," "faithful," "true," and "upright." In contrast, His "unworthy children" have "played Him false." He has been thus requited by a "crooked and twisted generation." This "dull and witless people" has forgotten that He is the Father who created them and fashioned them to endure.

Verses 7–9 draw on Israel's collective memory to recall how the Lord had first singled Israel out from the other nations and peoples. "Ask your father, he will inform you,/ Your elders, they will tell you"—that is, of how the "Most High" had "[given] nations their home," established "divisions of man" and fixed national boundaries "in relation to Israel's numbers." For Himself, the Lord took Israel as "His people" and Jacob as "His own allotment."

Verses 10–12 purport to give further details on the Lord's discovery of the early Israelites. Having found them (i.e., Jacob's line) "in a desert region," in "an empty howling waste," He proceeded to guard and guide them—much like the eagle that protects and guides its growing nestlings. This He did "alone," with "no alien god at His side."

Note D–159: I use "purport" because of this remarkable deviance from the Lord's traditional "calling" of Abraham to be the father of Israel.

Verses 13–15 tell of the abundance that the people knew under the Lord's protective guidance. From "atop the highlands" they "feast[ed] on the yield of the earth," with "honey . . . oil . . . curd of kine and milk of flocks . . . the best of lambs and rams, Bulls of Bashan and he-goats . . . the very finest wheat," along with "foaming grape-blood" to drink."

Verses 16–18 tell of the consequences of their good and easy life. "Jeshurun [i.e., Israel] grew fat and kicked." Having become "fat and gross and coarse," it "forsook . . . God . . . and spurned the Rock of his support." The people incensed their God with "alien things" and "abominations." They sacrificed not only to "demons" and "no-gods, but to "gods they had never known," to "new ones who came but lately." and who "stirred not your fathers' fears."

Verses 19–25 describe the Lord's wrathful response—in words and deeds— to what He sees as Israel's base perfidy. He "spurned his sons and daughters" and resolved to "hide His countenance from them." He saw them as "a treacherous breed . . . with no loyalty in them" (32:19–20). Just as they "incensed" Him with their "no-gods," so would He "incense" them with "a no-folk" (i.e., perhaps, with foes so cruel as to seem less than human) (32:21).

"For a fire that [had] flared in [His] wrath and burned to the bottom of Sheol," He will "sweep misfortunes" on Israel. Their lot shall be "wasting famine, ravaging plague, deadly pestilence and fanged beasts . . . to youth and maiden alike, the suckling as well as the aged" (32:22–25).

In verses 26–27, He considers the constraints that prevent Him from obliterating the Israelites, that is, from making "their memory cease among men." At first they are more a function of Lordly pride than Godly compassion. It is "for fear of the taunts of the foe, their enemies who might misjudge and say 'Our own hand has prevailed; none of this was wrought by the Lord.' "

In verses 28–31, He describes Israel's foes as "a folk void of sense, lacking in all discernment." Their fault is in their failure to grasp the reality (as known to the Lord) behind Israel's utter rout. Thus, "how could one have routed a thousand, or two put ten thousand to flight, unless their Rock had sold them [i.e., sold them out], the Lord had given them up? For *their rock* is not like *our Rock*."

Verses 32–35 proceeds as a segue toward Israel's ultimate "vindication." It is now fueled not by the Lord's greater love of Israel but by His greater contempt for its foes. "Ah, The vine for them is from Sodom, From the vineyards of Gomorrah . . . the venom of asps . . . the pitiless poison of vipers." The Lord will seal it all in "[His] storehouses." It will be His "vengeance and recompense, at the time that their foot falters." He declares "their day of disaster is near, and destiny rushes upon them."

In verses 36–43 the Lord's previous wrath gives way to what might appear to be a fundamentally irrepressible love of His people, unrequited though it may be. Thus, though lacking evidence of Israel's repentance, the Lord cannot rid Himself of hope. Indeed, so strong is His hope and expectation of repentance, that He speaks as if redemption were but a formality: "For the Lord will vindicate His people, and take revenge for His servants, when He sees that their might is gone, and neither bond nor free is left" (32:36).

In verses 37–38, the Lord gleans pleasure from what Israel will have learned about the utter futility of worshipping the ineffectual gods of their neighbors. With effusive sarcasm, He will ask, "Where are their gods, the rock in whom they sought refuge? Who ate the fat of their offerings and drank their libation wine? Let them come up to your help, and let them be a shield unto you!"

To conclude, in verses 39–43 the Lord vividly contrasts His own power with the fecklessness of all other gods.

"See, then, that I, I am He; there is no other god beside Me" (32:39a).

> Note D–160: The phrase "no other god beside Me" suggests the ahl panahyah of the Second Commandment (Exod. 20:3, Deut. 5:7). Here, however, the Hebrew is ain elohim imahdee. While RSV joins JPS2 in "no other god beside Me," JPS1 may better express the Lord's meaning with "there is no other god with Me." In context the Lord's likely point is that "I wield My power without need for aid from any other god.

He then continues: "I deal death and give life . . . none can deliver from My hand. . . . When I whet My flashing blade, and My hand lays hold on judgment, vengeance will I wreak on My foes, will I deal to those who reject Me. . . . I will make drunk My arrows with blood . . . Blood of the slain and the captive, from the long-haired enemy chiefs" (32:39b–42).

And finally, He speaks of His people. "O nations, acclaim His people! For He'll avenge the blood of His servants, wreak vengeance on His foes, and cleanse the land of His people" (32:43).

> Note D–161: Again the Lord is spirited away by His power. But given the historical context of the Song (see Comments D–40A and B), we can excuse Him for His need to restore Israel's morale and renew its hope. In any case, the final phrase is disturbingly ambiguous, with its possible suggestion that the land is to be cleansed of "His people." However, "of His people" merely describes the land to be cleansed for His people's use.

And so, with Hosea (i.e., Joshua) son of Nun, "Moses . . . recited all the words of this poem in the hearing of the people" (32:43). After doing so, Moses explained to the people the significance of all he had said:

Take to heart all the words which I have warned you this day." Enjoin them upon your children, that they may observe . . . this Teaching. For this is not a trifling thing . . . it is your very life; through it you shall long endure on the land which you are to occupy upon crossing the Jordan. (32:45–47)

Comment D–40B. On the possible author of the "Song of Moses," as revealed in the Song itself

Nothing in the words of the song, or poem, warrants altering the general conclusion of Comment D–40A that the Lord is meant to be identified as its author, whether by revelation or inspiration. Further support (of a different sort) for the Lord's creative role is found in its obvious references to the Babylonian conquest of Judah. Lacking the Lord's prescience, Moses could not have known of it in c.1300.

Such a contention, however, ignores the psychological insights of Jeremiah, as the putative author. He would not have expected his readers to assume that the song's many allusions to an "armageddon" were intended to describe the Babylonian conquest and ensuing exile. Rather, he would hope they might discern the obvious parallels in the events described. As written, therefore, the Song of Moses required neither human nor Godly prescience. In any case, I would be remiss not to note that traditional commentators attribute the "Song of Moses" to Moses himself.[29]

Deut. 32 closes with the imminent fulfillment of the Lord's sadly enigmatic decree regarding Moses.

That very day the Lord spoke to Moses. Ascend these heights of Abarim to Mount Nebo, which is in the land of Moab facing Jericho, and view the land of Canaan. . . . You shall die on the mountain . . . and shall be gathered to your kin, as your brother Aaron died on Mount Hor and was gathered to His kin: for you both broke faith with Me among the Israelite people, at the waters of Meribath-kadesh in the wilderness of Zin, by failing to uphold My sanctity among the Israelite people. You may view the land from a distance, but you shall not enter it. (32:48–52)

Note D–162: After noting that Deut. 32:48–52 repeats Num. 27:12–14, Friedman attributes it to R. His conclusion finds support in Deut. 10:6–7, in which D mentions Moserah, rather than Mount Hor, as the site of Aaron's death (see Comment D–24 and Notes D–50 and 61). As for the events at Meribah as the Lord's reason for denying Moses entry into Canaan, see Comments N–22 and 33. The death of Moses is discussed in Comment D–42.

Deut. 33 continues with the blessing of Moses on Israel's twelve tribes.

Note D–163: The source of the blessings is quickly brought into question by this first and sole appearance of Sinai in Deuteronomy (i.e., in place of Horeb) (33:2). Despite differences in time and place, the individual tribal blessings of Moses can be compared to those of Jacob (see Gen. 49 and Comment G–99).

The blessings, as such, are preceded by an encomium to the Lord from Moses, now identified as *"the* man of God" (33:1–5). They are followed by the vision of an idyllic relationship between Israel and its God (33:26–29).

First, the introduction:

This is the blessing with which Moses, the man of God, bade the Israelites farewell before he died. He said: The Lord came from Sinai . . . [to] Seir . . . [to] Mount Paran . . . [to] Riboboth-kodesh, Lightning flashing at them from His right./ Lover, indeed, of the people,/ their hallowed are all in Your hand./ They followed in your steps, Accepting your pronouncements, *When Moses charged us with the teaching*/ As the heritage of the congregation of Jacob./ Then He became King in Jeshurun [i.e., Israel],/ When the heads of the people assembled,/ The tribes of Israel together.

Note D–164: The sudden third-person reference to Moses, by Moses, casts doubt on who is speaking. Overall, Plaut characterizes verses 3–5 as "evidently a corrupt text."[30]

Now compare the vivid curses of Deut. 28 (as likely related to the destruction of the two kingdoms in c. 722 and 586 B.C.E.) to the sublimity that marks the close of Deut. 33:

O Jeshurun, there is none like God,/ Riding through the heavens to help you,/ Through the skies in His majesty. The ancient God is a refuge,/ A support are the arms everlasting./ He drove out the enemy before you./ By His command: Destroy!/ *Thus Israel dwells in safety, Untroubled in Jacob's abode,* In a land of grain and wine,/ Under heavens dripping dew./ O happy Israel! Who is like you,/ A people delivered by the Lord,/ Your protecting Shield, your Sword triumphant!/ Your enemies shall come cringing before you,/ And you shall tread on their backs.

At the core of Deut. 33 are the blessings of Moses.

Reuben—"May Reuben live and not die, Though few be his numbers" (33:6).

Note D–165: Cf. Gen. 49:3–4. As compared to "Jacob's" impassioned denunciation of Reuben, Moses is totally nonjudgmental. His simple wish (or blessing) is that the tribe of Reuben should survive despite its declining numbers.

Judah—"Hear, O Lord, the voice of Judah, And restore him to his people, Though his own hands strive for him, Help him against his foes" (33:7).

> Note D–166: Cf. Gen. 49:9–12. As for Judah, Jacob's passions were directed to praise for a son whose tribe, as a reflection of his character, was destined to rule. In his own essentially nonjudgmental view of Judah, however, Moses foresees that the tribe will be hard pressed by its foes and needful of help from others. Clearly, the author of Deut. 33 viewed the tribe of Judah at a different time, and under different circumstances, than J.

Levi—"Let your Thummin and Urim Be with your faithful one, Whom you tested at Massah, Challenged at the waters of Meribah; Who said of his father and mother, 'I consider them not.' His brothers he disregarded, Ignored his own children. Your precepts alone they observed, And kept your covenant. They shall teach your norms to Jacob, And Your instructions to Israel. They shall offer You incense to savor, And whole offerings on Your altar. Bless, O Lord, his substance, And favor his undertakings. Smite the loins of his foes; Let his enemies rise no more" (33:8–11).

> Note D–167: Cf. Gen. 49:5–7, in which Jacob condemns Levi and Simeon alike for the events at Shechem and foresees their being divided and scattered. In total contrast is the present author's fulsome praise of the tribe of Levi for placing its love of the Lord above all other conflicting concerns. Here, before the confusion wrought by P's Aaronide priesthood, the adult males of the tribe of Levi were Israel's priesthood (as in the Code of Holiness).

Benjamin—"Beloved of the Lord, He rests securely beside Him; ever does He protect him, As he rests between his shoulders" (33:12).

> Note D–168: Cf. Gen. 49:27, in which Jacob speaks only of the tribe's fighting prowess. Because Benjamin was a southerly tribe adjoining Judah, the special characterization of the tribe as "Beloved of the Lord" counters the possibly northern "bias" of the blessing on Levi. Of particular interest is why Benjamin should be so at peace while Judah is said to be threatened.

Joseph—"Blessed of the Lord be his land, With the bounty of dew from heaven, and of the deep that crouches below; With the bounteous yield of the sun, And the bounteous crop of the moons; With the best from the ancient mountains, And the bounty of hills immemorial; With the bounty of earth and its fulness, And the favor of the Presence in the bush. May these rest on the head of Joseph, On the crown of the elect of his brothers. Like a firstling bull in his majesty, He has horns like the horns of the wild ox; with them he gores the people, The ends of the earth one and all. *These are the myriads of Ephraim, these are the thousands of Manasseh"* (33:13–17).

> Note D–169: Cf. Gen. 49:22–26, in which Jacob concludes his praise of Joseph with the appellation "the elect of his brothers." And so, too, does Moses name Joseph "the elect of his brothers." Thus far, no characterization of a tribe or its founder in the blessings of Jacob and Moses is so consistent in evaluation and description. Moses alone, however, identifies Ephraim, the dominant northern tribe, and Manasseh, as sons and heirs of the Joseph/Jacob legacy.

Zebulun and Issachar—"Rejoice, O Zebulun, on your journeys, And Issachar, in your tents. They invite their kin to the mountain, Where they offer sacrifices of success. For they draw from the riches of the sea, And the hidden hoards of the sand" (33:18–19).

> Note D–170: Cf. Gen. 49:13–15. Zebulun's lands by the sea and Issachar's agricultural lands are similar in the two blessings, but Moses puts more emphasis on their wealth.

Gad—"Blessed be He who enlarges Gad. Poised is he like a lion, To tear off arm and scalp. He chose for himself the best, For there is the portion of the revered chieftain, Where the heads of people come. He executed the Lord's judgment, And His decisions for Israel."

> Note D–171: Cf. Gen. 49:19. As with Joseph, the blessings for Gad are basically in accord. Both portray Gad as a strong tribe under pressure, but well able to deal with its foes and command respect.

Dan—"Dan is a lion's whelp that leaps forth from Bashan" (33:22).

> Note D–172: Cf. Gen. 49:16–18. Although Jacob described Judah as a "lion's whelp," this author deemed the term more suited to Dan. Whether as Moses' "lion's whelp," or Jacob's "serpent by the road," or "viper by the path," Dan is described by both as a tribe capable of striking its foes fast and hard. Yet Moses, unlike Jacob, does not see Dan as "a [tribal] judge of Israel."

Asher—"Most blessed of sons be Asher; May he be the favorite of his brothers, May he dip his foot in oil, May your doorbolts be iron and copper, And your security last all your days" (33:24–25).

> Note D–173: Cf. Gen. 49:20. While Jacob anticipates Asher's prosperity, it is the subject of Moses' most earnest wishes, together with security. Presumably, Moses' wish that Asher be "the favorite of his brothers" is not meant to displace Joseph as "the elect of his brothers."

Simeon—For Simeon there is no wish, no blessing and no description. It is as if Simeon's tribe will have vanished.

> Note D–174: Cf. Gen. 49:5–7. In the context of Jacob's assessment of Simeon, the tribe's disappearance might seem fully deserved as an act of Godly retribution. But Jacob's castigation of Simeon was directed in identical words to Levi, so much beloved in Moses' blessing. Accordingly, we must attribute Simeon's tribal disappearance to factors other than the moral and ethical failings of its founder.
>
> It is widely accepted that after Israel's entry into Canaan the tribe of Simeon was gradually forced southward. In time the tribe was largely merged into Judah, while other remnants remigrated to the north. But the time at which it would have become so scattered as to lose its independent identity is historically uncertain.

Comment D–41. On the authorship and time of the Blessing of Moses

In confessing that I have no definitive answer to the time and authorship of the Blessing of Moses, I can plead in mitigation the varying views of life-long Biblical scholars. A case in point is whether the whole of Deut. 33 comes from a single source and time. Particularly in question is whether the opening and concluding verses (33:2–5 and 33:26–29) are from the same source as the core blessings.

Consider the following rather distinctive views.

33:2–5, 26–29. Almost certainly . . . [these] two elements of the poem were originally separate, the framework being taken from a psalm celebrating the kingship and triumphant power of the Lord God. . . . It must be of pre-exilic origin, but . . . unlikely . . . earlier than the building of the Jerusalem Temple.[31]

Because verses 2–5 and 26–29 contain no blessings, some scholars have suggested that these phrases did not originally form a part of the text. However, as in a covenant (on which the blessings are ultimately founded), an exordium and a matching conclusion are necessary. They frame the main text perfectly, and there is no convincing reason to suppose them to be later additions.[32]

The mood of well-being in the introduction and conclusion is not so different from the overall tenor of the blessings as to preclude the possibility of a single source. Conversely, however, the fact that Deut. 33 conforms to a prevailing literary structure does not preclude the possibility of the later addition of an introduction and conclusion. Thus, a final answer is not easily reached.

The matter of source is best approached by considering the actual blessings. The most striking differences in the blessings of Jacob and Moses involve those for Judah, Levi, Benjamin, Asher, and Simeon. Comparisons, of course, are inevitably affected by the facts of Jacob's passionate judgments of his sons and Moses' relatively objective views of the tribes. Yet, a pattern emerges.

Judah, the most praiseworthy of Jacob's sons (together with Joseph), who is destined to hold the "scepter" and the "ruler's staff" in Jerusalem, is described by Moses as a weakened tribe dependent on others.

Levi, together with Simeon, the most excoriated of Jacob's sons, is elevated by Moses to the priesthood of all Israel. His tribe becomes, in essence, the northern priesthood of Deuteronomy and the Kingdom of Israel, centered in Shiloh.

Benjamin, the "ravenous wolf" of Jacob, who consumes "the foe," is seen by Moses not as a tribe forever at war but as the "Beloved of the Lord," who does "ever protect him." This could well reflect the close premonarchical relations that were said to have developed between Benjamin and Ephraim, the dominant tribe of the north.[33]

Jacob's blessing of Ephraim is totally subsumed in his blessing for Joseph, in which neither Ephraim nor Manasseh, both prominent in the north, are separately mentioned. However, while Joseph is accorded no less praise by Moses than by Jacob, only Moses extols the legacy of Joseph in "the myriads of Ephraim" and "the thousands of Manasseh" (33:17).

Asher, also of the north, though prosperous under Jacob's blessing, is now seen and blessed by Moses as "the favorite of your brothers."

Simeon, of course, has been totally deprived of any continuing identity—perhaps as a consequence of having largely merged into the southern tribe of Judah, now in a hapless state, as described by Moses.

From their substance, therefore, may we not presume that the Blessings of Moses come from forerunners of E, with a clearly northern perspective?

The remaining question is when.

In theory, the main clues might come from Simeon and Judah. As for Simeon, however, there is no is fixed date to mark its "final" loss of identity. Nor is it known how much time may have elapsed between such loss and the writing of the blessings. Indeed, the implied extinction of Simeon may even have been a perjorative comment by northern authors on its close affiliation with Judah.

Judah, however, may offer a better basis for a time estimation. If the blessings were indeed by the forerunners of E, they were likely written amid the growing rivalries between the north and south during the tenth century B.C.E. Even more significant in the earlier Davidic portion of the century, however, was Judah's prolonged inability to dislodge the Jebusites, Hivites and other Canaanite tribes from the south. It was only after David took Jerusalem from the Jebusites and repulsed the Philistines that Judah began to rise to its later prominence as the site of the Temple.

David, of course, was himself a Judahite, whose removal of the sacred Ark of Shiloh to Jerusalem hardly endeared him to the northern priests. But more to the point, in the early tenth century B.C.E. the author of the blessings had a good factual basis for citing Judah's weakness, isolation and dependency.

To conclude, however, that the Blessings of Moses were written from a "northern" perspective by forerunners of E is to reopen the matter of the single authorship of Deut. 33. The problem, of course, is the sole "Deuteronomic" use of "Sinai" in 33:2, with its implications of a "southern" perspective (reflecting its use by J and P). We might wonder, therefore, if it was not R who added suitable psalmic verses to introduce and conclude the blessings. R's joinder of "northern" and "southern" materials in a single passage would be but one of many such countless joinders that, together, came to shape the entire Torah.

The Torah now concludes with the twelve verses of Deut. 34 that mark the death of Moses.

From the "steppes of Moab" Moses climbed to "Mount Nebo, to the summit of Pisgah, opposite Jericho." From there the Lord showed him the "whole land: Gilead as far as Dan; all Naphtali, the land of Ephraim and Manasseh; the whole of Judah as far as the Western Sea; the Negeb; and the Plain—the valley of Jericho, the city of palm trees—as far as Zoar" (34:1–3).

There the Lord assures him that as He had sworn to the patriarchs, "I will give it to your offspring." But as for Moses, himself, He adds, "I have let you see it with your own eyes, but you shall not cross there" (34:4).

"So Moses the servant of the Lord died there, in the land of Moab, *at the command of the Lord*" (34:5). *The Lord* then buried him "in the land of Moab, near Beth-Peor; and no one knows his burial place *to this day*" (34:6). When he died, Moses was "a hundred and twenty years old; *his eyes were undimmed and his vigor unabated*" (34:7). The "wailing and mourning" for Moses by the Israelites in the steppes of Moab continued for thirty days (34:8). Upon the death of Moses, and because "Moses had laid his hands on him," Joshua son of Nun "was filled with the spirit of wisdom." The Israelites then "heeded" him, "as the Lord had commanded Moses" (34:9).

The Torah then ends with a final eulogy to the greatest of the Israelites— but in terms which inadequately honor his fundamental human qualities, as revealed throughout the Torah:

Never again did there arise in Israel a prophet like Moses—whom the Lord singled out [or knew (y'dahoh)] face to face, for the various signs and portents that the Lord sent him to display in the land of Egypt, against Pharoah and all his courtiers and his whole country, and for all the great might and awesome power that Moses displayed before all Israel. (34:10–12)

Comment D–42. On the death of Moses

With its customary candor, the Torah reveals the death of Moses as a deliberate, albeit a Divine, killing. Thus he died "at the command of the Lord." Nor was it an act of mercy that after forty incredibly stressful years would at last allow a weary Moses a well-earned rest. To the contrary, "his eyes were undimmed and his vigor unabated." Nor was it to fulfil any other wish of Moses. Had the Lord not abruptly dismissed his plea to "cross over and see the good land on the other side of the Jordan?" (Deut. 3:23–28).

How, then, does the Torah explicitly justify the untimely death of Moses at the command of its own Lord God? It does so by entrapment. By clear implication, under conditions of great travail, it has Moses recall an earlier command to strike his rod on a rock, at a place sometimes known as Meribah, as the means of producing water (Exod. 17:1–7). When Moses then does the same at a second Meribah, contrary to the Lord's artfully contrived instructions, He promptly declares the fate of Moses (and Aaron): "Because you did not trust Me enough to affirm My sanctity in the sight of the Israelite people, therefore, you shall not lead this congregation into the land that I have given them" (Num. 20:2–11).

Surely it was not P's purpose to demean either the Lord or Moses (or Aaron). To that end, P gave the Lord God a just complaint of disobedience and gave Moses the moral justification of an unintended act of disobedience. (See Comment N–22.)

But why would author and redactor unite to bring Moses to a premature and deeply troubling death? Either they were governed by a compelling tradition that denied Moses entry into Canaan, or by a common belief that the unique intensity of the prophetic relationship between Moses and Israel's Lord God had served its purpose.

It is my own sense, however, that just as our journey through the Torah took root in an early myth regarding human free will, so was it meant to end. I thus view the untimely death of Moses as a logical ending to the Torah's most profound morality tale—a tale that began with Adam and Eve in a garden. How better can the Torah remind us of the heavy cost, but of the yet greater potential value to humanity, of the free will acquired in Eden through Eve's curiosity and courage? (See Comments G–4 through 9.)

As J's Lord of Creation II might have put His mythic case, "Through Eve, humanity sought free will, and for the sake of her bravery, I allowed humanity to gain it. But as part of the price of human free will, I decreed death as the inexorable fate of every human being. Accordingly, death can make no concession to human worth. It will come when it will to the most and the least worthy among you." And to this He might have added, "As for the most worthy, who can make My point better than Moses?"

Moses knew of and accepted the pact that had been forged in the Garden of Eden. But how ironic it seems that he must die before completing the very purpose for which he had been called. Yet, when told it had to be, he was never again heard to complain of his own personal price for human free will. Far from succumbing to anger at the Lord God's harsh priority of sanctity over compassion, Moses, in facing death, honored every remaining duty to Israel and to the Lord, its God. And thus, having descended from the great human exemplar that was Abraham, Israel was guided to its destiny by yet another—by Moses, who had faced and surmounted every challenge to body, mind, and spirit known to humankind.

CONCLUSION

PREFACE

We began our inquiry with a question: "What remains of the Torah when we accept that its God exists in the human mind alone, having been created by human authors as the means, *in their time*, of guiding a people toward its highest human ends?" To this we added a final question: In light of our initial answer, how might we now make fuller use of the Torah's humanist roots in pursuit of humanity's highest ends? In seeking answers in the Torah itself, we undertook a detailed reading based on the naturalistic premises of our questions and on modern scholarship regarding the Torah's human origins. Having completed our reading, we can now consider our answers.

ON THE ROLE OF GOD
AS A MEANS OR AN END

Underlying these answers are two distinct views of the Torah's God: that is, as a human end in Himself or as a means of guiding humanity toward its own worthiest ends. (See the final paragraph of Leviticus, p. 346.) In turn, the choice will depend largely on whether He is viewed (1) as a transcendent Being who first chose to reveal Himself and His earthly purposes through the Torah or (2) as the product of human authors whose nature and purposes were shaped and "revealed" by them.

It is premise (1), of course, that impels human beings to sanctify the unique Being of the Torah's God and to establish His will (as it is thought to have been revealed) as the highest human end. Conversely, it is premise (2) that looks to the Torah's God as a means of directing and inspiring humanity toward its own highest ends.

Why, we might ask, would the Torah's human authors have created their

561

God, if not as a means to human ends? Yet, since neither logic nor feeling are wholly immune to each other's demands, a question persists. Could the God of the Torah, as created or recreated, serve as a means to human ends without being viewed in some degree as an end in Himself? And in this question lies the roots of a major doctrinal tension in liberal theistic Judaism today.

ON MODERN VIEWS OF GOD WITHIN LIBERAL JUDAISM AS AIDS IN UNDERSTANDING THE TORAH'S GOD

It is likely to alleviate this tension that Reform and Reconstructionist Judaism, contrary to their reformulated god-ideas, retain the liturgy of transcendence (see introduction part 2). Even as each movement, in its own way, seeks to adapt the Torah's God to modern standards of credibility, they share a common recognition. Absent the liturgy of transcendence that exalts their God(s) above humanity itself, their Godly transformations may satisfy the minds, but not the hearts, of their *theistic* congregants.

Indeed, this perceived need to retain the liturgy of transcendence might be viewed with bemusement by the Torah's authors. Can we not hear them now? "Recreate our God as you will to satisfy human standards of credibility in your time. But you must know that without the imputed power of *our* God, your recreations will never succeed. All efforts to accommodate human rationality by changing the character and attributes of our God must fail in the absence of His emotional sustenance within your congregations."

If such is the case, why do liberal Judaic theistic scholars feel compelled to tinker with Godly transcendence? As suggested above, they do so in response to the force of human logic in the context of humanity's evolving knowledge and experience. Over a span of two and one-half millenia since the Torah's completion, such knowledge and experience sharply challenge the reality of Godly omnipotence, Godly concern, and, indeed, Godly existence. It is the force of these challenges that has compelled liberal theistic Judaism to adapt its concepts of God to new perceptions of reality.[1]

As to Reform Judaism, we might first recall Rabbi Plaut's concession to contemporary standards of reality in the matter of Torah authorship: "God is not the author of the text, the people are."[2] But closer to my present point is Rabbi Plaut's concession to the power of "human freedom" to limit God's presence on earth. It is the holocaust that brings him to the end of Godly omnipotence.

> The Holocaust could not be understood as the monstrous result of putative sins Israel had committed. There remained only one alternative—short of total disbelief or a defiant "Yet I will believe"—and that was to give up the idea of an omnipotent God. *Rather one needed to see Him as limited by human freedom. God*

is hidden as long as the world chooses to be alienated from Him. . . . Not God hides His face, we hide it.[3]

In similar vein, Rabbi Plaut later envisions a "God who suffered and wept with us during the Holocaust."[4] Thus, amid horrors that transcended the powers of his God, Rabbi Plaut would replace His omnipotence with a goodly portion of his own human compassion. In this, however, Rabbi Plaut offers an ironic scenario to explain his God's absence. Rather than responding to the innocent cries of the tortured, his God can only withdraw from the scene of despair. He must thus subordinate His own beneficent will to the depravities of the torturers and the suffering of the tortured.

Only when humanity itself had finally ended the horrors of the holocaust would this scenario allow the return of this tragically ineffectual God. But if He could neither prevent nor end the horrors of the holocaust, what beyond tears can we expect of Him in future tragedies? In truth, just as humanity alone could end the depravity of the holocaust, so must humanity alone deal with all earthly afflictions. And if all humanity were to "know" this truth, might it not rely more fully on its own resources to do so?

My purpose, however, is to understand rather than to demean such well-intended efforts to recreate the Torah's God in images of our own time. To that end I suggest that Rabbi Plaut's evocation of a recreated God of the Torah effectively addresses two needs of liberal theistic Judaism. The first is to recreate a God whose credibility can better withstand current perceptions of reality. The second is to endow Him with qualities appropriate to a God. True to this model, Rabbi Plaut recreates a compassionate God Who must, when challenged, subordinate Himself to a natural order beyond His control.

As a more radical response to questions of credibility, Rabbi Kaplan chose to eliminate God as a Being from the *formal* doctrines of Reconstructionist Judaism. Accordingly, his god-idea was transformed from a "Being" into "forces" or "relationships" that make for "cosmos rather than chaos;" or an inchoate "spirit" that promotes "righteousness." Was it with thoughts of the great Spinoza centuries earlier that Rabbi Kaplan sought to identify his God with nature itself?

But here we must ask, other than the human mind and spirit, what sources of moral and ethical substance can there be for a "god-idea" that is not in itself a "Being?" Except through human values and judgment, how do we distinguish between "cosmos" and "chaos?" And except by human standards how do we identify "relationships," "forces," and "spirits" that promote "righteousness?" In this, Rabbi Kaplan's God seems like an endlessly renewable mass of energy that awaits human direction for beneficial use. (See introduction, p. 31.)

The common dependence of their gods on humanity itself creates a kinship between Rabbi Kaplan's naturalism and Rabbi Plaut's post-holocaust vision of a less than omnipotent god. Taken together, their recreations of the Torah's God shed light on the human processes and purposes through, and for, which the Torah's God was first created.

564

SOME FINAL THOUGHTS ON THE HUMAN CREATION AND RECREATIONS OF THE TORAH'S GOD

To distinguish between a human creation and recreation of a god is not always easy. Every process of original creation is likely to draw on existing models of a god or gods. In turn, a process of recreation may introduce new godly qualities as innovative and portentous as those of the original creation. Consider the impact of Christianity and Islam on the persona and role of the Torah's God.

But consider as well these recreations of the Torah's omnipotent and vengeful God into (1) an impersonal system of naturalistic forces or (2) as a Being reduced to tears as His people are systematically slaughtered by human miscreants. Yet, even as I respect the self-perceived needs and imagery of Rabbis Kaplan and Plaut in recreating god-ideas for our time, I sense that their results were shaped more to satisfy standards of current credibility than eternal reality. Times change, as do human perceptions of reality. But if we are to put our faith in a universal Being common to all humanity, should we not expect greater stability in the essence and reality of His Being?

Yet, there is no unique fault in their efforts. A common aim of godly creation and recreation is to project a Being whose credibility, *in a particular setting*, finds support in existing human knowledge, experience, traditions and needs.[5] But just as we may view the Godly recreations of Rabbis Plaut and Kaplan in these functional terms, so, too, may we view the creation of the Torah's God.

The Torah's God projects a uniquely powerful presence. Yet, withal, it is a composite presence that borrowed (even as it recoiled) from the gods of the Sumerians, Egyptians, Babylonians, Hittites, and Canaanites. A commonality of their "god idea" is described as follows: "All of the ancient Middle Eastern people saw the agency of the gods in every aspect of life and nature. Everything on earth was regarded as a reflex of its prototype in the divine or sacred sphere, such as in the biblical description of the creation of man 'in the image of God'; God was viewed as the primary reality of the universe."[6] And for a striking model of monotheism itself, there was the vision of Amenhotep IV, Egypt's spiritually inventive king of mid-fourteenth century B.C.E.[7]

Nor did the composite nature of the Torah's God result from external sources alone. Beginning with His Name, He emerges as a composite Being drawn from differing internal traditions within early Israel itself. Was He "Elohim," "Yahweh," "El Shaddai," or, as revealed to Moses, "Ehyeh-Asher-Ehyeh"? And what manner of priests did the Torah's God anoint or select to guide His people in the critical task of sustaining His sanctity? Was it Aaron and his sons, as P would have it? Or was it a priesthood of all male Levites, as declared by the levitical priests of Shiloh (and duly recorded by D). And was He a God whom a human being could see and speak with, as portrayed by J (Gen.

18:1–8) and E (Exod. 24:9–11 and 33:7–11)? Or would the sight of Him, or His "face," bring death? (Exod. 33:12–23).[8]

Only persons with an unyielding faith in the reality of the Torah's God as Creator and Ruler of His universe can ignore the compelling evidence of His human origins.[9] Among the liberal Judaic theists who do so, however, how many more rely on tradition rather than faith to sense His Presence? In any case, for liberal theists who do sense the Presence of the Torah's God, a question remains. How would the Lord, as God of Israel, who slew two priestly sons of Aaron for violating His sanctity with an "alien fire," view their successors who openly deny the omnipotence from which His sanctity first derived? (See Lev. 10.)

In one of two ways, the question answers itself. As a tenet of faith within doctrinal orthodoxy, He remains omnipotent and unchanged. Although he may choose at will to manifest, or not manifest, particular attributes at any given time, His essence never changes. But absent such faith, logic suggests that such an omnipotent Being never existed—except as a human construct that must forever be readapted to evolving standards of human credibility.

I must agree, however, that to view the *Torah's* God as a human construct says nothing of the possible existence of some other purposeful transcendent Being. But were there such a Being other than the Torah's God, its existence alone would tell us nothing of its import for humanity. Whatever that import, however, the very existence of such a hitherto unknown Being, once established as true, would shake the doctrinal foundations of Judaism, Christianity, and Islam. In that the issue does not bear on the Torah's God, as such, I need add nothing to my earlier comments on the general subject.[10] Instead, we must finally turn to our unanswered questions. What remains of the Torah today when we view its God as a human construct created by humans as a means to human ends? And how might we use the Torah's humanist roots more fully in pursuing those ends?

WHAT REMAINS OF THE TORAH WHEN WE VIEW ITS GOD AS THE MEANS CREATED BY HUMAN AUTHORS TO SERVE HUMAN ENDS?

In viewing the Torah's God as a human construct, we at once eliminate any need for the rituals and paraphenalia of Godly sanctification and human obeisance. Their apotheosis was found in the Torah's arcane sacrificial system, with its core in Leviticus. As was inevitable before long in Israel's evolution, what remained of the entire system ended with the destruction of the Second Temple in 70 B.C.E.

Other quasi-ritualistic practices, however, which include mandatory expressions of obeisance to the Torah's God, also foster human sentiments that greatly enrich the ethos, traditions and worthiness of a people. Prominent among them were the festivals. In keeping with the protocols of the Torah, the festivals necessarily arose from Godly commands. But even without the imprimatur of its God, Judaism would have done well to honor their human origins. Together, the Torah's festivals reflect human impulses that enshrine some of the worthiest themes of human existence into Israel's communal spirit. We have considered them in Comments L–52, D–22 and Numbers 28 and 29 (see pp. 424–28). To recall their essence, I repeat some thoughts from Comment L–52.

> In discussing Israel's "spiritual character," as expressed in Lev. 23, I do not refer to that aspect of "spirituality" that bears on Israel's relations with its God. Instead, I refer to qualities of communal character that P/h may have sought to foster through the authority of its God. In speaking of Israel's "spiritual character," therefore, I refer to its ethos—that is, "the fundamental character or spirit of a culture, the underlying sentiment that informs the beliefs, customs or practices of a group or society." The solemn occasions and celebrations of a people tell us much of its ethos—and prominent among them are the "fixed times" and "sacred occasions" of Lev. 23.
>
> From those "fixed times" and "sacred occasions," four major themes emerge. . . . (1) A theme of introspection and contemplation (as expressed...in the weekly Sabbath) . . . ; (2) A theme of freedom as a people (as expressed in the Passover and the Feast of Unleavened Bread) . . . ; (3) A theme of harmony between humanity and its environment (as expressed in the Omer and the two harvest festivals) . . . ; and (4) A theme of communal responsibility, self-evaluation and atonement (as expressed in *rosh hashonah* and *yom hakippurim*).

To the timeless themes of the recurrent festivals, the Torah adds its equally timeless themes that relate to daily conduct. These are dispersed throughout the Torah in (1) the "codified" laws and rules of the Ten Commandments and the various social *mishpatim* of the four major sources, (2) other noncodified commands on particular subjects, and (3) the conduct of the great human exemplars of the Torah. As among the greatest I would cite Abraham, Joseph and Moses. Each possessed (Abraham and Moses), or came to possess (Joseph), the human decency, integrity, compassion, self-respect, and inner strength to fulfil their vital roles despite every human or Godly impediment.[11]

As for the Ten Commandments, I cite first and foremost the Third, in the form rendered by JPS2: "You shall not swear falsely by the name of the Lord your God; for the Lord will not clear one who swears falsely by His name" (Exod. 20:7). So stated, the Third Commandment provides a fitting foundation for the whole of the Torah's moral and ethical structure. Theologically, as related to God's sanctity, to swear falsely by the Torah's God is to abuse His authority or misrepresent His will. Ethically, however, its focus is on humanity's responsibility for its own conduct (see Comment E–56). (Consistent with such a purpose, this reading of the Third Commandment serves reciprocally to protect the Torah's God from becoming a scapegoat for human sin. The Third Commandment avails Him not, however, where, as in the rules of war, Israel's greatest human transgressions are in response to commands said to be given *by Him in His Name*.)

In regard to the great human *themes* of Commandments Five through Ten, see Comments E–58 through 63. Many of these same themes are also repeated in the codified *mishpatim* and other more "random" commands. Among the twelve themes that follow, the twelfth (as derived from the curses and blessings of Leviticus and Deuteronomy) comes closest to the Third Commandment in its overarching breadth.

First, however, I would separate the Torah's "*dated particularities*" from its "*timeless concerns*." The Torah's most vital "remains" today are too often obscured by those particularities. Our focus then must be on the on-going concerns of humanity that these particularities were meant to address *in their time*.

As among the most compelling and pervasive of these "timeless concerns," I suggest the following:

1. The unique value of life in the hierarchy of human values.
2. A general respect and concern for the human body and its health and well-being (with a special awe reserved for the processes of reproduction).
3. A respect for the purpose and power of human sexuality and of the need for its responsible use so as to fulfil its great potential for good and avoid its great potential for harm.
4. A respect for the family as the basic unit of social organization and as the primal nurturing source of well-being for all of its members.
5. A general respect for the inherent dignity and potential worth of every human being, whether "brother" or "stranger," and of whatever class or status.
6. A particular respect for one's immediate neighbors so that all may live peaceably and productively within their immediate communities.
7. An ingrained concern for the needs and well-being of the poor, the physically impaired, the stranger, the elderly and by necessary analogy, all persons subject to debilitating circumstances.
8. A special regard for the role of human empathy (that is, a heightened ability to sense the feelings of others) as the truest source of human compassion. ("Remember that you were a slave in Egypt.")
9. A recognition of the sentience of animals and of the consequential need to avoid the imposition of all unnecessary pain and suffering.
10. The central importance of a comprehensive system of law to settle disputes and to define and punish wrongdoing fairly, impartially, objectively and efficiently—free from the contamination of bribery, perjury, favoritism (whether with good or evil intent), and every other impediment to individual justice.

11. The need to deal honestly with every one in all matters, with special care to maintain these standards in the context of impersonal commercial dealings.

12. The duty of every member of the community to contribute to its overall moral and ethical worth and its general well-being.

The timeless relevance of these "documented" remains of a Torah written between thirty and twenty-five centuries ago would seem self-evident.[12] And with them we must include the great universal themes of the festivals, as discussed above. But the worthiest of human goals are of little consequence without a human commitment to fulfil them. It was in creating the Torah's God as both Israel's conscience and as the enforcer of its conscience that its authors in their time sought to develop the needed commitment in its people. In doing so, however, they also provided a moral and ethical system capable in time of vesting the Torah's collective conscience in each human being and transferring its enforcement to humanity itself.

Here I allude to what I have construed to be the mythic source of human free will in the Torah's complex morality tale of Adam and Eve in the Garden of Eden (see Comments G–4 through 9). Morally inseparable from our personal freedom to choose, however, is our personal responsibility for what we choose. We must be therefore judged not by what we ascribe to the Name of a God, but by what we do in our own names. This is the ultimate teaching of the Third Commandment (see Comment E–56).

And what is it above all that the Torah tells us we must strive to do? That obligation was first declared in the context of Creation I. It demanded nothing less of humanity than to strive toward perfecting its earthly existence—that is, to bring its common abode from a state of "very good," as created, to a perfection that could yet be. Having been created by the Torah's authors in the image of their God, humanity possessed "every quality of mind, spirit, and body necessary, or useful, to [its] earthly purposes" (see Comment G–1 and Gen. 1:1–2:3).

In that the Torah's authors looked to the fulfillment of humanity's obligation in perpetuity, they would have surely understood that humanity could not forever live by the Torah's wisdom alone. *By necessary implication, therefore, the Torah charges humanity with a continuing duty to avail itself of every potential source of knowledge and wisdom useful to its central purposes.* The Torah's own prescriptions are necessarily limited to the state of knowledge in its time. Central to that knowledge, however, are its "timeless concerns," which continue to offer humanity invaluable guidelines in its pursuit of earthly perfection. Under conditions of constant change, however, new societal needs are identified, and new knowledge developed with which to address them. The Torah thus charges humanity to identify those needs and to draw on all available sources of knowledge and wisdom that might contribute to their fulfillment and to the improvement of earthly existence.

In extolling the Torah's enduring virtues and worthy "remains," however, I can hardly ignore the character and conduct attributed to its God. All too often they mock rather than inspire these virtues and "remains." How can we possibly explain, let alone justify, His purposeful extermination of the whole of humanity other than for Noah and his family? Or His destruction of the innocent women and children of Sodom? Or His deliberate slaying of all the firstborn of Egypt, including the youngest among them? Or the litany of mayhem that continues through the utterly inhumane rules of war, as revealed by God to Moses in Deuteronomy? In the context of these and countless other cruelties, how can we look to the Torah's God as a fit exemplar for Israel and humanity?

In brief, we cannot. The Torah's authors did not create the Lord, as their God, to serve humanity as an exemplar. His manifestations of power, His wrath, His menacing threats and His propensity for the collective punishment of innocent and guilty alike were not contrived as models for human emulation. Just as the endless rituals of animal sacrifices were meant to reinforce His sanctity, so, too, was His distinctly Lordly conduct meant to strengthen His role as the means to gain Israel's adherence to the Torah's societal laws and ethical standards. *Thus, in reading the Torah, we must forever distinguish between* patterns *of Godly conduct and* standards *of human conduct.*

HOW MIGHT WE BETTER USE THE TORAH'S HUMANIST ROOTS IN SUPPORT OF ITS HUMAN PURPOSES?

To understand and better utilize the Torah's essential humanism we should first consider with an open mind the logical significance of its human origins. Just as human authors created the Torah, so, too, from varied perspectives, they created a composite *yahweh* as its God and chief protagonist. From this it follows that humanity was not created to serve *yahweh*, but that He was created to serve it. So that He might do so, His creators endowed Him with a persona that would serve most effectively *in the world they knew* as the means to their human ends. For this they drew on varied traditions of their own and other people(s).

Their common aim was to create a Being whose character and attributes would both compel and inspire obedience to His will. Largely through words and deeds attributed to Him, such obedience was identified as Israel's greatest good and ultimate end. Most significantly, the Torah's authors expressed His will through what I have termed "dated particularities" and "timeless human concerns." Through the former, they sought to develop a more benign complement to the role of fear as the prime impetus for obedience (as cultivated through endless portrayals of Godly wrath and omnipotence). Prominent among these "dated particularities" were highly structured and repetitive rituals and mnemonic devices that were meant to internalize a sense of His sanctity. These sources of internalization were in turn augmented by the Lord's occasional professions of His own abiding compassion. As a quality to be emulated by Israel, such professed compassion was exemplary. But as to *yahweh*, Himself, His compassion could rarely withstand his pride, anger, and quixotic recourse to plagues and collective punishments.

The highest purpose for which the Torah's authors sought obedience to the Torah's God, whether through fear, reverence or gratitude, was embodied in the morality and ethics of their *societal laws*. It is here that we find the Torah's "timeless human concerns." And it was through obedience to them, and the inculcation of their values into Israel's collective conscience, that the Torah's authors, in their time, sought to develop Israel as a worthy exemplar for all humanity.

Inevitably, my reading, interpretations, and conclusions have been influenced by my abiding secular respect for the humanist elements of Judaic culture and values. The impact of my nontheistic beliefs on the integrity of my inquiry I must leave for readers to judge. But whatever their verdicts, my inquiry has at least fulfilled my hopes in pursuing it. Through it, my initial sense of the Torah has become a conviction. As the well-spring of Judaism, the Torah can indeed be read, understood, and honored as an embodiment of many of humanity's highest purposes,

My approach to the Torah's God as a human creation, however, is not unique to Jewish humanism. As noted in the introduction (p. 30) and conclusion (p. 564), contemporary efforts within theocratic liberal Judaism to conform the Torah's God to modern views of reality reflect His necessary malleability as the intended means to human ends in an ever evolving world. Over the course of the twentieth century, Reform and Reconstructionist Judaism have sought to recreate either a Being (Reform), or a concept (Reconstructionist), that avoids the difficulties of a literal belief in the traditional God of the Torah. In essence, and somewhat akin to the Torah's authors before them, they have each sought to develop a credible god-idea as the means in their time for perpetuating Judaic values and culture.

If there is, therefore, a common doctrinal ground on which the theistic and nontheistic denominations of liberal Judaism can stand, it is the contemporary irrelevance of the Torah's God, as first created. However, as noted in the introduction (pp. 30–31), *doctrinal* irrelevance may not inspire a sense of *liturgical* irrelevance. Tradition and feeling within the human spirit does not always yield readily to reason. Thus, even in "knowing" the Torah's God (as created or recreated) to be a product of the human mind, many liberal theistic Jews continue to seek guidance and comfort within the formal framework of a god-idea.

Nontheocratic humanistic Judaism differs from theocratic liberal Judaism in its definitive rejection of the reality of the Torah's God, as created or recreated. Its goal is to enrich its members and society at large through the perpetuation of Judaism's humanist values and cultural traditions. To this end, humanistic

Judaism approaches its heritage as the product of human rather than Godly inspiration. In this it differs from Reform and Reconstructionist Judaism, not as to ends, but as to means.

Experience teaches that the distinction between God, or a god-idea, as a means or an end has consequences. Throughout history, religious strife among monotheistic religions and sects has been tragically exacerbated by a widespread view of God's sanctity as a human end in itself. Here the issue is not the reality of *a* God, but the reality of *whose* God. As the sanctified source of salvation, God can hardly be shared with one's enemies.

Less dogmatic, but still divisive, is the difference of views within liberal Judaism regarding the role of any god-idea in perpetuating the peoplehood, traditions and cultural values of Judaism. Nevertheless, from my gradual emergence as a secular humanist during a period of active membership in a vibrant Reform Congregation, I have a sense of the broad commonality of human ends among theists and nontheists within liberal Judaism. In my view it is a commonality that warrants intercommunal respect that looks beyond the role of a god-idea as the means to those ends.

In assessing the work of the Torah's authors today, I must confess to one regret. It is that the power of their imagery has so long obscured the intended role of their Godly creation as a means to human ends *in their time*. Centuries later, their literary eloquence continues to inspire many to view His sanctity as an overriding human end in itself. It is time, therefore, to lift at least a portion of the moral burden that the Torah's God must bear as a divisive force among the descendants of His creators.

We can do so by openly acknowledging that the Torah's God has been created and recreated by humans as a means to human ends. Today, it would seem that most liberal Jews still look to a god-idea for support in honoring the Torah's "timeless concerns" and in finding inspiration in its cultural heritage. What of the countless others, however, who honor these same ends, but who, from respect for their own convictions, reject the reality and role of any god-idea?

It is true indeed that the people of the Torah include nontheists as well as theists who seek to perpetuate its human values and the remarkable cultural heritage that developed in its great wake. To do so effectively requires every such person to relate to the Torah and its God in accord with his or her own informed judgment and personal conscience. But for all who view the Torah's God as the means created by human authors in their time toward fulfilling a people's worthiest human ends, there is a special obligation. It is to give greater heed in our time to those human ends that we share than to differences concerning the role of a god-idea as a means to those ends.

NOTES

A BRIEF PREFACE TO JUDAISM, THEISM, NATURALISM, AND HUMANISM

1. The Torah portrays its God as male. By convention, most English translations capitalize all references to its God. Hebrew, however, makes no use of capital letters.

INTRODUCTION

1. See Ramban, *Commentary on the Torah: Genesis*, trans. C. B. Chavel (New York: Shilo Publishing House, 1971), p. 7.

2. My textual references are mainly to the 1962/67 translation of the Jewish Publication Society (JPS2), as incorporated in W. G. Plaut, ed., *The Torah: A Modern Commentary* (New York: Union of American Hebrew Congregations, 1981). This volume includes Rabbi W. Gunther Plaut's commentaries, which I refer to and comment on frequently. I will also address various subtleties in Torah translations by comparing the excellent but often varied translations of JPS2, as rooted in Reform Judaism; JPS1, as rooted in Jewish Orthodoxy; and RSV, as rooted in the Christian tradition of the King James Version.

3. Ramban, *Commentary on the Torah: Genesis*, p. 7.

4. Ibid.

5. Plaut, *The Torah: A Modern Commentary*, p. xix.

6. *Encyclopedia of Religion*, 1987, s.v. "Reconstructionist Judaism."

7. These passages appear in M. M. Kaplan, *The Meaning of God in Modern Jewish Religion* (New York: Reconstructionist Press, 1962), p. 76, and E. S. Goldsmith and M . Scult, eds., *Dynamic Judaism* (New York: Schocken Books/The Reconstructionist Press, 1985), pp. 77, 95.

8. *Kol Haneshamah: Shabbat Vehagim* (Wyncote, Pa.: The Reconstructionist Press, 1994), p. 264. This prayerbook was compiled by a Reconstructionist Prayerbook Comission.

9. The following discussion of Torah authorship in light of the evolving Documentary Hypothesis draws on various sources. These include: R. E. Friedman, *Who Wrote*

the Bible? (New York: Harper & Row, 1989); Encyclopedia Britannica, 15th ed., s.v. "Biblical Literature and its Critical Interpretation"; Encyclopedia of Religion, 1987, s.v. " Biblical Literature: Hebrew Scriptures"; H. Minkoff, ed., Approaches to the Bible (Washington, D.C.; Biblical Archeology Society, 1986), chaps. 1, 2; B. Anderson, Understanding the Old Testament, 3d. ed. (Englewood Cliffs, N.J.: Prentice Hall, Inc., 1975), pp. 19–20, and index entries for J, E, D, and P sources; T. Mann, The Book of the Torah: The Narrative Integrity of the Pentateuch (Atlanta, Ga.: J. Knox, 1988), pp. 1–9; and E. Nicholson, The Pentateuch in the Twentieth Century: The Legacy of Julius Wellhausen (Oxford: Clarendon Press, 1998). Following a broad review of more recent literature critical of the theory, Nicholson concludes: "But the Documentary hypothesis should remain our primary source of reference, and it alone provides the true perspective from which to approach this most difficult of areas in the study of the Old Testament" (p. vi).

10. The use of a single letter would seem to suggest a single author for each "source." In some cases, however, the source may have included one or more redactors (or editors) who melded various subsources into an end product. Thus, a single letter designation might properly refer to a single author or to one or more redactors and subsources.

11. Most notably, see Plaut, The Torah: A Modern Commentary, pp. xxi-xxiv. He refers to the Documentary Hypothesis as "the theory which continues to command general scholarly adherence" (p. xxii).

12. In attributing Torah passages to particular sources, I will basically follow Professor Friedman's conclusions (see Who Wrote the Bible?). Notably among the "mainstream" authorities, he has prepared a systematic and comprehensive set of attributions of almost every Torah verse to one or another of the various sources (pp. 246–60). Although he does not specifically explain each of his attributions, they derive from the general principles of his basic text. On a rare occasion one might question one or another attribution. But the fact remains that Professor Friedman is a well-informed and resourceful scholar who has fulfilled his challenging task with true distinction. Where I might question a particular attribution, I will try to explain why.

13. David N. Freedman states, "No extant non-biblical records make reference to Moses or the Exodus, therefore the question of historicity depends solely on the evaluation of the biblical accounts." The Anchor Bible Dictionary, vol. 4 (Anchor, N.Y.: Doubleday, 1992), p. 909. To the same effect, see Encyclopedia of Religion, 1987, s.v. "Moses." Conversely, as to Joshua, who in the later Book of Joshua leads Israel into Canaan, I have found no similar assertions.

In Moses and Monotheism (New York: Alfred A. Knopf, 1939), Sigmund Freud speculates on the possible identiy of Moses as an actual Egyptian convert to the short-lived monotheistic cult of Amenhotep IV (or Akhenaton), c. 1353–36 B.C.E. (see Encyclopedia Britannica, 15th ed., s.v. "Akhenton." If such a Moses did ever live, it became his destiny to be incorporated into the Torah as a legend after his time. As for Joshua, however, his central role in the later Book of Joshua may have led to his appearance in the Torah as a legend before his time.

14. P. McCarter Jr., "The Patriarchal Age," in The Ancient Near East, 3d. ed. rev. (New York: W. W. Norton, 1965), pp. 1–29.

15. Useful insights from differing perspectives on how the Oral Law (of whatever origin) led to the Talmud is provided in the following books (among other sources): A. Steinsaltz, The Essential Talmud (New York: Basic Books, HarperCollins, 1976); J. Wein-

green, *From Bible to Mishna: The Continuity of Tradition* (Manchester: Manchester University Press, 1976); M. Adler, *The World of the Talmud*, 2d. ed. (New York: Schocken Books, 1963); J. Neusner, *The Oral Torah: The Sacred Books of Judaism, an Introduction* (Atlanta, Ga.: Sholars Press, 1991); and D. Zlotnik, *The Iron Pillar—Mishnah: Redaction, Form, and Intent* (Jerusalem: Bialik Institute, 1988).

16. Freedman, "Meal Customs, Jewish," *The Anchor Bible Dictionary*, vol. 4, p. 648.

17. L. Jacobs, *The Jewish Religion: A Companion* (Oxford: Oxford University Press, 1995), p. 345; see also *Encyclopedia Britannica*, 15th ed., s.v. "Judaism." An English translation of much of the original Midrash is provided in *Midrash Rabbah*, ed. H Freedman and M. Simon (London/New York: Soncino Press, 1983). Midrashism on the five books of the Torah are in volumes 1 to 7 of this ten-volume work. For a comprehensive introduction to the intricacies of Midrash, see B. Holtz, *Back to the Sources: Reading the Classic Jewish Texts* (New York: Summit Books, 1984), chap. 3.

18. J. Neusner, *Invitation to Midrash* (San Francisco: Harper & Row, 1989), p. 276.

19. Among the many sources that cite and explore these connections, the interested reader might consult the following books: N. Sarna, *Understanding Genesis* (New York: Jewish Theological Seminary of America/McGraw-Hill, 1966), and *Exploring Exodus: The Heritage of Biblical Israel* (New York: Schocken Books, 1986); C. L. Wooley, *The Sumerians* (New York/London: W. W. Norton, 1966); and C. H. Gordon, *The Ancient Near East*, 3d. ed. rev. (New York/London: W. W. Norton, 1965).

20. For a theistic view of Maimonides on these issues, see K. Seeskin, *Maimonides: A Guide for Today's Perplexed* (West Orange, N.J.: Behrman House, 1991).

1. GENESIS

1. For an explanation of my references to JPS1 and RSV in relation to those made to JPS2, see my introduction, p. 29 n. 2.

2. Plaut, *The Torah: A Modern Commentary*, pp. 30, 1539.

3. See *The Pentateuch and Rashi's Commentary: A Linear Translation into English*, ed. Abraham Ben Isaiah and Benjamin Sharfman (New York: S. S. & R. Publishing Co., 1976), p. 36. (The Torah translation in this case generally follows JPS1, with occasional departures to accommodate Rashi's text.) Rashi (1040–1105 C.E.) is widely regarded as *the* preeminent Torah commentator.

4. H. Orlinsky, ed., *Notes on the New Translation of the Torah* (Philadelphia: Jewish Publication Society, 1969), p. 63.

5. *The Pentateuch and Rashi's Commentary*, Genesis, p. 29.

6. Ibid., p. 38.

7. R. E. Friedman, *Who Wrote the Bible?* p. 256.

8. *The Pentateuch and Rashi's Commentary*, Genesis, p. 63.

9. Plaut, *The Torah: A Modern Commentary*, p. 116.

10. *The Pentateuch and Rashi's Commentary*, Genesis, p. 121.

11. See also Freedman, "Salem," *The Anchor Bible Dictionary*, vol. 5, p. 905, and Ramban, *Commentary on the Torah: Genesis*, pp. 188–90.

12. Plaut, *The Torah: A Modern Commentary*, p. 116.

13. *The Pentateuch and Rashi's Commentary*, Genesis, pp. 140–41.

14. Ibid., p. 143.

15. Ibid.

16. Friedman, *Who Wrote the Bible?* pp. 256–57.

17. *The Pentateuch and Rashi's Commentary*, Genesis, pp. 234–35.

18. Ramban, *Commentary on the Torah: Genesis*, pp. 307–308.

19. *Encyclopedia Britannica*, 15th ed., s.v. "Philistines."

20. *Encyclopedia Americana*, International ed., s.v. "Philistines."

21. See, for example, T. Dotham, *The Philistines and Their Material Culture* (New Haven, Conn.: Yale University Press, 1982), pp. 14–15.

22. *Encyclopedia Americana*, International ed., s.v. "mandrakes."

23. *Encyclopedia of Religion*, 1987, s.v. " Inanna."

24. *Encyclopedia Britannica*, 15th ed., s.v. "Baal."

25. *Encyclopedia Britannica*, 15th ed., s.v. "Lamarck," "Lysenko."

26. Gordon, *The Ancient Near East*, p. 129.

27. *The Pentateuch and Rashi's Commentary*, Genesis, p. 349.

28. All Torah names, including those in 36:31–39, are listed in *Who's Who: The Old Testament* by J. Comay (Oxford: Oxford University Press, 1993).

29. *The Pentateuch and Rashi's Commentary*, Genesis, p. 359.

30. Ibid., p. 364.

31. Ramban, *Commentary on the Torah: Genesis*, p. 462.

32. *The Pentateuch and Rashi's Commentary*, Genesis, p. 381.

33. Ramban, *Commentary on the Torah: Genesis*, pp. 511–13.

34. W. Durant, *The Story of Civilization: Our Oriental Heritage* (New York: Simon and Schuster, 1954), p. 202.

35. *Encyclopedia of Religion*, 1987, s.v. "immortality."

36. Gordon, *The Ancient Near East*. Cf. Comment G–83.

37. *Encyclopedia Britannica*, 15th ed., s.v. "Ramses."

38. Ibid., s.v. "Ephraim."

39. *Encyclopedia Americana*, 1993, s.v. "Ephraim."

40. Friedman, *Who Wrote the Bible?* p. 258.

41. *Encyclopedia Britannica*, 15th ed., s.v. "Reuben."

42. Ibid., s.v. "Simeon."

43. Orlinsky, *Notes on the New Translation of the Torah*, p. 63.

44. *The Pentateuch and Rashi's Commentary*, Genesis, p. 497.

45. *Encyclopedia Americana*, 1993, s.v. "Benjamin."

46. Friedman, *Who Wrote the Bible?* p. 258.

2. EXODUS

1. *The Pentateuch and Rashi's Commentary*, Exodus, p. 8.

2. Plaut, *The Torah: A Modern Commentary*, p. 383.

3. Ramban, *Commentary on the Torah: Exodus*, p. 14.

4. *The Pentateuch and Rashi's Commentary*, Exodus, p. 23.

5. Ramban, *Commentary on the Torah: Exodus*, p. 52.

6. *The Pentateuch and Rashi's Commentary*, Exodus, pp. 37–38.

7. Ibid., p. 40; Ramban, *Commentary on the Torah: Exodus*, p. 57.

8. Ramban, *Commentary on the Torah: Exodus*, p. 112.

9. Ibid., pp. 113–14. See also Comment E–31.

10. *The Pentateuch and Rashi's Commentary*, Exodus, p. 96.

11. Ibid., p. 106.

12. Plaut, *The Torah: A Modern Commentary*, p. 459.

13. *The Pentateuch and Rashi's Commentary*, Exodus, p. 115.

14. Plaut, *The Torah: A Modern Commentary*, p. 470.

15. See Ramban, *Commentary on the Torah: Exodus*, p. 150; *The Pentateuch and Rashi's Commentary*, Exodus, pp. 120–21; Plaut, *The Torah: A Modern Commentary*, p. 463.

16. Plaut, *The Torah: A Modern Commentary*, p. 462.

17. *The Pentateuch and Rashi's Commentary*, Exodus, p. 130.

18. Ibid., p. 133.

19. Ibid., p. 141.

20. Ibid., p. 184; Ramban, *Commentary on the Torah: Exodus*, p. 241.

21. Plaut, *The Torah: A Modern Commentary*, p. 506.

22. For a survey of the Amalekites' appearances in the books of the Torah and early prophets, see Freedman, "Amalek," *The Anchor Bible Dictionary*, vol. 1, pp. 169–71. Amalek will appear again in Numbers 13:29; 14:25, 42–45; 24:20; and Deut. 25:17–19. The likely concerns of Amalek to E (as author of 17:8–16) might be found in references to Amalek in Judges and 1 and 2 Samuel. A reference to King David's defeat of Amalek appears in 2 Sam. 8:11–12.

23. See Freedman, "Jethro," *The Anchor Bible Dictionary*, vol. 3, p. 821.

24. Plaut, *The Torah: A Modern Commentary*, p. 534.

25. Ibid., p. 535.

26. *The Pentateuch and Rashi's Commentary*, Exodus, p. 214.

27. Ramban, *Commentary on the Torah: Exodus*, pp. 288–89.

28. *New York Times*, 28 March 1996, Chicago Edition, p. 1, col. 2.

29. *The Pentateuch and Rashi's Commentary*, Exodus, p. 218.

30. Ibid.

31. Freedman, "Ten Commandments," *The Anchor Bible Dictionary*, vol. 6, p. 386.

32. Plaut, *The Torah: A Modern Commentary*, pp 562–63.

33. Ibid.

34. *The Pentateuch and Rashi's Commentary*, Exodus, p. 240.

35. Ibid., pp. 242–43; Ramban, *Commentary on the Torah: Exodus*, pp. 368–67.

36. *The Pentateuch and Rashi's Commentary*, Exodus, p. 256; Ramban, *Commentary on the Torah: Exodus*, p. 378.

37. Plaut, *The Torah: A Modern Commentary*, pp 577–78.

38. *The Pentateuch and Rashi's Commentary*, Exodus, p. 259.

39. See also B. F. Batto, "Red Sea or Reed Sea: What *Yam Sup* Really Means," in *Approaches to the Bible: The Best of the Bible Review*, ed. H. Minkoff, vol. 1 (Washington, D.C.: Biblical Archaeology Society, 1994), p. 291.

40. *The Pentateuch and Rashi's Commentary*, Exodus, pp. 225–26; Ramban, *Commentary on the Torah: Exodus*, pp. 338–40.

41. *The Pentateuch and Rashi's Commentary*, Exodus, pp. 225–26.

42. Ibid., p. 286.

43. See, for example, B. Metzger and M. Coogan, eds., *The Oxford Companion to the Bible* (Oxford: Oxford University Press, 1993), p. 214.

44. Plaut, *The Torah: A Modern Commentary*, p. 591.

45. Ibid.

46. *The Pentateuch and Rashi's Commentary*, Exodus, p. 284.

47. Ramban, *Commentary on the Torah: Exodus*, p. 428.

48. *The Pentateuch and Rashi's Commentary*, Exodus, p. 286.

49. Freedman, "Weights and Measures," *The Anchor Bible Dictionary*, vol. 6, p. 898.

50. Ibid., "Aaron," vol. 1, p. 5.

51. Ibid., pp. 3–6.

52. Plaut, *The Torah: A Modern Commentary*, p. 646.

53. Friedman, *Who Wrote the Bible?* p. 258.

54. J. R. Hertz, *The Pentateuch and Haftorahs* (London: Oxford University Press, 1936), pp. 228–29. Emphasis added.

55. Freedman, "Jeroboam," *The Anchor Bible Dictionary*, vol. 6, pp. 742–44.

56. *Encyclopedia Britannica*, 15th ed., s.v. "Kings, Books of."

57. *The Pentateuch and Rashi's Commentary*, Exodus, p. 413.

58. Ramban, *Commentary on the Torah: Exodus*, pp. 571–73.

3. LEVITICUS

1. *The Pentateuch and Rashi's Commentary*, Leviticus, p. 5.

2. Ramban, *Commentary on the Torah: Leviticus*, pp. 10–14.

3. *The Pentateuch and Rashi's Commentary*, Leviticus, p. 12.

4. Ibid., p. 19.

5. Ibid., p. 13.

6. Ibid., p. 25.

7. Plaut, *The Torah: A Modern Commentary*, p. 777. See also Orlinsky, *Notes on the New Translation of the Torah*, p. 208–209.

8. Plaut, *The Torah: A Modern Commentary*, p. 778.

9. *The Pentateuch and Rashi's Commentary*, Leviticus, p. 66.

10. Ramban, *Commentary on the Torah: Leviticus*, pp. 90–91.

11. Ibid., pp. 260–61. See also *The Pentateuch and Rashi's Commentary*, Leviticus, p. 178.

12. Similarly, in regard to the worship of Baal, see Jer. 19:3b–5. For a nonbiblical reference to child sacrifices in cultures surrounding the Israelites of this period, see N. Davies, *Human Sacrifice in History and Today* (New York: William and Morrow, 1981), pp. 61–65.

13. Plaut, *The Torah: A Modern Commentary*, p. 814.

14. *The Pentateuch and Rashi's Commentary*, Leviticus, pp. 109–10; Ramban, *Commentary on the Torah: Leviticus*, p.163.

15. *The Pentateuch and Rashi's Commentary*, Leviticus, pp. 136–37.

16. Freedman, "Leprosy," *The Anchor Bible Dictionary*, vol. 4, p. 281.

17. *The Pentateuch and Rashi's Commentary*, Exodus, pp. 222–23.

18. *The Pentateuch and Rashi's Commentary*, Leviticus, pp. 181–82.

19. Ibid., p. 182.

20. Ramban, *Commentary on the Torah: Leviticus*, pp. 292–94.
21. Ibid., p. 306.
22. *The Pentateuch and Rashi's Commentary*, Leviticus, p. 195.
23. Ibid., p. 196.
24. Ibid., p. 203.
25. Ibid.
26. Plaut, *The Torah: A Modern Commentary*, p. 905.
27. *The Pentateuch and Rashi's Commentary*, Leviticus, p. 232.
28. Ramban, *Commentary on the Torah: Leviticus*, pp. 90–91.
29. *The Pentateuch and Rashi's Commentary*, Leviticus, p. 295.
30. Ibid., pp. 305–306.
31. *Encyclopedia Americana*, International ed., 1993, s.v. "superego."
32. *Encyclopedia Britannica*, 15th ed., s.v. "superego."

4. NUMBERS

1. *The Pentateuch and Rashi's Commentary*, Numbers, p. 23.
2. Ibid., p. 30.
3. Ibid., p. 32.
4. Ibid., p. 34. See also Plaut, *The Torah: A Modern Commentary*, p. 1077.
5. *The Pentateuch and Rashi's Commentary*, Numbers, p. 85.
6. Plaut, *The Torah: A Modern Commentary*, p. 1081.
7. Ibid., p. 687. Emphasis added.
8. Freedman, "Amalek," *The Anchor Bible Dictionary*, vol. 1, p. 169.
9. Orlinsky, *Notes on the New Translation of the Torah*, pp. 232, 265–66.
10. Friedman, *Who Wrote the Bible?* pp. 221–22.
11. Ibid., pp. 253, 259.
12. *The Pentateuch and Rashi's Commentary*, Numbers, p. 193.
13. See, for example, Freedman, "Balaam," *The Anchor Bible Dictionary*, vol. 1, pp. 569–72.
14. Plaut, *The Torah: A Modern Commentary*, p. 1184.
15. *The Pentateuch and Rashi's Commentary*, Numbers, p. 268.
16. Ibid., p. 332.
17. Friedman, *Who Wrote the Bible?* p. 259.
18. Such a map is found in Plaut, *The Torah: A Modern Commentary*, p. 1106.
19. *The Pentateuch and Rashi's Commentary*, Numbers, p. 359.
20. Ibid., p. 360.
21. Ramban, *Commentary on the Torah: Numbers*, pp. 389–92.

5. DEUTERONOMY

1. Plaut, *The Torah: A Modern Commentary*, p. 1320.
2. Ibid., p. 1356.
3. Ibid., p. 1368.

4. *The Pentateuch and Rashi's Commentary*, Deuteronomy, p. 69.

5. Ramban, *Commentary on the Torah: Deuteronomy*, p. 101.

6. Friedman, *Who Wrote the Bible?* pp. 117–24.

7. *The Pentateuch and Rashi's Commentary*, Deuteronomy, p. 13.

8. Hertz, *The Pentateuch and Haftorahs*, Deuteronomy, p. 188.

9. Ibid., p. 190.

10. Freedman, "Tithe," *The Anchor Bible Dictionary*, vol. 6, p. 579.

11. In general, see 1 Kings 11:1–8. As for horses, see Plaut, *The Torah: A Modern Commentary*, p. 1458, and 1 Kings 10:26–29.

12. *The Pentateuch and Rashi's Commentary*, Deuteronomy, p. 164.

13. Ramban, *Commentary on the Torah: Deuteronomy*, pp. 208–209.

14. Plaut, *The Torah: A Modern Commentary*, p. 1476.

15. Ibid., p. 1483.

16. Hertz, *The Pentateuch and Haftorahs*, Deuteronomy, pp. 226–27.

17. Plaut, *The Torah: A Modern Commentary*, p. 1486.

18. *The Pentateuch and Rashi's Commentary*, Deuteronomy, p. 207.

19. Ramban, *Commentary on the Torah: Deuteronomy*, pp. 287–88. To similar effect, see *The Pentateuch and Rashi's Commentary*, Deuteronomy, p. 211.

20. Ramban, *Commentary on the Torah: Deuteronomy*, p. 297.

21. Friedman, *Who Wrote the Bible?* pp. 76–79.

22. Ramban, *Commentary on the Torah: Deuteronomy*, p. 304.

23. *The Pentateuch and Rashi's Commentary*, Deuteronomy, p. 224.

24. Ramban, *Commentary on the Torah: Deuteronomy*, pp. 317–18.

25. Friedman, *Who Wrote the Bible?* pp. 143–49.

26. See *The New Oxford Annotated Bible*, vol. 2 (New York: Oxford University Press, 1991), pp. 254–55, and *The New Interpreter's Bible*, vol. 2 (Nashville, Tenn: Abington Press, 1998), pp. 501–504.

27. *The Pentateuch and Rashi's Commentary*, Deuteronomy, p. 271.

28. Ibid., p. 283.

29. Ramban, *Commentary on the Torah: Deuteronomy*, p. 349. See also Hertz, *The Pentateuch and Haftorahs*, Deuteronomy, p. 386.

30. Plaut, *The Torah: A Modern Commentary*, p. 1569.

31. *The New Interpreter's Bible*, vol. 2, p. 534.

32. Plaut, *The Torah: A Modern Commentary*, pp. 1567–68.

33. Freedman, "Benjamin," *The Anchor Bible Dictionary*, vol. 1, p. 671.

CONCLUSION

1. I limit my definition of liberal theocratic Judaism to Reform and Reconstructionist Judaism. In the former we encounter a steady narrowing of Godly transcendence. In the latter we meet a God comprised entirely of naturalistic forces. Although my working definition of "liberal" might be disputed, I exclude Jewish Conservatism because of its lingering doctrinal adherence (in substance as well as liturgy) to Godly transcendence and revelation. See, for example, *Emet Ve-Emunah: Statement of Principles of Conservative Judaism* (New York: Jewish Theological Seminary, 1988), pp. 19–20.

2. Plaut, *The Torah: A Modern Commentary*, p. xix.

3. Ibid., pp. 1551–52. Here Rabbi Plaut draws on the theme of Martin Buber's wise rabbi of Kotsk (see Comment E–84). By definition, of course, the loss of any power means an end to omnipotence. *In theory*, however, the loss of omnipotence (i.e., the loss of *any* power) does not preclude the possible retention of *some* power to "transcend" the natural order.

4. "God Where Were You: Keeping the Faith After Auschwitz," *Reform Judaism* (summer 1998): 21–25.

5. For a brief overview of other efforts to reinterpret (or recreate) Israel's God, together with citations, see *Encyclopedia of Religion*, 1987, s.v. "God in the Hebrew Scriptures" and "God in the Postbiblical Judaism." For useful assessments of such later figures (among others) as Hermann Cohen, Franz Rosenzweig, Martin Buber, and Modecai Kaplan, see J. Agus, *Modern Philosophies of Judaism* (New York: Behrman's, 1941).

6. *Encyclopedia Britannica*, 15th ed., s.v. "Ancient Middle East Religions."

7. See introduction p. 35 n. 13.

8. From its own substance and apparent contradiction of Exod. 33:7–11, which precedes it, I am inclined to ascribe 33:12–23 to P. The critical verse is "But you cannot see My *face*, for man may not see Me and live." Even if we read "face" as a metaphor for God's "inner essence," does "Me" not include His physicality as well as His inner essence? In any case, Friedman attributes the whole of Exod. 33:7–23 to E (see Comments E–78, 91, and 92).

9. It is a faith, however, that warrants respect for its internal consistency—except when debased by invocations of Godly authority to justify conduct not justifiable by human authority. This is why I view the Third Commandment as the Torah's necessary restriction on the abuse of Godly authority (see Comment E–56).

10. See preface p. 28.

11. In the end, my profound regard for the mythic Moses reflects the totality of his conduct in his thankless role as mediator between his people and their God. Like the Torah's God, Moses himself is largely an original creation of its authors. It became his destined role to mediate between the pride and wrath of the Torah's omnipotent God and the human failings of a people from whom their impulsive God often expects too much. (For accounts of Moses' zeal both in protecting his people and in seeking to discern and implement his God's will, see Comment N–19 and 30. As to the latter, one can almost hear Moses give voice to his cumulative frustration: "Will the death of these Midianites finally appease the wrath of my God!"

12. As important (but not exclusive) elements on the Torah's "documentation" of these "timeless concerns" I cite the following verses (arranged in order of appearance rather than subject matter): Genesis—18:22–32, 44:18–45:15, 50:15–21; Exodus—20:12–14, 21:2–22:16, 22:20–26, 23:1–12; Leviticus—5:1, 5:21–26, 11:24–27, 12:1–8, 13:1–46, 14:1–32, 15:1–33, 18:1–30, 19:3a, 19:9–18, 19:29a, 19:32a, 19:33–36, 22:27–28, 25:2–17, 25:25–28, 25:35–37, 25:39–55 (but see Comment L–57), 26 (see Comment L–59); Numbers—5:11–31 (see Comment N–6), 35:6–33; Deuteronomy—5:11–15, 5:16–18, 15:7–17, 16:18–20, 17:6–13, 19:15–21, 21:1–21 (see Comment D–31 in regard to 21:18–21), 22:1–4, 22:6–8, 22:10, 22:13–29, 23:1, 23:8–21 (but see Comment L–57), 23:25–26, 24:1–22, 25:1–4, 25:13–16, 26:12–13, 27:16–25, 28 (see Comment D–38).